IN SITU

IN SITU

George Ranalli

WORKS & PROJECTS

Main text by George Ranalli
Edited by Oscar Riera Ojeda
Introduction by Michael Sorkin
Interview with Susan Szenasy
Project Descriptions by Anne Valentino

Essays by
Joseph Giovannini,
Paul Goldberger,
Ada Louise Huxtable,
Herbert Muschamp
and Anthony Vidler.

OSCAR RIERA OJEDA
PUBLISHERS

CONTENTS

PROJECTS

ESSAYS

APPENDIX

INTRODUCTION by MICHAEL SORKIN

The "heroism" of modernism is self-identified with rupture. Assuming a genuine isomorphism with the political revolutions that were so instrumental in defining its culture, we've been over-influenced by a particular – and particularly narrow – reading of both modernism's appearance and affect. Valorized by its proclamation to have produced an architecture like none that had gone before and by its resonantly insubordinate identification with a class of objects and production that were at once fascinating and innocent of architecture's hermetic arcana – whether the pure abstraction of a proun or the pure functionality of an aircraft – the emblematic forms of pre-war architecture proclaimed their triumph over the constricted refinements and corrupt aspirations of their predecessors.

Not so many buy into this nowadays: post-modernity (not to mention the war itself and its sad consequences for the sunny side of utopia) have rendered modernism either historical or simply one piece of a plural contemporary. Not such an impoverishment, really. By insisting on modernism's context, by refusing the absoluteness of its break, its horizons broaden. Robbed of materialist inevitability, the "functionalist" branch of the modernist taxonomy is forced to share the stage with a big family of talented and inquisitive siblings. On the other hand, the effort to dissociate modernism from its foundational insistence on the relevance of a project beyond mere architecture, a project in which the beautiful was not a complete description of the good and the true, has only supported a frantic – but ultimately flabby – basis for thinking about architectural quality. Here we are confronted with a contrived battle between the emptiness of rarefied aesthetic signifiers and the need to foreground architecture's inevitable role in the fate of the planet and the founding of equity.

In his lucid and persuasive introduction to this volume, George Ranalli makes an argument for the historicity of architecture that grows from both passion and learning.

Ranalli makes no fetish of discontinuity and his project is firmly situated at both a particular site in the body of modernisms and in a far larger view of architectural and urban history. Although his creations are strikingly original, Ranalli does not for a moment believe that any architectural work is created ex nihilo. And this is important: Ranalli's architecture grows very much from both a love of process – his is a maker's hand – and from a deep feeling for the facts of space. His work is filial rather than Oedipal (that murderous muse of modernity) and he is clearly happy to be part of a big and boisterous family. This sense of daily drama underlies the meaning of Ranalli's expansive evocation of musical ensembles as a source of his method of artistic invention and, more broadly, of his insistence that tradition, too, is retrospective, an individual invention.

Thus, the history Ranalli traces of the influential figurations and spatialities of masters like Wright, Scarpa, and Kahn – as well as of the architecture and urbanism of the Italian Renaissance – is neither inevitable nor universal. But they are unassailable as influences not simply because of their immanence in Ranalli's work (where they become truly indigenous, not the empty authority of the mere fact of authority) but because they're his choice, his taste. Because of his critical relationship to this body of work and experience, he authorizes us to look for its influence in his own project. This is clear not simply in the obvious craft and refinement, the sense of proportion and materiality, the artfully modulated light and volume that is everywhere visible in his elegant and lapidary work but in his primary insistence on the social value of building.

And let's be clear about this. What Ranalli's work affirms is the nesting of individuality in a structure of compacts. I've written before about Ranalli's affinity for the rituals of everyday life, his remarkable sensitivity to the experience of the materiality – the palpability of architecture and space at every scale. His architectural project is realized in the actualizations of contact, the hand on the handle, the breeze induced by lifting the sash, the coming around the corner to find the space shifted. This is an architecture of elegance and sobriety and it finds its politics in a sense of parity, the idea that no place should be unattended to, residual. Whether the organization of movement and the lush registration of tone and purpose in an office lobby, the elevating dignity imparted to a community hall in a housing project, or the capture of the possibility for privacy, complexity, and public celebration in the reorganization of a forgotten city block, Ranalli insists – his credo, really – that no space, no object, for human use deserves less than perfect care. In his uncanny ability to produce grandeur without grandiosity, Ranalli democratizes design, asserts that no object is too trivial to be loved. Nor any person who uses it.

The argument implied here is that the beloved Modernist idea of a deep, even epistemological, break is both dangerous to the environment and that Modernism is misrepresented if this idea is taken to define it. What Ranalli critiques in his text is an idea of modernism held captive by a cadre of hegemons who distorted the presence of an unparalleled era of creativity that embraced many voices, many forms, many ways of making. While Ranalli may seem to lay the sins of a greedy and idiot brood at the feet of fathers whose failures were, let us say, those of too Olympian a view rather than mistakes in the particulars of art, his feeling of desertion in his survey of the consequences is entirely sympathetic. There is an architecture all around us that really has gone astray, a mechanized, soulless, building-on-the-cheap, insult to our minds, our bodies, our freedoms.

I don't mean to overstate the character of the resistance in Ranalli's work, simply to say that it inheres in an attentiveness that is thoroughly inclusive. In his work, there is no class system and – in both his practice and his decades of teaching – he has always insisted on the search for perfection, for individuality, and for inquiry – Le Corbusier's "patient search." Ranalli alludes, in his introduction, to the influence of Sibyl Moholy-Nagy and Eduard Sekler (whose lectures I also had the pleasure of attending way back when) and his work surely cannot be discussed outside a sense of architecture's history, of the past-in-present. Nor, I think, outside the passionate enthusiasm of these two historians for their subject, their ability to convey architecture's weight and its power to accumulate ideas in mass, material, light, motion, construction, and representation. We cycle back to an idea of seriousness that must be judged – however eccentric the genius that may have produced it – in a context that always exceeds its physical envelope.

In siting his practice both intellectually and formally, Ranalli departs from Modernism's preferred metaphors of mechanism and technology, favoring instead biological and musical analogues as well as Alberti's idea of reciprocity between building and city. These are not deployed methodologically – Ranalli would have little patience with the justification by procedure with which practitioners have lately sought to elevate a mechanization of parametric design (as if all architecture weren't the outcome of its parameters!) or aleatory techniques or any of the other late spawn of functionalist self-regard and aspirations to an objective architecture. Nor would he have much patience with the equally authoritarian classicists, those architectural originalists who believe architecture to have been born, fully formed, on a sunny day in Rome a couple of millennia ago.

Ranalli, rather, delights, in evolution, the idea that – like the human subject – the architectural object is riddled with DNA, encoded with sources of continuity and singularity both, and produced, generation after generation, by breeding, not parthenogenesis. Like music, another "practice" that evolves within an envelope – the human ability to hear – architecture is a cooperative, inseminating, enterprise and one built on a repertoire of tones and rhythms that are at once infinite in their possibilities and clearly defined by the abilities of the listening or inhabiting subject to process and feel them and, ultimately, to collaborate in what they do. The great architect, like the great musician, is the one who offers us the pleasures not simply of recollection or communion or pleasure made accessible but of exceeding what we thought were our own limits in understanding the new, teaching us some fresh truth about enjoyment. Ranalli has never been content with mere novelty, knows in advance that architecture always rests on a foundation of convention driven by the body's own capacities and by the forms of cooperation and lived-life that building supports.

Which brings us back to the city, especially to those masterpieces of urbanity – New York, Rome, Sienna, among others – that are such an indispensable referent for George Ranalli. Like Alberti, Ranalli sees building as a kind of urbanism, a supple structure of organization for movement and repose, for privacy and society, for the experience of a rich variety of spatial and material patterns and densities. Having known him for well over three decades, I can say he is very much a man about town and we've strolled and sipped cappuccinos and taken in the life of many great urban places together. Given that my most emblematic and beloved view of George is across a café table, I was somewhat abashed a few years ago when he acquired a country place. Of course, he has a family and does dote on the domestic and its rituals and summer in the city can be nasty and he does like to drive and kids need sunshine and fresh air. But mowing the lawn? The unvarnished quietude? The simple life? Nothing to be seen but trees. The potentially nasty spontaneities of nature, the chiggers and the Lyme disease?

"George," I asked him one Monday when he was just returned, "how can you stand it?"

"It's on the main drag. It's in the town. There's an excellent cafe across the street!"

Eternal values.

IN SITU: PEOPLE, HISTORY, PLACE by GEORGE RANALLI

Works

My architectural practice evolved in a dense urban setting, making the city my natural starting point for inserting new buildings, spaces, and interiors into the landscape. As I began to work on my own projects, I noticed that many older buildings had a quiet power belied by the casualness with which they were often torn down. The elaborate narrative that is New York's cultural story is cradled in all the millions of façades, streets, and interiors that make up this fascinating, textured cityscape.

Working on projects forced me to confront the question of how to modify cities and landscapes of whose strong presence I was keenly aware and appreciative. Each project felt like a laboratory for investigating some aspect of urbanism, building design, or interiors that I found in need of re-visioning. For example, closely examining contemporary urban spaces revealed problems with how such spaces are sometimes made. In New York, many projects have left large swaths of urban space unaccounted for: the spaces between large urban complexes and nearby small-scale buildings have tended to become barren wastelands, windswept dustbins not configured to any civic purpose. Outside the city, too, I was struck by the indiscriminate way buildings were carelessly deposited on the landscape, apparently without concern for their effects on adjacent properties and buildings.

Institutional settings seemed the most dramatically affected by such architectural impositions; university campuses, in particular, have been the scene of some fairly unpleasant new architecture. Sometimes new buildings have even been contrapositional by design, deliberately at odds with their host environments, indifferent to the specificities of place. While discussing potential projects with institutional clients, I listened to the criticisms of such projects that some of them had. I formed my own responses, too, since I have spent a great deal of time on campuses and in other institutional settings.

My interest in the question of how detailed elements make any setting unique was piqued by these settings, and I found myself recalibrating my theoretical position, thinking more carefully about what motivated my own designs. The encounter of my evolving ideas with the environments I was working on in my practice further clarified and transformed my thinking. I came to feel that contrapositional architecture was unreasonable and unnecessary: every project offered such rich associations with setting and history that I felt moved to strike a balance between project and setting rather than making something so novel that its difference was its primary agenda. This is not to say that contextualism makes design. Rather, I have sought a middle way, a place where both sides of the question—difference or belonging?—can be asked and answered. And it is indeed possible, as I have found in practice, to design a unique and original building while making direct, necessary, and complex associations to the setting, all without jeopardizing the theoretical clarity of the project.

The craft of architecture—the actual construction of buildings, from bulk structure to finest detail—has also had an enormous impact on my approach to design. My office is arranged to incorporate selection of materials, details, and ornaments from the very beginning of the process so that all these elements can be effectively developed and made integral to the design. Conversations with artisans are an essential part of the process, and figure directly into the evolution of each project as it is studied and developed. Delving into actual methods of construction allows finishes, surface treatments, and other effects to be chosen with an eye not only to immediate effect but also to withstanding the ravages of time. It also enables my office to maintain responsible cost-tracking, which is essential to incorporating all details and craft techniques on budget. Although elaborated over the life of the firm, this approach was in fact present with its very first project over thirty years ago, when I made a deliberate decision to ensure that the preliminary design could be maintained throughout the construction documents process. If this higher-level view is incorporated early enough in the design process, then executed projects can reliably incorporate all desired design factors without breaking the bank.

We use a varying mix of drawings, photography, computer imaging, and models, but it is three-dimensional physical models that have most expanded our design of space and form and most enabled full comprehension of each building's architectural strategy. More than other study methods, models offer an enveloping experience that fosters understanding of many aspects of a building simultaneously. Drawings offer particular views such as sections, elevations and plans, so multiple images are necessary to specify form and space completely; in a model, opposite sides of a building can be simultaneously represented and evaluated in relationship to each other.

and to the interior. Modeling multiple speculations in the development of the building generates ideas of greater complexity and ultimately offers more complete understanding. Thus, a portion of the design process is performed directly in the model. A study model may be accompanied, at first, by no drawings other than a sketch: the idea resides in the model itself, which becomes a generative device to produce spatial relationships or more complex formal strategies. Models provide tectonic proximity to the sense of real architecture. Coupled with full architectural drawings, they offer the best synthesis of the architect's imagination short of the completed building. The drawings tend to reveal the pleasing intricacies of joints, details, and other small-scale features of the building's fabric, while the model's intensity of presence anticipates the physicality of the actual building. In some cases, when a project is not completed, the drawings and models are the final result, the sole record of the content and artistry of the design.

Over the years it became increasingly clear to me that there is a relationship between the craft of one's design methods and the craft of building the building. Lavishing time on a beautiful drawing naturally focused one's attention to the artisanal efforts of the craftspeople working on a project. Drawing and modeling to design astonishing finishes transposes into the sensuousness of materials, surfaces, joinery, and texture in real construction. The fabrication of the models reaches a zenith in the construction and finishing techniques necessary to make a superbly executed miniature of the building; the model is then photographed and stripped into a site image to make a photomontage that can suggest an in situ experience. The photomontage has featured consistently in my work ever since my undergraduate thesis. Before Photoshop, a montage was made by carefully cutting the model photo out, slipping it onto a site photo, and re-photographing the whole. The end result was several generations removed from an original negative. Through computer technology, however, especially Photoshop, montages can be assembled with no image degradation—a pleasing advance.

My understanding and knowledge of such tools has deepened over time, and the daily activities of architectural design have had a significant impact on how I work with the people entrusted with the actual construction of projects.

I began my practice in 1976, in the daunting aftermath of a recession. After being employed by several firms, I received a commission for a small shop on upper Lexington Avenue in New York. The scope consisted of renovating the second floor of the building and adding a new façade linking the second floor to the existing first floor. This was a chance to build on the street in Manhattan, an opportunity rarely accorded a young architect. The significance of this was not lost on me, and I embarked on exploring the design.

Careful analysis of Lexington Avenue showed that a number of extensions had been built out to the lot line on the street side. The new store, The First of August, could also claim this space, moving the building envelope forward via a two-story addition. The new façade was built of steel tee sections with the stem of each tee arranged outward so the surface of the resulting gridded box was heavily textured. Shaped and sculpted, the new form made associations with the existing brownstone façade: inflections taken from the proportion and arrangement of the original exterior made a strong relationship between the old and new. The completed project was an essay in material sensibility, an elaborate spatial design feeling far larger than the small dimensions of the actual space. Color and light were used to transform the store from reflective material solid in the daytime to a transparent, glowing block of color in the evening. Often compared to Otto Wagner's Die Zeit telegraph shop and to Hans Hollein's Retti candle shop and Schullin jewelry shop, the design resonates with both New York's contemporary built landscape and local traditions of architecture and design.

While travelling in the Midwest in the summer of 1978, soon after the First of August project, while gazing out at the apparently unending, unbroken, flat line of the earth, I came across a manmade canal cutting a swath through a long expanse of land. Struck by the powerful presence of this arrangement, I began documenting the variables that produced it. Eventually I produced a series of drawings exploring the relationship or nexus of a waterway and path intersecting amid a larger site. The place where the axes met struck me as the perfect location for a building. I considered many ideas as the design unfolded, drawing a series of sketches that meditated on variations of site and landscape.

At this time I was contacted by Ace Frehley, of the rock group Kiss, about a house in the Connecticut countryside. He expressed his need for a dwelling that would provide some respite from waking up to find fans pressing their noses against his windows. The house I was already developing seemed ideal for solving the problem of Mr. Frehley's boundary-challenged fans. We looked for a site in Connecticut and found a parcel where a large arc of river allowed for a bypass canal to be cut into the landscape. The house would sit surrounded by canal water with access through an underground passageway leading to stairs cut into the foundation wall. It could be readily built on this site and would meet all the programmatic needs of the client and his family. Although the Frehley House (designed 1979) was not built, the project remains, for me, rich in ideas about the interrelationship of building forms and nature. It was also part of my ongoing research into historic buildings and landscapes such as the Loire Valley houses, with their water systems and gardens, and certain castles in Scotland and elsewhere, with their moats, waterways, and protective encasements. One of the most powerful of these, for me, is the 13th century Caerphilly Castle in Wales, with its island fortress, moat, lake, and other defenses. The Frehley House was my first opportunity to think about the connection of brand-new buildings to landscapes across time.

On the heels of the Frehley House I received a commission for a project that was to further shift my understanding of modern architecture. The Callender School Renovation (1980), the largest project in my office up to that time, transformed my thinking about the role of history in architecture, particularly the way contemporary buildings avoid connection to the history of cities, and indeed to history itself. The client, William E. Boggs, called me one afternoon to say he had purchased the Callender School House, a National Register Landmark Building in Newport, Rhode Island (formerly a school). To complicate matters, he had already interviewed a noted New York architect who had told him and his wife that their collection of original seventeenth- and eighteenth-century furniture would not fit with his plans for the structure and therefore would have to go. On reflection, they decided that the architect should go instead. I was hired after a lengthy interview process.

The clients wished me to reference certain buildings as points of departure for the project: they named the Davanzati Palace (c. late 1400s) in Florence and the Isabella Stewart Gardner Museum (1903) in Boston as especially representative of their interests and desires. I was familiar with both structures, but this was a significant challenge: though I had studied history of architecture with Sibyl Moholy-Nagy, who stressed the importance of architecture being part of its environment, as well as Eduard Sekler, utilizing historic precedents so vigorously had not been part of my academic studio training or my professional apprenticeship.

Upon visiting the Callender School itself, I was compelled by its qualities. First, the building possessed an obvious ability to defy time—no mean feat, after having been exposed to the sea-salty winters of Newport since 1862. Second and more importantly, it had a surprising, quietly eloquent power and authority that arose largely from the weight and heft of its materials. I was not prepared for the impact the Callender School had on my sensibilities. Its commanding presence recalled historic buildings I had seen in Europe, but this was a building I was working on in my office!

When the old interior had been removed, the raw structure of brick, timber, and stone became even more impressive. I had not sensed such gravitas in the presence of more transient materials. At this point I began to move toward an interior design that would acknowledge the power of the original building and remain sympathetic to its sense of history, neither alienating nor diminishing it. The structure itself was forcing me to think about history's role in architecture in a way I had not anticipated.

In addition to its material impact, it stood in a remarkable setting in the city of Newport on the corner of Third and Willow Streets, in a neighborhood of spare but eloquent eighteenth-century wooden houses in the old Point Section. The Callender School fit this context but also stood out as a distinctive public building. I did not fully absorb the lesson it had to teach until somewhat later, but encountering this confluence of town and building and this transition from building to interior was a powerful learning experience that began my reorientation toward the synchrony between buildings and their environments.

The Callender School's newly opened interior volume could, I saw, be converted into an inventive set of apartments that would meet my clients' particular requirements (furniture included) along with five units to be sold to other owners. The final design bridged the original structure with an interior vision that evoked ideas about the history of architecture and how designs originating over time can coexist. I made a set of lush pencil drawings for the project, blending building and landscape into a synchrony of space, time, landscape, and feeling. The interior façades of each unit, designed to resonate with the older portions of the structure, became the living room walls. The owner, Mr. Boggs, played a crucial role in developing the project, provocatively urging his own programmatic requirements and historic references. In every interaction he was a good client—rigorous in his assessment yet totally supportive in seeing the project through to completion, playing a critical role in elaborating the project.

A series of apartment and loft projects followed the Callender School. In almost every case the existing building was a formidable piece of design, usually built at the end of the nineteenth century. In each project I pursued themes of material density, often by using inexpensive materials such as skim-coated drywall. In several projects, more precious materials were included in the material palette. One New York apartment (1982), for example, included a verde antique marble tabletop on a raw steel base. In this early (perhaps first) use of raw, welded steel in open residential space, the table base is fabricated from sheets of steel folded on a press brake machine, welded, and ground smooth. A lacquer finish prevents rust while revealing the steel's mill scale and ground surfaces as the final effect. Juxtaposing raw steel to polished, almost jewel-like green marble heightened my sense of ornament and design in a new and surprising way. This would emerge in subsequent projects as much more elaborate ornamental ideas unfolded.

In the 22nd Street loft project (1986), a dense enclosure, crenellated and fenestrated for views from within and without, was positioned in the existing space to define a master bedroom and study. Although this new enclosure provided the privacy necessary for both spaces, its skim-coated plaster shapes were, in isolation, devoid of the fine-grain detail needed to stand daily review for years to come. To balance these smooth, unornamented forms I suspended a hinged and winged metal canopy above the master bed. The canopy is constructed of uncoated sheet bronze to provide a hint of golden light otherwise lacking in the north-facing loft and is held together by several thousand screws whose exposed heads form a pattern both functional and decorative. The canopy is supported at the wall end on delicate-looking steel posts and above the foot of the bed by stainless-steel cables dropped from the ceiling. Its two wings or sheets, stiffened by internal frames, are hinged and supported lengthwise by a steel tee that runs above the center of the bed and is connected to the sheets by brackets. In the rest of the apartment, the design involved furniture, tables, serving shelves, and other domestic equipment.

The 22nd Street loft thus deepened my engagement with the ornamental aspect of the materiality of buildings. Ornament extends the principles of design to small-scale surface treatments, often utilized to obscure joints and to provide building surface textures. The loft's bronze bed canopy is an investigation of ornament in an interior setting: the screws holding the bronze sheets to the frame also serve as decoration, invigorating the surface and allowing the inhabitants to see the logic and poetry in the arrangement of fasteners. Viewed through the openings of the plaster enclosure from the living room or kitchen, the canopy is seen glowing and as if poised in mid flight.

Each new project has brought to the fore, to be scrutinized and investigated, a different aspect of the dialectic between design and setting. In additions and renovations such as the 22nd Street loft, I have explored the relationship between additions and existing structures. A 1987 project, the G House addition in Scarsdale, New York, expanded the space around a ground-floor living room and kitchen by adding a family room and breakfast room. Calibrated to the rear elevation of the house, the addition makes specific references to the original Westchester, New York structure in a garden-like setting. Terraces are accessed from the master bedroom and hallway leading out to the roof of the new addition. In the Barn Renovation in Redhook, New York (designed 1988, unbuilt), two large forms inserted into a nineteenth-century barn provide family and guest quarters for the owner. Surrounded by hand-hewn structural timbers, these two forms define a variety of spaces, the most dramatic being the living space pressed between them and rising almost thirty-five feet into the rafters. The two separate elements also give form to the building's program, that is, the owner's desire to have one enclosure for the family and another for guests. The two structures were to be raised on columnar elements so that the main living level would appear unencumbered by walls, two floating structures situated amid the structure of the barn.

The strategy for weaving the new design into the structure of the barn was to blur the boundary between old and new. Integration of new and existing forms fused the spaces within, recognizing the experiences of all the building's inhabitants across time without distinction as to which came first. The architecture thus allowed the history of the building's users to take precedence by setting a stage for the unfolding stories, narratives, and histories that have and will take place. Memory became fused with location, a pairing of event and room.

Around 1990, my office received a commission to restore and renovate a 23-story building in the Garment District of Manhattan. At first the project appeared to be a straightforward modernization of a tower on Seventh Avenue that had been in the owner's family since being raised by his grandfather in the 1920s. The Fashion Center Building was built in a Romanesque style with red brick and red terracotta trim. Investigation at the job's outset rediscovered ornate exterior trim that horrible renovations in the 1950s had either destroyed or covered over with bland granite blocks, lowered ceilings, and dull, unadorned material. The first uncovering was a shock; when the workman pulled away the coverings we saw that behind, entombed in the walls, were magnificent ornamental terracotta ornaments, bronze window frames, and other historic artifacts.

The original design was by noted turn-of-the-century architect Henry Ives Cobb. In 1902 Cobb, having completed important works in Chicago, including the University of Chicago campus and many exceptional houses, embarked on the final phase of his career in New York City, which included the zoning studies that would give form to the New York skyline. While in New York he also completed two commissions. The first (1909) was a slender tower of glazed white terracotta on Liberty Street in downtown Manhattan; the second was the Fashion Center Building (1925). The latter supplied rentable garment-center loft spaces filled with milliners, sewing rooms, hat makers, and other garment-related businesses.

Photographs were discovered that revealed some of Cobb's interesting spatial devices, obscured or destroyed since their construction. The original entry sequence featured a large, public open space with soaring ceilings set into the body of the building, just off the sidewalk. This had been boxed in with marble walls covering large windows into commercial spaces, low ceilings, and Herculite glass doors in 1950. The original open-air room had provided a generous space of transition, a respite from the hustle and bustle of Seventh Avenue—a place where colleagues could converse, where friends could arrange to meet, or where one could put up an umbrella before braving a soaking rain. It was the beginning of an elegant entry sequence that was continued by an intermediate lobby and then a radiant main lobby, both also high-ceilinged. A distinguishing feature of this sequence was the outstanding transparency into and through the shops flanking the entrance, which allowed light and visibility into the deep recesses of the lobby. The windows on the street were repeated in the interior walls of the main lobby, allowing light and view-lines to pass from the lobby out onto Seventh

Avenue. After consulting at length with the owners, Marian and James H. Cohen, we decided to restore Cobb's original entry design. This would entail replacing elements both on the ornamental entry arches and in the lobbies, which had been rich in ornamental plaster.

The photos we had found, taken just prior to the 1950 renovation, proved essential to completing the restoration. At times my office looked like a scene in the 1966 Antonioni film Blow-Up, adorned with fragments of the photos enlarged over and over so that particular decorative elements could be seen and drawn. We even enlarged an area of a photo that revealed, reflected in a pane of glass, an animal frieze on the back of an arch.

The most tantalizing part of the project was that here, unlike the Callender School, where the new portions of the project were neatly contained by preexisting walls, history had to coexist in the same rooms. Restorative and contemporary elements had to be deployed without the luxury or artifice of physical separation; both layers of the design would be experienced simultaneously. In the outdoor vestibule, for example, where no evidence remained of the original floor design, the walls and ceiling were filled with decorative red terracotta and large windows opening into shops, making lighting a challenge. I decided to embed the lighting in the new terrazzo floor so that the space would be up-lit at night. New and old thus worked together to produce a memorable effect.

The intermediate lobby was lined with expansive glass and cream- and purple-colored marble, fortunately still intact. Beneath the awful 1950 renovation, many fragments of the original Cobb plaster detailing were also intact. We used these to create a drawing set enabling recreation of the original plaster wall details, ceiling beams, brackets, and arches at the end of each hall.

The main lobby presented the largest challenges of the project. At the each end of this large, long room were identical low-slung arches with ribbed soffits. Reproducing the arch from photographs was complicated, as its low, elliptical curve was unusual and there were few fragments remaining on the walls. The ceiling featured varied decorative floral panels set within beams and brackets held up (visually) by paired columns set against the walls. These columns proved to be the most difficult element of all to reproduce. Ultimately, reproductions were first elaborately drawn, then fabricated using period techniques. The original design was carved in clay, a rubber mold was made of the clay, and the final plaster elements were cast in hemp-reinforced plaster.

The lobby's new focus is a reception desk at the back of the hall. Built of sheet bronze fastened over a frame, the desk presents a varied form, with a highly ornamental texture of screw fasteners and raised lines of bronze culminating in a silver orb in the center of the composition.

When the project was completed, the building's tenancy changed almost overnight. Major players in the garment industry moved in, such as Nicole Miller, Badgley Mischka, Carmelo Pomodoro, and Elie Tahari, to name a few, making the Fashion Center a nexus for some of the most prominent fashion designers on Seventh Avenue.

In the 1990s, several projects came to my office that offered interesting contrasts in scale and completion time. The Union Hardware Company of Osaka, a large hardware firm in Japan, invited me to design a line of architectural hardware for the twenty-first century. The developed line featured three scales of door hardware to be used, respectively, on large front doors, apartment or office doors, and mid-size conference-room doors. These were to be mass-produced in metal, so it was necessary to understand the casting and machining processes that would be used to manufacture the pieces. The design process began in drawings but quickly evolved into cardboard and plaster models, then wooden models, all completed in the office. The designs were submitted to the factory, which also produced a series of models with varying degrees of detail, first in painted wood and then in nylon. Each model varied thicknesses, dimensions, and tolerances, anticipating the needs of manufacture. Finally the first castings were fabricated and sent to us for inspection. The difference in heft between the models and the metal pieces was palpable and important. Small adjustments were made, and the three designs were put into production.

Although this process sounds painstaking, the transition from idea to material seemed nanosecond-fast compared to the making of whole buildings. The rich, rapid feedback from fabrication produced a faster learning experience than the more linear growth of a paper-based building design. Over the years, design projects for hardware and other objects have thus provided a more fluid exchange between idea and execution in a timeframe that allows more comprehension and development than the building process.

For example, I have often designed cabinetwork and furniture as an extension to building and interior designs. These objects are intimately connected to the larger-scale ideas of their environment, and enable me to fulfill a project to the most intimate level of detail. They participate in a family of forms that works across the breadth of a project, from the most expansive scale to the most intricate sensibilities of joinery and craft. These iterations of form are not mere copies or mimicries, but specific shapes developed for their necessary tasks. A good example is the Valentine #2 chair, designed for the G House addition. While the addition was never completed, the chair was fabricated as a prototype. As part of an ensemble including right- and left-hand variations and a table, it was to sit inside a breakfast room connected to an elegant window/skylight configuration. The prototype was first exhibited in a small gallery in SoHo, New York, then incorporated into the permanent Modern and Contemporary Art collection of the Metropolitan Museum of Art in New York.

I have occasionally completed a project by extending its ideas of spatial organization into tableware. In several lines of dinnerware designed for interior projects, I explore the space of the table as a decorative environment. White porcelain plates edged and ornamented with gold leaf give a formal, elegant sense to the dining experience. Among many such investigations, the most extraordinary of these designs arose from an invitation to create a wine goblet for the Murano Glass Factory in Venice, Italy. The glass was designed on a slightly oversized scale to establish a presence at the table. Hand-blown by Venetian artisans, it is encrusted with amethyst chips that provide both texture to the touch and an opulent sensation to the eye as liquid is poured. Each such project is an opportunity to explore form, space, and fabrication at a faster pace than buildings generally allow. The rapid, exploratory design process opens new and exciting possibilities for the product, provides feedback about form and material, and allows for excursions into areas not possible with buildings or interiors.

My work includes many furniture designs for apartments, lofts, and office interiors; in some cases, though a space was not completed or has since been changed, prototypes still exist. For example, in 1986 I was invited to participate in the XVII Triennale di Milano expo. This exhibit, held in Milan's vast Palazzo dell'Arte exhibit hall (by Giovanni Muzio, 1933), was structured to question the new domestic landscape: architects and designers were asked to design new domestic space for the coming millennium. A chair I designed as a prototype for a loft residence in New York and put into limited production in Udine was placed on view in the Triennale domestic exhibit. I also designed a residential space for the Triennale itself. This space was an essay on the notion of converting old industrial space, the "loft," into a new residential model. Instead of bringing an alternate reality into the gallery, I utilized the gallery's actual space, building a program on the enclosure, openings, and circulation of the gallery to fabricate a dwelling within its confines. The exterior was hermetic and protective, while the interior had rooms and furniture integrally designed to be more open and expressive and to take advantage of available windows and natural light. The exhibit offered me an opportunity to step back and deepen my thinking about architecture, interior design, and furniture as a simultaneous experience. After the exhibit finished its course in Milan, the residence and chair were shipped to Udine for permanent installation.

Exhibit design has been an important component of my practice. On several occasions I have been not only an exhibit designer but a member of the curatorial team, and these have been particularly stimulating. In the Frank Lloyd Wright exhibit at the Whitney Museum of American Art in New York and the Carlo Scarpa exhibit at the Canadian Center for Architecture in Montreal, my office built a series of analytic models to interpret both built and unbuilt works of each architect. For the Wright exhibit, models of Wright's work indicated his startling capacity to visualize his architecture in the immense scale of the American landscape. In some cases there were only fragmentary sketches to work from and the models were constructed from sketches on topographic maps, small perspectives, and other fragmentary information. Rendered in drape-molded wood veneers, they were produced to an exacting degree of craft and finish because we felt it important that the interpretive models have the same elemental power as the architectural concepts they were representing.

The Scarpa models were larger, illustrating the exquisite care with which Scarpa inserted his additions, renovations, and new buildings into the ancient cityscapes of Italy. These models paid particular attention to the exacting nature of Scarpa's detail, joinery, and ability to reinterpret history. In the two installations the galleries were treated very differently, for each gallery space is a site, that is, a condition of space to be reckoned with in particular terms. The space of each museum thus helped to determine the approach taken to the exhibit design. Exhibits are wonderful moments to think about design strategies that can be executed in real space quickly, convincingly, and with direct material sensibility.

In 1995 my office began work on a loft apartment on West 15th Street, the K Loft. The owners, artists Robert Kirschbaum and Jacque Metheny, had lived in the loft for some time without much alteration to the original space. While the loft was spatially expansive and rich in heavy masonry, the couple found themselves facing a space problem, like many other couples expecting a child. Should the apartment be carved into little private spaces, or should a more expansive vision be preserved? The couple's directive was clear: accommodate the programmatic necessities of domestic privacy while maintaining the openness of the loft.

Windows appeared only at the front and back, the apartment's long, narrow volume being framed by solid brick walls and a vaulted brick ceiling. I began the dialogue between the brick container and the volumes to be placed within it by choosing a warm palette of materials that would enable each element to complement the other. Skim-coated plaster volumes would define new living spaces, pierced by frosted-glass infills to allow for perception of the spaces within while preserving privacy. The project includes plywood panels, applied predominantly to plaster corners both for protection and to alter the scale of the forms. These panels are cut in an interlocked pattern to develop a finer grain of scale with the space and are applied to the walls with four-quadrant screw fastener sets. The process of merging the new design with the powerful brick room was a delicate operation that ultimately counted on the depth and density of the masonry to anchor the lighter, more open aspects of the new enclosures.

Public projects have always held a strong position in my office. Several have taken the form of competitions inviting investigation of the private citizen's relationship to public space; these have included The Peak, the Paris Opera Competition, and the Times Tower competition. In each project we have explored the architectural program as an instrument of social change. In 1999, for example, the New York City Housing Authority awarded me a commission to design an addition to a community center at the Saratoga Houses in Brooklyn. David Burney, then the Housing Authority's Director of Design, was looking to award projects to design-minded firms with the goal of delivering quality buildings to underserved populations. For my own part, to design public buildings for New York City was a longstanding goal of my practice; New York's legacy of public buildings is a proud heritage, and these buildings are often the first contact persons have with any city institution.

Several ideas drove the design of the Saratoga Avenue Community Center from the outset. Small buildings had inhabited the original site but were demolished in the 1960s to make room for a 16-story slab-housing block. As at many such sites, the rupture between superblock and small-scale city texture had been a jarring occurrence: a barren, windswept space had been left between the new building and its neighbors, and over the next 40 years had not improved. If anything, it became an ever more indefensible, unguarded space subject to being overrun and abused. In stark contrast, the next block over had Saratoga Park, a magnificent, block-long, public green space filled with huge oak trees and surrounded by brownstones. To revisit and re-imagine the condition of this site, where a residential superblock had been imposed on the small-scale urban fabric, was a wonderful occasion to revise a clumsy twentieth-century intervention.

Although the size of the new Community Center was relatively small, it was possible to use the new structure to heal the wound the superblock had created in the city and to enhance the presence of Saratoga Park. The new building is close to Hancock Street, allowing the establishment of a large, public, semi-enclosed garden at the rear of the complex, while Saratoga Park sits comfortably surrounded by three and four story row houses a block to the west. The new garden thus makes a strong landscape connection to the surrounding area by linking up with the existing park. The client (David Burney) and I had many discussions about the necessary adjustments, inflections, and specific references to the varied conditions of the site that the Community Center might make. He was skeptical that such a small building could achieve all this. However, after he visited the finished site, he remarked at the building's agility in fulfilling all the premises I had discussed with him.

Among its other roles, the new building was to be part of the legacy of public buildings that have traditionally symbolized the City of New York. This meant designing it to be recognizable as part of the historical continuum. In so doing, I revisited the idea of a building's expression and stature as defined by the material, position, composition, and ornament that create its essence.

My basic strategy for the Saratoga Community Center was to have the building fully define the street. It would feature a small-scale outdoor courtyard in the front, while the back elevation would open onto a large semi-enclosed garden that would merge with Saratoga Park. As the design took shape, I provided a large public room, clearly visible from both inside the building and out, as the main focal part of the composition. This room accommodates the project's key program functions. At the entry on Hancock Street, a small courtyard accommodates the people entering the building from both the street and the main housing block. The smaller rooms of the program are located on this elevation both to provide security for the entrance and to reduce the scale of the building on this more intimate space. The Director's office is placed in front of the larger mass of the main social room and on axis with the entry, providing both security and a smaller-scale space. On the garden side of the building, the elevation is much longer and is fitted with two entrances. There is a small set of doors opposite the Hancock Street entry so that tenants and visitors can enter from both sides. Two very large doors allow the main room, which is often used for parties, celebrations, and other activities, to open onto the outdoor space in good weather, enabling events to use the garden. From these doors one can see the edge of Saratoga Park, permitting users—mostly tenants—to see their garden as an extension of the larger public park space.

The Saratoga building is clad in masonry materials chosen to evoke the feel and tone of a public building. Elongated iron-spot, buff-colored brick is the main exterior material, with a limestone base and glass-fiber-reinforced casting-stone copings, lintels, and ornamental features to lend the structure a presence that satisfies the cultural norm for public architecture. Fully visible beams and columns of structural steel accentuate the free-floating effect of the roof as seen from outside, strongly suggesting the space and light within the main room. This is the building's dominant feature, around which smaller volumes situate the building in its place. These spatial gestures may seem small, but in fact transform what would be an otherwise awkward and ungainly volume into a connected, contextually situated set of forms, communicating that the building is at once public and neighborly. This compositional device—which was common practice in previous generations of architects—can be utilized to mitigate the differences between small-scale residential environments and the larger, institutional, and somewhat more abstract nature of public buildings.

The Saratoga Community Center brings a new vision of the positive role of public architecture into a community setting. The structure both represents the City of New York and gives credibility to the community's program and sense of self. During the design process there were direct meetings with the residents, often led by Damon Fuseyamore, President of the Saratoga Village Association. He and the Association's other members were extremely helpful as well as excited to be working with such enlivened ideas of urbanity and public construction. In addition to drawings and elaborate models, we often brought material samples to meetings for tenants to see and feel. Association members were thrilled at the final results, affirming the structure as an important contribution to revitalization of the neighborhood and to the community's effort to establish a strong, positive residential presence in the area.

The Saratoga Community Center supports its community by enriching its members' lives and honoring their presence. It meets the needs of the inhabitants' everyday activities while providing a central symbol that represents them with grace, dignity, and distinction.

Completion of the Center opened a new chapter in the work I have pursued over the last thirty years, a chapter that blends my experiences in music (which I discuss further below) and architecture in ways both surprising and exciting. Saratoga gave me a chance to rethink ideas that had been circulating through my work at the urban, architectural, and interior levels. It prompted me to seek a still clearer alternative to architecture that is out of touch with, or in open defiance of, its historic environment. It strengthened my conviction that this is the right time to re-imagine the premises of Modernism vis-à-vis how we respond to our cities and how buildings ultimately fit into them. Many of these premises have had, it seems to me, a deleterious effect on that sense of place which hitherto so clearly imprinted itself upon our built world. But if we abandon them, where do we go next? There must be a place free from the polarities of architecture's current theoretical landscape, a middle ground between historicism and compulsive novelty, a way to remain connected to both the present and the historic continuum of culture and form.

The notion of a middle ground between historicism and compulsive novelty seems like an appropriate starting point for a new body of theory and practice, one that will bridge the world of the past to the promise of the future. The job will not be easy; it is always difficult to make a fresh contribution to architecture while remaining connected to history.

Teaching

Through all my time in practice, I have also held an academic position in an architecture school. The academy has enabled me to isolate particular projects or parts of the learning experience and put them in experimental settings in order to study and develop them further.

As I reflect on my experience of design while preparing curricula, it is clear that at least two agendas—an "inner," creative agenda and an "external," theoretical agenda—are, in practice, always in simultaneous operation, and that each needs to be examined individually before being integrated into a unified work of architecture. The art of architecture requires that the designer oscillate between the inspirational and the analytical modes with dexterity. My teaching approach, therefore, is to focus on both internal creative principles and external theoretical issues. Studio assignments can be particularly effective at focusing attention both on the internal experience of learning a complex craft and on the social, political, and theoretical issues touched upon by a project, so I focus on these assignments as a teaching tool. Certain studio problems are deliberately geared to the exposure of architectural, theoretical, or social concerns.

In learning music, a student is not asked to compose a symphony and then perform it publicly in the first year of music education. There are studies in composition and music theory, and kinesthetic exercise—practice—is critical. These elements are finally synthesized into coherent works of music. In architectural education, similarly, the student must practice both the individual tasks and the integrative acts of making architecture. To externalize design ideas, it is crucial to first become aware of compositional techniques while acquiring manual dexterity in drawing and model-making. These techniques can be explored through basic exercises in form, composition, space, structure, and other compositional themes that foster the making of spaces.

Next, the architectural program, the idea of utility, must be folded into the methodology. A simple program is introduced into the formal exercises, forcing the student to come simultaneously to terms with two of the basic parameters involved in the essence of architecture. With each new study, more criteria are included—technology, structure, construction, budget—until the student can accommodate all the parameters involved in producing architecture.

Previous architectural education systems, such as that of the École des Beaux Arts, addressed the historical dimension of architecture by having students visit ancient sites, measure the ruins, and accurately draw what they saw. They were then required to depict the original, un-ruined structures and to speculate on the history and program of the architecture. This approach, rooted in historical accuracy, worked quite well to incorporate the history of architecture into an adaptable methodology that could serve the contemporary programs in the nineteenth century. Similarly, I felt that in modern architectural education it was imperative for a form of historical analysis to take place, but not as an isolated history lesson: rather, it should occur as a vibrant part of the architectural studio sequence. Therefore, early in the study sequence, I introduced historical analysis to bring the creative process into alignment with the idea that architecture is a socially and culturally derived art form, part of a centuries-old continuum, that must reconcile itself with society.

At the beginning of each semester, then, each of my students is assigned a masterwork of architecture loosely related to the project they would ultimately design. The student makes a full set of documenting drawings and then builds an elaborate three-dimensional model, usually with some analytic operation performed to make visible an otherwise hidden aspect of the project. The analytic model is crucial to helping students understand what essential characteristics make these works extraordinary, enabling them to comprehend fully the spatial, structural, and hierarchical relationships present in the masterwork. The exercise banishes all ambiguity and focuses the student's attention on the exceptional resolution of these works. It also initiates students into the intense craft of exceptional objects: as the students struggle with the task of building a comprehensive yet sensual model, there is a hidden transmission of what it takes to make extraordinary objects by hand.

The analytic model exercise thus serves at least two pedagogical purposes. First, it moves the students to a level of production that is free from pressure to be creative but where manual dexterity, craft, and observational skills can be developed and a thorough understanding of a master-level work can be achieved. Second, it implicitly sets a standard for the student's own work by presenting a model of excellence and encouraging them to perceive it—through grappling with the dimension, measure, and scale of its components—more deeply than could be achieved by listening to lectures and looking at photographs and plans. The masterwork is demystified, in the sense that the student comes to understand exactly what makes the work so successful.

The next phase of the semester involves one or several form problems that are again loosely tied to the site and program of the student's upcoming project. The exercise is designed to facilitate two important aspects of the studio. First, the students are required to define a real and substantial relationship to the given site of the exercise. Although the project is a 1:1-scale exercise in pure form, not an architectural design project per se, the assigned "site" does bear a striking resemblance to a city building site, and the existing shapes are tectonically similar to buildings. The students are directed to work on solutions to these programs, usually a spatial sequence or structural hierarchy, while paying definite attention to material, craft, and joinery to ameliorate the differences between the given context and their projects. This helps ensure their attention to situating their project comfortably in a city setting. Second, the students are required to provide a closure or a façade for the site, which again has to respond to the adjacent property (part of the given landscape).

Having been armed by the masterwork study and the form problem with two key aspects of the design process, namely historical memory and creative problem-solving, students are now prepared to design an architectural work. That is, they are equipped to think in architectural terms; they can grasp the manifold, dynamic forces at play in such work. I now assign a complex program, usually an institutional building, to start students on the journey of working out a comprehensive solution to a bona fide architectural problem. I choose the site, usually urban, for its architectural relevance and the directly adjacent presence of a major historical building. This analytic provocation, coupled with the previous masterwork-analysis exercise, encourages the students to implicitly think of their own work as on an equal footing with the masterworks. Juxtaposition with an historical building also prompts the student to consider resolving their project to a higher level of detail (possibly including ornament), reflecting that of the precedent building. I select the analytic subjects to illustrate how previous architects fit their buildings comfortably into their environments.

Although never stated explicitly, the goal of historical analysis is to infuse the student's own architecture with the qualities of the analyzed works. In practice, each student extrapolates from the reference buildings that motivate and excite him or her. The results are never merely imitative but always poised in a new direction, informing the student's production throughout the semester.

Externalizing an architectural idea is a lengthy and sometimes circuitous journey. Multiple studies, nuanced variations, careful analysis, and inspirational moments are in dynamic interplay, constantly shifting in emphasis and relationship depending on where one is in the process. The longer I teach, the more clearly I see that students tend to show up with strongly held beliefs and desires at the level of theory, but intellectually outpace their manual ability. Many students are predisposed to "think through" an architectural challenge in the abstract; it takes them a good part of each semester to learn that it is essential to make, view, and evaluate drawings and models, "thinking" through making and seeing as well as through an intellectual process. I therefore direct students to complete each physical task, evaluate it, speculate afresh, and then make a new set of drawings and models.

As I discovered in my own design process, the model is a key item in the arsenal of design tools. Designing in the model is difficult but worth the effort. Each student grapples with three-dimensional studies, sketch plans, and modeling, but always with the model providing the primary ideas of the scheme. Following this approach, ideas proliferate geometrically, rather than linearly. Multiple design studies produce an explosion of material in a short period of time, and more complex and well-resolved projects appear earlier in the semester. This enables students to complete a more finely worked-out project in the same number of weeks.

For students from excellent but academically driven schools, and those who do not have art backgrounds, this can be a novel and frustrating process of discovery. Once they engage it, however, they make great leaps as they master a method that allows them to access their vision and externalize it fluently.

Early in my career as both teacher and architect I struggled to devise a teaching methodology that would help me come to grips with my own design process while helping my students tap their own inner premises to fashion an architecture belonging to their unique vision. Observing real buildings is integral to theoretical speculation within the discipline, and an inherent component of the architectural learning process; deep, analytic assessment transforms one's ideas of social, artistic, and technical theory in ways that can be applied to new designs. In learning to teach, which entailed repeated reassessment of existing buildings, I was therefore inevitably reorganizing my own theoretical position. Constant participation in critiques of contemporary architecture in institutional and historical settings, coupled with my own observations of the built legacy of the last century, caused me to reevaluate early on how we place buildings in settings.

Thoughts on Recent Architecture

At Harvard, I spent many hours as a graduate student in the Carpenter Center (1962) by Le Corbusier (1887–1965). Time after time I found myself standing on Carpenter's ramp, yet consumed by a building on the other side of Quincy Street, Sever Hall (1880) by H. H. Richardson (1838–1836). The presence of the building, already about a century old, was stately and profound. Thousands of molded bricks formed many of the simple yet potent details that marked the building as exceptional, especially the broad arch that opens generously toward Harvard Yard—and, of course, no Richardson building would be complete without the low, slit-window roof openings that he made so popular. What is more, Sever Hall stood in remarkably good condition, unharmed by the freeze-thaw cycles of many harsh Boston winters.

I would stand transfixed by the apparition of this building, engulfed by its power to be both eminently of its time and yet a harmonious part of present-day Harvard Yard. Carpenter Center, behind me, still did not fit comfortably into its surroundings after more than 40 years, having been deliberately rotated out of alignment with the other buildings in the Yard. It was materially dissonant, too, being made of cast concrete that had already taken on the stained, gray, drab color that concrete cannot escape. Despite Carpenter's formal intensity, I felt bereft of feeling for the building. It was totally and deliberately out of sync with its environment.

Much other architecture I observed in the 1980s and 1990s also seemed unsettling and unsatisfactory. In visiting many revered modern buildings, I came away feeling unsympathetic and disappointed. This compelled me to revisit my understanding of architecture's symbolic, formal, and social nature, beginning with the work of several architects who had found a way to relate to the urban and landscape context without either sacrificing originality or mimicking context. Among the architects I began to re-evaluate were H. H. Richardson, Louis Sullivan, Frank Lloyd Wright, Louis Kahn, and Carlo Scarpa. All these architects had designed works linked to the specifics of place through a style of composition that was casual—almost picturesque—yet rigorously clear in organization and form. They offered an important alternative to the oppositional mode exemplified by some of the later works of Ludwig Mies van der Rohe and by works of architects who applied Mies's theories with less rigor and success than the master. These architects cast crystalline forms into urban settings in direct opposition to the stone buildings around them—their glass skins ever cheaper, their details ever fewer.

Further study of Richardson and the others revealed not only conceptual clarity but a deep interest in texture and detail. In each of their structures there are expressive moments, rich elements of ornament, detail, and pattern, that reflect on the history of architecture while yet being startlingly new. Unification of structure with site was achieved in large part through alertness to those small interventions that can fit a structure comfortably to its place. These rely not on mimicry or material association, mere sameness of color, texture, or detail, but on an ability to keep the overarching concept clear while taking subtle cues from the particularity of each site.

Over years of observation and reflection, I thus came to feel that there is a deep dichotomy in modern architecture: on one side, what impressed me as the object-dominant ideology of a majority of Modernists, and on the other a more sophisticated and complex program, an attempt to extend the historical continuum in situ.

Foremost among the modern architects who have struck me as having a particular genius for the latter type of architecture is H. H. Richardson (1838–1886), whose work was inventive yet proved remarkably compatible with other buildings of the era and of subsequent decades, though at the time it may have appeared disparate. Richardson worked assiduously to rework, transpose, and transform his architecture by combining Beaux Arts planning with medieval forms, the result being a personal vocabulary of form. He reinvented the language of architecture, transforming the moribund designs of his day into the enlivened, rich, and highly ornamented style often referred to as Richardson Romanesque. Several of his works exemplify a planning methodology that adjusts the staid symmetry of a main space or building to the asymmetry of a site by means of ancillary or secondary structures and spaces. One such project is Trinity Church in Copley Square, Boston (1877).

The site, an irregular trapezoid, posed a unique challenge: how to accommodate the radically different dimensions of narrow front and wide back. Richardson's deft solution transitions from highly formal central spaces and building forms to more casual and asymmetric, almost picturesque, spaces. The main church is poised on axis with Copley Square, presenting an elegant main façade to the urban plaza. Moving clockwise around the building, the main axis of the church remains legible as one approaches the parish house and sacristy, whose forms are utilized to fill out the wider portion of the eccentric site. A colonnaded stair cascades up and around the parish house to its foyer. Moving still further, one sees, tethered by the stair on the front and a cloistered arcade at the back, a small courtyard that separates the church from the smaller outbuildings.

This exemplifies Richardson's method of accommodating highly organized axial spaces to eccentric site conditions and complex contexts by means of seemingly casual, random, and picturesque assemblages. Many of Richardson's buildings, both residential and institutional, manifest these compositional devices, though not all feature extended outbuildings. A subtle example is Austin Hall on the Harvard campus, where the placement of a stair and tower just to the right of the multi-columned entry provides a counterpoint to the axis and symmetry of the façade. This counterpoint keeps the building from feeling overly formal without simply defying the many serious-minded buildings of Harvard. This light touch has worked well for the building, as the college campus becomes an increasingly informal space. More precise and classical buildings now feel overbearing, while Austin Hall does not.

Richardson's strategy is worked out in exquisite detail in the Glessner House (1887), a single-family dwelling in Chicago that perfectly exemplifies the architect's incredible capability to resolve the split between formal and informal. Situated on the corner of South Prairie Avenue and East 18th Street in Chicago, the building occupies a corner-lot position in the cityscape. The site strategy was to provide a hard edge to the two streets while defining a softer interior courtyard of undulating, curved shapes. The distinct character of the exterior walls versus the courtyard walls heightens the building's contextual relationship: rough-hewn exterior granite relate to adjacent buildings

while the interior court is faced with softer, rounded-brick forms. The U-plan house presents a main entrance on one of its short sides, the left-hand stem of the U. From this side the house appears at first glance axial to S. Prairie Avenue, with a rustic arch above a heavy center door flanked by symmetric arrays of windows and openings; however, there is an extra bay of openings at the far left of the elevation, breaking the symmetry. Circling to the right on East 18th Street, one perceives that the house has a long side elevation (the bottom of the U). This exterior street façade, like its partner on South Prairie Avenue, is fabricated of heavy cut stone penetrated by a number of fenestrations. Along this side of the house there is also an asymmetric arch, which offers an opening into the wall but then diverts the caller to a flight of stairs, within the body of the house but still open to the outside, which ascends to the second floor. Directly on the opposite side of this wing, Richardson organizes one of the main rooms of the house at the midpoint of the long wall of the courtyard (recalling the church façade at the Certosa del Galluzzo). Here and in other projects he utilizes every compositional device to expand and enliven the journey from the street to the interior, and so roots his buildings in their immediate surroundings.

Louis Sullivan (1856–1924) developed Richardson's compositional strategies in many works, including the Auditorium Building (1889) and Carson, Pirie, Scott and Company Building (1904) in Chicago, the Guaranty Building in Buffalo (1894), and others. In a series of "jewel box" bank buildings designed toward the end of his career, Sullivan excelled in the use of ornament, detail, and associative design. These banks—the People's Federal Savings and Loan (1917) in Sidney, Ohio, the Merchants' National Bank (1914) in Grinnell, Iowa, and the National Farmer's Bank (1908) in Owatonna, Minnesota, to name a few—are remarkable triumphs of design, each occupying a corner site in a small town and utilizing ornamental motifs to make a significant and effective association between structure and setting. Sullivan clearly establishes a connection to the town while elevating the symbolic power of the bank as an ornamented, protective enclave of citizens' money at the community's center.

Merchants' National Bank in Grinnell is one of the clearest examples of this eloquent urban and architectural strategy. Though only two stories high, the building appears larger and is filled with expressive power. The design presents a large-scale brick block on a corner defined by the long and short sides of the building. On the short side, a large, square, ornamented figure of buff terracotta elements is affixed in the middle of an otherwise blank wall above the main entrance. Within the square there is a circular shape and within that a rotated square, all ornamented with Sullivan's floral motifs.

On the long side of the bank, also a large brick mass, a rectangular incision is made and a row of golden columns appears. Within this field there is a beautiful, leaded window-wall of pale white, blue, and green translucent glass that sheds multicolored light on the banking room inside. Around the top of the building, unifying the two elevations, a red terracotta cornice connects the bank to adjacent existing structures despite its originality of design. With this dual strategy firmly in place—outstanding, yet connected—the building is free to oscillate between the background and foreground of the townscape, to be at once connected to the town of Grinnell and transported by a few deft and remarkable elements into the exceptional range of architecture.

Frank Lloyd Wright (1867–1959), evolving the ideas of Richardson and Sullivan, surpassed even his brilliant predecessors in fitting each project to its situation, playing off symmetry and asymmetry with astonishing results. One only need look at such projects as the Unity Temple (1906), Midway Gardens (1914), or Robie House (1910) to see Wright's ordering principles at work. Despite the formally axial overall appearance of each design, all these buildings develop asymmetric, more casual associations to their entry conditions or nearby buildings. In the Robie house, for example, seen straight on from outside, the plan makes the living room and dining room appear axially connected in a direct and formal relationship. As seen from the street corner, however, the house appears untethered or floating. Moreover, at the back of the house a cascade of rooms, corridors, and a motor court lies cheek by jowl with the next house over, right up to the property line. Wright had a profound understanding of how to use context to create not only an iconic building but a structure that appeared to have grown out of its place. His ability to delicately site each building in an appropriate and mediated relationship to its context is manifest throughout his diverse career.

Let us tie together what has been said so far. It has seemed to me, throughout my career, that there are two basic strains of modern architecture with distinct attitudes toward the relationship of buildings to their environment. The dominant strain, typified by the work of Mies van der Rohe, takes an oppositional or contrapositional stance. In many American cities, new buildings have appeared that are out of sympathy with a local sense of place carefully constructed over generations. In my opinion we are still in the throes of this approach, heavily involved in making object-buildings with little regard for the places where they are built and the outdoor spaces that they shape. Current theoretical positions seem to prefer searching for forms that are purely formal, and to have a bent toward novelty as such. The resulting buildings have a difficult time making civic connections in Boston, Chicago, San Francisco, and other places having clear local identity. Over five decades or so, the effect has been to infuse a certain sameness into many American cities and institutional settings. In almost any city, one may see a vast difference between the architecture of decades past and that of many newer buildings, which demand recognition of their novelty. I do not advocate for nostalgia, but for a theoretical position that can better accommodate issues of continuity, engaging in dialogue with the historic past while remaining inventive and original in its concepts of form, space, and program.

Starting in the late nineteenth century, architects belonging to what I think of as the Richardson-Sullivan-Wright lineage, the second basic strain of modern architecture, produced unique buildings that explored novel programs and structural forms while paying close attention to setting and incorporating ornament as an integrative element. By the mid twentieth century, however, exponents of such architecture were fewer. Perhaps the most important in this period were Louis I. Kahn (1902–1974) and Carlo Scarpa (1906–1978). Kahn tried at first to embody the values and principles of modern, light, thin, glass curtain-wall architecture, but the results were not, in my opinion, particularly well resolved. His early buildings were ungainly and unsure and did not project a strong feeling about their materials. Nor did this work embody the Beaux Arts education that Kahn had received at the hand of the noted architect and teacher Paul Philippe Cret (1876–1945). It was after a stay at the American Academy in Rome that Kahn discovered the sensibility he longed for, a way of recasting the history of architecture in an idiosyncratic modern-classic language while linking his buildings to a timeless tradition. His great later works were able to incorporate a strong sense of timelessness, reflecting the full weight and maturity of his metaphysics of space. In re-creating and re-inventing the meaning of public space, he succeeded in linking modern forms to the elemental past.

Hearing Kahn make his argument about the "servant" and "served" spaces of architecture could often be baffling, but his built projects made the idea crystal clear. As he grappled with the messy and often disruptive structural and mechanical-services aspects of buildings, he saw that these could produce the thickness, mass, and density he so desired. Instead of trying to hide these mechanical and structural aspects in corners and crevices, he gave them weight and presence and used them to help organize his architecture. Although such mechanical systems are typically hollow, Kahn expressed them as thickened parts of the structure, organizing the mass of the architecture into a palpable, opaque presence, mysterious yet light-filled—as had existed in all the timeless buildings from the Pantheon forward. In Dhaka, the shade devices provided by the concrete enclosing screens defined interior voids of light. Although his architecture has often been criticized for the opaqueness of its elevations, said to be mute or to lack expression other than as a by-product of structure and service, it did argue for a reconsideration of modern theory in favor of an architecture connected to the continuum of history. Kahn left the question of how to relate the idea of façade to the structure of the building largely unanswered in any symbolic sense, but it can be argued that in the Dacca Complex (1974) he brought a degree of ornament to the surface of the government assembly building, with marble inlays relieving the otherwise brutalist concrete finish and large triangular cutouts.

Contemporary with Kahn was Carlo Scarpa, whose architecture resolved the question Kahn had implicitly tried to pose. Scarpa not only excelled to an astonishing degree in imbuing façade with significance but was also a master of interior space and of situating his buildings within profoundly important historical contexts, as shown by the Olivetti showroom (1959) in the Piazza San Marco, Venice and by the Banca Popolare (1973) in the Piazza Nogara, Verona. In both these projects, Scarpa linked interior to façade and endowed the outside surface of the building with a lyrical power that, though striking on its own terms, was yet very much in conversation with the façades around it. While Ignazio Gardella, Carlo Aymonino, and later Aldo Rossi were busy exploring social politics and housing, Scarpa was investigating a poetics of space, form, and surface that was both more contemporary and yet more rooted in the craft of eras gone by.

One of Scarpa's earliest projects, yet also a work of exceptional maturity, the Castelvecchio Museum (1959–1973) in Verona was predominately a renovation of a highly modified fifteenth-century castle built on Roman ruins. Scarpa surgically transformed each part of the structure, imparting a sense of order and particularity. For example, typical gallery designs of the period featured mostly neutral backdrops, but Scarpa placed vibrantly colored Venetian fresco plaster behind antique art works. By challenging the supposed objectivity of the bland, he was able for the first time in decades to deliver a new sensibility to ornament in modern design. This sensibility was also manifested in Scarpa's other projects of this period, as he brought back texture, color, pattern, and figure to the vertical surface. The sheer amount of time that Scarpa lavished on the elevation of a project as an expressive agent in architecture is clear in his luscious elevation study drawings.

Scarpa's Canova Plaster Cast Gallery (1957) in Possagno is elegantly situated among its historic neighbors. Folded against the original Canova exhibit building, the new wing adjusts itself to the larger structure while also forming the edge of the town and a new piece of a street. Scarpa's approach succeeded most impressively in the Banca Popolare in Verona and the Brion Cemetery (1972) in San Vito d'Altivole. In both projects Scarpa, unlike most practitioners of his day, brought history to the fore. The Brion complex is embedded in a row of mausolea at the back wall of the cemetery of San Vito d'Altivole; the new design extends the existing cemetery yet transcends its mundane organization, reinterpreting the stereotyped landscape of death and eternity into a pure poetry of material, form, and surface. The interplay between life and death in many aspects of the composition bespeaks Scarpa's desire to communicate with the depths of the psyche in every detail. In addition, the clients, Giuseppe and Onorina Brion, were owners of the noted Brionvega industrial design company in Italy, which produced some of the landmark design objects of the twentieth century. Scarpa designed headstones and objects that were truly astonishing in their finish, form, and meaningfulness in association with the Brion family.

In contrast, the Banca Popolare presents a startling façade on the Piazza Nogara. While the Castelvecchio project entailed small-scale contemporary additions to an ancient building, the Banca Popolare is a compelling new building with dual façades, one facing a public square and the other a garden. Scarpa was allowed to build this new building in one of the most sacred of Italian cities, where modern construction is not casually permitted to disturb longstanding traditions. He achieved a profound balance, bringing a powerful historical memory into the present through a complex method of associative meanings. By attending to the ornamental features on the façade, he delivered a building that resonated with the architecture of Verona. The most outstanding feature of the design is an exquisite stucco façade impregnated with Verona red marble dust, an immediate link to the region. Embedded in the surface and crossing the façade horizontally is an intricate three-dimensional molding made of Verona red marble. Above this is a set of rectangular windows, and above that five circular windows, all designed to lyrically denote the thickness of the wall and provide light to the interior. The focus of the wall, however, is the moment where the molding drops down to make way for the totemic entry door. This large, bronze, sliding panel is set within the composition of the façade and asymmetrically located. Overall, the façade is magical in its recuperative ability to align this striking contemporary design with the values and integrity of Verona. Scarpa was able to present an invigorated building that is at once new and old, able to sit within the cultural context of a historic city.

Inspirations

The feeling that there are two basic types of modern architecture, a place-defying type and a collaborative or integral type, has struck me with special force in light of my musical experience. From 1963 to 1974, before becoming an architect, I worked as a professional jazz and pop percussionist. Ensemble playing, as I learned from my performances with Toots Thielemans, Etta James, and others, is an intense group experience: a number of highly trained individuals with great creativity and technical prowess must blend their talents to make music. Familiar songs or melodies establish a base for communication between players, but as the music cooks along, each musician is encouraged to perform innovative solos. These are held together by the rhythm section or by the piano's comping chords, which provide bottom and feeling. It is an electrifying, intoxicating sensation to compose with other musicians on site, as it were—on the bandstand, in real time. A sort of spontaneous combustion is sparked by the signals that pass between musicians: sometimes a mere wink is the cue to fill a space or to lay back, eliciting a response that enlarges and develops the composition. Balance between the individual and the group is key.

Unfortunately, it is not a given. Over the years I worked with a number of technically competent musicians who could not swing or who, despite their high level of musical invention, could not connect to the audience or the ensemble. For my own part, I tried to remain aware of the need not only to improvise as an individual, but to be present in the room and remain intimately connected to the group.

In retrospect, it seems clear that in learning to be an architect I was drawn to a compositional dynamic similar to that of live music. The connection between music and architecture is, for me, in that dynamic linkage of individual to group, often mediated by slight cues or details, which allows a high level of personal invention while still enabling the group to make a unified sound. Given my musical background, I could not but question the underpinnings of much modern architectural theory, especially its refusal to connect new designs to existing cities and landscape features. A building should collaborate with the players around it, not ignore or override them. The structures of a campus or city should swing together, not raise a cacophony of clashing solos. Music is performed best when everyone is both a soloist and background musician in alternating patterns; architecture is at its best when each building can be both idiosyncratic and an integral part of the dynamic cityscape.

The importance of such collaboration became even more apparent to me, early in my career, as I explored the cities and landscapes of Europe, especially England and Italy, reexamining the built legacy of our culture. In particular, the pertinence of site and context to new institutional buildings became intensely clear. I saw an amazing range of complexes where new public buildings had been integrated into beautiful vernacular environments, and was constantly struck by the obvious ability of their architects to marry disparate entities into cogent and clear city forms.

Siena, for example, is constructed almost entirely of light-brown (sienese) brick. Out of this pile of warm masonry rises the Duomo or cathedral (1263). The Duomo is casually composed into the city fabric on two sides, while its front, covered in a rich composite of religious statuary and ornate decorative relief and textured in a white and green horizontal marble pattern, is open to a small public space. The building's vibrant pattern, texture, and color immediately set it apart from the vernacular, yet some of its horizontal striping is wrapped around lower portions of adjacent structures, pulling it into the city fabric. Thus, although the Duomo is instantly legible as the primary religious building of the city, pains were taken to reconcile its color,

material, and form with the texture of its surroundings. So seamless is the transition that when you stand in the piazza it is hard to see exactly where church ends and city begins.

The Duomo of Pisa (1092) occupies a quite different but equally satisfying position in the city texture. The Piazza del Duomo, at the heart of the city, is an open public space partly covered by a grassy lawn, unusual for Italian cities. Backed against one of the old city walls, the piazza complex is primarily defined by the Campo Santo, containing 84 Roman sarcophagi and other works. A long, blank, stone wall of the Campo Santo organizes the partly grassy public space directly before it. In front of this wall are the Duomo and the Baptistery, placed on a common axis that approximately parallels the Campo Santo wall and is marked by a white marble path. Crossing this axis are two paths that lead to the entry to Campo Santo. On the far side of the church from the Baptistery stands the famed "Leaning Tower." The rest of the piazza is bounded by low walls and buildings that are part of the city fabric.

Most famous for the folklore of the structurally compromised tower and its inevitable failure, the complex is a magnificent composition of pure white stone buildings set into the irregular lawn against a backdrop of the city's brown brick. The complex accepts its irregular edge and stands in an intimate, inviting, embracing relation to the cityscape. For example, a key element of the Baptistery roof is its split material design. Seen from the Duomo, the roof is white marble, unified with the striking white forms of the church, tower, and burial building. When one migrates to the city side of the building, the material shifts to a terracotta tile that links the Baptistery roof to the traditional roofs of the city's vernacular buildings. This is a sophisticated use of design to situate a building distinctively while simultaneously fitting it into a city's fabric. The Baptistery and its companions in the Piazza del Duomo are pure and symbolic, yet wedded to the commonplace utility of the city.

The Certosa del Galluzzo monastery in Florence (1341) is another striking example of both high formal planning and subtle asymmetric adjustment. Built over time, the monastery incorporated diverse strategies for social and political expression as its composition grew. Visits to this building have put me in particular awe of the care taken with scale, from the most public aspects of the complex to the monks' most private spaces. For example, I am struck by how the design has been tuned to magnify the church's presence while subsuming its mass into the complex. This consists of three main courtyards around which public, semi-public, and private functions are arranged. The first courtyard doubles as the main public assembly space and the forecourt of the church of San Lorenzo. It is organized in a long, horizontal manner with the church facing across the narrow space from the center of one façade—an unusual location for this most public function of the complex. The clear entry sequence, with the church's façade at the cross axis of the rectangular space, places the church formally in the court but not necessarily in the position one would expect. More typically it would have stood at one end of the long, narrow space, providing the drama and sense of power usually associated with a church and courtyard space of this extent.

From this main courtyard one may transition into two semi-public squares. The first, the chiostrino del colloquio, is adjacent to the basilica. From here one can clearly read the pilaster structure of the church and the beautiful formal garden within the cloister. Passing through this space, one achieves the most private square of the monastery: a perfectly square, serene, manicured lawn bounded by a colonnade. Light and shadow play on the yellow plane of the stucco bounding wall, which is virtually blank except for oak doorways leading into the monks' private apartments. These are spare yet commodious; the only surprise is that each communicates with a small personal garden set between the residential blocks and open to the landscape beyond, crenellating the complex's outline. Each of these encapsulated gardens belongs to the private realm of a monastic cell, imparting a texture of individuated ownership to the architecture despite its institutional scale.

Conclusion

As student, architect, and teacher, I have been forced to reconsider the well-worn assumption that new work must be glaringly different, must stand out from its host location. This lesson has been literally all around me: in the academic environments where I have spent most of my professional life, the dissonance between buildings in collegiate gothic (or equivalent) style and the jarringly disruptive buildings of the mid-twentieth century forward has been chronically painful. Furthermore, many latter-day buildings have been built with materials having a 20-year life cycle, with the result that much of this work is already failing or in poor condition. The 20-year material life cycle is one of the less successful ideas in architecture and the building arts today. The time is right to reevaluate the compulsive construction of buildings that defy their settings and are designed and built as cheaply as possible.

As I begin to formulate my next body of work, I seek a timeless architecture in the middle ground—that space, occupied by so many works both modern and premodern, where a new building can be steeped in distinctive craft and novel design while respecting its environment, thus contributing to an ever-deepening sense of place. And my musical experience remains key to my thinking about individual and setting. Just as one can be both a soloist and a member of a group making beautiful music, so it is possible to create buildings that are both distinctive and at home. If we are to have an architecture capable of buildings not only iconic but fitting—iconic partly because they are fitting—we must respond lovingly to the specificities of place.

METROPOLIS MAGAZINE INTERVIEW by SUSAN S. SZENASY

On November 18th George Ranalli will receive the prestigious Sidney L. Strauss Memorial Award for 2010, from the New York Society of Architects. Dean of the Bernard and Anne Spitzer School of Architecture at City College, Ranalli also practices architecture in New York City, where he grew up. Since 1950 the award has been given to such important figures in architecture and urbanism as Ada Louise Huxtable (1970), still the strongest and most thoughtful voice in architecture criticism (now at the Wall Street Journal); Robert Moses (1976), the powerbroker who built modern New York; and Robert A.M. Stern (2004) who was instrumental in making us aware of our rich architectural history (now dean of architecture at Yale). Knowing about George's meticulous preparation for everything he does, his ethics, his interest in history, his love of craft, and his attachment to New York City—all of it somehow related to his commitment to Modernism—we wanted to know what he's thinking as his big day of celebration nears.

Susan S. Szenasy: So, George, in thinking about the amazing company you'll keep as a Sidney L. Strauss Memorial Award recipient, as a long-standing architecture dean at City College, and as head of your own architecture practice, what goes through your mind as you make notes about your acceptance speech?

George Ranalli: I am very honored to be in such illustrious company. Although the past honorees do not fit into one ideology, they can variously be described as free spirits, visionaries, and pathfinders. That's not bad company.

You are very kind to ask me what has been going through my mind these days. My mind has been filled with oscillations and analogies. In my own architectural practice and as the dean of a school of architecture, I continuously think about balancing innovation and stability, often on my walks to the office in Manhattan's flower district. The place where I practice is in a loft building on a street filled with hustle and clamor. Merchandise spills from doorways, pots of trees line sidewalks. Trucks park in the middle of the streets, and dozens of workmen shout in different languages. The flower district reminds me every workday of a city that stays the same as much as it changes, and that balance is what I am always seeking to find in my work.

As the dean of a school of architecture, my thinking about how to educate the next generation of architects is probably more divergent than that of many educators; at the same time, the architectural education at my school stands solidly on the traditional mission and vision of City University of New York. At school-wide gatherings, the faculty and students gather to pledge service to the city. It is a key positive moment of every school year for me.

I am a modernist architect who loves to fold architectural history into the process of making architecture. I never think of creativity and consistency in an inverse relationship. When things go well for architecture, the work is always a substantial, craft-intensive, meticulous balance between the old and the new. This is what moves the architecture field forward. Architecture is an exciting phenomenon because the momentum never reaches an end point; rather, the synthesis becomes the next thesis, until architecture takes another step forward.

SSS: It is no accident that when Mildred Friedman asked you to curate the Carlo Scarpa show at CCA in 1999, she also asked you to design the installation and build the models for the show. You have had a life-long conversation for Scarpa, during his lifetime and seemingly posthumously. How much has your work, at all scales, been influenced by Scarpa? Are you continuing, and evolving, his famously enigmatic symbolism?

GR: Actually, it was Frank Lloyd Wright who made me first want to become an architect. The moment of clarity came on a Sunday evening when I was about thirteen-years-old. My father was driving the family through Central Park. I was dozing in the back seat. Then suddenly, through the trees, there was the Guggenheim Museum. It was still under construction, surrounded by scaffolding. In the half-light of dusk, the building had an incredible presence. I had never seen such an amazing sight! This is my earliest memory of an exquisite building paired with the excitement about construction and, of course, the beginning of my life-long enchantment with modernism.

As a fledgling architect, Scarpa's work exercised an incredibly powerful influence on me, especially his methodology. In 1998, Mildred Friedman and I made a wonderful trip to Scarpa's archive to research the CCA show, more than twenty-years after my initial accidental pilgrimage to Scarpa in the late 1970s. Having recently completed my graduate studies, architecture seemed adrift. At the time, American architecture was all about metal and glass, even though Louis Kahn had designed amazing buildings, from simple materials, like brick and concrete, into striking geometric, luxuriously textured, light-filled forms, which were so compelling to me as a student.

An interview with George Ranalli before his reception of the prestigious Sidney L. Strauss memorial award for 2010, from the New York Society of Architects.

NOVEMBER 2010

I wrote a travel grant, which afforded me the opportunity to research stone and masonry construction in European buildings. By 1976, I was traveling through Italy researching masonry construction. The highpoint of a visit to a Milanese furniture factory had been a newly fabricated table, made from large layers of hefty plywood and a gorgeous, ebony top. The chief designer conducting the tour explained that an Italian architect, I had most likely never heard of, had designed the table, which was about to be shipped to the owner. Shortly afterward, my colleague pointed me toward Verona, and the work of an Italian architect, Carol Scarpa.

The work by Scarpa in Verona marked my introduction to ingenious contemporary design within the fabric of an ancient city, and it was nothing less than a revelation. I was certainly "young" then, compared to Scarpa, but I trusted that my own eyes had found something very special. Encouraged by my colleague, I arranged a visit to Scarpa's studio in Vincenza. I had expected to find myself in a prestigious architecture studio. Instead, I had arrived at Scarpa's home. He was dressed in a black smock, and he looked like a quintessential European artist. What's more, he was a modernist architect living in the carriage house of the Villa Rotonda, which was built in the 1500's.

Scarpa's office was even more of a surprise. Located in the cellar—more like a catacomb—the drafting desks were nestled into a space created by spindly stone columns. It was an exceptionally beautiful old room, but I kept saying to myself, "We're in the basement of a carriage house." Scarpa and I spent the day together, and we continued our discussion into the evening. His wife invited me to stay for dinner, and it was then that I found myself sitting at the same ebony table I had admired weeks earlier at the Bernini factory in Milan.

SSS: One of the most memorable aspects of your work is your use of light and how surfaces reflect and bounce this ephemeral (and yes, we can say, spiritual) builder and revealer of space. In your candid judgment, which of your works is the most successful in rendering that special quality of light you're after? What makes it so?

GR: Light is an essential component in the formulation of buildings and interiors. I always employ light –natural and artificial –to enhance space for its occupants. We can look at these phenomena through the example of the Saratoga Community Center in Brooklyn, New York. On the building's exterior, the movement of light across the recesses and framed elements accentuates the building's mass, and therefore its resilient durability. Ornamental elements encased in the mass also define the outer edges of the wall as it meets the sky. The overall experience is a variable kind of vibrancy around the larger volume of the building in its place on the street.

The interior, by contrast to the exterior, is a light filled volume allowing natural light through carefully placed irregular openings in the masonry. Windows were arranged to capture the maximally positive atmospheric effects of daylight. The shape of the ceiling inside and the artificial sources of light, set in the delicate openings of the surface create another kind of special effect after sundown. The design elements befit the various events that take place in the large room. The daytime functions involve recreational programs for young children, teenagers, and senior citizens. On weekends, community members use the room for special events and celebrations, such as weddings, birthdays, anniversaries, and holiday parties. The quality of light is an essential ingredient to achieve the different atmospheric qualities supporting all these activities and occasions.

Our most precious memories of special events are usually organized around our experience of the physical qualities of the spaces that resonate with the heightened positive feelings about a wonderful time of life or a special day. Building interiors, especially the interiors of public buildings, either support or hinder the construction of key positive life experiences. I am very gratified to hear from the community about the ways in which the physical environment at the Saratoga Community Center reflects and enhances their personal experiences there.

SSS: Your architecture, as well as your small scale works like door handles and furniture, have a kind of handcrafted quality to them, but they are also very industrial in their material and form. How do these small-scale objects symbolize or reflect your architectural thinking?

GR: Design objects allow materials to be the star of the show. When I design an object, I do think about weight, heft, texture, natural colors, and other intrinsic qualities of materials. Form is equally important. A familiar object, in an unfamiliar form, engages people in particularly interesting ways. Materials tie form and design together.

One example is my Valentine Chair # 2. This chair is a reconsideration of the use of a building material, typically a flat surface finish, to make a chair with an atypically complex, luxurious, comfortable, geometric form. The Valentine Chair # 2 does not have a stereotypical form, making it difficult to categorize as anything other than modern. Although it also nudges the expectation that modern furniture design is spare. When I design an object, I think about decorative modernity, which is form that is functional and decorative through the innovative use of complementary materials. This process is exciting to me because it offers me as a designer the opportunity to incorporate what is often an optimal amount of novelty into everyday experience.

SSS: If a master builder like Robert Moses were around today, what would you tell him about building 21st century New York?

GR: My home, with my wife and two children, for the past thirty years has been in the same old lower Manhattan neighborhood, on the same block, in the same old apartment building. We share a deep affection for home, which begins with our neighborhood, and then moves to our block, then our building, and finally our apartment. Our neighborhood is uniquely special for many reasons, including its status as an epic social and political battleground.

In 1960s Mr. Moses advanced the idea of urban renewal, which meant bulldozing so-called "blighted" areas, enormous high-rise rebuilding, and ever-expanding highways. Mr. Moses became a rapidly spreading trend. Ms. Jacobs said, "Stop" by arguing a completely different view of the same city districts, she described as appealing, complex, socially vibrant places full of self-rejuvenating, and self-sustaining potential through community development, neighborhood rehabilitation, and historic preservation. Mr. Moses talked about what cities did badly. Ms. Jacobs pointed out what cities did well.

The skirmishes waged by New York's most articulate, energetic civic activist Jane Jacobs against New York's most formidable planning czar Robert Moses, over proposals like the lower Manhattan Expressway, took place right outside my front door. The debate inspired large numbers of everyday New Yorkers to participate, and when the dust settled, people had an understanding of urban economies and ecologies, and a lasting interest to participate in local planning and development—a newfound wisdom about the nature and functioning of cities.

These days, neighborhood and community altering proposals continue to come forward – and it happens quite regularly–the process is not what it was before the great clash of Robert Moses and Jane Jacobs. There is no large-scale visionary planner or master builder like Robert Moses, and this speaks volumes about 21st century New York City. The city has become an ascendant composite of progressive zones offering more of something for everybody, since more of everybody participates in the process. As New Yorkers shift away from old ways of living and reasons for living that way, like the automobile culture of Mr. Moses' projects, toward citizen-led community groups of bicyclist, historic preservationists, and community environmentalists, local people remain involved in a public process. And their architects consider how a project, through its qualities of design, fits into an existing commercial, cultural, and residential activities, and at the larger scale, what is the lifecycle of a building, particularly its uses or misuse of materials and energy. Now, architecture has even more potential to reflect, enhance, and facilitate 21st century New York City life by contributing more fully to the genuine expression of the city's interesting and delightful diversity as a human setting.

SSS: As dean at the Bernard and Anne Spitzer School of Architecture, what are your students teaching you about the future of the architecture profession?

GR: The students of the Bernard and Anne Spitzer School of Architecture are outstandingly successful young architects. Some have been recently selected as one of twenty finalist groups to compete in the U.S. Department of Energy's Solar Decathlon. The City College submission for a solar roof pod is unique for its adaptability to urban rooftops, and it is a beautiful, environmentally innovative idea. Given that the surfaces of buildings in cities retain the sun's heat and create urban heat islands that as the EPA estimates may increase the city's average air temperature by 1 to 3 degrees Celsius as the expected one-million-plus new residents settle here, the students have innovated an idea for an increasingly urgent environmental problem. Our newly launched student architecture journal, Informality, was recently awarded as a student architecture publication by the Washington DC Chapter of the AIA. These are just two ways to illustrate my undeniable opportunity to learn from my students.

The most important lesson, as always, is in the medium. City College students teach me about the advantages of a public school architectural education that cultivates competence, knowledge, creativity, principals of best practice, and innovation in a school setting that is one of the country's most diverse. Thomas Edison remarked, "Genius is one percent inspiration and ninety-nine percent perspiration." No one even disputes this statement, but people tend to focus on inspiration.

My students remind me every day about the hard work of making architecture: the work of tolerating ambiguity, categorizing concepts broadly, defining and redefining challenges, uncovering the heuristics of novel ideas, making decisions, and expressing complex ideas clearly, simply, and convincingly.

My students astonish me with their intellectual vigor and curiosity, their civic mindedness, and their tenacity for social justice. As they near the end of their schooling, they develop a passionate love for the work, affirming, over and over again, that the labor of love aspect of architecture is very important. After all, what's more appropriate for a Modernist architect who loves history than to nurture architecture's future to embrace its past?

PROJECTS

RESIDENTIAL

project name	Park Avenue Renovation
location	Park Avenue, New York City
year of design	2005
client	Name withheld at owner's request
lot size	25' x 100'
project size	2,550 sq. ft.
architect	George Ranalli
associates	Aaman & Whitney Structural Engineer; Aaman & Whitney, Mechanical Engineering
design team	Hollace Metzger, Hayden Marrero

Park Avenue Renovation

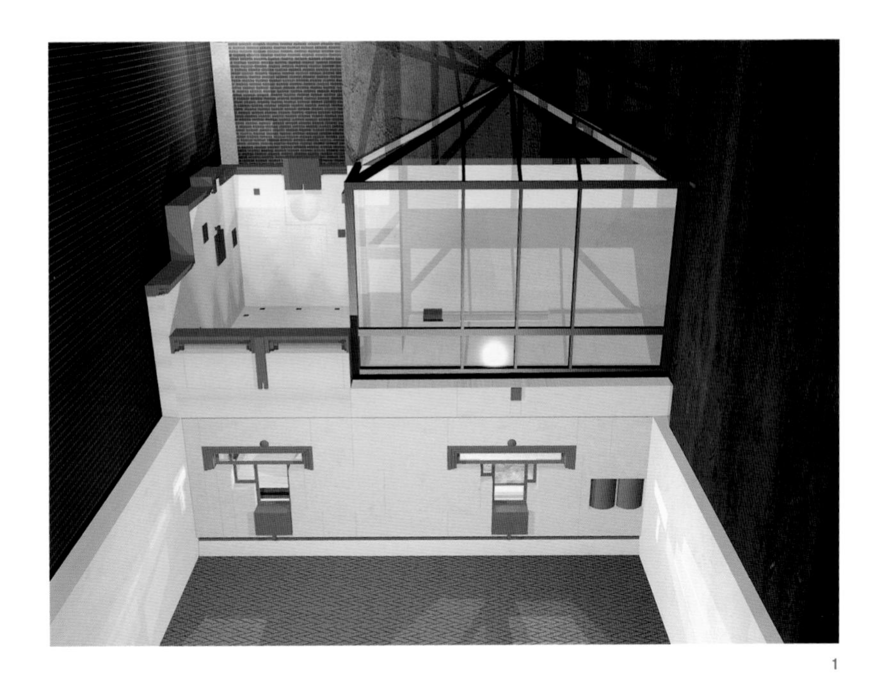

1

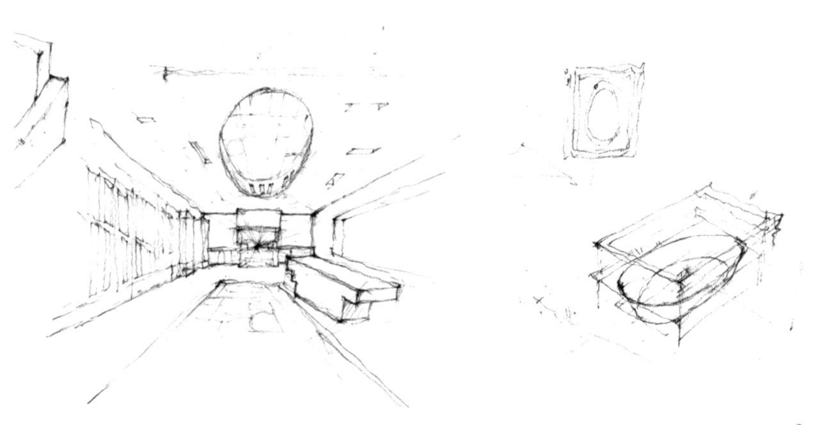

2

By the time the owner of this four-story, single-family Carnegie Hill home sought to renovate in 2004, the building had come a long way from its humble origins. Built in 1884–85 as one of four speculative row houses, it originally stood beside the cinder and steam of the Park Avenue locomotive transit. Andrew Carnegie's 1899 purchase of two-block fronts in the area, followed by the State legislative mandate for electric-powered trains on Manhattan in 1903, repositioned Park Avenue as the Upper East Side's quintessential residential boulevard. In 1923, an affluent owner hired architect Emery Roth to redesign the exterior façade in the same modern-classical style as a neighbor's house down the street. Removing the porch and street stair made way for a classically inspired, centered entrance and service door in a little courtyard paved to match the new black-and-white marble floor of the interior hall. All that remained after clearing off the decorative brackets, molding, ironwork, window balconies, and multi-pane casements was a simple stone cornice and parapet wall, a sleek limestone façade, and a set of large, square-headed, upper-story windows.

The classical unity of the building's exterior was no match for the accumulating eccentricities of the interior. Under various owners, including a film star, the building went through a series of renovations and interior conversions that created a hodgepodge of broken-up spaces and gardens. A mid-1930s renovation introduced a four-story expansion at the back to house servants' quarters and physical plant. French doors leading to a scrolled iron gateway and trellised patio (later enclosed in glass) were added to the second-story drawing room. At one time the lower two floors were even connected to the adjacent house.

The clients wanted to renovate the lower floors, converting a barren space beneath an existing solarium into a new dining room, breakfast room, and terrace. While the program seemed simple, the complex structural reality of the building required the addition of columns, beams, and new walls in critical locations to achieve the desired spatial results. The owners also requested a twelve-foot dining table, fabricated in onyx, to host their frequent celebratory events.

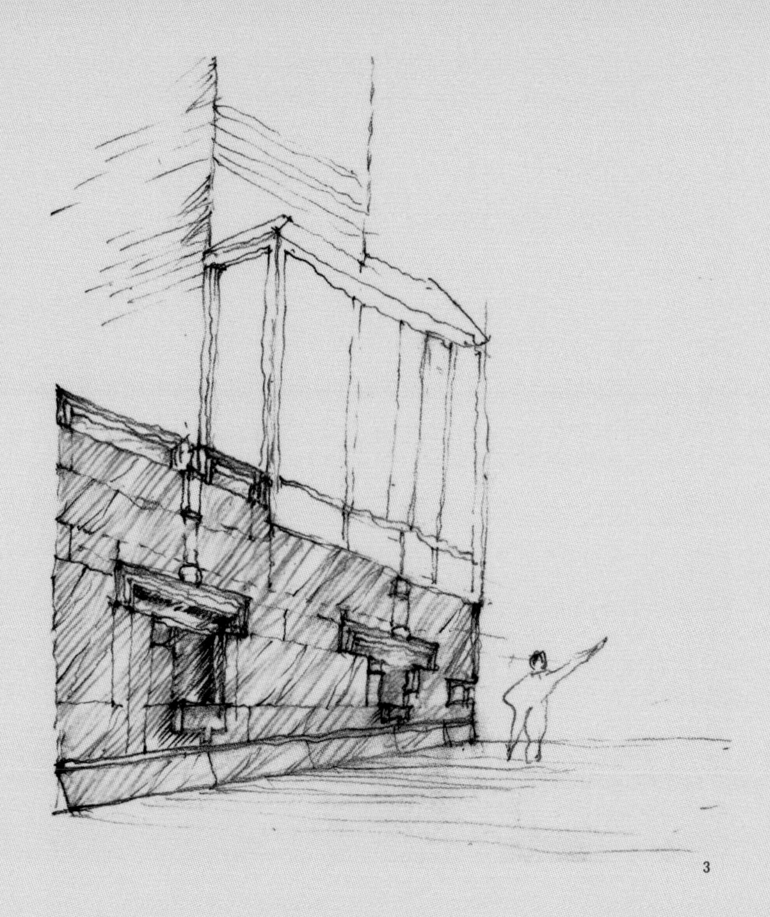

3

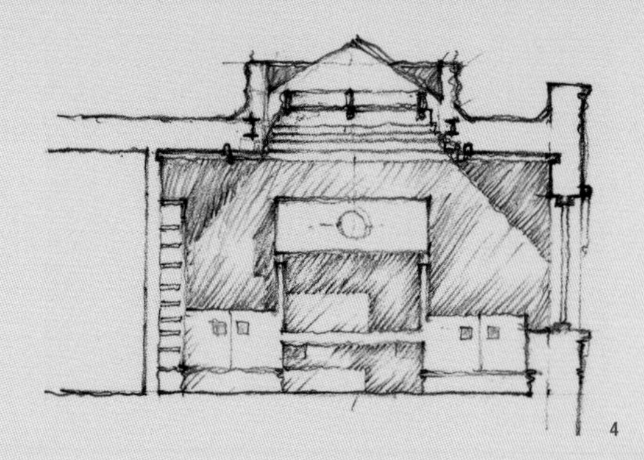

4

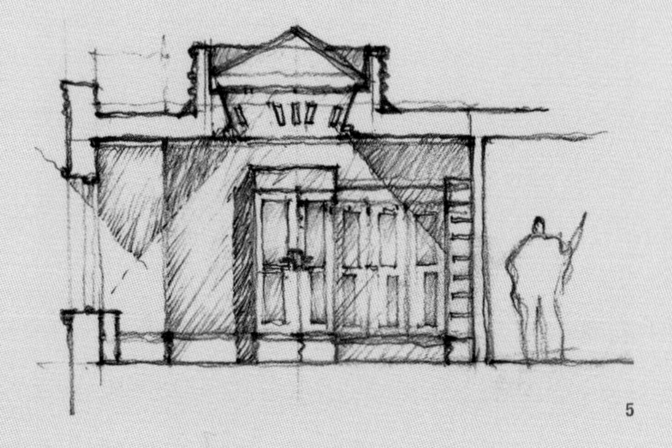

5

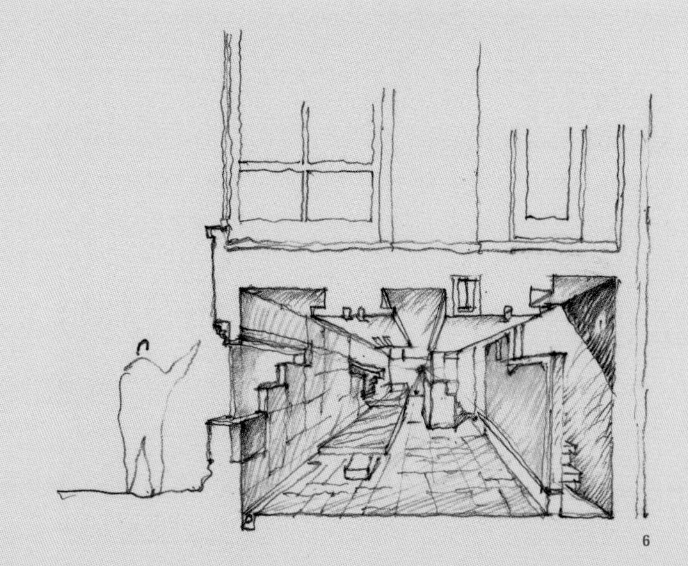

6

1 Garden view showing existing glass sunroom on right
2 Sketches of the fourth floor library
3 Sketch of the garden wall
4 Library elevation looking south
5 Library elevation looking north
6 Perspective of the dining room

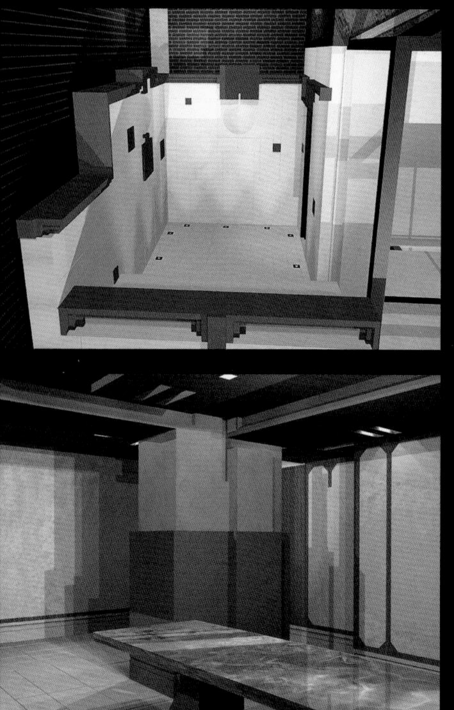

The proposal made space for a formal dining room, sunny kitchen with ample pantry storage, breakfast room, upper-story library under a skylight, and an inviting outdoor garden patio. The new exterior façade walls expand the back of the house, incorporating the open space beneath the sunroom-gazebo to shape an open air volume and terrace.

This project explores a return to dense stone construction for both its environmental and architectural rationale. The possibility of an ornamental approach to the stone construction was included in the client's list of desired results. The new enclosing exterior wall in the rear of the house is made of Valders Buff dolomite with Pietra Serena accent stones in various locations.

The lower-story breakfast room or sunroom enjoys a skylight that admits additional sun. Adjacent to it, the dining room comprises misty green Venetian plaster and pear-wood trim that peels back at the top to hint at a stair rising along a party wall to the second-story sunroom. During the day, the room's lighting is shaped by the glow from the terrace skylight at the back and by light from magnificent mahogany windows that look out to a garden. In the evening, the smooth Indiana limestone floors and onyx stone tabletop gleam under artificial lights. Finally, a plaster ceiling opportunistically contoured around equipment and an existing steel beam creates an ethereal quality.

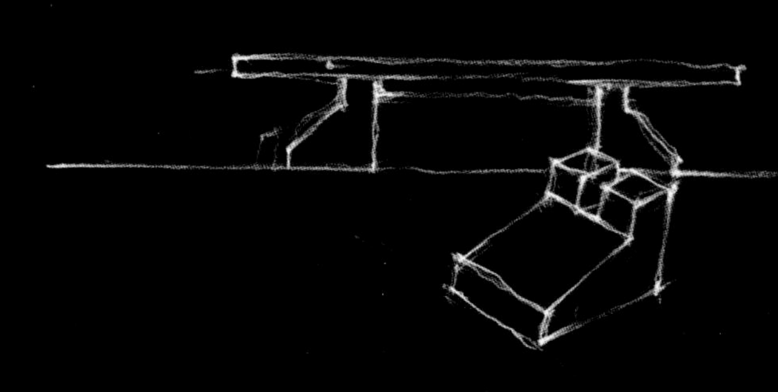

1 Computer model views of the terrace, breakfast room and dining room
2 Sketch of the table and table pedestal
3 Computer model view of the garden wall

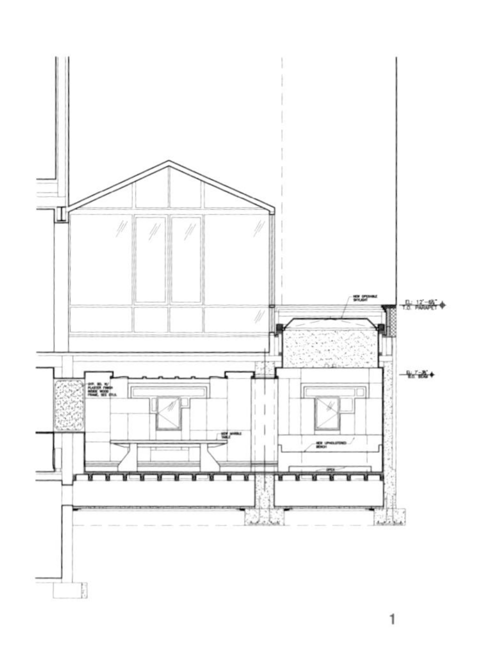

1

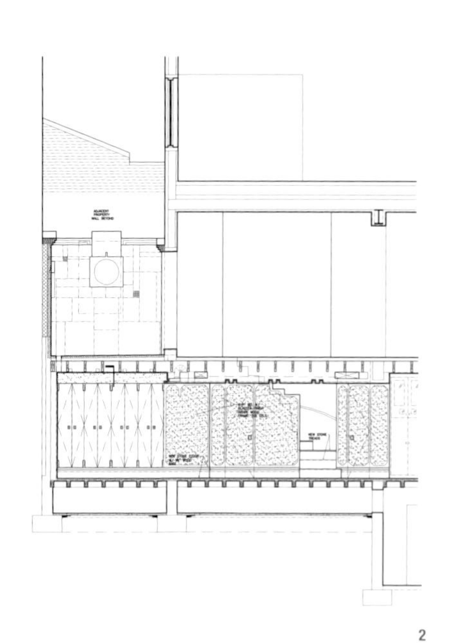

2

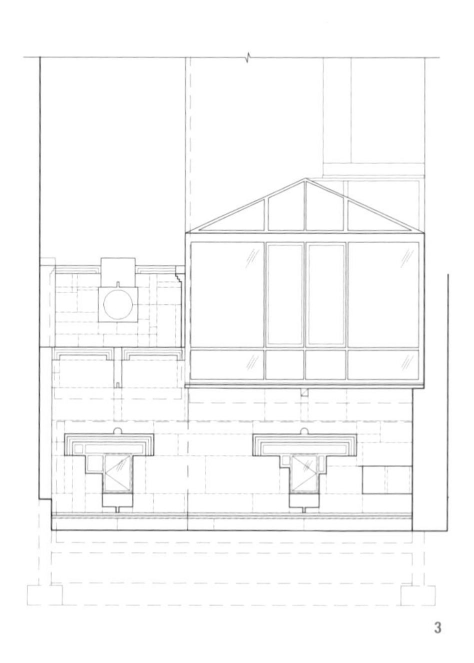

3

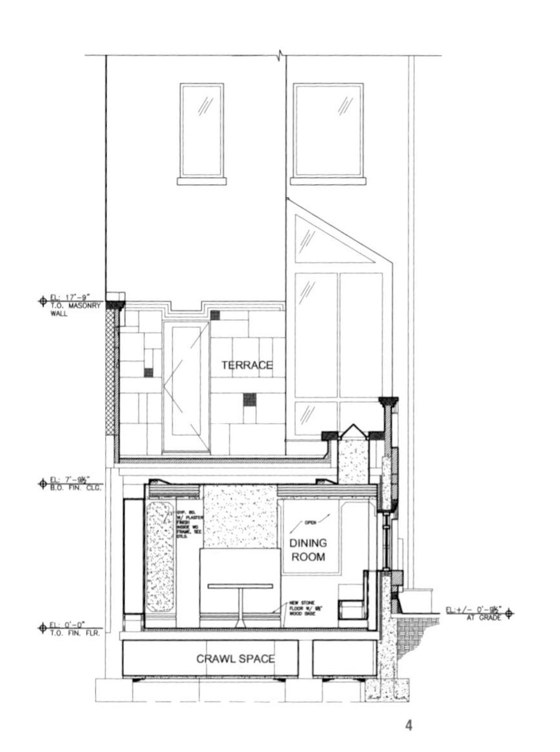
EL: 17'-9"
T.O. MASONRY WALL
TERRACE
EL: 7'-9½"
B.O. FIN. CLG.
DINING ROOM
EL: 0'-0"
T.O. FIN. FLR.
CRAWL SPACE
EL: +/- 0'-9½"
AT GRADE

4

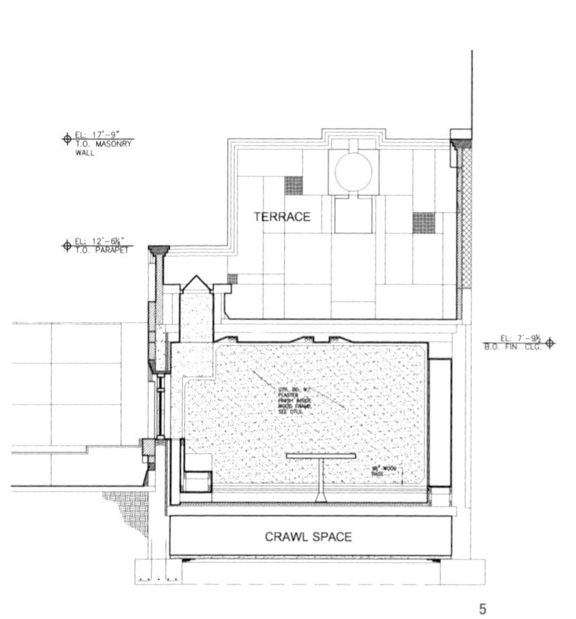
EL: 17'-9"
T.O. MASONRY WALL
EL: 12'-6¾"
T.O. PARAPET
TERRACE
EL: 7'-9½"
B.O. FIN. CLG.
CRAWL SPACE

5

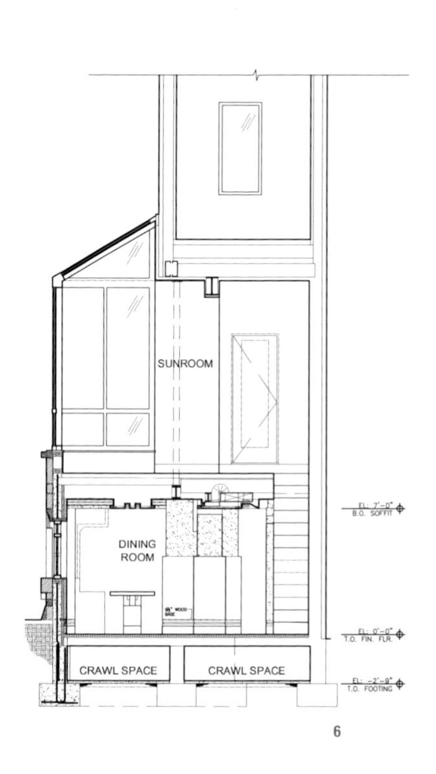
SUNROOM
DINING ROOM
EL: 7'-0"
B.O. SOFFIT
EL: 0'-0"
T.O. FIN. FLR.
CRAWL SPACE
CRAWL SPACE
EL: -2'-9"
T.O. FOOTING

6

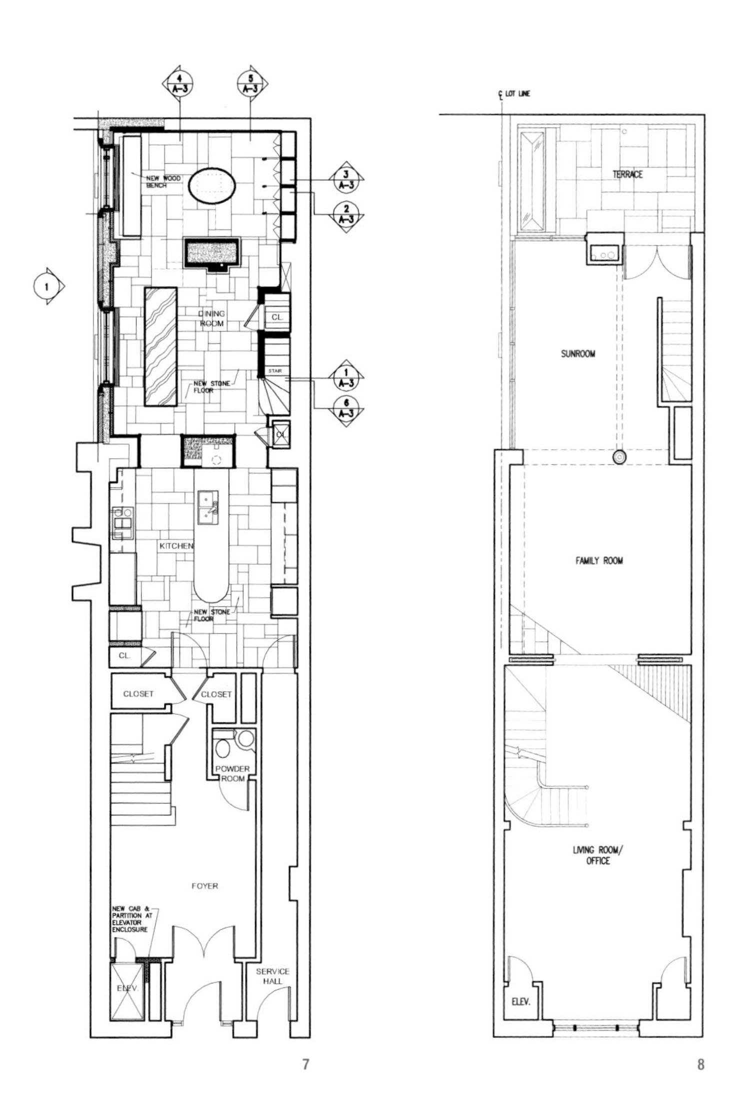

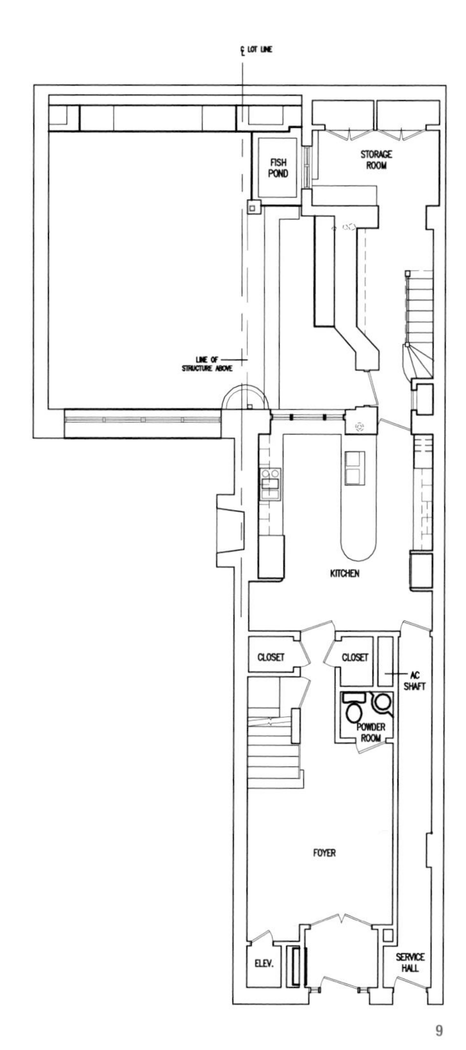

1 Section through dining room and breakfast room
2 Section through terrace and breakfast room
3 Garden elevation with new stone wall and existing glass sunroom
4 Cross section through terrace and breakast room
5 Cross section through the terrace and breakfast room below
6 Cross section through the existing sunroom and breakfast room below
7 New ground floor plan
8 Existing condition second floor plan
9 Existing ground floor plan
10 New terrace plan

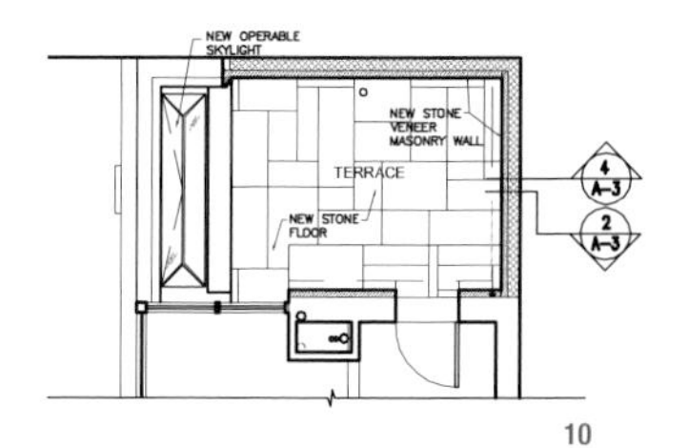

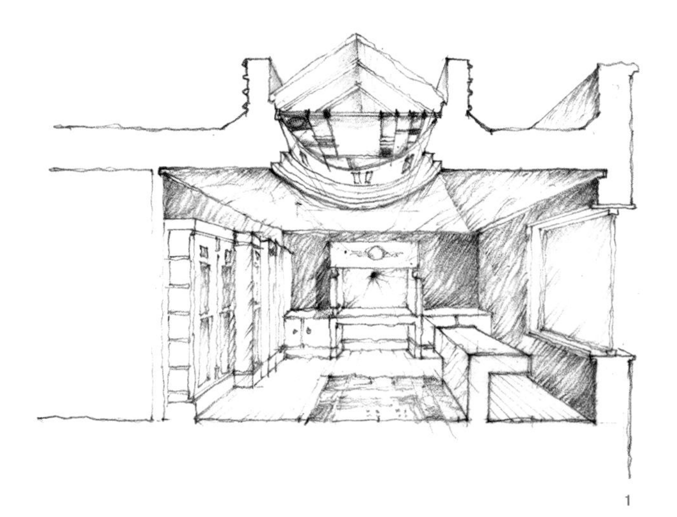
1

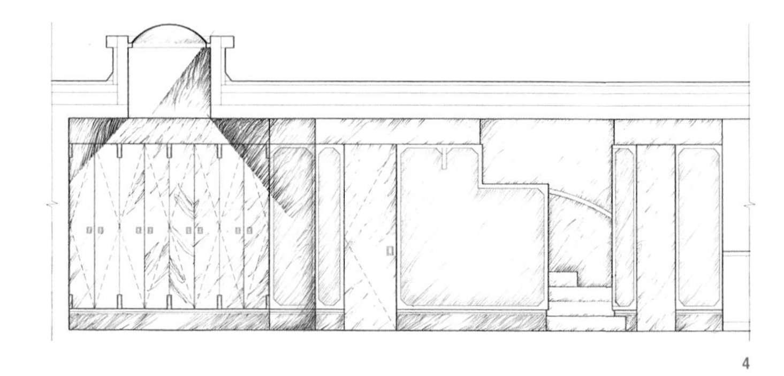
4

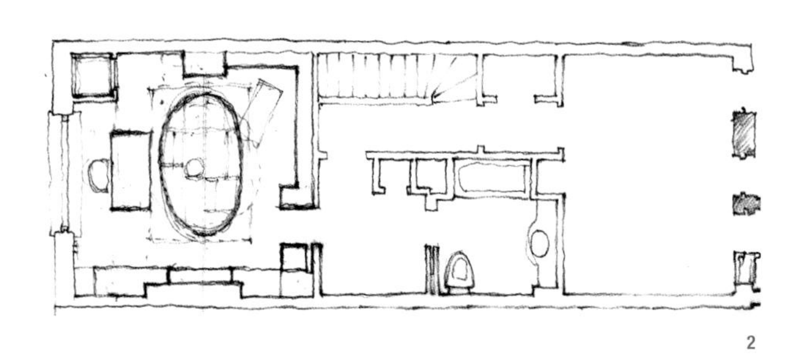
2

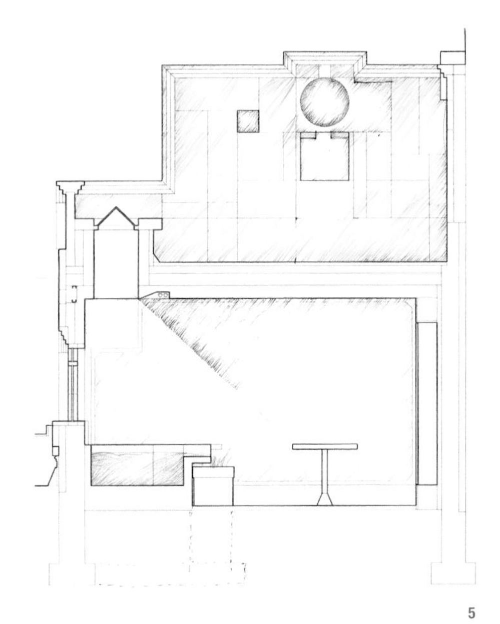
5

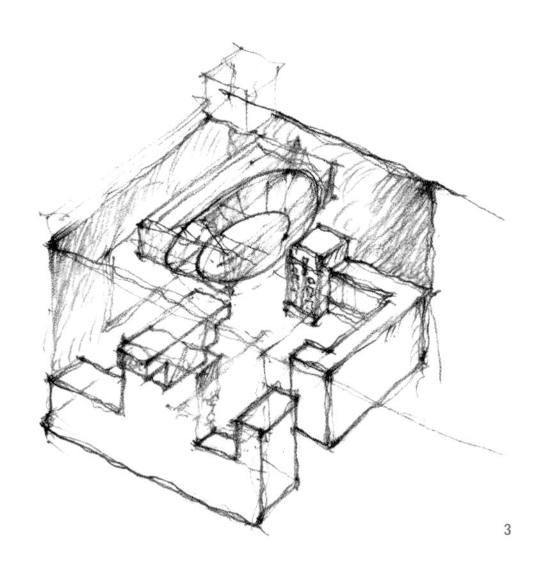
3

1 Perspective sketch of the fourth floor library
2 Sketch of the fourth floor plan
3 Sketch of the library with oval skylight and cabinets
4 Section through lower level closets and color infused plaster wall
5 Study section through the breakfast room and terrace above
6 Study section through the dining room and breakfast room
7 Sketch of the onyx table pedestal
8 Detail sketch of the stone work in the exterior wall
9 Perspective sketch of the dining room
10 Study elevation of the garden wall showing new stone work and existing glass sunroom above

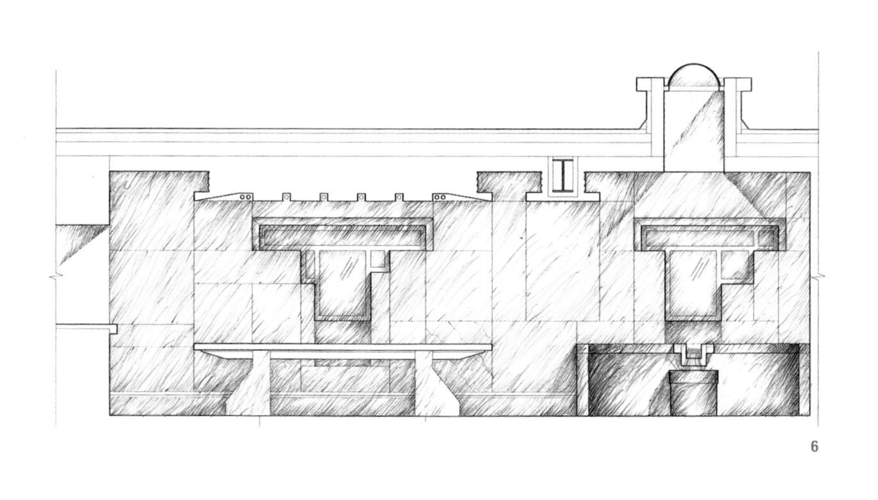
6

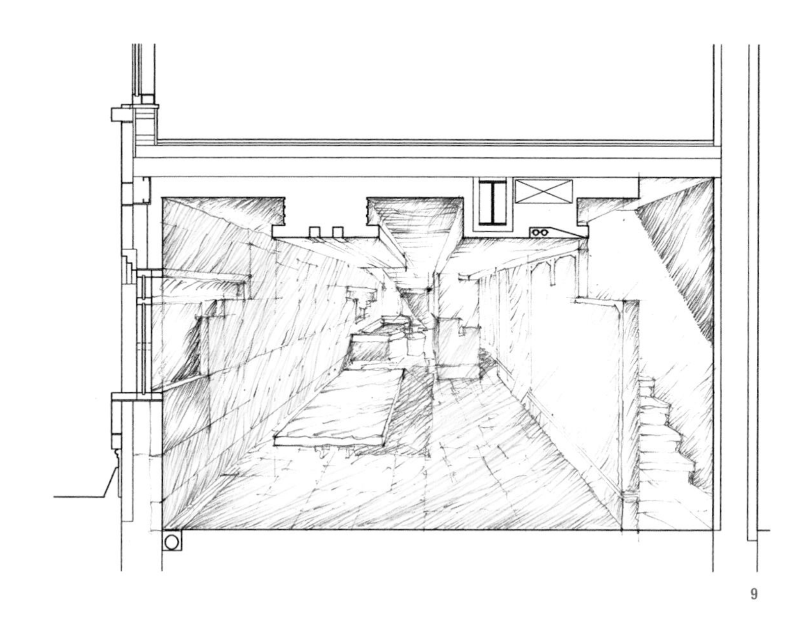
9

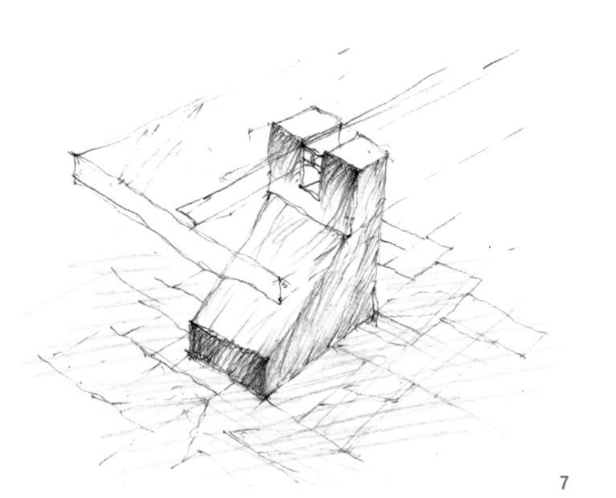
7

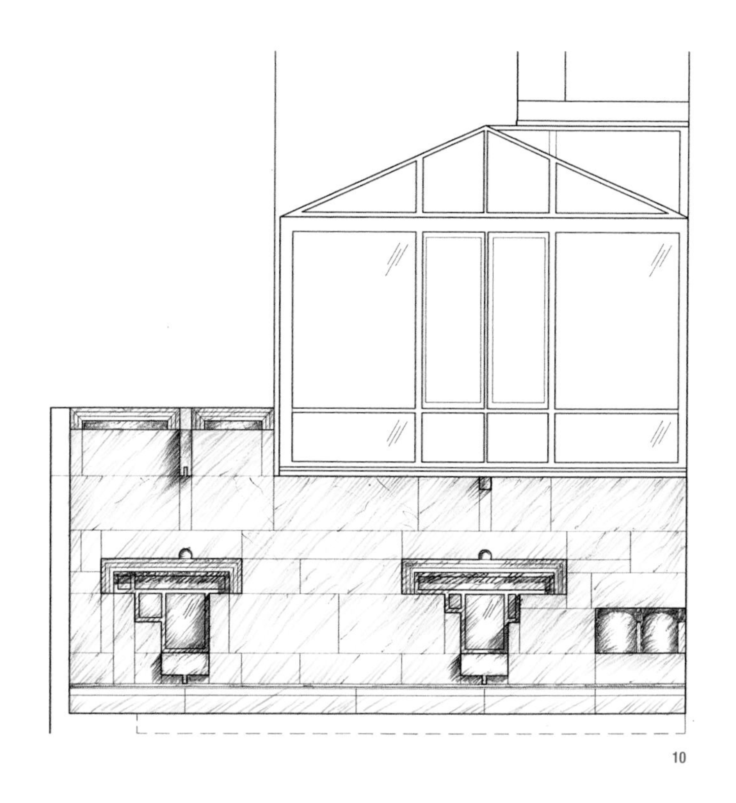
10

8

project name	Chatham House
location	Chatham, New York
year of design	2002-2003
client	Name withheld at owner's request
lot size	4.25 acres
project size	6,800 sq.ft.
architect	George Ranalli
associates	Robert Silman Structural Engineer
design team	Mario Gentile, Kimberlae Saul, Hayden Marrero, Hyungjin Lim

Chatham House

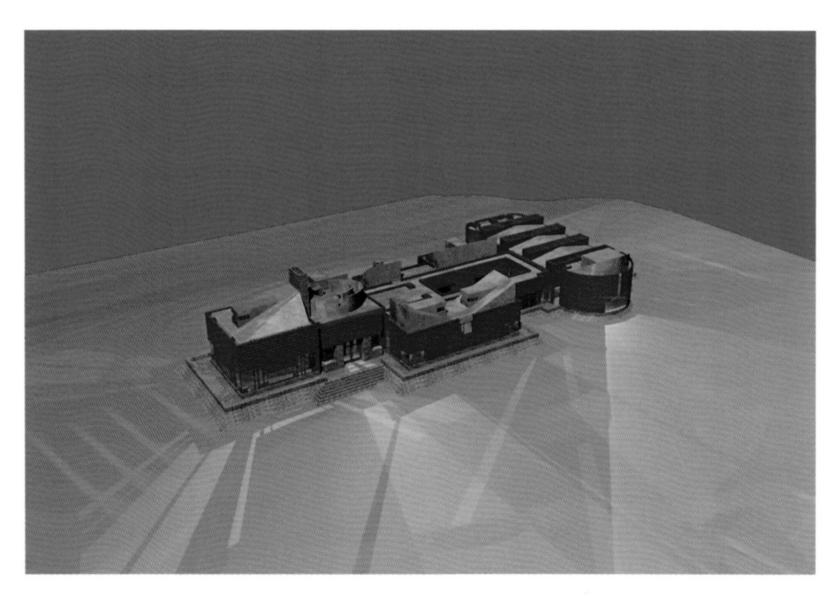

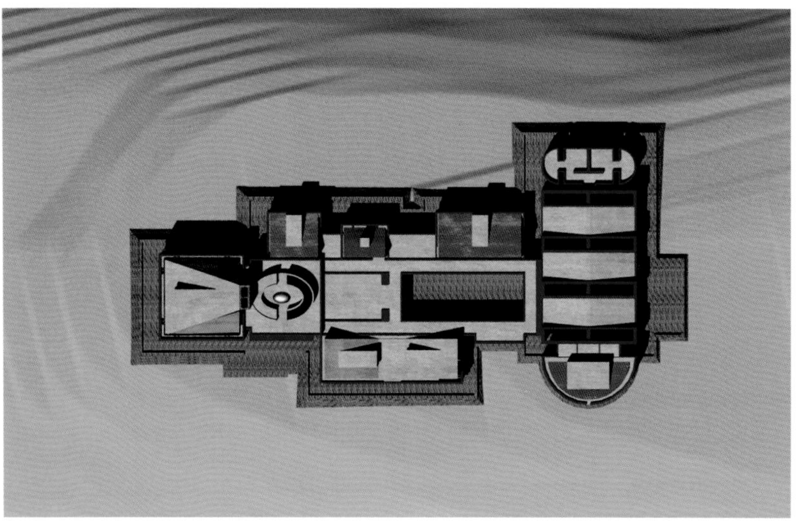

1

The house is set on a four-acre site amid rolling green hills outside the village of Chatham, New York, at the northern end of Columbia County. Originally named Groat's Corners, Chatham was incorporated in 1869 and by 1900 was a bustling center of rail traffic from New York to Albany and Boston. Although most rail traffic has long since been routed elsewhere, trains still pass thru the town daily, giving it the aura of a still-vital transportation hub, and the memory of the station stop lingers in the town structures. The house site is just outside this setting, a short distance into the landscape, with spectacular views of the Catskill and Berkshire mountain ranges.

The clarity of form expressed in the house's organization interprets the owner's desire for serenity and calm. The design balances the highly defined specific program requirements of the client and an appropriate environmental response, setting a strong, clear form of weather-resistant stone, wood, and copper into the bucolic site. Each space within the house exploits the opportunity to create a unique and specific design for a particular function. At the entry to the house, for example, there is an oval reception room with small, enclosing stone walls and spindly columns supporting a copper enclosure above. This room has a hidden stair that takes one up to an observatory at the tallest point in the house. A large living hall just off the oval entry partakes of the magnificent view yet has a striking sense of enclosure and material finish. An outdoor courtyard at the center of the plan, designed as a space of contemplation, is fitted with two cypresses at each end.

One of the most elaborate sequences of spaces is the large indoor pool and Jacuzzi spa. Finished in exquisite materials including color-infused plaster, pear-wood trim, and copper elements, these rooms offer a strong sense of place while providing a magnificent glimpse of the outdoors. Beauty is a driving desire of the client, and the building embodies that dream in its materials, forms, and detailing.

2

3

4

5

6

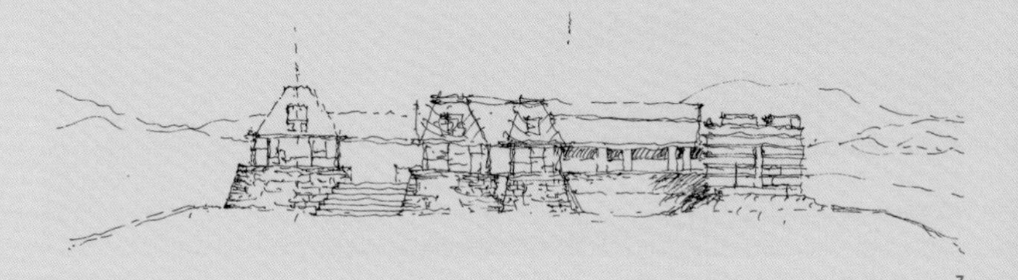

7

1 | Aerial view above and site plan view below
2 | Photomontage of the house in the site
3 | View of the lower stone work and the copper reception hall
4 | View of the master bedroom exterior
5 | View of the copper roofscape
6 | Exterior view of the swimming pool
7 | Sketch elevation of the entry side of the house

1

1	Computer model and site photo of the great hall end of the house
2	Sketch of the courtyard, children's bedrooms and pool
3	Sketch of the plunge pool and main pool roof
4	Aerial view of the courtyard, children's bedrooms and pool
5	Master bedroom and kitchen sketch
6	Early sketch of the children's bedroom massing and roof section
7	Great hall and copper entry hall
8	Sketch section of the pool roof
9	Study of the great hall room
10	Sketch elevation of the great hall
11	Elevation of the children's bedrooms
12	Perspective sketch of the courtyard
13	Alternate view of the children's bedrooms
14	Oblique drawing of copper entry hall observatory stair

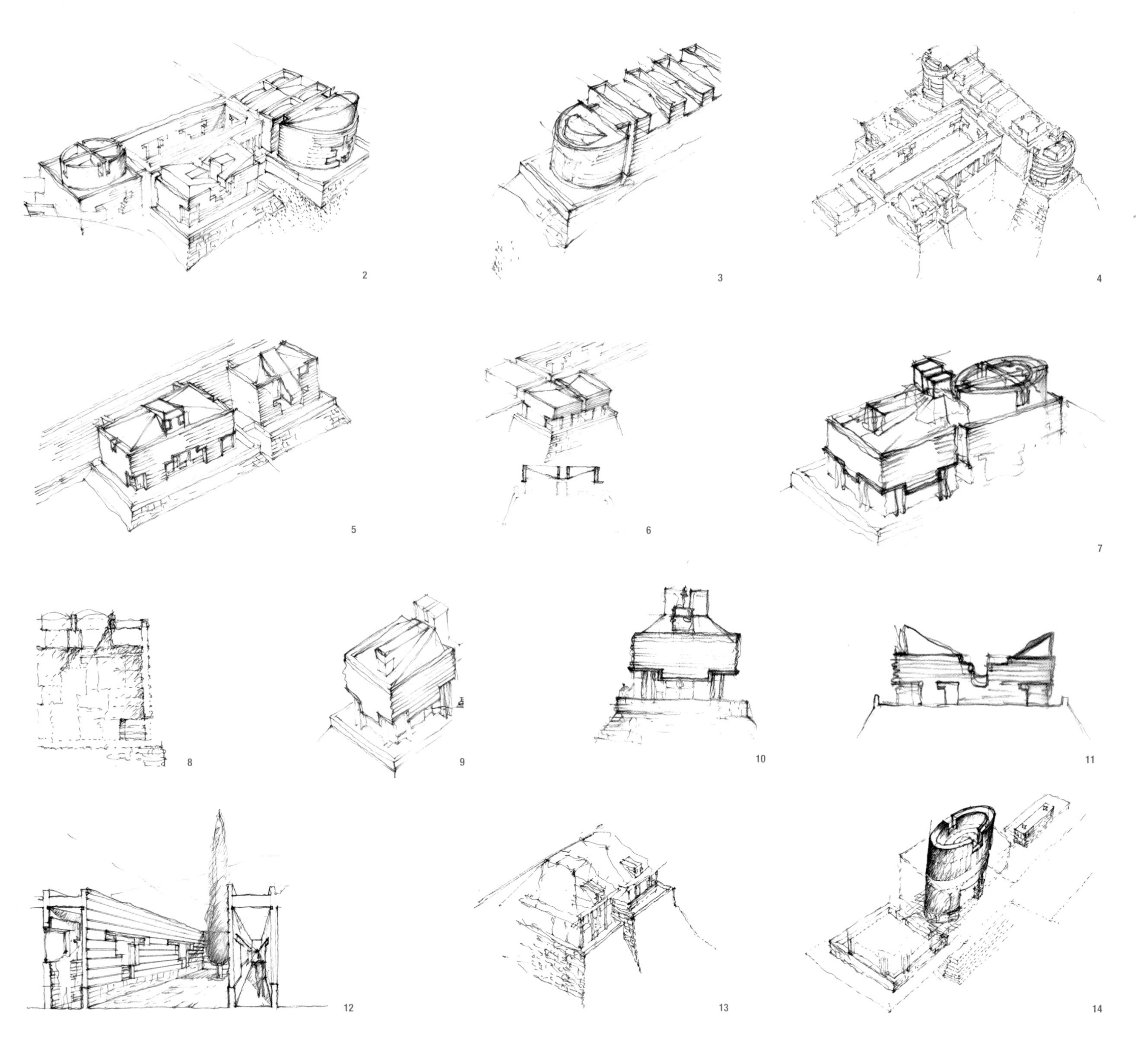
2
3
4
5
6
7
8
9
10
11
12
13
14

1

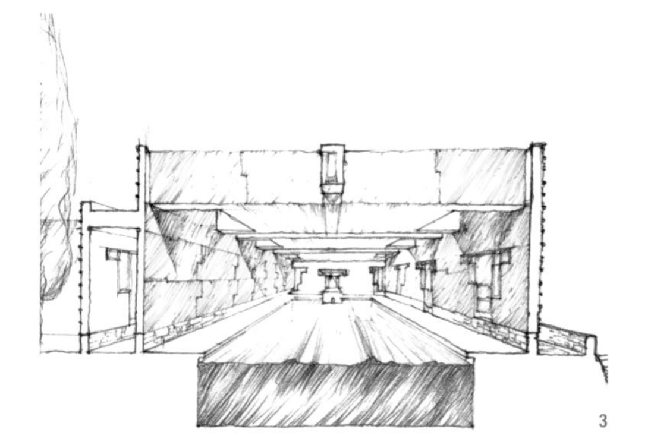

3

As scientists have come to appreciate, sustainability in building is primarily a function of the long-term durability of the building itself. Construction that proposes a long time-line is thus critical to a concerted and deliberate sustainability effort; buildings that can remain viable for a century or more offer a real contribution to the ecological balance between the natural and the manmade. This house is made to withstand the ravages of time through its selection of materials, detailing, and other appropriate responses to a cold, snowy climate.

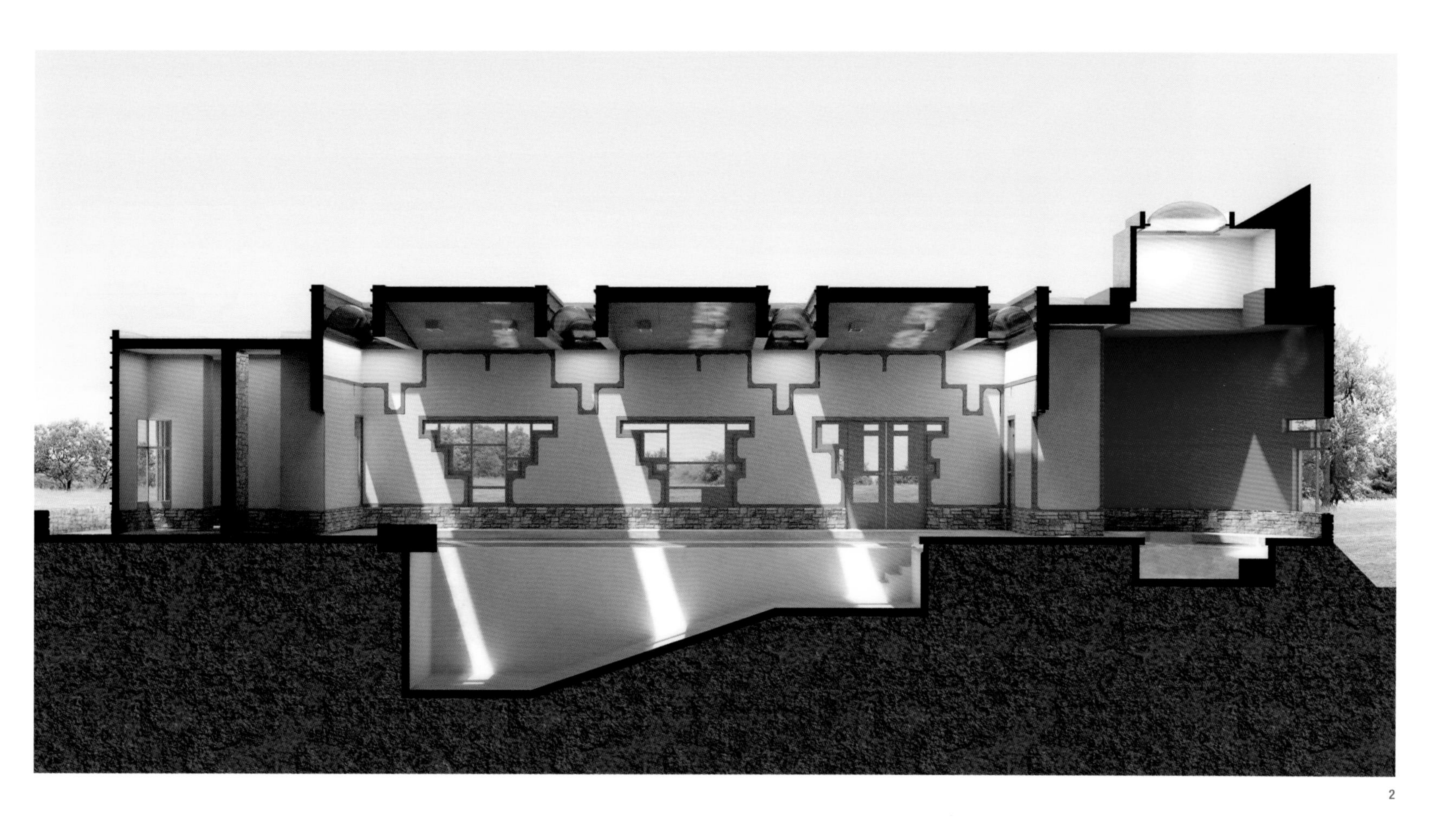

2

4

1 Section through the pool looking toward the house
2 Section through the pool looking to the landscape
3 Sketch section of the pool
4 Cross section of the pool looking toward the plunge pool
5 View of the main pool looking toward the plunge pool (following spread)

5

1

2

1 View of the model from the entry side of the house
2 View of the model on the master bedroom side
3 View of the model from the great hall end of the house

3

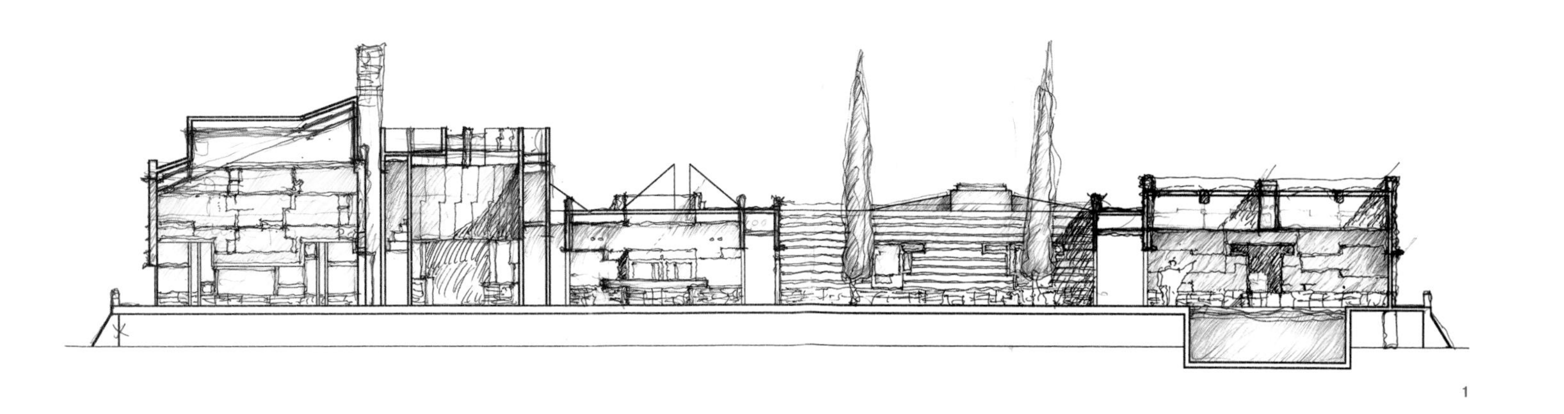

1

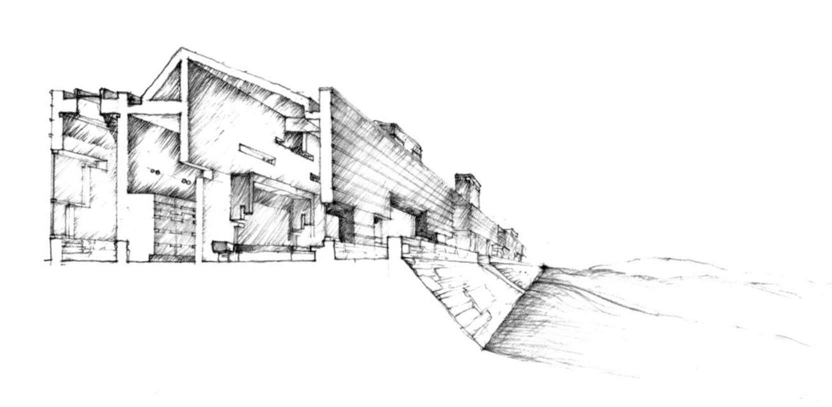

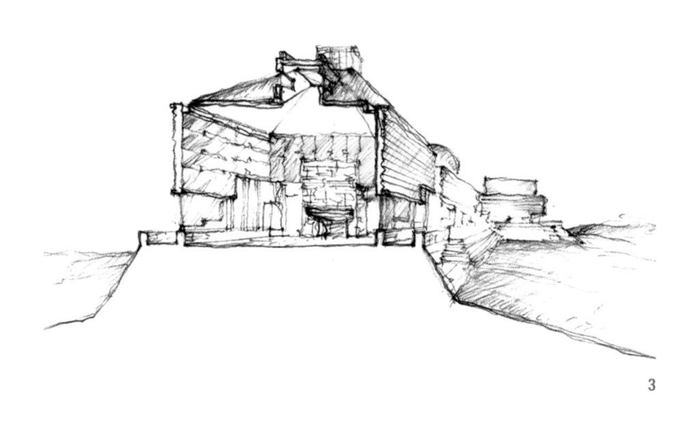

3

2

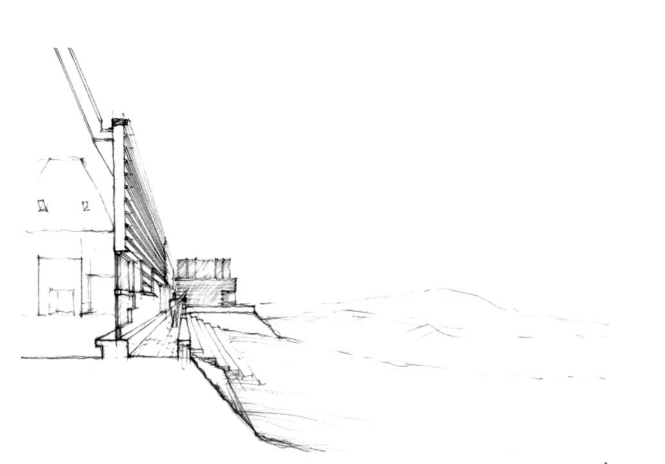

4

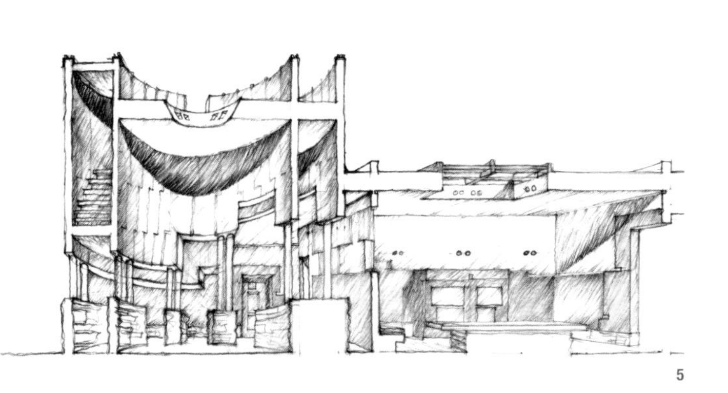

5

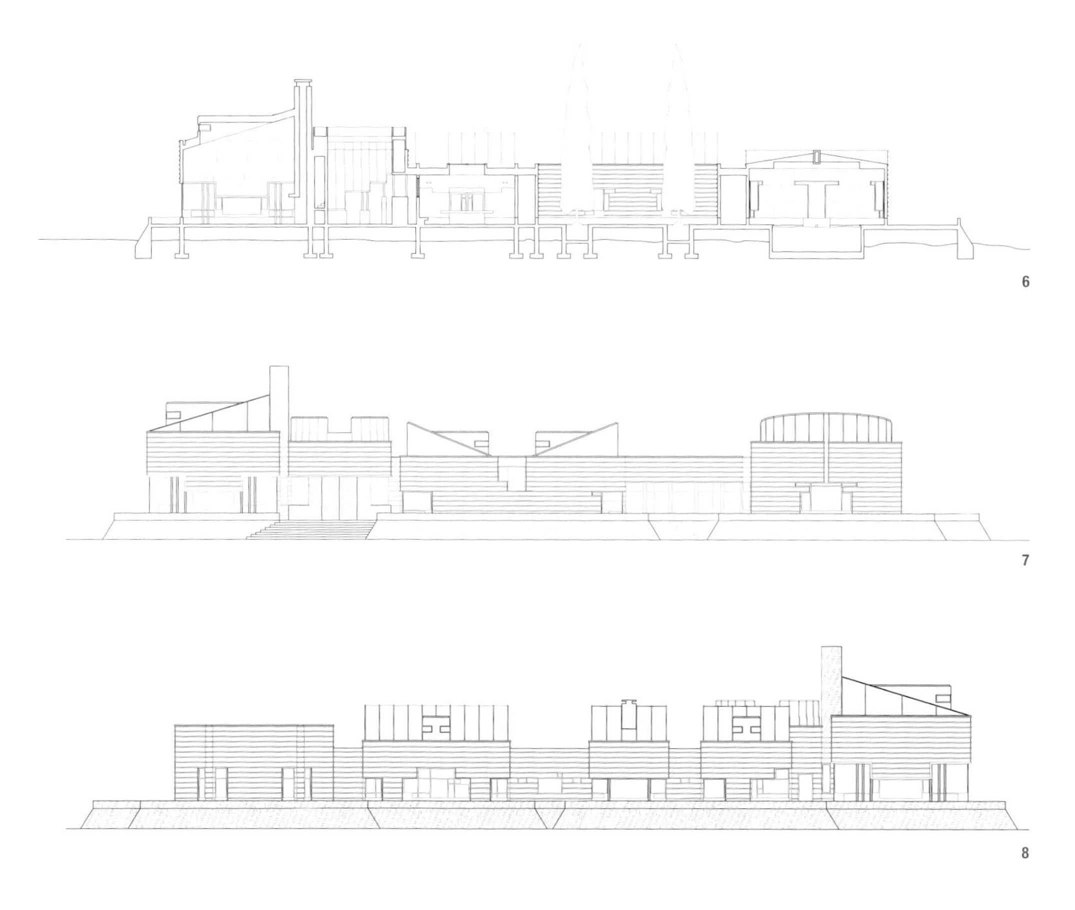

6

7

8

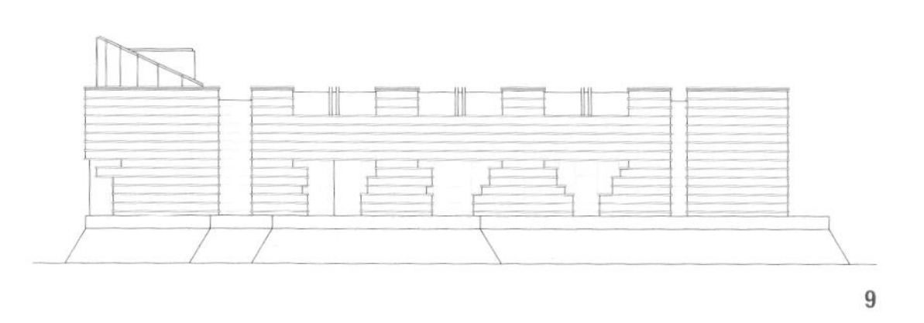

9

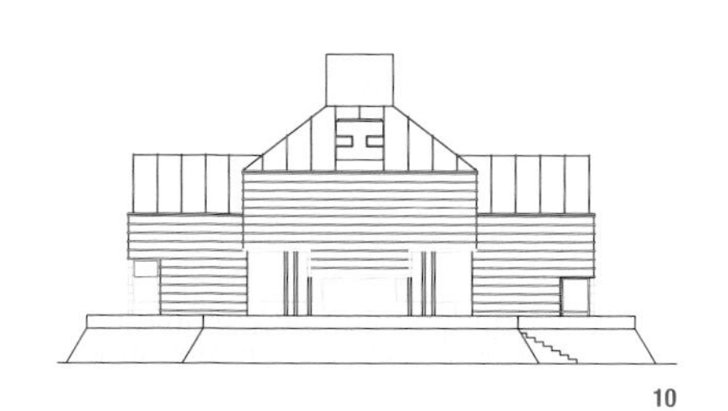

10

1 Study section through the house
2 Section perspective through the master bedroom
3 Section perspective through the great hall
4 Study drawing of the exterior wall
5 Sketch through the oval copper entry room and dining room
6 Section through the length of the house
7 Elevation of the entrance side of the house
8 Elevation of the master bedroom side of the house
9 Elevation of the indoor pool and plunge pool rooms
10 Elevation of the great hall end of the house

1

2

3

1 | View of the indoor pool looking toward the landscape
2 | Detail of the pool steps
3 | Detail of the pool edge

project name	Helmick Renovation
location	New York City
year of design	2002
year of completion	2003
client	Dan Helmick
lot size	50' x 100'
project size	725 sq.ft.
architect	George Ranalli
associates	Robert Silman Structural Engineer
design team	Mario Gentile, Hayden Marrero

Helmick Residence

1

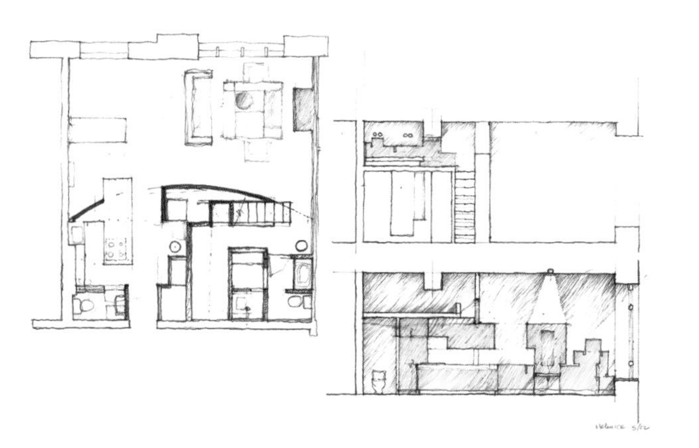

2

Situated in an 1892 building in the Chelsea section of New York City, the Helmick renovation project combines two studio apartments into one large two-bedroom apartment. Chic silhouettes and a sumptuous color palette characterize this residential interior for a professional couple, in which geometric abstraction, vibrant lines, veils of color, and sumptuous materials define a stylishly faceted and functional space.

The removal of the demising wall between the two studio units created a large, horizontal room floodlit with a soaring ceiling and natural light from oak-framed, north-facing industrial windows. This space is bounded on one side by the heart of the design—a sweeping, crimson-infused plaster wall that separates the living and dining area from two sleeping lofts above master bath, dressing room, kitchen, and powder room.

An entrance in the curved wall leads past storage tucked behind custom wood doors to the powder room, featuring crisp white ceramic tile and blue slate flooring, and a well-put-together kitchen. The latter, appointed with flaxen-wood grain pantry, cabinets, cupboards, and work surfaces of rose and cream marble, carves a spacious bay through the large volume defined by the crimson wall. Its sense of intimate efficiency notwithstanding, the energetic impetus of the kitchen design projects the marble topped element, peninsula-like, into the large dining area and majestic living room. A functional component of the dining area, this vivacious protuberance of wood and marble parts the luscious crimson façade.

The dapper master-bedroom suite consists of a spa-style bathroom. The spacious bath includes custom wood wainscoting, a vanity supporting a ceramic sink and a unique double-sided oval mirror. The travertine stone soaking tub and shower features lavish "cocktail" steps. The design extends to an elegant dressing room, customized with a delicate rise of wood stair, to the bedroom perch, above an inset wall concealing the wooden doors of a wardrobe.

3

1 View of the large curved red wall and living room
2 Sketch plans and sections of the apartment
3 View of the living and dining space looking toward the curved red wall

2

2 3 4

The occupants use the large space comprising a main living/ dining room for intimate occasions or large festive events. The design thus provides a backdrop for a whole range of experiences that take place in the apartment.

1 View of the curved living room wall with kitchen island projecting through
2 View from the kitchen into the living room
3 Detail view of custom designed wooden living room chair
4 Detail view of the custom cabinet media wall

1

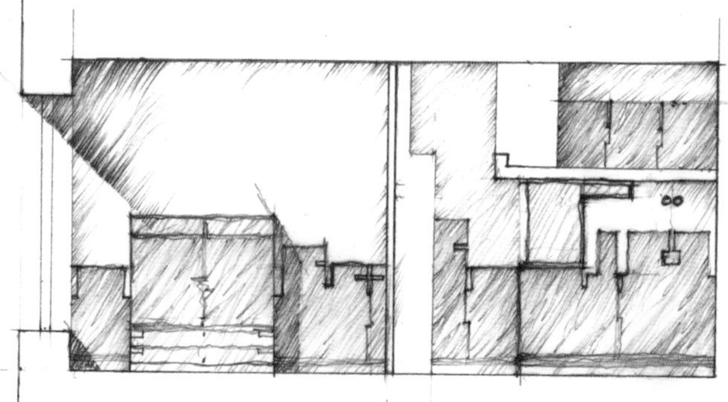

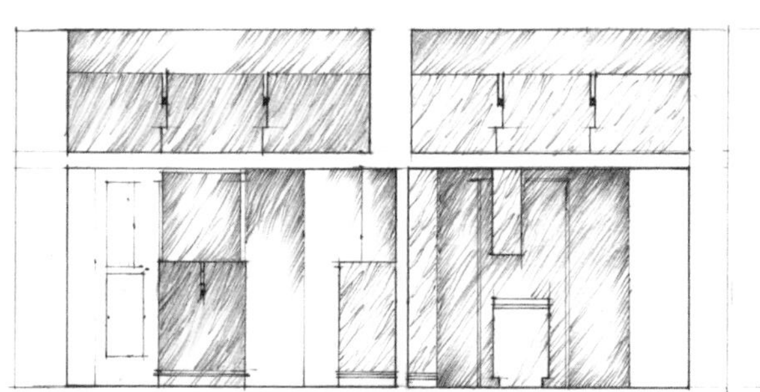

2

1 | Section through the apartment from the exterior wall through the curved red wall looking east
2 | Study section drawings of the wall woodwork
3 | Section through the apartment showing the bedroom lofts above the dressing room
4 | Floor plan

3

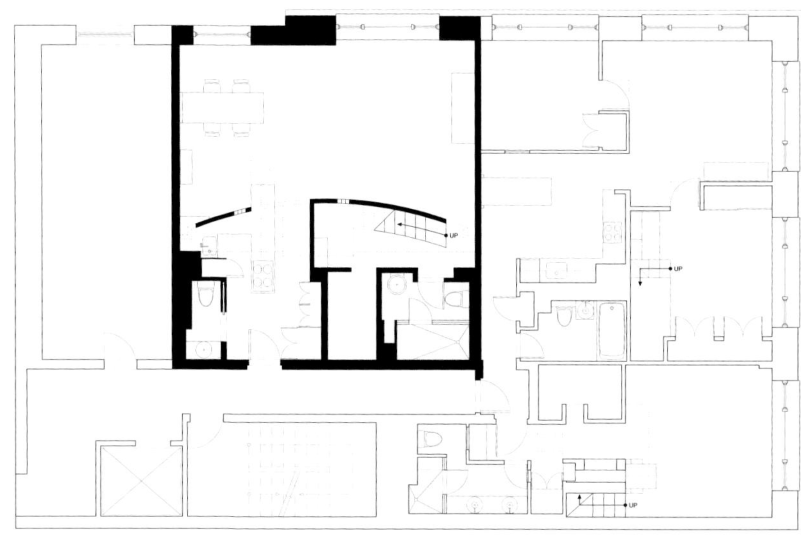

4

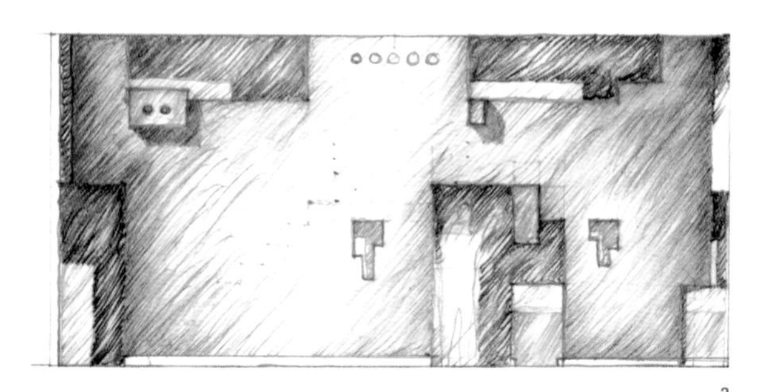

3

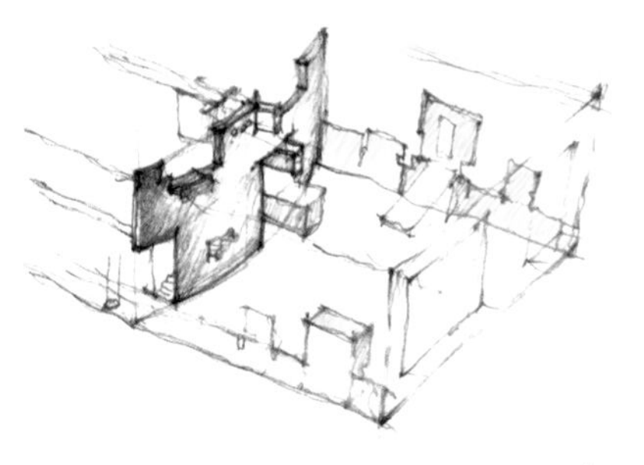

4

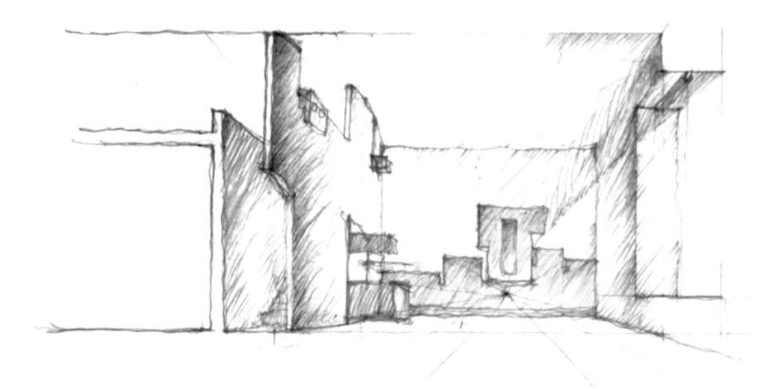

5

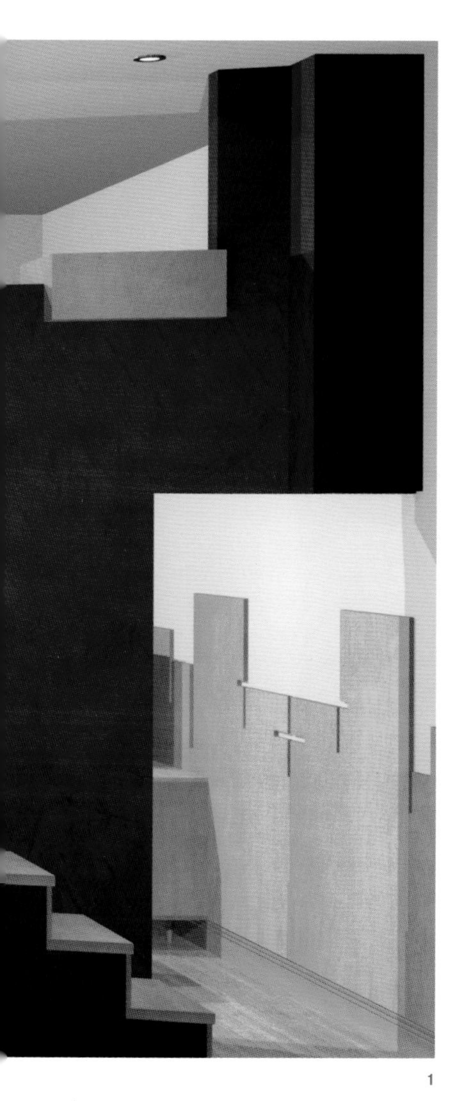

1

2

1 | Section through the kitchen and stair up to the bedroom lofts
2 | Detail view of the dining table with the red living room wall beyond
3 | Study elevation of the curved red living room wall
4 | Sketch illustrating the space of the apartment
5 | Section perspective sketch of the living room space
6 | Detail sketch of the curved red wall with the projecting kitchen counter

6

project name	Glocer Renovation
location	New York City
year of design	2002
year of completion	2003
client	Maarit & Thomas Glocer
lot size	100' x 100'
project size	1,800 sq.ft.
architect	George Ranalli
associates	Robert Silman Structural Engineer
design team	Brock Danner
photographer	George Ranalli

Glocer Renovation

1

In a stately, elegant Emory Roth building on Manhattan's upper east side, the redesign of a 1,200 square foot apartment recalls the occupants' sleek Scandinavian home. Although achieving simplicity is never simple, the architectural design for the project reconfigures existing space into two levels, which provides three good-sized bedrooms, connected by a tower stair to a living room cum guest room, for a family of four. The spacious light filled terrace facing penthouse features a honey colored line of wood, forming doorframes, corner guards, and windows, and enclosing cables and accessories, while subtle design cues define spaces within, for a functionally minimalist city home.

An unrealized phase of the project, scheduled for 2017, features an upper storey addition for a master bedroom suite, and two smaller rooms. Sets of interconnecting prisms, topped by partially cropped conical roof lights, flanking a terrace, compose a new copper clad roof, extending the apartment skyward. This harmonious topography of cresting gables is designed to reflect the expressive tops of the surrounding cityscape.

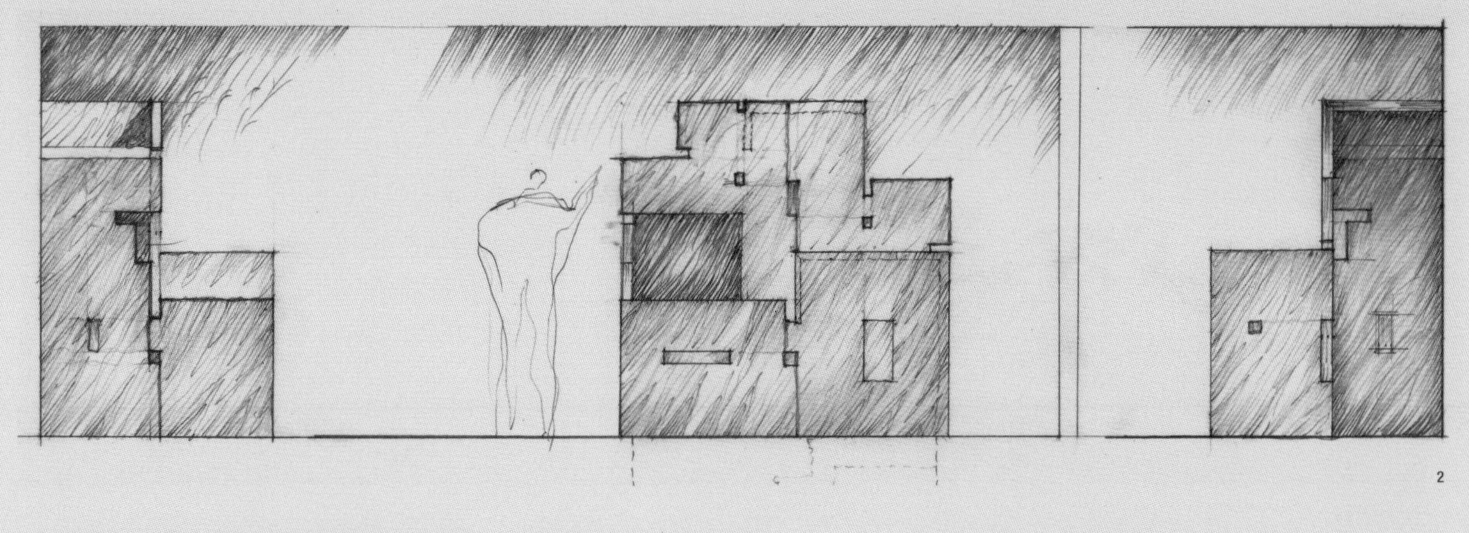

2

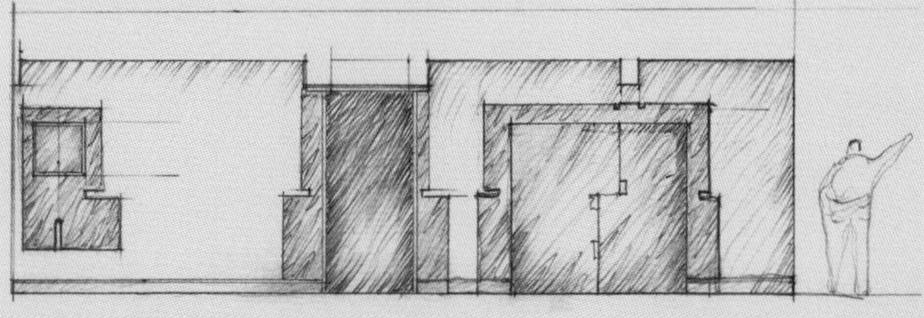

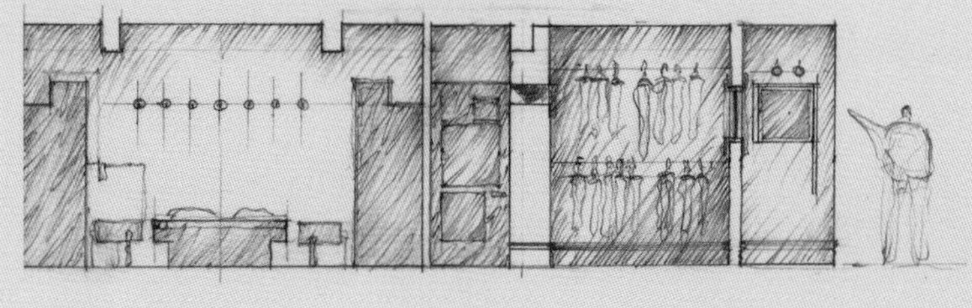

3

4

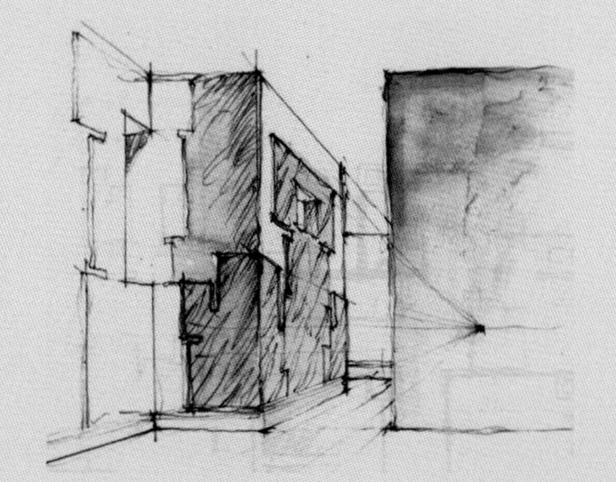

5

1 Stair detail photo
2 Study elevations of the stair bulkhead
3 Elevation sketches of the bedrooms
4 Base detail sketch and section through the stair connecting the penthouse to the lower bedroom floor
5 Sketch of the bedroom entry hall

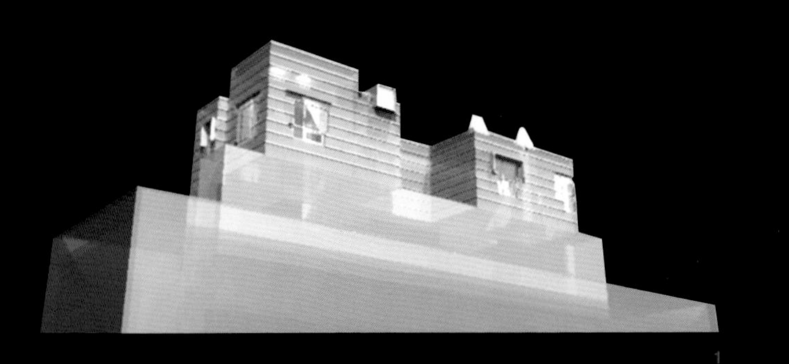
1

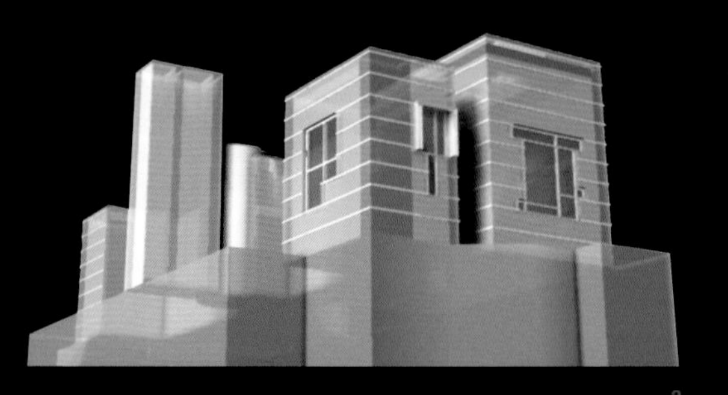
2

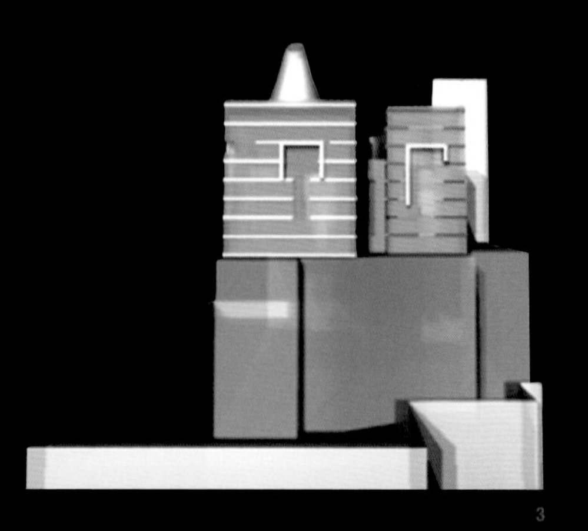
3

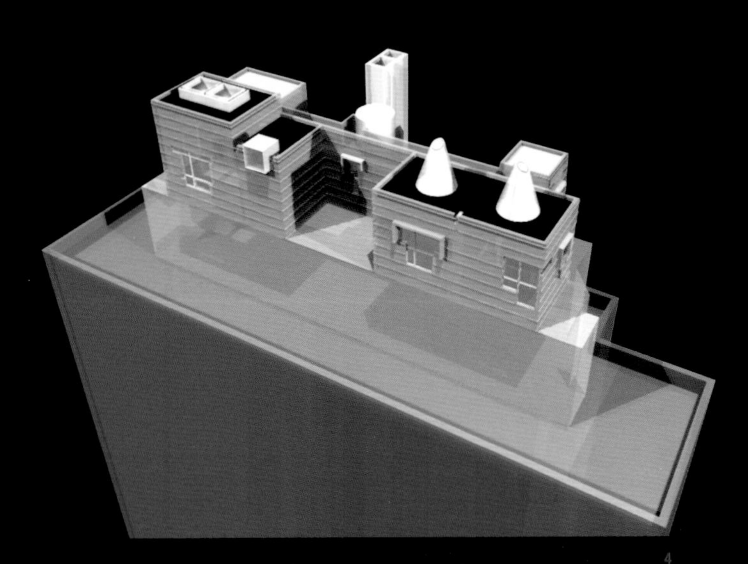
4

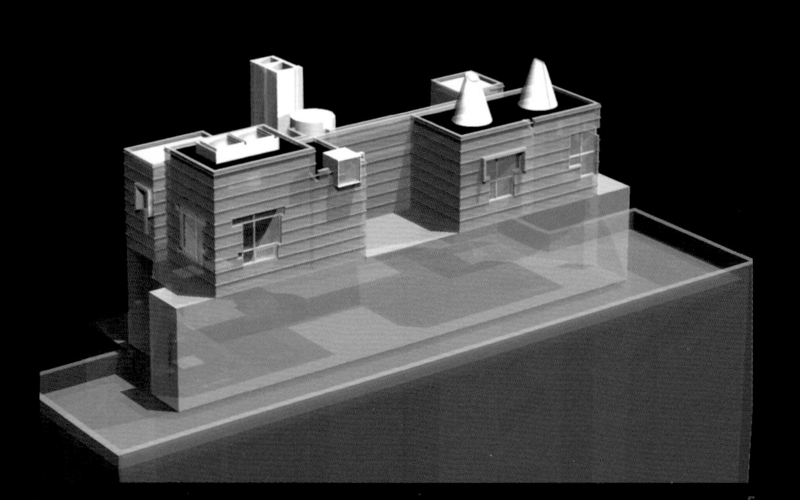
5

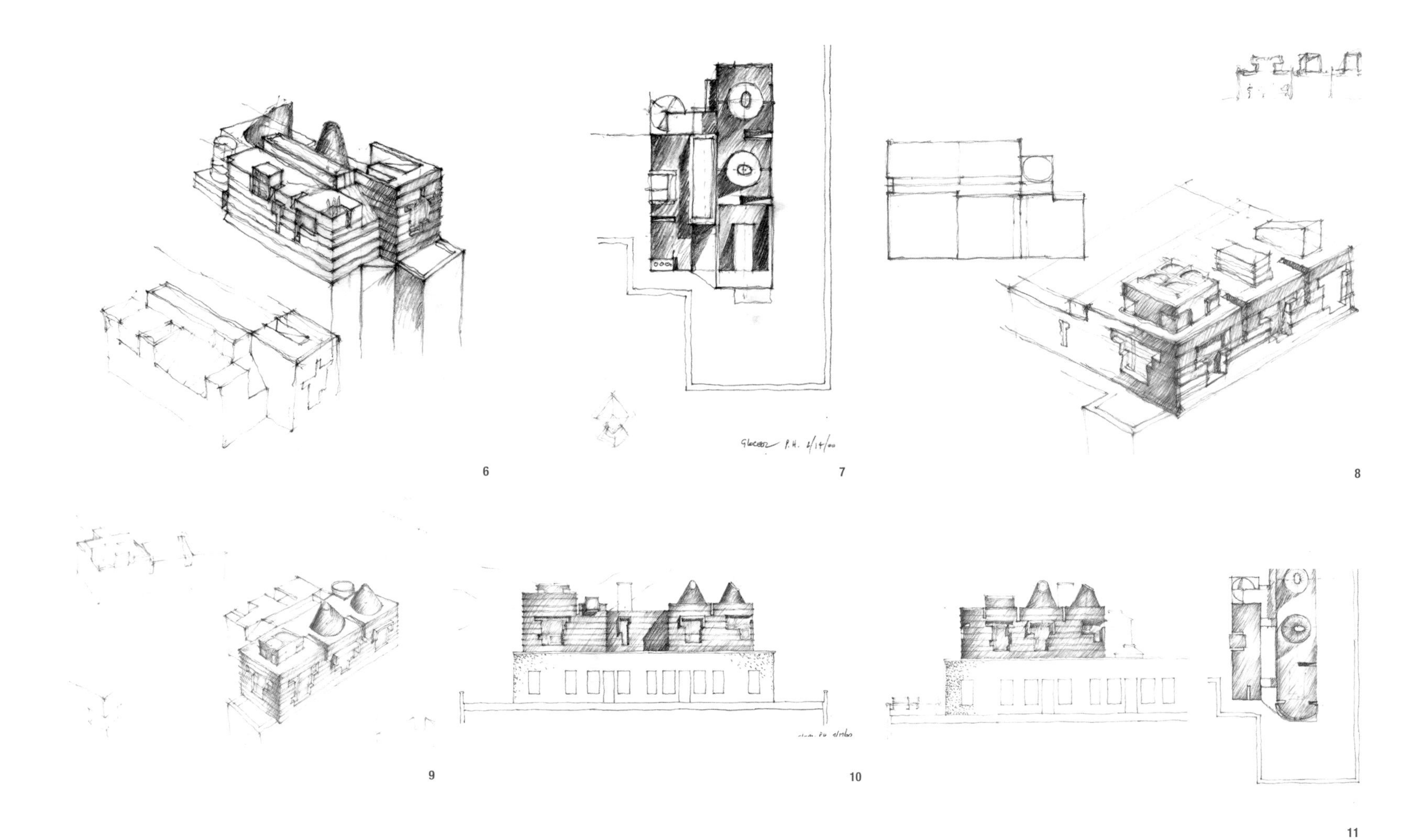

1 Model of the penthouse addition from below
2 Model of the back side of the penthouse addition from below
3 Children's bedroom end of the addition
4 View of the addition from above
5 View of the addition from above with the master bedroom on the left
6 Sketch of the massing
7 Roof plan
8 Massing study sketch
9 Sketch of the bedroom side
10 Sketch elevation of the new addition on top of the existing penthouse
11 Study elevation and roof plan

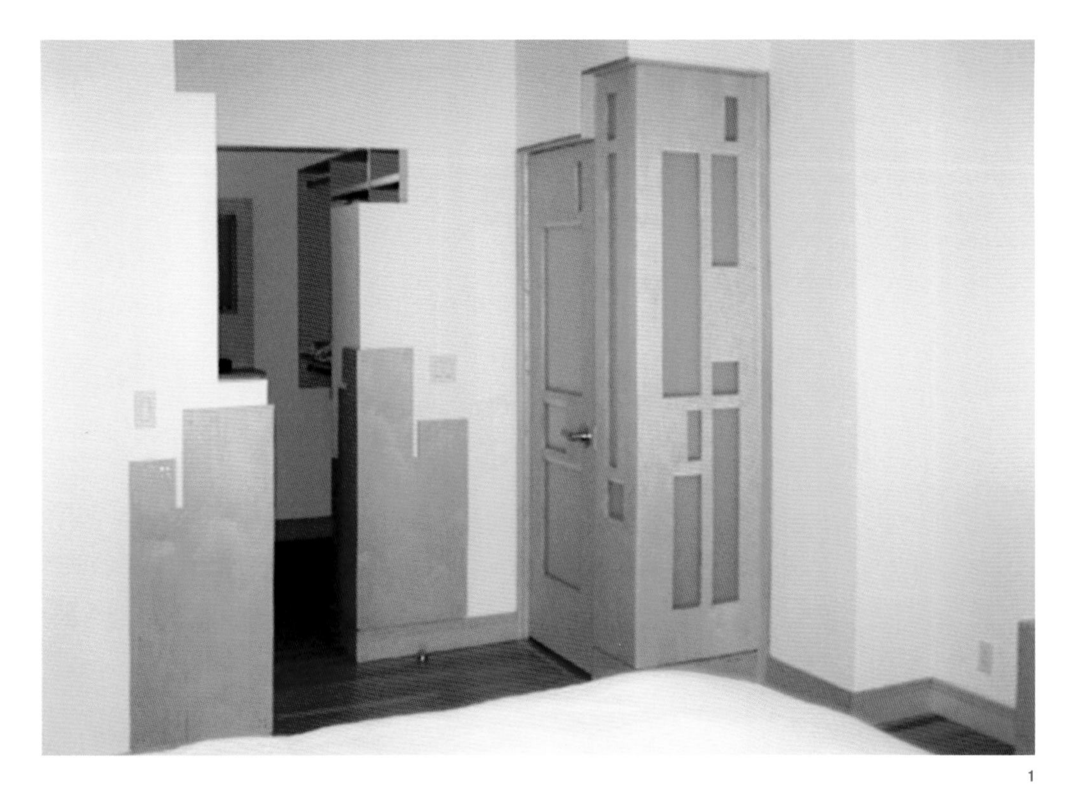

1

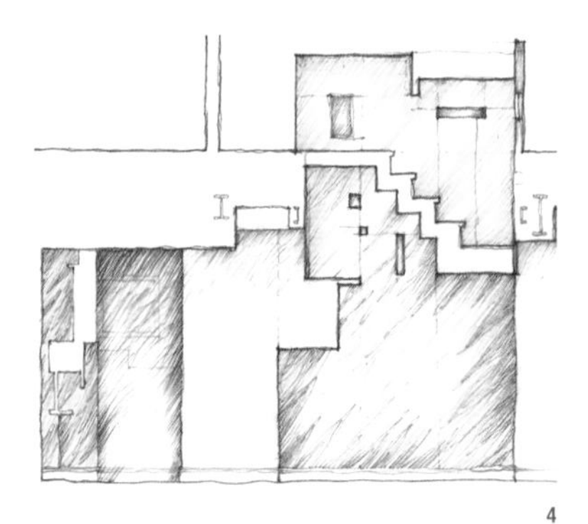

4

2

3

1 | Photo of the master bedroom
2 | Hallway between the bedrooms
3 | Child's bedroom
4 | Section sketch through the stair
5 | Entry door to the child's bedroom
6 | Stair enclosure detail
7 | Hallway windows into master bathroom
8 | Entry hall from the bedrooms
9 | Entry hall from the stair

5

6

7

8

9

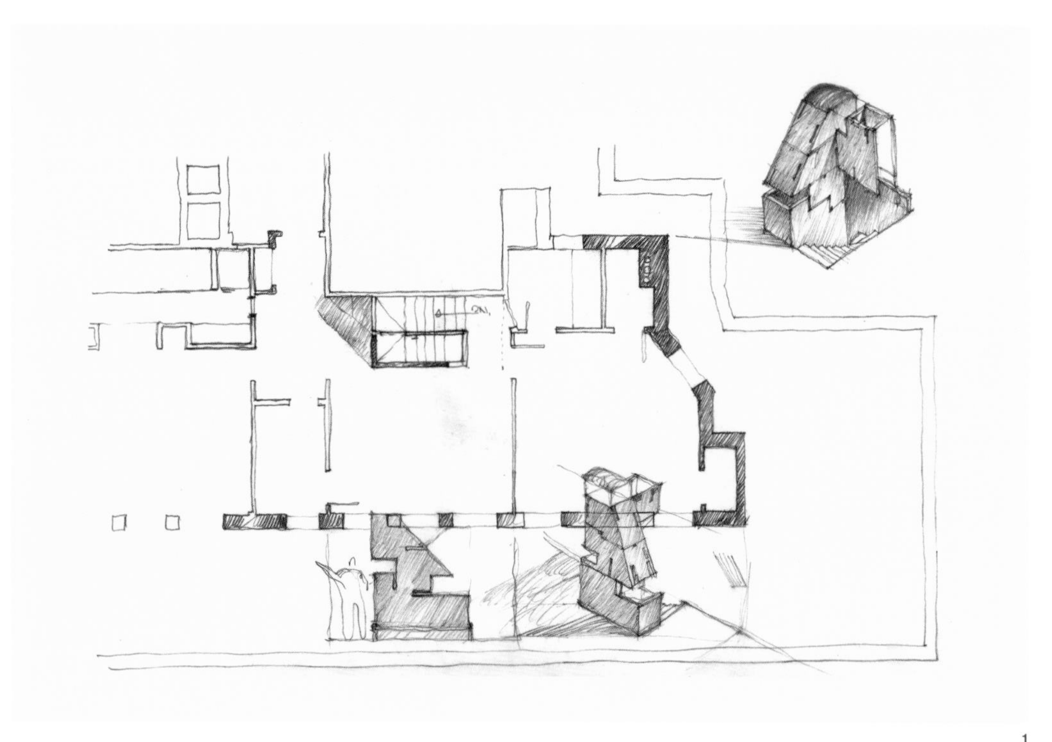

1

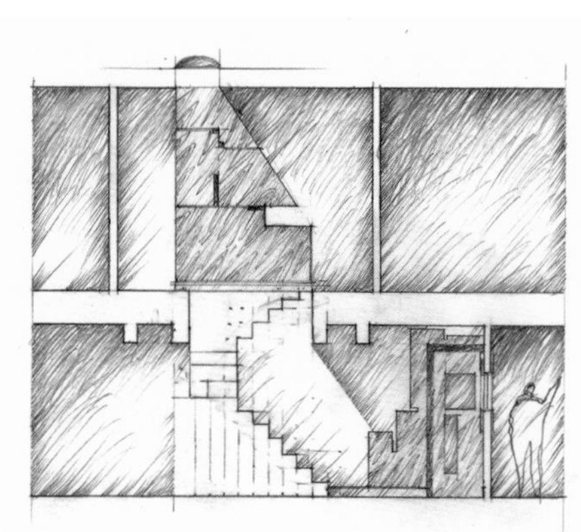

2

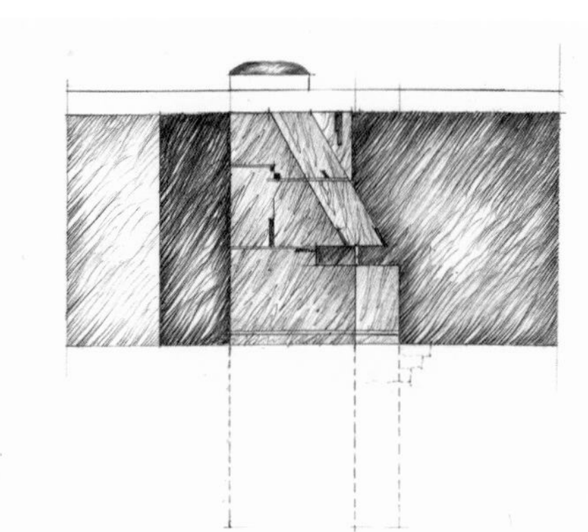

3

1 | Study drawing of early bulkhead design
2 | Sketch section drawing of the new stair and bulkhead
3 | Living room view of early bulkhead design
4 | Model view from the back side
5 | Study model from the bedroom side
6 | Study model showing the new addition on top of the existing penthouse
7 | Study model from the master bedroom and bathroom end
8 | Study model from the children's bedroom end

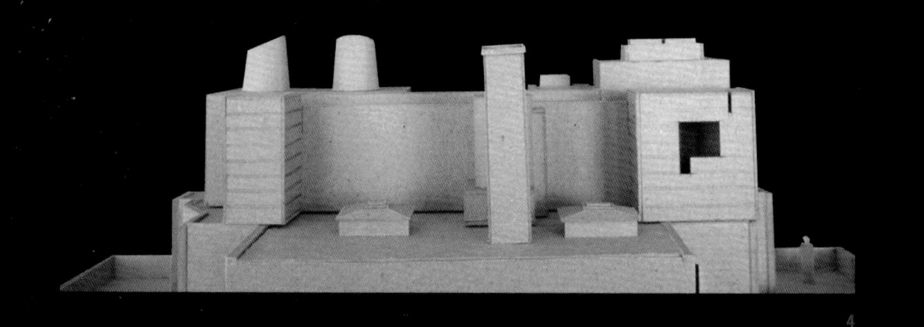
4

5

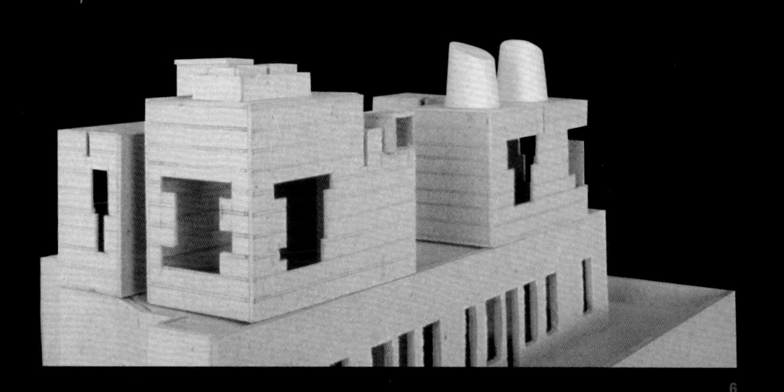
6

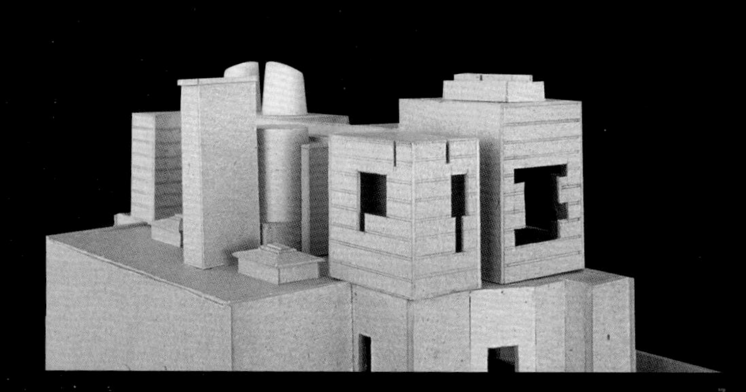
7

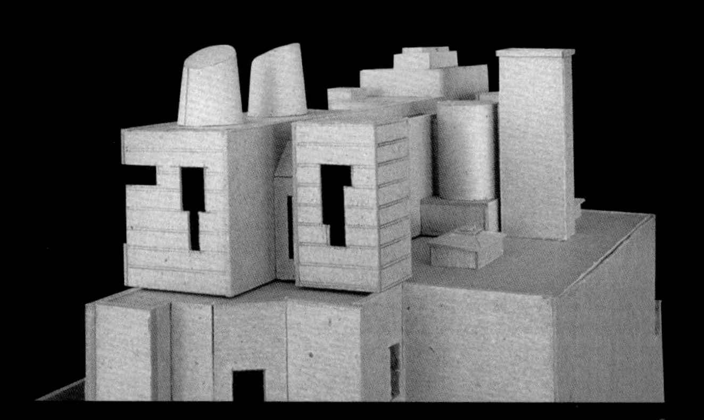
8

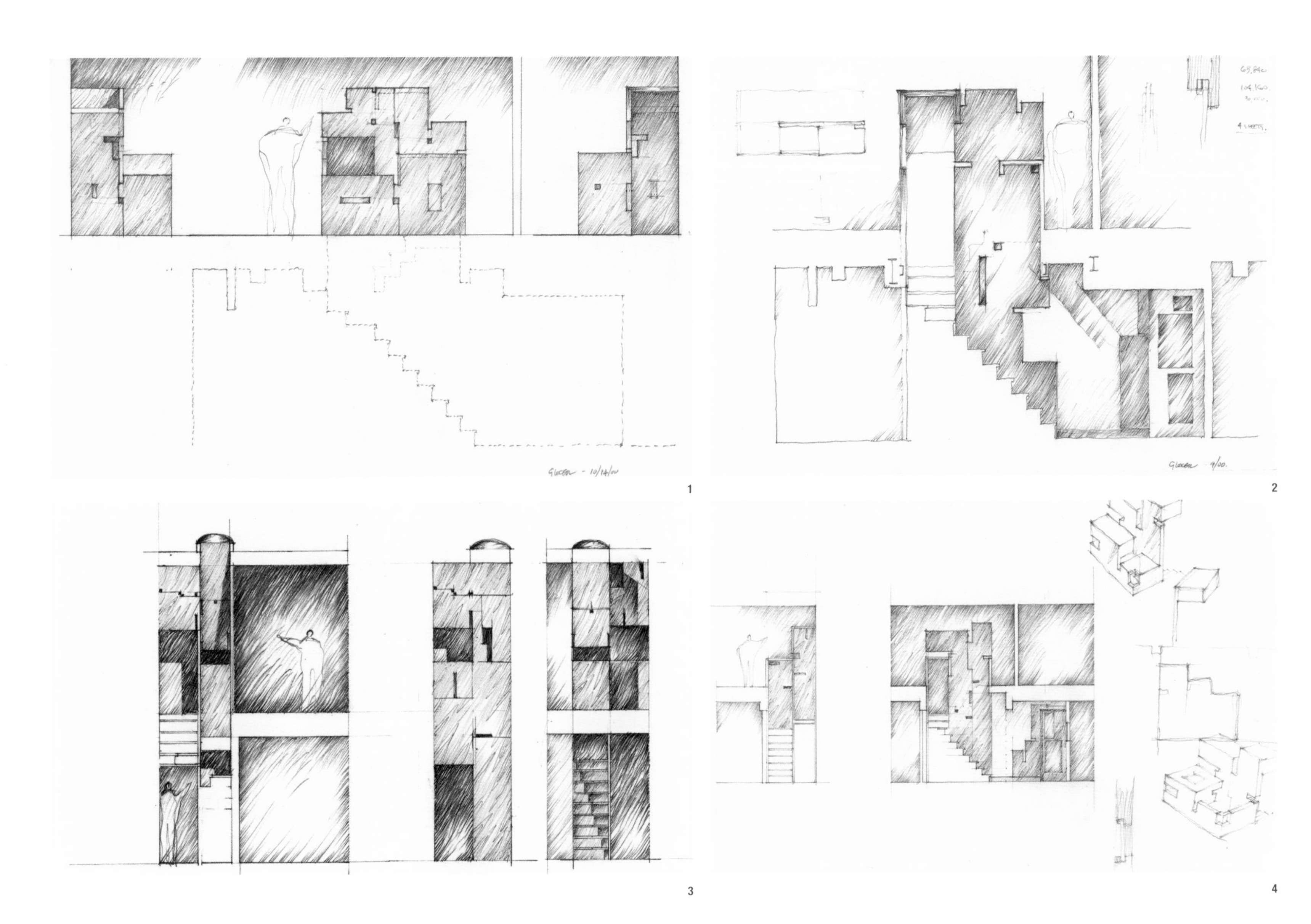

1

2

3

4

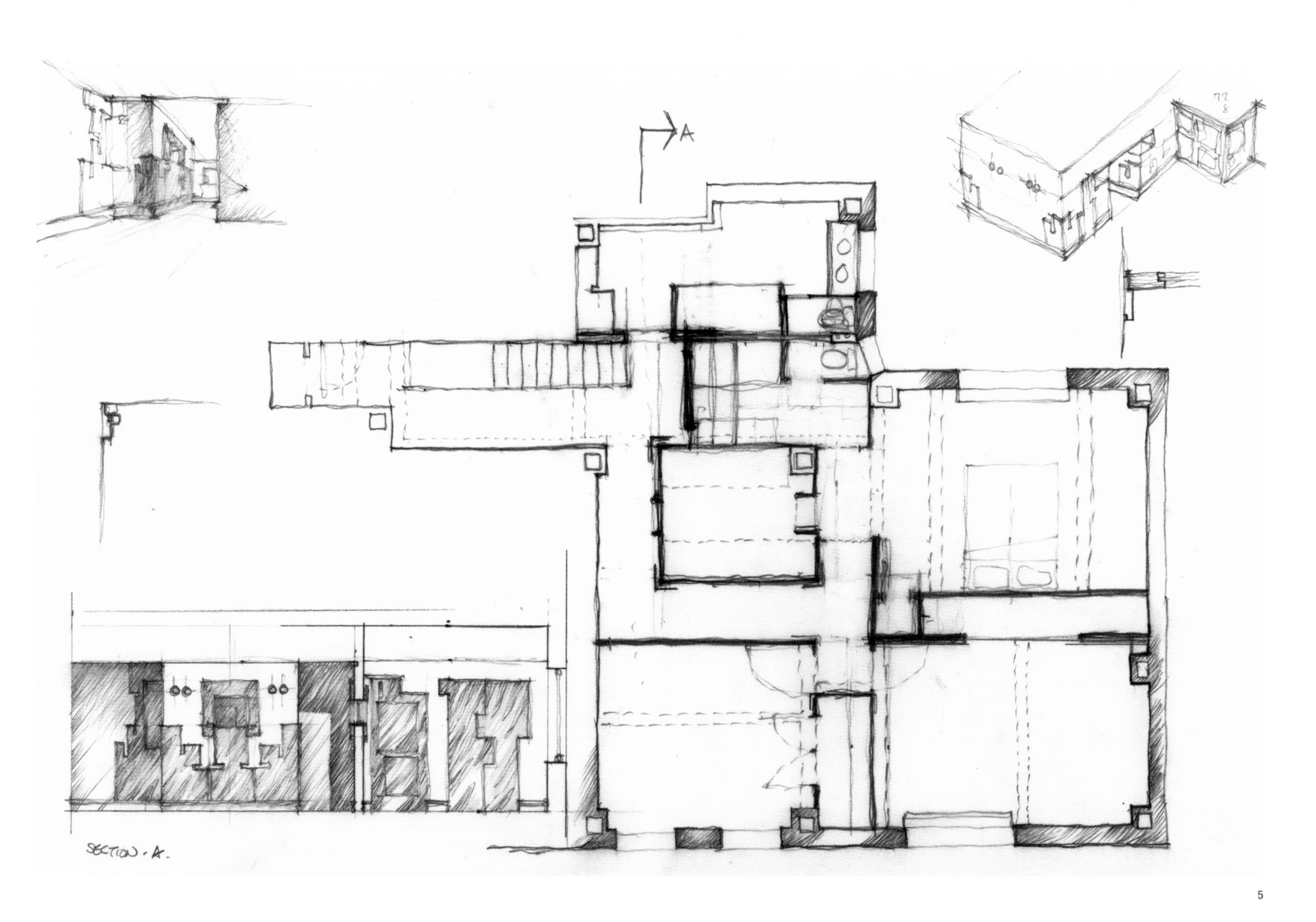

5

1 Early sketches of the stair bulkhead
2 Sketch section of the new stair and bulkhead
3 Bulkhead study section sketches
4 Stair sketches
5 Bedroom floor plan sketch with hall and elevation studies

project name	Blumenthal Renovation
location	Mt. Kisco, New York
year of design	1999
year of completion	2001
client	Wendy & Lawrence Blumenthal
lot size	¼ acre
project size	650 sq.ft.
architect	George Ranalli
associates	Robert Silman Structural Engineer
design team	Alexandra Porter, David Gissen, Mario Gentile
photographer	George Ranalli

Blumenthal Renovation

1

The owners of a tiny shingle-style bungalow home in northern Westchester County, New York sought an architectural remedy for their house. Notwithstanding its cozy depth, the rooms at the back never felt quite right. A dreary atmosphere in the ground-floor kitchen, dining room, and library drifted upstairs by way of a scrappy staircase.

Built in the 1930s, the timber-sided "saltbox" originally housed one bedroom, a bathroom, a living room, and a kitchen beneath a gabled roof. In the 1980s, a previous owner added a two-story stucco block at the end of the house, which featured a second floor master bedroom and bathroom, and at the other end of the original house a ground level, open porch.

The remedy for back of the house was to re-imagine the rear wall as a window, providing a more open interior in communication with the lush landscape. By removing the existing rear wall of the house, and replacing it with a wall of mahogany doors, a projected dining bay, with large picture windows, overlooks mature trees and flowerbeds and beautiful new limestone patio. This architectural engagement with the back wall permits sculpting sunlight to filter into the space previously drab, near claustrophobic space, amplifying the otherwise elusive aspects of the kitchen, dining room, and study. Pristine mahogany is composed around doorways, transoms, and windows. The revisions incorporate the preexisting porch, now screened in.

Soft interior lighting and a precise arrangement of flaxen-grain wood cabinetry transform an incommodious passageway into a generously proportioned and stylish dressing area, companionable with newly designed bedroom furniture, resulting in a brighter, more spacious and functional bedroom suite.

All these elements are seamlessly distributed into the multiple architectural styles of the original house, solving preexisting spatial problems while adding a new range of architectural expression.

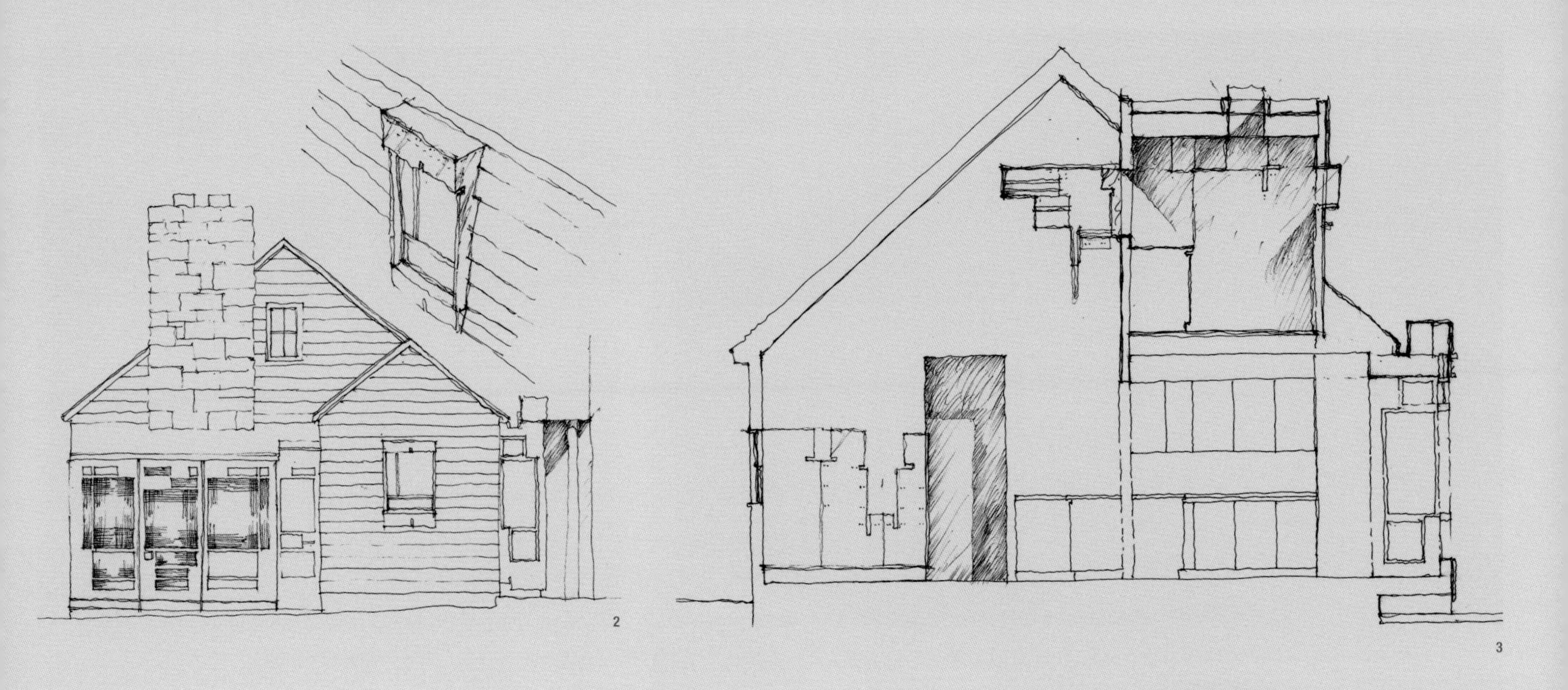

2

3

4

5

1 View of the new rear wall, limestone stairs, dining bay and copper scuppers
2 Pen and ink sketch of the screen porch and window
3 Pen and ink section sketch
4 Side of the house with screen porch and dining bay
5 View from Lakeside Road

1

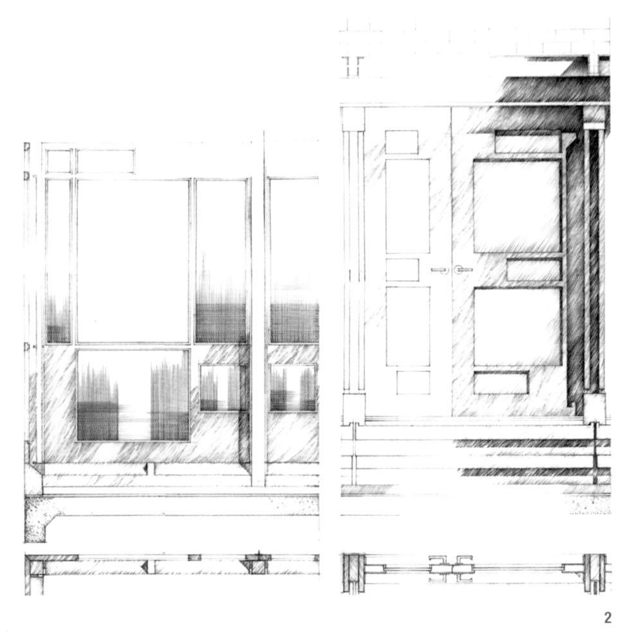

2

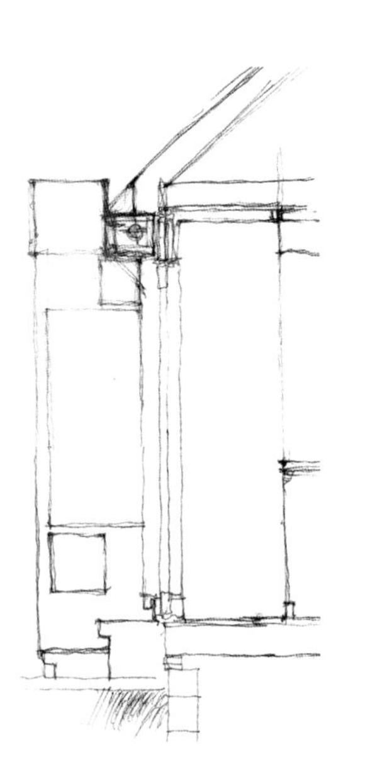

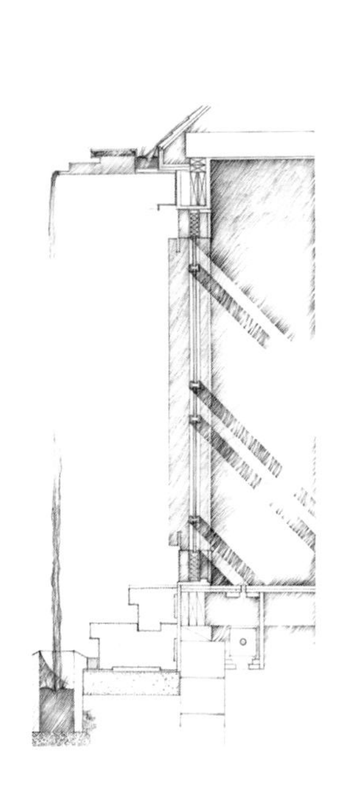

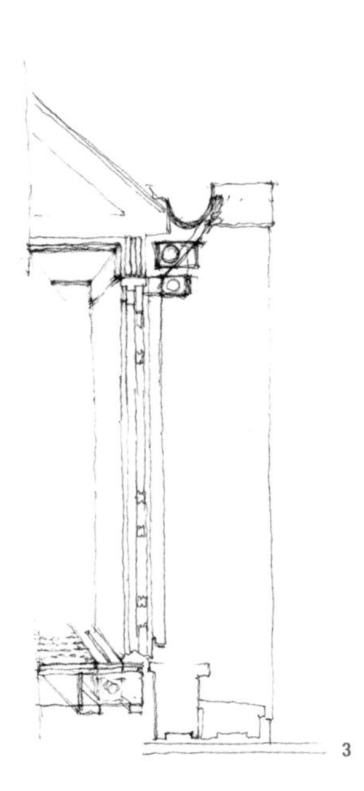

3

4

5

6

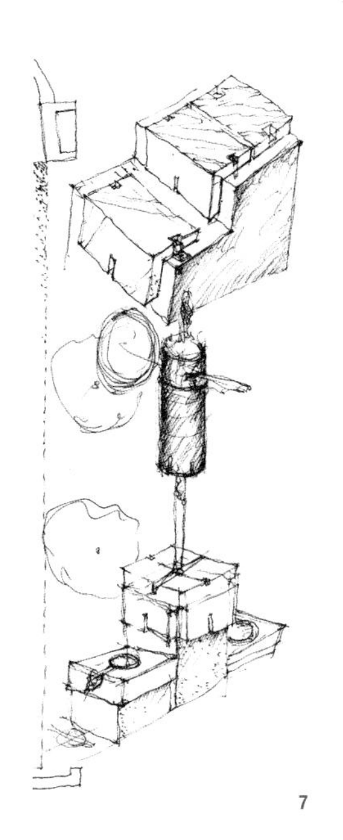

7

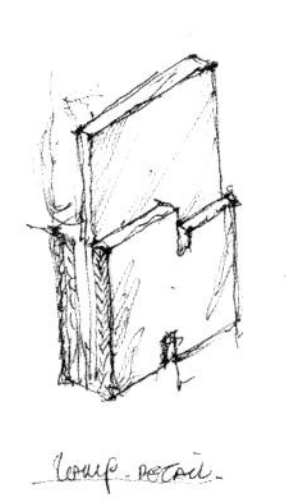
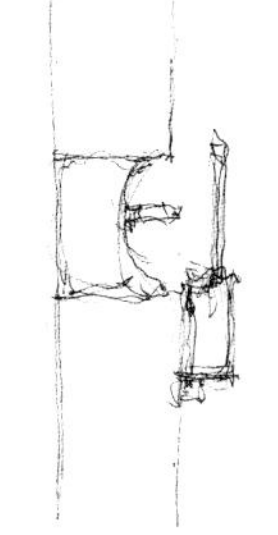

8

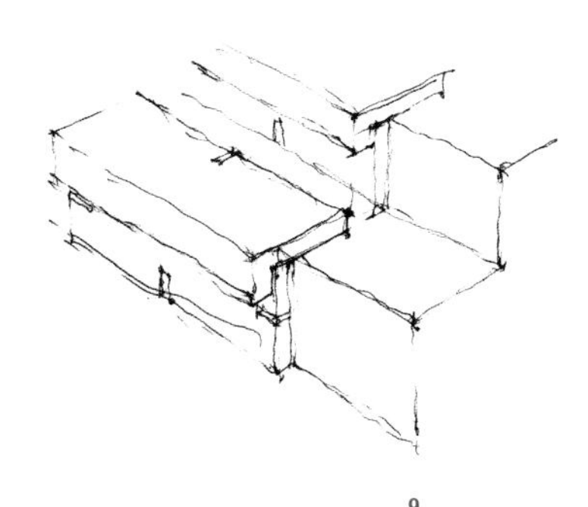

9

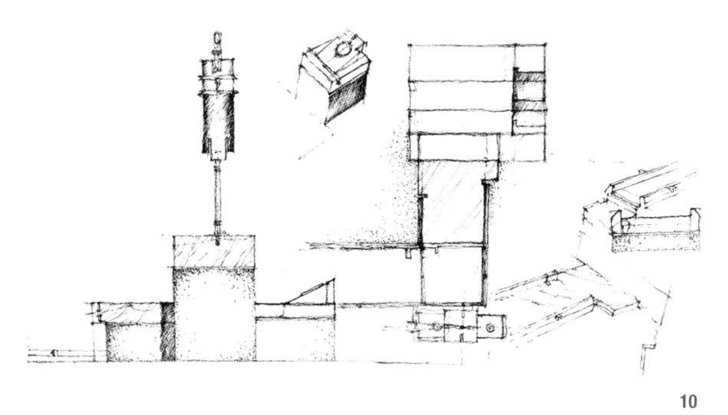

10

1 View of the rear wall with new mahogany doors, limestone steps and copper scuppers
2 Study drawing of the screen porch and rear door assemblies
3 Study sections of the rear wall
4 Detail view of the mahogany dining bay
5 Limestone stairs and limestone water basins
6 Rear wall detail view
7 Sketch of the weather vane and outdoor stairs
8 Lamp sketch
9 Screen porch stair detail sketch
10 Landscape sketch
11 Screen porch stair detail sketch

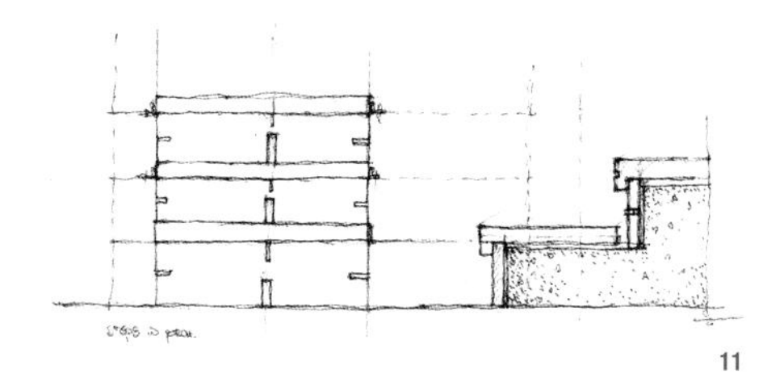

11

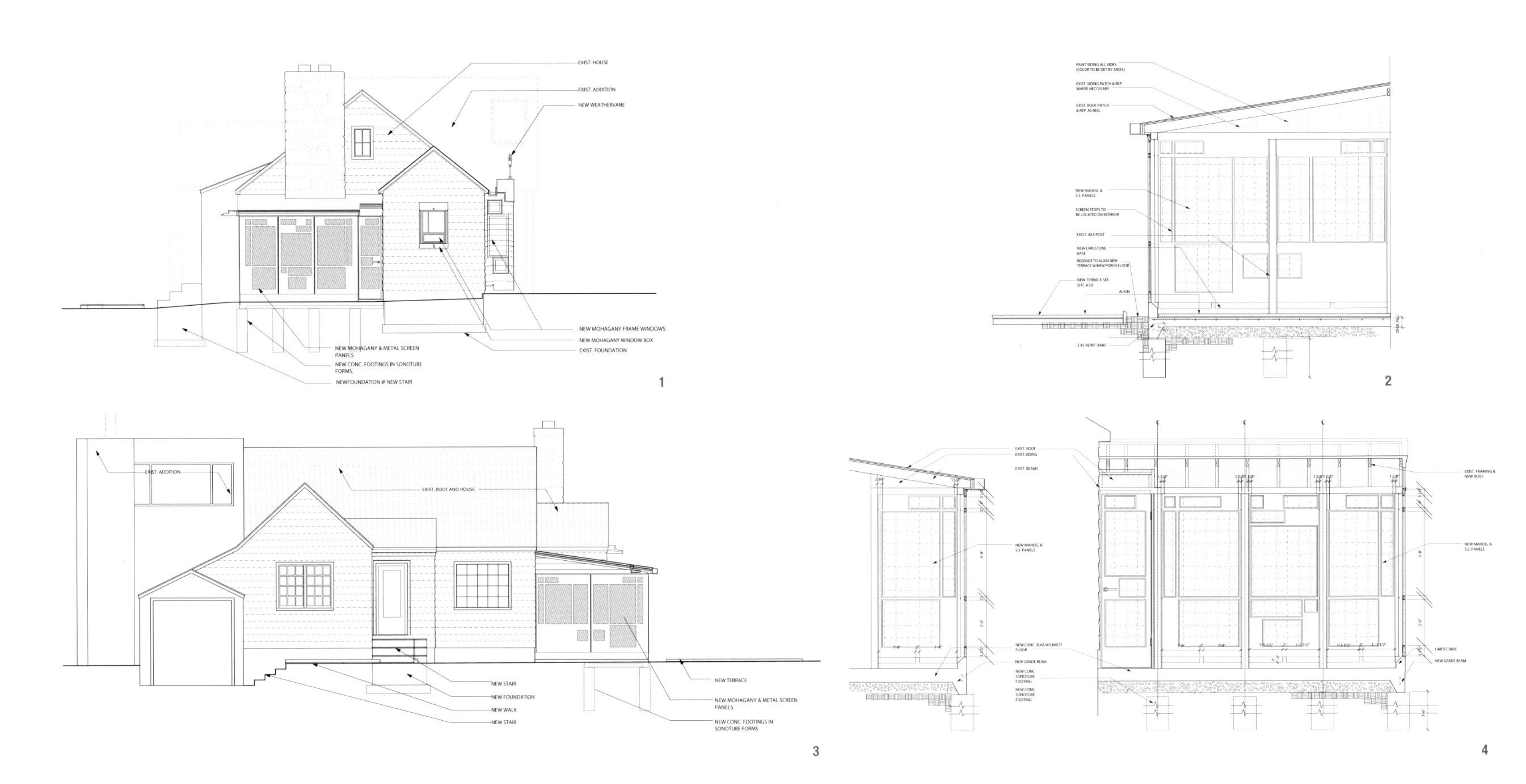

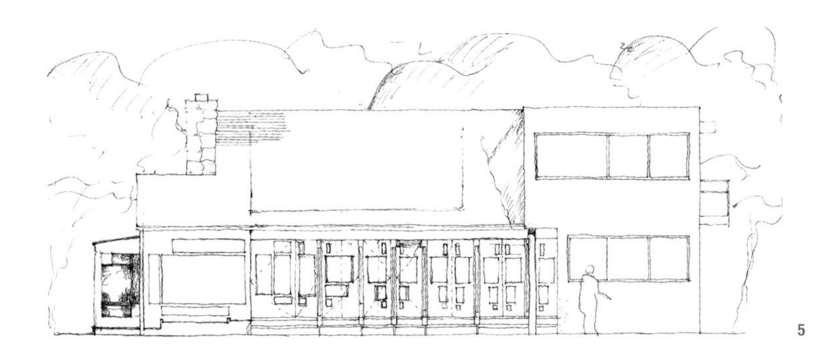

The added elements are fabricated in a set of distinctive and highly visible material choices to enhance the existing building while expanding the range of design. Each new element, such as the copper scuppers or white limestone catch basins, solves a technical problem while also extending the inside-outside relationships to a higher degree of resolution. For example, the stonework and catch basins containing water from the new attending copper scuppers project the space of the house beyond its previous scale, more fully engaging with the site and landscape beyond. Water in the catch basins is returned to the ground, making this an early environmental design.

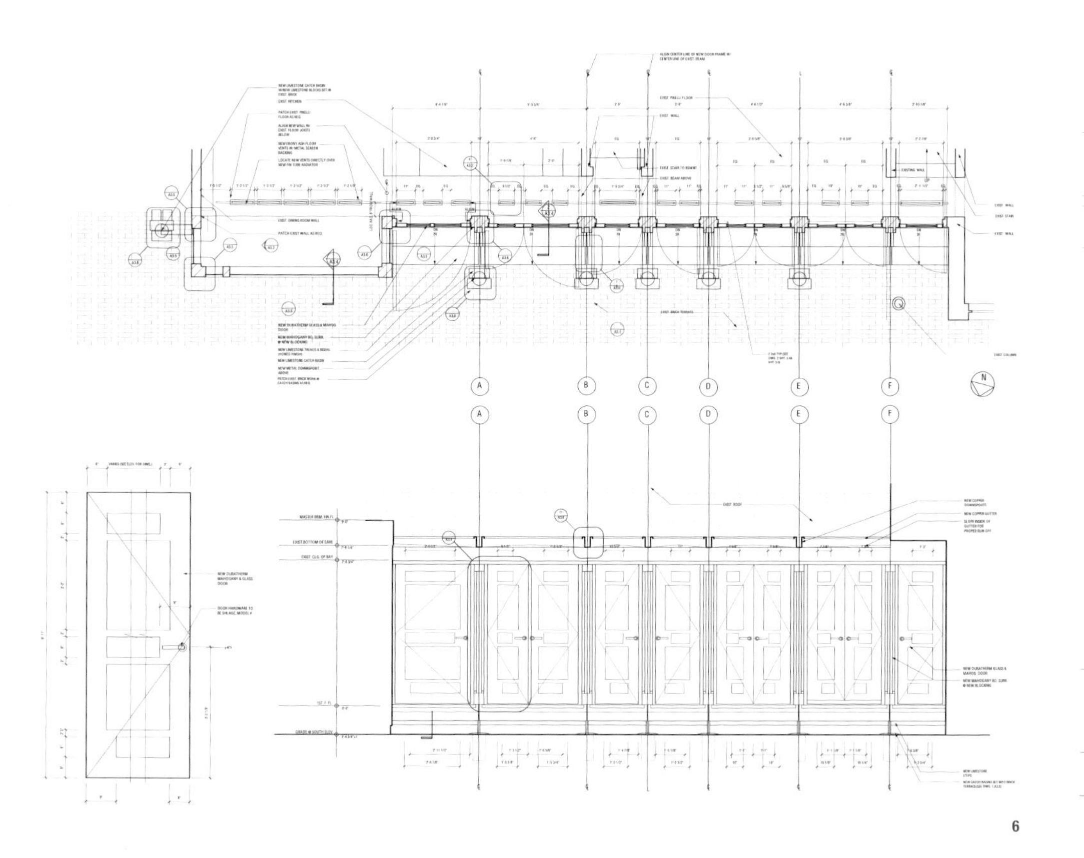

6

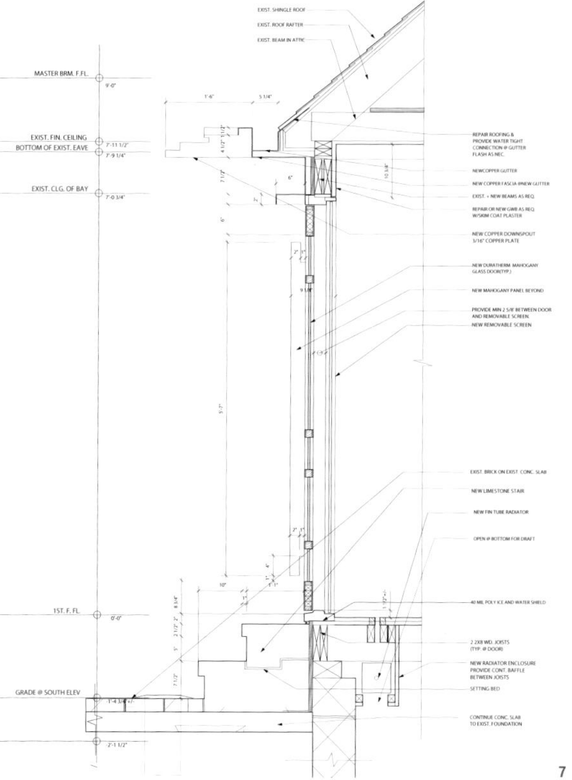

7

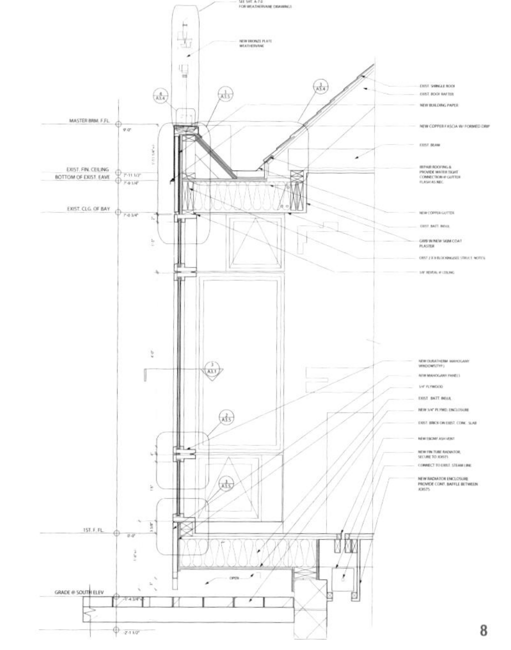

8

1 Construction drawing for the elevation of the scree porch and dining bay
2 Cross section of the screen porch
3 Construction drawing for the front of the house side elevation of the screen porch
4 Construction sections through the screen porch
5 Sketch elevation of the new rear wall and existing house
6 Construction plan of the rear wall with new columns & doors and construction elevation of the columns and doors of the new rear wall
7 Section through the doors, stairs and scupper assembly
8 Dining bay section showing the construction assembly and alternate location of the weather vane

1

2

1 Detail of the drawers
2 Dressing room area with the varied size drawers
3 Pen & ink sketch of of the closet doors with inlaid wood
4 Pen & ink sketch of the hallway elevation in the dressing room area
5 Sketch elevation of the drawers
6 Corner of the hallway in the dressing room
7 Custom designed lamps
8 Lamps and drawer details

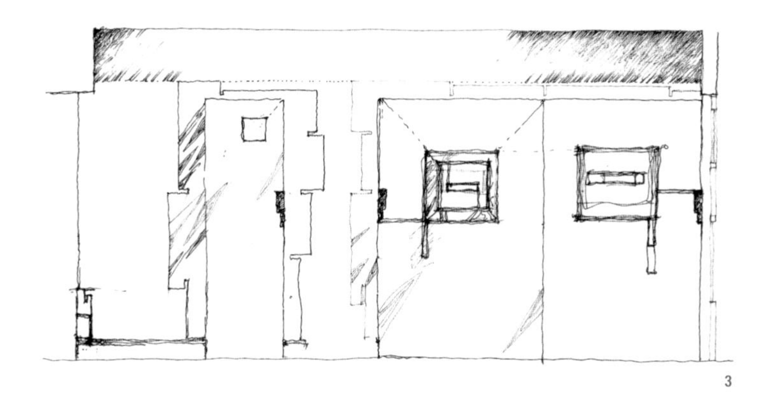

3

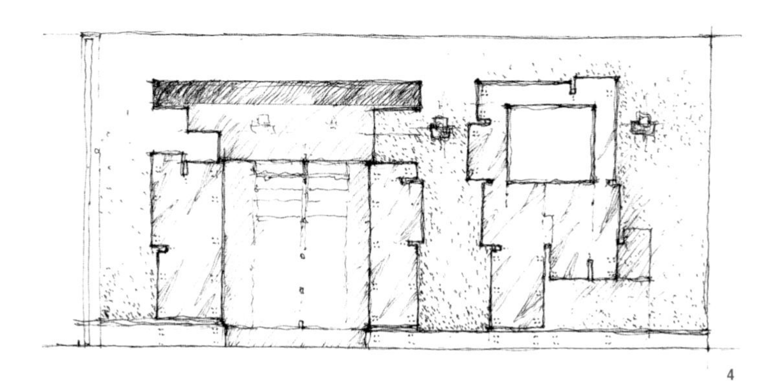

4

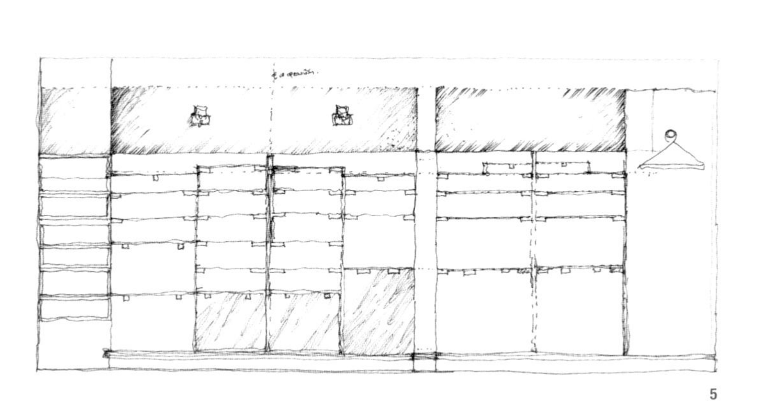

5

6

7

8

project name	75th Street Renovation
location	East 75th Street, New York City
year of design	1997
client	Name withheld at owner's request
lot size	5,000 sq.ft.
project size	20,000 sq.ft.
architect	George Ranalli
associates	Robert Silman Structural Engineer
design team	John Butterworth, Donald Hearn, Nathaniel Worden, Daniel Joo, Eugene Park, Lawrence Bekkerman

75th Street Renovation

1

The project is a restoration and renovation of a five-story, double-bay building on East 75th Street in Manhattan. Most of the building was gutted down to the structure as a result of decades of changing clients. The existing landmark building structure features an elegant façade built in 1912–1914. In the interior, a historic, stencil-painted wood stair moving through three floors was preserved.

The program for the new project is a residence for a couple occupying the full 20,000 square feet of the building. There are public and private aspects to the space in the building. On the first floor, a large reception hall and screening room accommodates the owner's professional activities. The second floor presents a large-scale living room and dining room connecting to an outdoor sculpture terrace. This floor also includes a kitchen and service area. The third through fifth floors are the couple's private quarters.

The design carefully integrates new elements set delicately into the fabric of the original building. The street façade is restored, as required by the Landmarks Preservation Commission of New York City. On the second floor, the main reception/living room opens onto a garden, with newly designed fountains, sculpture pedestals, and surface treatments. On the third floor, a new three-story atrium rises up to the roof, capped by a magnificent oval structure and skylight. Behind the elaborate atrium walls, suites of rooms contain custom cabinets. The design for each space attends to particular functional requirements and spatial characteristics.

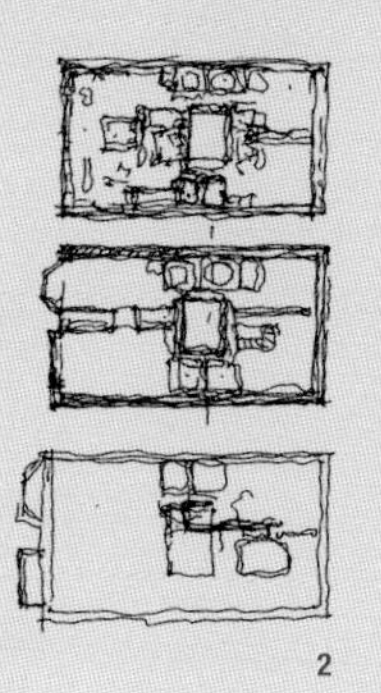

2

3

4

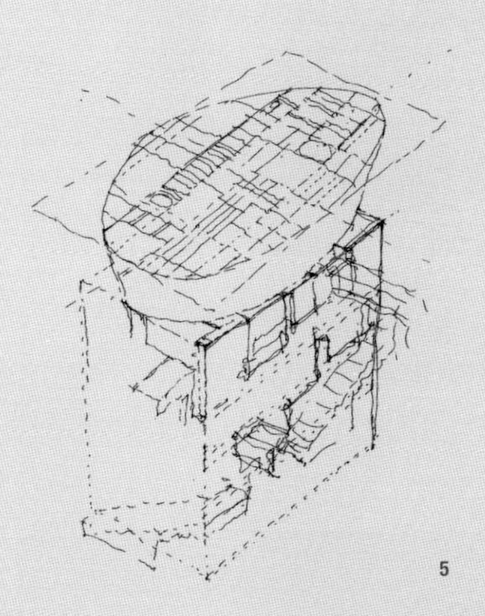

5

6

7

1 Photo of the existing building
2 Plan sketches
3 Pen and ink section study drawing
4 Perspective sketch of the atrium
5 Sketch of the atrium from above with the oval leaded glass skylight
6 Model photo, section of the upper floors
7 Model photo, exterior wall and upper copper roof enclosure

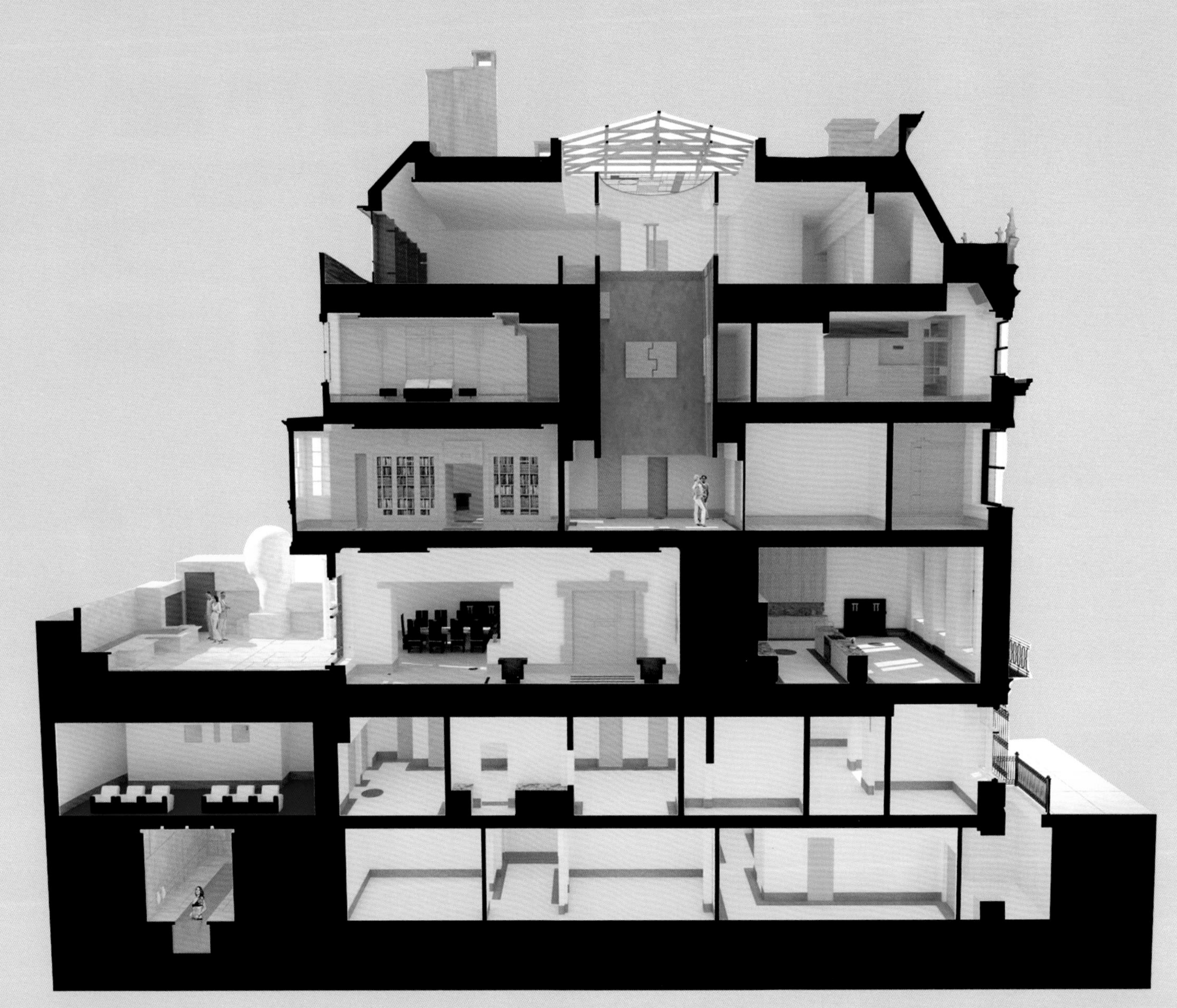

1

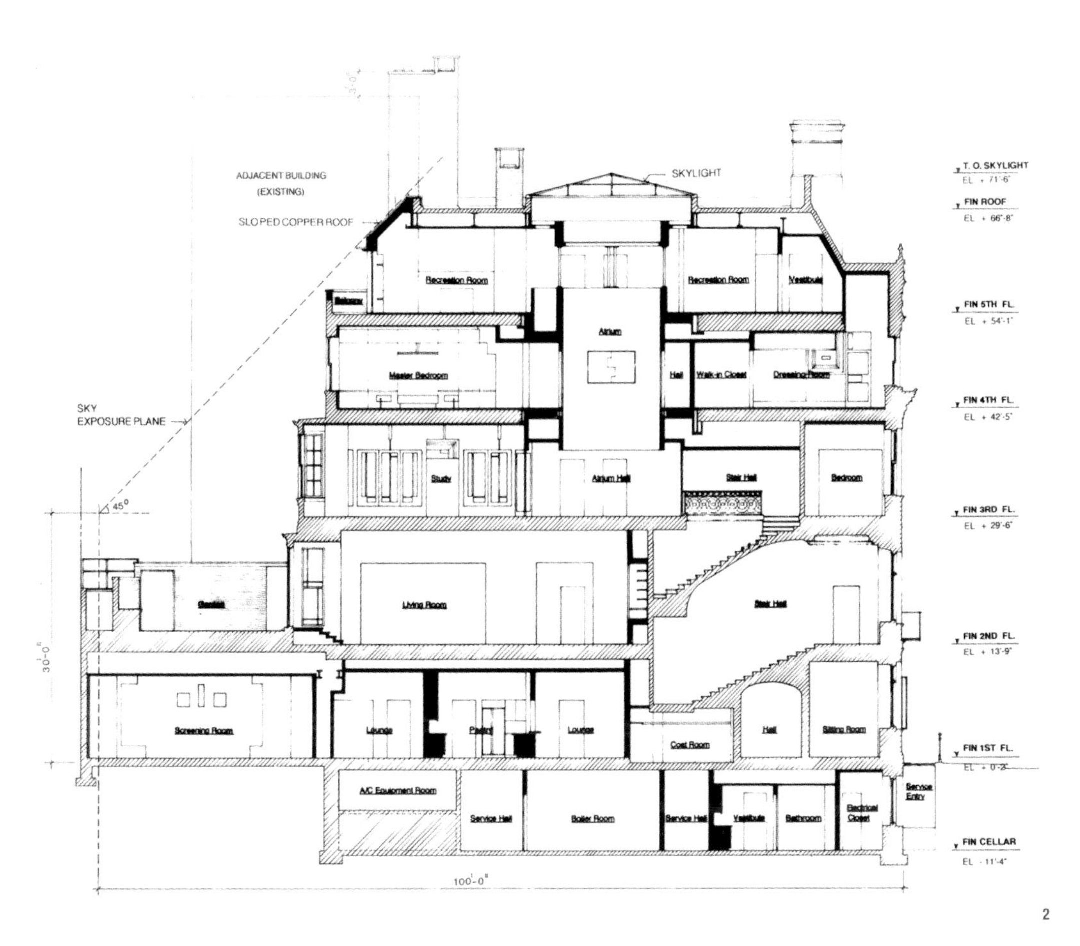

2

3

4

5

6

1 Computer model of the full building section
2 Section drawing
3 Living room and entry door, model photo
4 Library bookcase and entry door sequence, model photo
5 Master bedroom, model photo
6 Master dressing room cabinets and storage wall, model photo

1

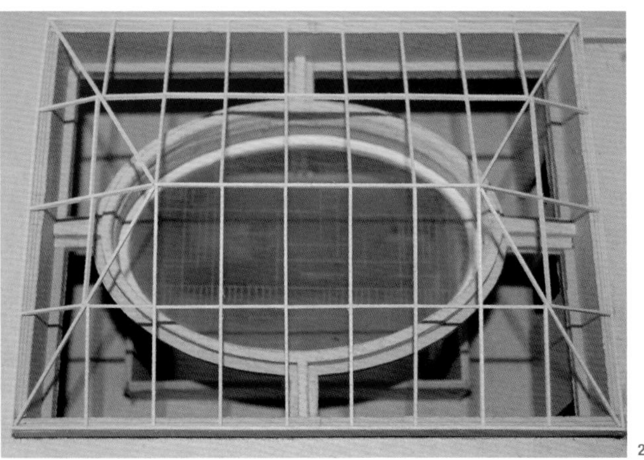

2

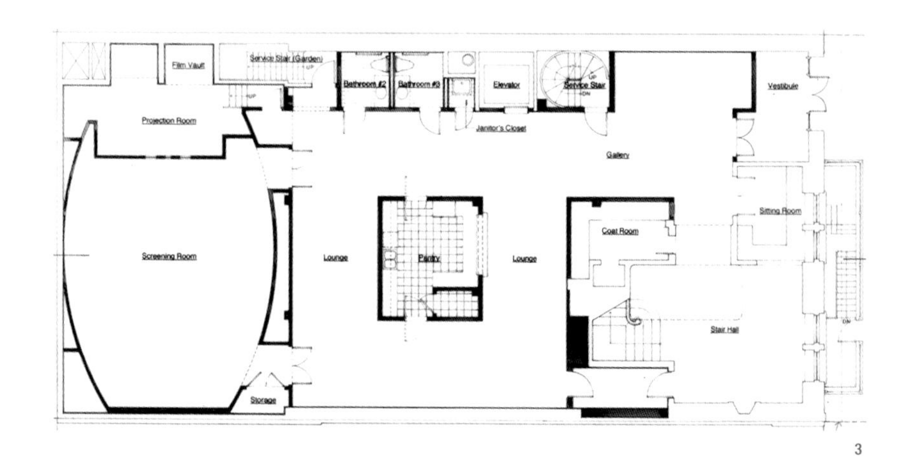
Film Vault
Service Stair (Garden)
Bathroom #2
Bathroom #3
Elevator
Service Stair
Vestibule
Projection Room
Janitor's Closet
Gallery
Sitting Room
Coat Room
Screening Room
Lounge
Pantry
Lounge
Stair Hall
Storage

3

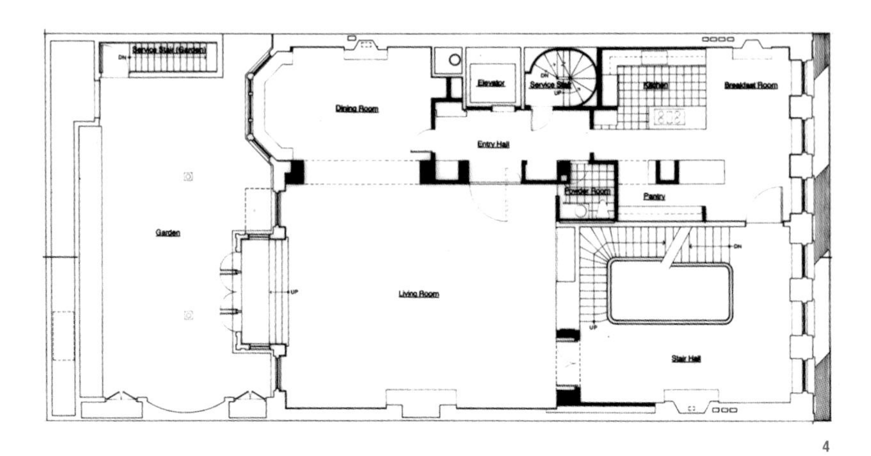
Service Stair (Garden)
Elevator
Service Stair
Kitchen
Breakfast Room
Dining Room
Entry Hall
Powder Room
Pantry
Garden
Living Room
Stair Hall

4

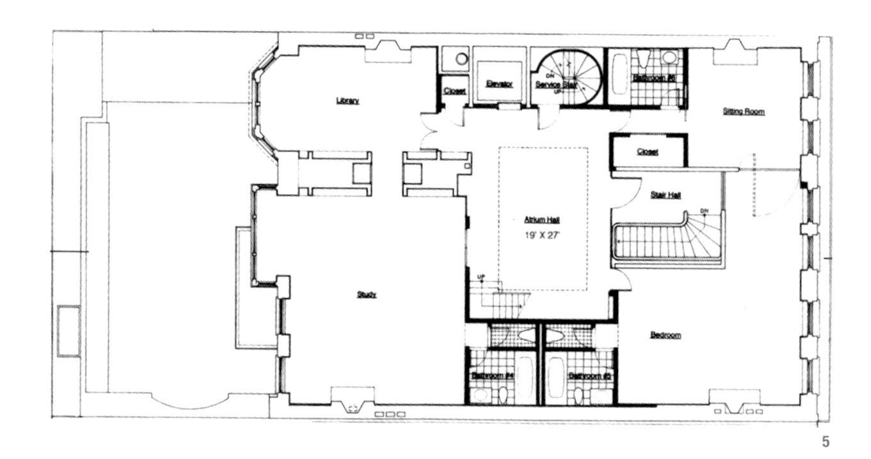
Library
Closet
Elevator
Service Stair
Sitting Room
Closet
Stair Hall
Atrium Hall
19' X 27'
Study
Bedroom

5

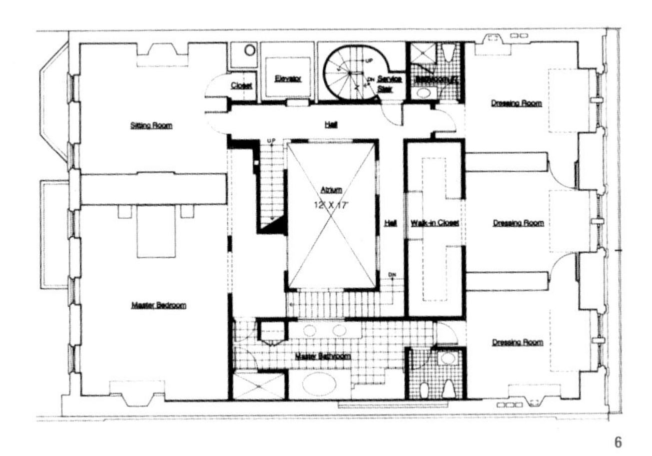

6

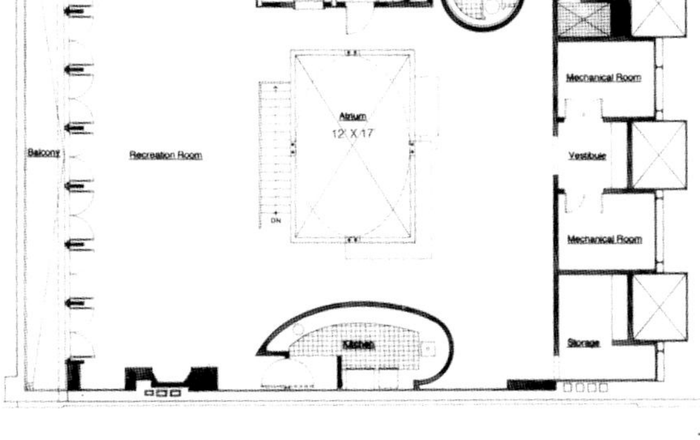

7

8

1 Computer model of the copper roof enclosure of the rear wall and skylight
2 Skylight enclosure model with the oval leaded glass atrium ceiling below
3 Lower floor plan with the screening room at the rear
4 Living/dining room floor
5 Library and reading room floor
6 Master bedroom floor
7 Upper lounge floor
8 Computer model of the rear garden wall with new mahogany doors in the living room and copper roof assembly and mahogany wood terrace doors on the lounge floor at the top

1

2

3

4

5

1 | View of the library with custom designed furniture and book cabinets
2 | Dining room with custom designed chairs and table
3 | Dressing room with custom designed cabinets
4 | Master bedroom wall, bed and night tables
5 | Living room and dining room beyond

project name	K Loft
location	New York City
year of design	1993
year of completion	1995
client	Jacque Metheny/ Robert Kirchbaum
lot size	2,500 sq.ft.
project size	2,250 sq.ft.
architect	George Ranalli
associates	Robert Silman Structural Engineer
design team	John Butterworth, Stephanie Rinaldi
photographer	Paul Warchol

K-Loft

1

The renovation of a residential Chelsea loft preserves the lofty expanse of existing space, while providing its occupants, two artists and their child, with two bedrooms, two bathrooms, a combined living and dining area open to a large kitchen, and workspaces for sculpture and printmaking. The architectural resolution centers on a unifying spatial theme not unlike a traditional courtyard house. The central spatial feature of two large sculptural elements is elaborated by architectural variation, within a soaring barrel-vaulted space.

Inside the 2,100 square foot rectangular loft, at the front, a central foyer leads into an artist's studio, with a new bathroom expanded from its original configuration. A separate entrance leads to a piazza-like interior for living and dining, which includes a large open kitchen. Nestled at back are the family's private quarters, including two spacious bedrooms, and a large bathroom. An antechamber outside the bedrooms, spacious enough for a private moment, or conversation, improvises space between more personal areas and the large expanse of living room.

Sculptural forms, defining the design of the kitchen, bathrooms, and bedrooms, undulate rhythmically beneath an existing vaulted brick ceiling; geometric spaces, within cabinetry, provide sculptural movement across transitive surfaces. A balance of materiality, extended further by honey-colored wood furniture, light fixtures, and cabinetry, moves across walls, and around doorframes, emphasizing and protecting corners and edges. Each interior design element echoes the planar inflections of the architectural design, fabricated at the same high-level of craftsmanship, producing a composed atmosphere. A combination of delicate lighting against the substantial brick ceiling, smaller lateral light sources, and tinted transom windowpanes, introduce an essence of the ephemeral into an otherwise solidly constructed space.

2

3

1 | Detail photo of the kitchen wall and pantry cabinet beyond
2 | Existing building exterior
3 | View of the living room from the entry

1

2

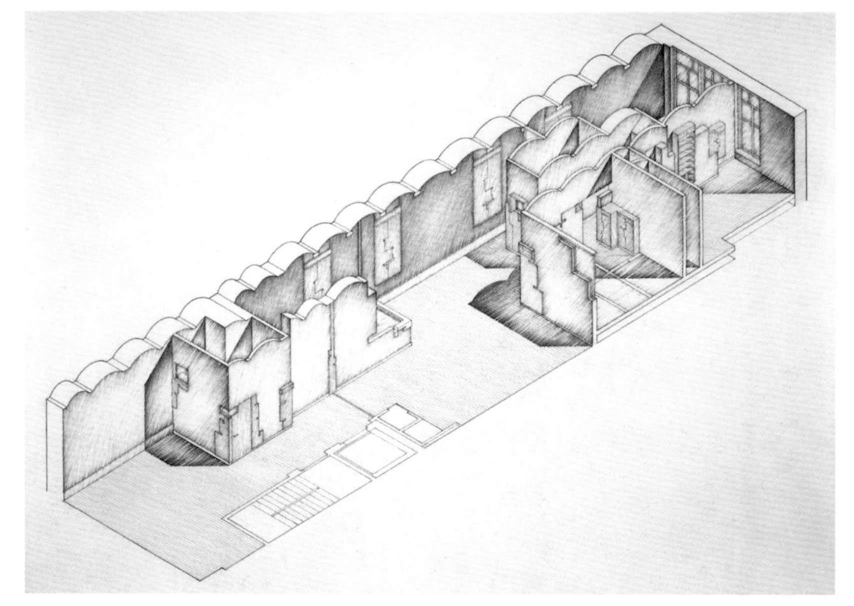

3

1 | Living room, dining room and kitchen from the entry to the master bedroom
2 | Model with the east wall and ceiling removed
3 | Axonometric drawing indicating the elements' materials

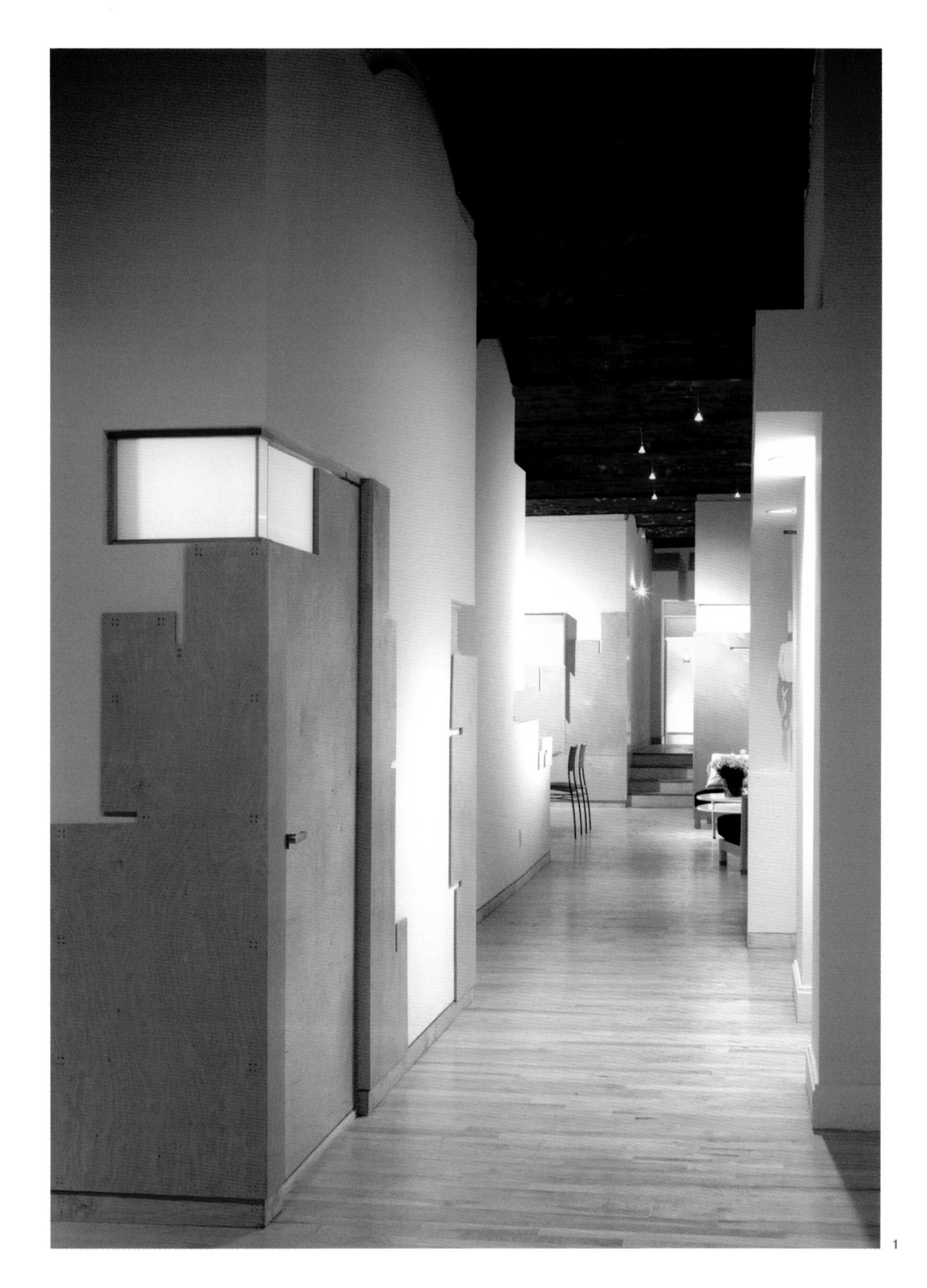

1

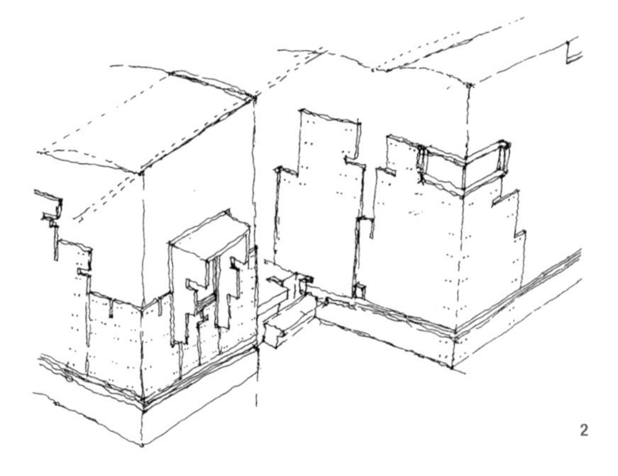

2

1 | View from the front gallery looking toward the living room area
2 | Pen and ink sketch of the new stair and master bathroom walls
3 | Model view of the east elevation and front view
4 | Floor plan
5 | North-south section looking east

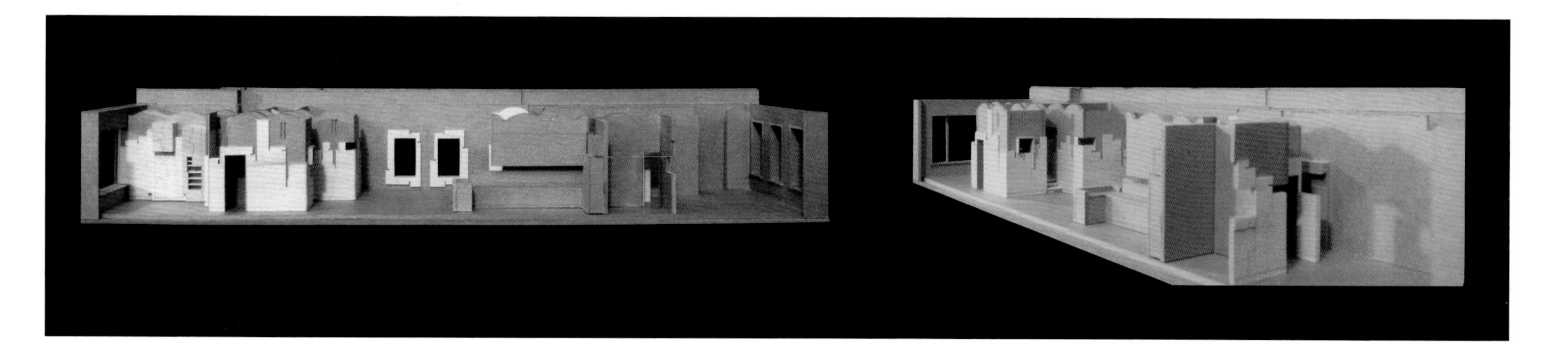

3

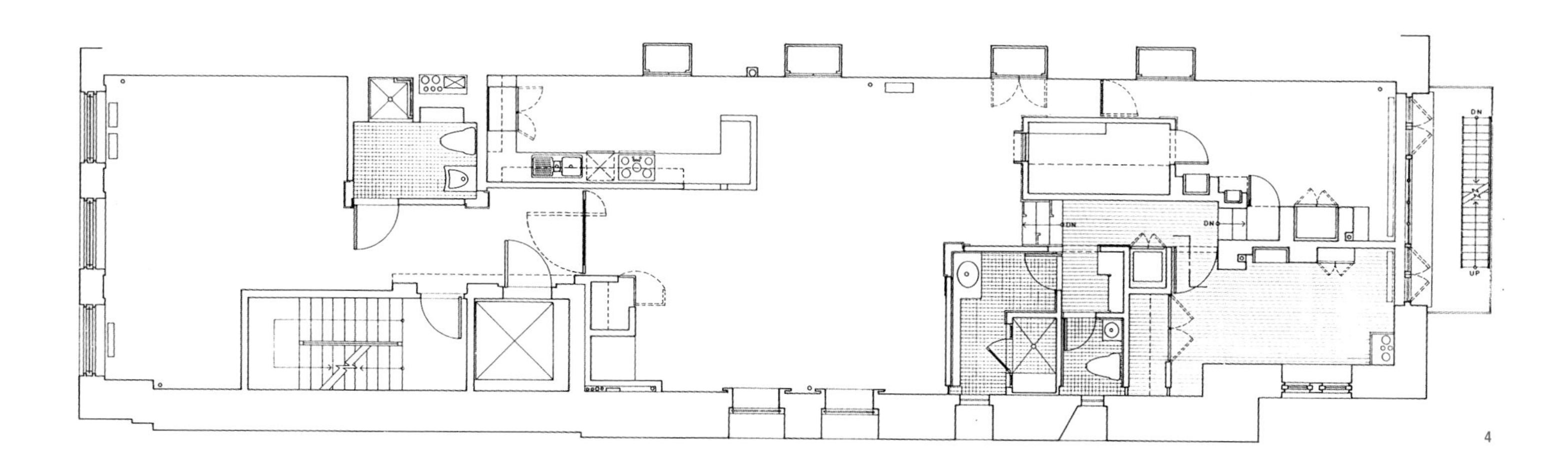

4

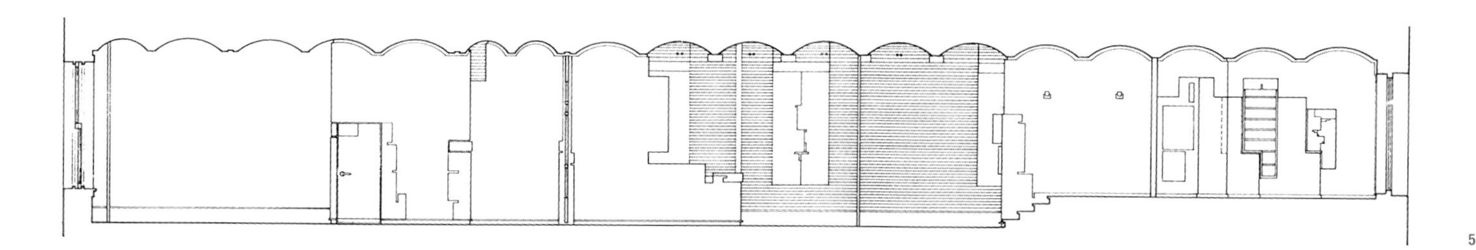

5

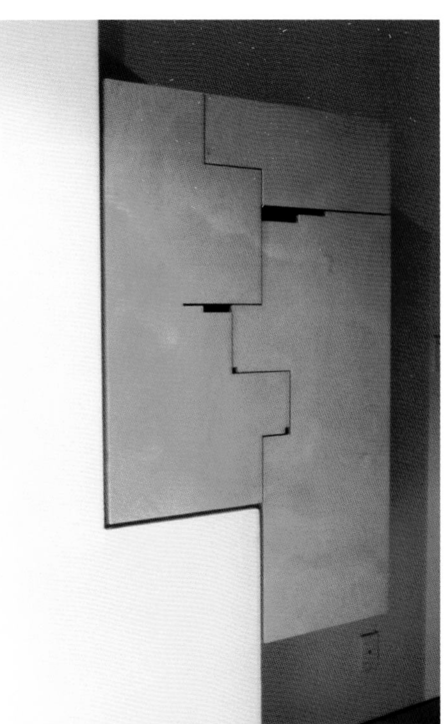

1

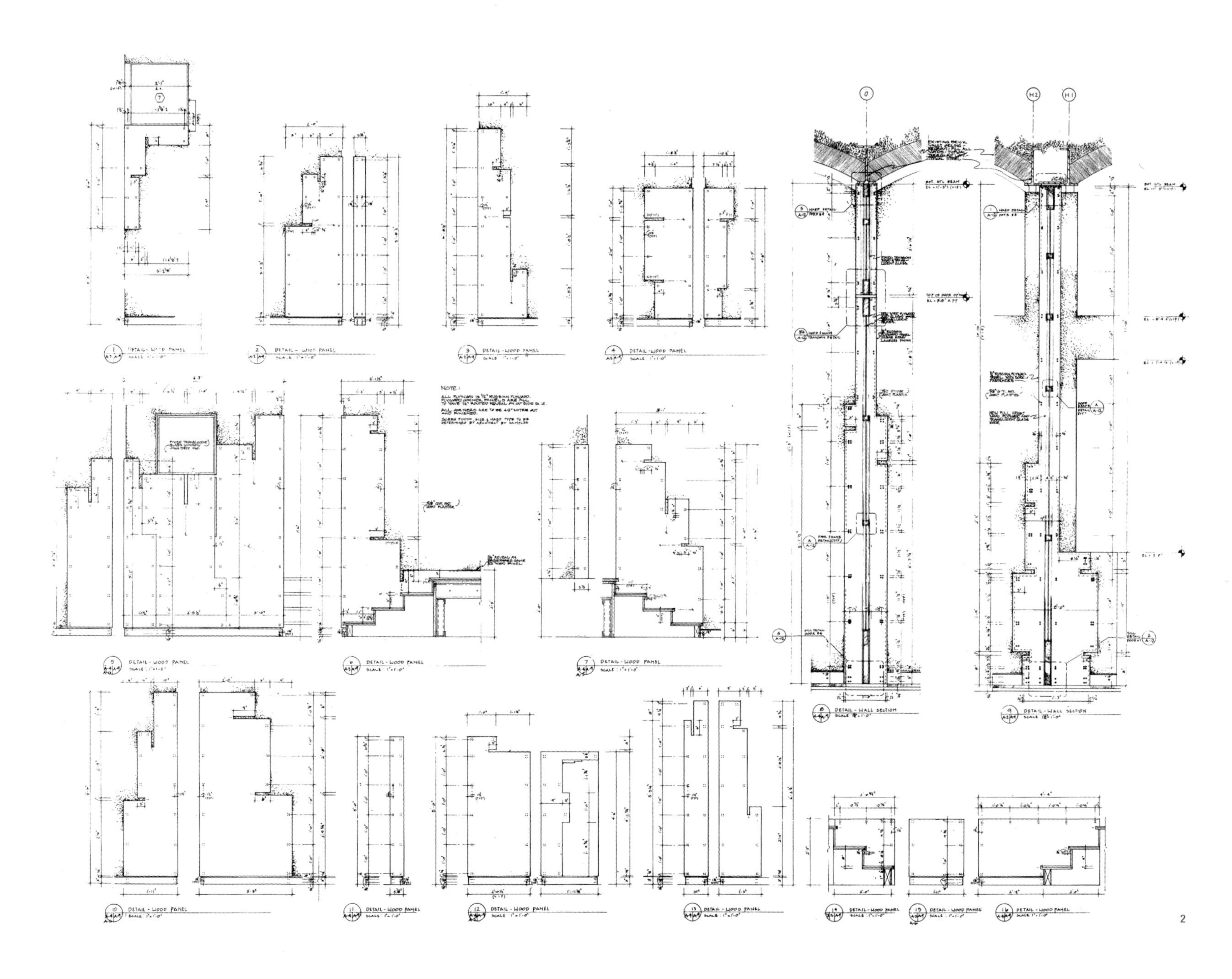

2

1 Various wood cabinets and details
2 Construction drawings of the woodwork corner panels, stair and door

1

2

3

1 View from the master bathroom entry looking toward the front of the loft
2 Stair detail at the entry to the master bedroom
3 Master bedroom passage on the left and the boy's bedroom door on the right
4 The kitchen with the open counter as a gathering space

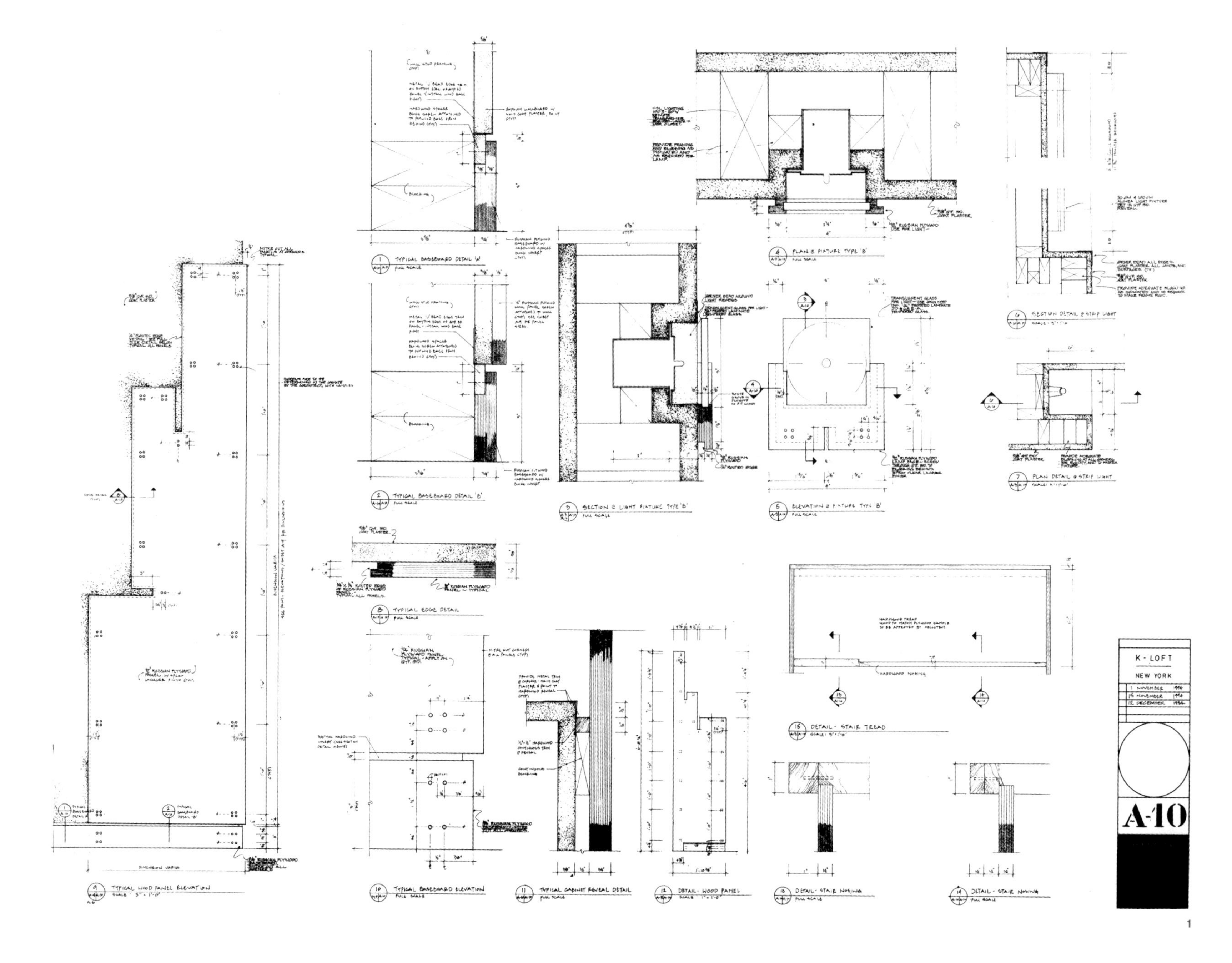
TYPICAL BASEBOARD DETAIL 'A'
FULL SCALE
TYPICAL BASEBOARD DETAIL 'B'
FULL SCALE
SECTION @ LIGHT FIXTURE TYPE 'B'
FULL SCALE
PLAN @ FIXTURE TYPE 'B'
FULL SCALE
ELEVATION @ FIXTURE TYPE 'B'
FULL SCALE
SECTION DETAIL @ STRIP LIGHT
PLAN DETAIL @ STRIP LIGHT
TYPICAL EDGE DETAIL
FULL SCALE
TYPICAL WOOD PANEL ELEVATION
TYPICAL BASEBOARD ELEVATION
FULL SCALE
TYPICAL CABINET REVEAL DETAIL
FULL SCALE
DETAIL - WOOD PANEL
DETAIL - STAIR NOSING
FULL SCALE
DETAIL - STAIR NOSING
FULL SCALE
DETAIL - STAIR TREAD
K - LOFT
NEW YORK
A-10
1

2

3

1 Construction drawing of the corner panel and custom lamps
2 Entrance into the toilet room on the left and bathing room on the right
3 Entrance to the bathing room

1 | Master bedroom with custom bed detail and custom night tables
2 | Master bathing room

2

1

2

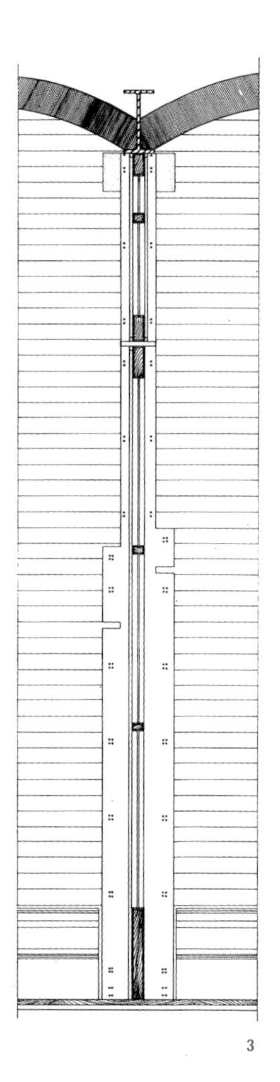
3

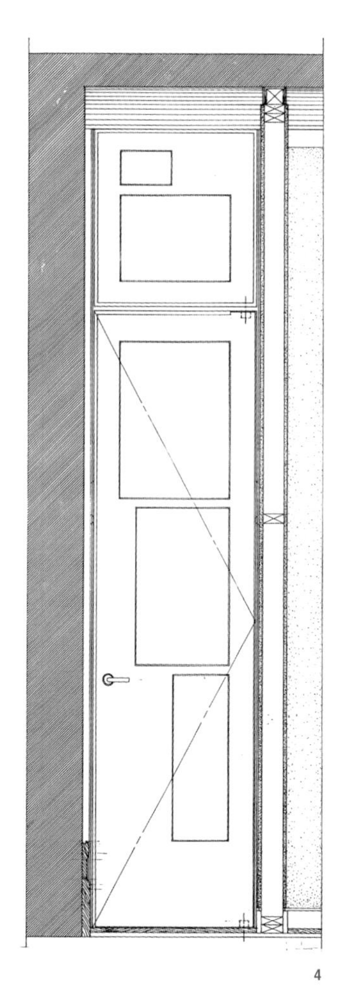
4

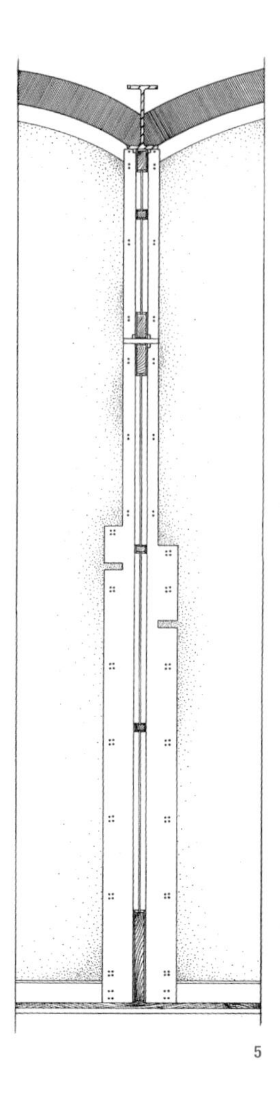
5

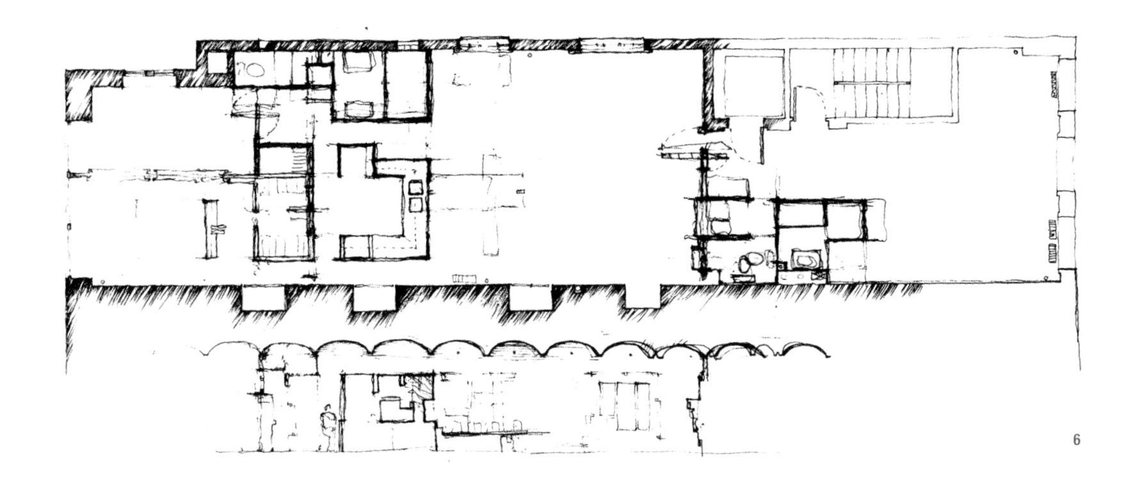

6

9

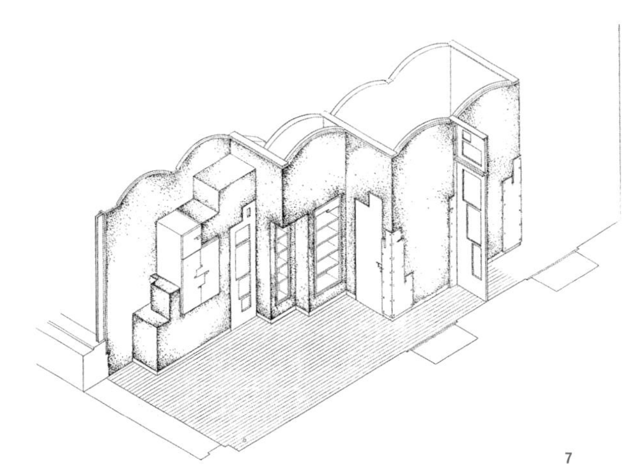

7

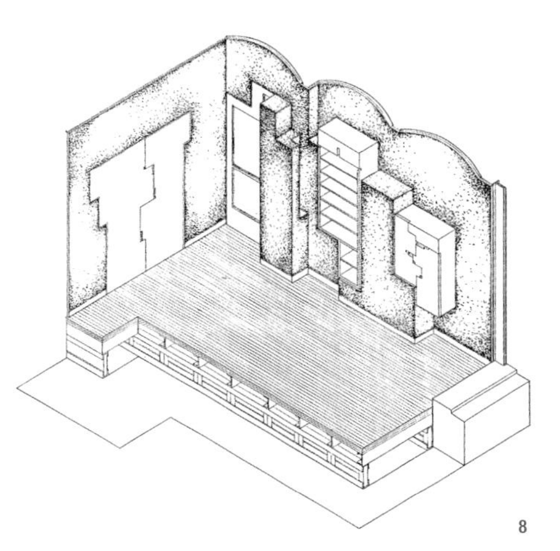

8

10

1 Stair detail at the entrance to the master bathroom
2 Ceiling detail at the entry to the master bedroom
3 Section of the new master bedroom door and existing brick wall
4 New master bedroom door elevation
5 Wood panel on the opposite side of the hall from the brick wall
6 Pencil sketch of an early plan and section
7 Drawing of the master bedroom design
8 Drawing of the boy's bedroom
9 Master bedroom door and television cabinet
10 Master dressing room with the entrance to the master bedroom on the left from the dining room

project name	Indoor Lap Pool Building
location	Kent, Connecticut
year of design	1993-1994
client	Name with held at owner's request
lot size	4.5 acres
project size	1,350 sq.ft.
architect	George Ranalli
associates	Robert Silman Structural Engineer
design team	John Butterworth, Nathaniel Worden
photographer	model photos George Ranalli

Indoor Lap Pool Building

1

The residents of Litchfield County, Connecticut occupy an enclave of hardwood and pine forests that rise to wooded hills, with a central valley, tranquil lakes, and wide-open sky. The area is home to a community of sculptors, painters, musicians, and writers. One resident, a novelist, who swims as physical therapy for a chronic back problem, commissioned a pool house adjacent to an eighteenth-century clapboard farmhouse, on 25 acres, bordered by low walls of dry stone. Writing for long hours, the owner wanted the lap-pool room to be as open and exciting as possible for his mandatory swimming ritual.

From the main house, a footpath leads through a large field of wildflowers and mature trees to the writer's office, another old building, once the chicken coop. Extending from the office, the new building lies between old stonewalls. The buildings of the whole complex thus complement each other in a dialogue of new and old.

The design for a new 1,350-square-foot pool house provided room for a 66-foot swimming pool, dressing area, and Jacuzzi plunge bath, all accessible through the eastern side of the rectangular structure. As one enters the new building, the pool extends the length of the space, pressed to the windowless west side. The pool house features large skylights and East-facing windows and pivot doors that provide the owner with expansive views of sky and the historic site's open landscape. The stepped cross-section of the interior roof maintains ample height above both the pool and the walking lane beside it, while the centric skylights over the plunge pool impart a feeling of stability to the space.

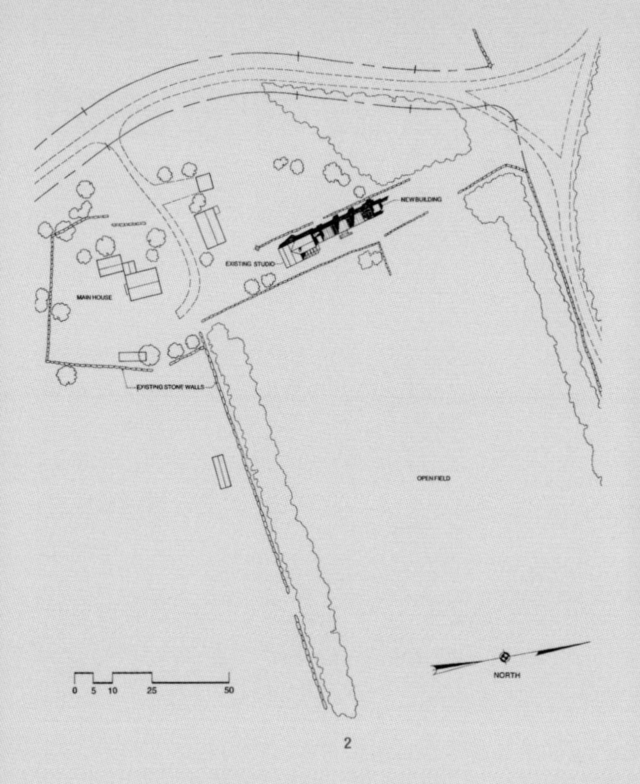

2

3

4

1 Section model through the pool and building
2 Site plan
3 Section perspective through the indoor pool building
4 Photo montage of the model and site photo

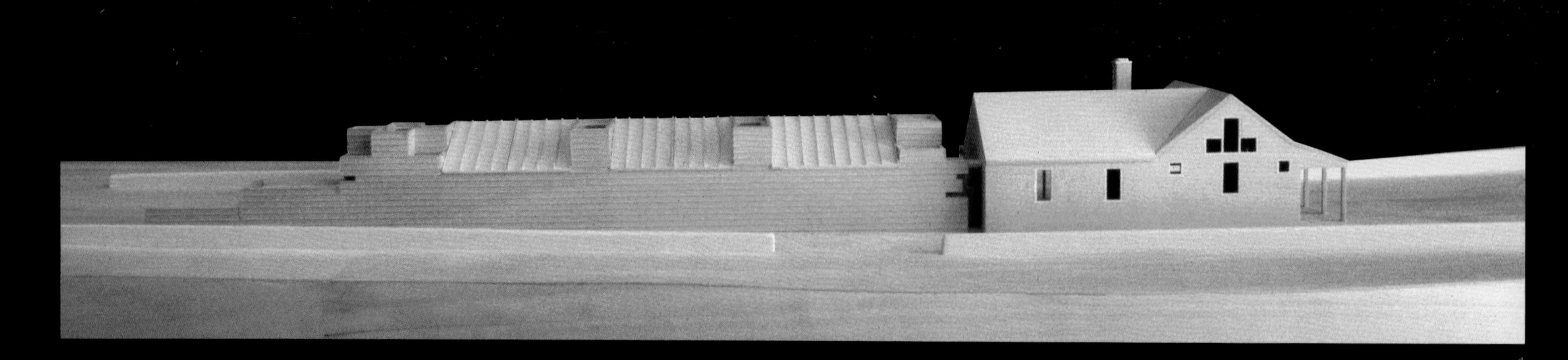

1

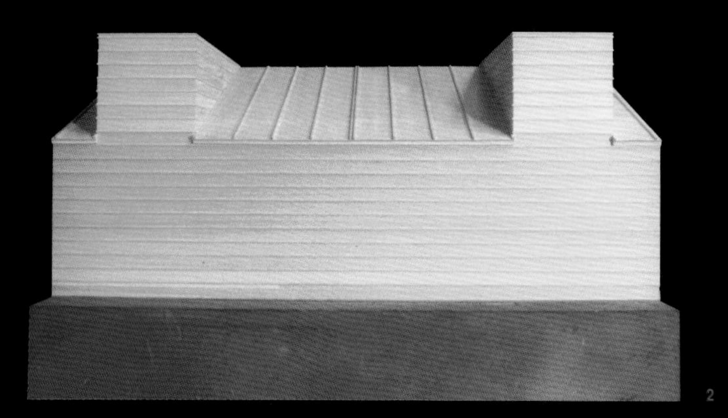

2

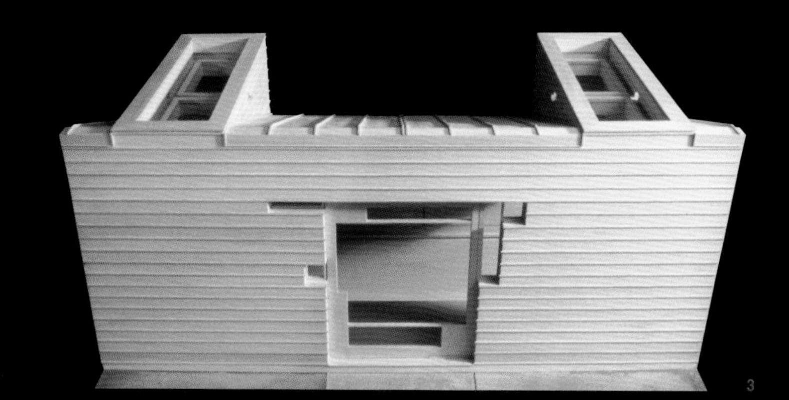

3

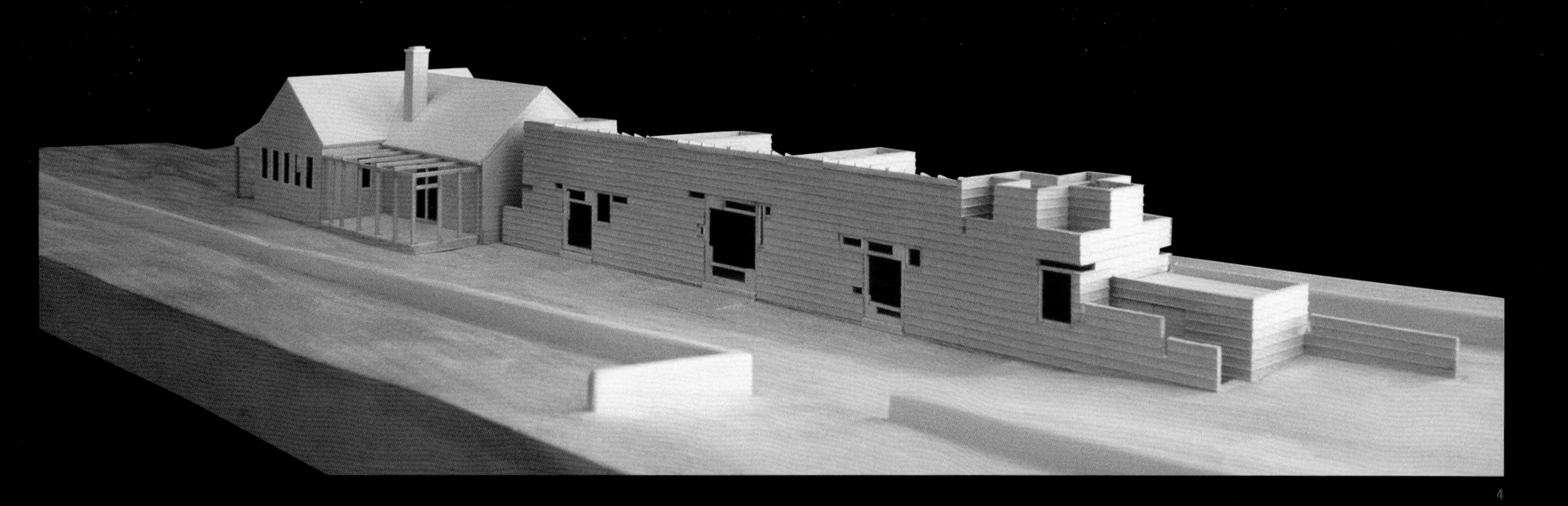

4

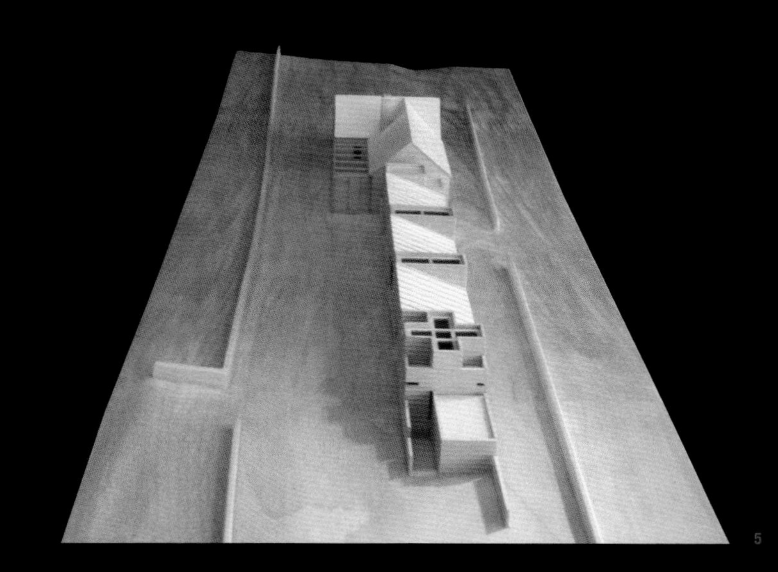

5

The building is designed to explore the various conditions of wood-frame construction and wood cladding on both the exterior and interior. A roof of sheet copper over horizontal Douglas fir board-and-batten accommodates the east side's wide composition of windows and pivot doors. Since the road is extremely near on the west side, the owner required that side be closed down, so the west elevation shows only the wood cladding and roof. Inside, the design of the large windows and pivot doors explores what is possible with wood framing and gives the owner an expansive view of the landscape while swimming. As the interior system of marine plywood sheets (from a durable, fast-growing tropical hardwood) meets the external board and batten, the windows and doors absorb and join these movements.

An interior palate of honey-colored marine plywood and travertine stone tile echoes the subtle hues and sumptuous textures of the natural landscape. The building's mass is a response to climatic necessity, and the number of openings is restricted so as not to cause large heat loss in winter or difficulty cooling in summer.

1 West elevation model view
2 Detail model west side with wood siding and copper roof
3 Aerial view of the east side middle door and skylights
4 Model view from the large open meadow
5 Aerial view from the north end of the site

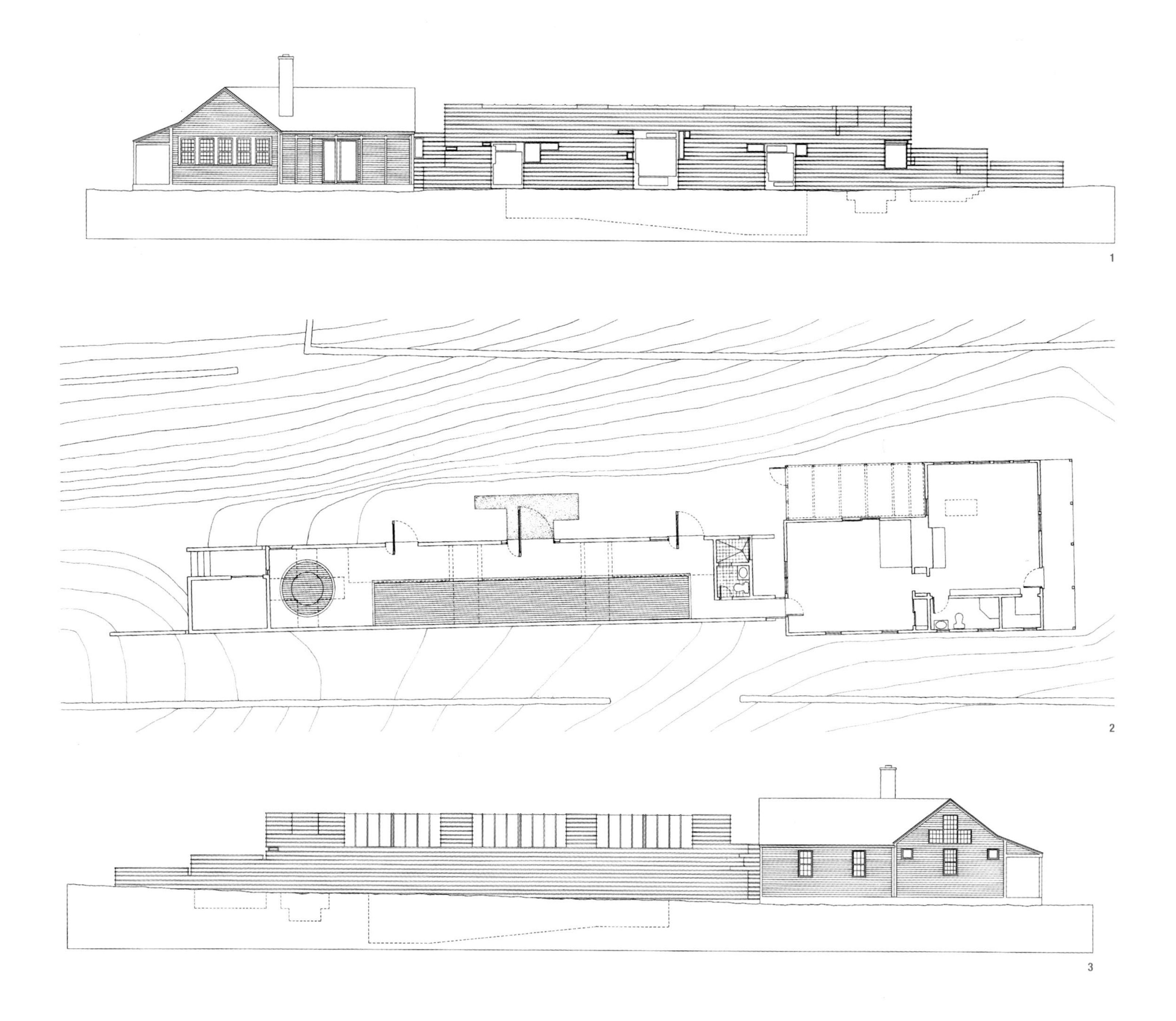

1 | East elevation drawing with existing writing shed on the left
2 | Floor plan
3 | West elevation drawing
4 | Detail model of the middle entry door on the east side of the building

4

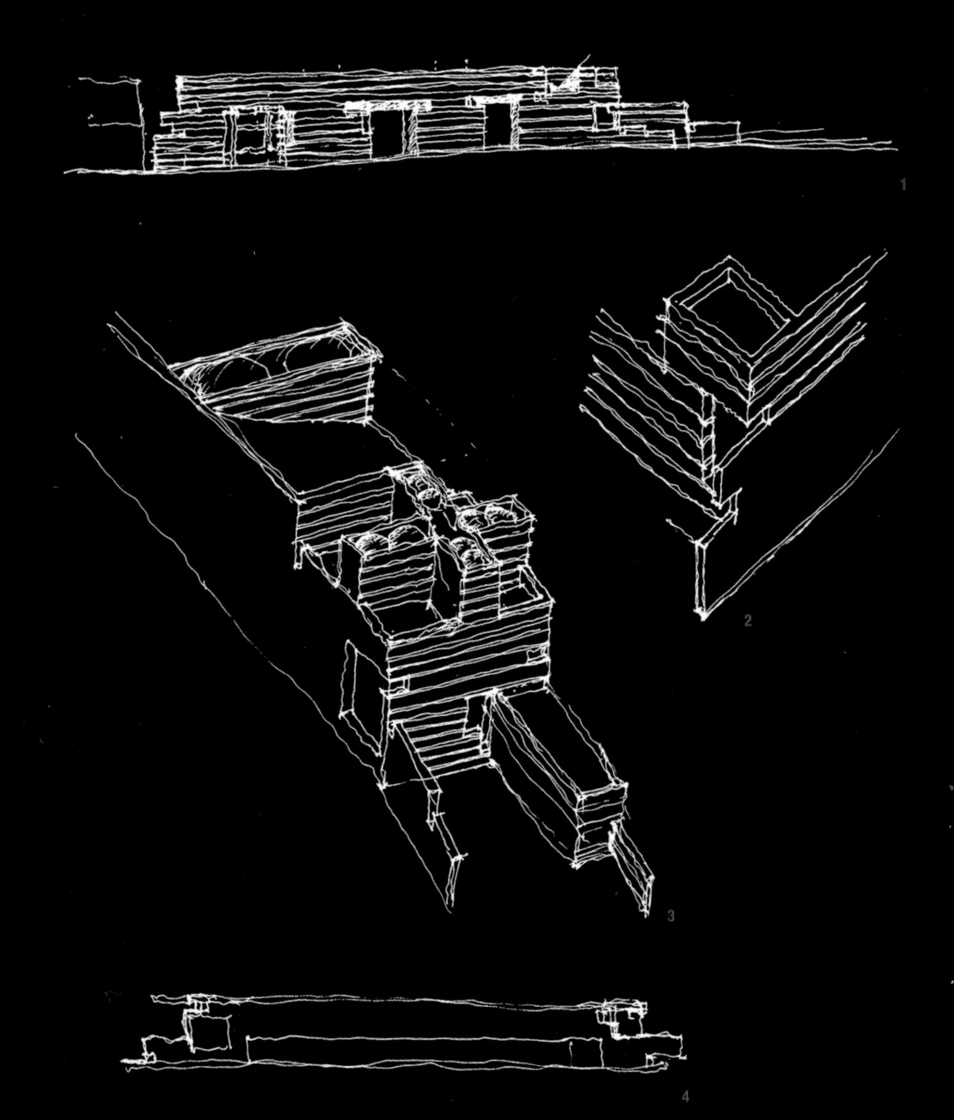
1
2
3
4

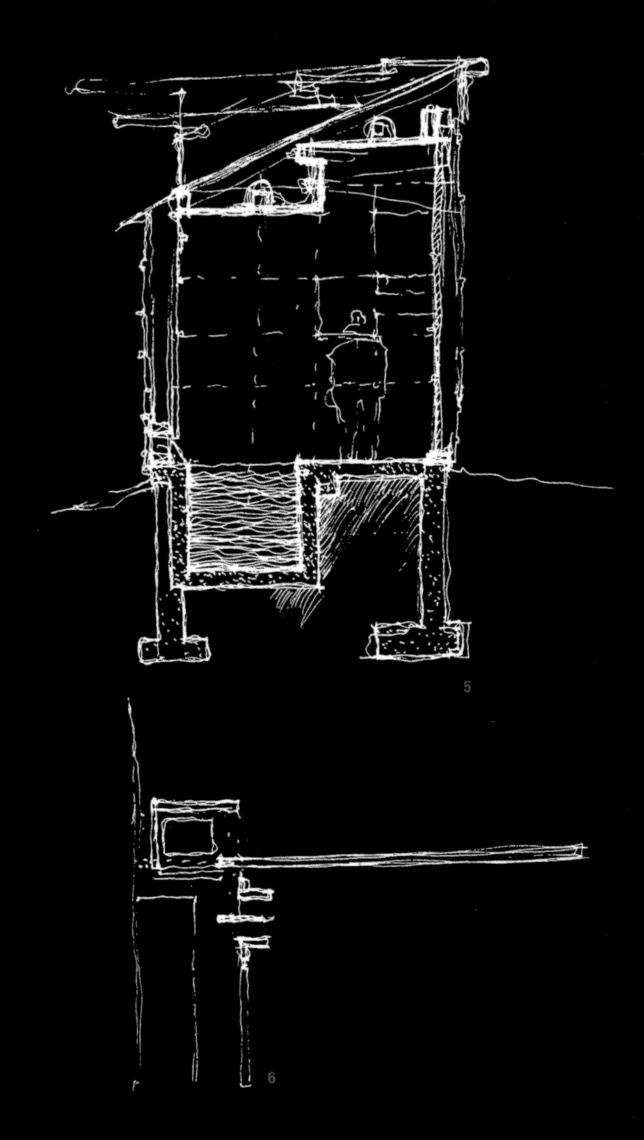
5
6

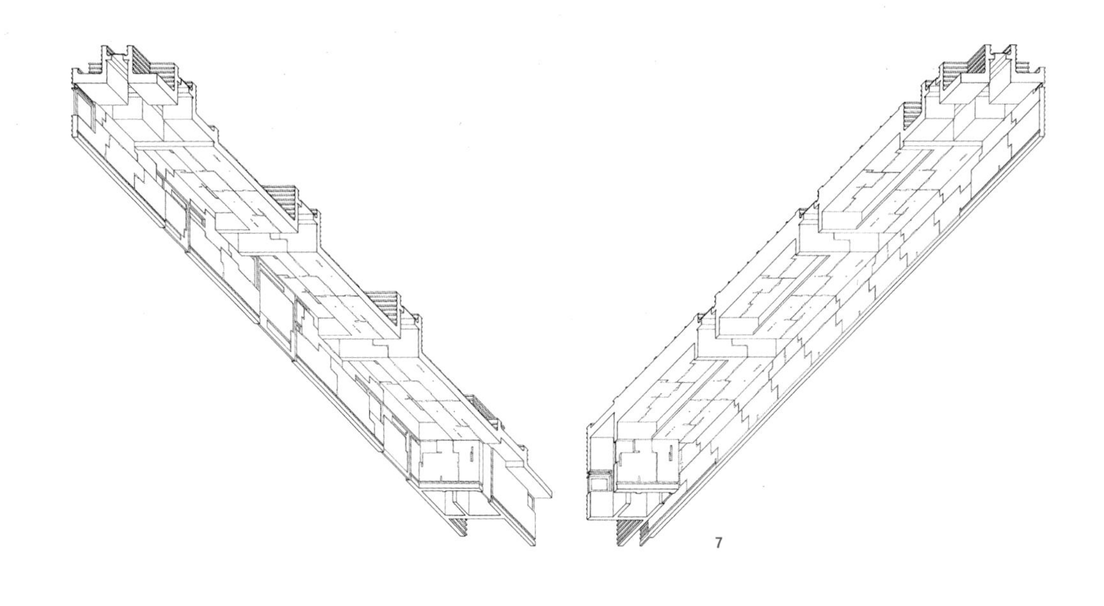

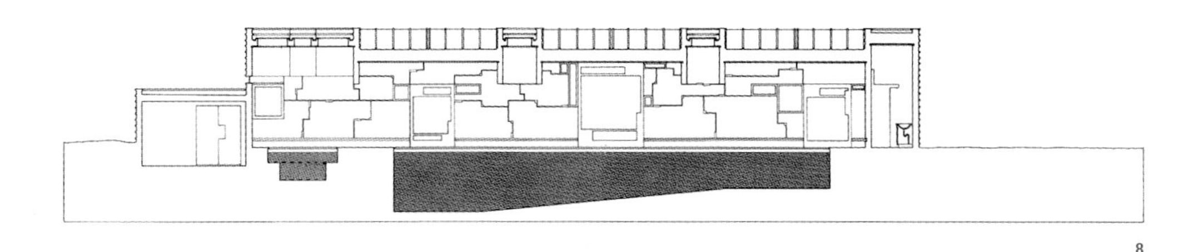

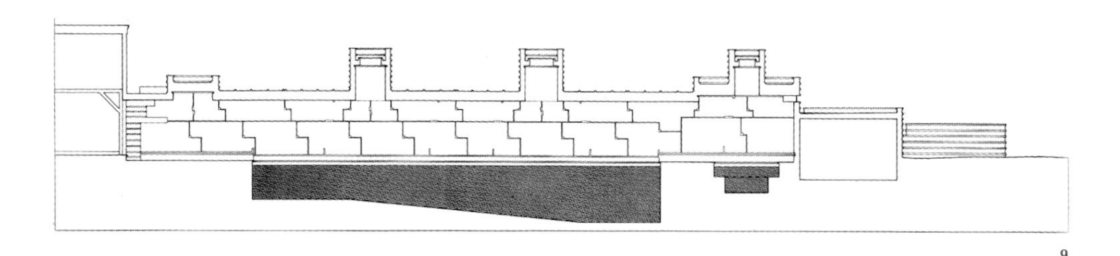

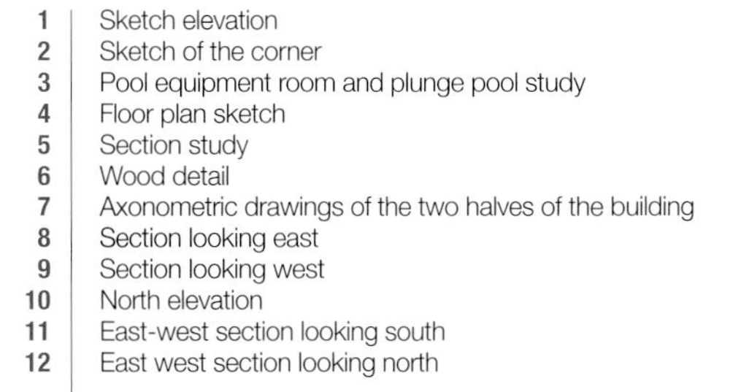
1 Sketch elevation
2 Sketch of the corner
3 Pool equipment room and plunge pool study
4 Floor plan sketch
5 Section study
6 Wood detail
7 Axonometric drawings of the two halves of the building
8 Section looking east
9 Section looking west
10 North elevation
11 East-west section looking south
12 East west section looking north

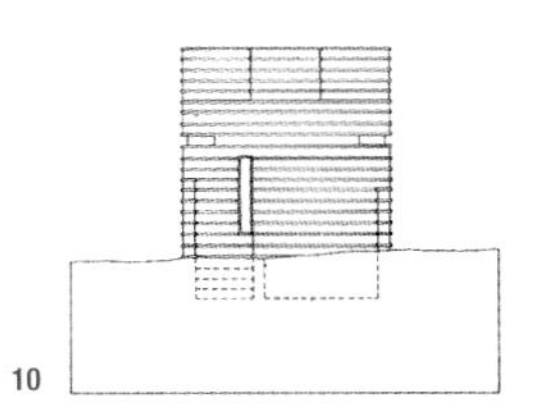

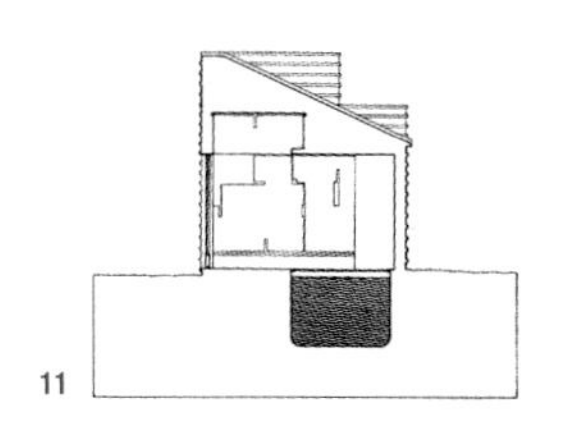

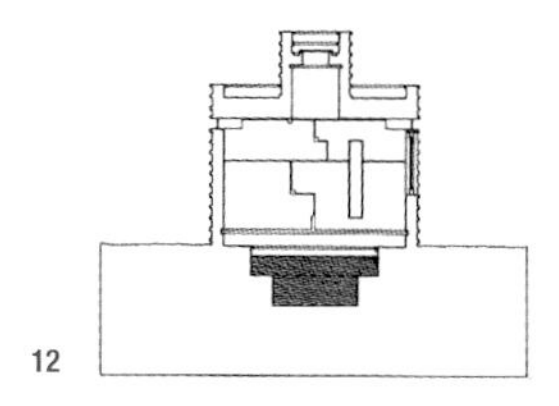

1

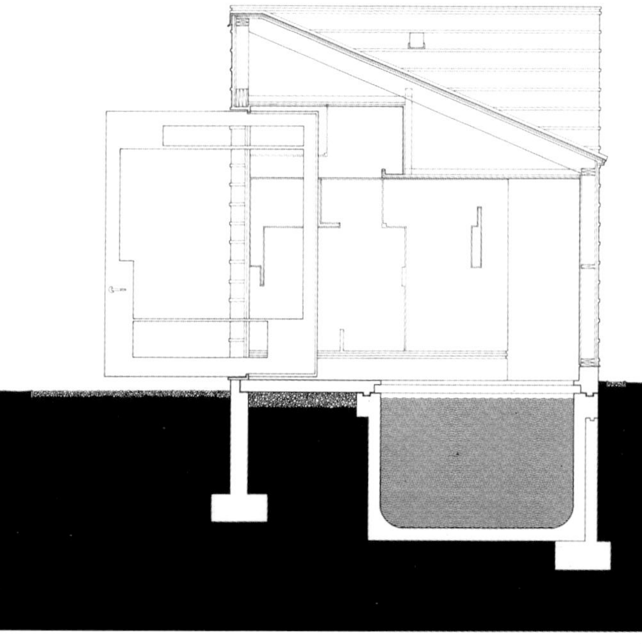

2

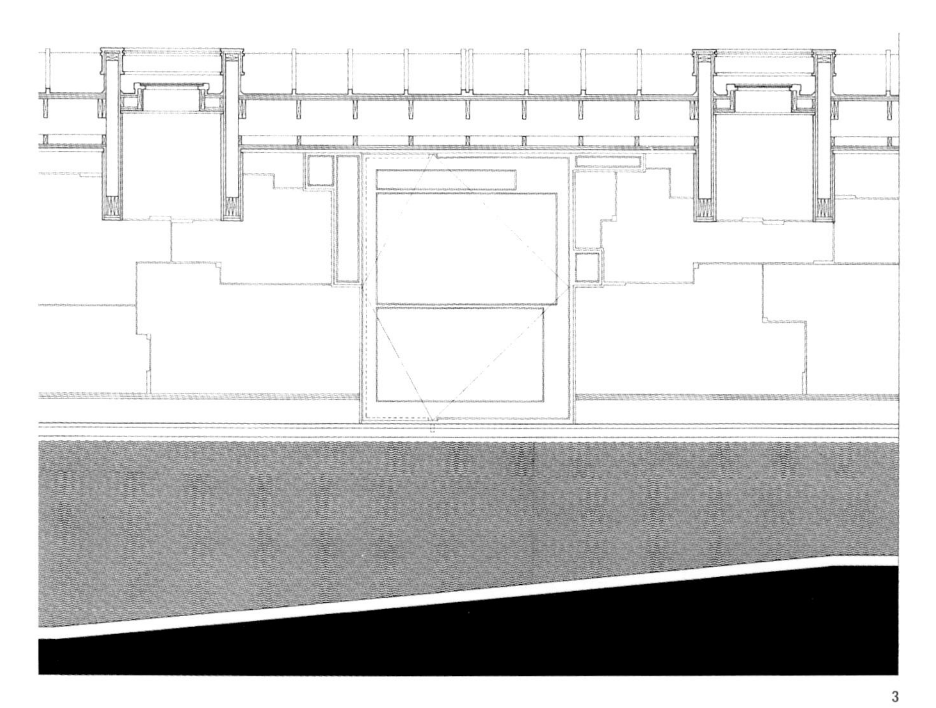

3

4

1 Large scale model indicating the marine plywood panels, walnut inlays and structure at the skylights
2 Detail of east-west section looking south
3 North-south section looking east
4 Exterior wall detail model view with the window-door configuration

project name	Pool & Pool House for "C" Family
location	Amagansett, New York
year of design	1991
year of completion	1993
client	Marian & James H. Cohen
lot size	2.5 acres
project size	2,500 sq.ft.
architect	George Ranalli
associates	Robert Silman Structural Engineer
design team	John Butterworth, Nathaniel Worden
photographer	Carla Breeze

Pool & Pool House for "C" Family

1

In a woodsy seaside village, two precocious aesthetes filled their sturdy summer retreat with intriguingly beautiful contemporary art and sculptural furnishings. No matter the flourishing out-of-doors, the owners of the house went on framing works by Cindy Sherman and Robert Longo, until family and friends compelled them to locate the middle ground, and the couple commissioned an outdoor pool and pool house pavilion.

By filling a precipitous slope behind the house, the site provided a two-and-a-half acre terrace overlooking woodlands of mature trees and thick ruffs of wild flowers. A mahogany fence, stained spindrift white, with watery green copper features, encloses a stone covered patio that is the color of the inside of a seashell. A low circular soaking tub relaxes alongside a glistening swimming pool. From the tub's edge, a gentle lisp of flowing water strikes a note of languor. Wide "cocktail" steps guide an assortment of swimmers to varying depths for lounging, swimming laps, and diving, across an iridescent arrangement of blue, green, and gold Italian mosaic glass tiles.

The design for a swimming pool pavilion of wood, glass, and copper accommodates a spacious multi-purpose room and full bath. The pool house design extends out from one end to shape a large covered patio. Delicate copper-clad domes, rising above the pool house roofline, filter sunlight and echo the seashore, creating a sense of distinction.

2

3

1 Fence detail and the main pool beyond
2 Section perspective drawing looking toward the existing house
3 Section oblique drawing of the landscape, pool and pool house

1

2

1 | View of the pool from an upstairs window
2 | Lap lane of the pool from the deck of the house with new fence work on the right side

1

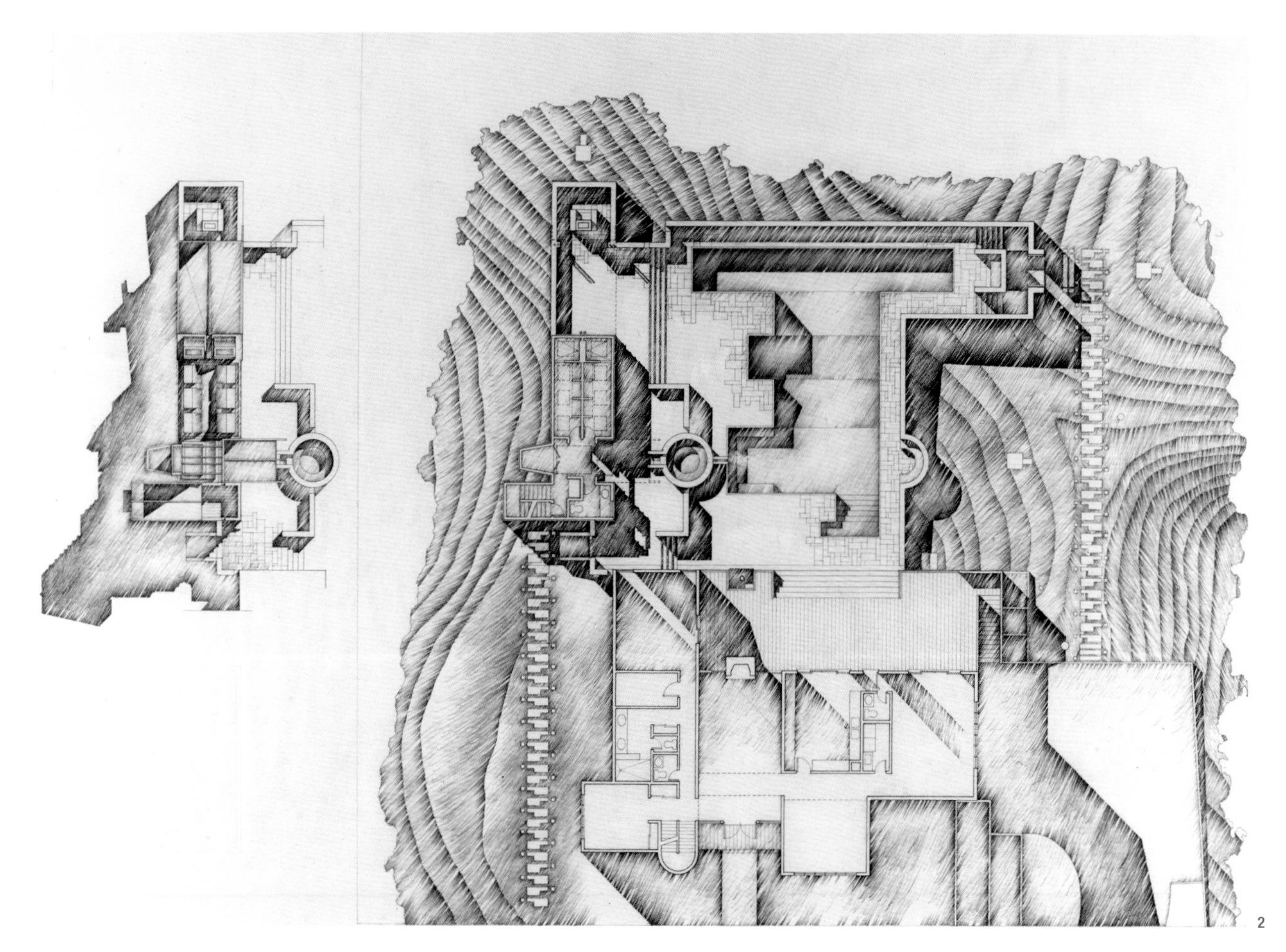

2

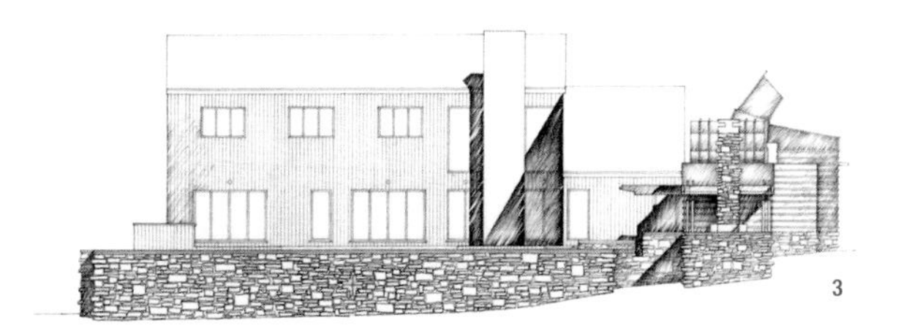

3

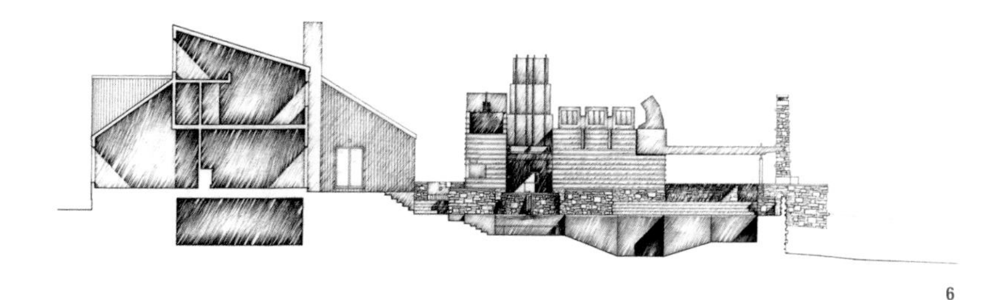

6

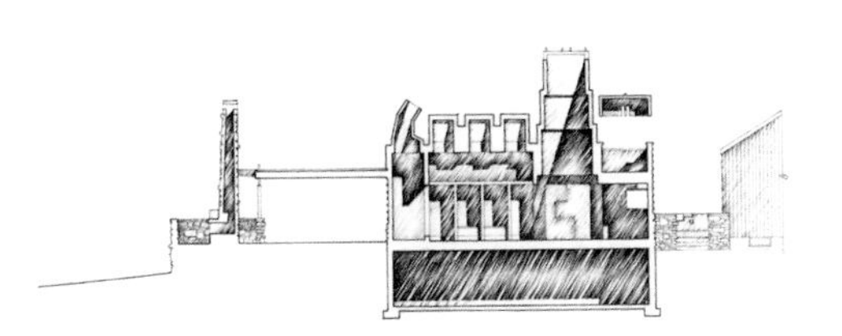

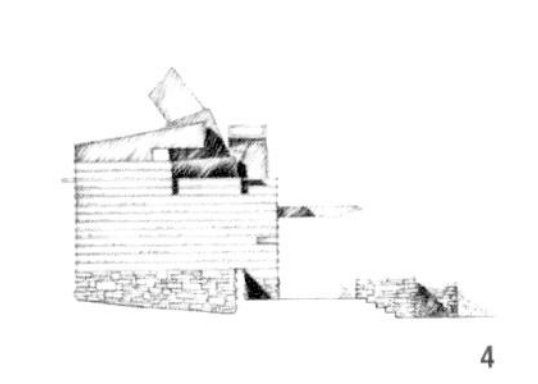

4

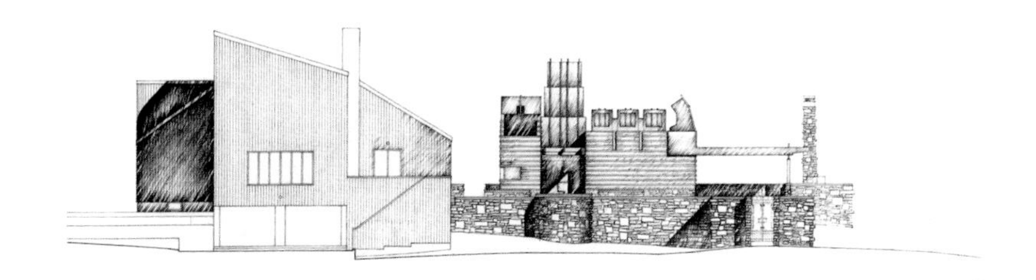

7

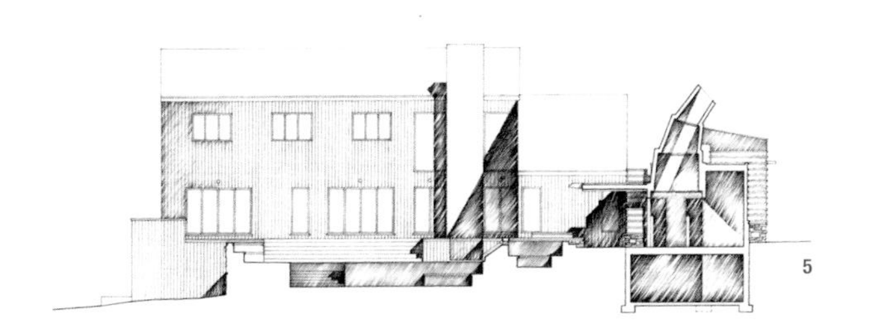

5

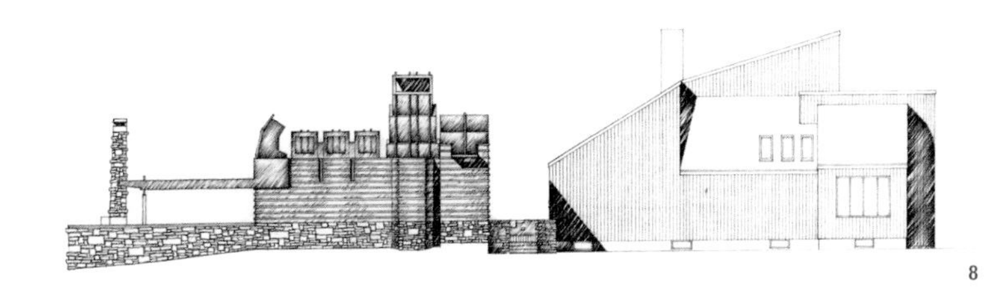

8

1 Section oblique cut-away drawing of the first scheme
2 Roof plan and plan of scheme one
3 South elevation, scheme one
4 South-north section looking west, scheme one
5 West-east section looking south, scheme one
6 East-west pool section looking north, scheme one
7 South elevation, scheme one
8 North elevation, scheme one

1

2

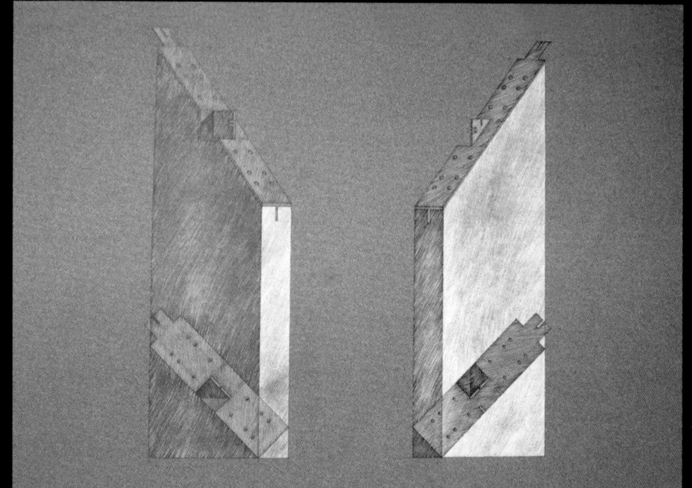

3

4

6

5

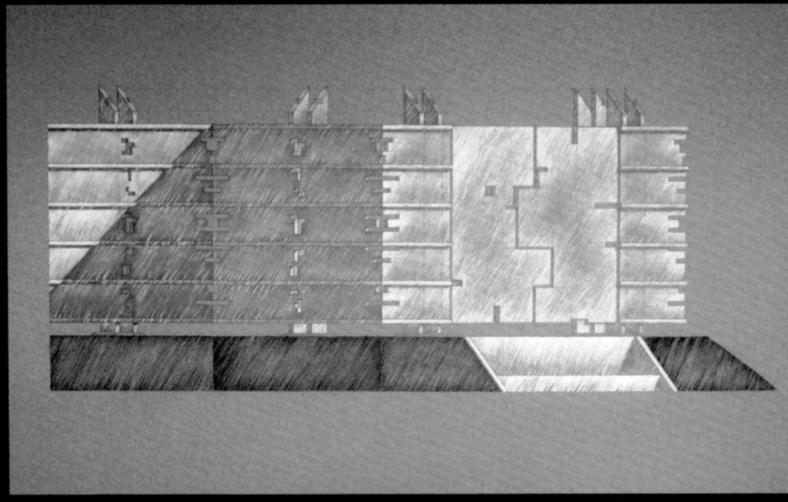

7

1 Detail of the new fence corner, gates and landscape
2 View from the existing deck
3 Fence structure detail drawing, plans and elevation. Color pencil on color paper
4 View of the new fence, landscape berm and stairs down to the site
5 Model of the project illustrating existing house and new landscape design with pool and pool house
6 Detail photo of the landscape stair and entry gates
7 Color pencil drawing of the fence and gates on color paper

1

2

3

1 Plunge pool plan and elevation drawing. Color pencil on color paper
2 Limestone spill way from the plunge pool to the main pool
3 Entry stair to the jacuzzi pool

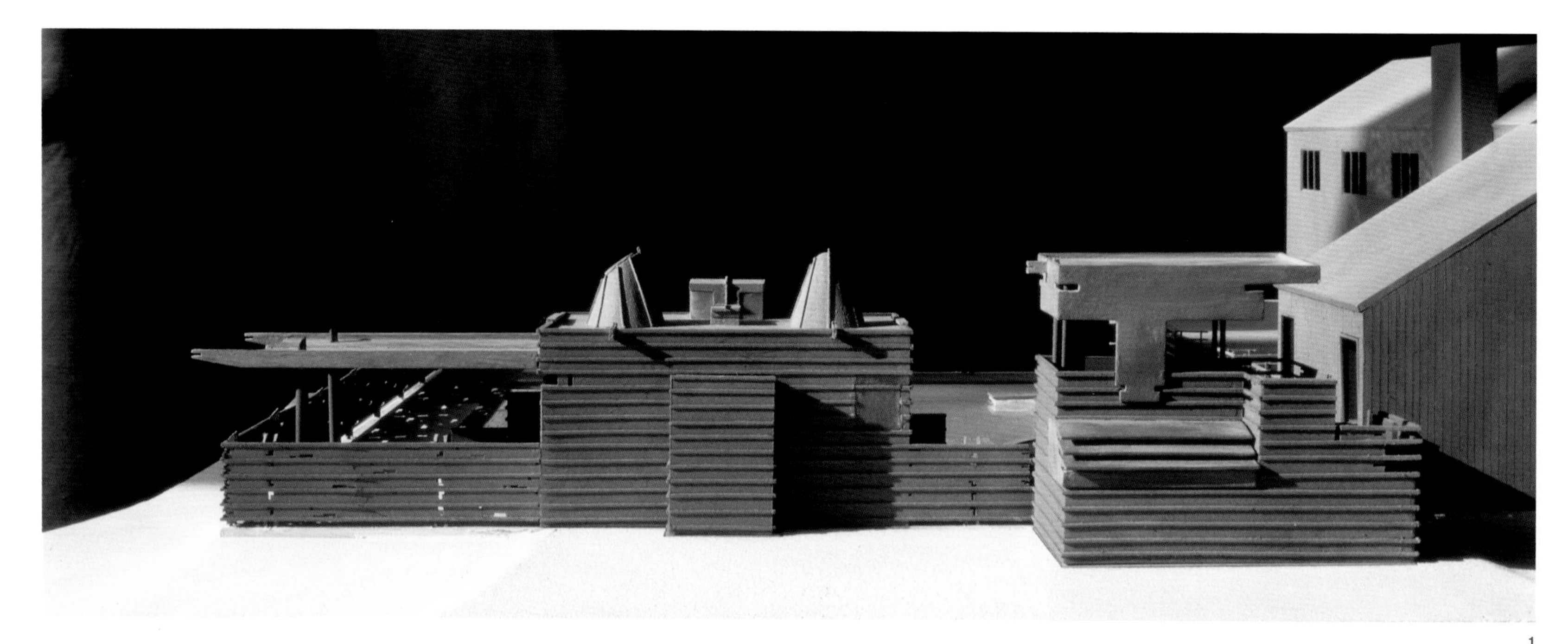

1

2

3

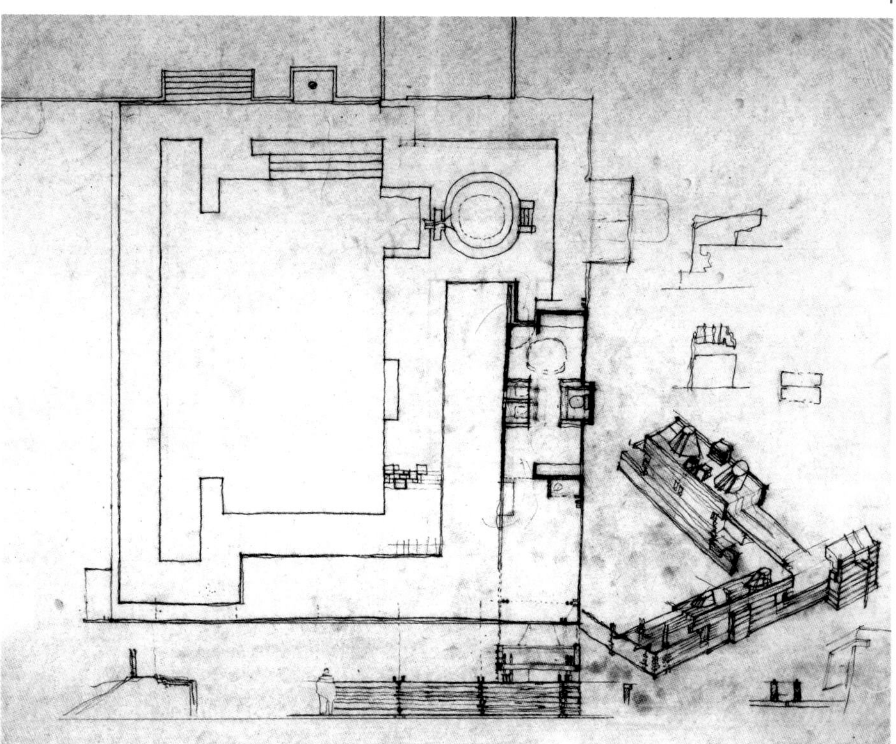

4

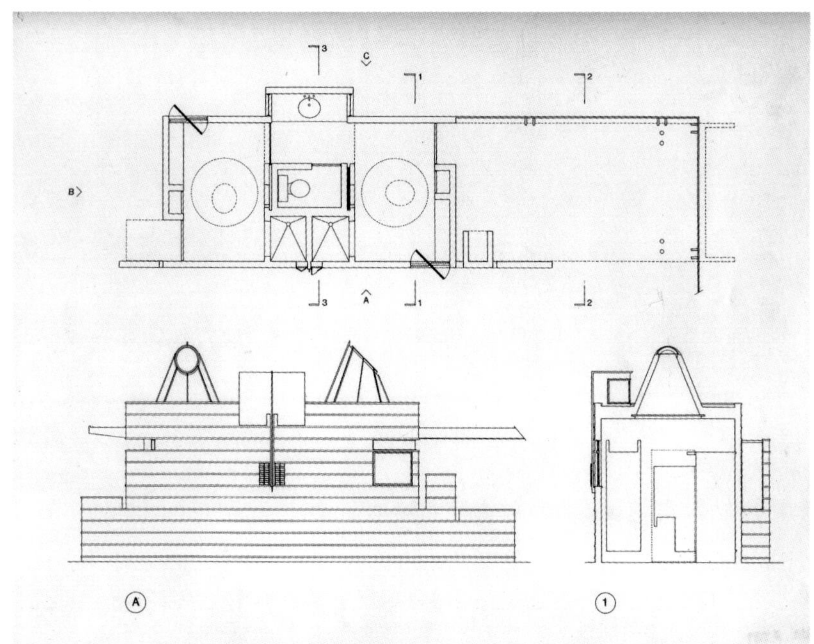

5

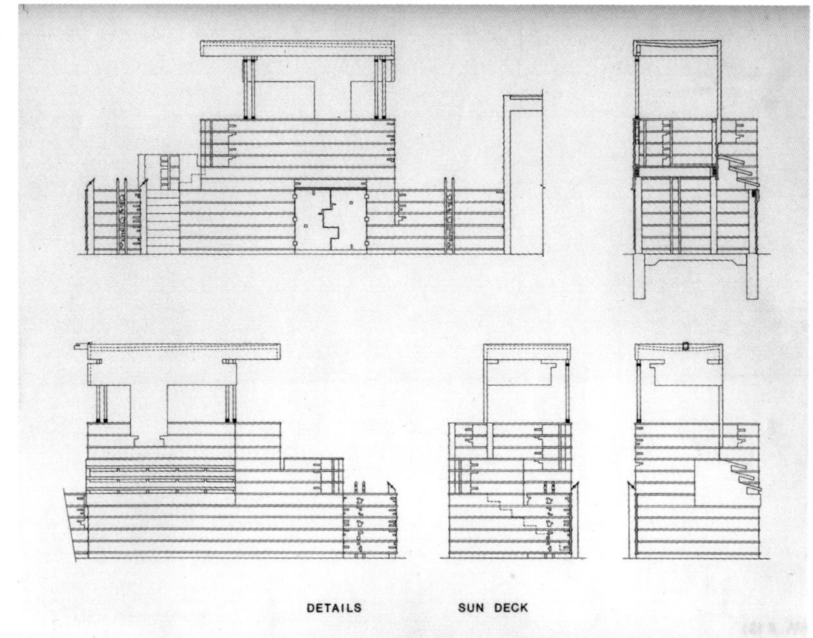

6

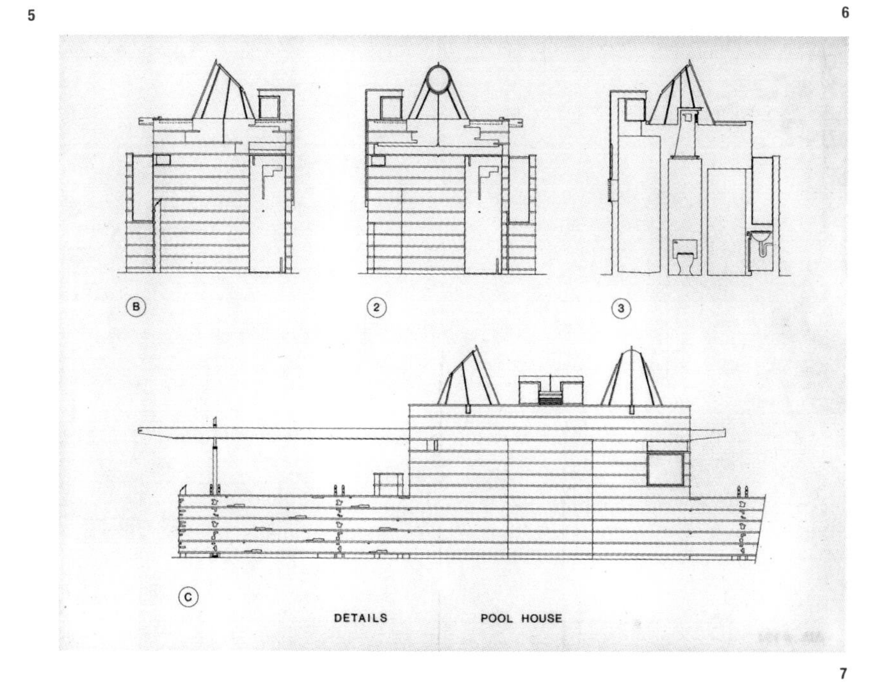

7

1 Model of the pool house and sun deck complex seen from the north side
2 Early pencil sketch of the pool and pool house
3 Model of the new addition from the south
4 Pencil plan study and other details
5 Plan, section and elevation of the pool house
6 Sun deck elevations and section
7 Elevations and section of the pool house

1

2

3

1 | View through the landscape gates
2 | Pool and lap pool lane seen from the modified existing wood deck
3 | View across lap lane, main pool and plunge pool on the other side

project name	Renovation to Barn for "A" Family
location	Red Hook, New York
year of design	1988
client	Name withheld at owner's request
lot size	2.5 acres
project size	6,500 sq.ft.
architect	George Ranalli
associates	Robert Silman Structural Engineer
design team	John Butterworth, Nathaniel Worden
photographer	Model Photos: George Ranalli

Renovation to Barn for "A" Family

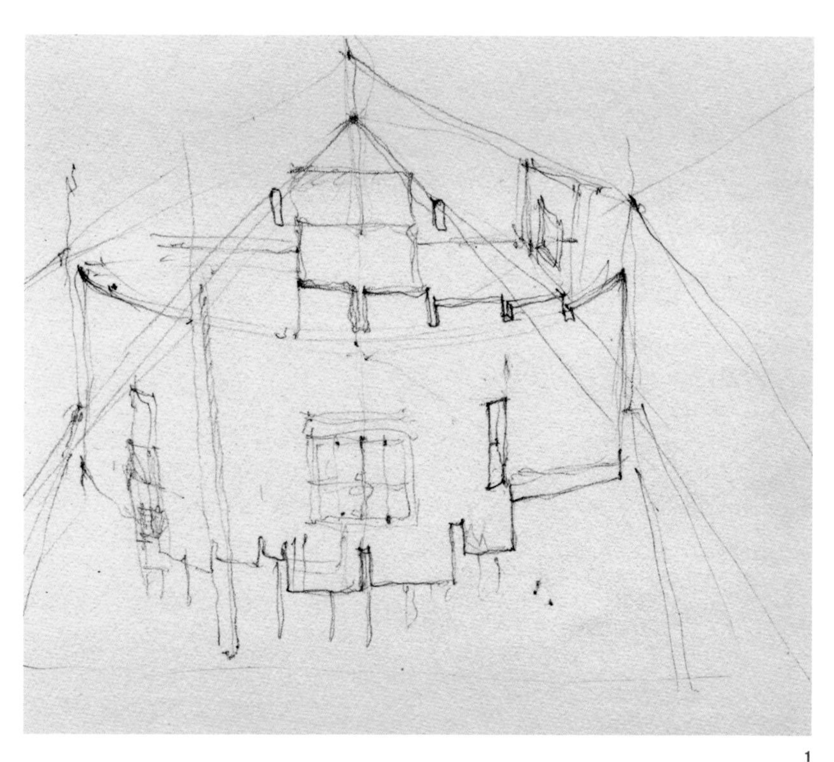

1

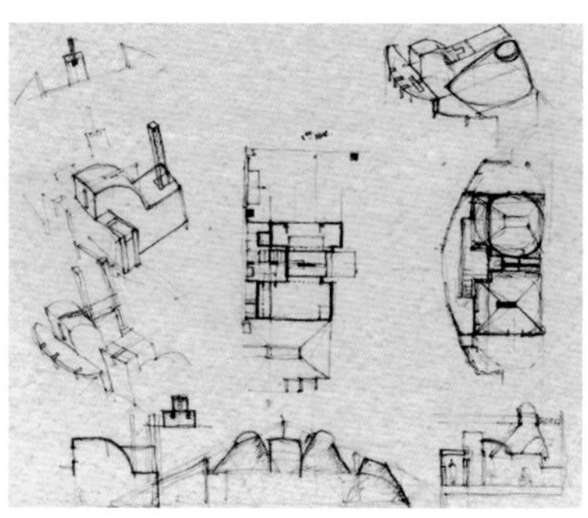

2

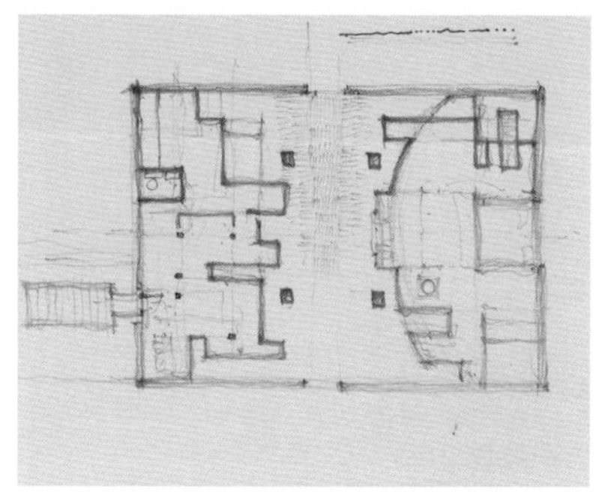

3

In pastoral upstate New York, an old barn in a rolling landscape inspires the architectural imagination. The reverie of massive posts and rafters over a high-peaked timber frame, softened by the century-old patina of rough hand-shaped beams, creates a desire for spatial particularity in what is essentially a massive blank room, originally meant for tractors and horses. This project adapts an old rustic dairy barn for reuse as a residence for a family of four weekenders from the city. The remarkably intact, energy-efficient, and weather-tight interior of the one hundred-year-old structure, fashioned from handmade hatchet-hewn timber construction, preserves the character of the old barn.

The architectural design introduces two differently configured, three storey sculptural volumes—one for the owners, and another for their guests—to shape 6,000 square feet of space inside the old barn. Thirty eight feet high columnar supports define a central area, with a large open kitchen, a dining area, lounge, and plenty of room for indoor recreation and entertainment. The densities and transparencies of the two color-tinted plaster forms incorporate existing structural elements, the timbers, and particularly the rafters, into an intimate geometry of interior spaces. Private rooms for sleeping, bathing, yoga, and reading orient around gently moving passageways, and a central stair, which offers vistas to the landscape, and views of the expansive interior.

4

5

6

1 Pencil sketch of the guest wing structure
2 Pencil sketches of the plans and sections of the two units
3 Plan sketch of the family and guest quarters in the existing barn
4 Existing barn with the milking shed on the left
5 Existing barn entrance
6 Model showing the family quarters on right, guest quarters on left and existing barn structure

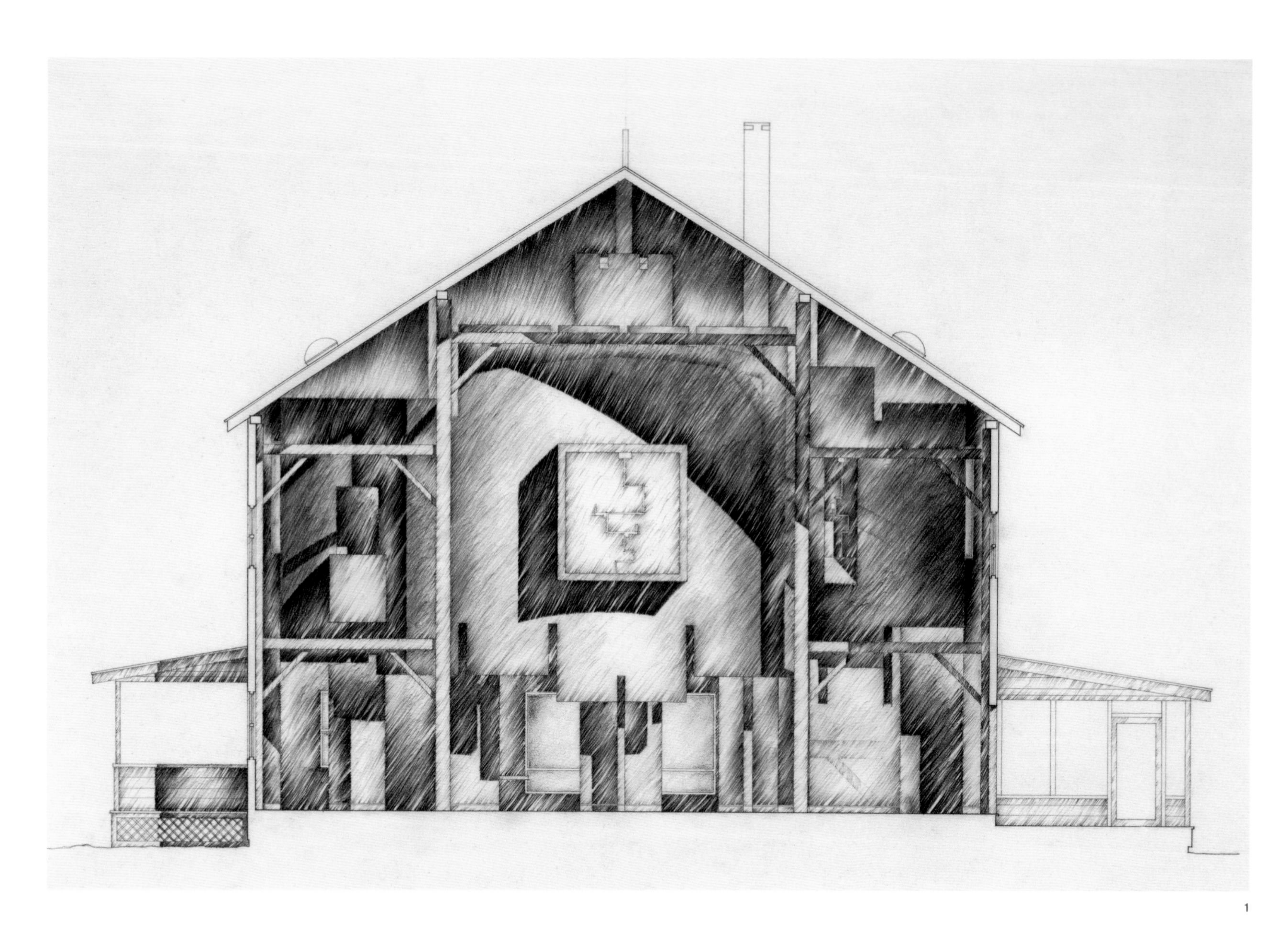

1

2

1 Pencil and color pencil on vellum section through the existing barn looking at the guest quarters
2 Pencil and color pencil on vellum section through the existing barn looking at the family quarters

1

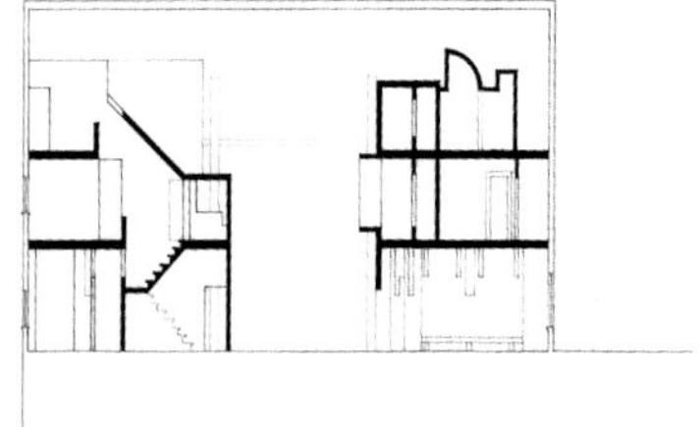

2

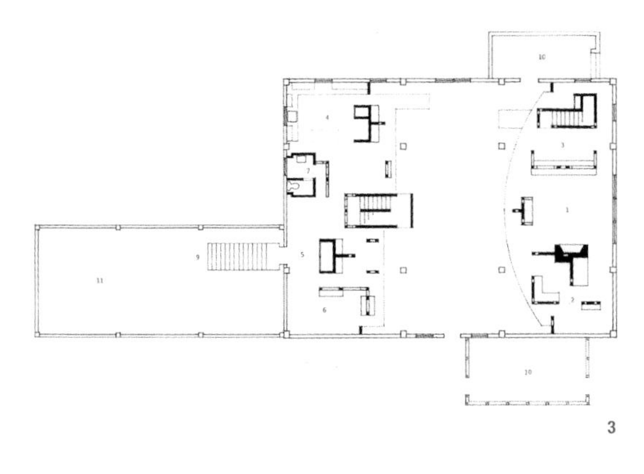

3

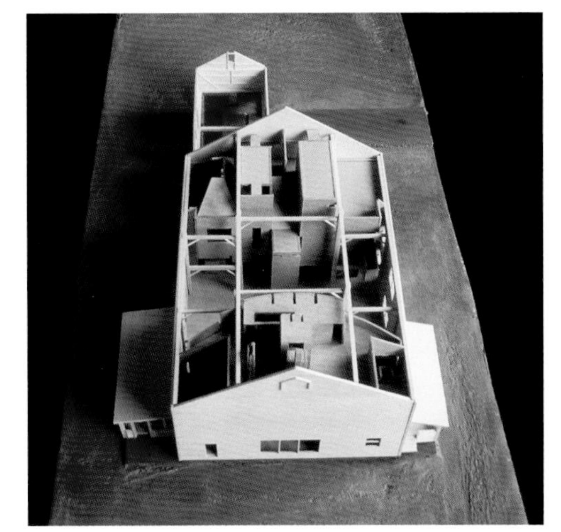

6

7

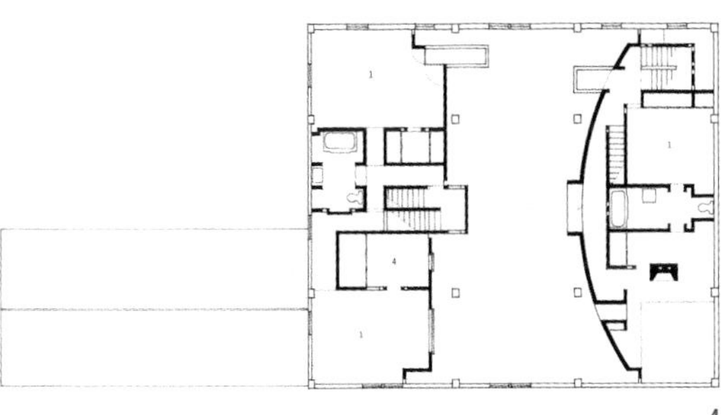

4

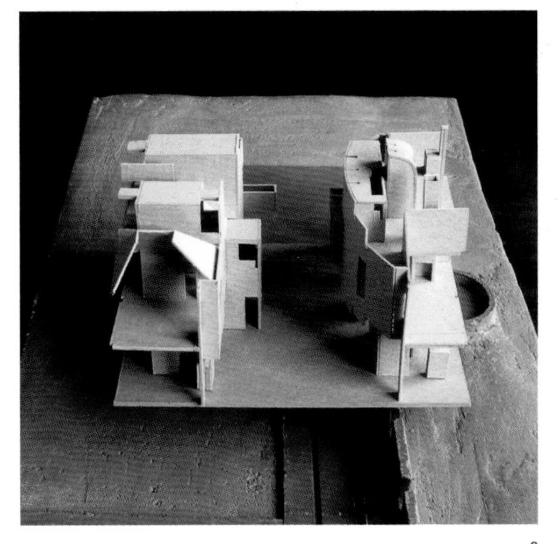

8

9

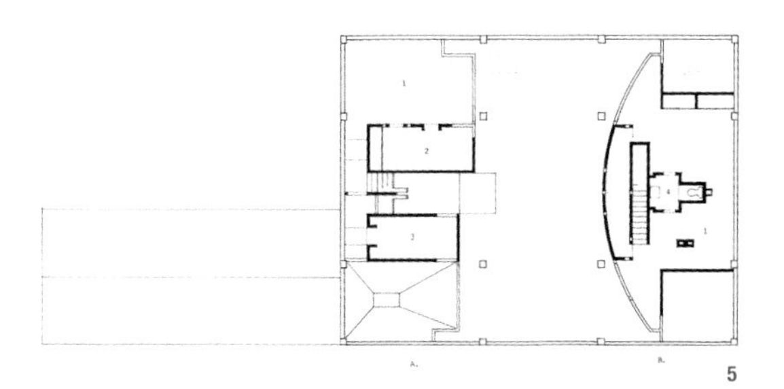

5

1 Pencil and color pencil on vellum perspective drawing of the three story space of the living room between the family and guest quarters
2 Cross section through the barn and family/guest quarters
3 First floor plan
4 Second floor plan
5 Third floor plan
6 Model view from above
7 Aerial view of the project showing the entrance through the existing milking shed with a new stair
8 Family quarters and guest quarters removed from the model
9 Guest quarters model removed from the barn

project name	Addition to "G" House
location	Scarsdale, New York
year of design	1987-1988
client	Name withheld at owner's request
lot size	1/2 acre
project size	750 sq.ft.
architect	George Ranalli Architect
associates	Robert Silman Structural Engineer
design team	Nina Hofer, Donna Cohen
photographer	Model Photos: George Ranalli

Addition to "G"House

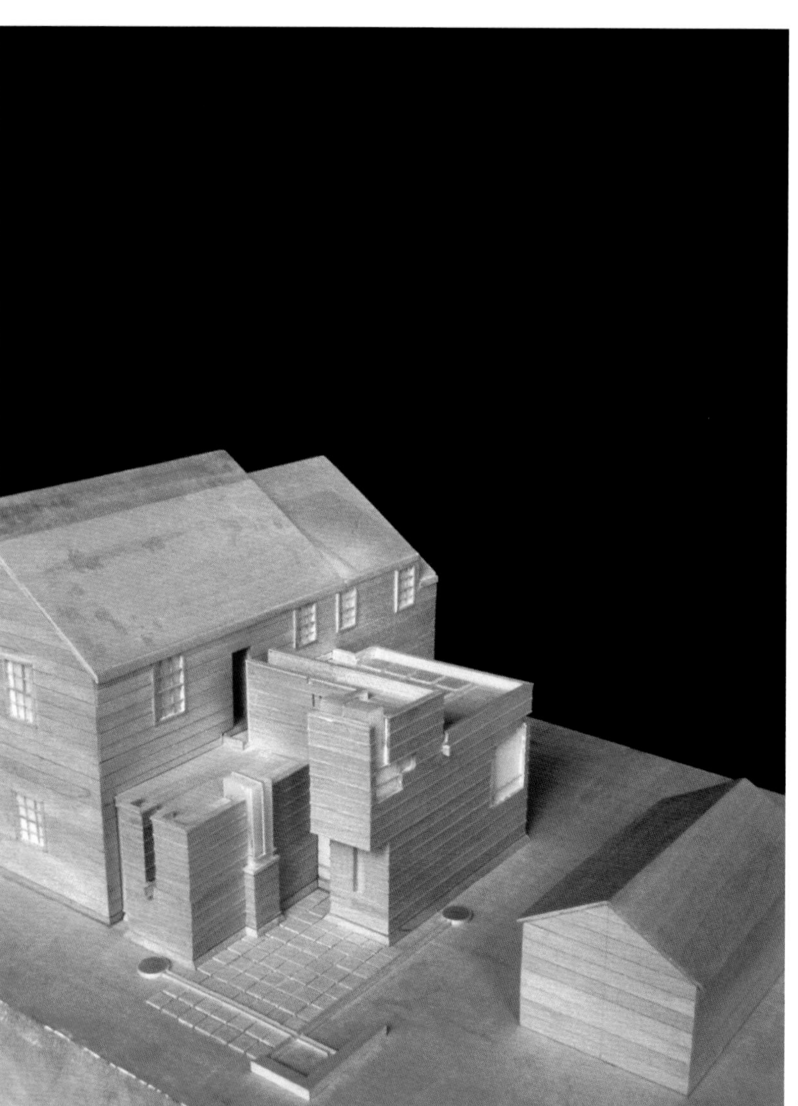

1

There are few locales less compatible with modern architecture than a colonial village. Yet in one such leafy suburb, a couple sought modern architectural relief for the discomforts and inconveniences of their beloved 1920s Garrison colonial, which included limited storage space and insufficient natural light.

Located in Scarsdale, New York, the house is a modest but stately building situated amidst houses twice or three times its size. The surrounding landscape is verdant and punctuated with spots of color provided by magnificent flowers. The house is set in the middle of the lot, and presents itself to the street with three dormers on axis and a more casually disposed assortment of windows and doors below the dormers. The existing rear of the house was even more casual, suggesting an extension to remedy the family's need for additional room. Expansion is constrained by the fact that the tiny lot was already at maximum allowable coverage.

The project proposed a larger, brighter kitchen, a new family room, an upper-story study, and a landscape design for a garden patio. The new second-story element relates to the existing board-and-batten structure in size, scale, and materiality (for example, its exterior aligns with the existing horizontal batten). Inside, the new design liberates the tiny, dark kitchen from its previous service function, providing it with space enough for casual dining beneath a gazebo-like stretch of skylight and with windows open to natural light and garden views. A spacious new family room shimmers in reflected daylight through an arrangement of tiny windows that animate the walls and ceiling with sparkle. In addition to the new upstairs study near the master bedroom, the design provides for a private rooftop terrace accessed by way of a hush-hush interior stair.

The exterior boundaries compose a figural field. An alcove links the passageway between parking garage and kitchen door; a niche door in the family room opens onto the patio-garden. The landscape design includes a water element, as rainwater falling from whimsical copper roof scuppers fills stone basins before flowing through delicate stone troughs into a central cistern.

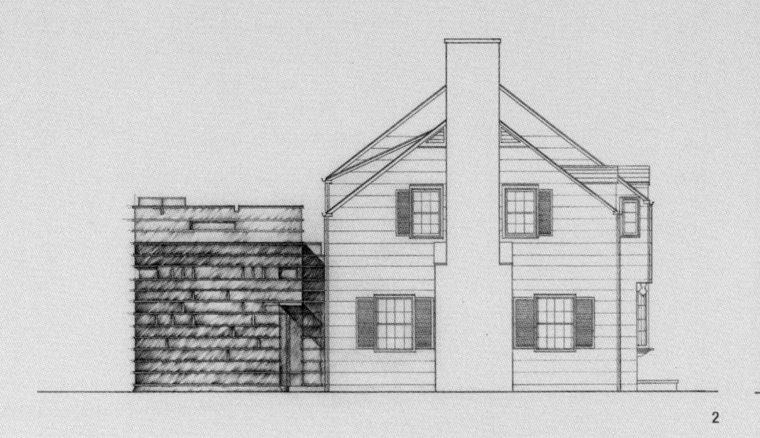

2

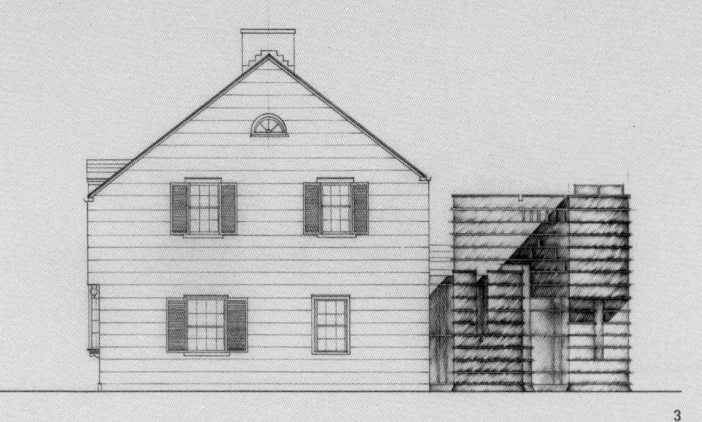

3

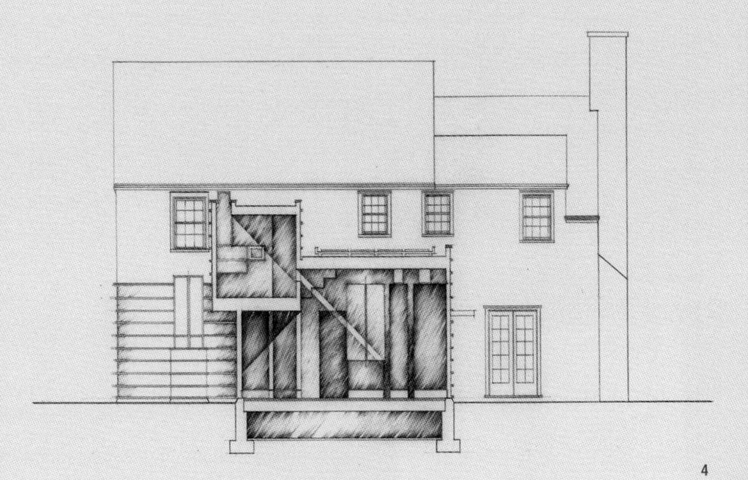

4

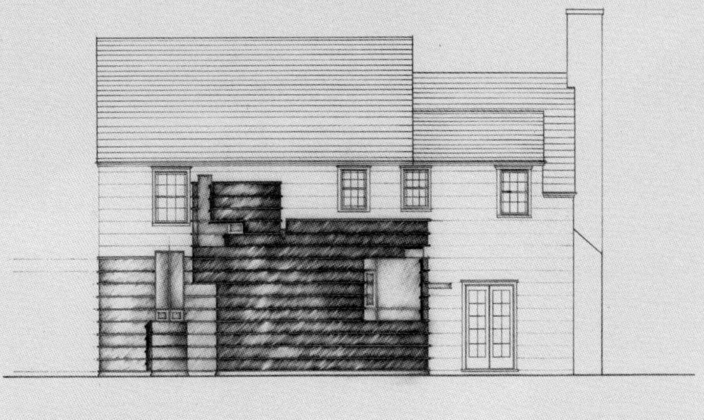

5

6

1 Model of the addition at the rear of the house
2 South elevation
3 North elevation
4 North-south section looking east
5 West elevation
6 Front of the existing house

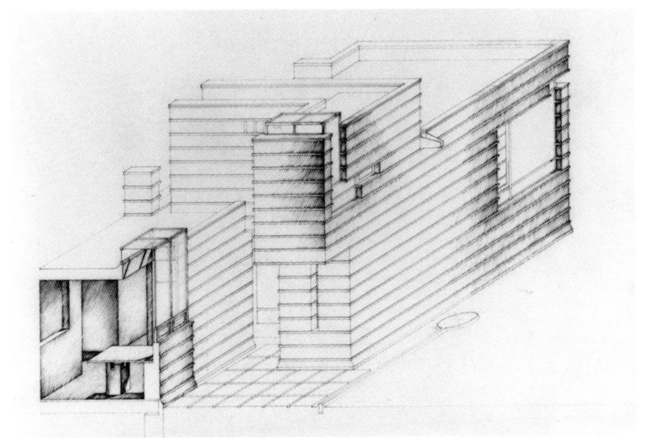

2

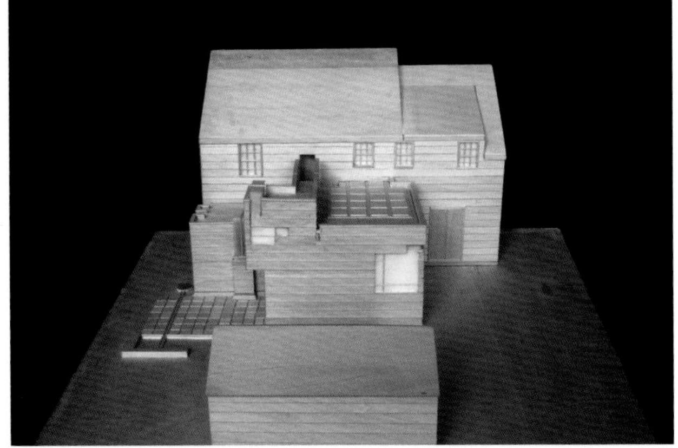

4

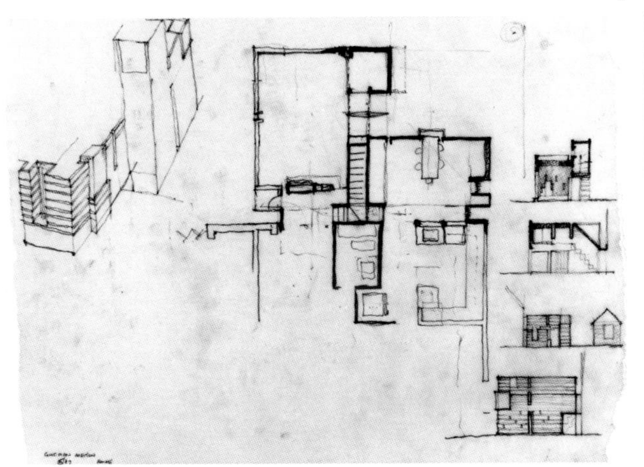

3

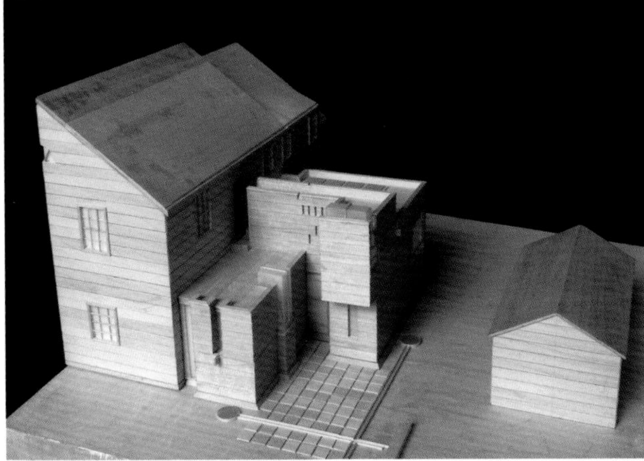

5

When a family loves the sense of stability that comes with an old house, but not the discomforts, an architectural remedy must consider what is essential to home life. In order to renew the reciprocity between home and family, old and new, elements are merged through subtle interconnections that neither juxtaposition of old and new nor simply replicate the vernacular. In this case, crucial to linking the structures is the establishment of a balance between the rhythm and order of old and new by a careful alignment with existing openings and with the general block volume of the house. The addition also organizes the garden space and includes the landscape in the total composition.

The Valentine Chair 2, (seen on page 416), was originally designed as breakfast-room furniture for "G" House.

1 | Model view from the northwest
2 | Section oblique drawing cut through the breakfast room
3 | Sketch studies of plan, sections, elevation and massing
4 | Aerial view of the model from the west
5 | Aerial view of the model from the northwest

1

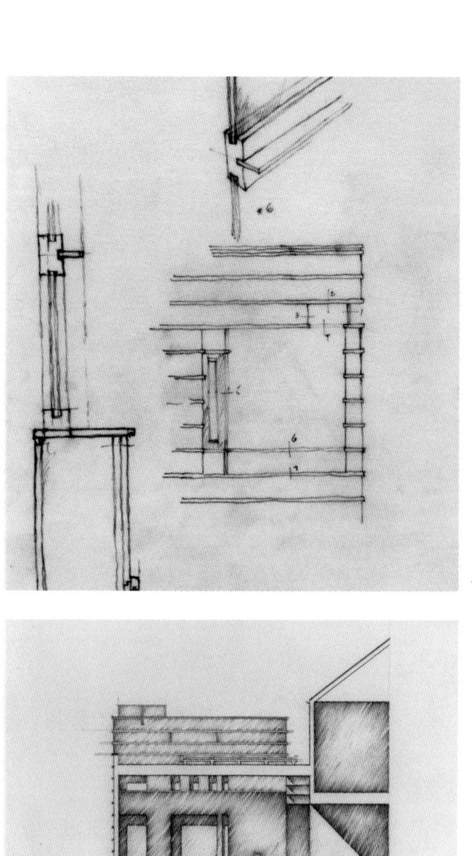
1

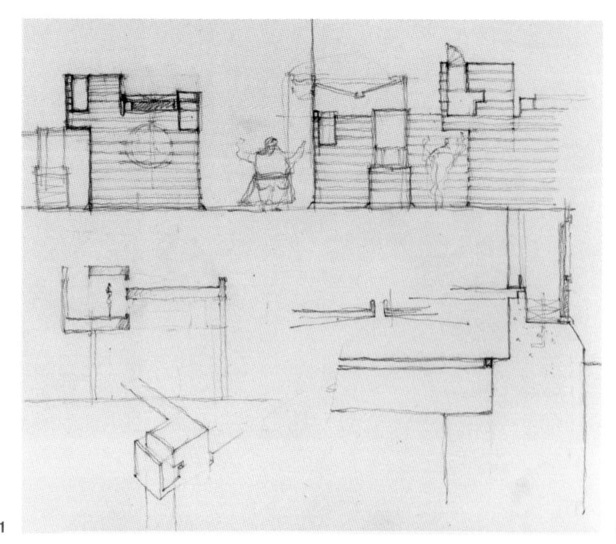
2

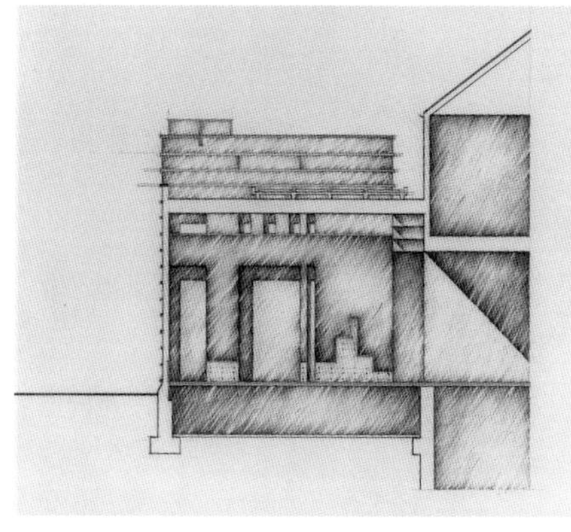
3

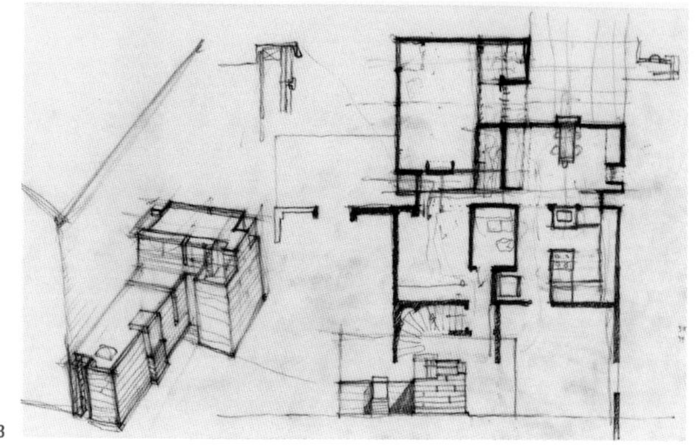
4

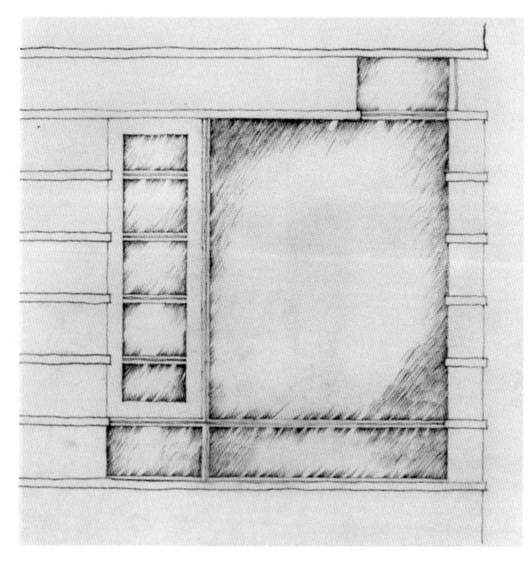
5

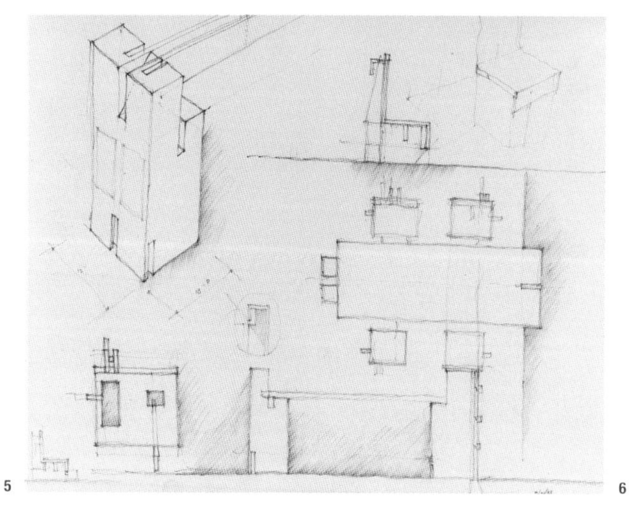
6

1 Window and woodwork detail sketches
2 Elevation studies and details
3 East-west section looking north
4 Plan and massing studies
5 Window sketch
6 Table and chair studies for the breakfast room
7 Model view from the southwest
8 First floor plan
9 Second floor plan
10 Breakfast room table and chairs

7

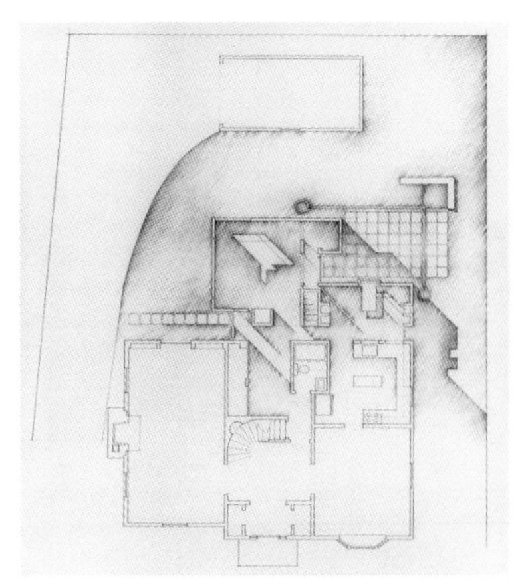

8

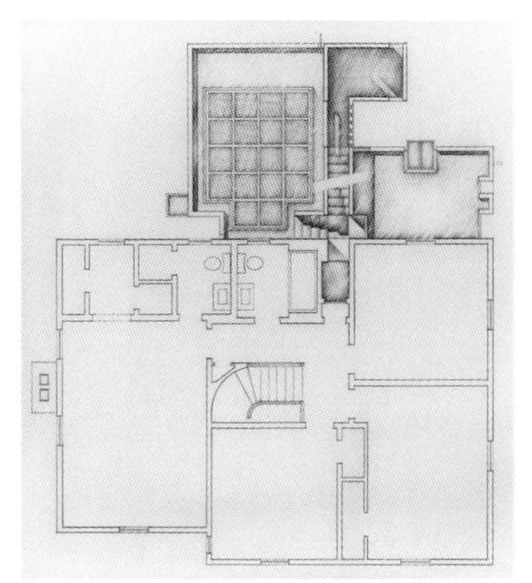

9

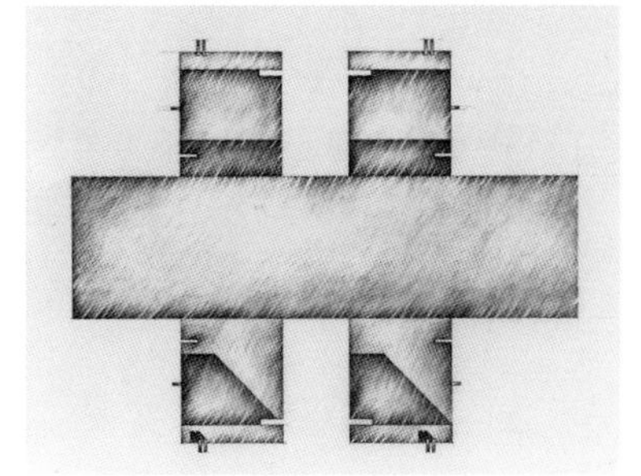

10

project name	22nd Street Loft
location	New York City
year of design	1985
year of completion	1986
client	Anita Pagliaro/ Bill Hayward
lot size	100' X 100'
project size	2,500 sq.ft.
architect	George Ranalli
associates	Robert Silman Structural Engineer
design team	Nick Dermand
photographer	George Cserna

22nd Street Loft

1

Even in the up-and-coming neighborhoods, it's never a small accomplishment for architecture to transform a dilapidated industrial loft into a family home. In the case of a Chelsea, New York apartment renovation, the achievement applies, without exception, for two cosmopolitan owners seeking a meticulously appointed urban residence that somehow retained the "old feeling." By means of geometric abstraction, the architecture invokes a delicate transposition, simultaneously referencing the idiosyncratic and the familiar.

By letting go of some customary divisions of household space, and maintaining others, the design introduced two orderly forms unifying a compact arrangement of private rooms and an approachably open living and dining space. From the public hallway, one form composes the antechamber outside a compact library, nestling a writer's desk surrounded by a chunky wall of bookshelves. The library all but conceals a confidential rise of four stairs, to a bedroom suite, fashioned between a double wardrobe-cum-dressing room, on one side, and deep-set closets, on the other. A companion form, inserted alongside the bedroom suite, partners in establishing a wide hallway into a large open room. Midway across the hall, the smaller of the two new forms makes a neat enclosure around a spacious kitchen, which features cabinetry and storage, a double sink, appliances, and spacious work surfaces.

Disposed by adjustments of surface modeling, and brightened by strong sunlight through the windows of the old loft, density transforms. The design of numerous slots, alcoves, and niches, heightened by shade and reflection, evokes an enigmatic condition. Overhanging lanky metal adornments, and a glimpse of a brass-winged canopy, hovering above the bedroom, imbue the living and dining spaces with illusion. At the smaller scale, a coherence of form and materiality appointing the architectural elements shape handcrafted lighting and household furnishings for comfortable, sculptural seating and elegant dining for eight. The residence embodies the illusory atmosphere of artistic poise.

2

3

1 View from the living room
2 Exterior view of the loft building on 22nd Street
3 Entry hall view toward the living and dining room

1

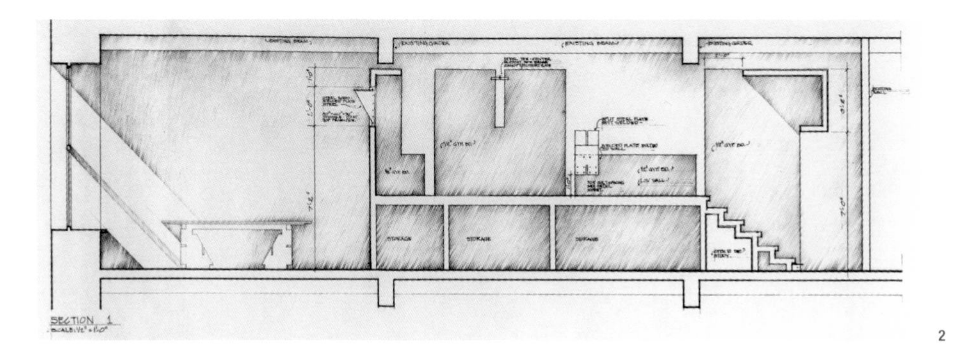

2

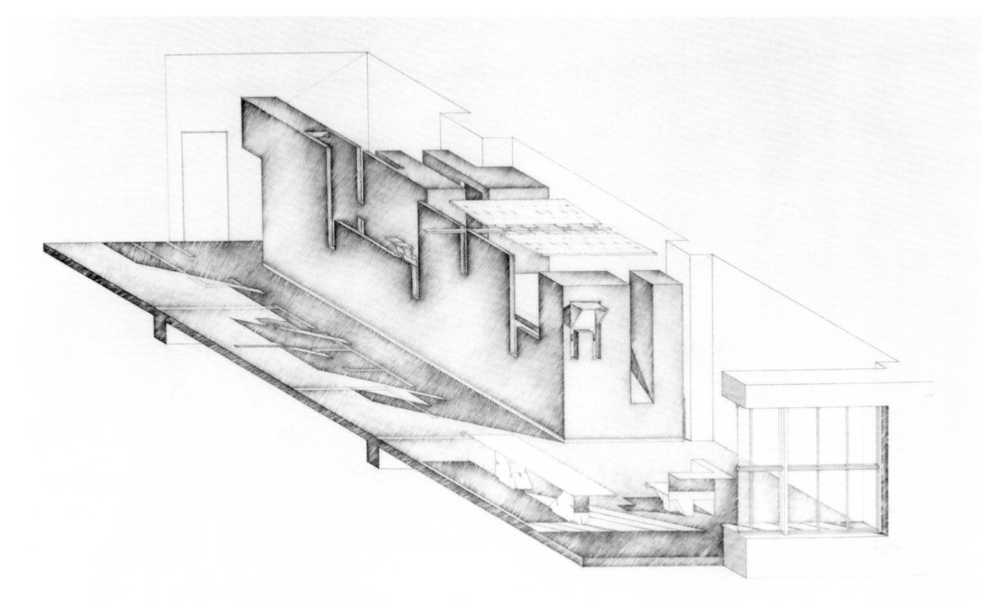

3

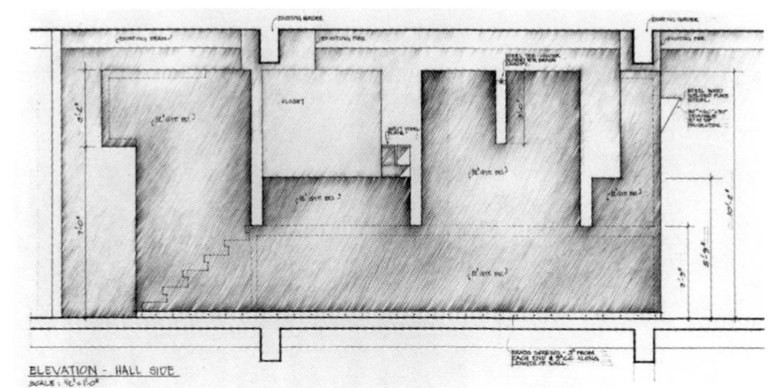

4

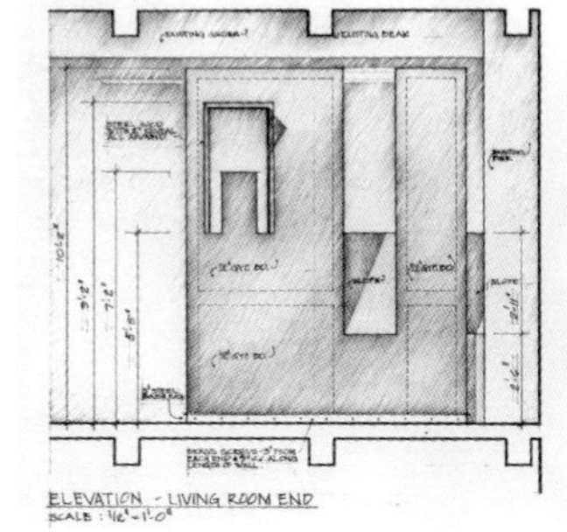

5

1 | Living room and dining room
2 | Section through the bedroom and loft
3 | Pencil and color pencil on vellum section oblique drawing
4 | Hallway elevation
5 | Living room elevation

1

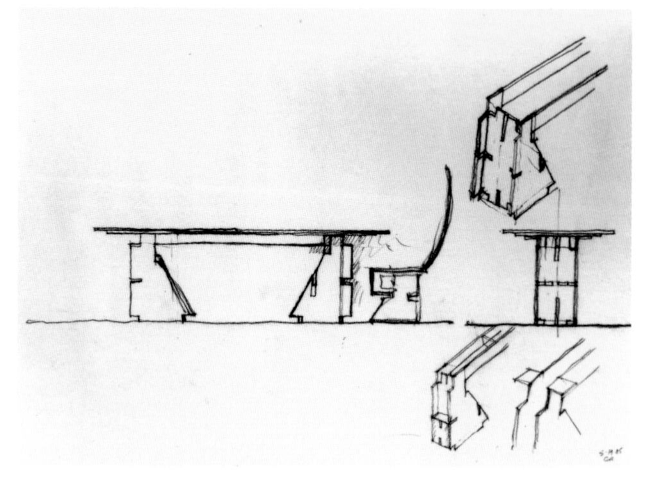

2

3

1 | Detail view of the living room wall and furniture
2 | Sketch of the dining chair and table
3 | Steel and leather side chair and sofa

1

2

3

4

5

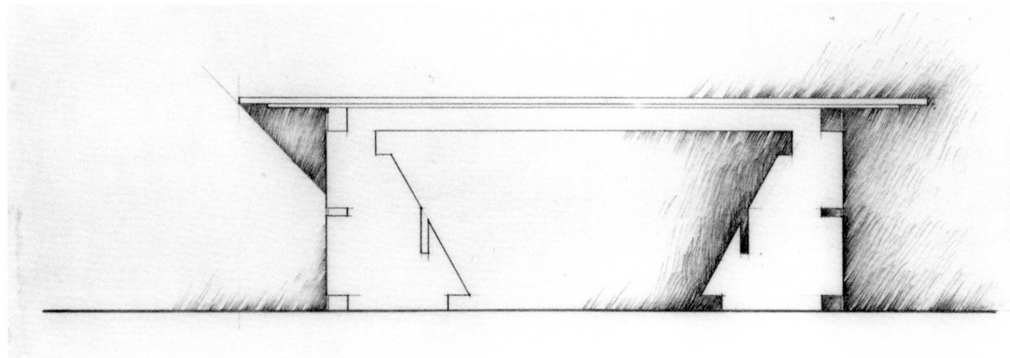

6

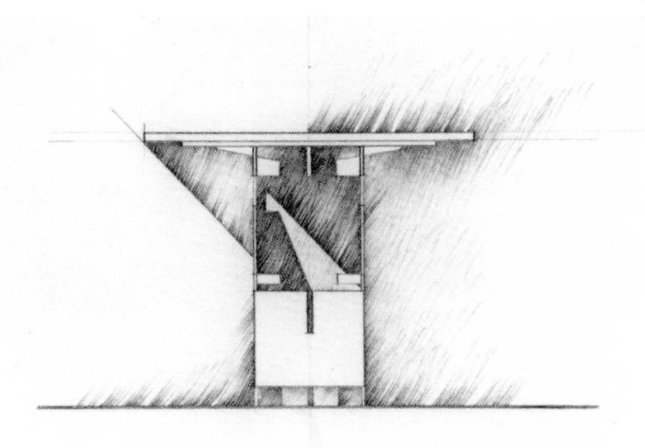

7

1 Shop fabrication of the steel side chair and table base
2 Steel side chair without the leather cushions
3 Steel side chair elevation drawings
4 Table base before the marble top was installed
5 Elevation drawing of the table
6 Table base pedestal at fabricator
7 Section through steel and marble table

1

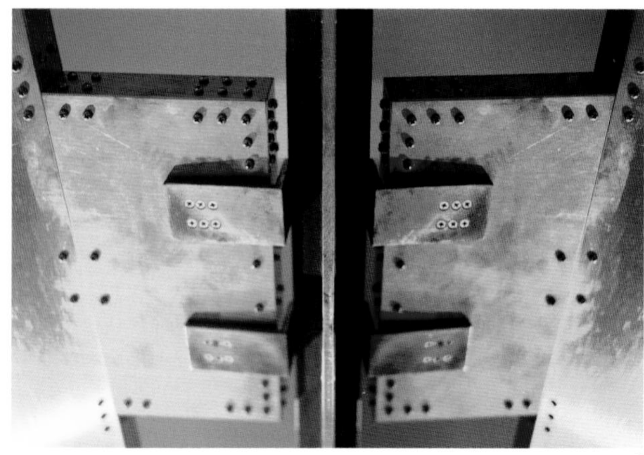

2

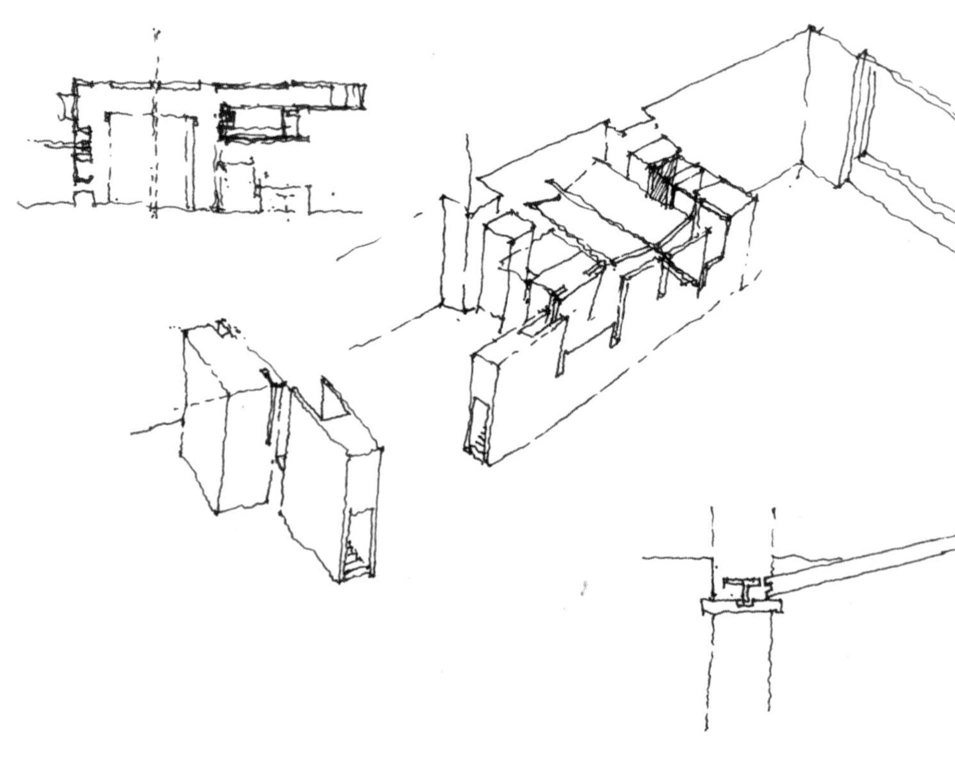

3

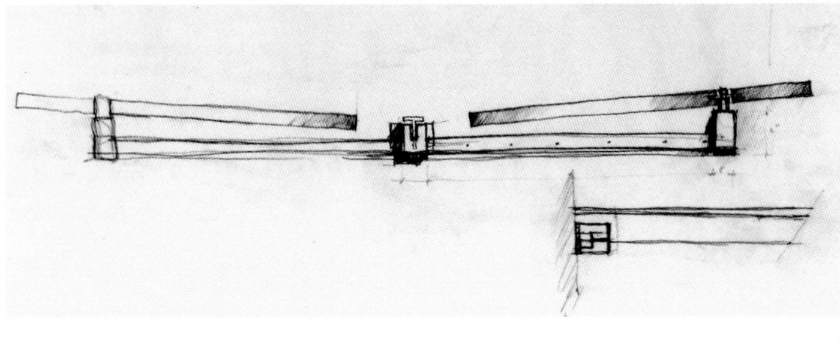

4

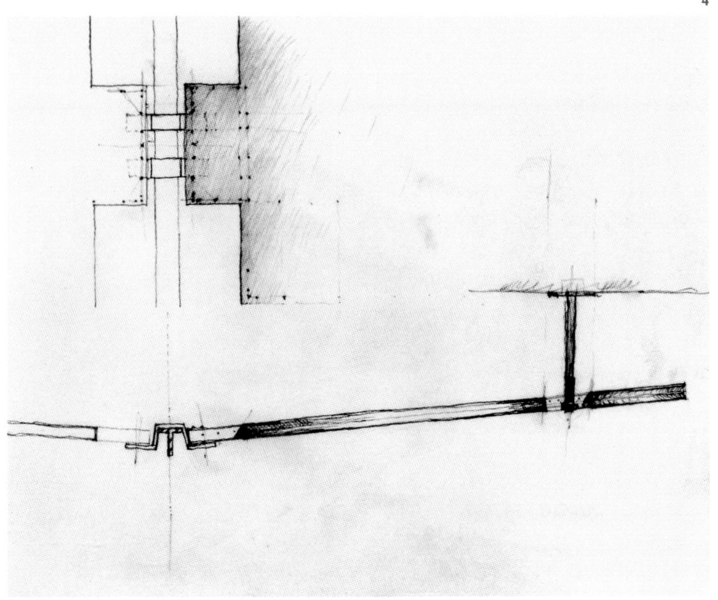

5

6

1 | Canopy seen from the entry hallway
2 | Detail of the canopy supports and screw assembly
3 | Pen and ink sketch of the loft design
4 | Pencil and color pencil study for the brass canopy
5 | Plan and section drawing of the brass canopy
6 | View of the bedroom with custom steel lights, brass canopy and steel side tables

project name	Ranalli Studio Apartment
location	New York City
year of design	1974
year of completion	1975
client	George Ranalli
lot size	50'x100'
project size	400 sq.ft.
architect	George Ranalli
associates	Robert Silman Structural Engineer
design team	Paula Beall
photographer	George Cserna

Ranalli Studio Apartment

1

In a light-filled apartment, the design, a chalky bi-level element, composes an entry foyer leading to a tidy recessed kitchen space and a bathroom. The geometry also frames a view from the front door across a hallway of well-worn oak floor, into an open living space. Walking toward a large window of city views, the narrowness expands with the presence of a dinette space. A slightly elevated platform offers space near the kitchen for a table between chic upholstered banquette benches. The seating neatly conceals tableware storage. Above the cozy dining nook, a delicate circular line of light charms the evening meal. Further inside the main room, magically, an arabesque of a staircase, flanked by alcove bookshelves, ascends toward a cozy nest of a spacious loft bed, resting calmly beneath a shady geometrical canopy. The cantilevered sleeping berth crowns the dining space, and overlooks a pleasant double-height living room, with a large oak wood arch frame window, an element of utility from the old factory, now domesticated beneath a translucent sailcloth stretching from the top of the windows to a tall handcrafted wooden work desk. The diaphanous fabric defines an open study underneath, while shading the sleeping berth above, and filtering sunlight throughout. The design for a small apartment renovation is a process of abstraction which liberates and incorporates portions of existing conditions, and instigates an interplay of reflection and shadow among the bright white perimeter walls and ceiling, softer gray facets of the sculpted element, and the warmth of wood floors and factory window frame, to register impressions of comfort, function, and beauty in a living space.

1 View of the new construction in the large room of the studio
2 View from the work area of the stair up to the loft and the library

2

1

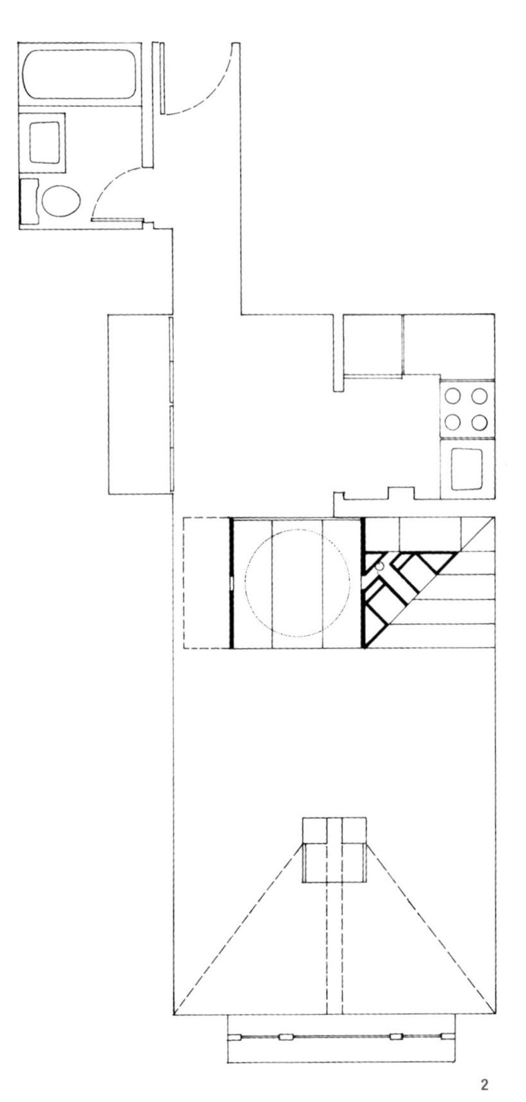

2

1 | View from the entry with the red neon light in the dining booth
2 | Floor plan
3 | Plan oblique view from the entry side
4 | Plan oblique view from the studio side
5 | Detail of the bedroom space
6 | Detail view of the library and stair with neon light hidden within

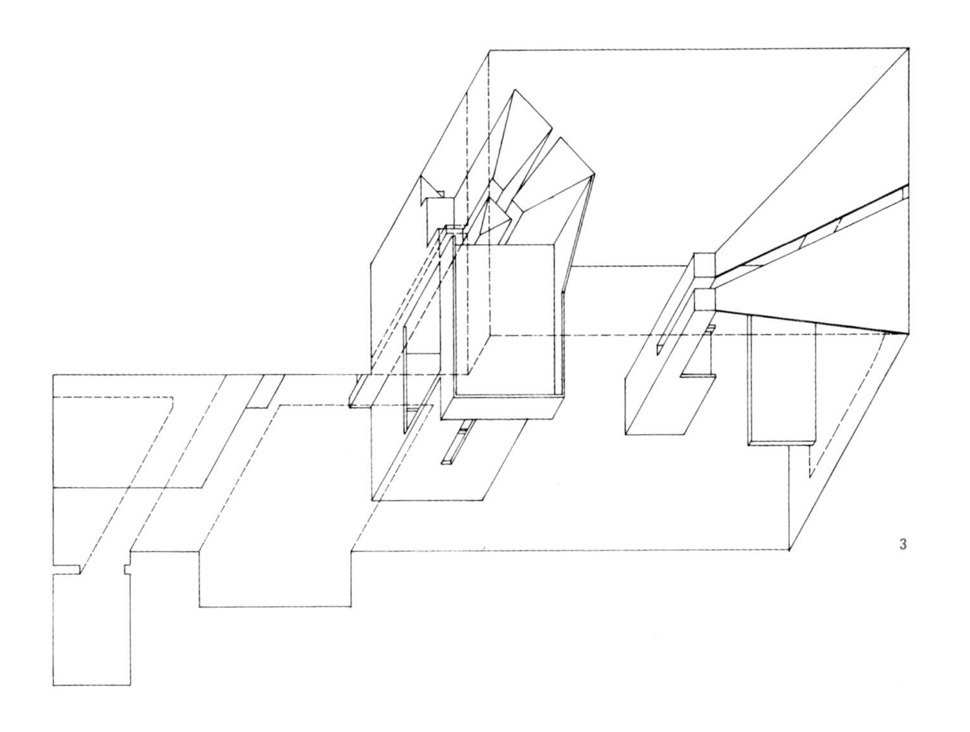

3

5

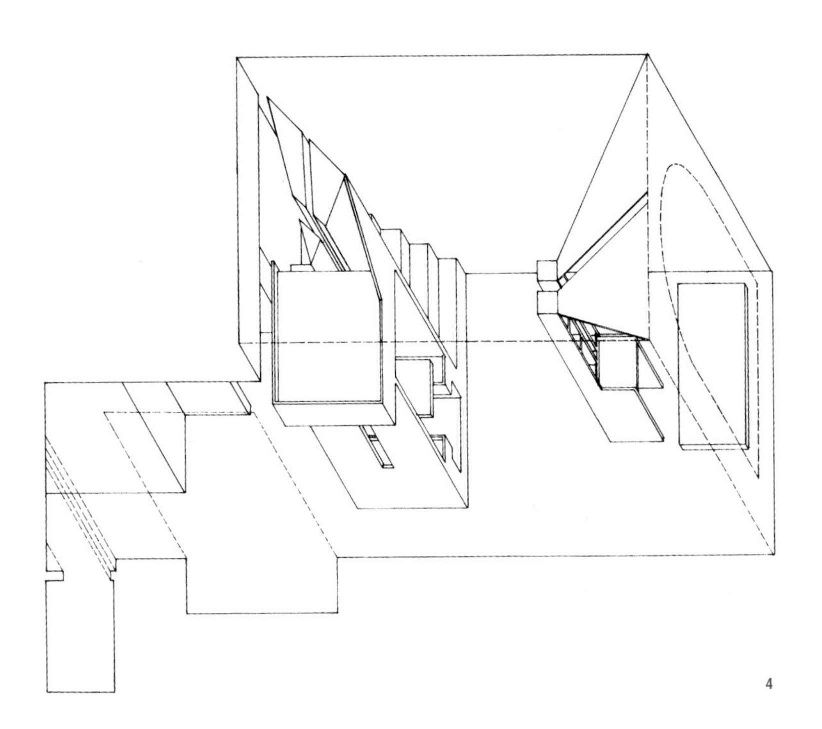

4

6

project name	Callender School Renovation & Restoration
location	Newport, Rhode Island
year of design	1979
year of completion	1980
client	William Boggs
lot size	50'x 100'
project size	21,600 sq.ft.
architect	George Ranalli
associates	Robert Silman, Structural Engineer; Kiley Engineers
design team	Paula Beall, Turan Duda, Mark Mascheroni
photographer	George Cserna /Nick Wheeler

Callender School Renovation

1

The Callender Schoolhouse, a National Historic Landmark in Newport, Rhode Island, was reborn when the client, William Boggs, commissioned a renovation to convert it into housing. The project incorporates the exterior restoration of the elegant Italianate schoolhouse with the creation of six architecturally compelling apartments.

The original building, built in 1862, is in one of the oldest sections of Newport. The primarily residential neighborhood is located between the town cemetery and the sea, with this stately masonry building set amidst seventeenth-century wood cottages.

Structurally, a brick cavity wall sits on top of a foundation of granite and sandstone. The building was constructed in two sections over a twenty-year period, and some unique conditions developed during that time, which were incorporated into the new architectural design. Most notable were the wood roof trusses on the second floor, left over from the original A-frame roof, and the two cast-iron columns on the first floor that help support the second. Both the size and quality of the interior spaces, as well as the powerful historic exterior, demanded a solution that would preserve the original exterior.

The project restored the exterior of the building to its original condition, with all moldings, cornices, and details matched and replaced where necessary. The existing interior stair hall was included in the renovation, but an effort was made to keep the feeling and quality of the school, so in this space the memory of the school is felt strongly.

To resolve complex zoning and local building-code requirements, all new construction is gathered toward the center of the building, allowing the major living spaces to occur in the space between the shell of the old building and the new dwelling units. These spaces are faced with a façade behind which are all the small-scale private rooms of necessity. The collective assembly of these façades, grouped around the public space of the central hall of the old school, forms a city within the building that is symbolic of the community of dwellers that exist within.

2

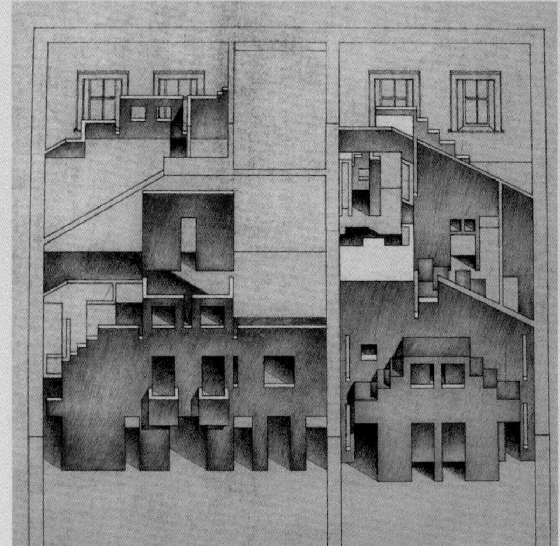

3

4

1 View of the triplex unit on the second floor with the original roof truss incorporated into the new design
2 Restored exterior of the building
3 Elevation oblique of the second floor north side
4 View of the ground floor triplex living room

1

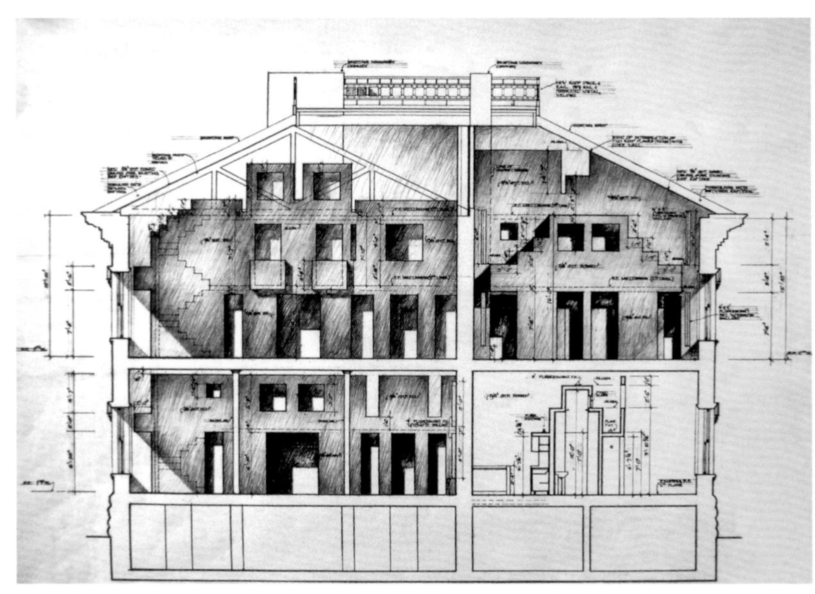

2

3

The metamorphosis of the space required removing the second-floor ceiling and many interior walls and recombining portions of basement and attic. Restored stairwells remain central to common access of laundry facilities, a sauna, and storage. The original classroom doors act as front and back entryways for each apartment, and the old classrooms become the living quarters for the new domiciles.

The design for each apartment centers on a large living room/dining room on the first level with a soaring, 23-foot ceiling. A large sculptural form inserted into each apartment contains a kitchen, informal dining area, large walk-in pantry, and laundry room. The living room has built-in shelving, designed lighting, and a full bathroom. The second level provides a cozy inglenook around a fireplace and a master bedroom with full bath. Up a few stairs, a loft space is well suited for use as a family room or home office. The design borrows from the visual trickery of Cubist painters, by creating an interplay of color from a multiplicity of perspectives.

1 Owner's living room looking toward the entrance
2 East-west section facing north
3 Owner's living room with their collection of antique furniture

1

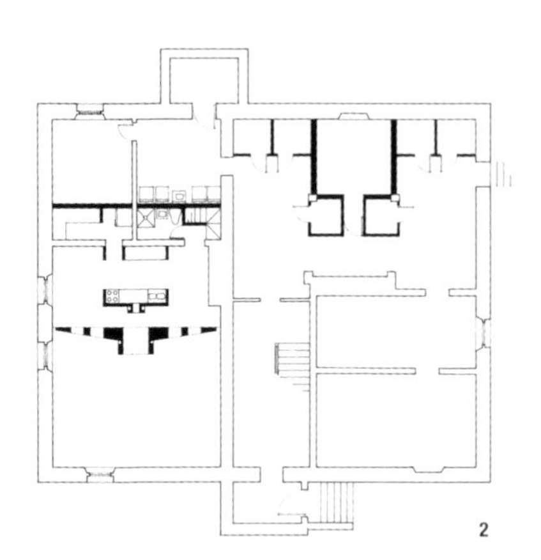

2

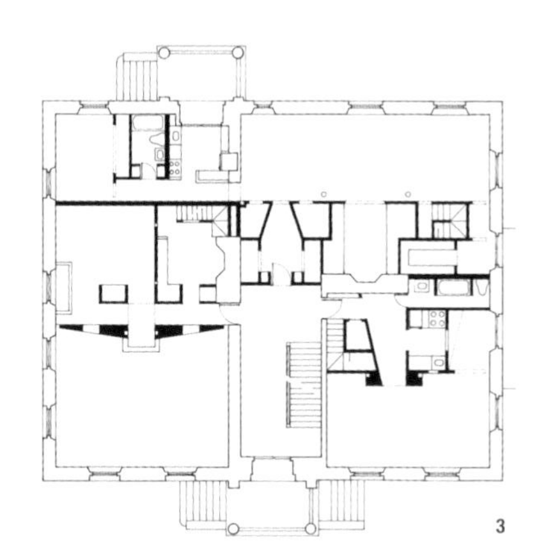

3

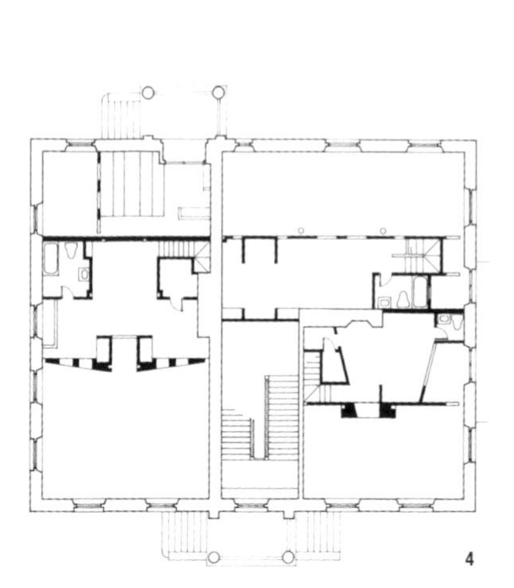

4

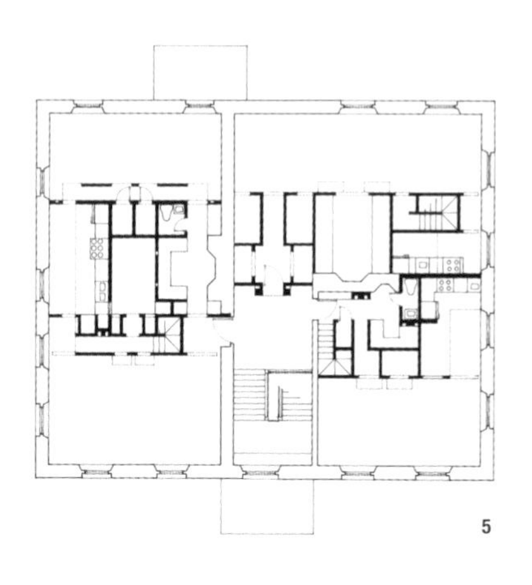

5

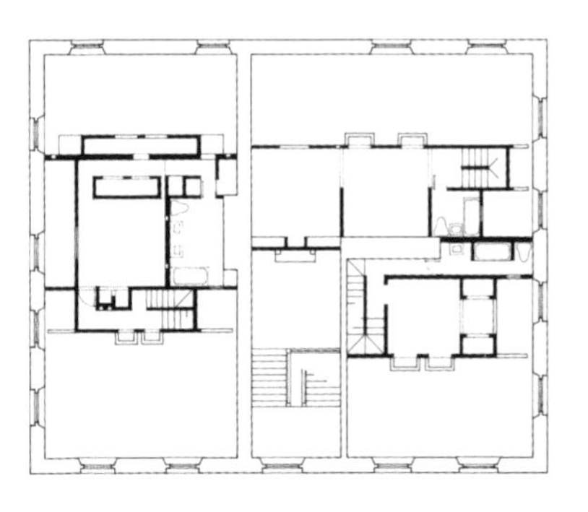

6

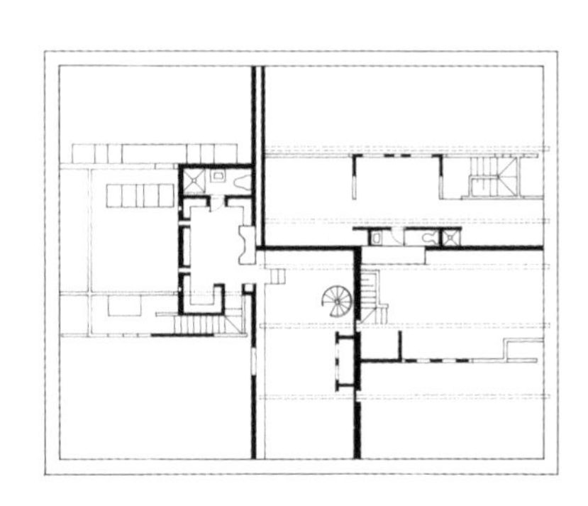

7

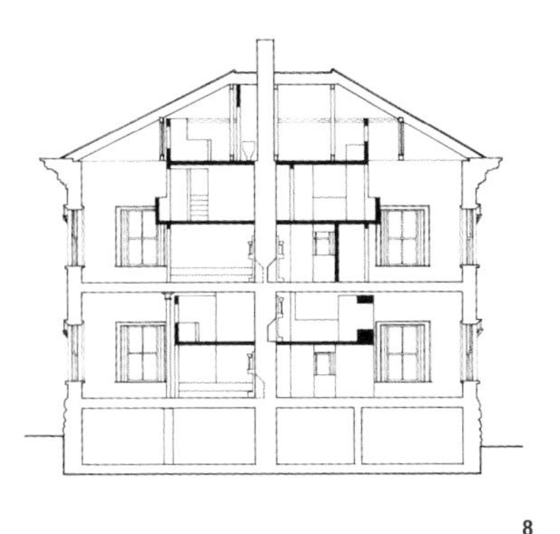

8

10

11

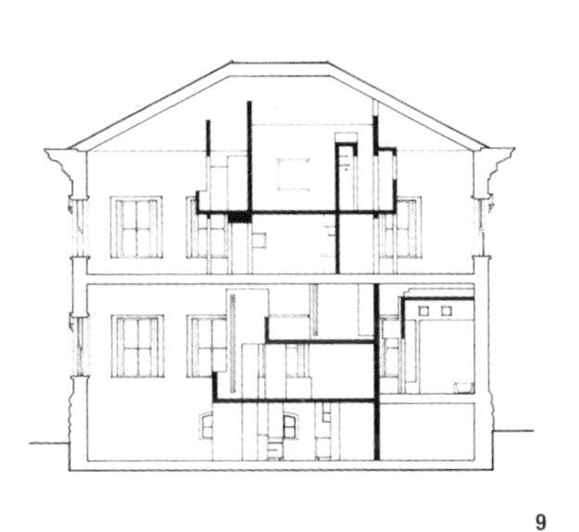

9

12

13

1 Owner's stair hall looking down from the third floor
2 Basement floor plan
3 First floor plan
4 First floor mezzanine plan
5 Second floor plan
6 Second floor mezzanine plan
7 Third floor plan
8 North-south section looking east
9 North-south section through owner's unit on second floor looking west
10 Model view of the second floor north side
11 Model view of the second floor south side
12 South side model removed from the building
13 North side model removed from the building
14 Existing floor plan
15 Existing building prior to the renovation

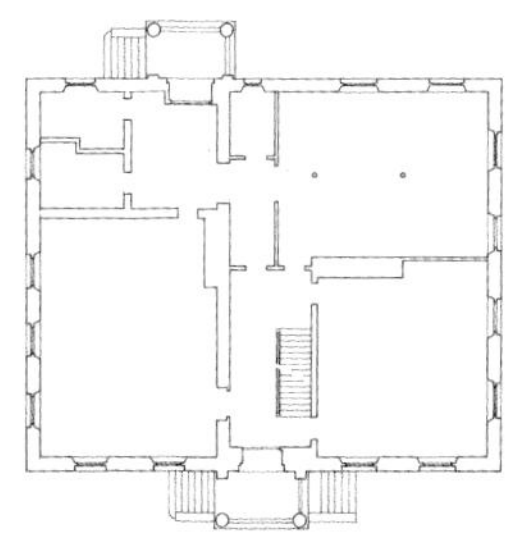

14

15

1

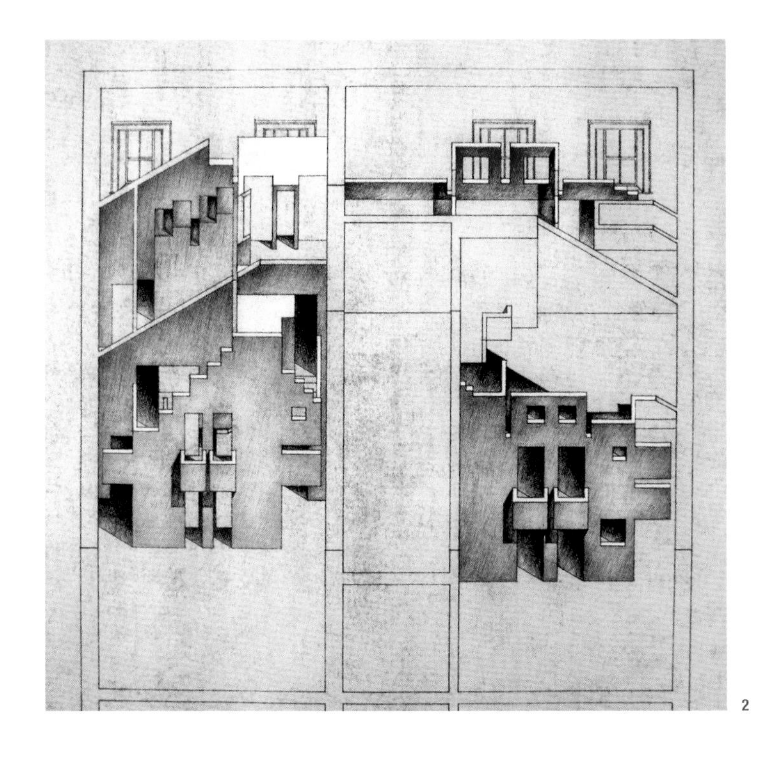

2

4

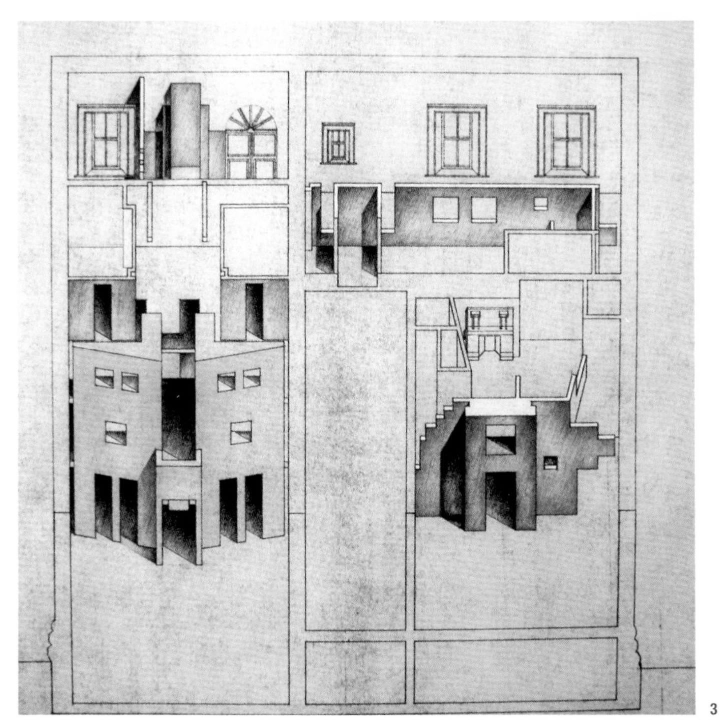

3

1 | Owner's living room from third floor study
2 | Elevation oblique drawing second floor south side
3 | Elevation oblique drawing first floor south side
4 | Detail of the balconies on the owner's façade

1

1 | Owner's dining room with windows from the dressing room and the table set for dinner
2 | Owner's kitchen
3 | Owner's master bedroom
4 | Stair hall in the Owner's apartment looking up toward the third floor

2

3

4

1

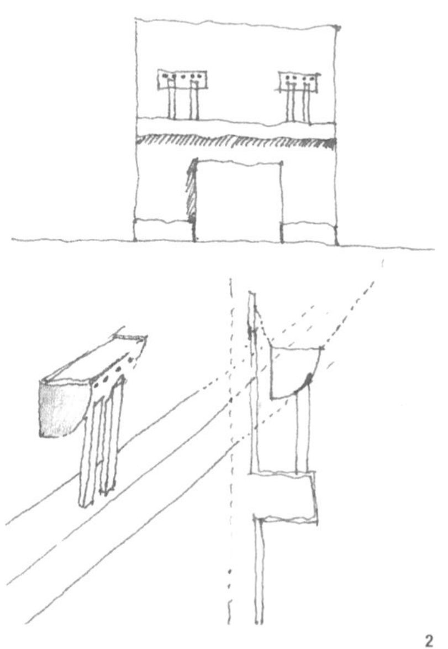

2

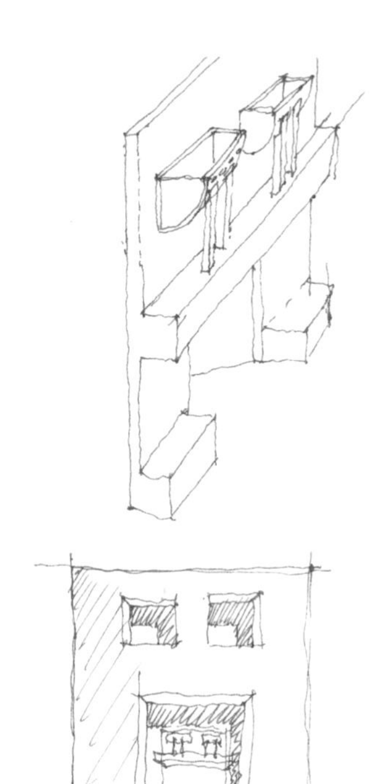

3

4

5

6

7

1 Fireplace sitting room in the second floor duplex apartment. Existing cast iron columns hold up the second floor
2 Pen and ink sketch of the steel fireplace mantle elevation and lights
3 Sketch of the inglenook and fireplace design
4 Second floor duplex with existing cast iron columns
5 First floor duplex apartment from the entry side
6 First floor duplex apartment
7 Triplex apartment on the second floor with the wood timber truss from the existing roof

1

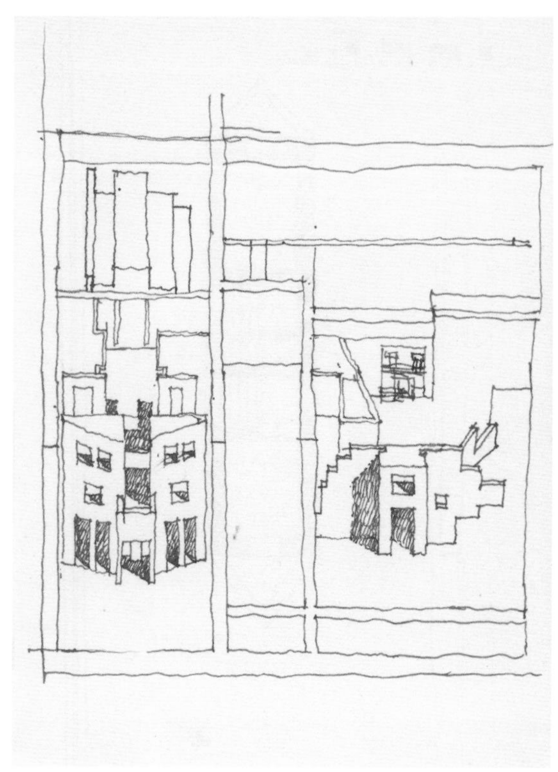

2

1 Large triplex façade on the ground floor
2 Sketch of the triplex and duplex apartments on the first floor south side
3 Pen and ink and color pencil study of the triplex apartment ground floor
4 Triplex apartment living room on the ground floor south side
5 Stair hall inside the renovated and restored building
6 Exterior of the building night view with new apartments visible

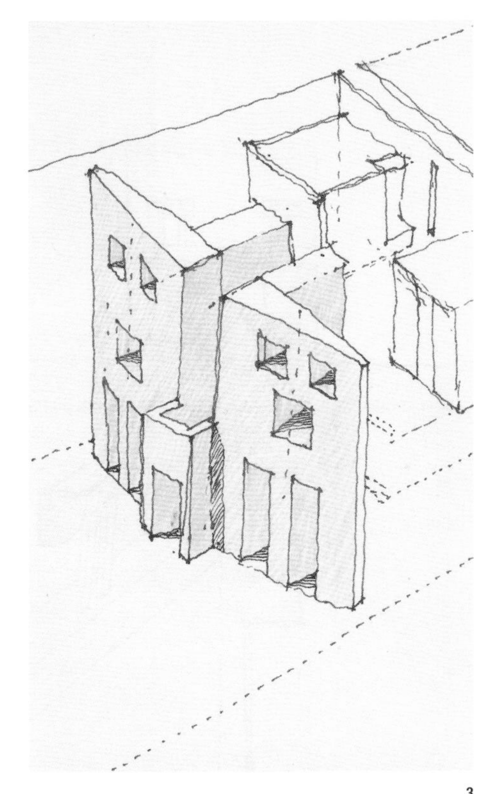

3

4

5

6

project name	Frehley House
location	Stratford, Connecticut
year of design	1978
client	Ace Frehley
lot size	7.5 acres
project size	6,400 sq.ft.
architect	George Ranalli
associates	Robert Silman Structural Engineer
design team	Paula Beall, Mark Mascheroni, Turan Duda, M.T. Chang
photographer	Model Photos: George Ranalli

Frehley House

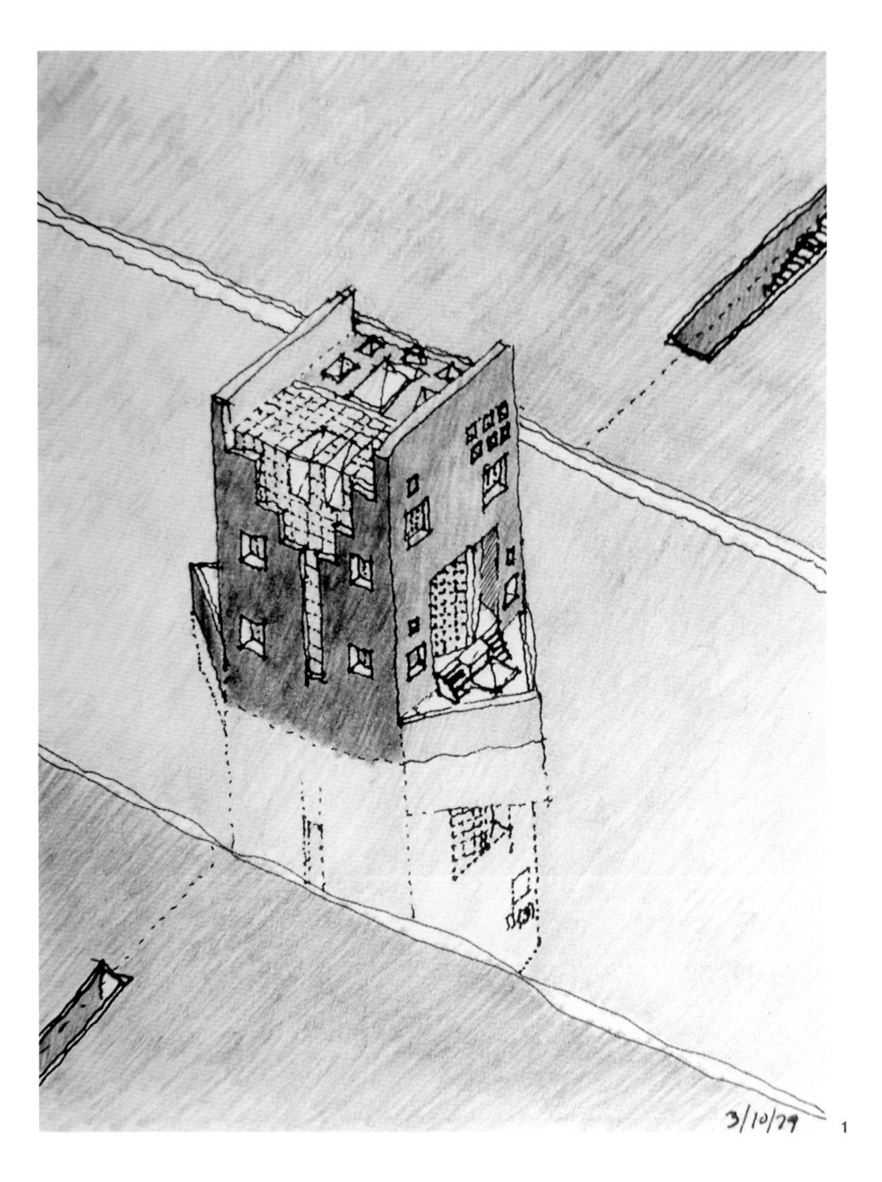

1

After a decade of continuous motion across the world's stage, a natural born vagabond and entertainment icon longed for home. To make matters worse, the public could not get enough. Tasked with the burdened to hold back the sea, a request for contemporary architecture specified a paradoxical place of idyllic tranquility, neither nostalgic, nor humdrum, with a touch of the psychedelic.

The verdant and vast site for a new residence spreads across a velvet green. By providence, natural and civic resources allow a diversion of water from a nearby river, all the way through a large man-made canal, before returning to its source. The illusory setting brings into play a sloping underground passageway, embedded in the landscape, at cross-axis with the canal, as well as a house, and several smaller buildings, set into the succulent countryside. When viewed from above, the way in appears to dissolve into the landscape, as a passage underground leads to the main entrance through the foundation of the house, anchored to the concrete base of the canal.

The house is a cubic composition of stone, glass, and steel. Fifteen feet below grade, light through a glass bock ceiling clarifies the central entrance, which orchestrates the way into a spacious, temperate, top-lit spa. The 18-foot high courtyard rises up through the center of the house, orienting space for a drawing room, dining room, kitchen, three bedroom suites, and a library. Flights of stairs, one at the front, and another at the back of the house, arrange passage through three levels. Up from the subterranean, the courtyard gives direction to the drawing room on one end, and the dining room on the other. Each room opens up onto a large triangular terrace. A slow drift of sunlight and soft air moves from two large faceted doors, and four operable pyramids of glass on the rooftop, through the atrium, to refresh the surrounding space, while continuously changing light creates various architectural effects. On the upper levels, vertical and lateral openings delineate the main architectural characteristic of the space. Equally, the stone exterior lightens on the way up. The step-gable pattern of a traditional canal house, in reverse, becomes a device for relatively more transparency on the southern side.

2

5

3

4

6

1 | Pen and ink and color pencil sketch of the house in the canal
2 | An existing canal
3 | Front elevation of the house
4 | Rear elevation of the house
5 | Views of the front of the house, wood model
6 | Canal view of the house, wood model

1

2

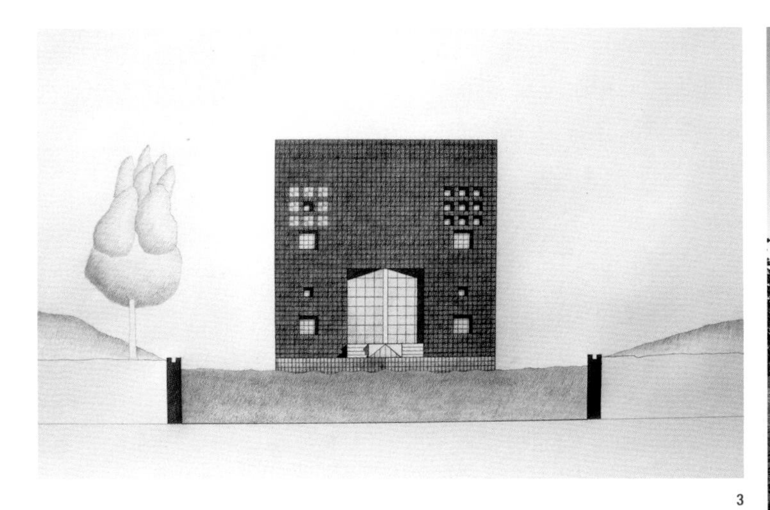

3

4

1 | Computer model view of the canal elevation
2 | Canal elevation
3 | Pencil drawing of the canal elevation
4 | View of the canal and rear elevation of the house

1

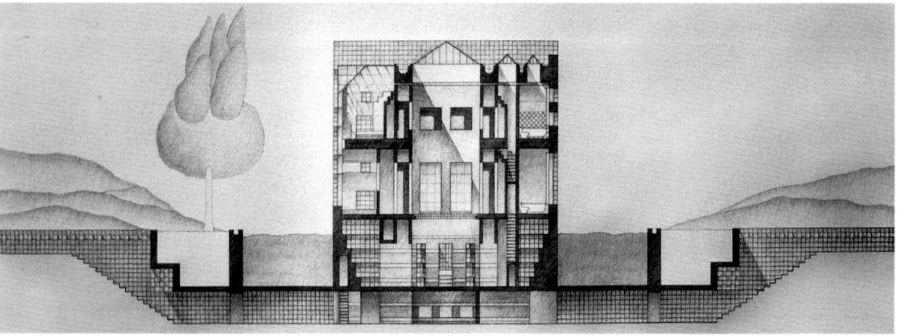

2

1 Sketch of the house in the landscape
2 Section through the entry sequence
3 Sketches of the entry and canal sequences
4 House study, pen and ink and color pencil
5 Computer model of the entrance to the house
6 Entry level plan
7 Lower court and exercise level
8 Living and dining level
9 Bedroom level

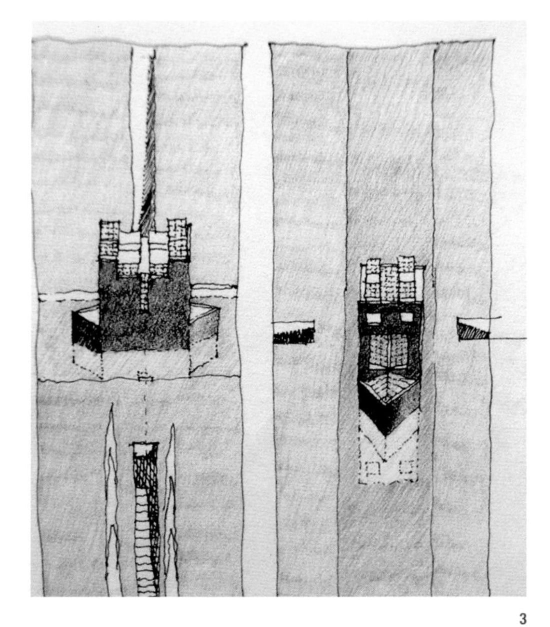
3

4

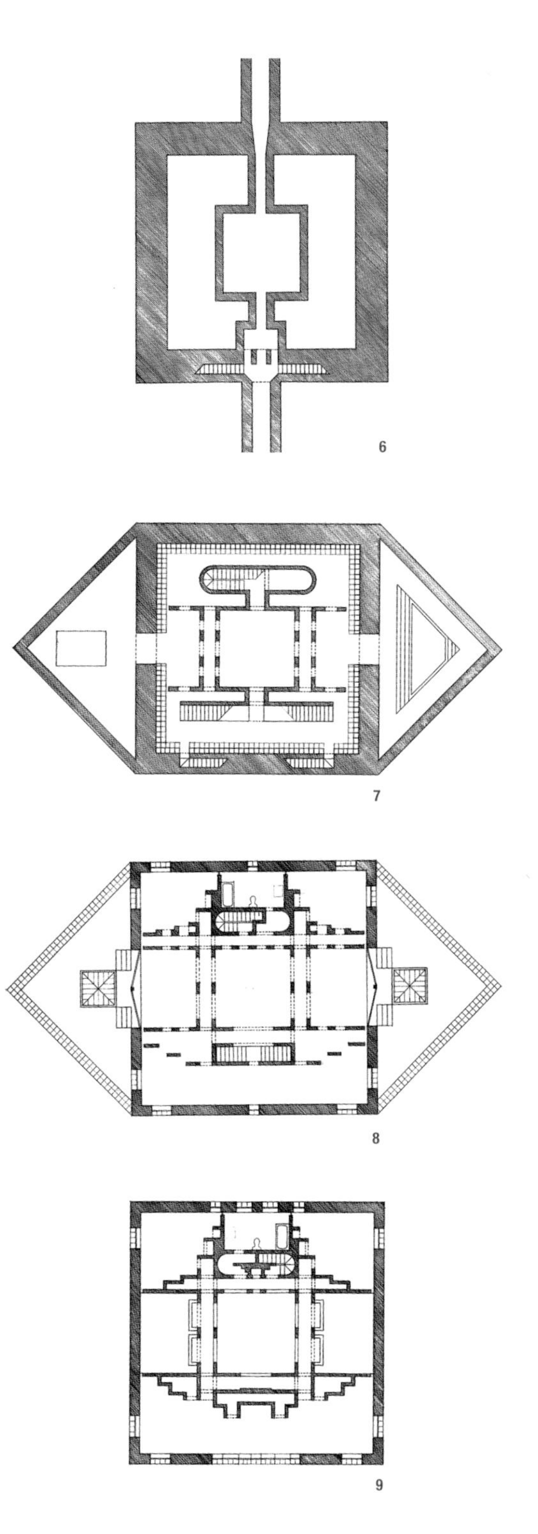
6

7

8

9

5

1 | Computer model section through the entry sequence and central court

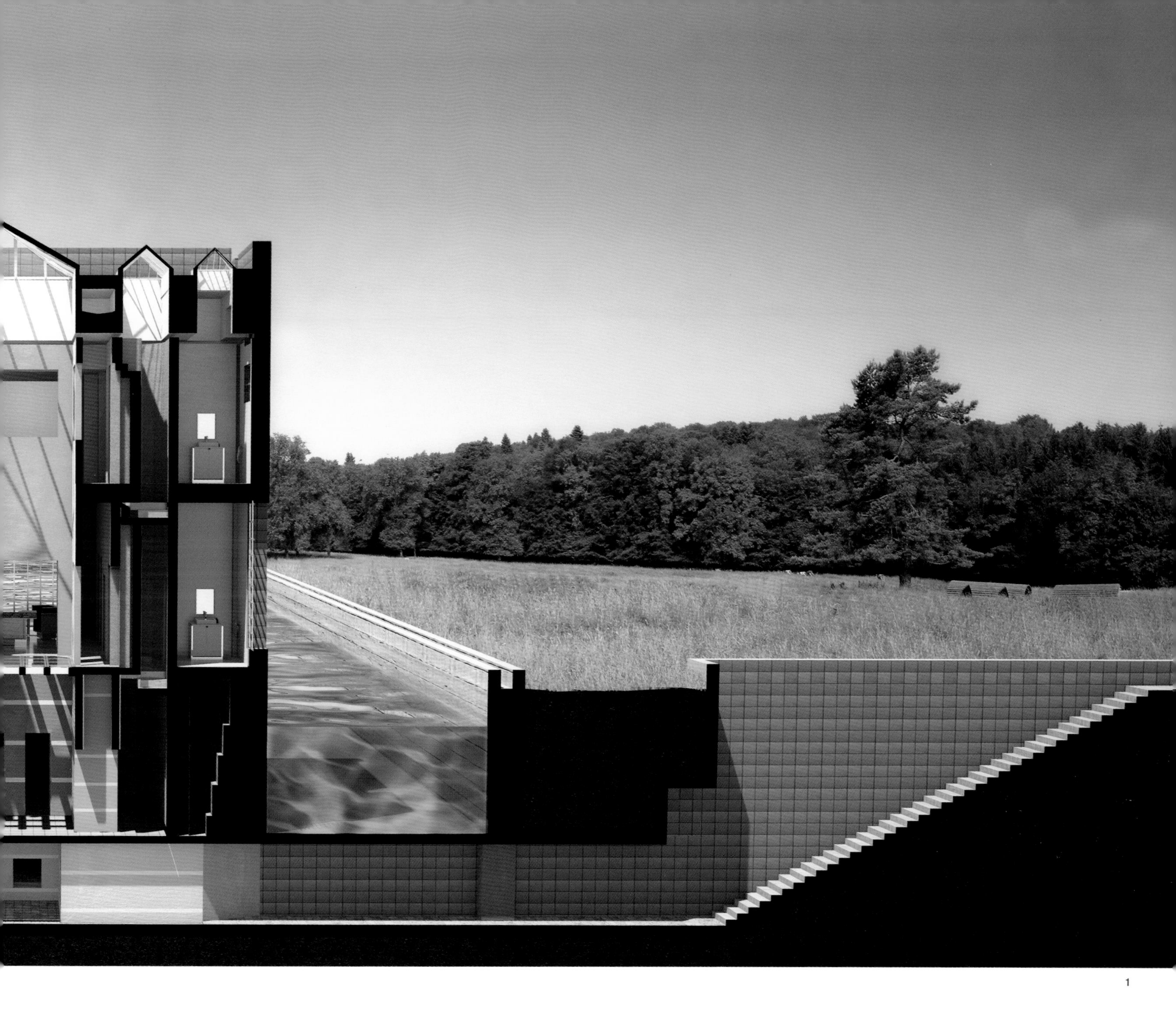

1

1

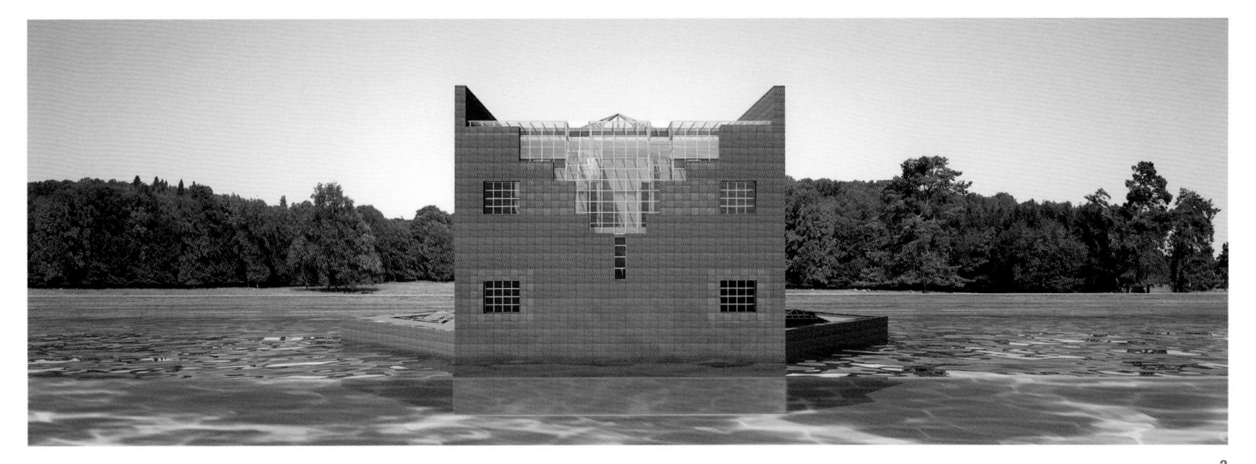

2

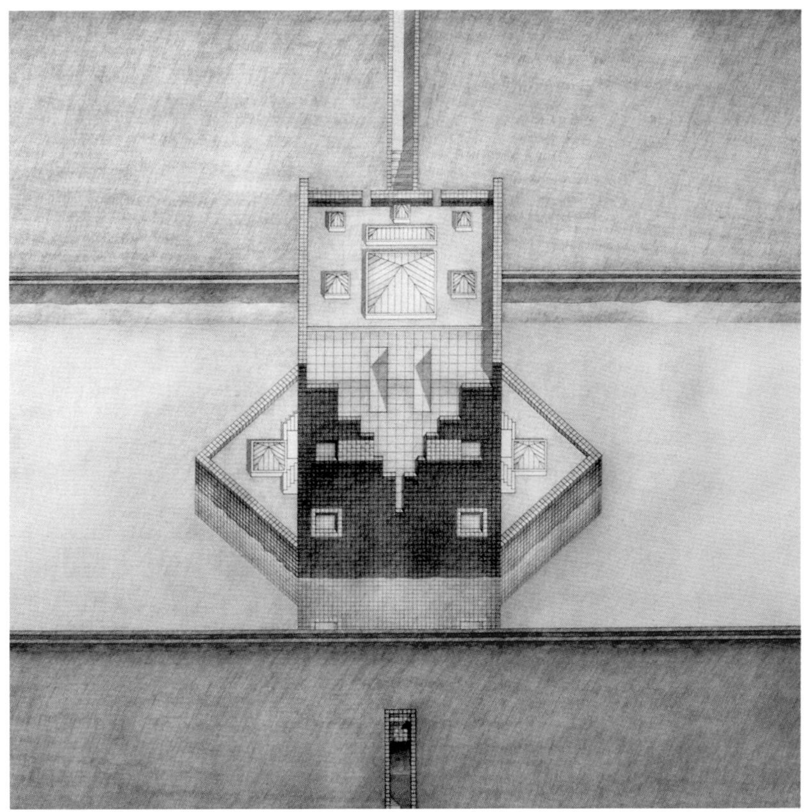

3

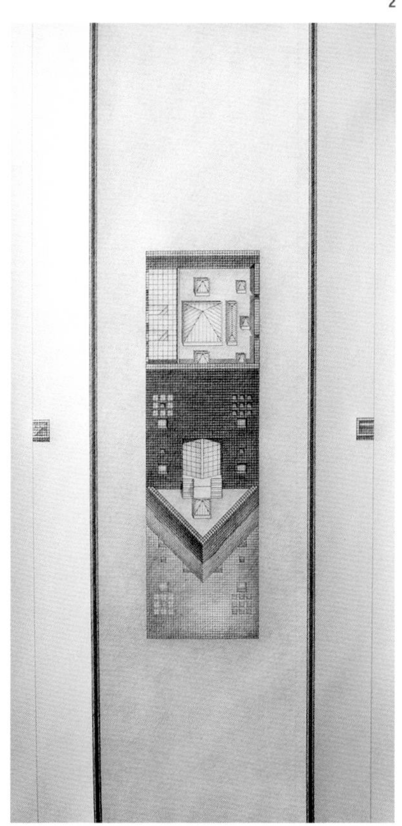

4

1 | Aerial view of the house and landscape
2 | Entry elevation
3 | Pencil and color pencil on paper, elevation oblique drawing on the axis of the entry sequence
4 | Pencil and color pencil on paper, elevation oblique drawing on the axis of the canal
5 | Section through the building and the canal (next spread)

5.

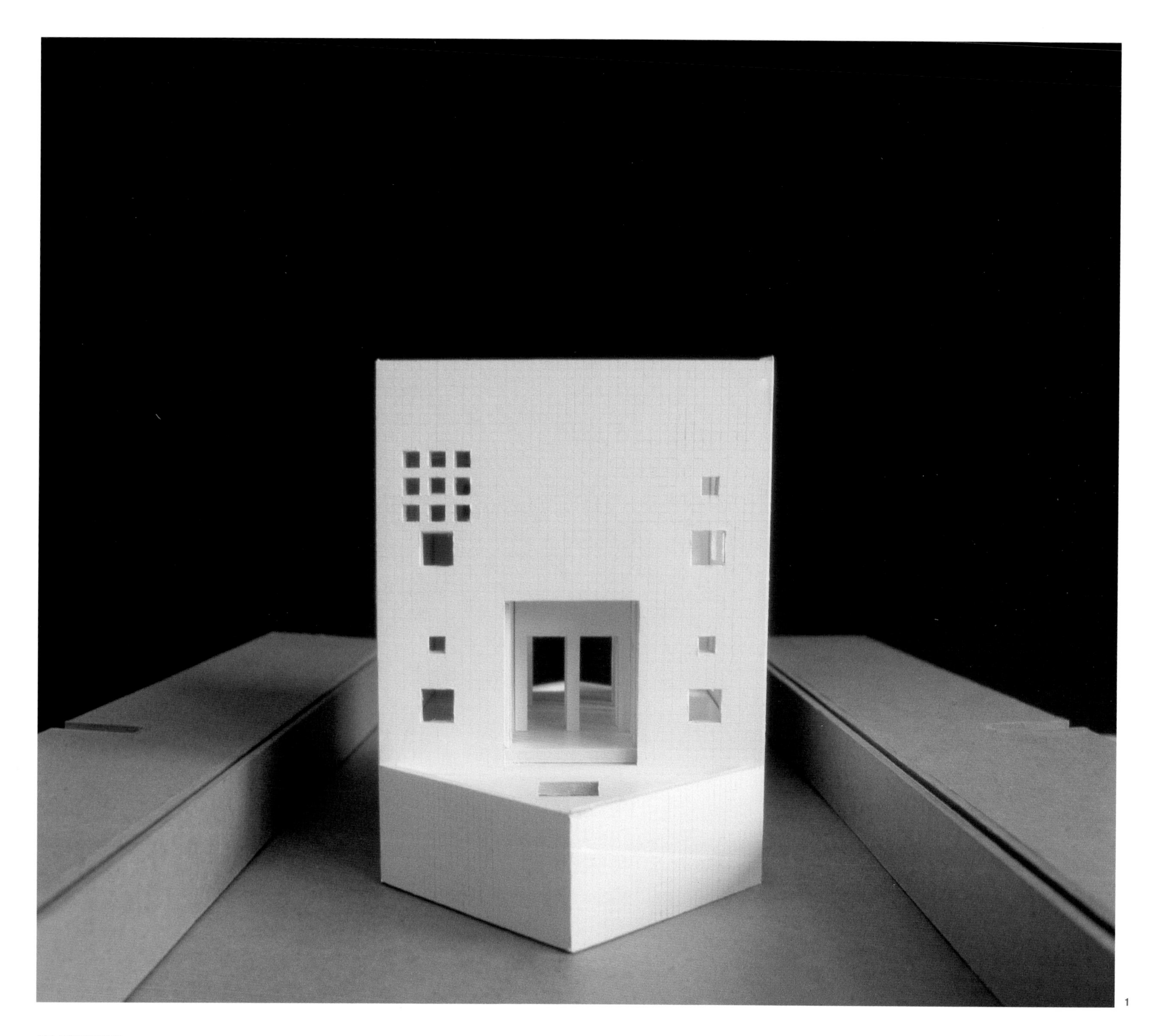

1

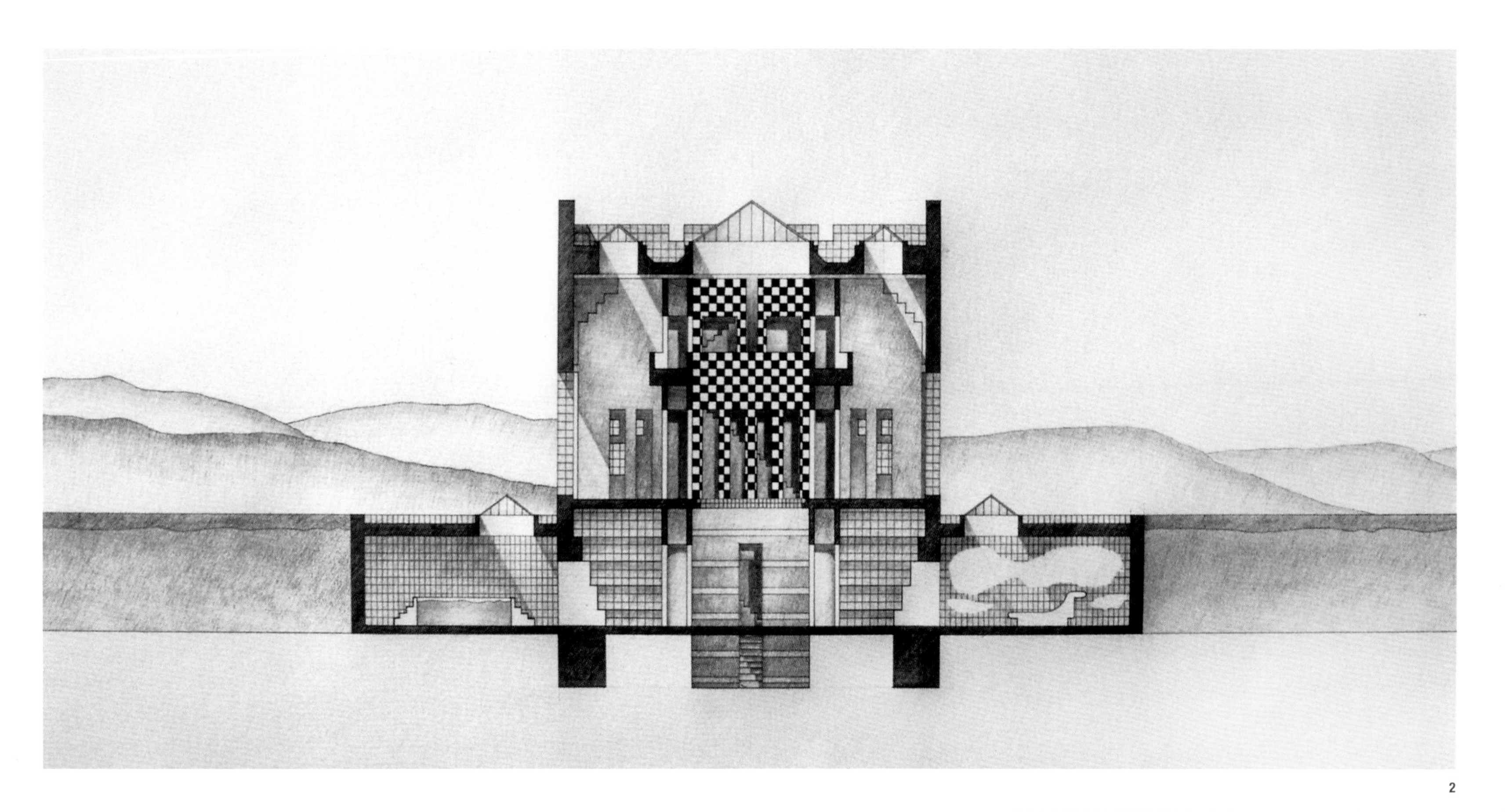

2

3

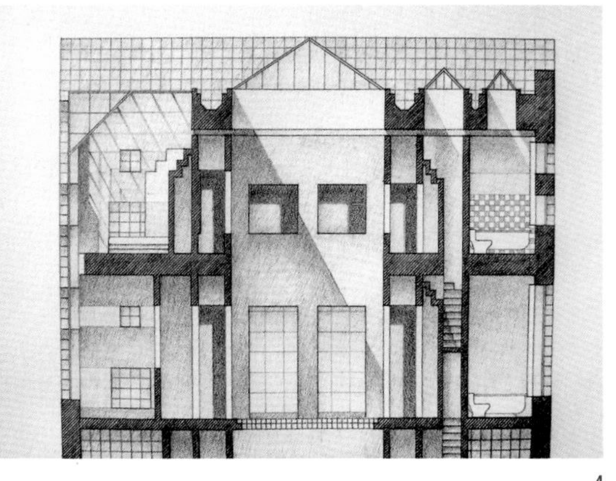

4

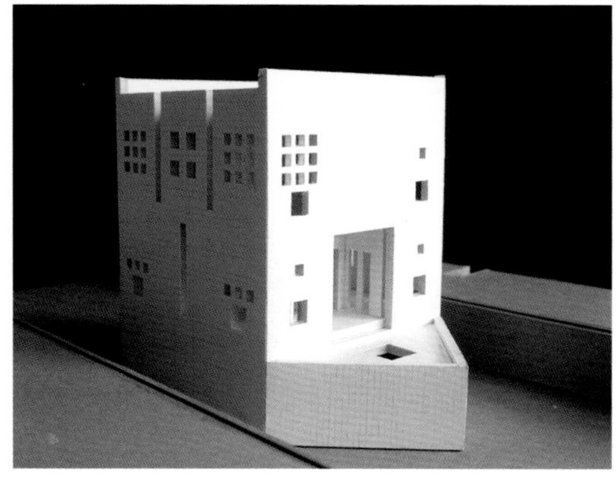

5

1 | Study model sitting in the canal
2 | Section through the building and the canal
3 | Early study model in chipboard and plastic
4 | Detail of the cross section, upper floors
5 | Study model looking at the back and side of the building

1

1 | Computer model view of the living room and landscape beyond
2 | View of the master bedroom

2

1

2

1 Dusk view at the entrance
2 Night view along the canal side of the house

project name	15th Street Apartment
location	New York City
year of design	1983
year of completion	1984
client	George Ranalli
lot size	50' x 100'
project size	1,250 sq.ft.
architect	George Ranalli
associates	Robert Silman Structural Engineer
design team	Andrew Formichella, Mario Gentile (second phase), Hayden Marrero, Eugene Park
photographer	George Cserna /Michelle Agins

15th Street Apartment

1

The project for the 15th Street Apartment in New York was built in two phases spanning over 10 years. The first phase involved the south portion of the short end of the building. A large block was installed in the almost two-story main room, thereby freeing up the other bedroom to be used as an office and study. The constructed block provides an hideaway bed upstairs, an anchor for a green dining table downstairs, and a bathroom and kitchen sequestered at the back. A wood-covered staircase with brass detail ascends from the lofty main area to a surprisingly spacious and restful sleeping space with walk-in closet below. The elevation of the cantilevered bedroom berth secures privacy behind sumptuous silhouettes—a vibrant backdrop for an open dining and living space. The outer wall of the 1892 building has large, nine-foot-square windows with different sections of operable and fixed glazing set in hulking wood frames. The heft of the frames provides a strong presence for a most open moment.

On the first level, one end of a long, green marble table, grand yet simple, rests on a shiny brass projection while a singular leg of bent metal supports the other. Vintage Bertoia chairs surround the table. Artful, durable, functional furniture design thus becomes part of the whole package.

2

3

1 View looking up into the bedroom space
2 Existing building exterior view
3 Renovation of the apartment, first phase

1

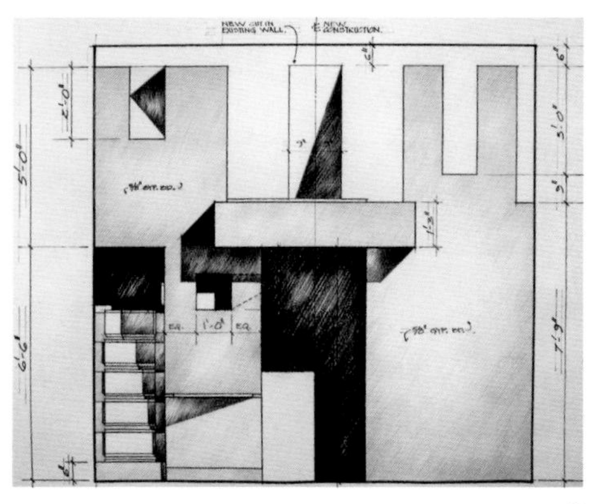

2

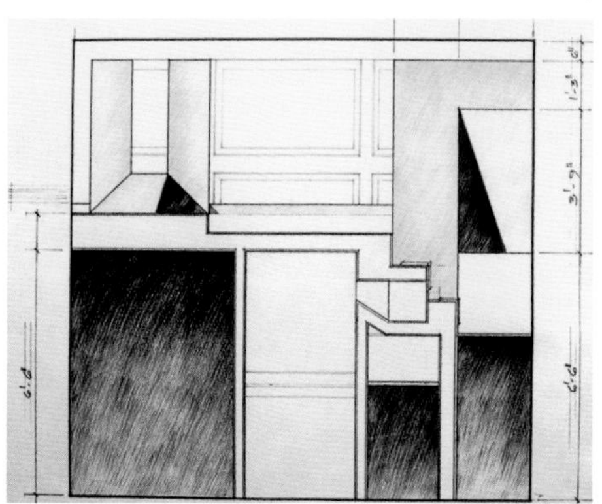

3

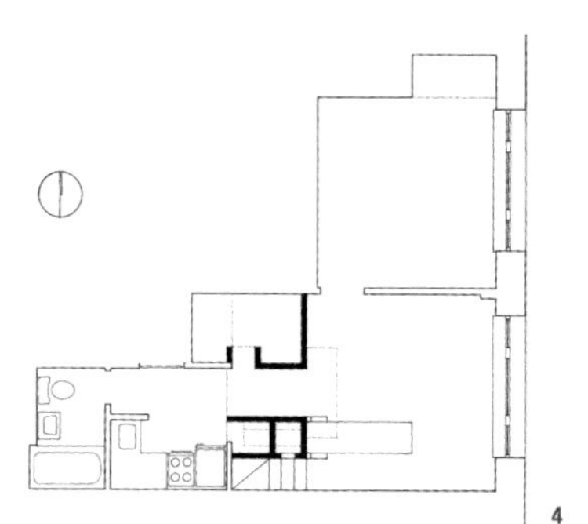

4

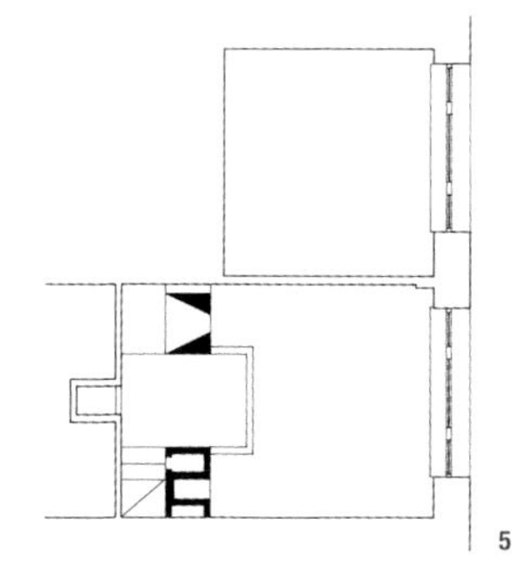

5

A decade later, a second apartment is added on, filling out the corner of the building with the new combined apartments. A full renovation transforms two former one-bedroom apartments into a three-bedroom apartment, complete with master bath, and second bathroom, each in custom-designed marble mosaics, a new kitchen, and three beautiful, sun-filled bedrooms. Tight floor area, although vertically spacious, accommodates cabinetry designed to maximize the use of storage and utility. In the kitchen, a deft geometric arrangement creates a clean line of cabinetry and appliances; a white respite from the profusion of grainy flaxen woodwork throughout the rest of the apartment, while optimizing floor-to-ceiling storage. The design provides convenient, proximate storage of utensils and cooking ingredients above and below the countertops near chopping and mixing stations and the stove, and locates day-to-day dishware near the dining table.

Each new room is keyed to a large nine-foot window for maximum light. Frosted-glass windows in walls and doors, along with mirrors, in key locations, create an illusory game that makes one feel open and airy.

The apartment features an intricate geometric wood wall covering originally exhibited by The Denver Art Museum, US Design 1975-2000, (seen on seen pages 410-411). Also, the custom designed door hardware Lock-it, included in the apartment renovation, is seen on pages 424-433.

6

7

8

1 Section oblique drawing in pencil and color pencil of the outer masonry wall and new interior
2 Main elevation drawing
3 Section through the bedroom looking east
4 Floor plan, first phase
5 Loft plan, first phase
6 View of the new structure and existing room, first phase
7 Elevation oblique drawing in pencil and color pencil of the existing building and the new interior
8 Photo of the original design with the green marble table supported on the bed structure and steel base
9 Views of the steel table base

9

1

2

1 | Renovation of the original living room into the master bedroom, second phase
2 | Master bedroom and sitting room, second phase

1

2

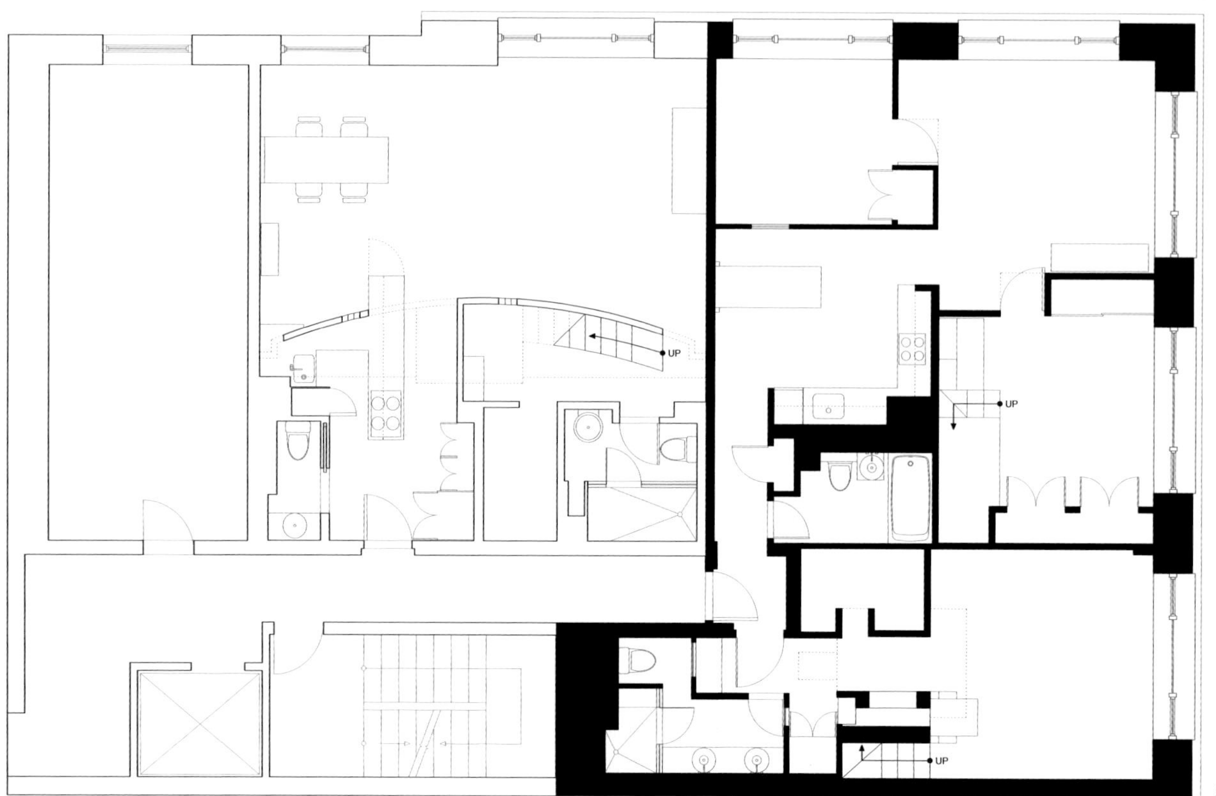

3

1 Detail view of the bedroom stairway
2 View of the living room looking north
3 Floor plan of the phase 2 renovation
4 Computer model of the phase two master bedroom
5 Section through the length of the apartment, phase two with the master bedroom on the left, small bedroom in the middle and living room on the right

4

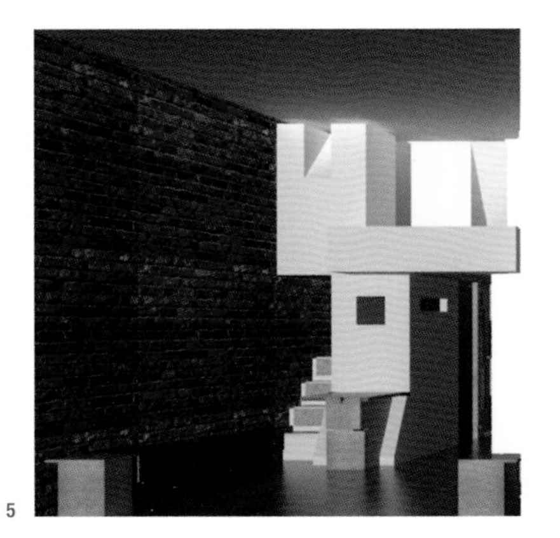

5

1

2

3

1 | Photo of the dining area
2 | Computer image of the dining room
3 | Computer view of the dining room from the living room
4 | Computer view of the small bedroom entry
5 | Section through the living room, small bedroom and the Helmick apartment next door
6 | Computer image of living room wall and furniture cabinet

4

5

6

1

2

3

4

1 View from the master bathroom window
2 Master dressing room cabinets
3 Computer view of the storage element for the master bathroom and window into the bathroom
4 Lock-it lever handle

1

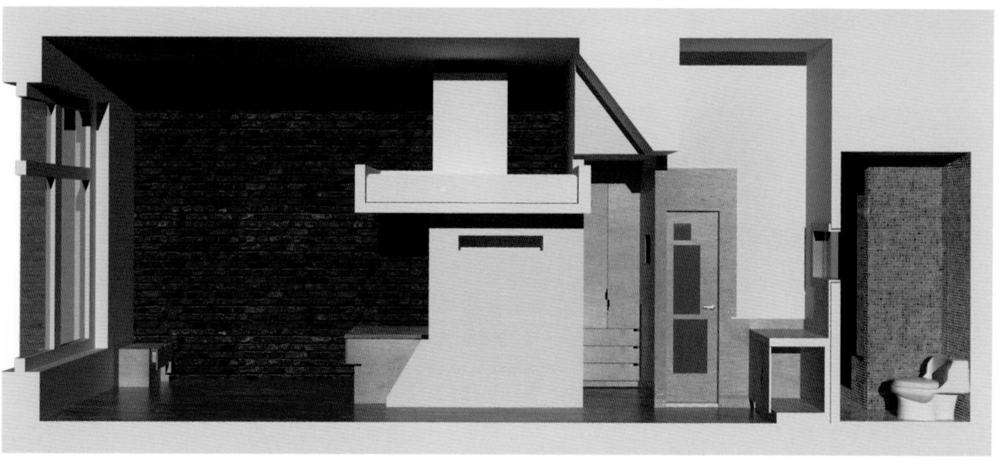

2

1 View from the master bed
2 Section at the master bedroom, loft bed and master bathroom
3 Small bedroom photo
4 Section through the living room and small bedroom
5 Computer view of the small bedroom woodwork and fixed windows

3

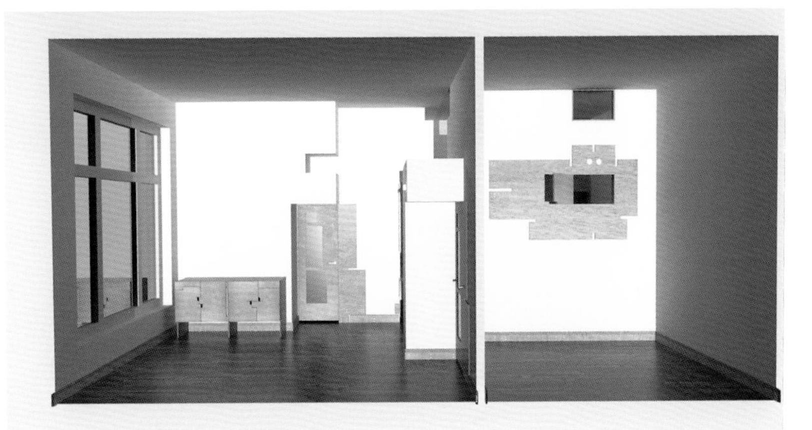

4

5

1

1 | Middle bedroom photo with built in storage elements, closet doors and furniture
2 | Computer view of the middle bedroom storage and furniture
3 | Section through the middle bedroom and kitchen
4 | Computer view of the middle bedroom with closet doors open

2

3

4

1

2

3

1 Small bathroom computer view
2 Photo of the master bathroom
3 Computer view of the master bathroom

1

2

1 Night view of the apartment with all large windows illuminated around the corner
2 Photo of the night view of the exterior

COMMERCIAL

project name	Amtrak Tower
location	New York City
year of design	2006
client	HOK/ Amtrak
lot size	50 x 100
project size	168,936 sq.ft.
architect	George Ranalli
associates	HOK, Robert Silman Structural Engineers
design team	Hollace Metzger, Hayden Marrero

Amtrak Tower

1

Established by Congress in 1970, Amtrak is a nationwide, high-speed, intercity, passenger-rail service traversing over 500 destinations; 46 in the United States, and three Canadian provinces. Nearly thirty million passengers a year travel on Amtrak commuter rails.

In 2005, Amtrak commissioned a study to optimize an old power plant, located on Manhattan's 31st Street, between Seventh and Eighth Avenues. The building sits mid-block among a row of 19th Century loft structures. The project proposes the renovation of the existing building for use as Amtrak's northeastern headquarters, and a 16-storey boutique hotel expansion.

The design provides a new central entrance area, with a café for occupants and visitors, below a contemporary bridge, connecting a newly designed lobby space to the preexisting building. Inside, the proposed renovation of the existing building provides Amtak, the busiest railroad in North America, with custom workspaces, state-of-the-art communication systems, and imaging technologies. The design transforms a soaring core space inside the old power plant, previously the coal hopper, into a dramatic triple-decker symposium facility, which includes a 30-seat auditorium, a large seminar and banquet room space, and a floor of quiet offices, ringed by a striking spiral passageway.

A small yard alongside the eastern end of the existing building offers a geometric fluke enough of a space for a 16-storey hotel tower. The exterior design for the hotel composes an active arrangement of horizontal casting stone and wood frame windows, and advantageous 1,800 square foot floor plates for ample natural sunlight and views. The tower design features two conical, copper-clad rooftop spaces for dining and gathering. Each skypod is positioned to capture the dramatic vistas of the downtown Manhattan skyline.

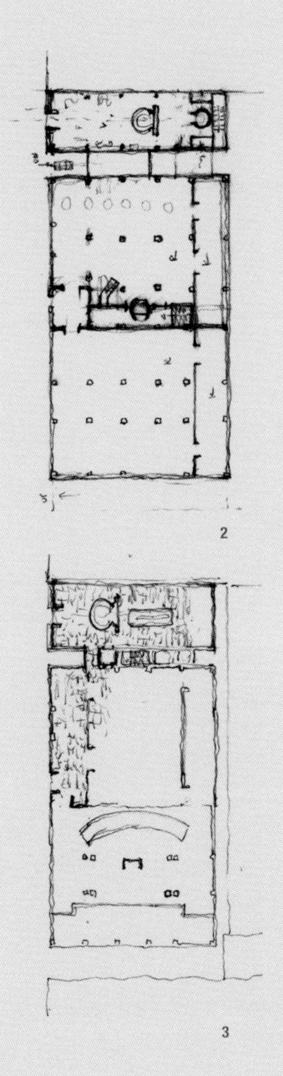

2

3

4

5

1 View of the new building looking up from 31st Street
2 Sketch floor plan
3 Alternate sketch floor plan
4 View from Seventh Avenue
5 Aerial view of the new building

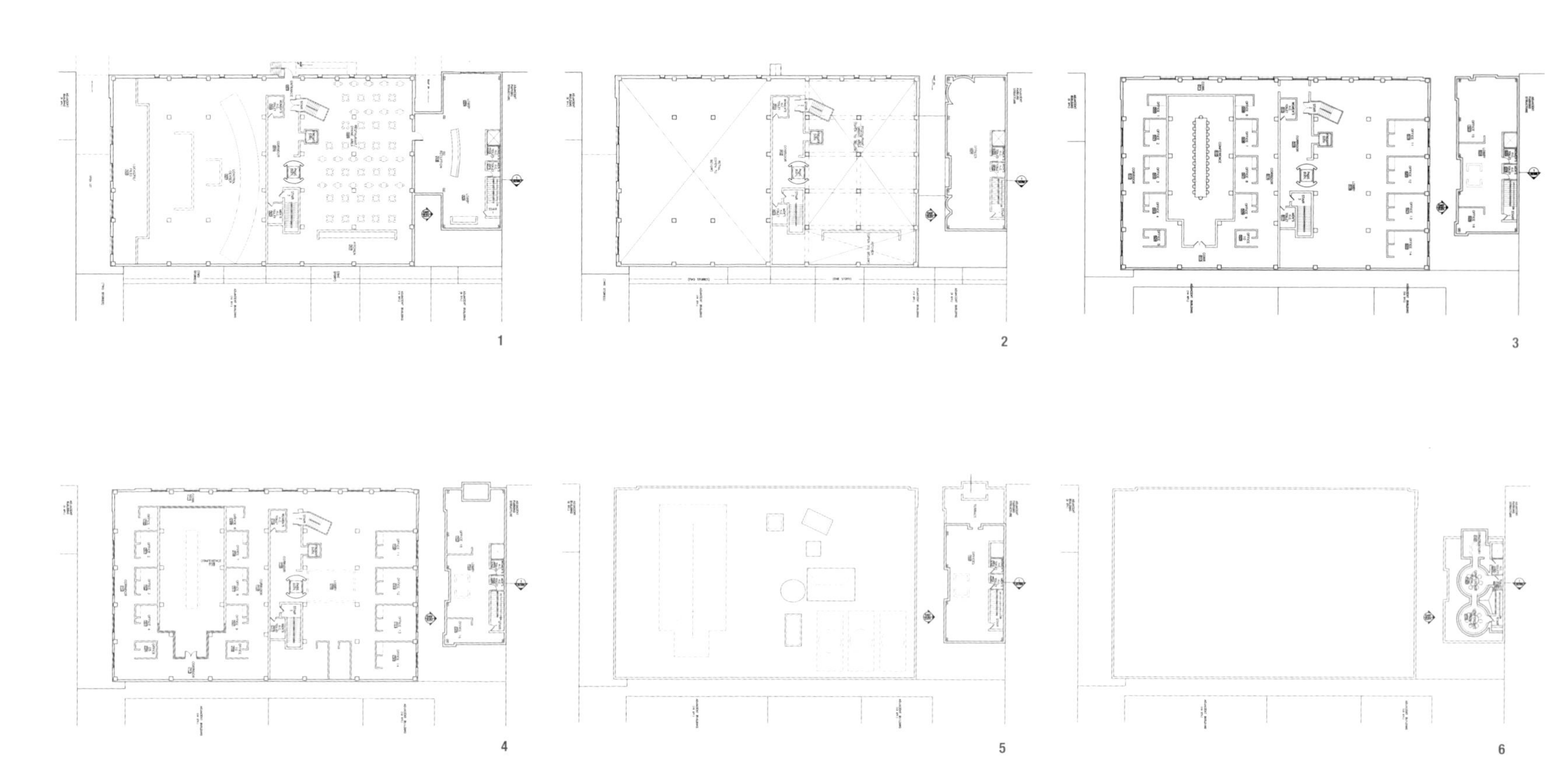

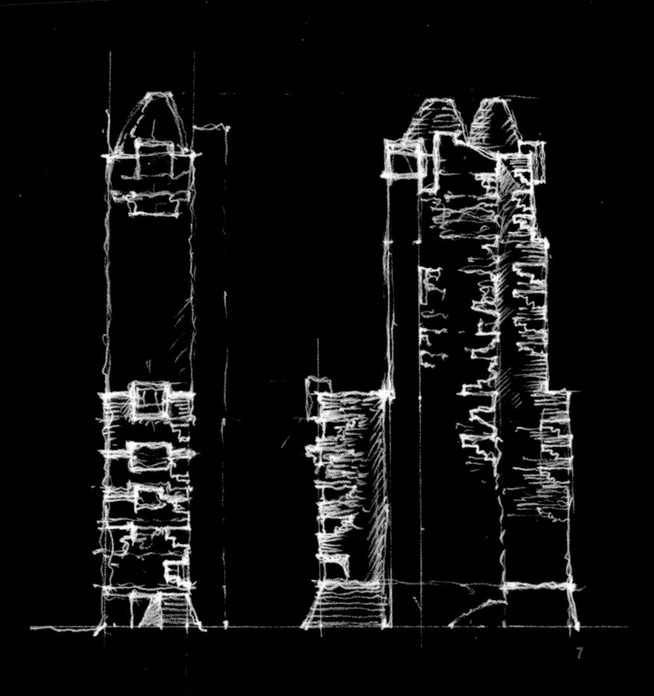

7

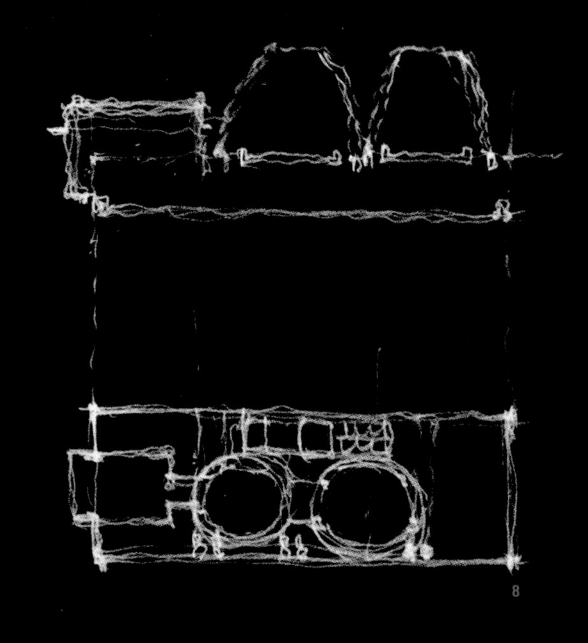

8

9

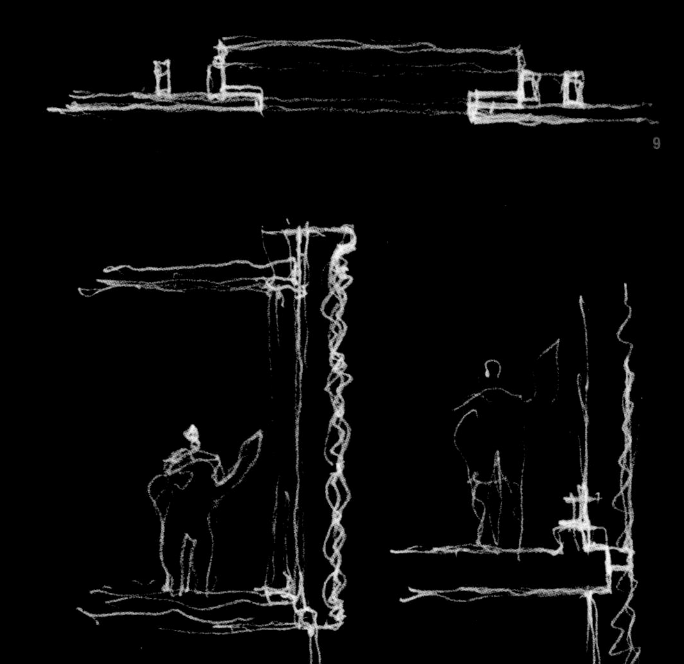

10

1 | Ground floor plan
2 | 2nd floor plan
3 | 3rd-5th floor plan
4 | 6th floor plan
5 | 7-10th floor plan
6 | 12th floor plan
7 | Sketch elevations of early scheme
8 | Rooftop conference rooms section and plan study
9 | Wall detail
10 | Wall panel assembly study

1

1 | Computer view of the power plant building on the right and the new hotel
2 | View from the front
3 | View from Eighth Avenue
4 | Elevation of the hotel and power plant
5 | Side elevation of the new hotel building

2

3

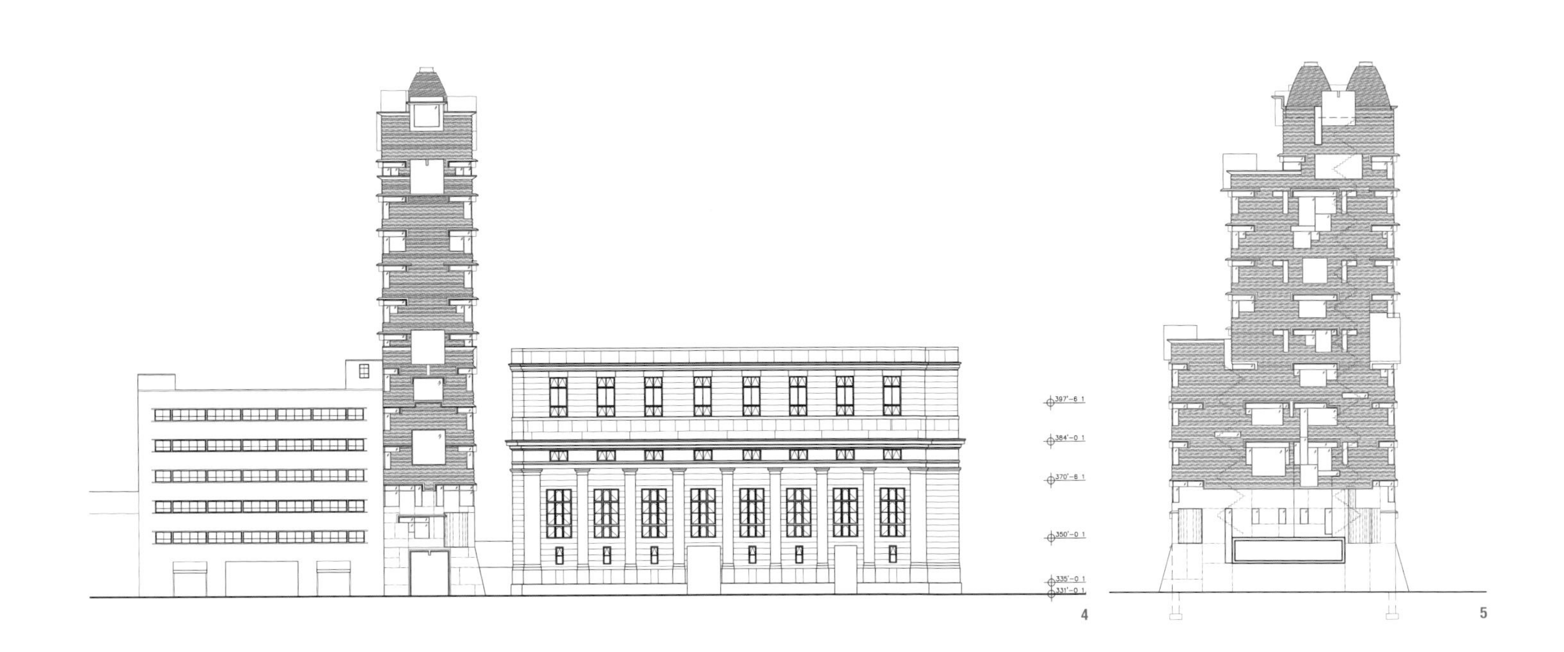

4

5

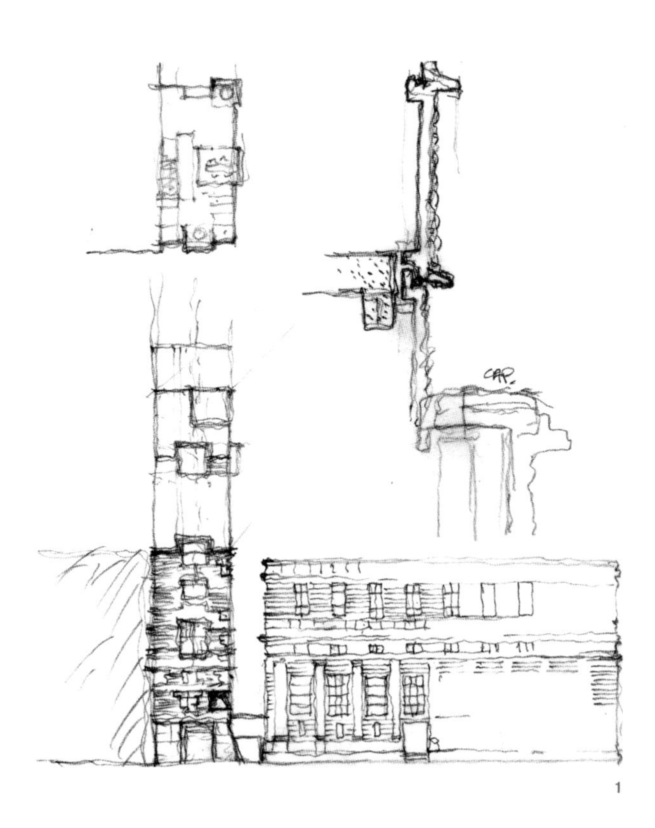

1

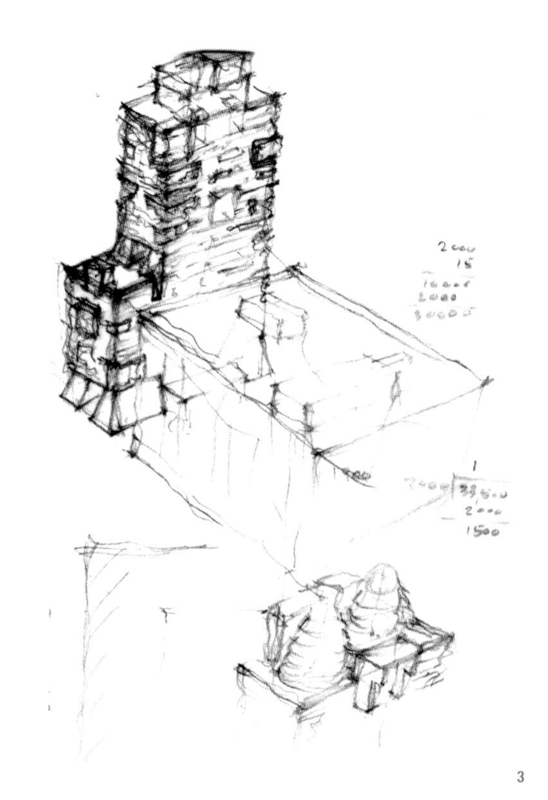

3

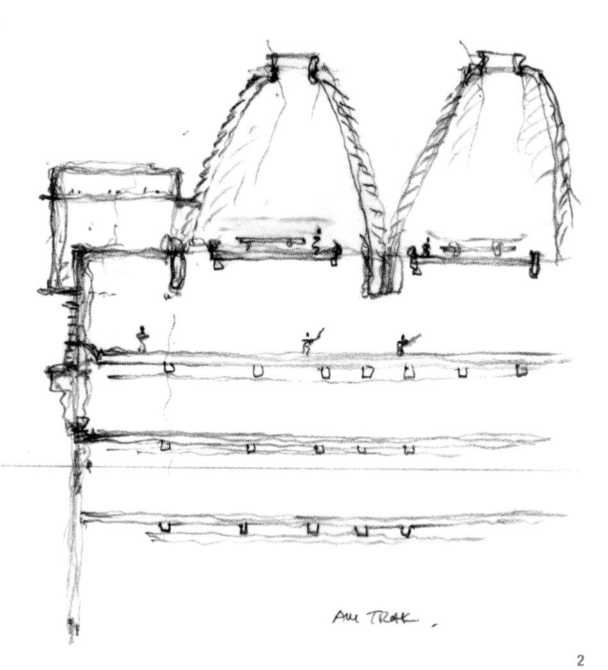

2

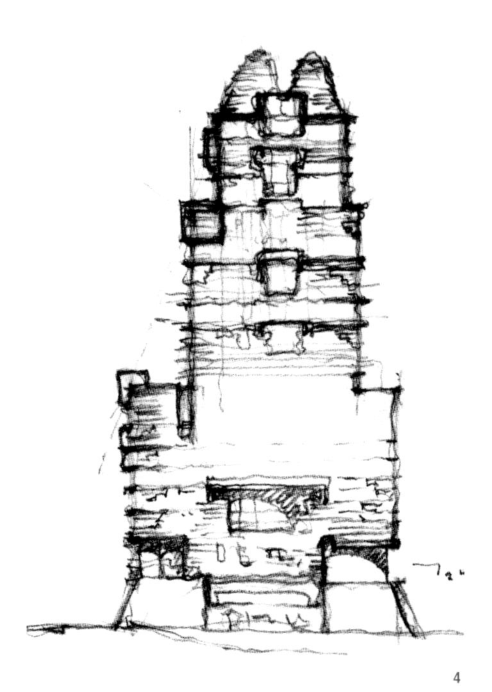

4

1 | Plan, elevation and detail sketch
2 | Sketch section through the top of the building
3 | Massing and rooftop sketch
4 | Study elevation
5 | Computer massing from the front
6 | Computer massing study from the corner

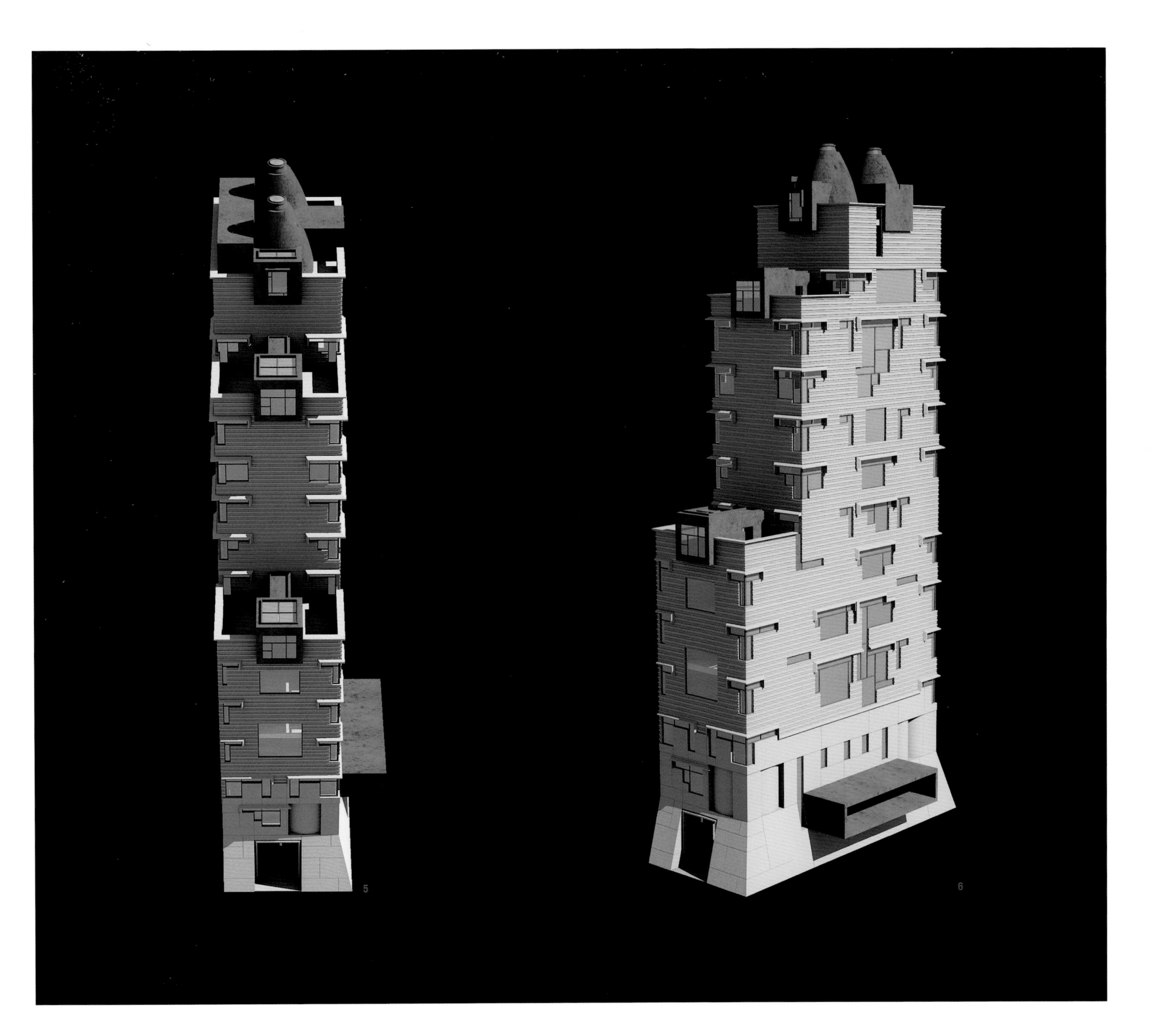
5
6

MILLROSE GAMES
FEB 4
PARK N LOCK
SUBURBAN
PENNSYLVANIA PLAZA
NYC
100
SWITCH TO THE BEST

1

2

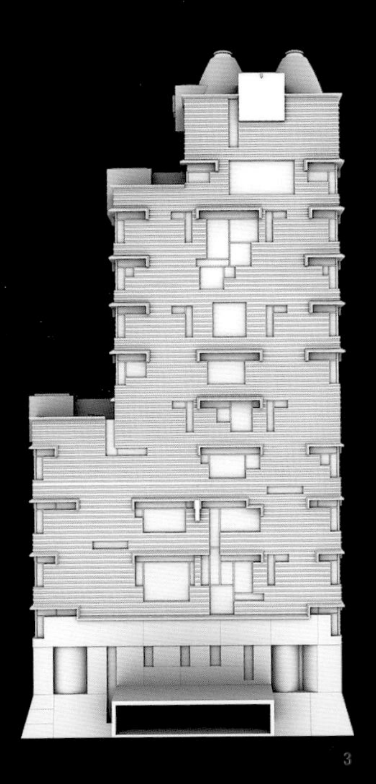

3

1 | View of the new design from Eighth Avenue
2 | Detail of the rooftop conference rooms
3 | Computer model of the side view of the hotel

project name	Yale University Commercial Building
location	New Haven, Connecticut
year of design	1999
client	Yale University
lot size	50'x 100'
project size	11,000 sq.ft.
architect	George Ranalli
associates	Robert Silman Structural Engineer
design team	Mario Gentile, Price Harrison

Yale University Commercial Building

1

Yale University commissioned a 3,500-square-foot commercial building on Broadway in New Haven as part of an initiative to repair the fabric of the downtown New Haven. Three sites were selected for projects by three different architects, located down the street from the 1920's Sterling Memorial Library complex designed by James Gamble Rodgers. The formidable stone library is a grand building, with highly formal spaces at the center and less formal spaces as the complex approaches Broadway and York Streets. The commercial program of the new building includes retail shops on the ground floor, commercial office space above, and other appropriate venues.

The challenge was to find an architecture that would facilitate connections to the Sterling Memorial Library, while making a unique statement. The design, a 42-foot-wide by 42-foot-high building, begins with an investigation into masonry construction techniques that recapitulates the heft and weight of the precedent library buildings, and other historic architectural markers, in the vicinity. Multiple façade studies explored various ideas with masonry that would facilitate a dialogue with the main library. A metal-and-glass version was explored, at the client's request. In the end, a limestone, copper, and mahogany-window version is selected as the appropriate design for a new building placed into a row of existing structures on Broadway.

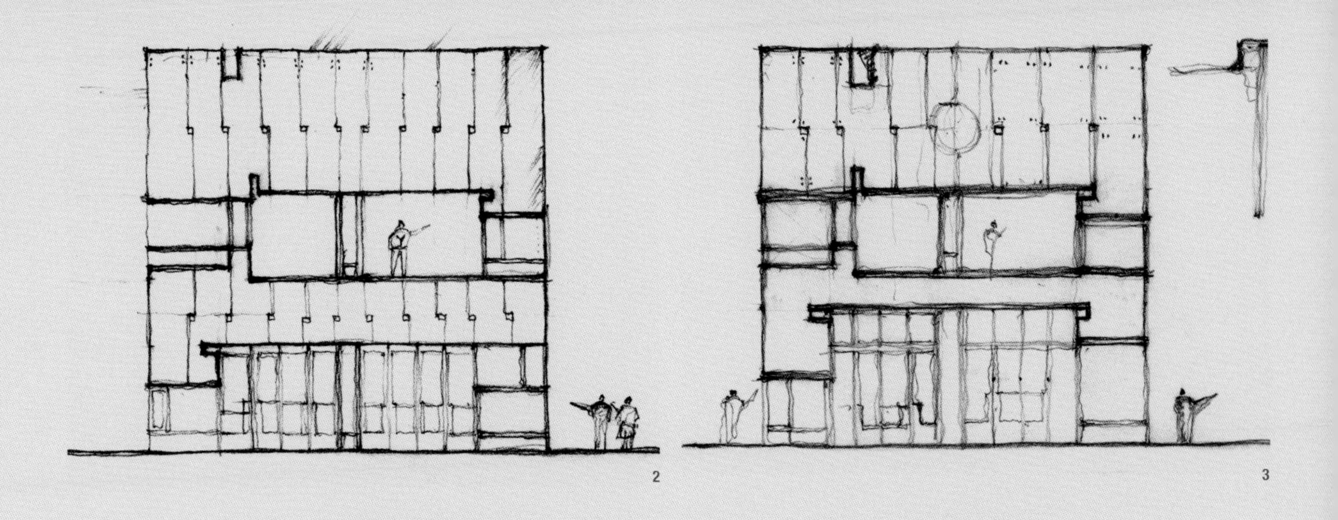

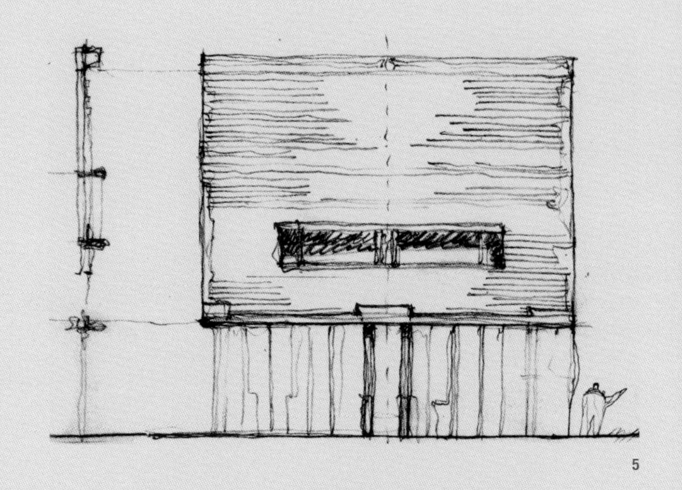

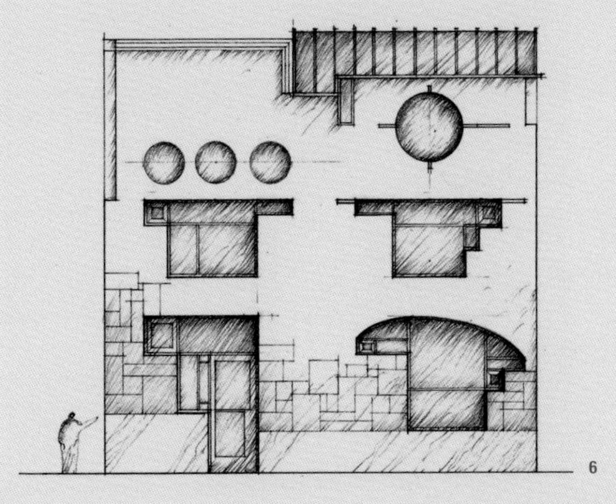

1 Study of the limestone and casting stone façade on Broadway
2 Metal panel scheme sketch
3 Alternate metal panel sketch
4 Color infused plaster scheme
5 Brick façade study
6 Limestone, casting stone and copper scheme

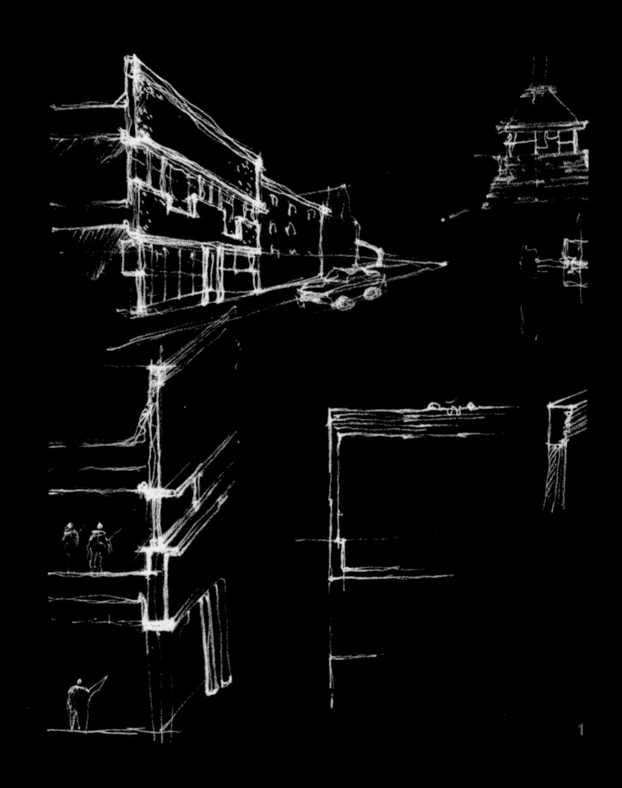

1

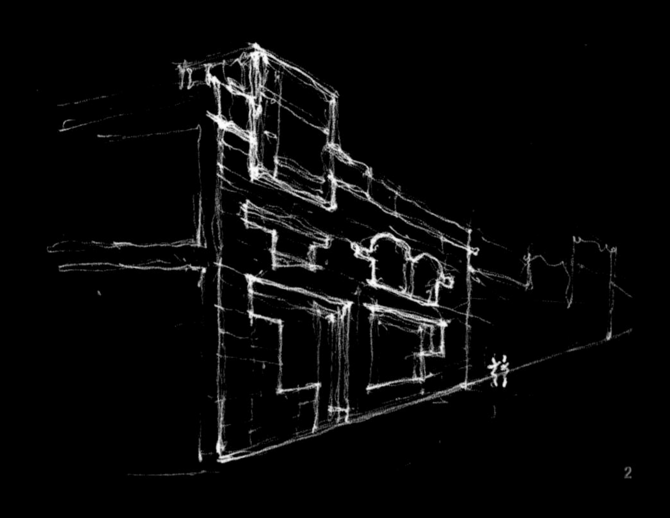

2

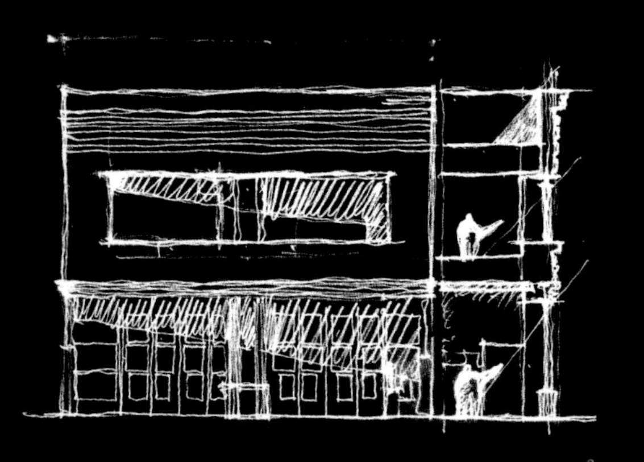

3

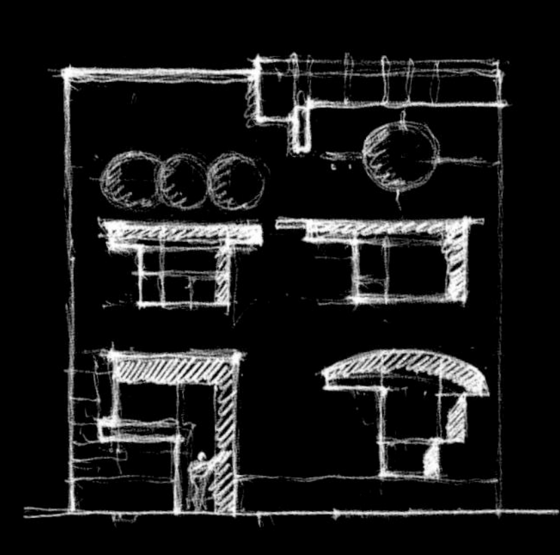

4

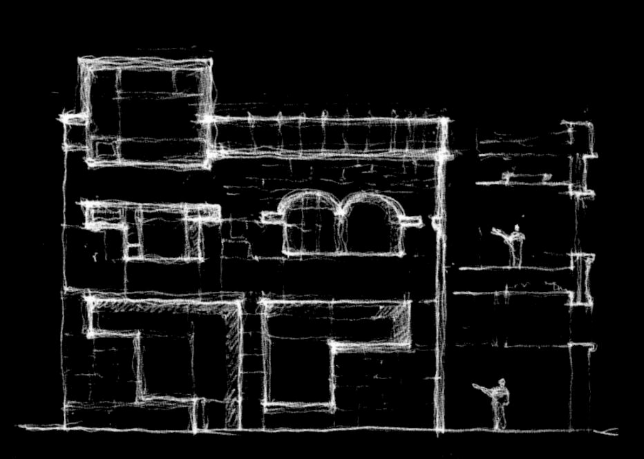

5

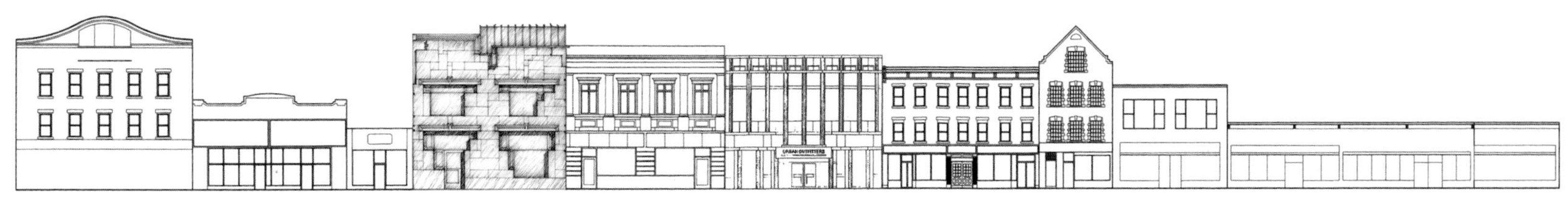

6

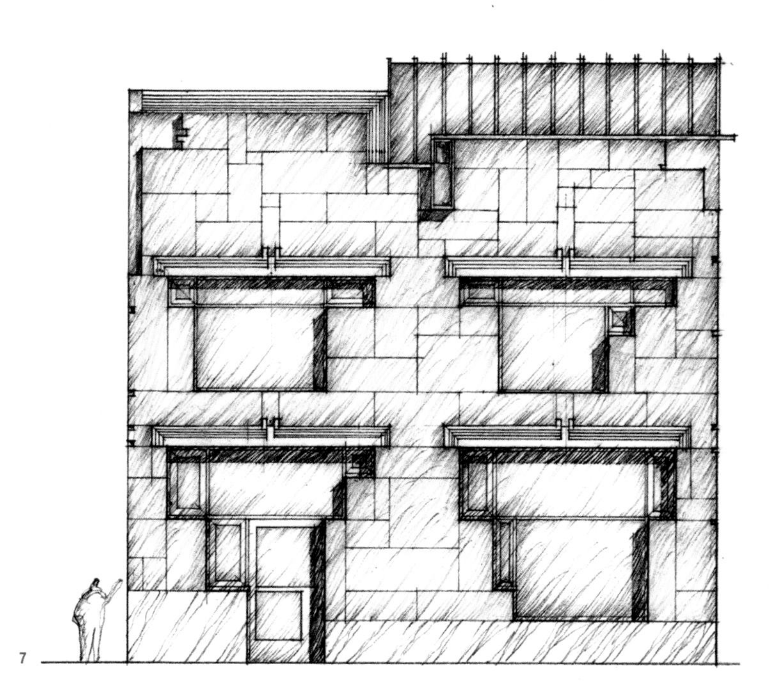

7

1 Perspective sketch view and details
2 Perspective view along Broadway looking east
3 Brick elevation study with section
4 Early limestone study
5 Later limestone study and section
6 Elevation study of final scheme of the north side of Broadway
7 Final version of the limestone, casting stone and copper façade

project name	Formica Office
location	New York
year of design	1995
client	Susan Lewin, Creative Director/ Formica Corp.
lot size	50' x 100'
project size	525 sq. ft.a
architect	George Ranalli
associates	Robert Silman Structural Engineer
design team	John Butterworth
photographer	model photos George Ranalli

Formica Office

1

Designed for the Creative Director's office of the Formica Corporation in mid-town Manhattan, this small arrangement of custom-designed furniture is a showcase for Surell, a material produced by the Formica company, previously used in earlier projects, the culmination, one of which was the prototype The Valentine 2 Chair. This space takes earlier ideas further.

Surell, primarily used as a high-end residential kitchen countertop material, holds more varied possibilities worthy of exploration. The new office design includes a worktable, sofa, cabinets, vertical lighting, and other custom-designed elements necessary for small, bright and functional work space. Answering to the translucency of the material, each component of the design achieves a sculptural elegance with rich surface engravings and texture for the delicacy befitting a showcase.

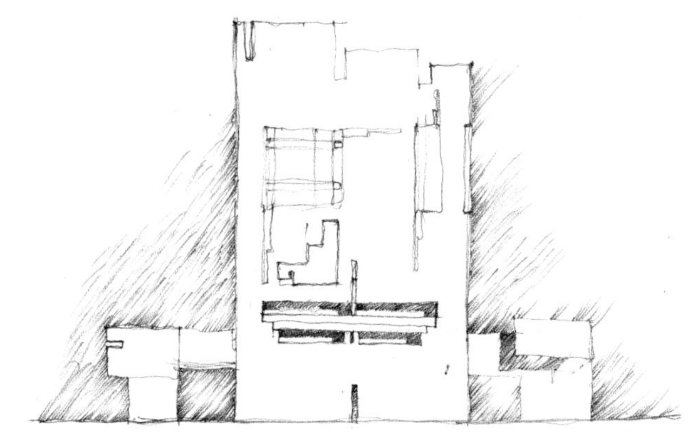

2

1 | Model view
2 | Sketch of the tall cabinet
3 | Elevation of the tall cabinet and the furniture in the room
4 | Section through the entry door
5 | Perspective view of the room

3

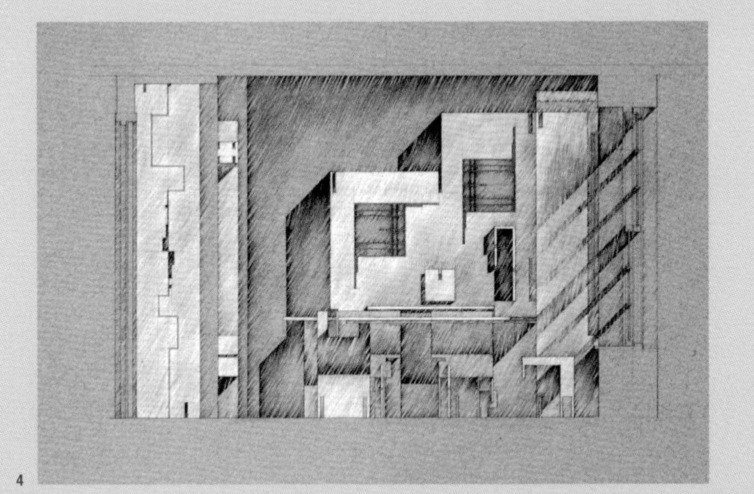

4

5

1

2

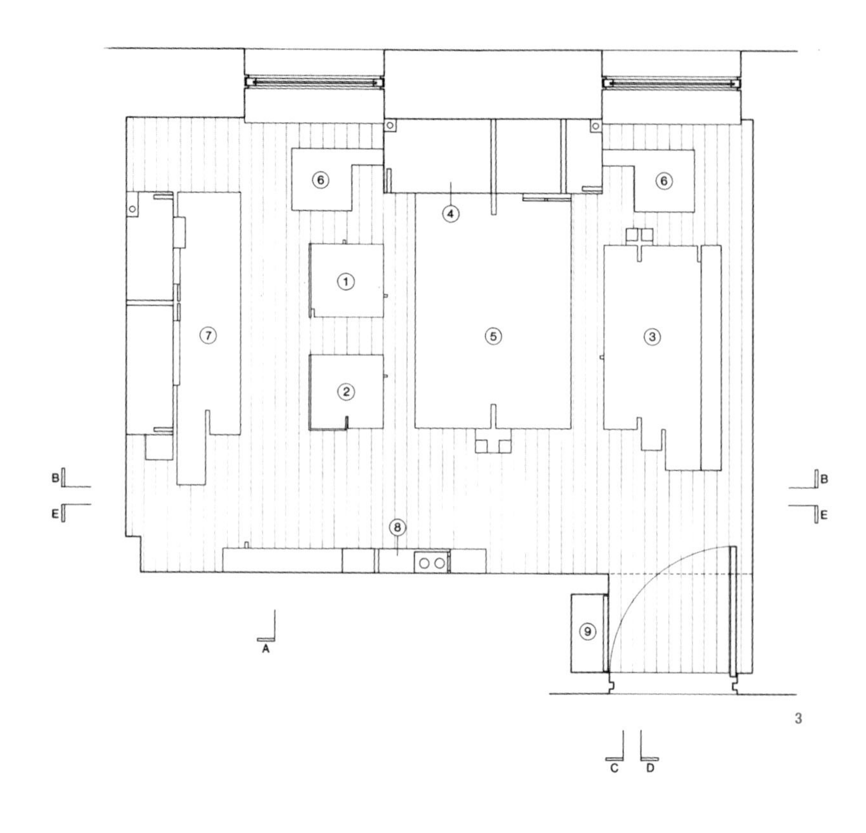

3

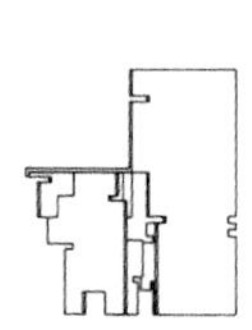
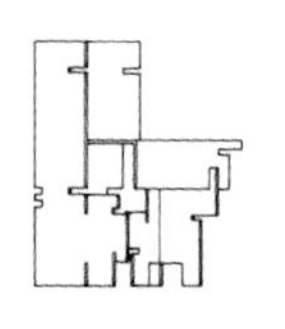
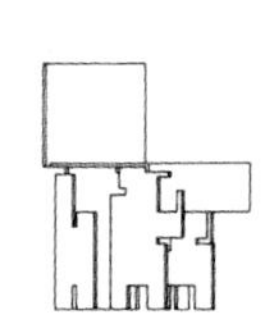
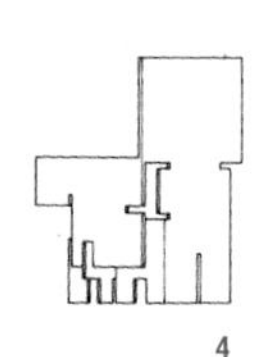

4

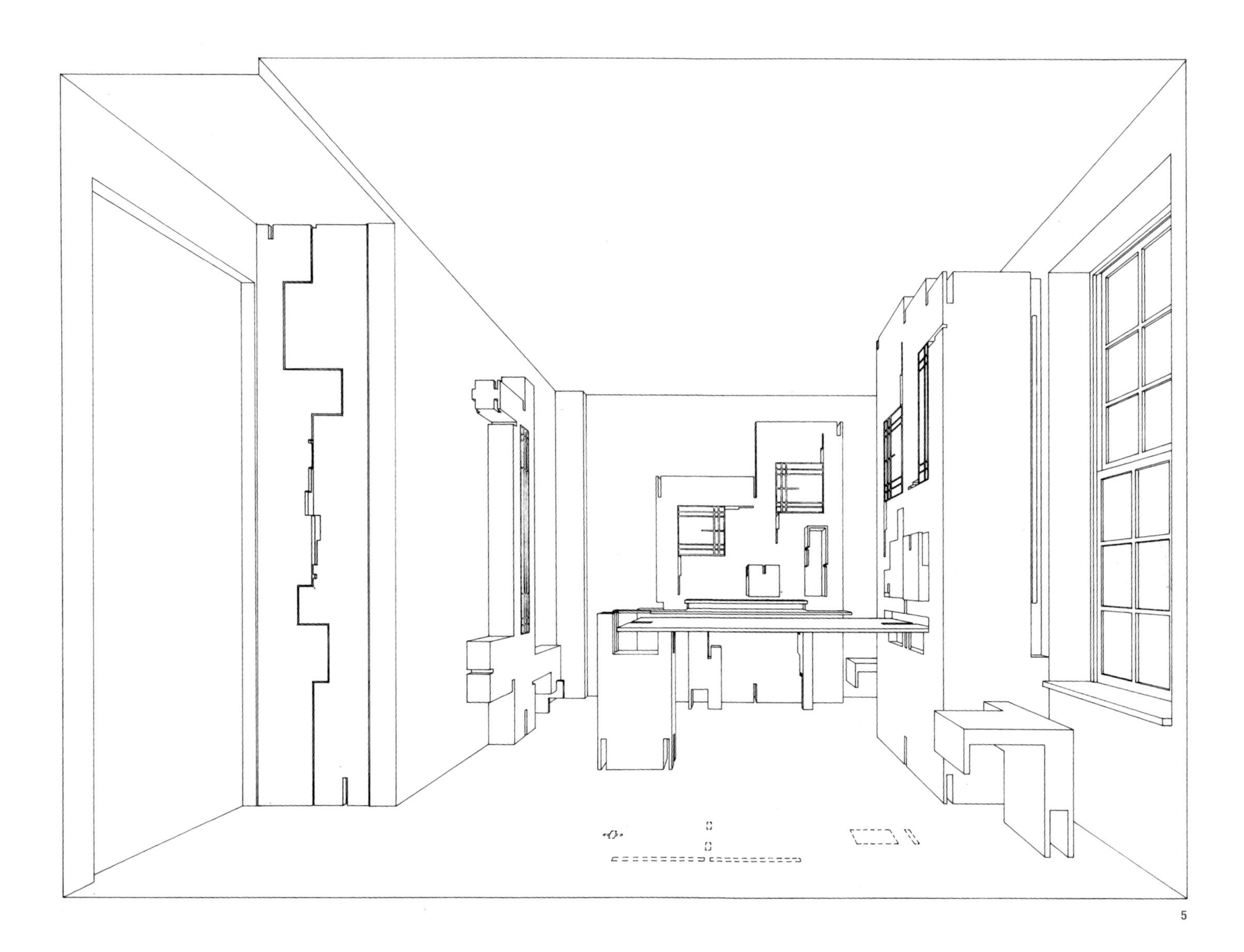

5

1 | Model view from above
2 | Model view from the side sofa pictured in front
3 | Office plan
4 | Rotated elevations of the side chair
5 | Perspective view of the office

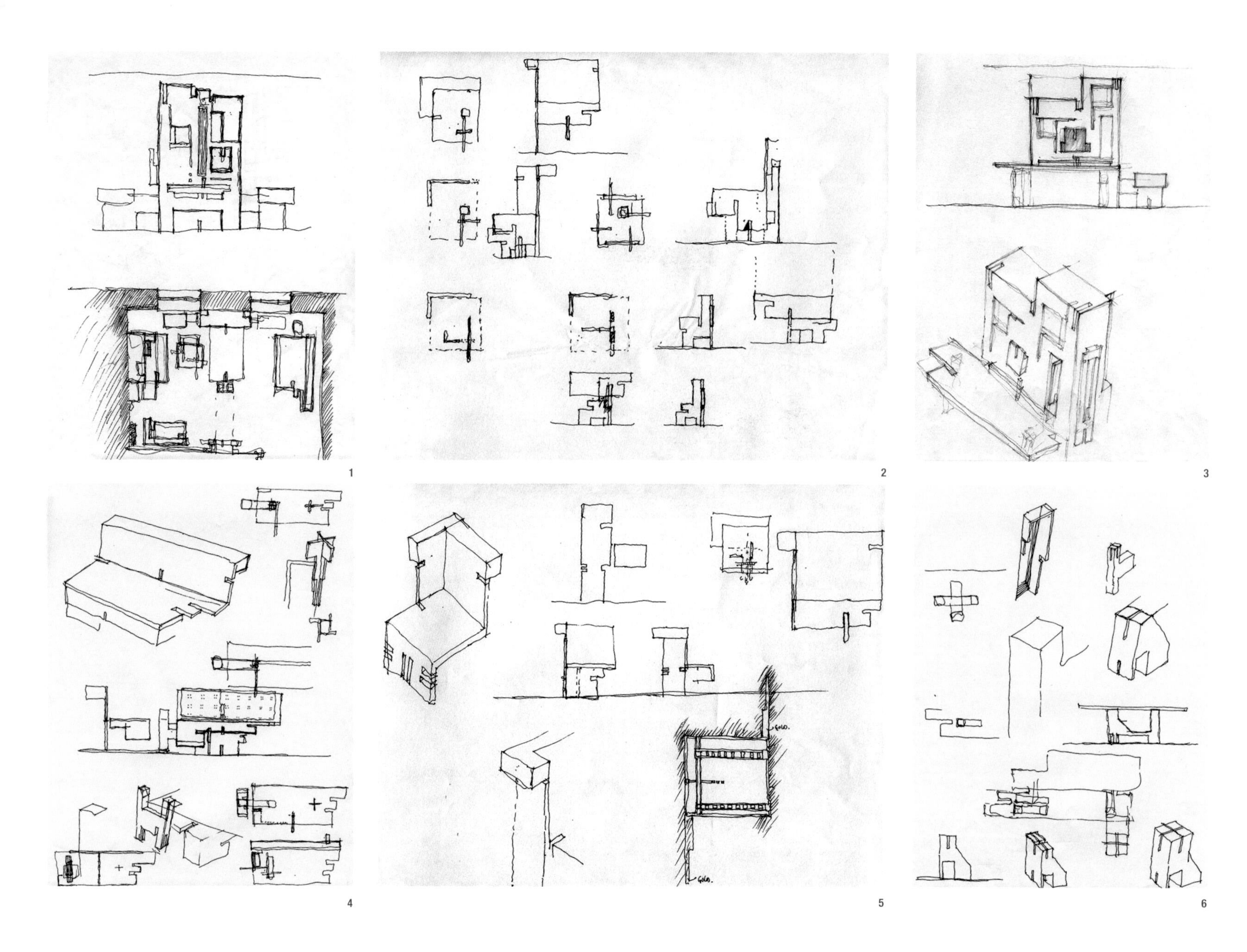
1 2 3 4 5 6

7

1 Plan and elevation sketch of the office
2 Side chair studies
3 Sketches of the smaller cabinet with a work table
4 Studies for the small sofa
5 Corner chair sketches and cabinet glass door detail
6 Table base study
7 View of the model

project name	Fashion Center Renovation / Restoration
location	New York City
year of design	1990
client	Marian & James H. Cohen, Fashion Center Bldg. Corp.
lot size	20,000 sq.ft.
project size	460,000 sq.ft.
architect	George Ranalli
associates	Robert Silman Structural Engineer
design team	John Butterworth, Ursula Kyle, Giovanni Pagnotta
photographer	Catherine Bogert

Fashion Center Building Renovation/Restoration

1

In the early 1990s, two of a small group holding title found themselves the improbable stewards of a benefactor's vision for the Fashion Center, a 23-storey Romanesque Revival structure in New York's historic Garment District. Two of the owners, sensing an opportunity, despite the building's shabby condition, and rent revenue, resisted the inclination of the others to hang up the "For Sale" sign, despite the buildings sluggish appearance and lackluster rent rolls. Instead, the pair, an art critic and an entrepreneur, sought consultation about possible alternative family plans for the building.

A genealogical investigation revealed that a prominent American Architect, Henry Ives Cobb, designed the building in 1924, although subsequent changes had left it beyond recognition. The details follow the storyline of many of New York's old buildings and neighborhoods during the decades of so-called "urban renewal." Evidently, the Fashion Center's terra cotta and cast plaster ornamentation was carried off along with much of the "fabric" of old New York's garment district. The excavating the fragments of a once splendid lobby, plans commenced to revitalize Fashion Center for a new tenancy.

1 Renovated entry from the sidewalk
2 Existing building photo c. 1925
3 Building entrance with the 1949 renovation
4 Newly restored and renovated outdoor entry space

2

3

4

1

By restoring the portico, previously sealed-off behind large glass doors, the building regained the distinctive appeal of a refreshing passageway from the public street. In the 'al fresco' entrance, a new terrazzo floor and ceiling further enhanced impeccably remade terra cotta and wrought iron elements. In the lobby, modern lighting hidden inside original fixtures illuminated the dramatic beauty of a recreated floral plaster cast ceiling, and sumptuously restored cream and purple marble walls, with delicate gold and black accents. A companionable bronze reception desk positioned alongside restored bronze window frames, heating grills, and elevator doors introduced a striking contemporary element to the old lobby.

On an upper floor, a new design offered modern variation on the geometry of the lobby. Light fixtures set inside recesses in the ceiling illuminated a new terrazzo floor. Milled aluminum brackets offered a modern reference to the contemporary city skyline, while protecting the walls from careening carts of merchandise.

Nearly twenty years ago, the contemporary renovation and historic restoration of Fashion Center preserved the aura of an ethereal past, while assuring a long future for the building. The project introduced the economically and environmentally advantageous architectural solution of bringing along the older building into the present.

2

1 | Seventh Avenue elevation illustrating the restoration and renovation
2 | Photo at the corner of 7th Avenue and 38th Street just prior to the restoration and renovation
3 | Ground floor plan with the new floor design for the exterior lobby space

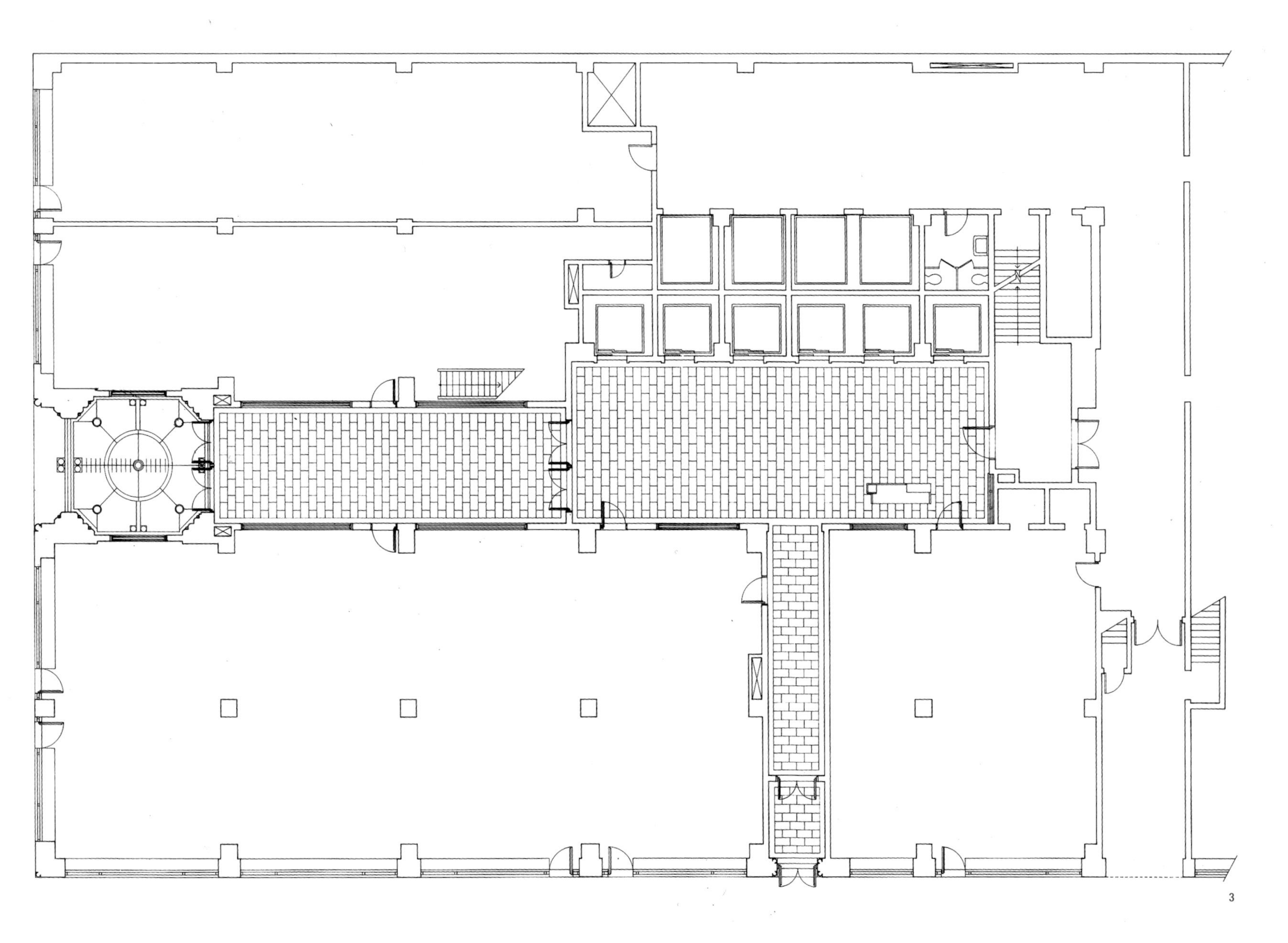

3

1

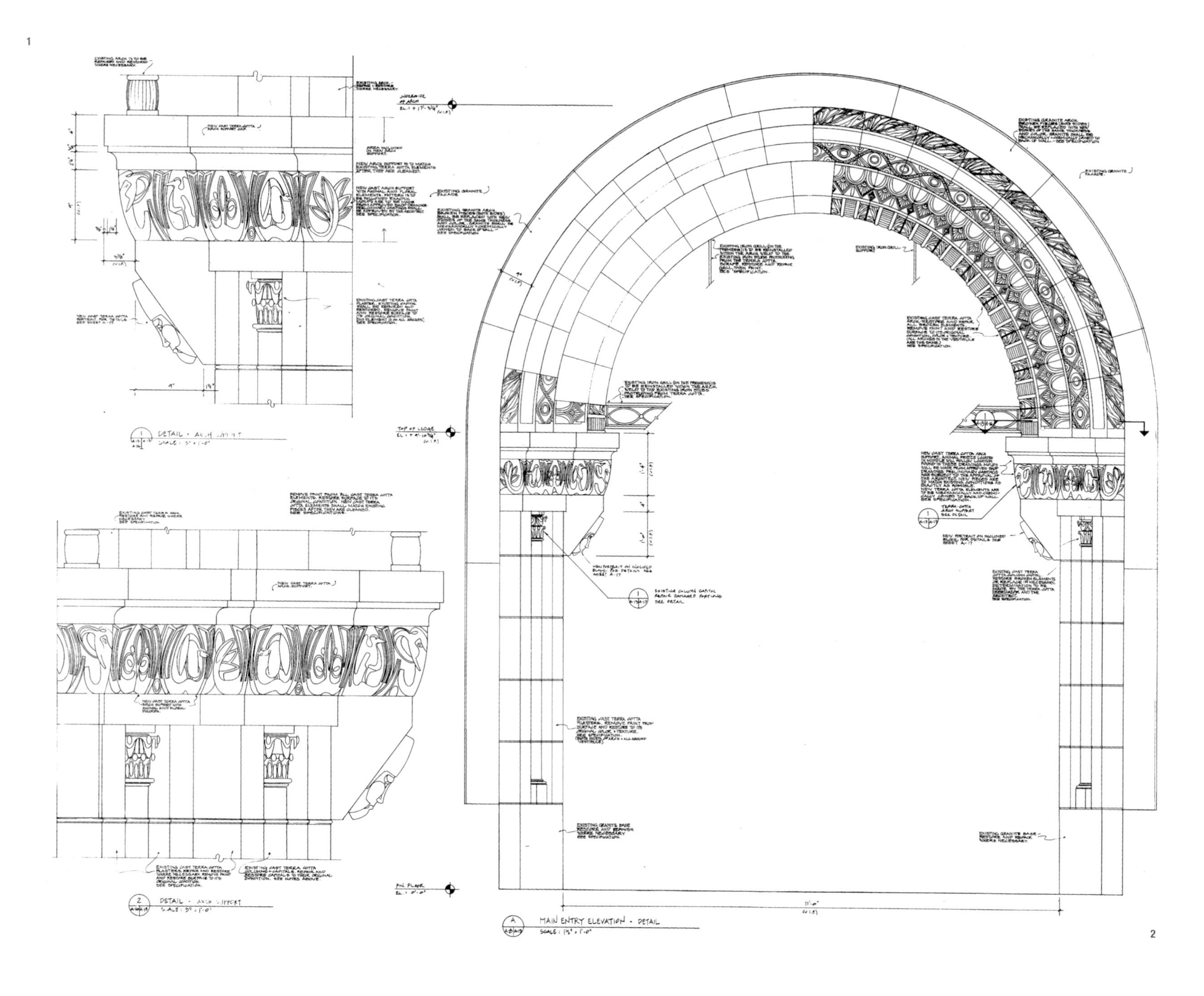

2

1 | Detail photo of the restored animal frieze and restored grill work
2 | Construction drawings for the terracotta frieze and elevation of the full entry arch

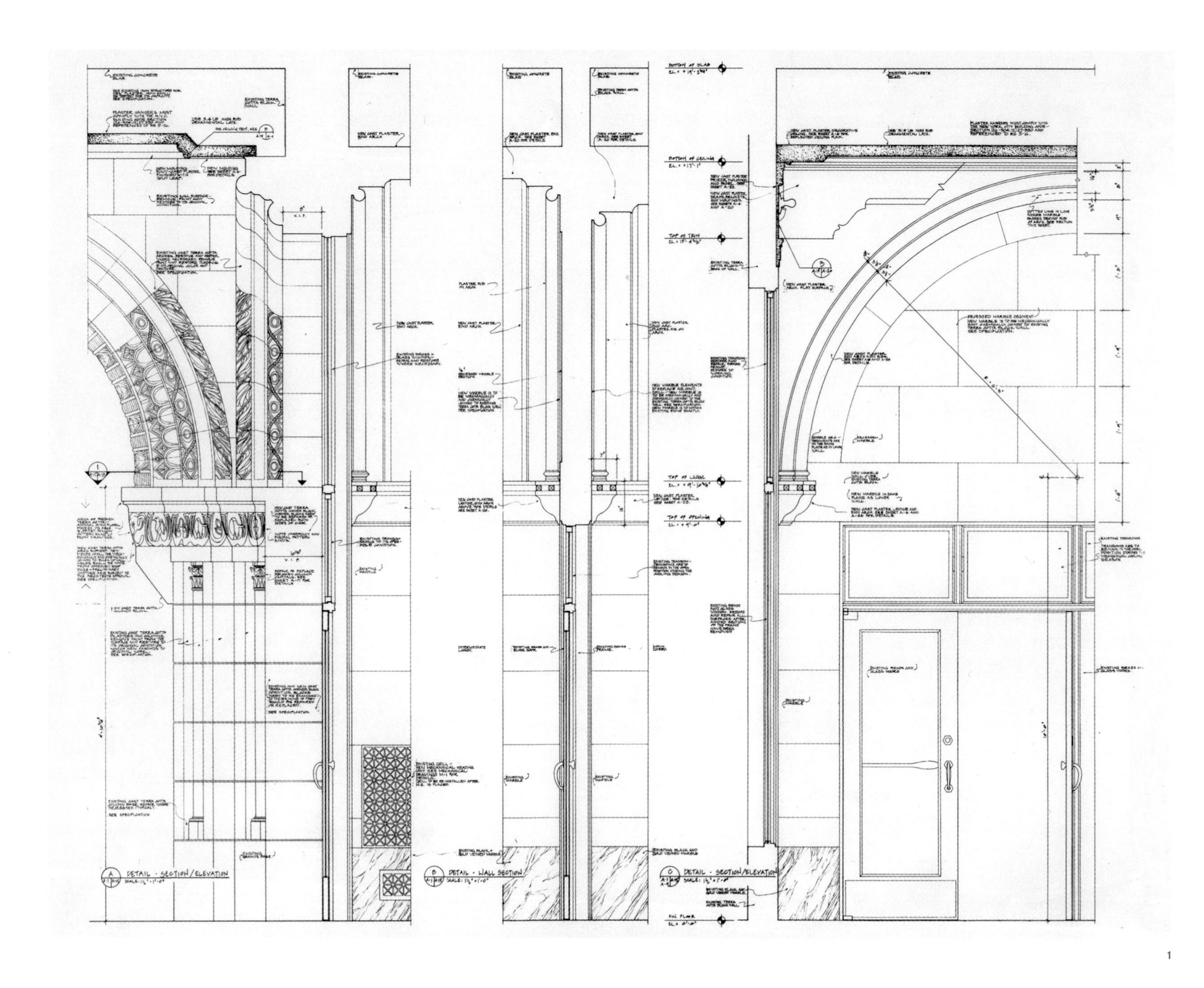

1

1 | Wall sections through the entry, intermediate and main lobbies
2 | Intermediate lobby looking toward the street entrance
3 | New cast plaster ceiling light enclosures
4 | Intermediate lobby looking toward the main lobby

2

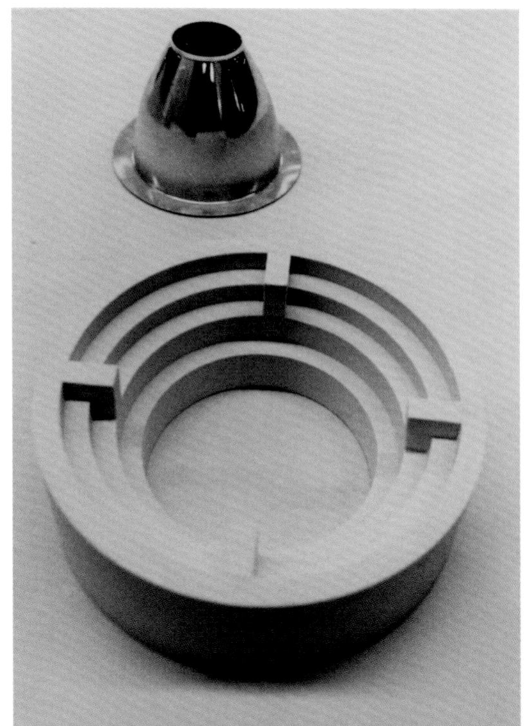

3

4

1

1 Clay carving of one of the ceiling panels waiting for the rubber to be placed in the form to make the mold
2 Reflected ceiling plan of the main lobby
3 Ornamental ceiling panel, type B
4 Ornamental ceiling panel, type A

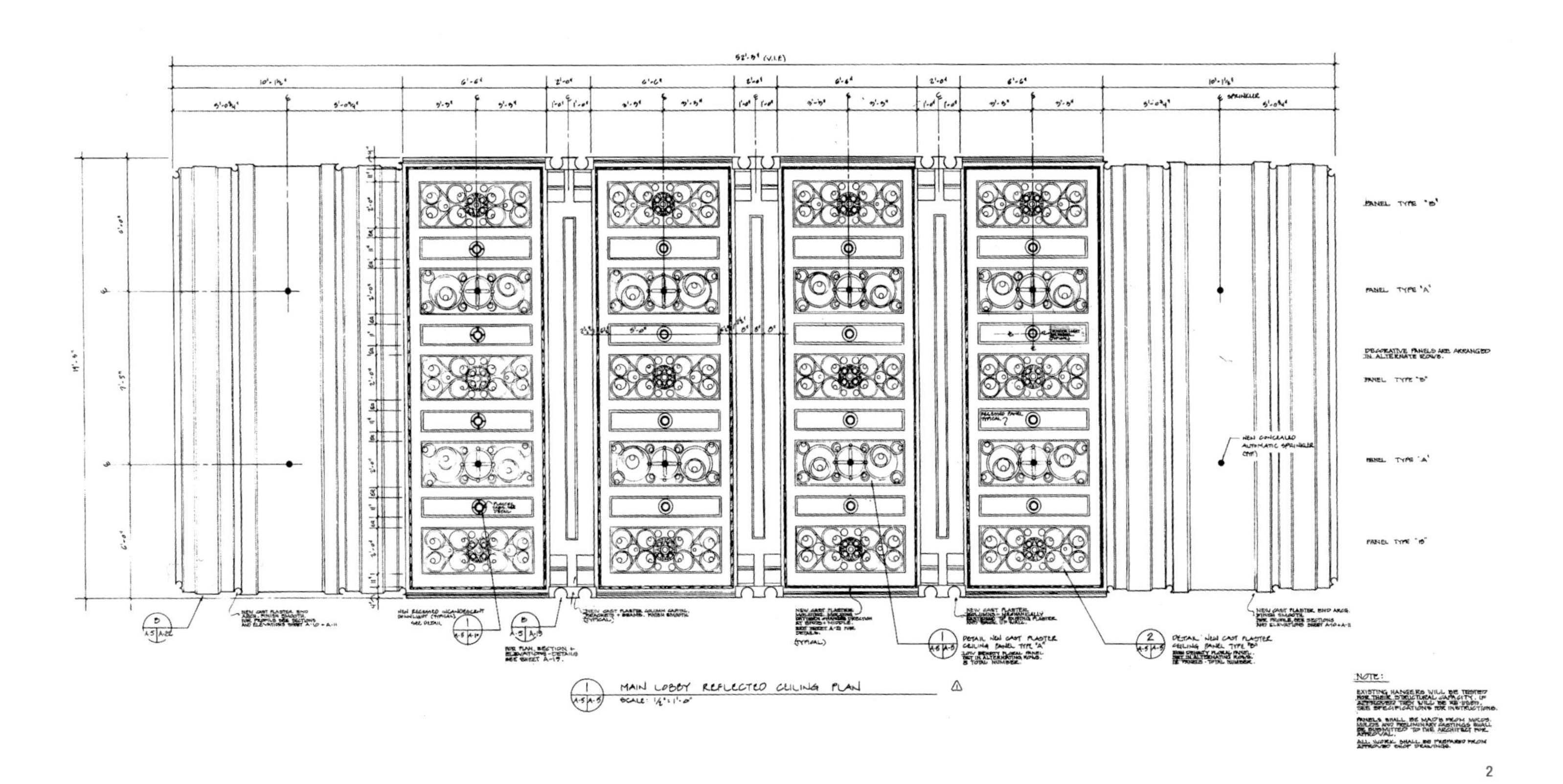
PANEL TYPE "B"
PANEL TYPE "A"
PANEL TYPE "B"
PANEL TYPE "A"
PANEL TYPE "B"
MAIN LOBBY REFLECTED CEILING PLAN
NOTE:

2

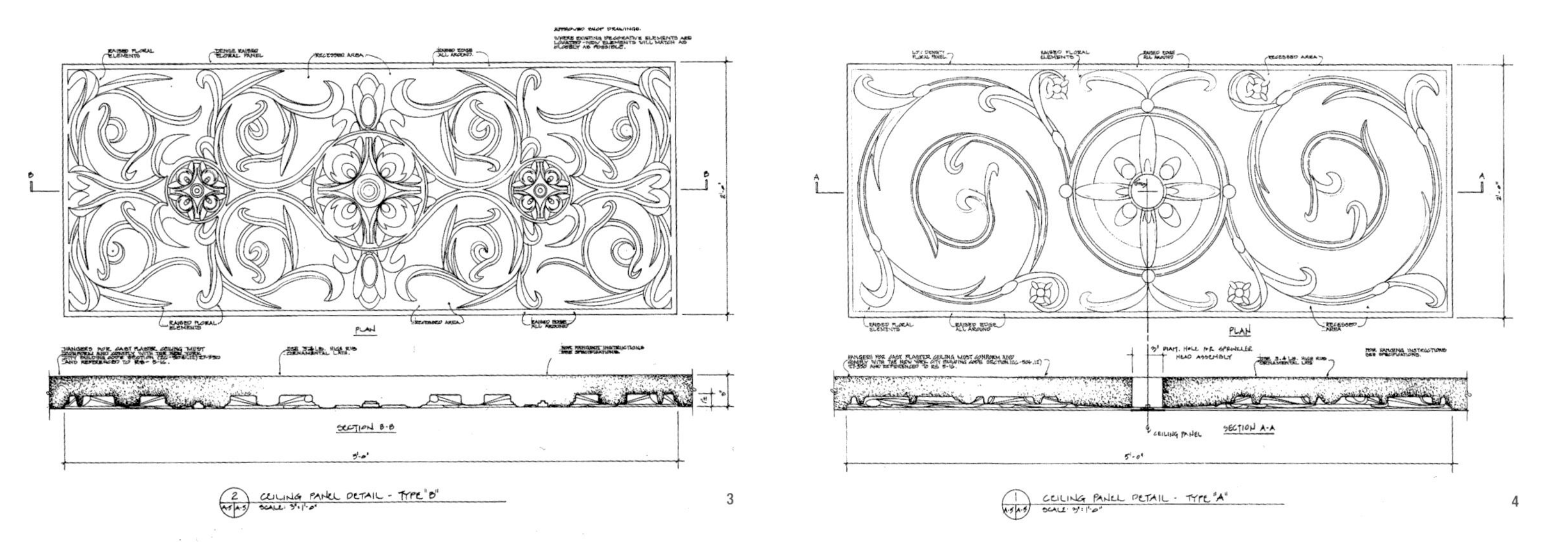
PLAN
SECTION B-B
5'-0"
CEILING PANEL DETAIL - TYPE "B"
PLAN
SECTION A-A
CEILING PANEL
5'-0"
CEILING PANEL DETAIL - TYPE "A"

3

4

1

2

3

4

5

1 Main lobby looking toward the back of the building
2 Main Lobby looking toward the 7th Avenue entrance
3 Side lobby entrance leading out to 38th Street
4 Main lobby prior to the renovation and restoration looking toward the 7th Avenue entrance
5 Main lobby prior to the renovation and restoration looking toward the rear of the building

1

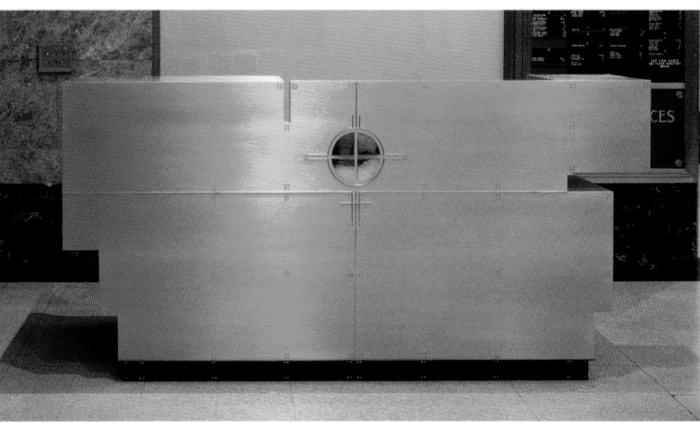

2

3

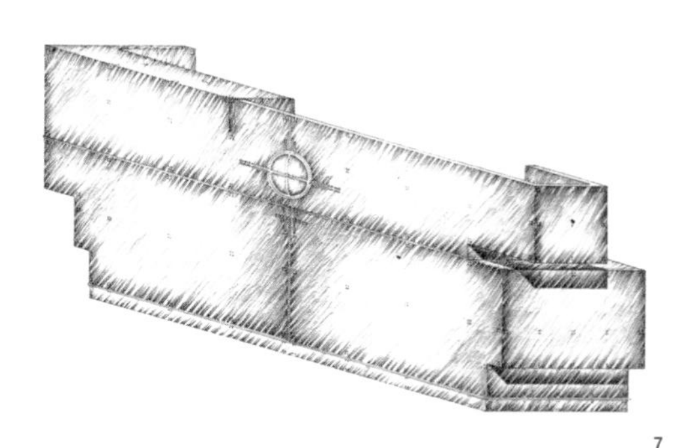

7

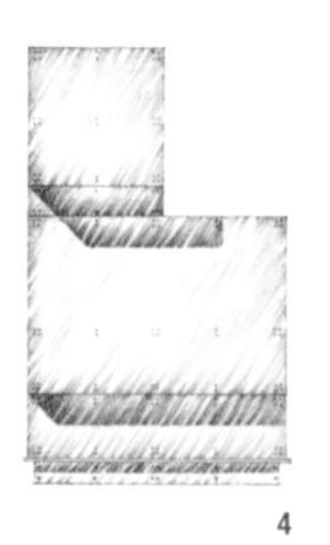

4

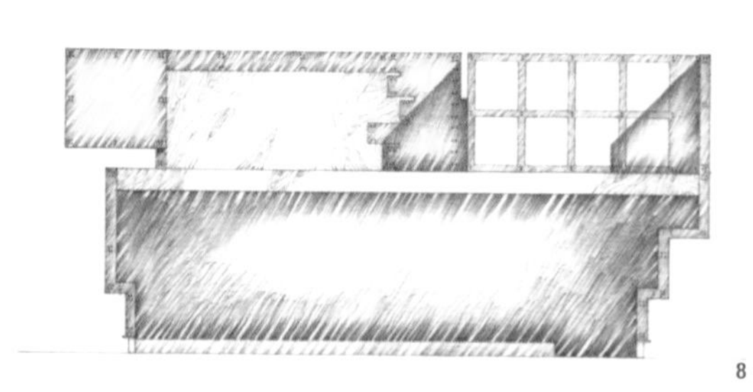

8

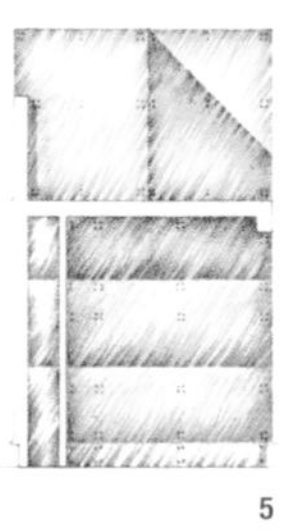

5

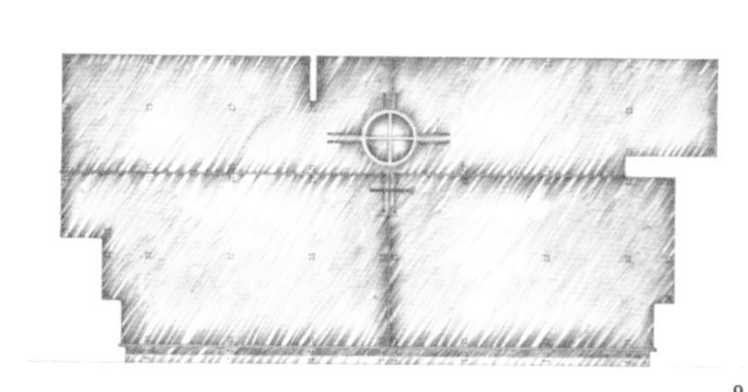

9

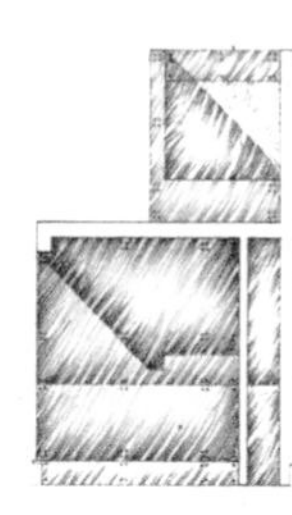

6

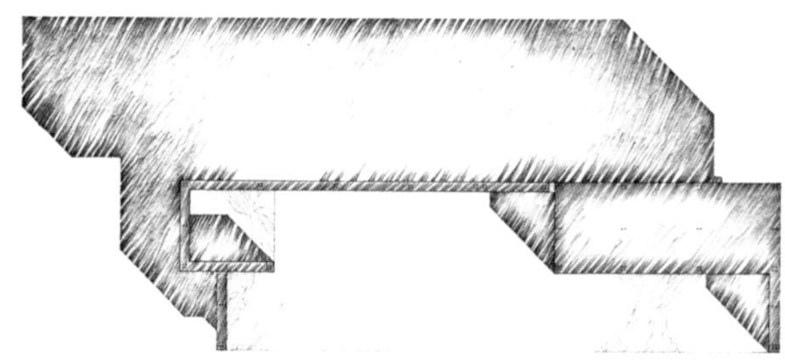

10

1 Side view of the lobby reception desk
2 Front elevation of the lobby reception desk
3 End elevation of the desk
4 Entry end elevation
5 Desk section looking toward the tv monitor end
6 Desk section looking toward the phone box
7 Elevation oblique drawing of the desk
8 Back of the desk
9 Front elevation
10 Plan of the desk
11 Detail view of the front of the desk showing screw assemblies, raised brass details and silver circle

11

1

1 | Craftsman working on the plaster column for the main lobby
2 | Construction document drawings of the paired ornamental columns in the main lobby in elevation, side elevation, plan and reflected ceiling plan

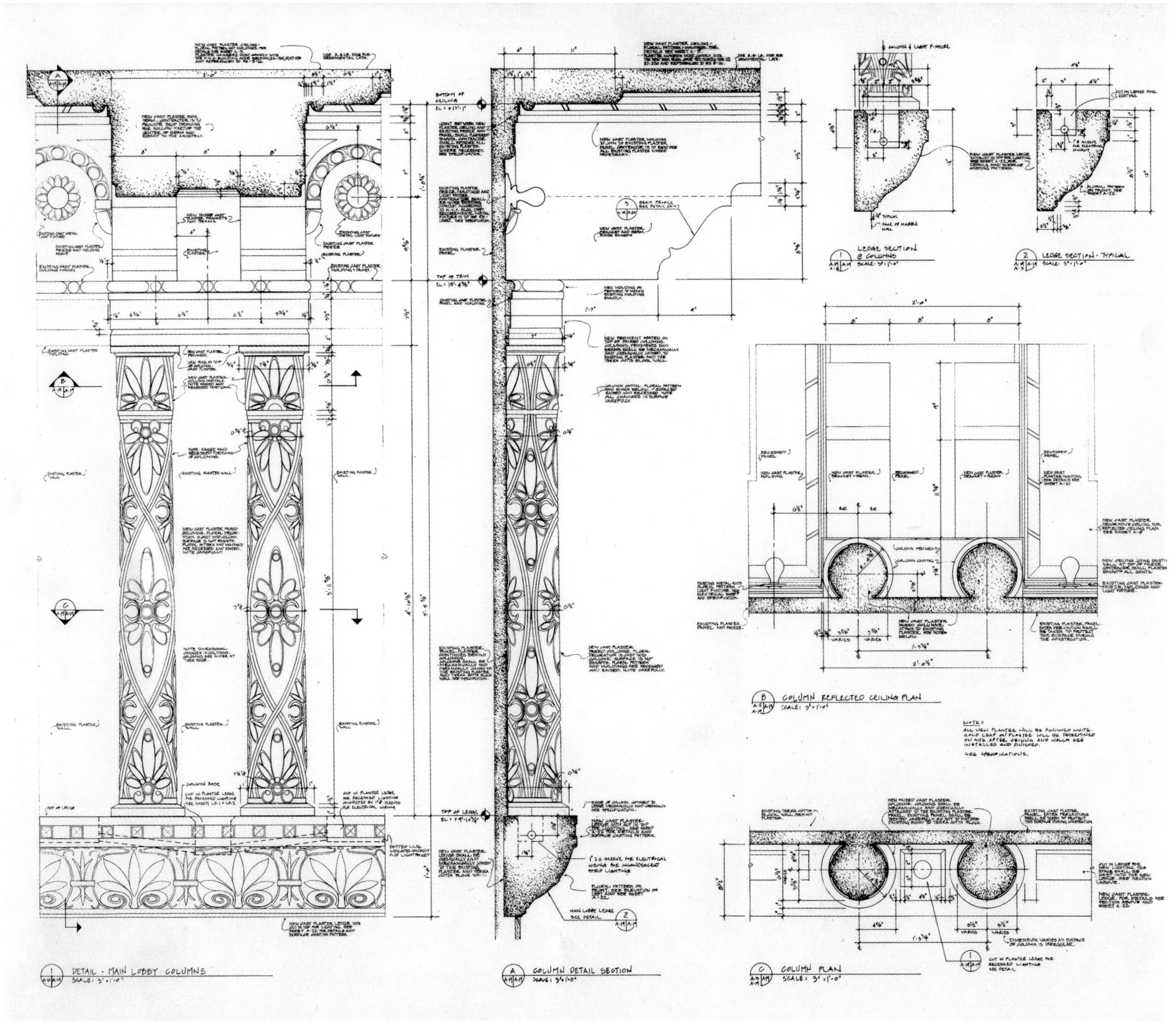
LEDGE SECTION @ COLUMNS
SCALE: 3" = 1'-0"
LEDGE SECTION - TYPICAL
SCALE: 3" = 1'-0"
COLUMN REFLECTED CEILING PLAN
SCALE: 3" = 1'-0"
NOTE:
ALL NEW PLASTER WILL BE FINISHED WHITE. GOLD LEAF ON PLASTER WILL BE DETERMINED ON SITE AFTER CEILING AND WALLS ARE INSTALLED AND FINISHED.
SEE SPECIFICATIONS.
DETAIL - MAIN LOBBY COLUMNS
SCALE: 3" = 1'-0"
COLUMN DETAIL SECTION
SCALE: 3" = 1'-0"
COLUMN PLAN
SCALE: 3" = 1'-0"

2

1 | View of the plaster columns in the main lobby
2 | Section oblique drawing of the plaster columns in the main lobby
3 | Detail view of the lighting cove, paired columns and side entry out to 38th Street

1

2

3

1 Typical new hall at the corner
2 Main hall in front of the elevators
3 New corner leading to the side hall with steel corner guards, steel base and new terrazzo floor
4 Isometric drawing of the corner guard and end condition
5 Electrical cabinet doors
6 Elevation drawings of the two side halls
7 Elevation of the elevator wall

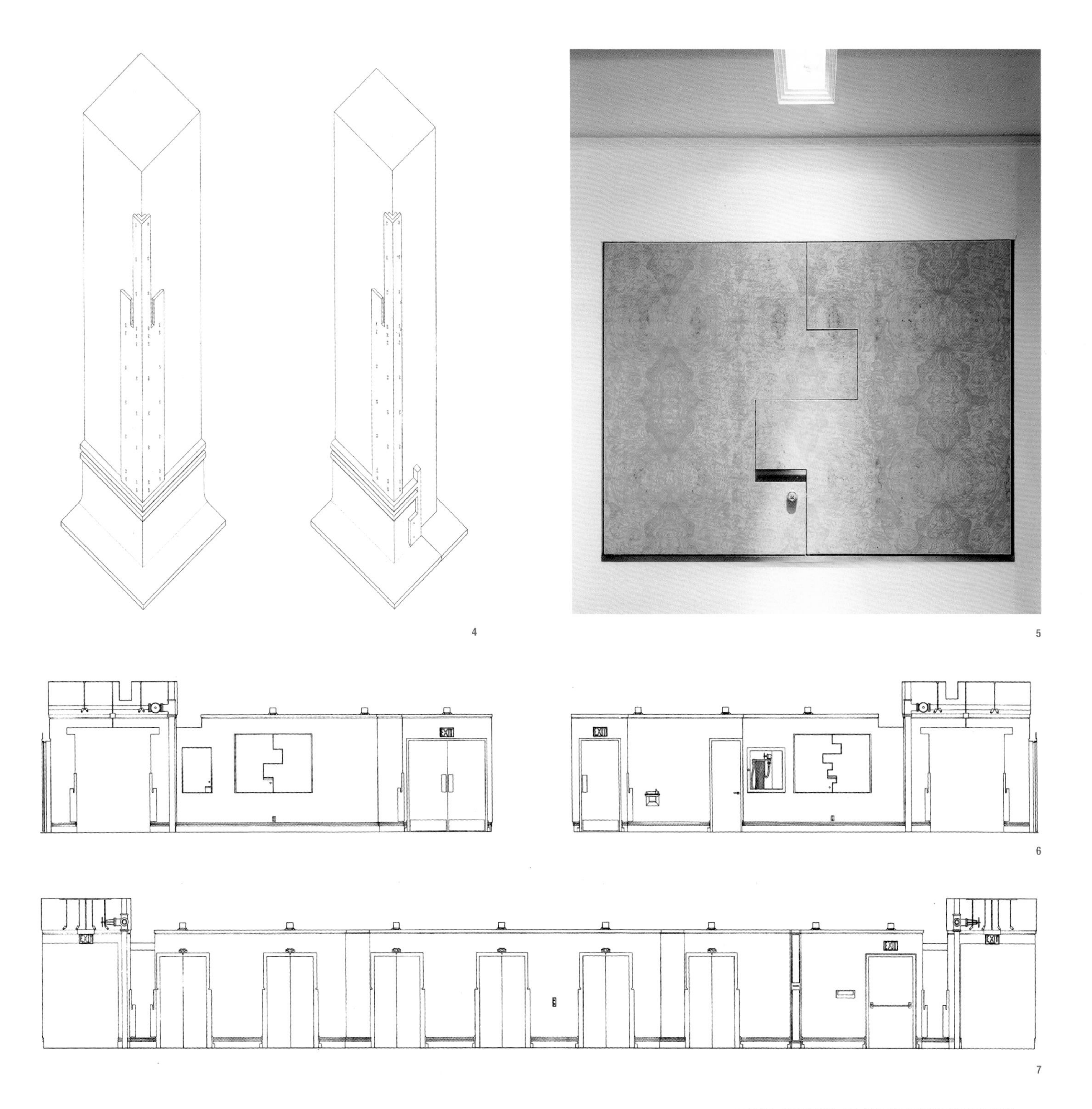

4

5

6

7

project name	Tower of Silence
location	Tokyo, Japan
year of design	1990
client	Toyota Motor Corp.
lot size	9,500 sq.ft.
architect	George Ranalli
associates	Robert Silman Structural Engineer
design team	John Butterworth, John Pagnotta, David Jon Rush
photographer	model photos George Ranalli

Tower of Silence

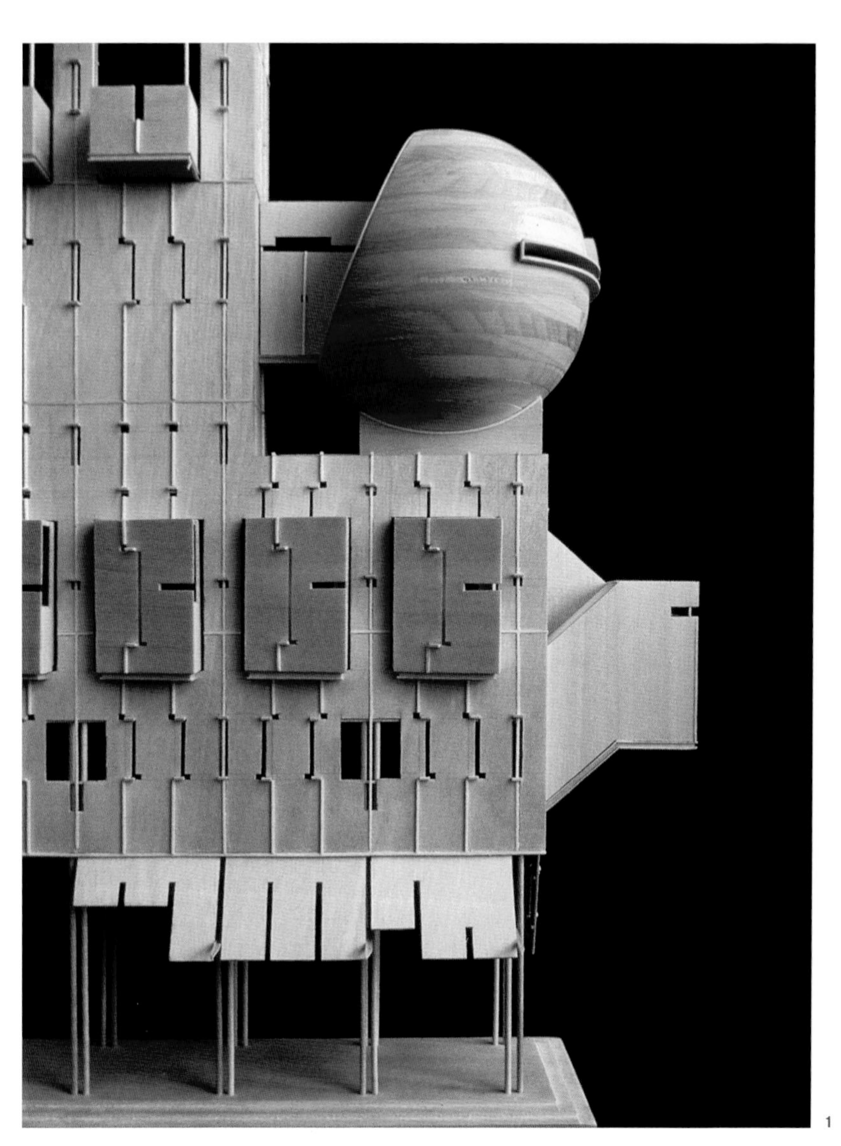

1

In 1989, the Toyota Motor Corporation commissioned Tower Of Silence, an architectural study to stimulate the development of corporate philanthropy in the arts. The program did not assign any special function to the monument except that it symbolize the company in its form, potential use, and material. The resulting design, Tower of Silence, is intended to stand in the multi-story atrium for a new Tokyo corporate headquarters. It addresses to people visiting the building, and moving throughout the six floors of automobile showrooms, surrounding the atrium.

The design proposes a contemplative environment within the lobby space: an enigmatic composition of panels, some folded outward like awnings at the bottom and others outlining niches, porches, and stairs, as well as a spherical concert hall for small audiences, all projected from the object's façade and emphasizing the human scale.

Tower of Silence offers a respite from the activity of the busy showrooms and atrium. The tower can be entered at various levels in order to accommodate people on each floor. People move on bridges across the void of the atrium and into the interior of the tower. Once inside, an individual may roam throughout a series of chambers, which protrude beyond the skin of the structure, or sit in privacy, looking out upon the city beyond. Small groups may gather for collective activity, including karaoke, in the spherical theater, situated at the middle of the structure.

Tower of Silence is supported by a series of paired steel columns, with horizontal supports. At various levels, the tower is covered with sheets of white 2000X material, by the Formica Corporation, cut and mounted to the frame with small horizontal steel elements that extend through the skin. Vertical ribs of 2000X add stiffness. The spherical shape is cast from liquid, in a formwork provided by Formica.

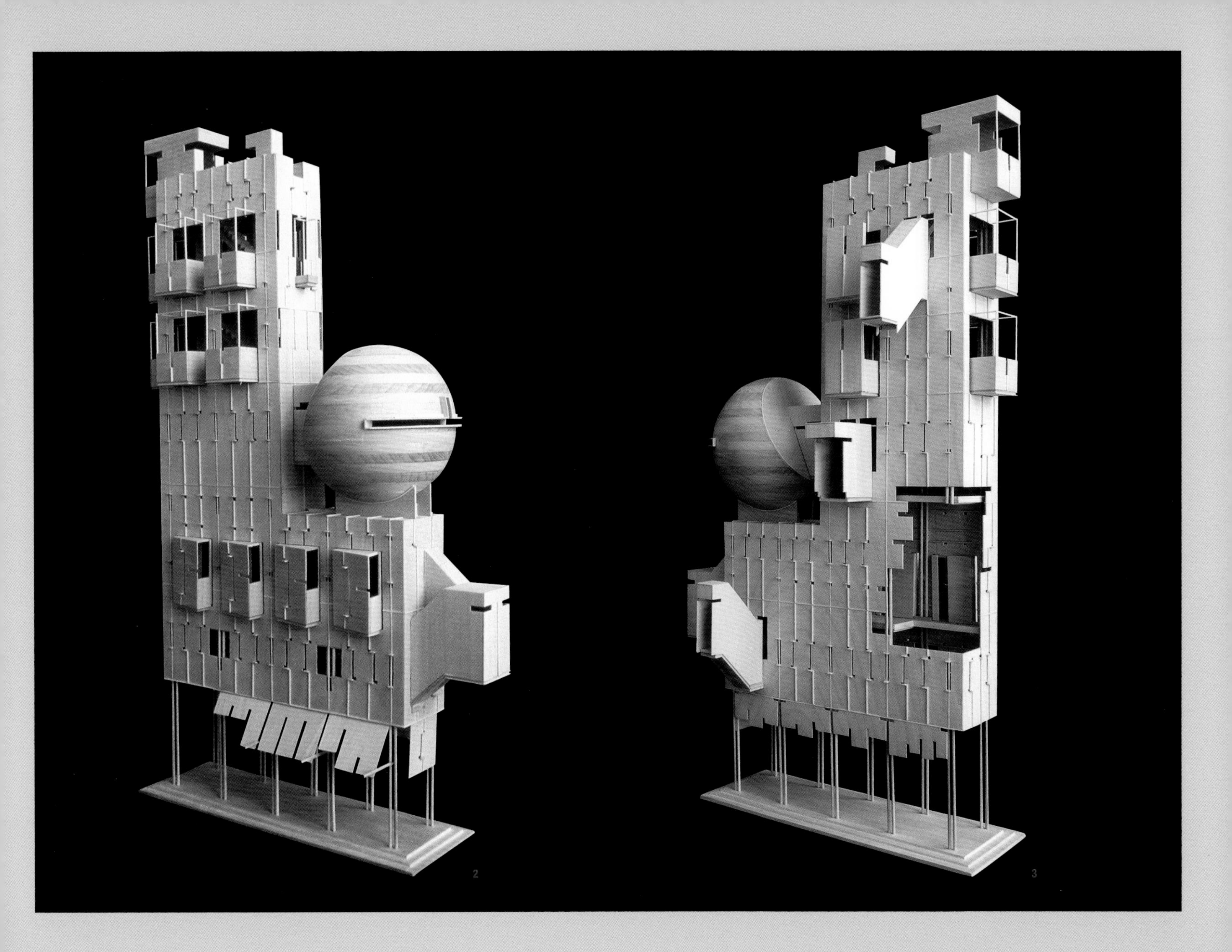

1 Detail view of the tower model
2 View of the detail model from the theater end
3 View of the detail model from the entry side

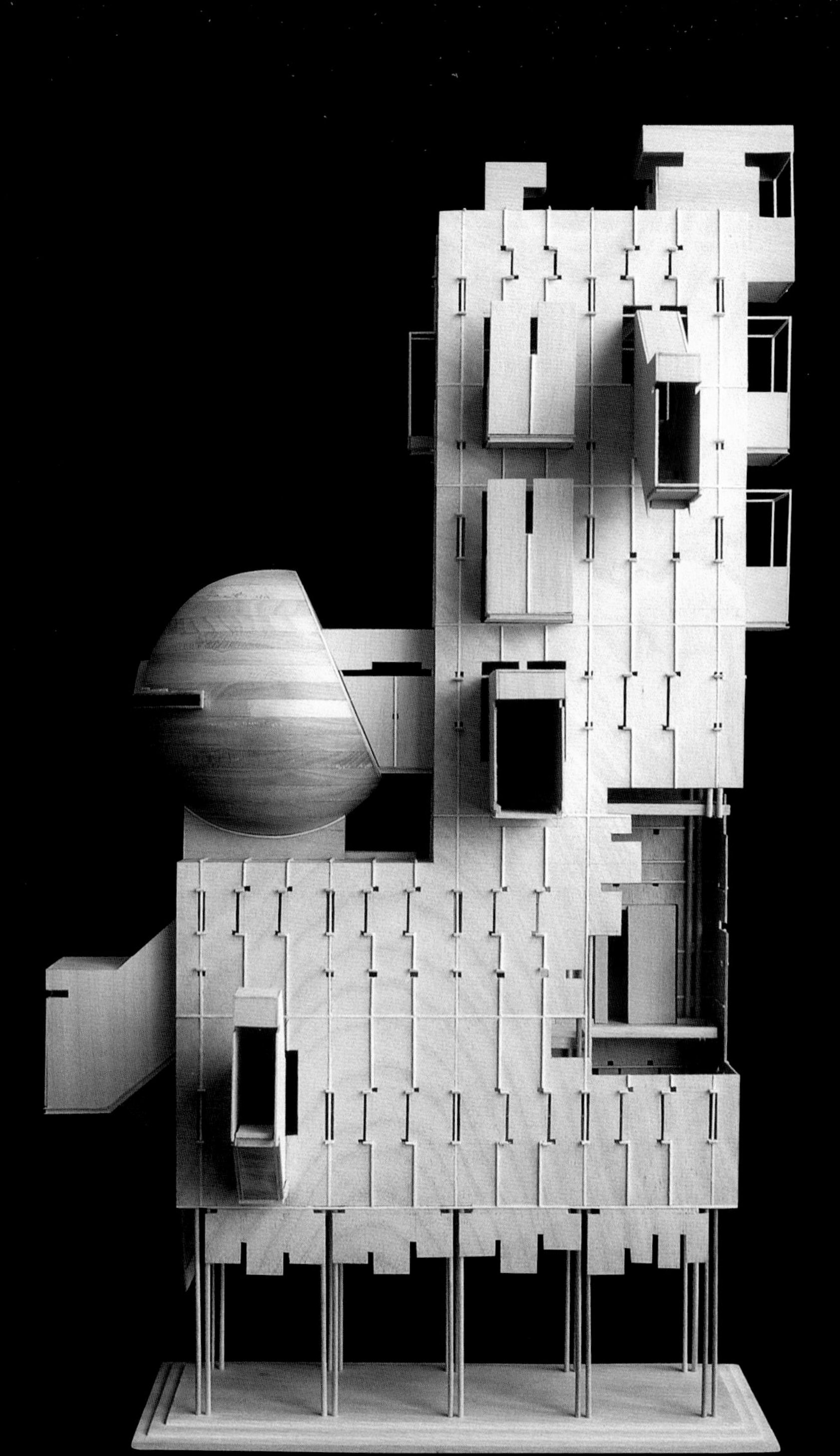

The project offers a multinational corporation an architectural case study on solitude and human interaction through which to explore the arts, philanthropy, and individual creative expression. Tower Of Silence investigates the complex notions of accessibility and contemplation as central components of creative spontaneity. Tower of Silence also examines interrelatational functions, which encourage autonomy and human relations. The project, expressing positive relationships between its inhabitants and product manufacturers, stands as a symbol of the Toyota Company, and of the people who occupy the tower. As an inhabited monument, Tower of Silence metaphorically belongs to the people who use it. Finally, as a construction, it fuses structure, form, program, and material into a synthesis of beautiful public space.

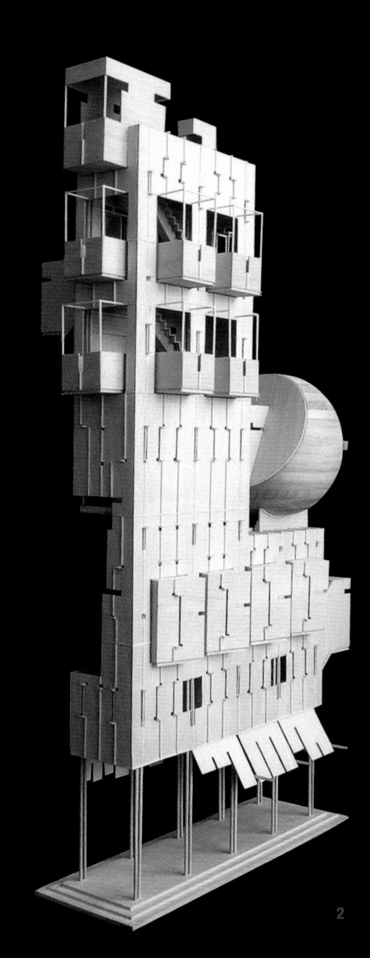

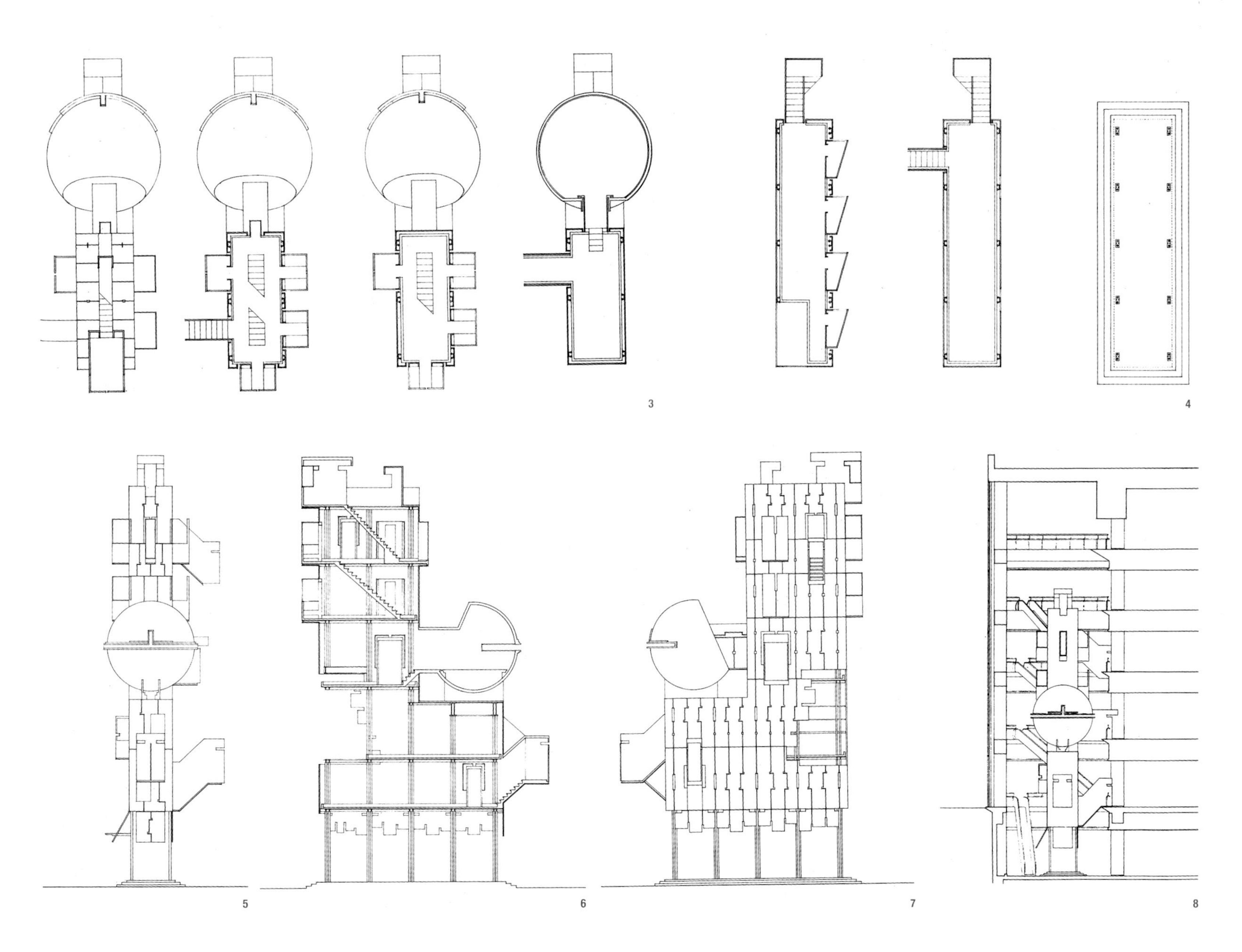

1 Detail model view of the entry side
2 Detail model view from the front corner
3 Plans levels 1-3
4 Plans levels 4-7
5 Theater end elevation
6 Section looking toward the entrance side
7 Elevation drawing facing the street side
8 End elevation of the tower in the main atrium space

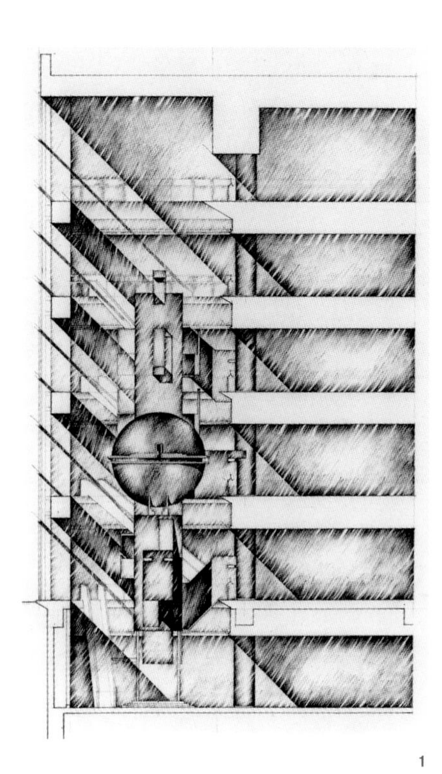

1

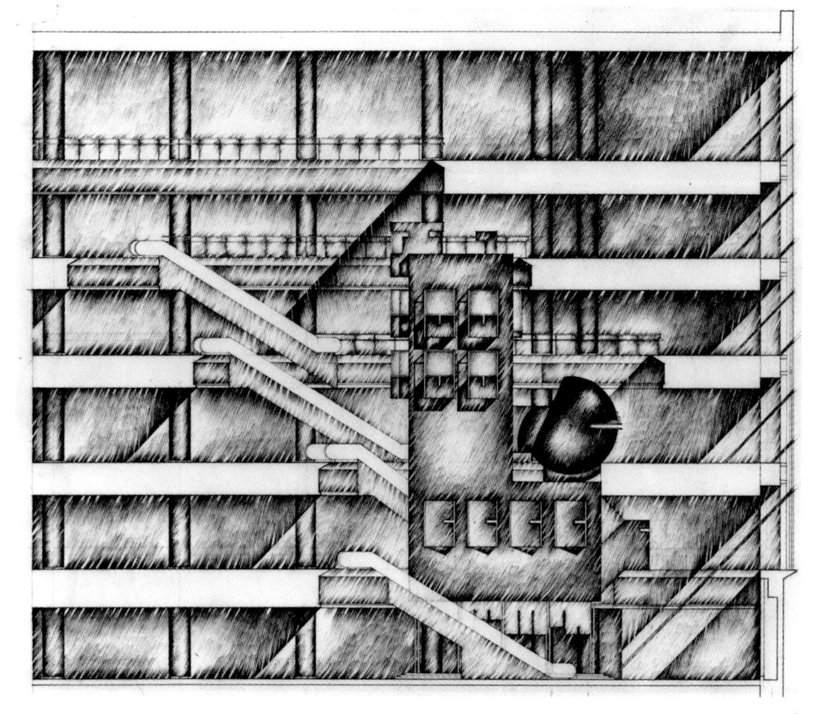

2

1 End elevation of the tower in the atrium space
2 Side elevation drawing illustrating the new tower in the larger atrium with the escalators passing through the end of the tower
3 Sketch of the theater end and skin construction
4 End elevation studies
5 Entry elevation massing study
6 Front elevation massing study
7 Early section drawing
8 First sketch of the project
9 Plan studies
10 Massing sketch
11 Theater section study

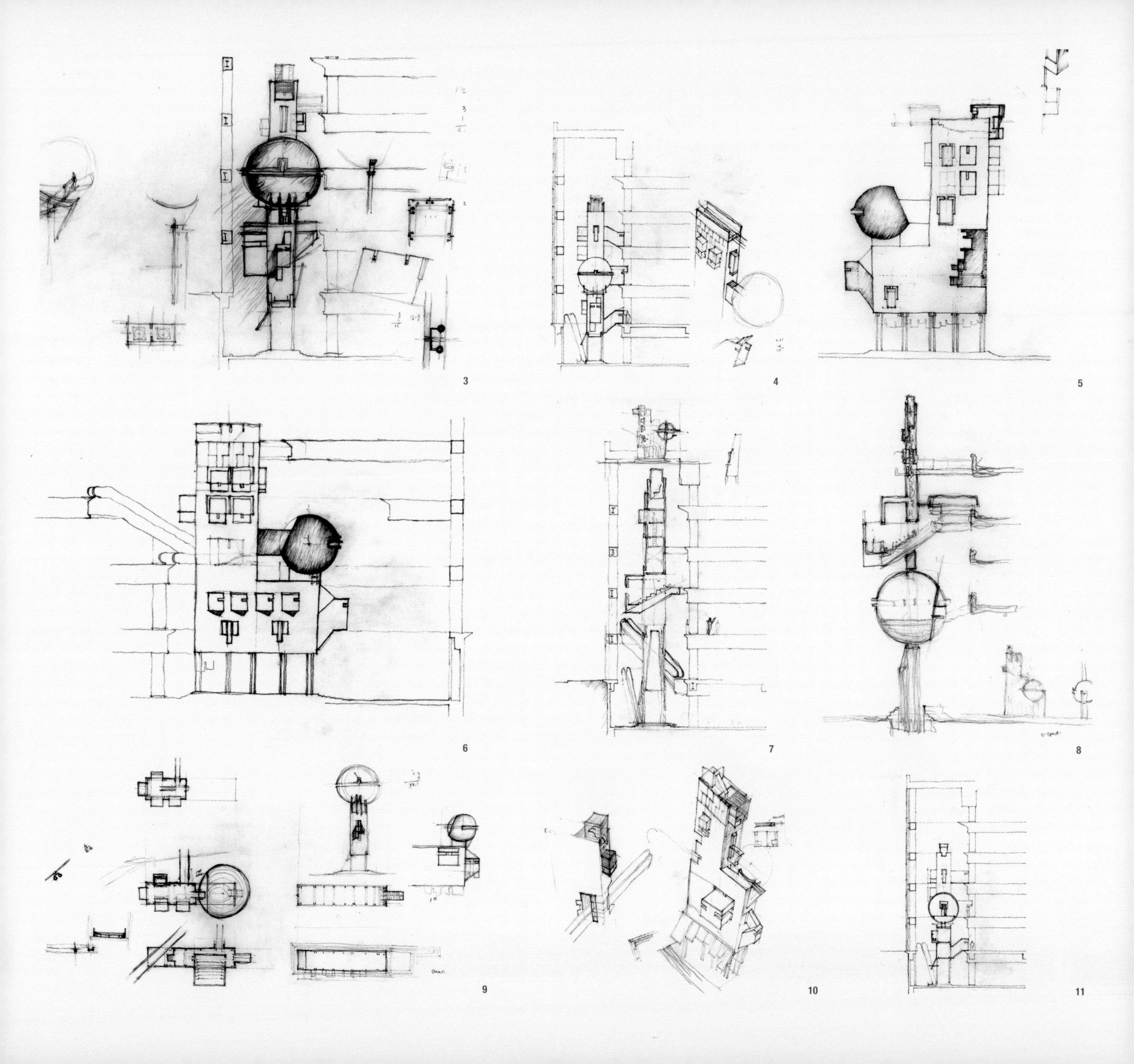

3 4 5 6 7 8 9 10 11

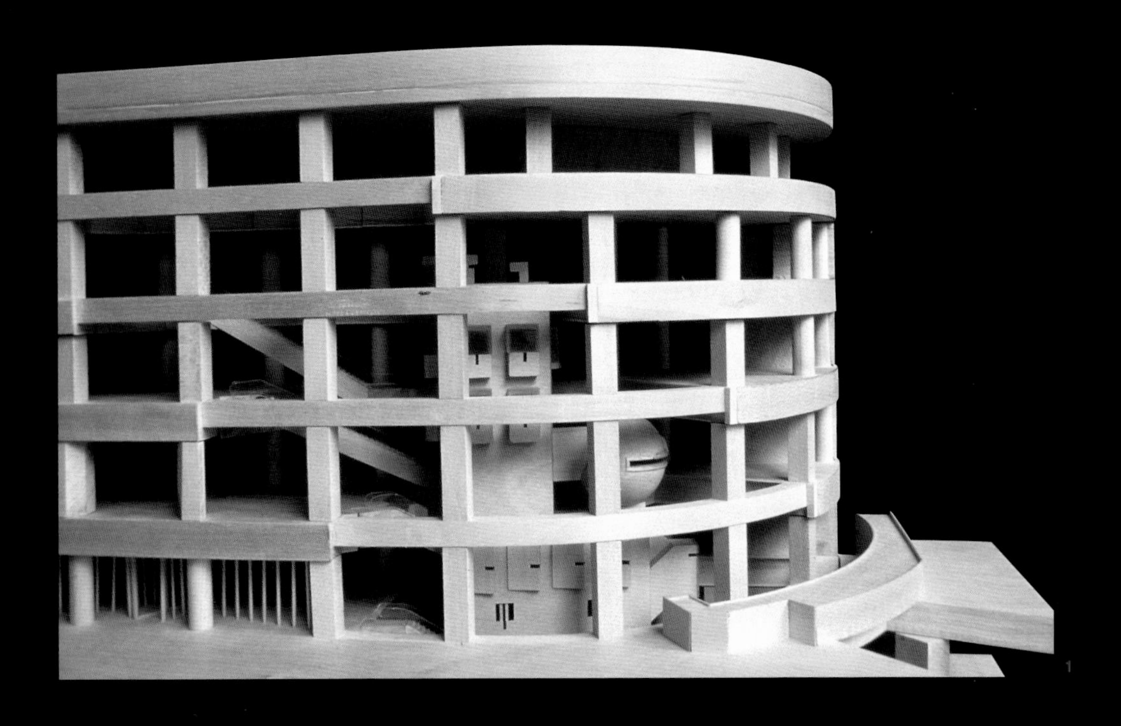

1

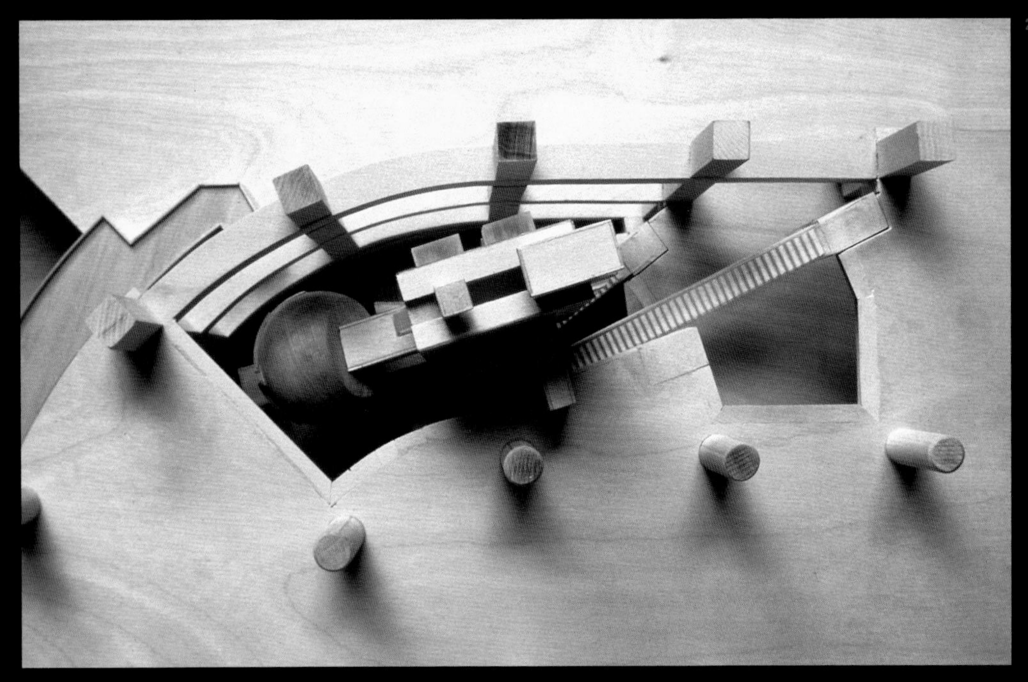

2

1 | Model of the tower inside the larger building
2 | Plan view of the model of the tower inside the main atrium space showing the escalators passing through the end of the tower
3 | Small model of the tower inside the atrium with several floors removed

3

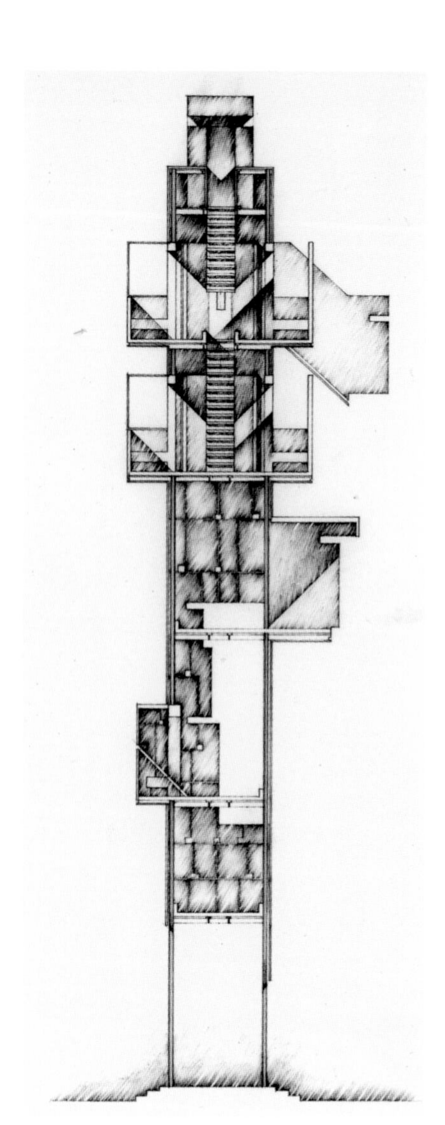

1

2

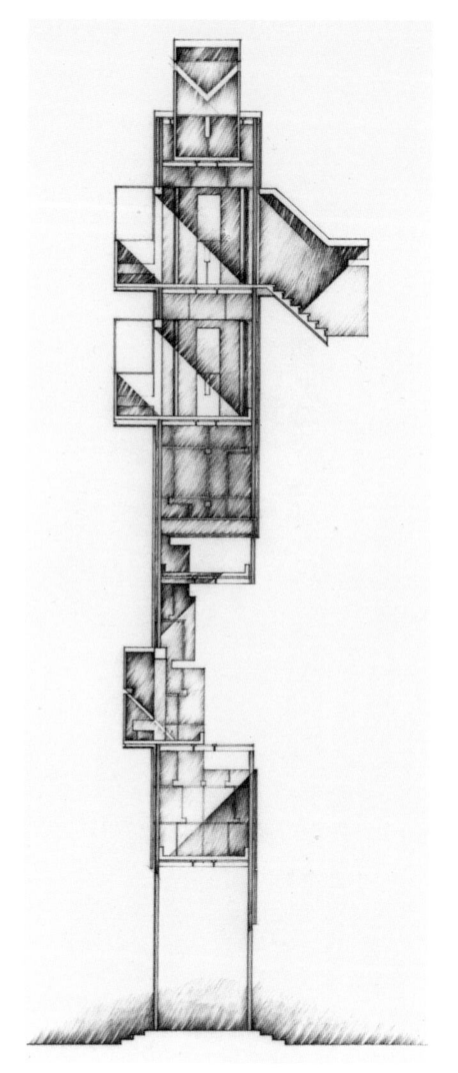

3

1 | Section through the small spaces of silence
2 | Section through the small theater
3 | Section through the end stair entry and cabins of silence
4 | End model view where the escalators pass through the tower
5 | Theater end elevation of the model

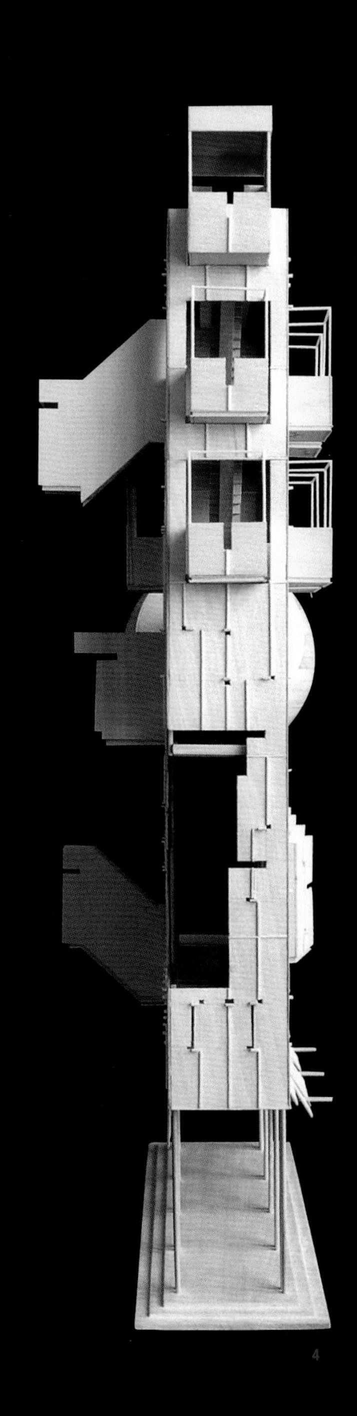

4

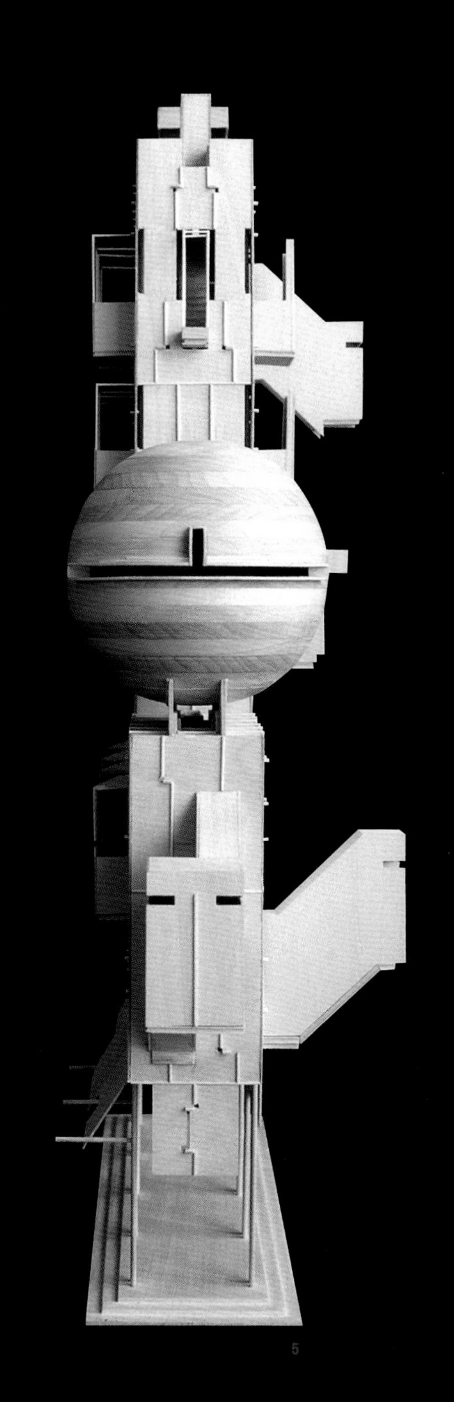

5

project name	New York Times Tower Competition
location	Times Square, New York
year of design	1987
client	Municipal Art Society
lot size	7,500 sq. ft.
project size	150,000 sq. ft.
architect	George Ranalli
associates	Robert Silman Structural Engineer
design team	John Butterworth

The New York Times Tower

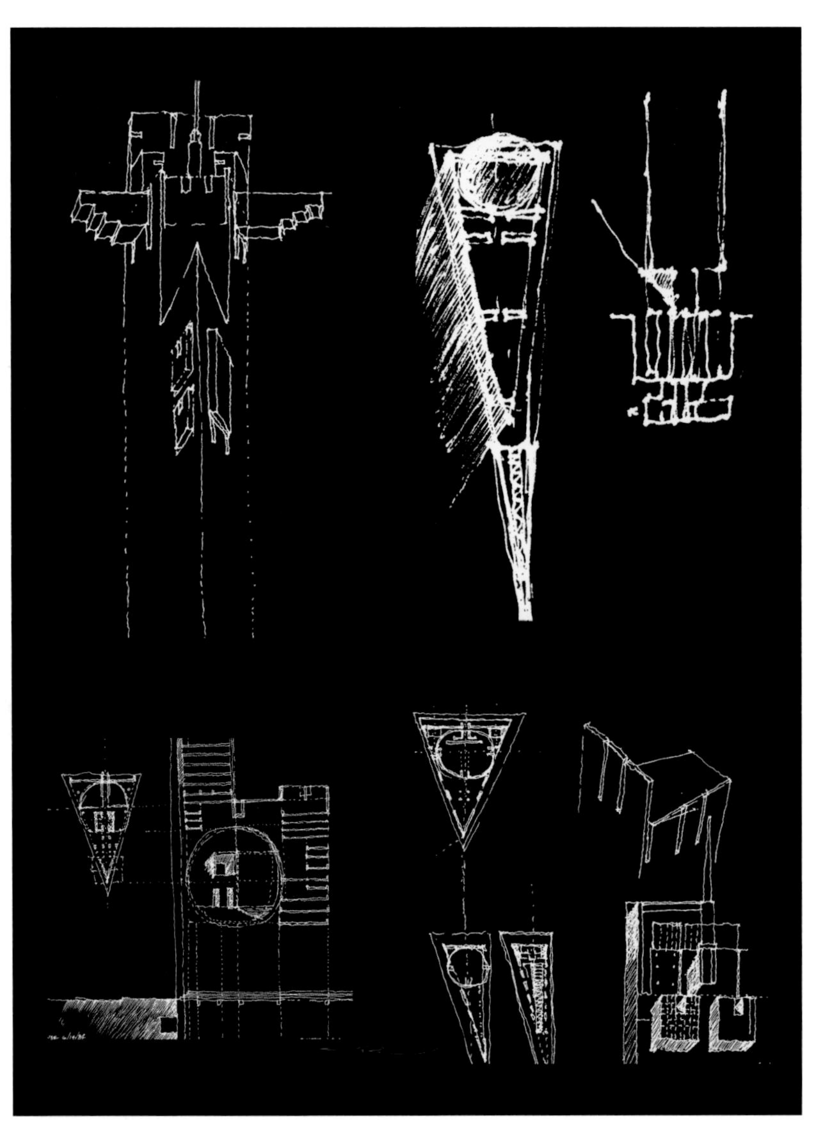

1

Since 1893, the Municipal Art Society has galvanized the efforts of architects, artists, and civic leaders on behalf of New York's public spaces, municipal buildings, landmarks, and historic districts. In the 1980s, the Society campaigned against the city's massive proposal to transform the fabric and social identity of the Times Square theatre district, in which Times Square itself, the city's famous "Crossroads of the World," simply vanished. In partial response, the Society sponsored a reconsideration of the iconic Times Square Tower, the old Allied Chemical Building (also variously known as One Times Square, 1475 Broadway, and the New York Times Building), soliciting ideas on how to reclad the existing triangular building as part of the reconstruction of Times Square. This competition began a major redevelopment that transformed this formerly seedy, honky-tonk part of the city into the major family-oriented entertainment capital of New York. Broadway theaters have never been so popular, and can now be visited as part of a safe, vibrant, and electrifying experience.

Although noted for the celebratory ball dropping at midnight on New Year's Eve, the original structure was quite ordinary in every other way. The concept design for the Times Square Tower aimed at creating the impression of timeless vertical space, resonating with historic context to enhance the building's positive civic identity. It simultaneously fulfilled programmatic requests for performing arts space and for renovation of the 42nd Street subway station.

At the base of the building, the design proposes an enlarged ground-level lobby space over a larger 42nd Street subway station entrance. Above the lobby, a distinctive sphere-shape provides space for an arena theater in which the stage is placed slightly lower than the audience. This design suits popular high-energy performances and classical stage productions equally. The sphere adjoins to upper floors where space is provided for rehearsal and production, screenings, gallery exhibitions, and educational facilities. At the top of the building, two wing-like projections are cantilevered from a faceted shaft, each offering space for a traditional proscenium theater with accommodations for state-of-the-art stage design that include a flexible proscenium arch, main and rear stages, orchestra pit, and dock-to-stage loading.

A vertical collection of theaters is thus assembled into the altered structural frame of the existing building, their forms protruding from a triangular enclosure that follows the boundaries of the site. These replace some of the exceptional theaters that have been demolished in the Times Square area of New York City over the last fifteen years or so.

2

In Memoriam
American Theater
Avon Theater
Belmont Theater
Empire Theater
Forty-Eighth Street Theater
Helen Hayes Theater
Maxine Elliott's Theater
Vanderbilt Theater

3

4

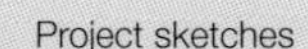

1 | Project sketches
2 | Existing building at Times Square
3 | Sketch study with protruding theaters
4 | Final competition drawing of the renovated building

project name	The Peak Competition
location	Victoria Peak, Hong Kong
year of design	1982
client	Private Developer
lot size	29 Acres
architect	George Ranalli
associates	Robert Silman Structural Engineer
design team	Nick Dermand, Ed Weinberg
photographer	Model Photos: George Ranalli

The Peak Competition

1

Victoria Peak is the highest mountain on Hong Kong Island, rising to an altitude of 1,811 feet. Its steep gradient traverses pine and bamboo forests, unfolding vistas so sharp that buildings appear to lean. The Peak, as it is locally known, is one of the most prestigious addresses in the global residential marketplace.

In 1982, a private developer sponsored the Peak Competition to elicit an architectural design for a residential complex at this prime site. Overgrown with lush local vegetation, the Peak was a breathtaking location for the owner's complex program of time-shared apartments, owner's houses, and club facility with dining room, library, recreational facilities, and swimming pool complex.

A winding roadway ascends to 32 granite-clad duplex townhouse-style apartments, a parking facility, large outdoor recreational plaza, and eight private residences. Orientation and materiality inspire unique features in alignment with the path of the sun as well as cascading vistas of sky, hillside, harbor, and city.

The design's dominant mode arranges the housing along the east-west length of the property. The duplex apartments are stacked in double height, each pair marked at its northern and southern end by a sentinel-like bedroom tower. Ground-floor apartments adjoin gardens of flowering hibiscus and other native vegetation and garden terraces topping second-story dwellings. Both first- and second-story apartments offer a dramatic, double-height main space and magnificent panoramas.

The townhouses' linear pattern is repeated on the highest portion of the site for the individual houses, although these are maneuvered to accommodate requirements differing from those of the time-shared housing.

In the middle of the composition, a restorative sanctuary is defined by shared program elements that include a 2,500-square-foot piazza, airy fitness studios, a light-filled library, and an al fresco dining and concert hall. This enclave also acts as a bulwark to retain earth for an infinity pool that extends the composition into the South China Sea in the distance.

2

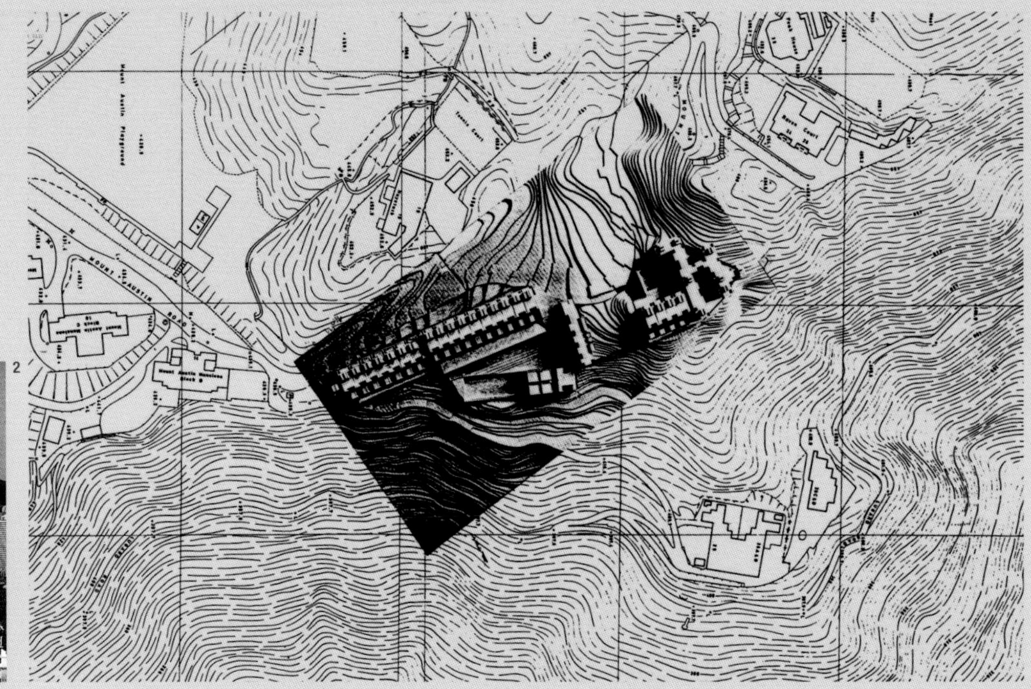

4

3

5

6

1 View of the model from the Owner's apartments end of the complex
2 Photo of the site on top of Victoria Peak in Hong Kong
3 View of the complex from the lower end of the site
4 Photomontage site plan
5 Section through the time shared housing units
6 Elevation oblique drawing of the time shared housing block with windows facing the view down the mountain

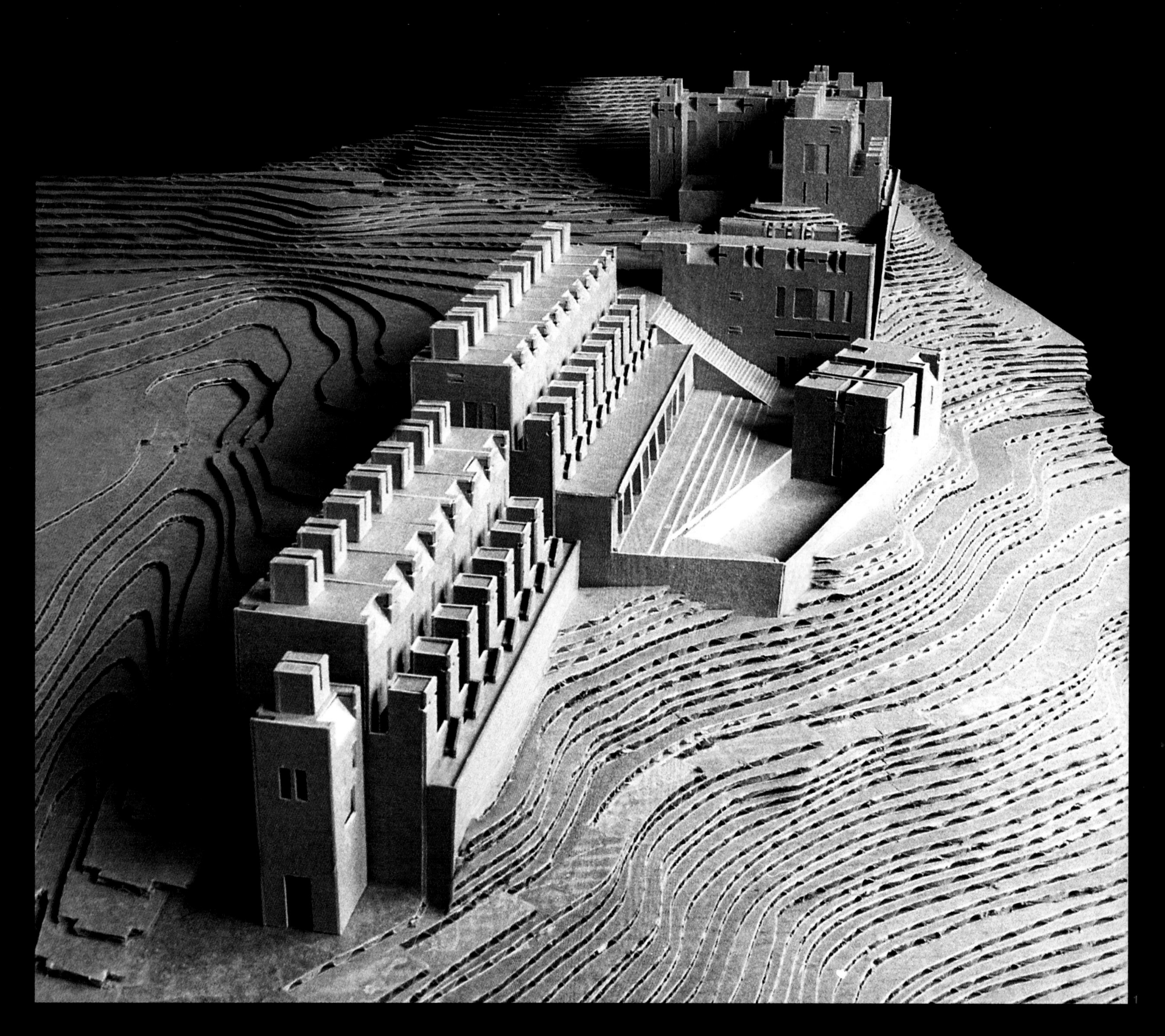

1

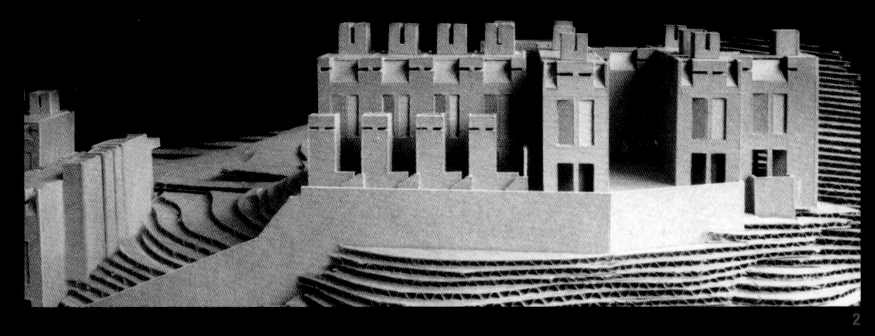

2

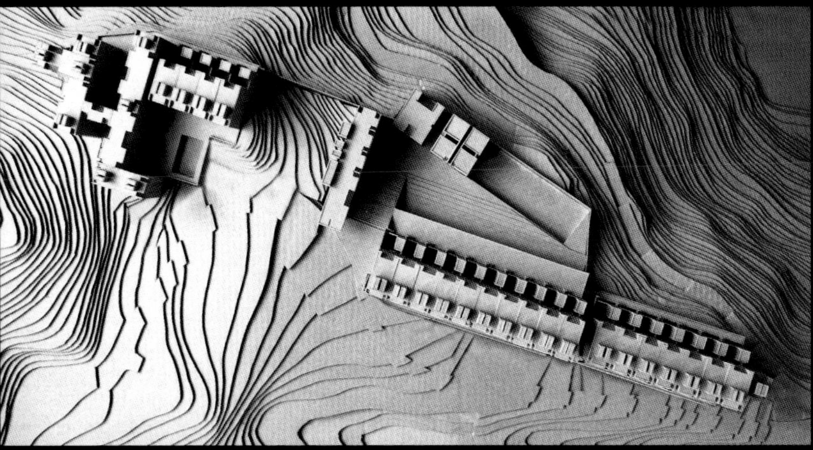

3

4

With its terraces, outbuildings, and towers, the overall design recalls the magic and mystery of building forms of eons ago.

In 2006, The Peak was built as a residential development by Sun Hung Kai Properties Ltd., with 22 townhouse-style apartments and accompanying recreational area. The completed project attests to the old adage, "Imitation is the sincerest form of flattery."

1 | Model view with the time shared units closest and the swimming pool and club facilities at the center
2 | Owner's apartment complex
3 | Site plan model view
4 | Road and entry side elevation

project name	Chicago Tribune Tower-Late Entries Competition
location	Chicago, Illinois
year of design	1979
client	Museum of Modern Art, Chicago Il.
lot size	100 x 100
project size	350,000 sq.ft.
architect	George Ranalli
associates	Robert Silman Structural Engineer
design team	Paula Beall

Chicago Tribune Tower Competition: Late Entries

1

In 1922, the Chicago Tribune newspaper hosted a competition to design its headquarters. From over 260 international entrants, the winner was the Gothic revival skyscraper by John Mead Howells and Raymond Hood that still stands on Michigan Avenue. The competition marked a turning point in American architecture, revealing the divergence between the stripped-down modernism soon to be ascendant and the winning design, which clearly sought to make a bridge to the history of architecture.

Nearly sixty years later, Chicago architects Stanley Tigerman and Stuart Cohen, with art dealer Rhona Hoffman, invited architects to submit contemporary "late entries" to the original contest. The designs were exhibited in a namesake exhibition and later published in a book. The Late Entries competition, like its original, occurred at a pivotal moment of American architecture and revealed similarly unresolved differences between many of the entrants.

The Ranalli Tribune Tower entry is a concept design that aims to fulfill the sponsor's mandate to enhance civic beauty. The multi-use high-rise tower includes superior commercial office space with spectacular skyline views, a central theater complex, and a lower-level village-like retail and production centre. The composition of elements brings a diverse mix of occupants to the building. As the building moves skyward its materiality moves upward in stepwise progression, from a broad masonry base that refers to the surrounding monumental architecture of the district, to a prow-like bay window elevation, to glass vaults. Midway, a deft 90-degree rotation reorients the building.

The submission attempts to give the employees the most celebrated spaces of the vertical building. Offices are distributed throughout the structure, bathed in light and natural ventilation. Glass volumes projecting through the masonry encourage occupants to experience living and working high above street level. The cube and sphere projecting through the front and back at the middle of the building are used for theatrical performances at lunchtime and early evening. The lower sections of the building

2

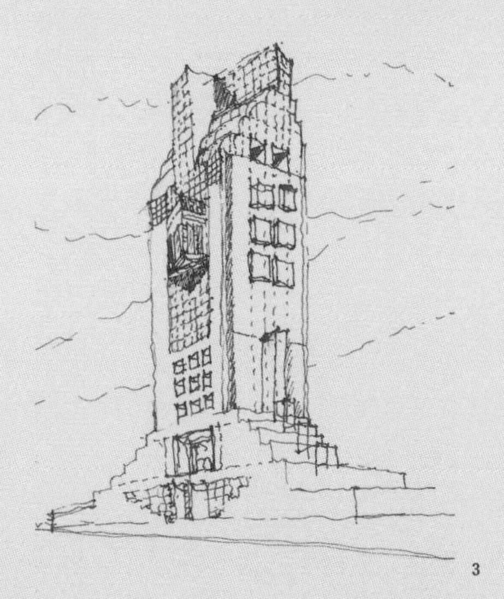

3

4

1 Sketch of the back side of the building attached to the printing room
2 Site showing the original Tribune Building
3 Sketch of the design
4 Final drawing submitted for the Late Entries Competition

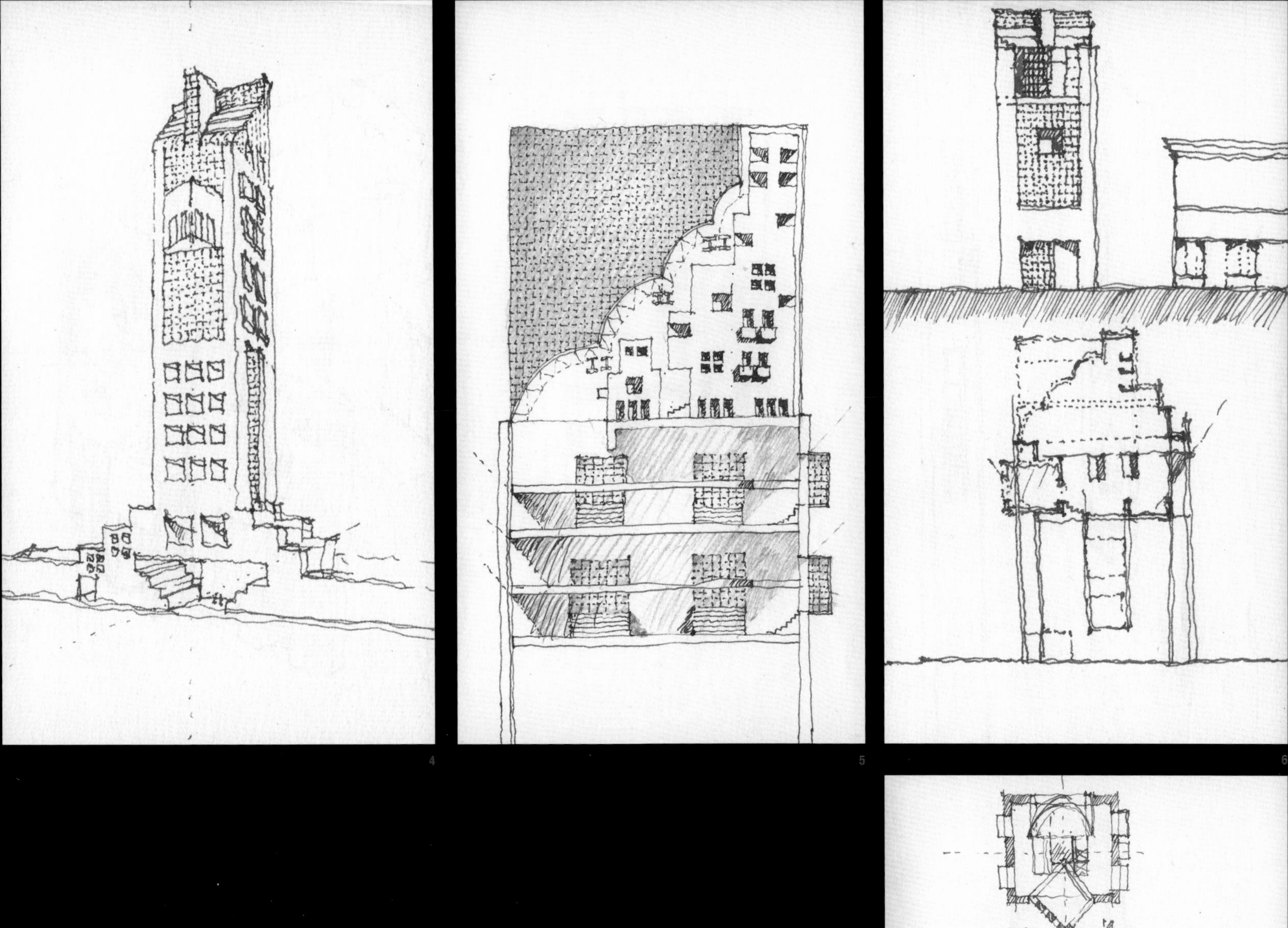

4

5

6

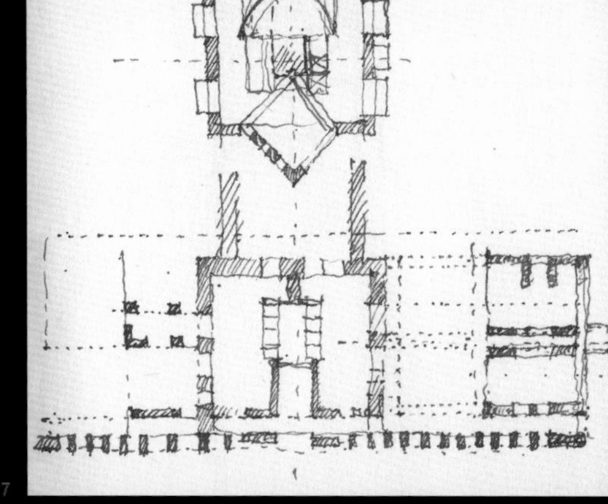

7

1 Sketch of the cascading glass at the top of the building
2 Study section through the building
3 Sketch from the rear of the structure
4 Early sketch of the main elevation
5 Section through the terraces and private offices at the top of the building
6 Study elevation and section
7 Plan studies

project name	First of August Shop
location	Lexington Avenue, New York City
year of design	1976
client	Ira Kent
lot size	25' x 100'
project size	3,750 sq.ft.
architect	George Ranalli
associates	Robert Silman Structural Engineer
design team	Michael Monsky
photographer	George Cserna

First of August Boutique

1

First of August Shop is a one of a kind environmental fit for a chic New York City district and stylish offerings. An early attempt at tailoring a retail shop towards a lifestyle theme, (think Urban Outfitters), this project with its fresh geometric façade and second floor renovation interacts with the old brownstone, existing first floor, and neighboring buildings. Calling upon recollections of small-pane shops with fronts that are more dense than transparent, inspired the dimension and scale of a new façade, and provides a necessary association with other city shops.

A forward extension of the shop into a zone of allowable space is accomplished by enveloping the outside wall of the old brownstone with a glass and steel lattice façade. By doing so, the interior of the building expands. Now there is room for an agreeable entryway for upper-floor residents, and suitable circulation between the first and second floors. At the top, notches in the new façade, made by inclining segments of the outer wall, define the depth of spatial connection between the old and new parts of the building.

Structurally, a tee-section frames the new façade. The tee is simply reversed so that the stem protrudes outward. The thickened tee form makes the steel dominant, rather than the glass.

3

2

1 Late afternoon view of the completed shop
2 Photo montage of the model superimposed onto the site photo
3 Detail view looking up at the shop and brownstone wall

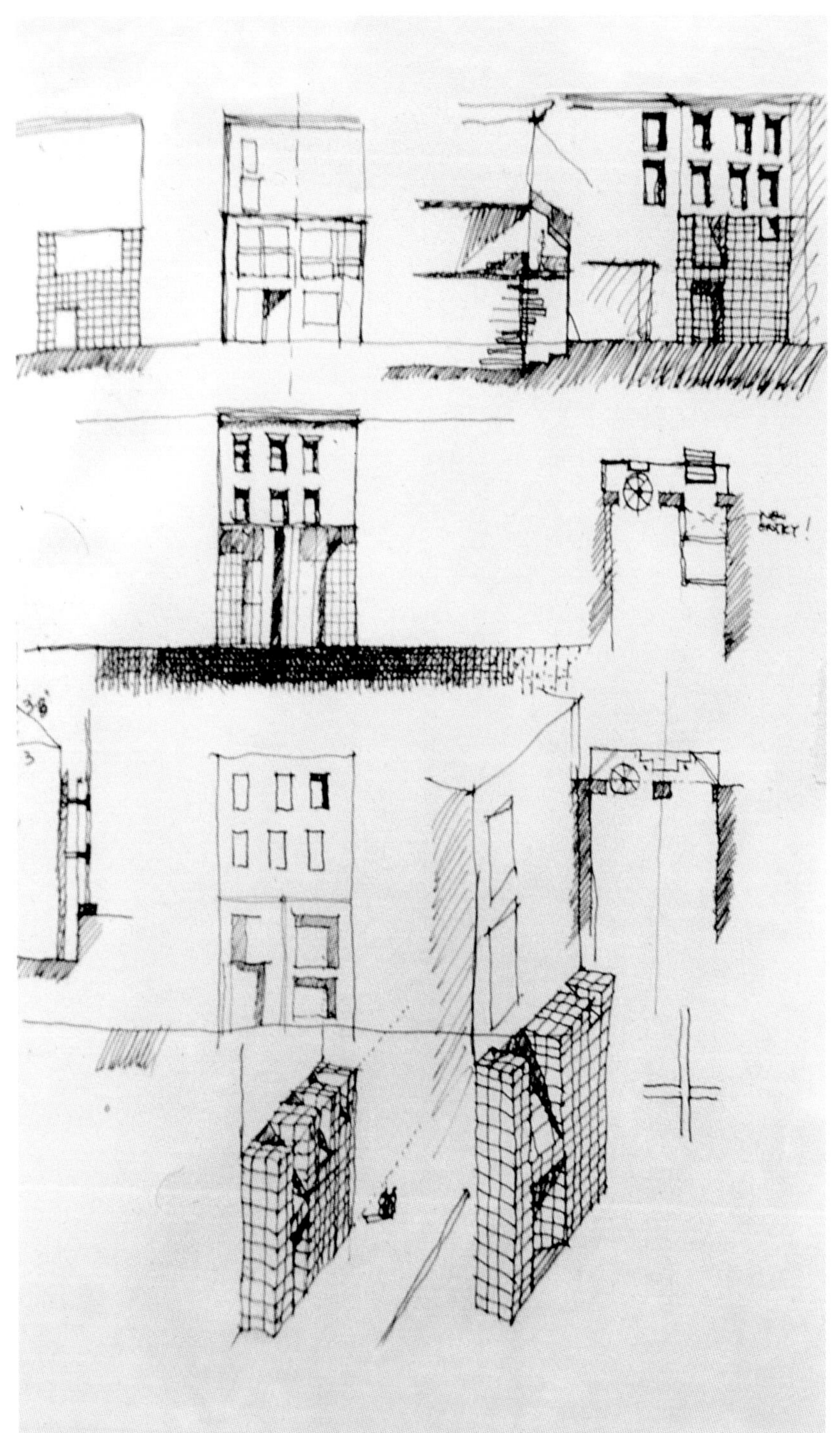

1

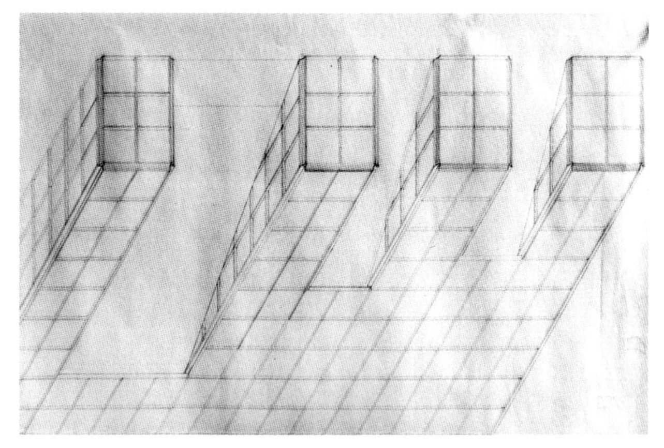

2

The new facade allows the shop owner maximum visibility for displaying a fine selection of women's apparel on a prime retail shopping avenue, and color and light are woven into the design that produces an evening transformation. As daylight fades away, a play of reflections is particularly visible to the passerby. Once the transition from daylight to darkness is complete, the façade reveals the brilliant undercoat of the colorfully hued interior design. When viewed from the nocturnal street, the building resonates with the cityscape.

The design for the shop interior included display areas, private dressing rooms, and a beauty care salon. The project maximized the use of mirrors in key locations to provide an expansive sense of space, color, and light. From entryway, through storefront, and on into the salon, movement is choreographed by a combination of artificial and natural light.

Neither perforated solid, not transparent container, the façade is a lattice patterned solid; with transformational properties of sturdiness and transparency responsive to varying conditions of natural and artificial light.

The old brownstone is wrapped and unwrapped through the use of old and new elements, which share an awareness of each other. Three walls- a new façade, an old brownstone front, and an interior—capture maximum exposure to the street, reorganize circulation throughout the building, and reconfigure the second floor, synchronously, for a distinctively urban architecture.

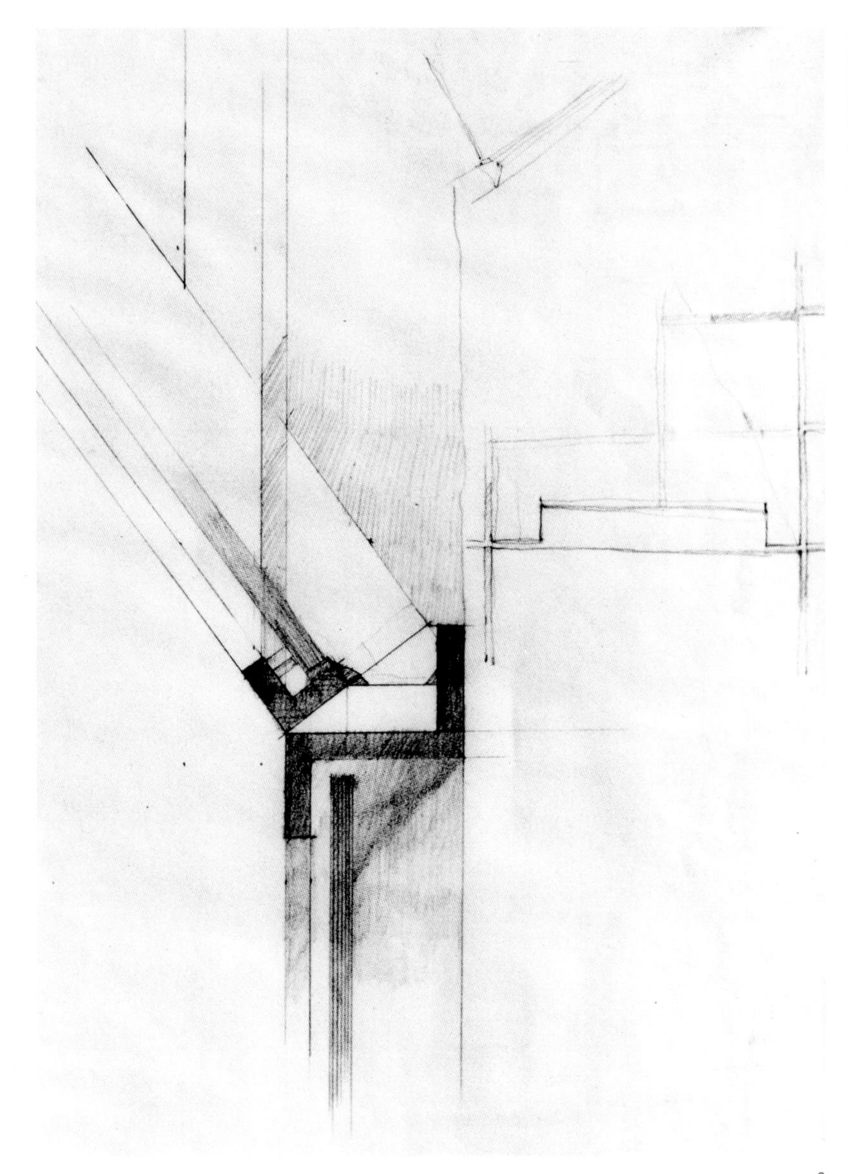

3

4

5

6

7

8

1 Early pen and ink studies of the design
2 Development drawing of the steel towers
3 Steel detail study drawing
4 Construction photo prior to the glazing
5 Gridded storefront shop fabrication
6 Shop fabrication of the upper section with the inclined segments
7 Steel shop fabrication of the inclined sections
8 Steel grid

1

2

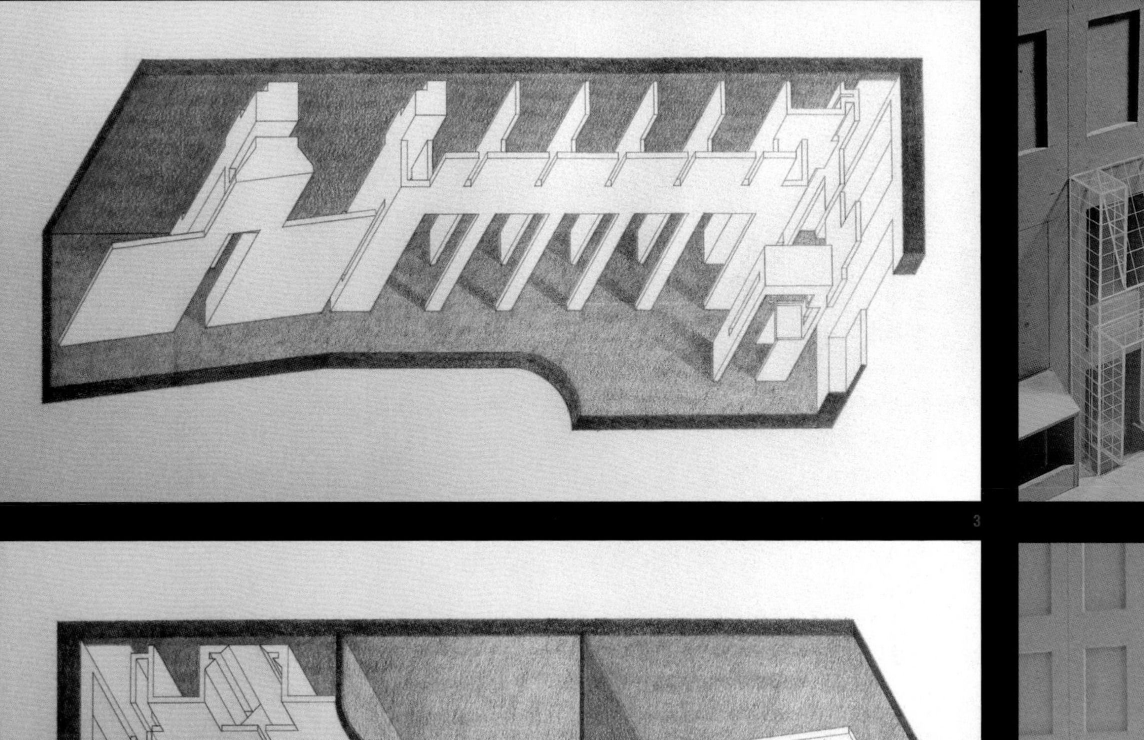

3

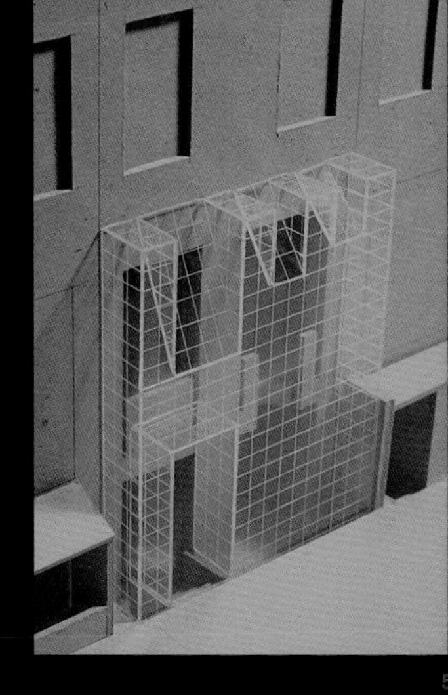

5

4

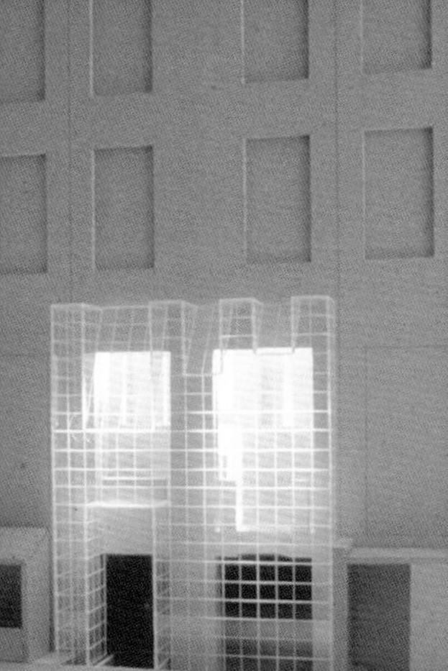

6

1 | View at the top of the spiral stairs on the second floor
2 | Interior of the second floor looking toward the shop front
3 | Floor plan of the second floor
4 | View at the rear of the shop with the more private beauty care functions on either side looking toward the shop façade

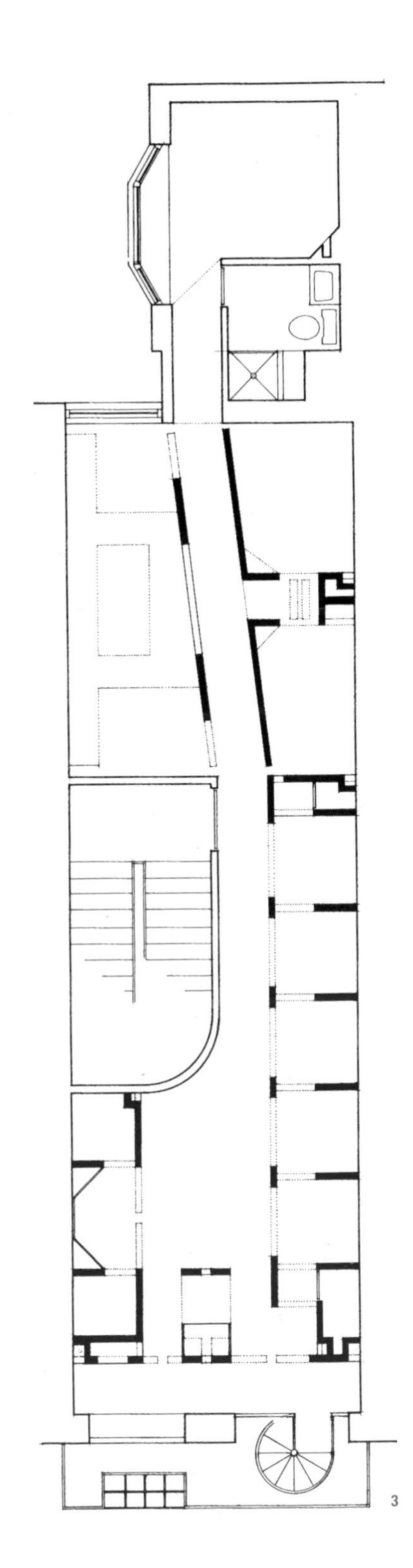

3

4

1

2

1 | Detail view up over the beauty care rooms with hidden lighting
2 | Upper section of the dressing room enclosure with strip light coves and mirrors

1

2

3

4

5

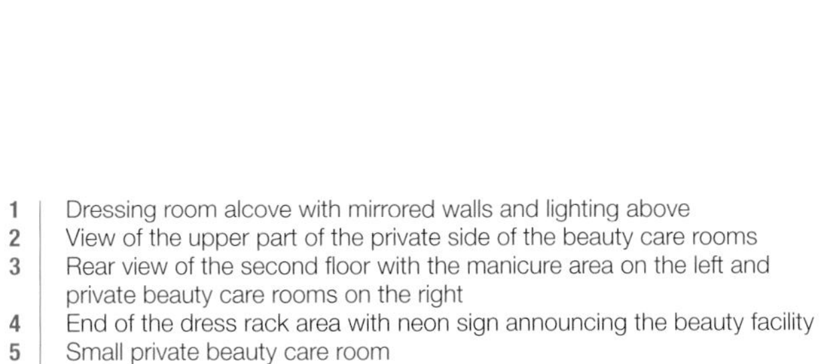

1 Dressing room alcove with mirrored walls and lighting above
2 View of the upper part of the private side of the beauty care rooms
3 Rear view of the second floor with the manicure area on the left and private beauty care rooms on the right
4 End of the dress rack area with neon sign announcing the beauty facility
5 Small private beauty care room

INSTITUTIONAL

project name	Chelsea Day School
location	Fifth Avenue, New York City
year of design	2006
client	Chelsea Day School
lot size	50' x 100'
project size	12,500 sq.ft
architect	George Ranalli
associates	Robert Silman Structural Engineer, Laszlo Bodak Mechanical Engineers
design team	Hayden Marrero, Hollace Metzger, Hyungjin Lim, Sean Ellis, Clement Sjauw
photographer	George Ranalli

Chelsea Day School

1

Over its more than three-decade history, Chelsea Day School is a premier nursery school serving the residents of the Chelsea section of Manhattan. Starting in a small row-house loft building, the original school comprised a small, intimate, and interwoven set of classrooms and play spaces that developed over time, constantly added to and encrusted with activities and local history. Children's artwork filled the walls and the entire environment was joyous. Eventually the school moved to a new space, but remained there only a few years. In 2008, economic forces compelled an unwelcome relocation to a five-story commercial building on hectic Fifth Avenue.

The program called for the renovation of 12,000 square feet of second- and third-floor space for 10 classrooms, a flexible open room, administrative offices, a staff room, and a rooftop playground. Environmentally responsive design strategies include the use of energy-efficient construction methods and green features such as super-insulation; paints, flooring, and adhesives lacking volatile organic compounds; formaldehyde-free millwork; optimal natural sunlight; and a forced-air circulation system using less than half the energy of a typical HVAC system. Perhaps, most importantly, the architectural design reflects recognition of early childhood as a crucial developmental period, and the educational vision offering children a steady place for exploration and friendship. The spaces, rooms, and play areas provide a full range of interests to occupy and stimulate the development of the imagination of children.

The two floors of an industrial building, approximately 12,000 square feet of space, were fitted out to accommodate an array of classrooms, sitting areas, and large public rooms for group events. From the public street, after traversing an anonymous alleyway, children and adults reach the second-story entrance either by exterior staircase or private elevator. The design shapes a casual foyer with a cavernous storage room for prams, to one side, and a welcoming reception desk on the other. Beyond, the school opens up into piazza-like space where natural light reflects from a palate of honey yellow, eggshell, and cork.

2

3

1 View of the 2nd floor classroom hallway with the stair bulkhead on the right side
2 Existing red brick building with the school occupying the second and third floors of the building
3 Classroom view at the corner of the building
4 Hallway wall of the classroom with window views into the classrooms

4

1

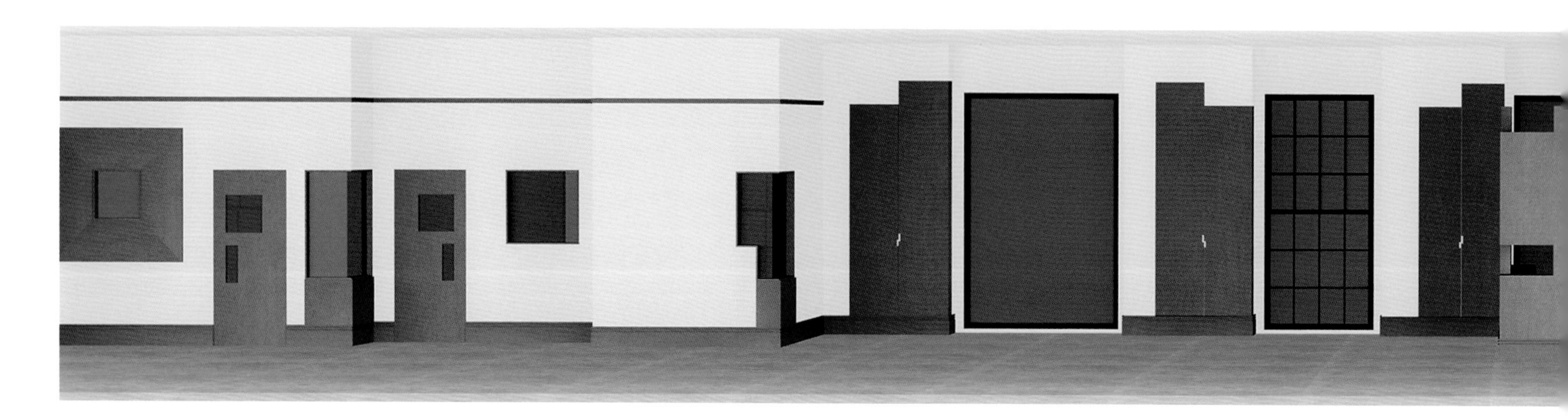

This great, sunny room can function as an auditorium, school library, or rainy-day gymnasium. A broad interior staircase, at the center, connects the second floor to the third, and doubles as stadium-style seating, podium, and choir loft.

The third floor contains classrooms, which are designed in conjunction with a meandering hallway to accommodate the circulation of teachers and children, and to provide spaces for casual conversations amongst staff, parents, and students. The shape of the hall provides a series of seating nooks where teachers or parents have intimate chats with a child, or children begin a new friendship.

A faculty room with enough space for a full kitchen and dining table facilitates meetings in the form of round-table discussions. Storage closets and cabinetry, hidden behind operable honey-grain wood panels and beneath hinge-topped furniture, harbor all manner of miscellanies while protecting the school from the perils of urban clutter.

Passageways meander toward atelier-style classroom spaces, intermediate spaces offer cozy seating and views into nursery rooms, each of which is equipped with a kitchen and pantry, ample space, and large windows with views of neighboring buildings that glint in sunlight one moment and disappear behind thick fog the next. Throughout, the architecture speaks to utility, durability, and youthful sensibilities.

2

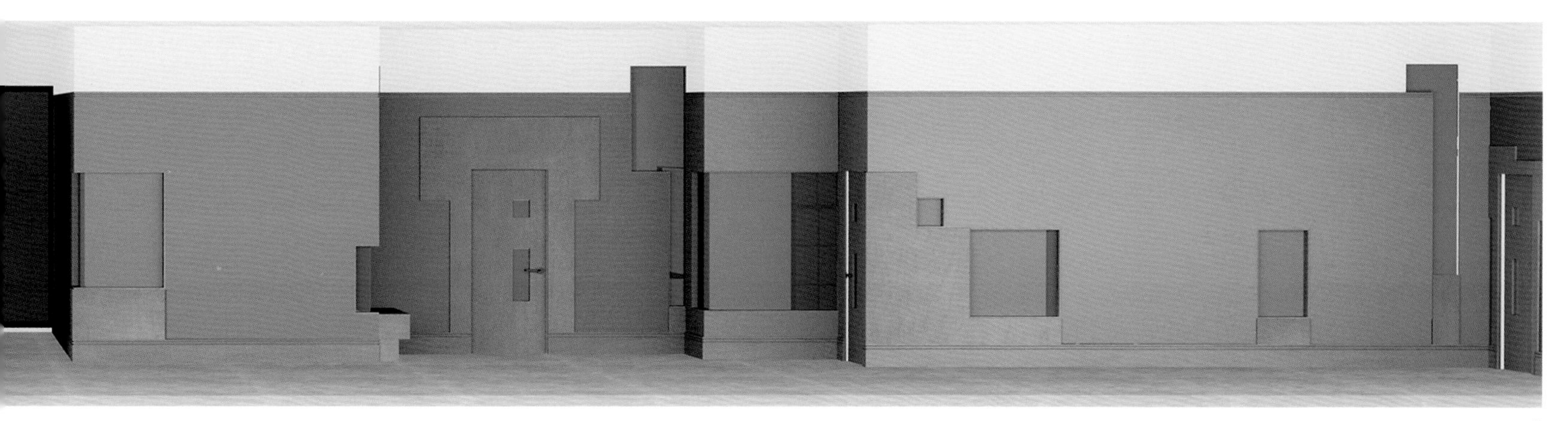

3

1 | Computer model view of a small assembly area for gathering
2 | Computer view of one of the classroom entries
3 | Section through the entire lower floor of the school

1

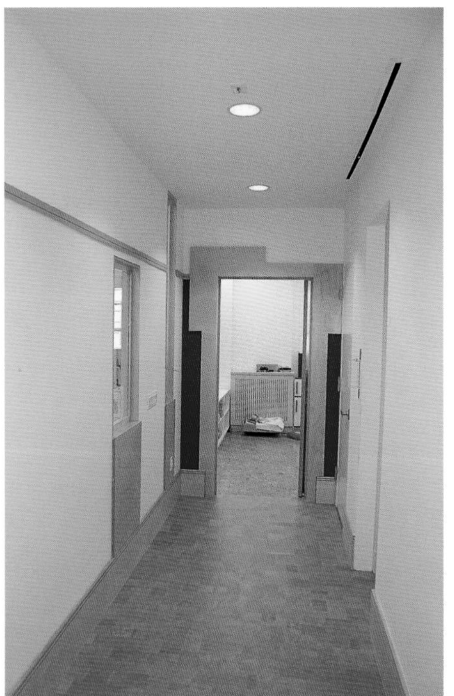

2

1 Small window detail
2 Lower floor hallway
3 Roof plan
4 Main entry level plan
5 Second floor of the school plan
6 Main floor wall
7 Mobile library elements

6

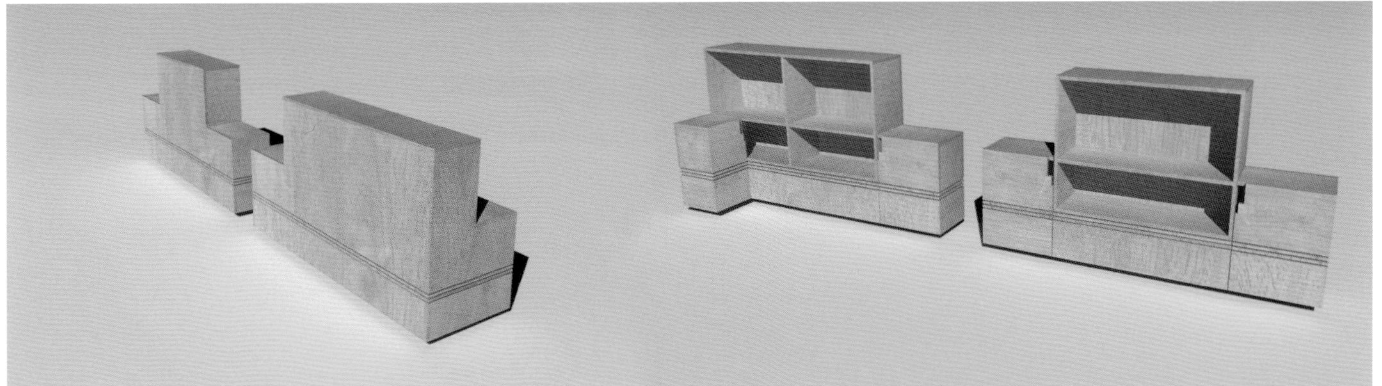

7

1

2

1 | Upper floor hallway with seating outside the classroom
2 | Window detail on the upper floor
3 | Hallway looking west with paired windows into the classrooms
4 | Stair bulkhead
5 | Computer models of the woodwork surrounding doors and classroom windows

3

4

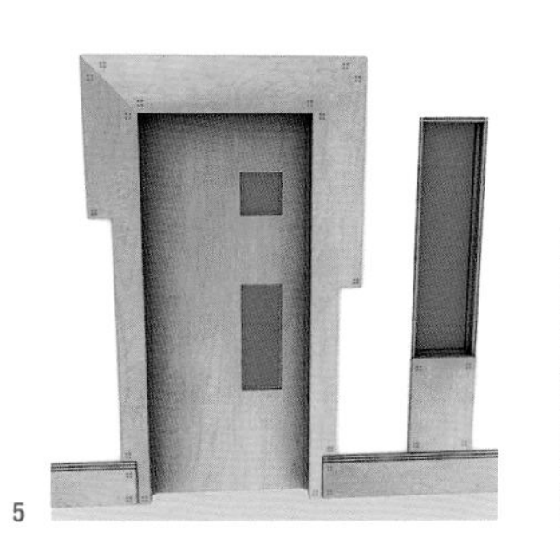
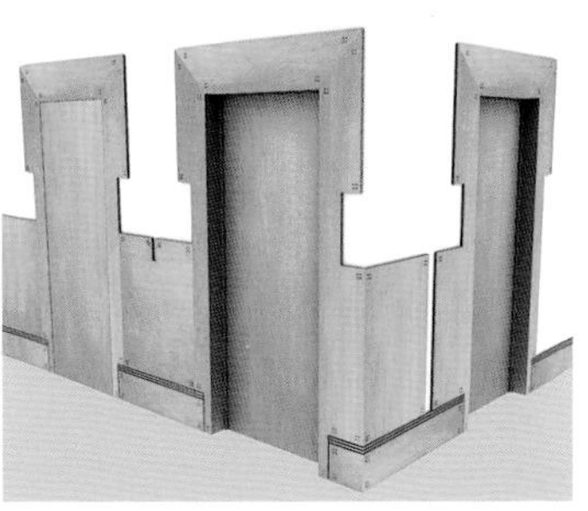
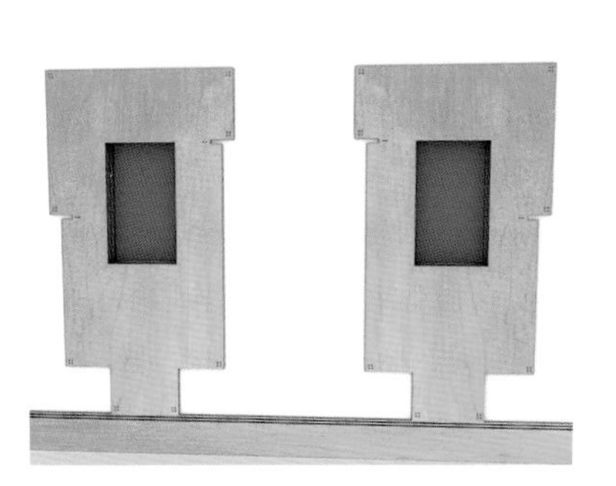

5

1

2

3

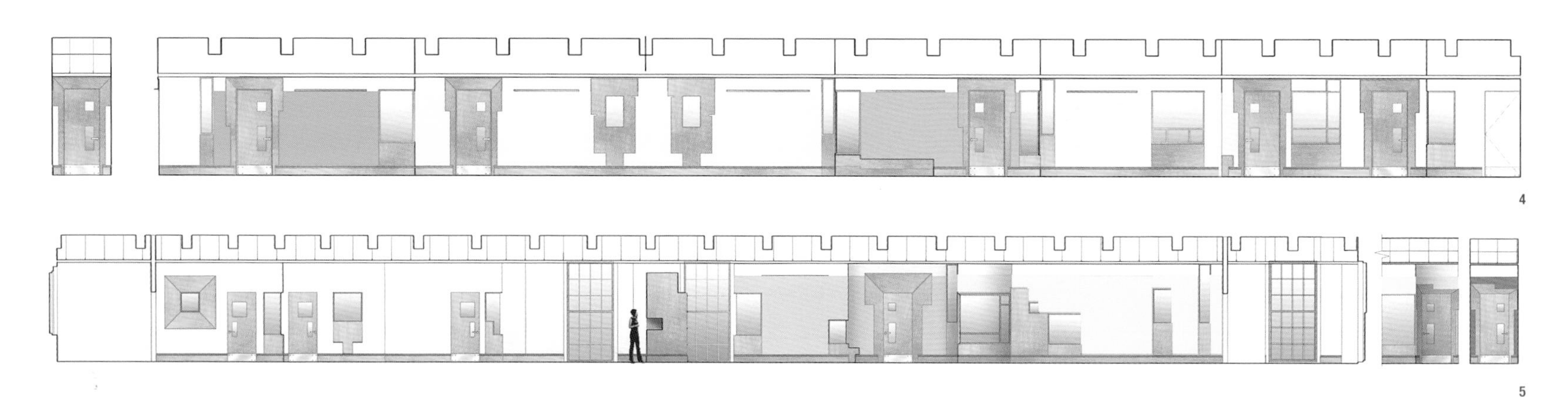

4

5

1 Main floor corner window into a classroom
2 Hallway off the main assembly room leading to classrooms
3 Vertical window into the classroom from the main floor hall
4 Elevation of the upper floor hall with the color study
5 Elevation of the lower floor hall with the color study
6 Performance stage and internal stair leading up to the second floor
7 Computer illustration of the main performance space
8 View of the main performance space looking west

6

7

8

1

1 View down the stair from the second floor of the school
2 Openings in the stairway wall from the hallway

project name	Wellington Arts Complex
location	Wellington, Florida
year of design	2004-2005
client	Wellington Cultural Trust
lot size	13 acres
project size	167,000 sq. ft.
architect	George Ranalli
associates	Robert Silman Structural Engineer
design team	Kimberlae Saul, Eduardo Benamor Duarte, Yuel Lee

Wellington Arts Complex

The Wellington Cultural Trust commissioned a master plan for an arts complex in Wellington, Florida. The complex is located on 10 acres of mature trees and rolling fields that slope toward a 99-acre lake, on one side and, woodland hiking trails on the other.

The plan embraces a harbor, lagoon, and scenic recreation amid grand stretches of green space to offer a community facility for people of all ages, social, and cultural backgrounds actively engaged with the arts. There are three theaters, two museum/gallery buildings, a parking structure, and outdoor dining and recreational facilities.

The plan explores the relationship between the buildings in the arts complex and the Florida landscape, inviting the community to discover a realm of formal geometry, simplicity, and beauty. Ground-level arts pavilion buildings, restaurants, shops, and other amenities are arranged amid a network of copper-shaded footpaths. Courtyards accommodate public gatherings before and after performances, while outdoor courts are graced by sculpture. Sweeping terraces provide generous, leisurely areas for promenades and for experiencing the lakefront. The geometric simplicity of footpaths and landing points compose lines between buildings and frame open space.

The museum/gallery buildings offer space enough for resident artists, education programs, and innovative contemporary art exhibits of all mediums. The theaters, however, are the main focus of the design: a black-box theater, first-class auditorium seating one thousand, and outdoor theater for live music events occupy primary locations in the site plan and are designed with strong forms, both to reinforce their essential positions in the plan and to provide strong interiors for program events.

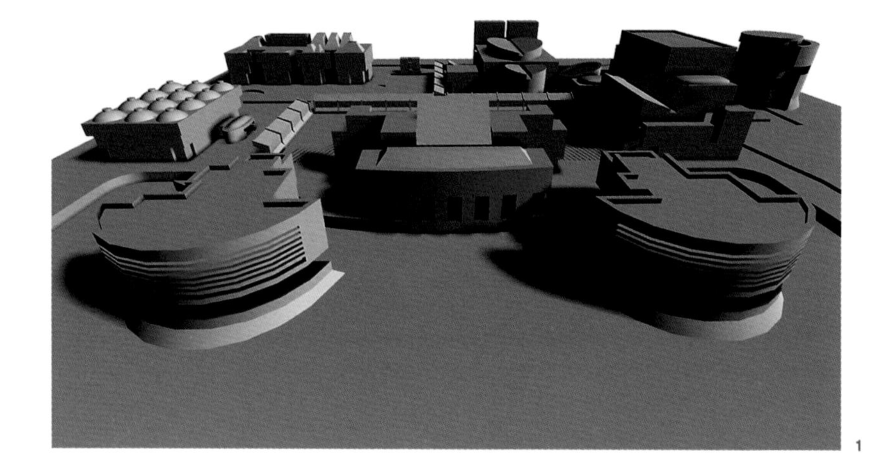

1

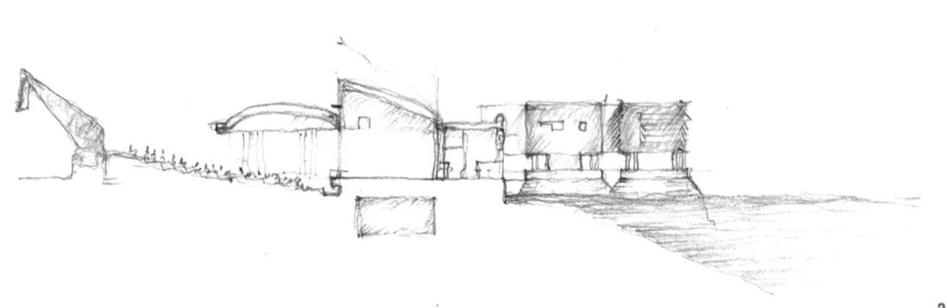

2

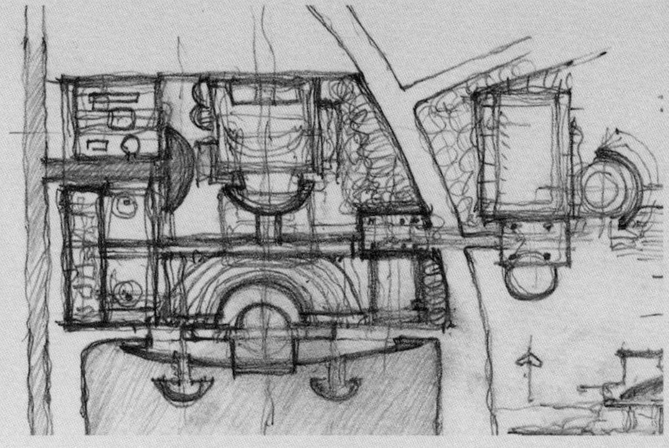

3

4

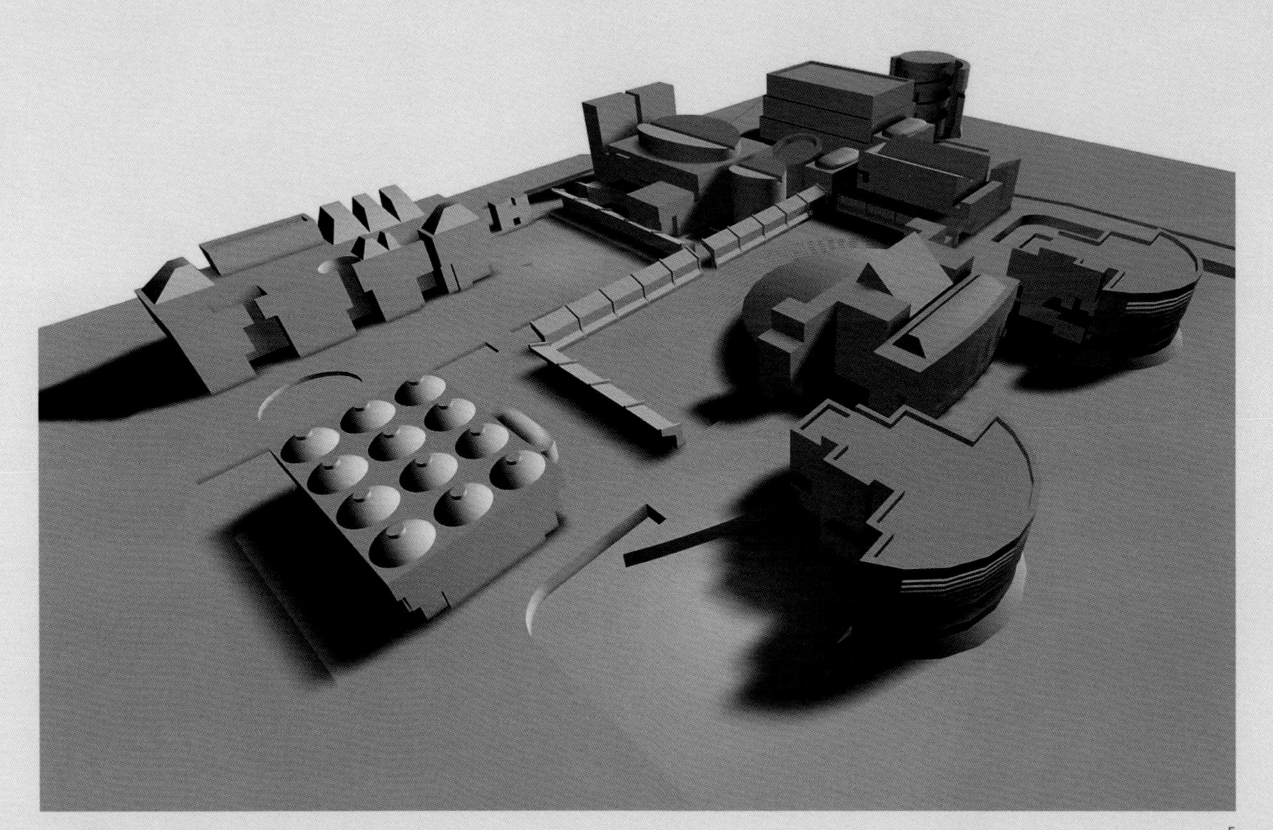

5

1 | Model from above taken over the lake
2 | Sketch section through the outdoor theater looking at the copper cafés
3 | View of the site and the lake
4 | Early sketch site plan
5 | Model view of the arts complex

1

2

3

The programmatic mandate to link the project to the lake is of paramount importance. An enchanting water strategy therefore captures and filters lake water through inland waterways, filling reflecting pools and fountains before returning the water to the lake. Two cafés, edged by stone balustrades, sit in the lake beneath large copper sunshades, producing a magical lakeside-dining locale. Sunlight filters through veils of translucent, adjustable copper, creating a delicately resilient atmosphere capturing magnificent lakeside views. The cafés function as part of the arts complex and as a separate commercial entity.

Climate-sensitive strategies allow passive cooling and reduction of the carbon footprint while new lighting technologies provide an array of colors and intensities. The water system, both active and standing, has a natural cooling effect on the overall landscape design. The durable, low-maintenance copper footpath shades provide shelter from glare and occasional rain while remaining open to seasonal variations of wind, rustling leaves, and the scent of blossoms.

5

6

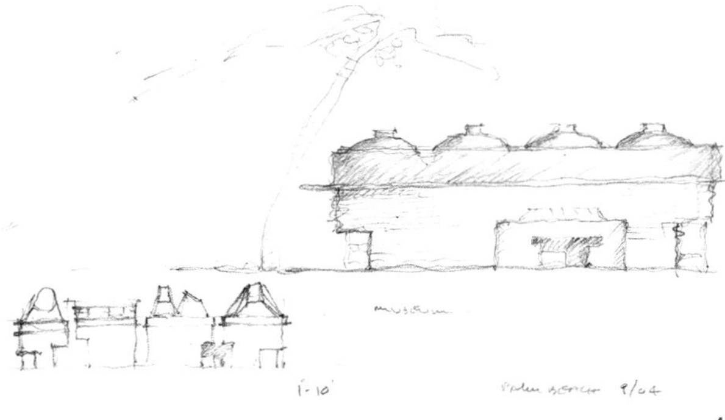

4

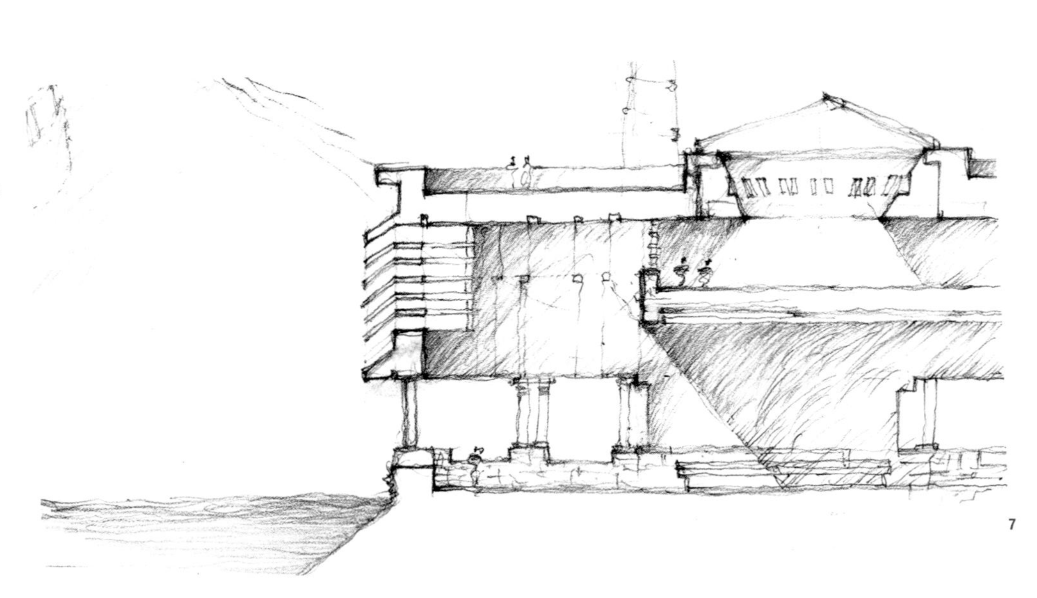

7

1 Drawing of the arts complex from above
2 Sketch of the copper sun shades
3 Sketch of the outdoor theater
4 Study drawing of the museum
5 Site section through the copper café
6 Cross section looking at the outdoor theater
7 Section study of the copper cafe in the lake with copper air louvers and upper restaurant

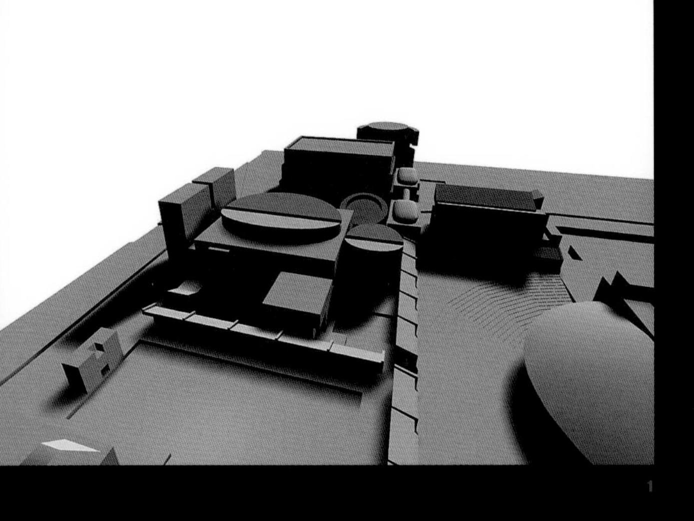

1

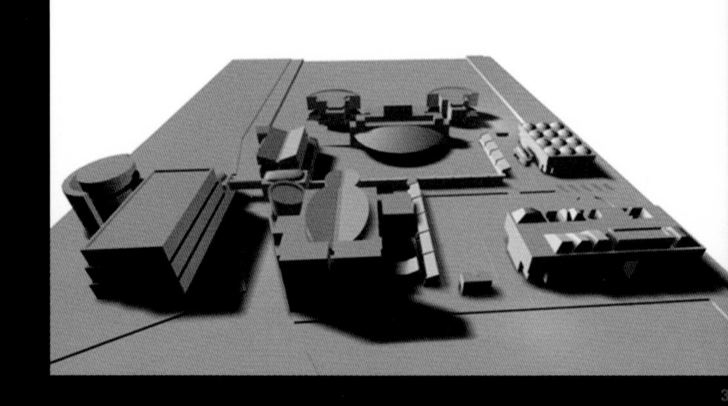

3

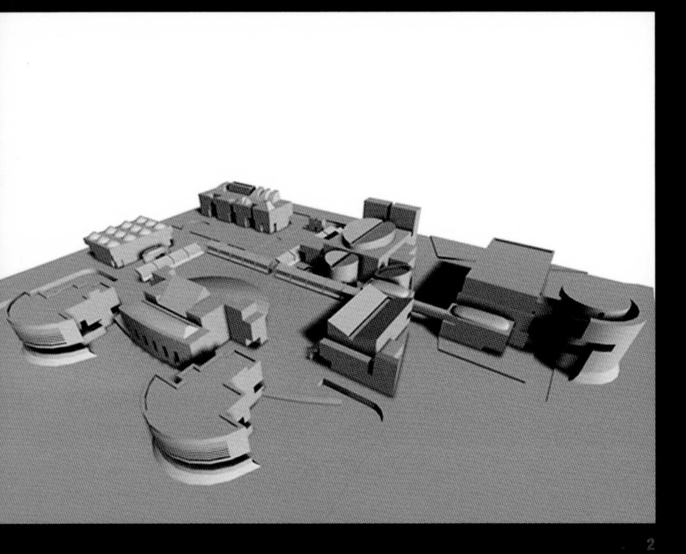

2

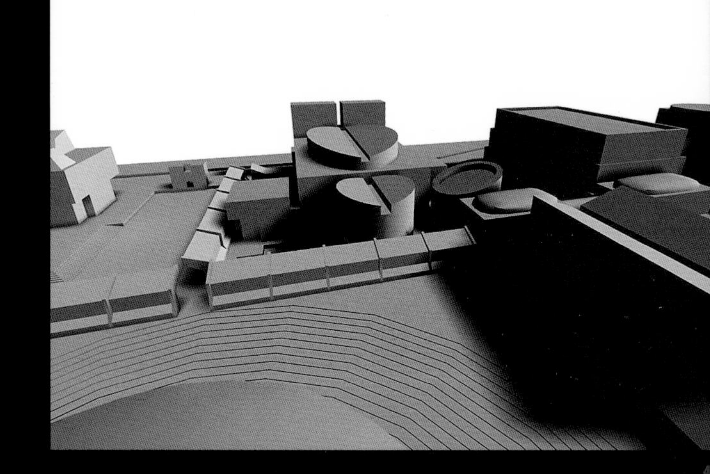

4

1 | Computer model view of the indoor theater
2 | View from above with the cafés sitting in the lake
3 | View from above looking toward the lake
4 | View of the main indoor theater from the roof of the outdoor theater

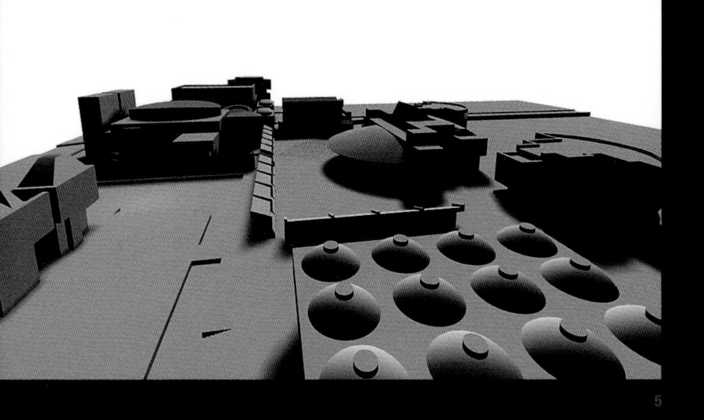

5

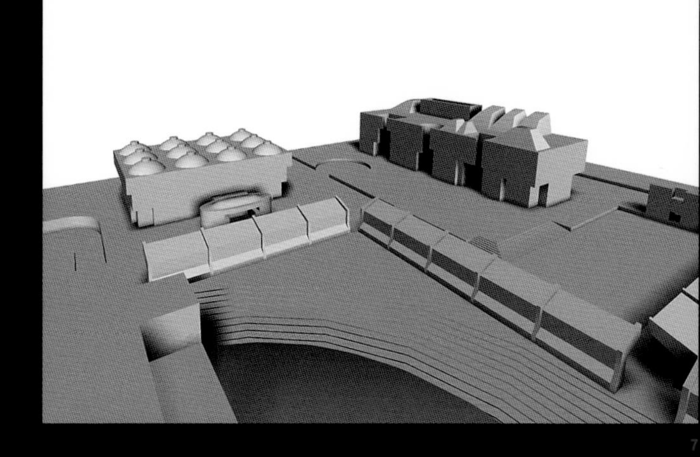

7

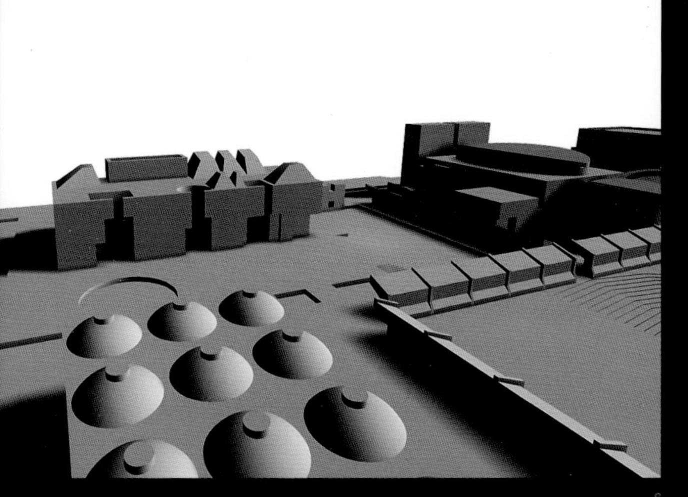

6

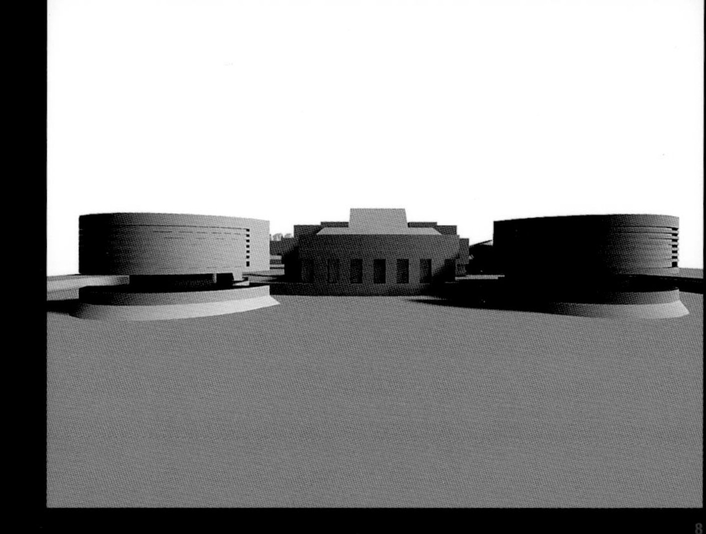

8

5 Museum roof in the foreground
6 Museum in the foreground and small museum beyond
7 View of the two museums
8 View from the lake of the two copper cafés

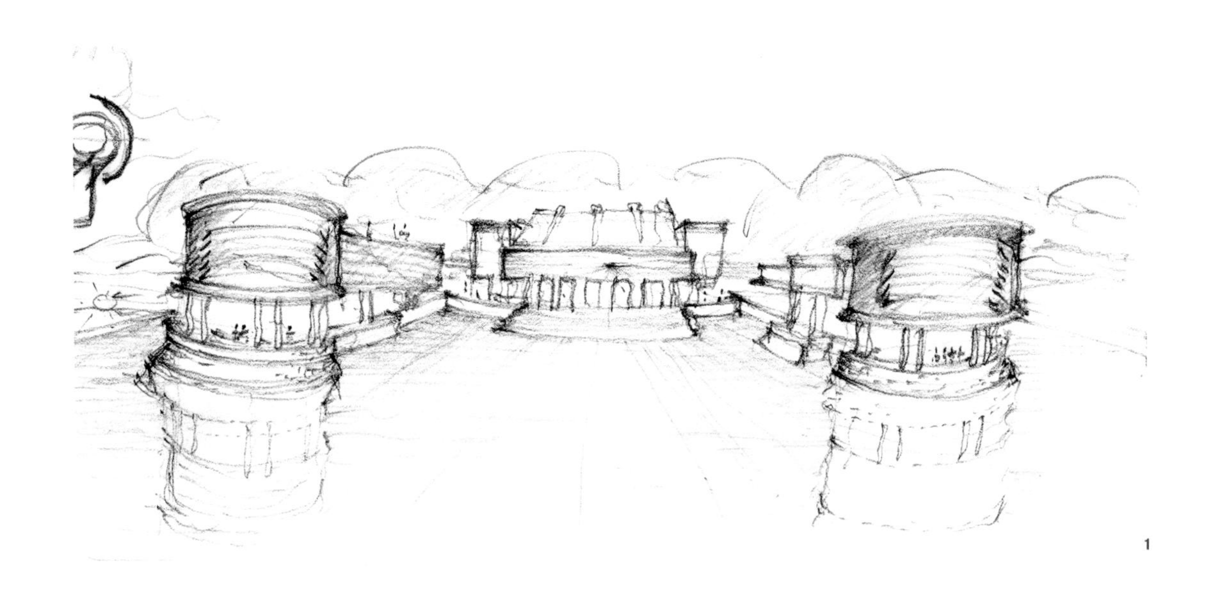

1

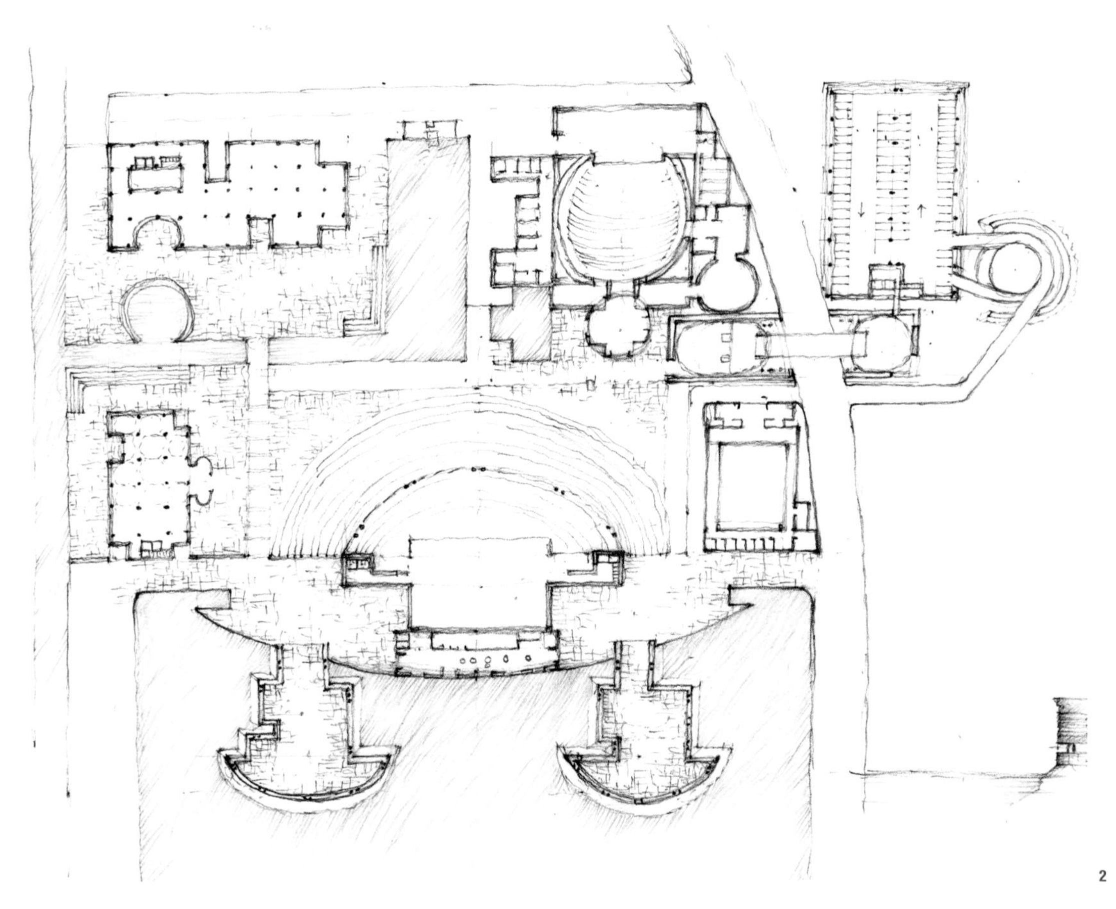

2

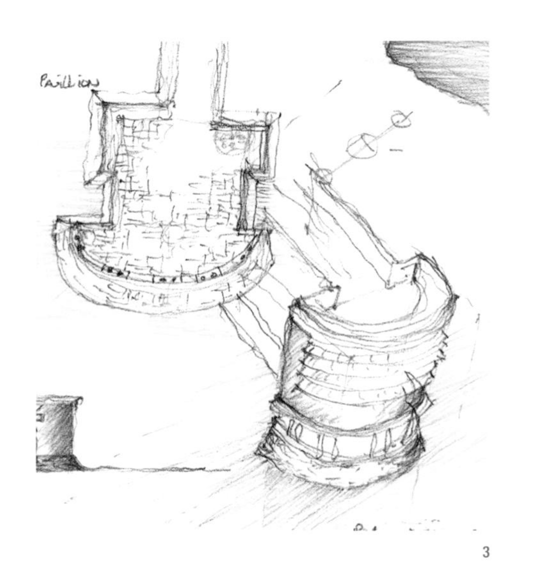

3

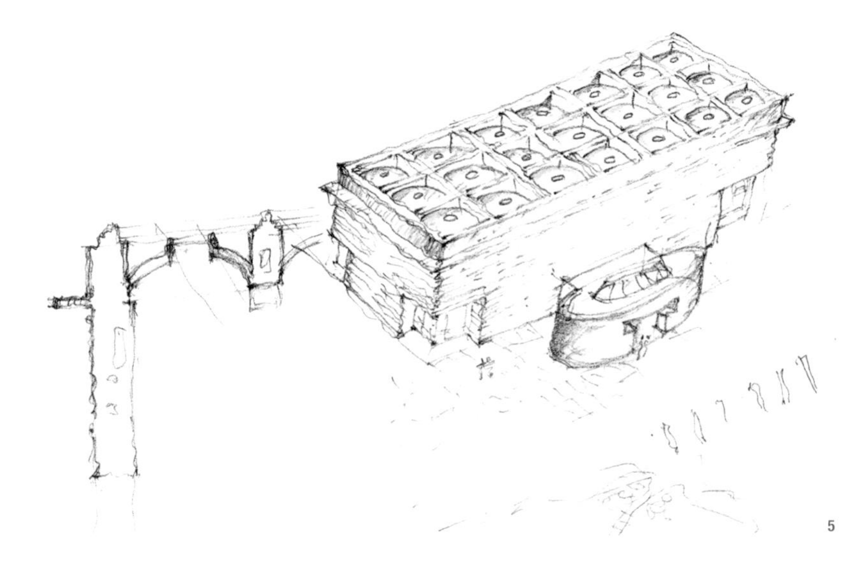

5

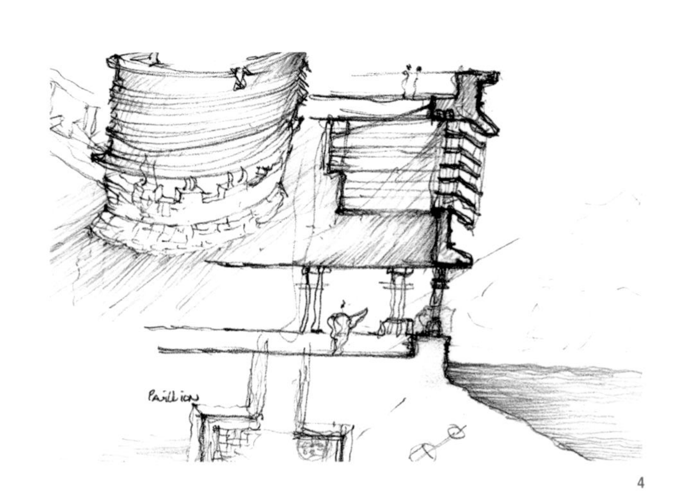

4

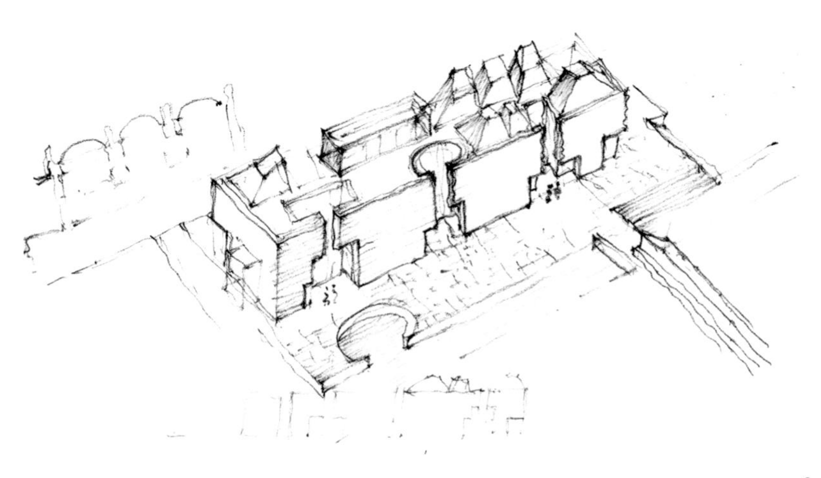

6

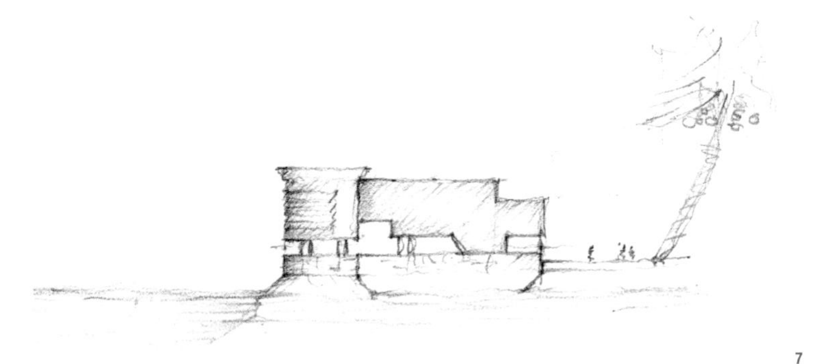

7

1 Sketch from the lake of the copper cafés and the back of the outdoor theater
2 Site plan of the arts complex
3 Copper café plan and massing view
4 Sketch and section of the copper café
5 Study for the large sculpture gallery
6 Sketch of the small museum
7 Site section of the copper cafés sitting in the lake

project name	Master Plan City College of New York
location	New York City
year of design	2005
client	City University of New York
lot size	35 acres
project size	450,000 sq.ft.
architect	George Ranalli
associates	Aaman Whitney Consulting Engineers, Langan Engineering
design team	Kimberlae Saul, Eduardo Benamor Duarte, Nadia Ostrovsky

Master Plan for the City College of New York

This Master Plan for the entire 36.5 acre City College of New York campus located at 135th Street and Convent Avenue, commissioned by City University, was based upon an evaluation of the existing campus in relation to the Strategic Plan. The goal is a building program plan for the next 20 years.

The Master Plan is divided into three phases of work, namely the Existing Conditions Assessment, the Programming Phase, and the New Proposal Phase. Included is the addition of new elements to the college, such as a Student Center, new Science Center, dormitories, a new high school, and other program pieces that will come out of a planning process, which includes faculty, administration, and students.

The site is divided into a north campus, which contains the original historic, gothic, collegiate buildings by George B. Post, and a south campus that sits atop St. Nicholas Terrace overlooking the east side of upper Manhattan and the midtown skyline. The south campus, with its large, rolling topography, largely empty of buildings, is an ideal landscape on which to situate program elements. New buildings are spatially organized for the intended program uses and to produce powerful images viewed from a distance. The scheme illustrates a large dormitory complex of undergraduate housing, and a graduate residential tower, with a highly differentiated set of rooms and suites.

1

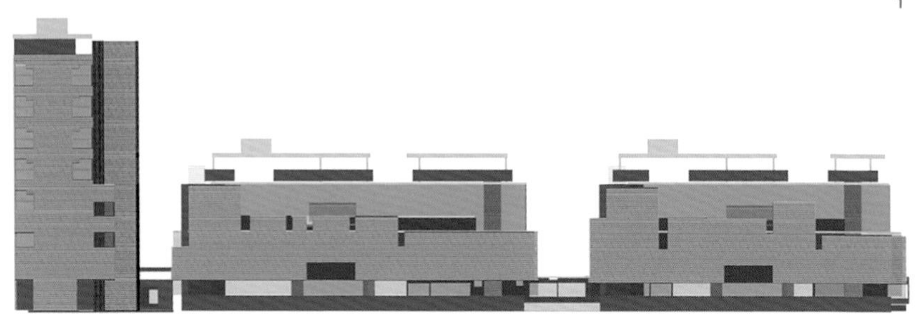

2

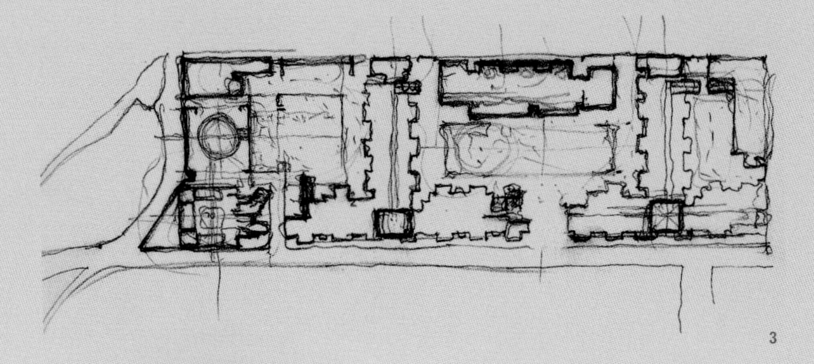

3

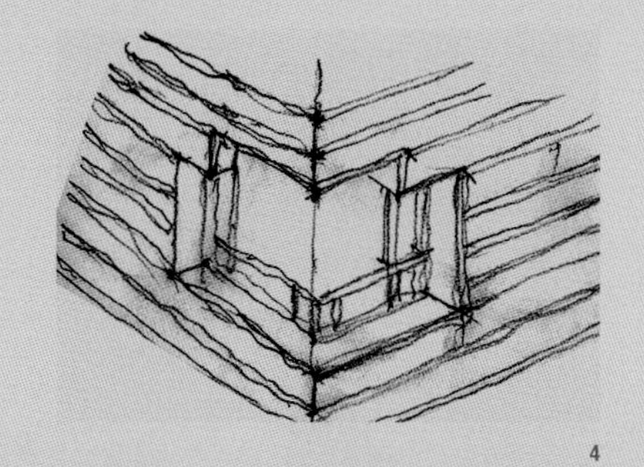

4

5

6

1 | Site plan of the south campus
2 | Elevation of the dormitory study
3 | Sketch plan of the dormitory study on the east side of the south campus
4 | Window detail on the graduate housing tower
5 | View of the proposed dormitory for the south campus featuring a graduate housing tower in the foreground and undergraduate courtyard housing beyond
6 | Aerial view of the campus in West Harlem

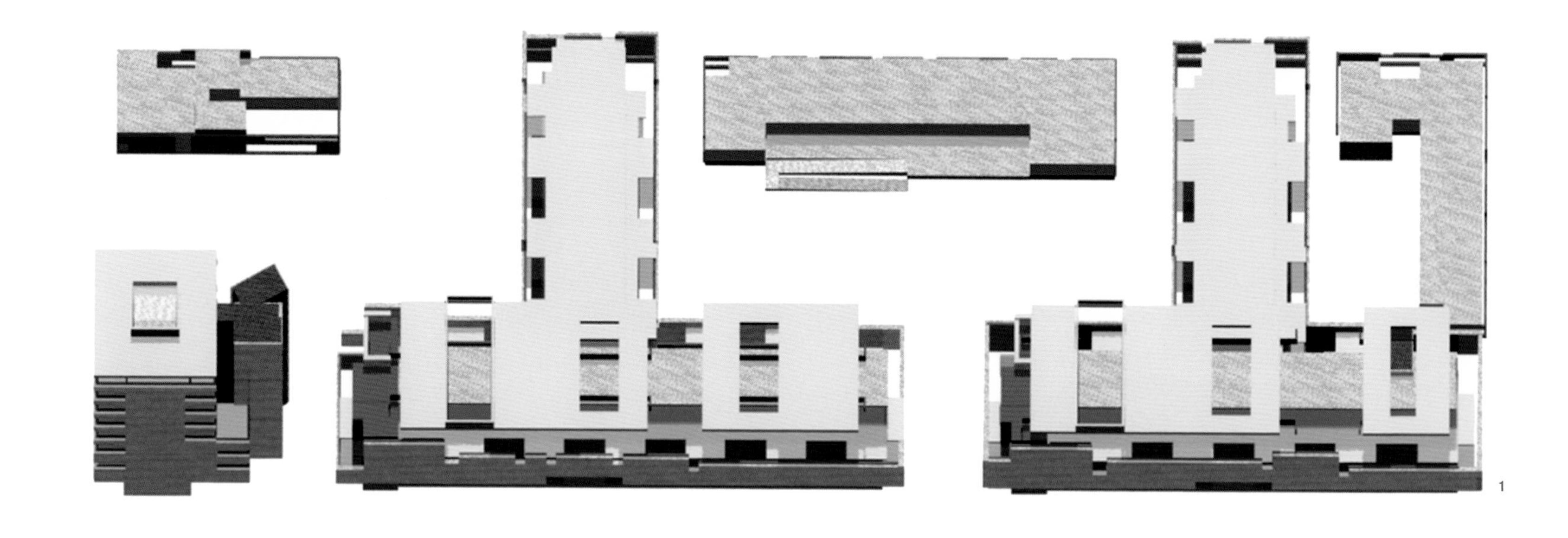

1

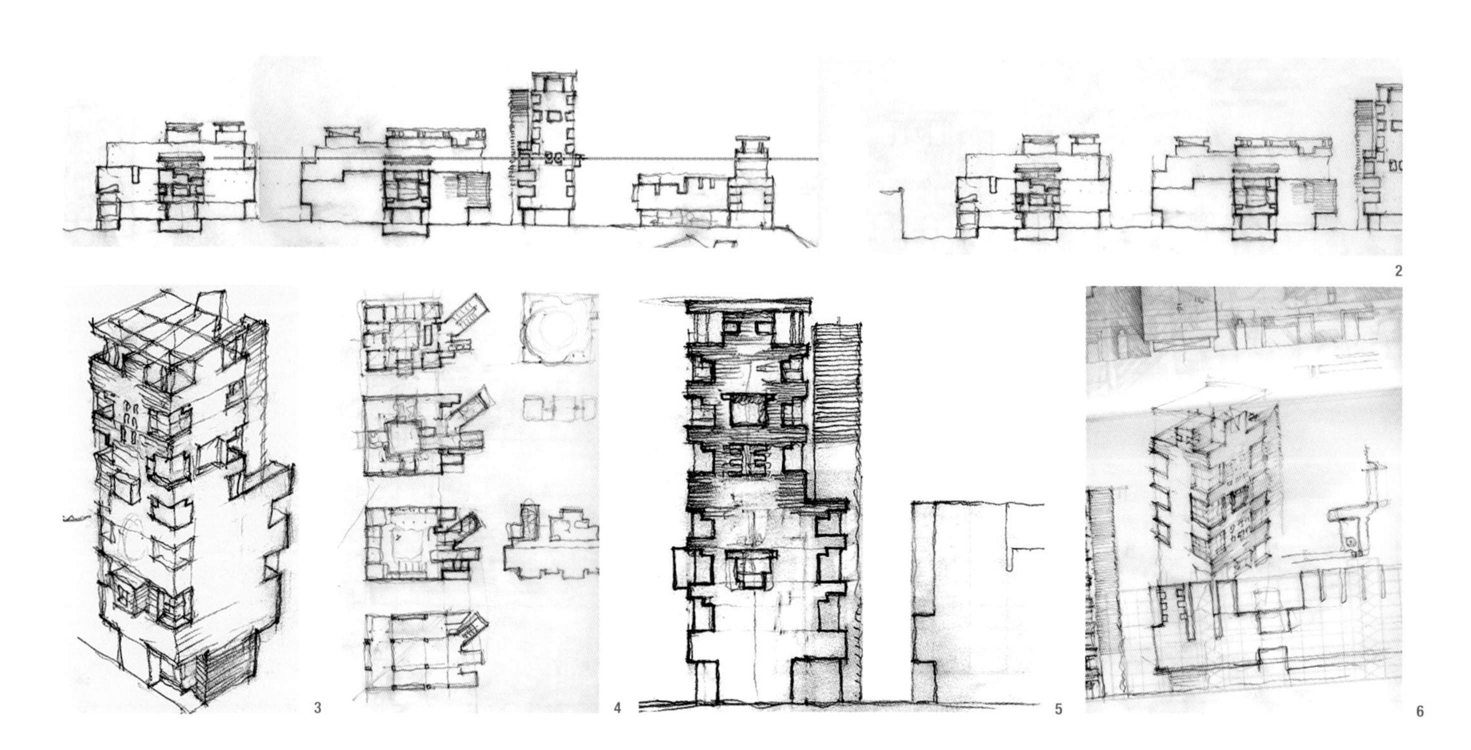

2

3

4

5

6

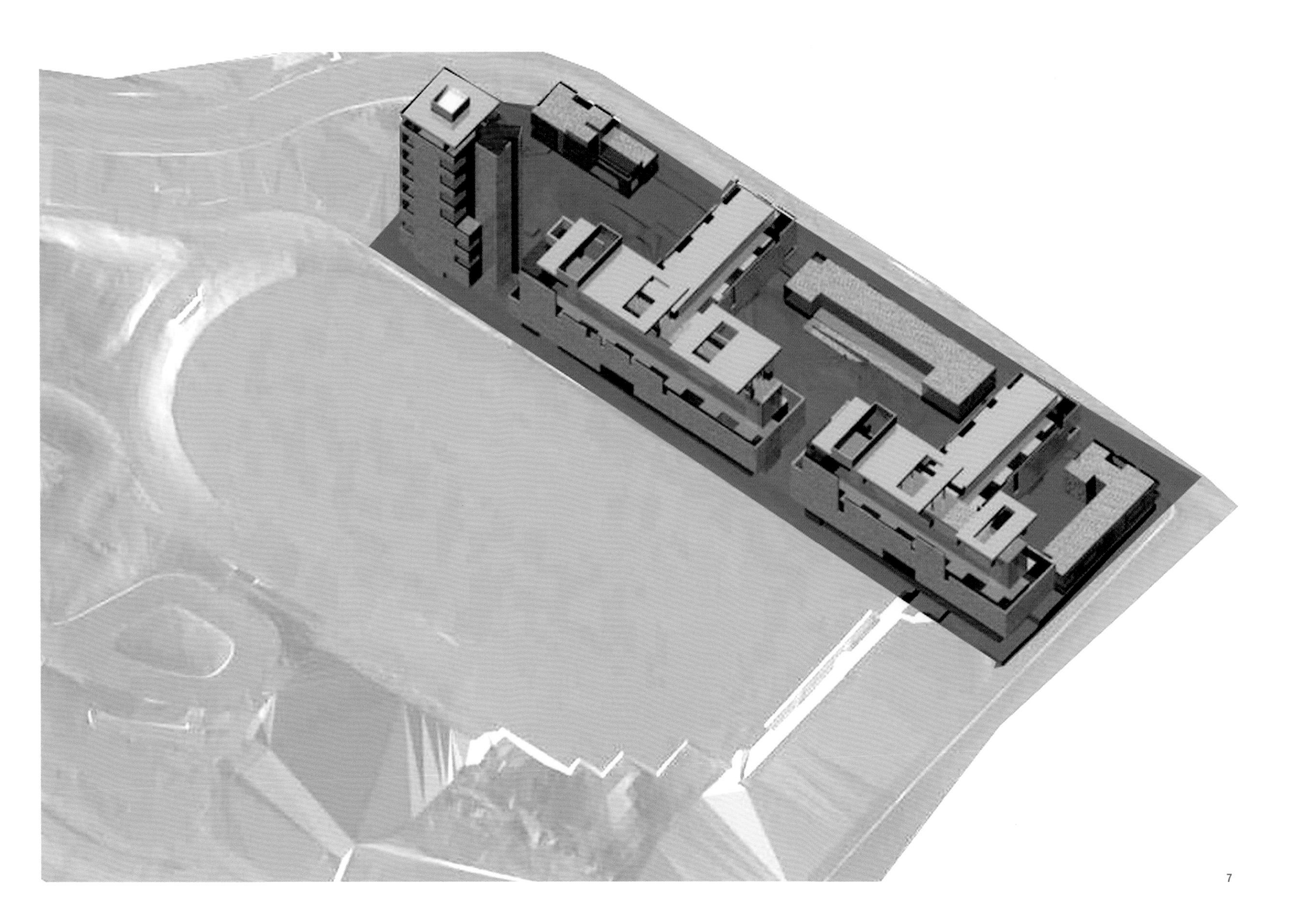

7

1 Computer model of the tower and the courtyard blocks
2 Sketch sections and elevations of the lower buildings
3 Tower sketch
4 Plans of the graduate tower suites
5 Sketch of the graduate tower
6 Studies of the tower
7 Computer model sketch of the dormitory on the south campus
8 Computer model of the dormitory seen from the playing fields on the south campus (following spread)

8

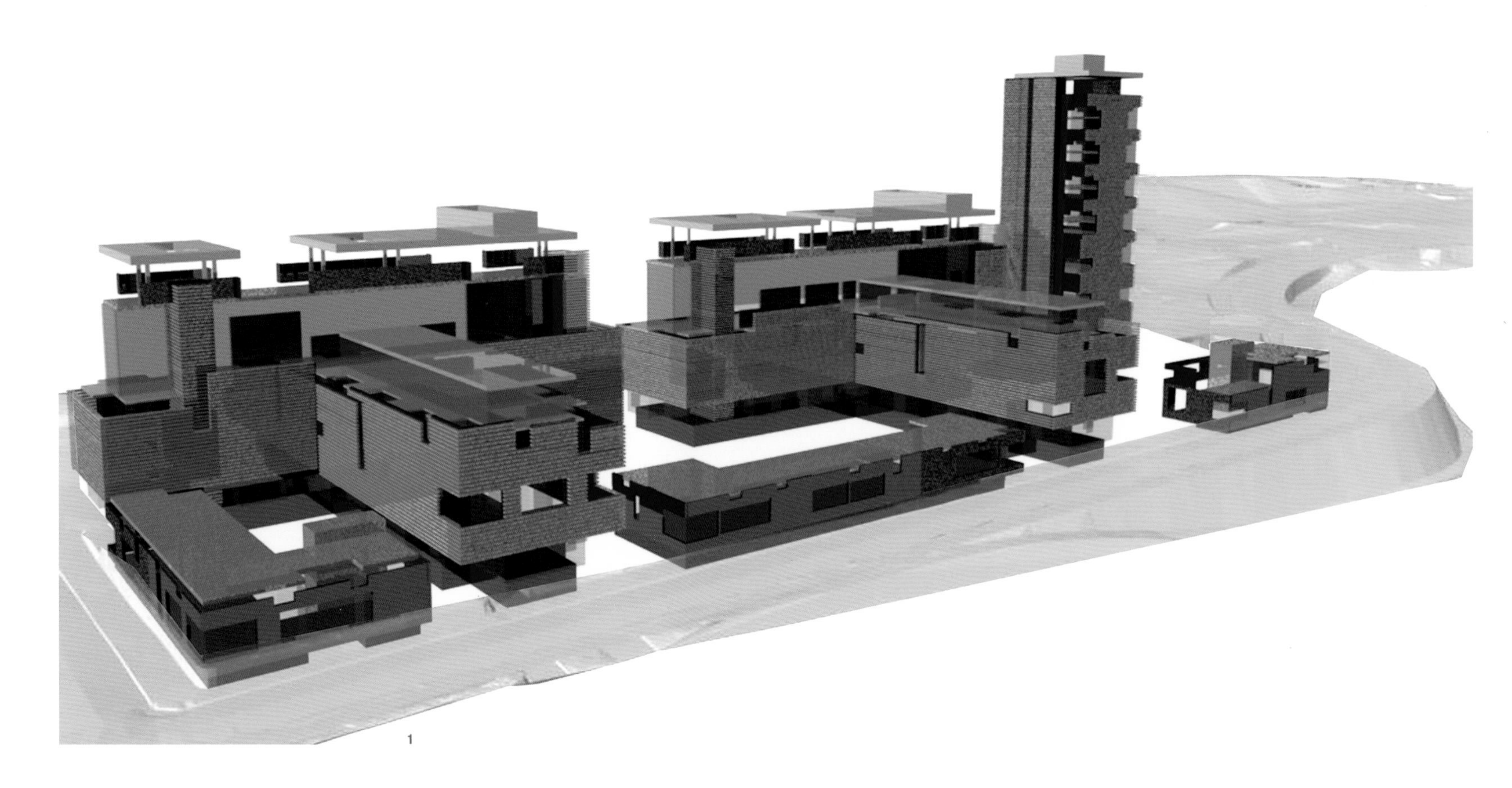

1

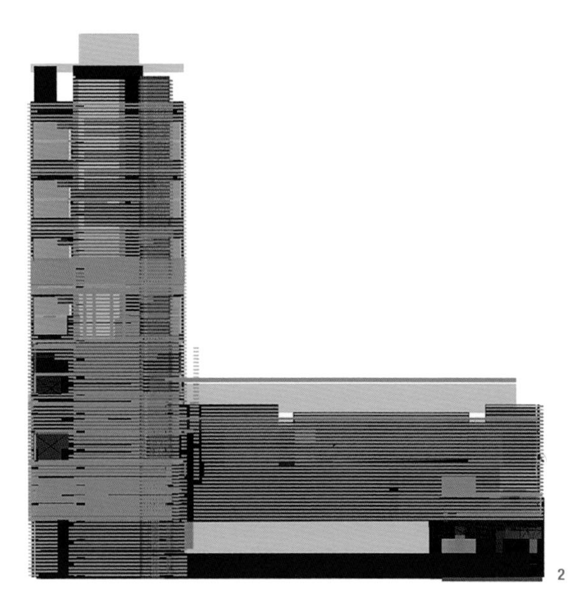

2

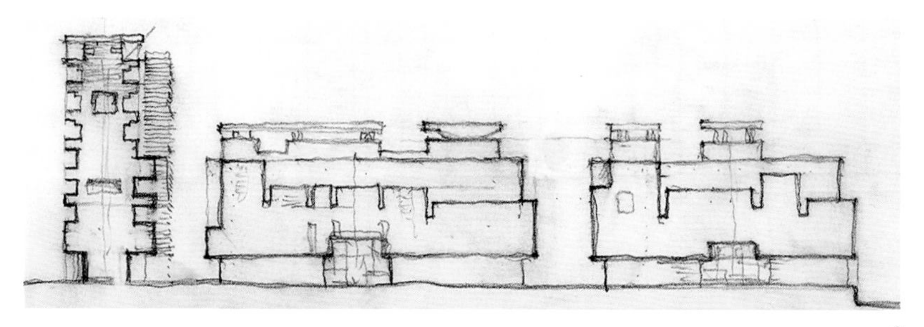

3

1 Computer model view from St. Nicholas Terrace
2 Elevation study
3 Elevation study drawing
4 Second floor plan
5 Ground floor plan
6 Site plan of the entire campus
7 Upper level plan

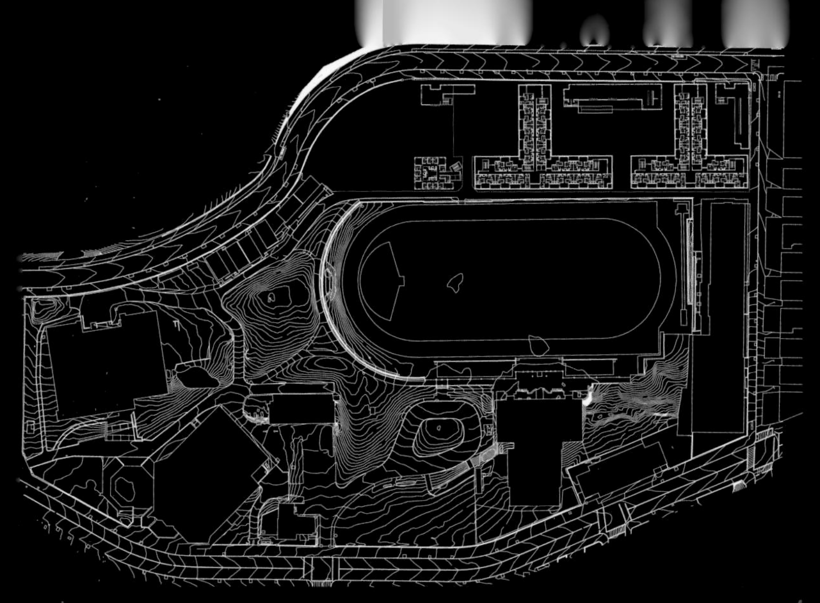

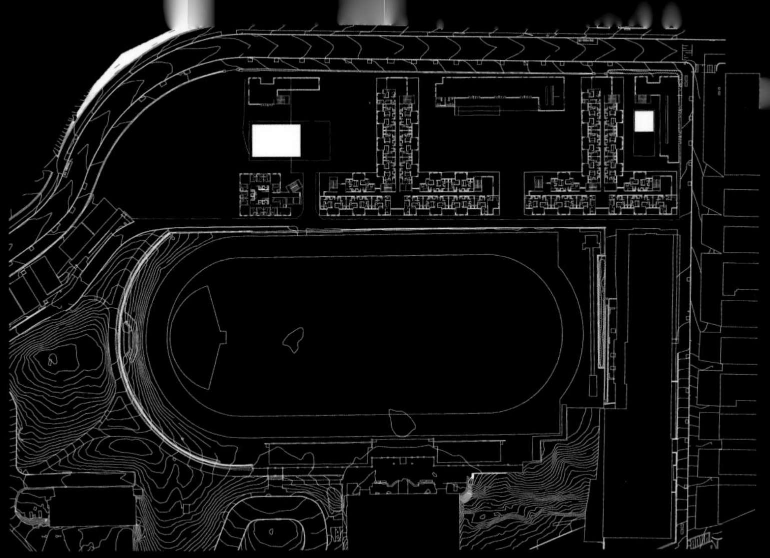

4

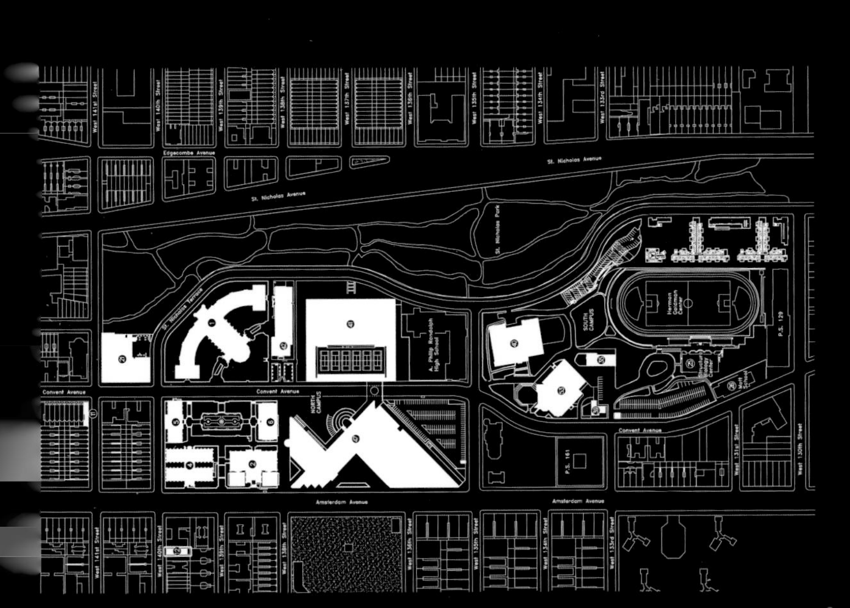
West 141st Street
West 140th Street
West 139th Street
West 138th Street
West 137th Street
West 136th Street
West 135th Street
West 134th Street
West 133rd Street
Edgecombe Avenue
St. Nicholas Avenue
St. Nicholas Avenue
St. Nicholas Park
St. Nicholas Terrace
A. Philip Randolph High School
SOUTH CAMPUS
Herman Goldman Center
P.S. 129
Structural Biology Center
Mott School
Convent Avenue
Convent Avenue
NORTH CAMPUS
Convent Avenue
P.S. 161
West 131st Street
West 130th Street
Amsterdam Avenue
Amsterdam Avenue

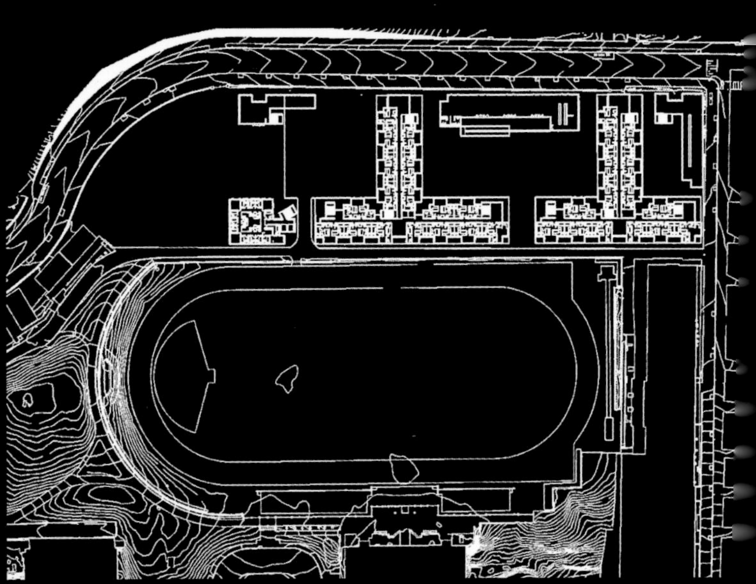

6

location	Brooklyn, New York
year of design	2000
year of completion	2008
client	New York City Housing Authority, David Burney, Director of Design
lot size	4.75 acres
project size	7,000 sq. ft.
architect	George Ranalli
associates	Robert Silman Structural Engineer; George Langer Mechanical Engineer; Stephen Falk, Specifications; Joe Di Bernardo, Lighting
design team	Mario Gentile, Hayden Marrero, Hollace Metzger, Oliver Calderari, Brock Danner, Price Harrison, Fran Leadon, Nadia Ostrovsky, Kimberlae Saul, Texer Nam
photographer	Paul Warchol

Saratoga Avenue Community Center

1

A community expressed interest in a facility of excellent design to accommodate civic events, parties, and education and arts programs. The project, sponsored by the New York City Housing Authority (NYCHA), would remodel 1,500 square feet of ground-floor space in the 16-story Saratoga Village Apartments building and add a new, 3,500-square-foot facility as an all-purpose community space with commercial kitchen, bathrooms, director's office, and other amenities.

The Saratoga Community Center posits an alternative to the contemporary lament that public architecture built by public agencies inevitably yields bland, stark buildings remote to occupants. This project transforms a solitary housing block into a residential housing complex of elegance and distinction. The orientation and design of the new building, the redesign of the ground floor of the existing high-rise tower, and the surrounding landscaping work together to brighten the formerly bleak apartment-block environs.

At the eastern end of the site, a newly designed hallway connects the apartment tower to the new community center; the adjacency frames the grounds in a sheltering street wall. A smaller volume in the new community center, for the director's office, balances the composition to the west. The design elements define two inviting outdoor spaces, one bordering Hancock Street and the other outside the community center's main entrance. In a metrical progression from either the street or the adjoining apartment building, visitors pass through a compact entryway into the soaring, 23-foot-high main space. There an expanse of hardwood floor, buff-white walls, and large mahogany-framed clerestory windows compel the view upward. A ubiquitous adjustment of scale and ornamentation frame the atmosphere of any activity or special occasion occurring within the space.

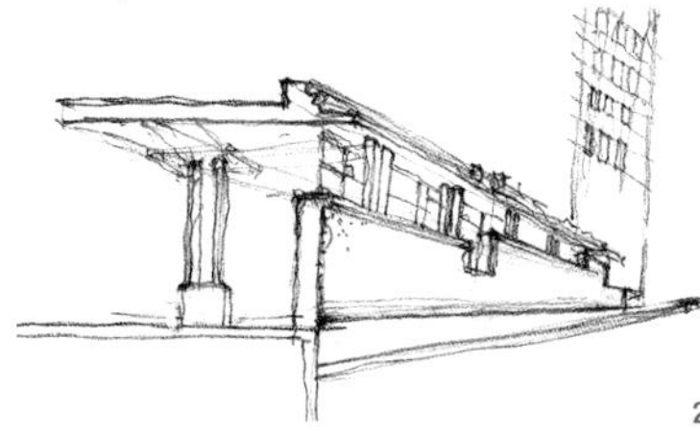

2

3

1 Detail of the large doors leading into the garden
2 Early sketch of the Hancock Street side
3 View of the entrance on Hancock Street

The design may look expensive but is as economical as it is beautiful. The total project, including site preparation, landscaping, and actual construction, met NYCHA's customary expenditure limits while heeding NYCHA guidelines that prohibit low windows and prescribe bulletproof glass. An exterior material palate of speckled roman brick over a limestone base connects comfortably to the tan brick of the existing housing block, while contrastive materials, transparencies, and densities invigorate the site. Innovative construction strategies, such as the use of precast concrete sections surrounding recessed, mahogany-framed window and doorways, cost no more than featureless brick and stainless steel. Similarly, the buff-white plaster interior walls are lined with superstrong, easily replaced, decorative panels that provide protection from daily wear and tear while providing a play of reflections that echoes the rhythm of the daylight hours with variations of light, and at night responds to the delicate interior-lighting design that fills the room with sparkle.

Saratoga Community Center represents the contemporary architectural application of traditional allusions to communal space. Its design, as the old phrase goes, began in delight and ended in wisdom. On budget and in balance, its golden-brown masonry and interwoven mahogany frame windows and doorways emit the vibrant composure proper to a public work of architecture.

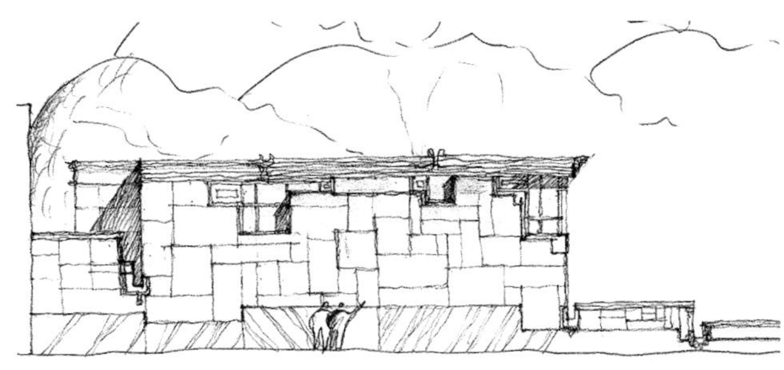

2

3

1 Aerial view of the project with Saratoga building in the foreground and Brooklyn and Manhattan beyond
2 Study elevation on Hancock Street
3 View along Hancock Street looking toward the entrance

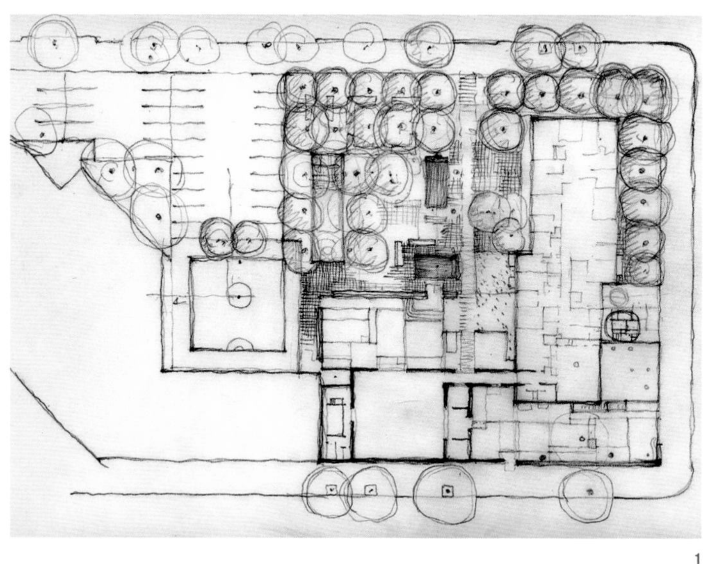

1

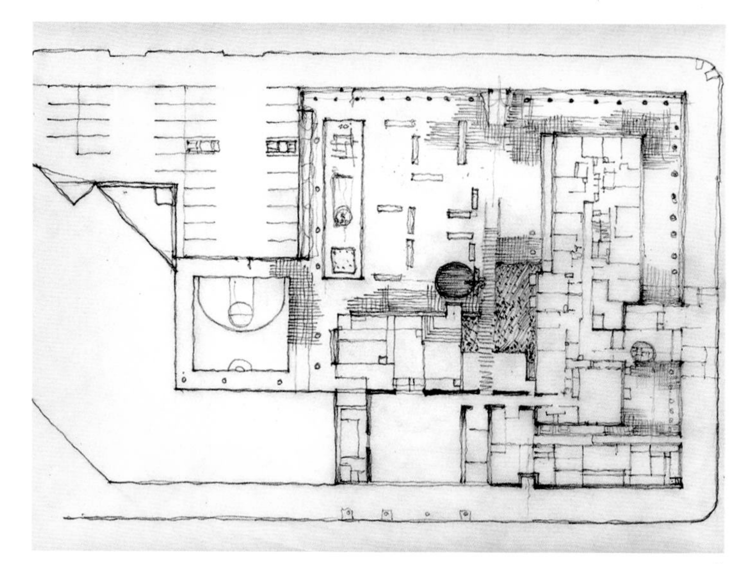

3

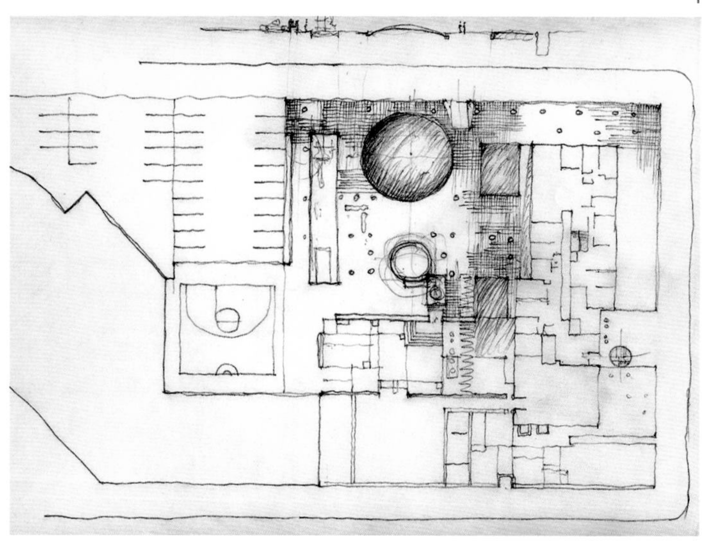

2

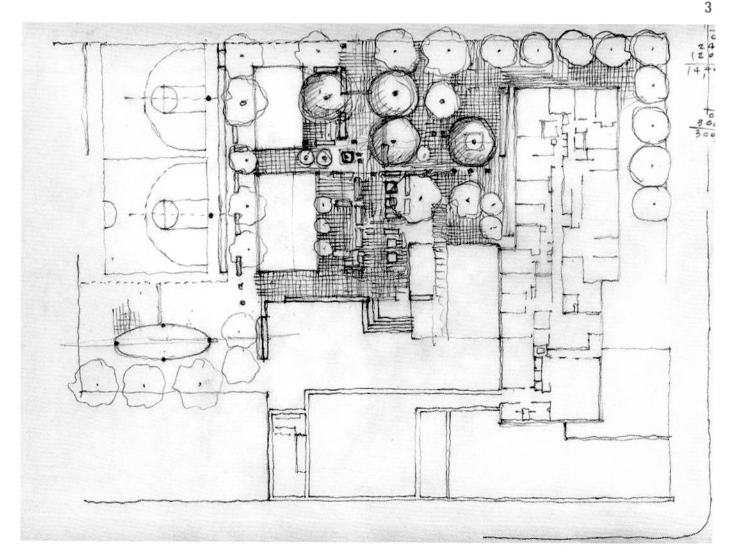

4

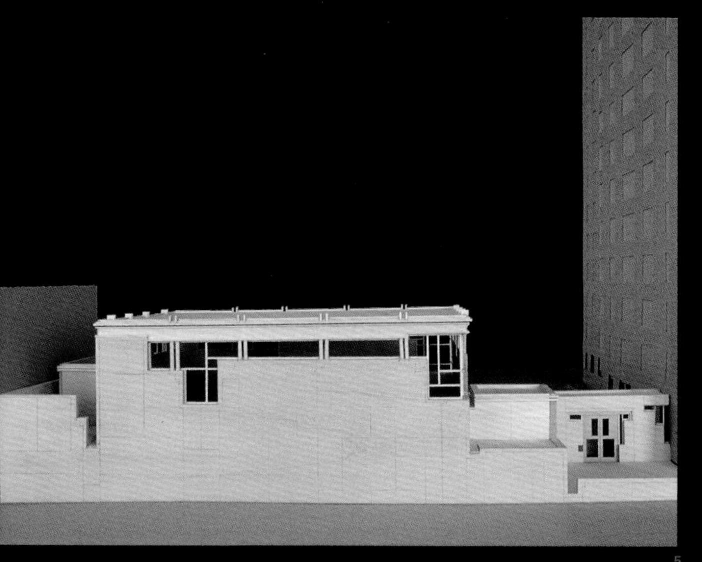

5

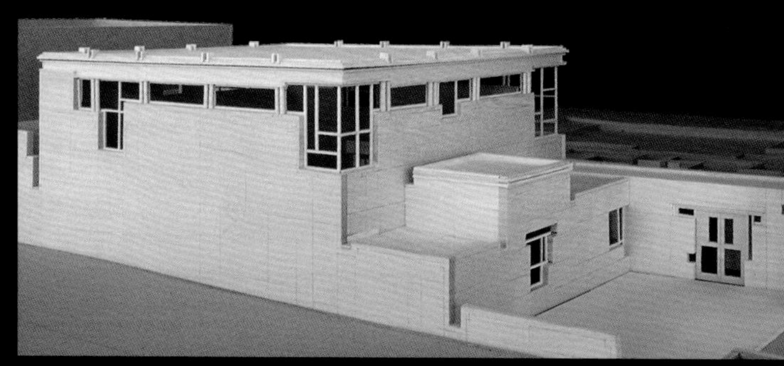

7

6

8

1 | Site and landscape design for the garden, with large trees
2 | Site design with larger paved area study
3 | Landscape design with multiple bench seating
4 | Final landscape study with oval water spray, sitting areas and play equipment
5 | Model view from Hancock Street

1

1	View of the new building and the housing tower and the entrance
2	Site plan
3	Plan of the existing building and the new community center
4	Photo of the existing site with the green color indicating the location of the new addition
5	Early computer study of the new building
6	Computer view of the garden side illustrating the courtyard design

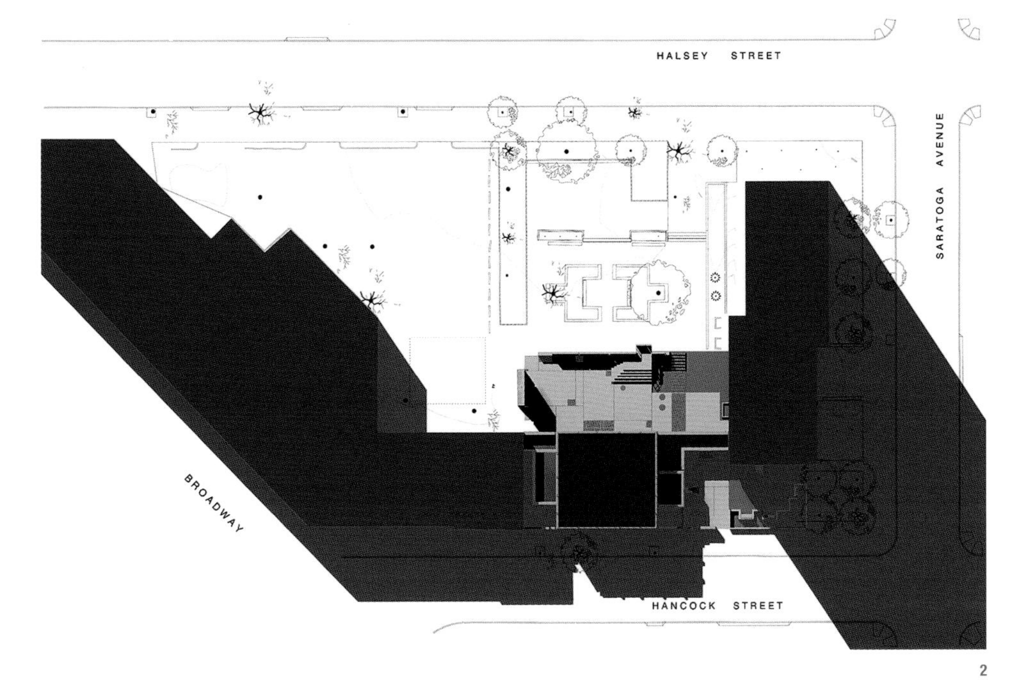

2

4

5

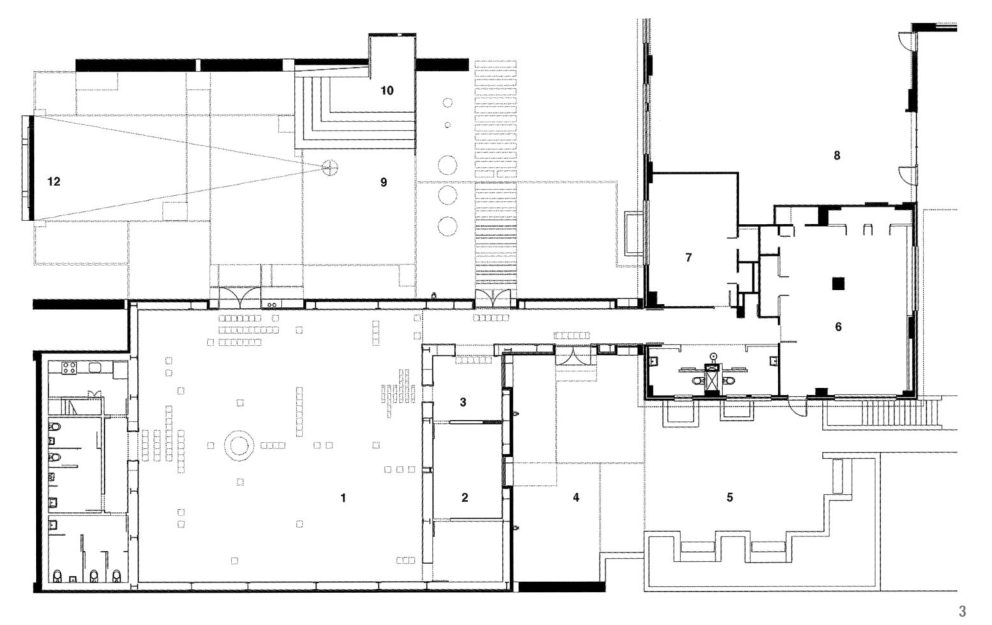

3

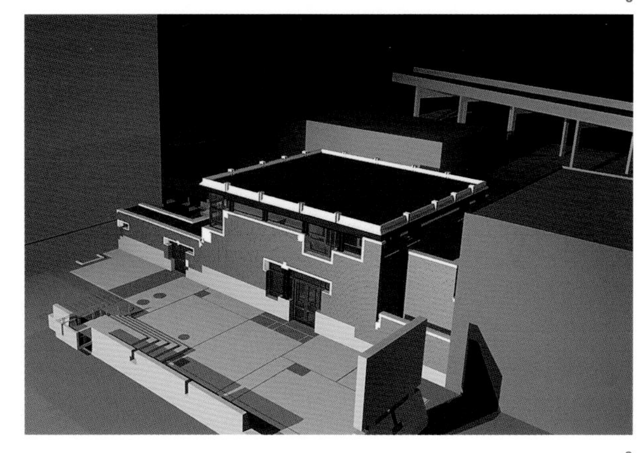
6

1. Community room multi-purpose
2. Director's office
3. Assistant Director's office
4. Entry court
5. Existing court
6. Game room multi-purpose
7. Reading room
8. Entry for existing building
9. New courtyard
10. Overlook
11. Existing courtyard
12. Cinema screen

1

2

3

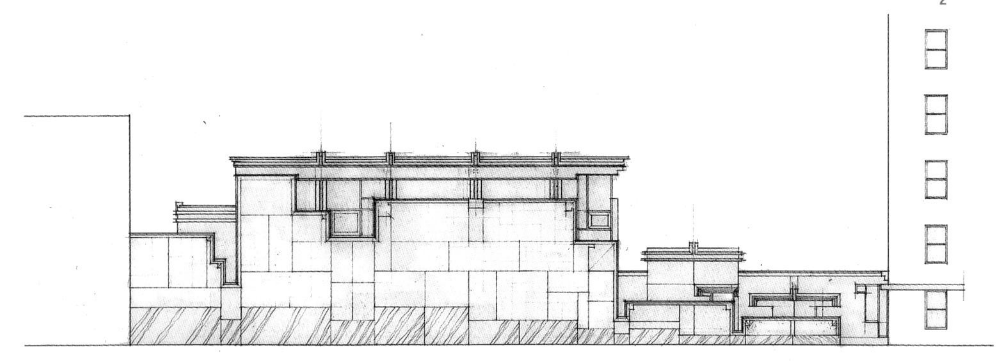

4

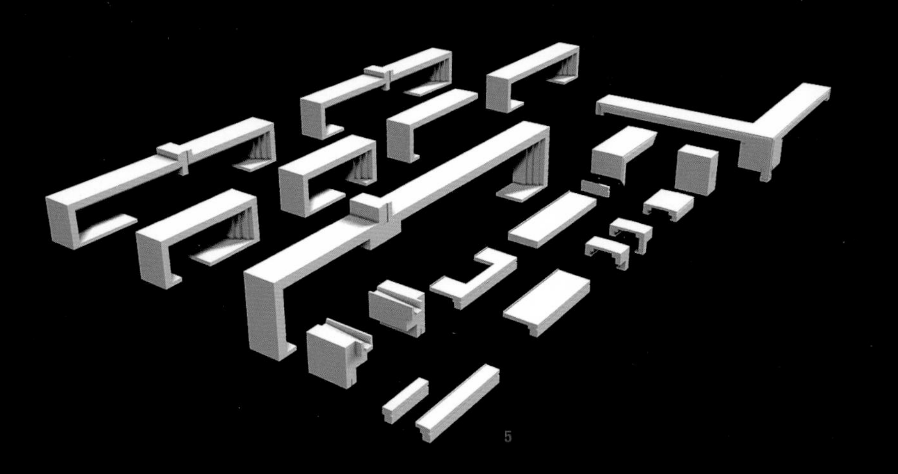

5

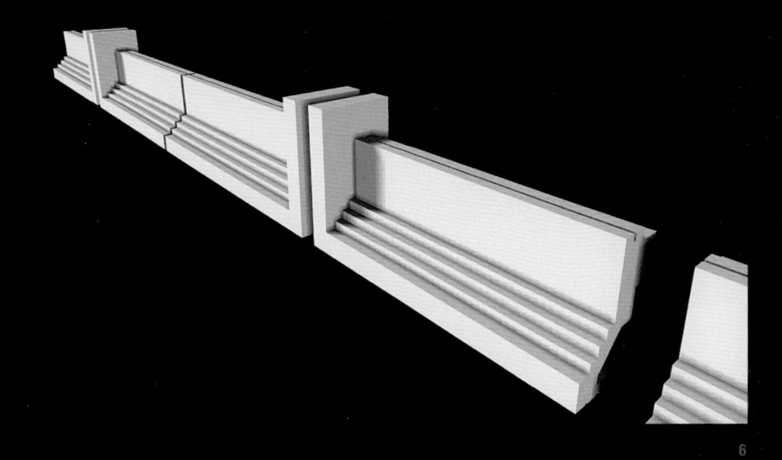

6

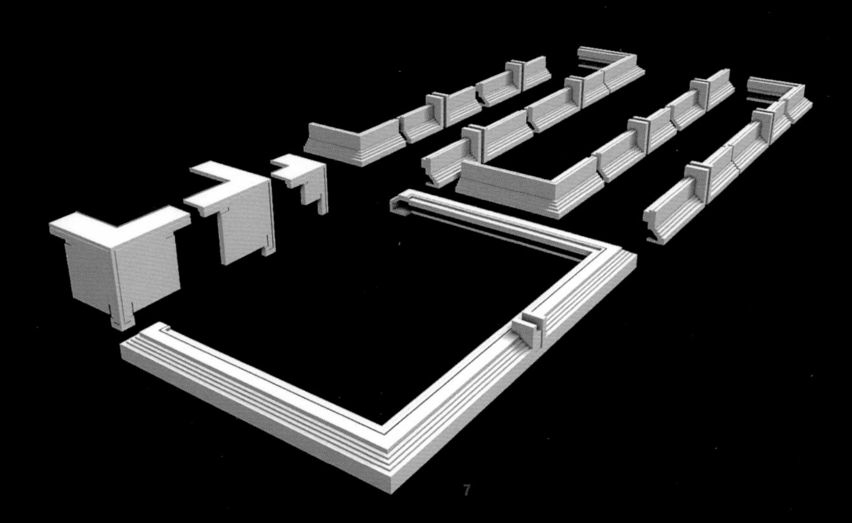

7

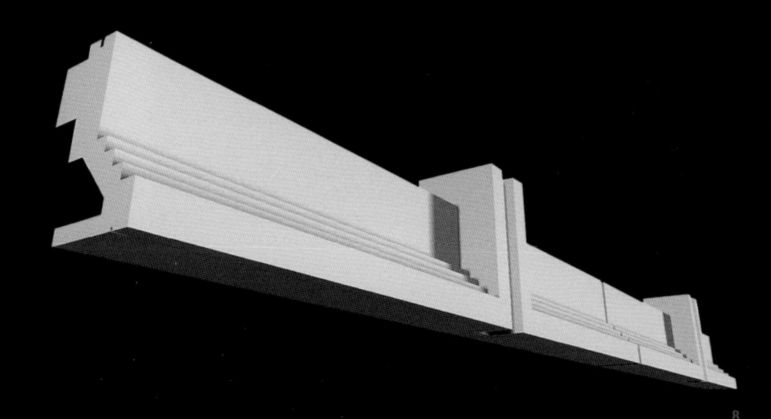

8

1 Computer montage of the building and the site photo
2 Computer study from the subway station on an existing photo
3 Computer image of the new entrance
4 Hancock Street elevation study
5 GFRC window, door and scupper details
6 Upper cornice detail from above
7 Cornice, director's cornice and corner details
8 Upper cornice detail view from below

1

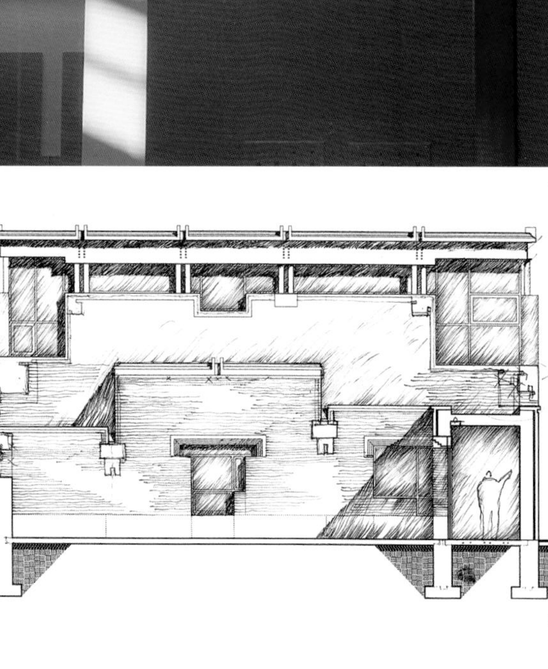

2

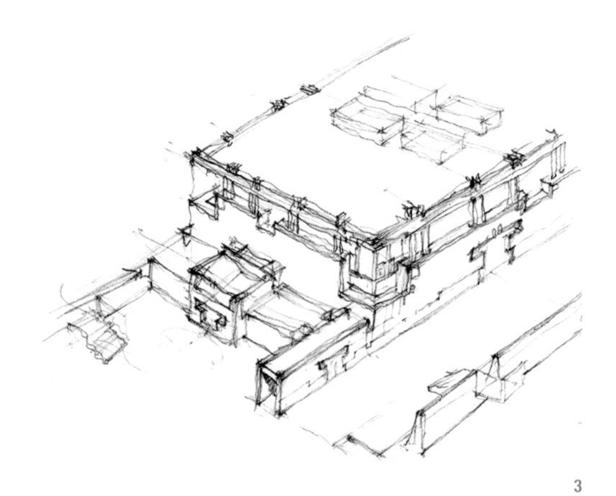

3

4

1 | Entry window detail
2 | Elevation study of the small courtyard entrance
3 | Early study sketch of the massing of the building
4 | View of the small courtyard from the main entrance

1

1 View of the Director's office from Saratoga Avenue
2 Building cross sections
3 Building long sections
4 Detail view of the Director's office

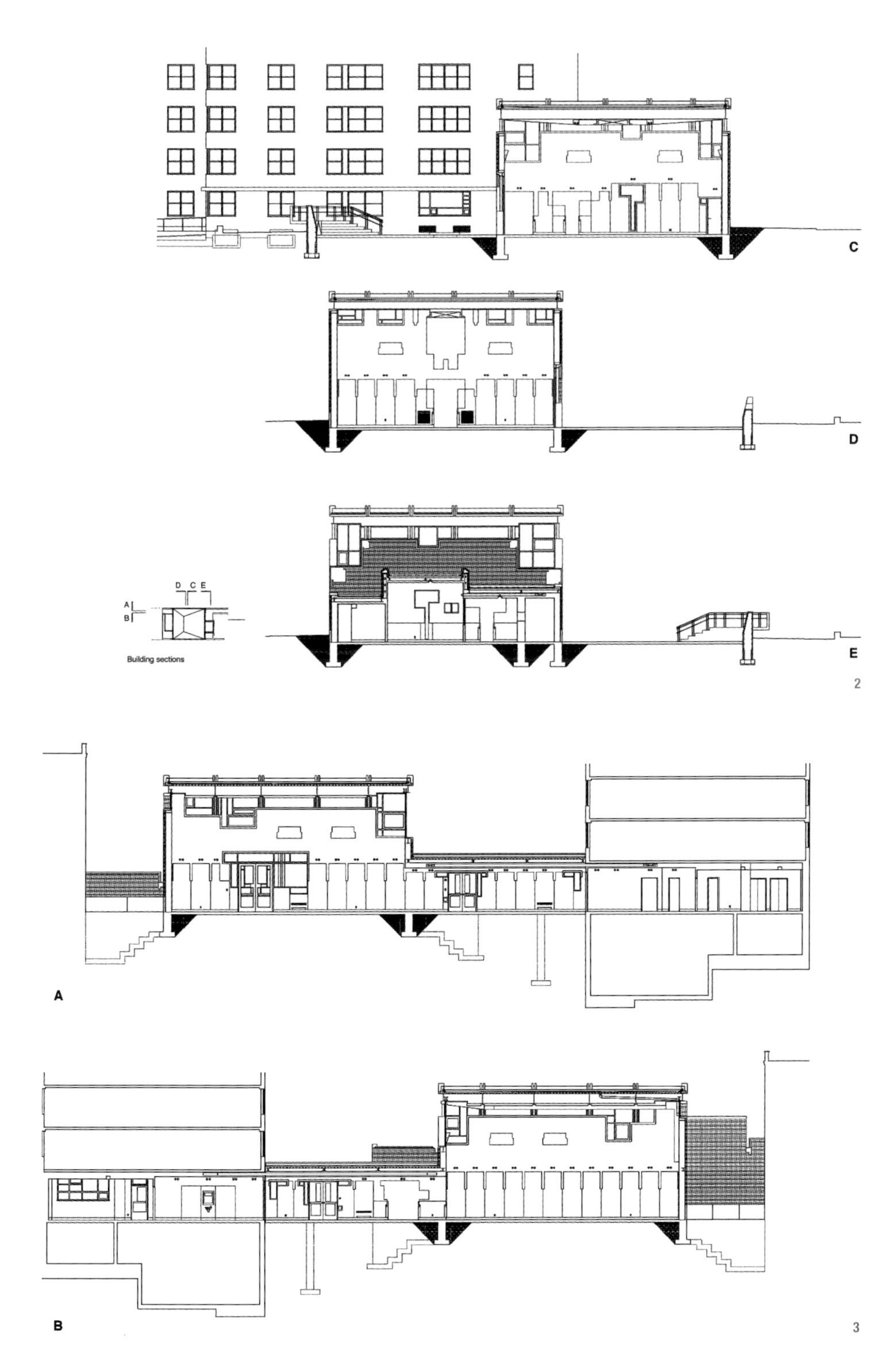

Building sections

2

3

4

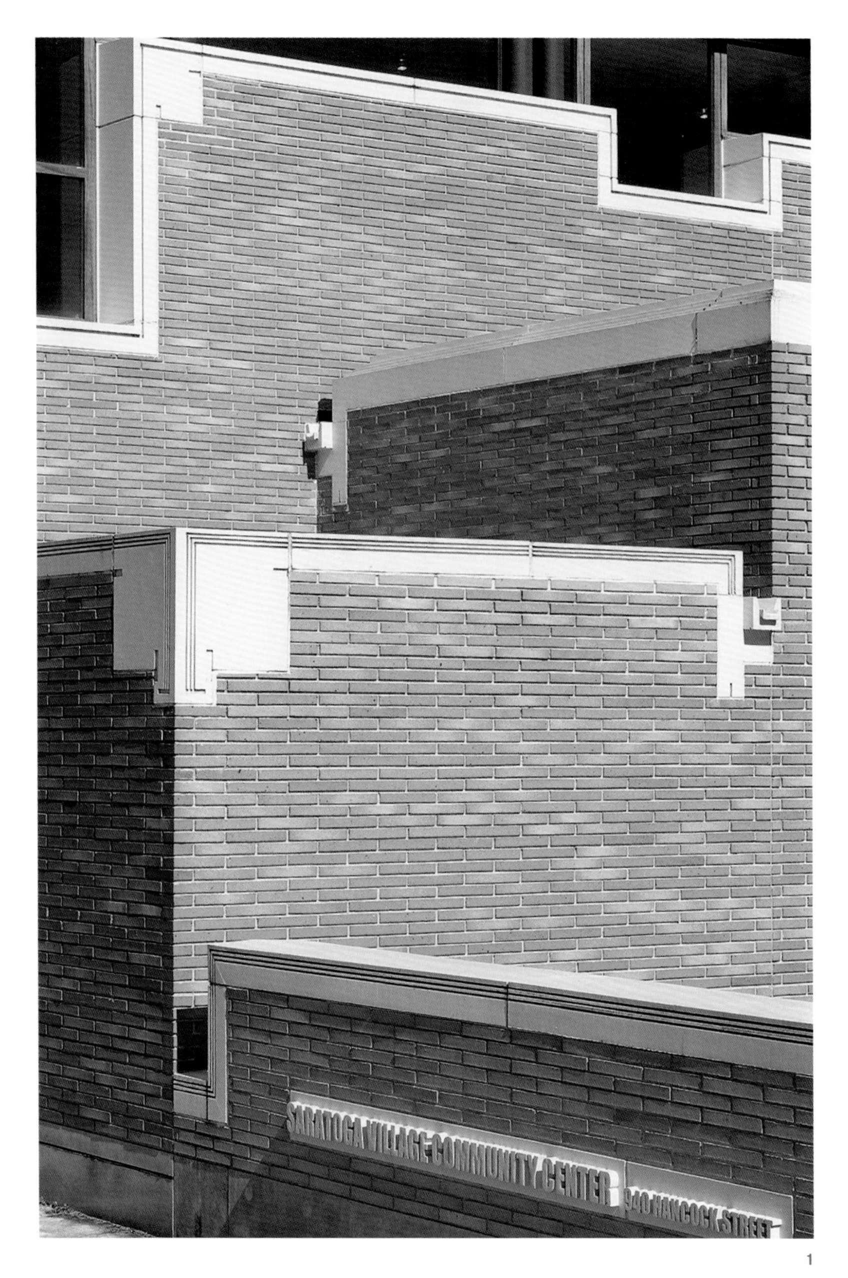

1

2

1 | Detail view at the entrance
2 | Scupper detail
3 | Section through the scupper
4 | Elevation drawing of the scupper
5 | Splash block detail
6 | Scupper and corner detail

3

4

5

6

1

1 | Large window in the main assembly room
2 | Director's office detail

2

1

2

1 | Detail of the Director's window
2 | View into the interior through the Director's office window
3 | Entry window and entry doors with main assembly room beyond

1

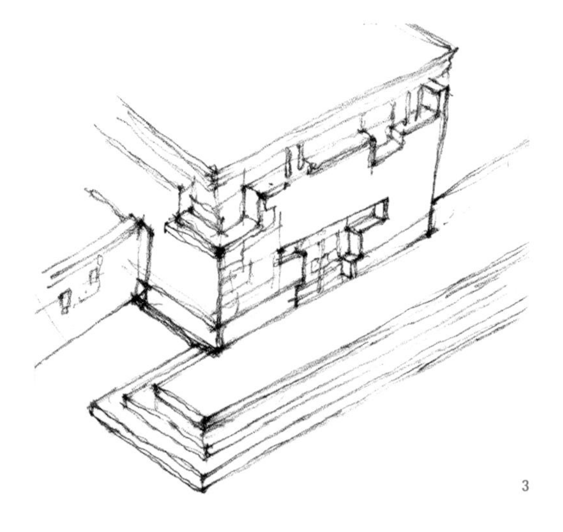

3

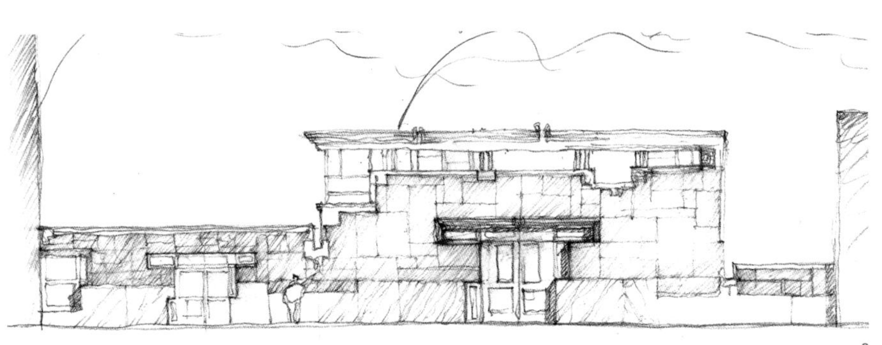

2

4

1 | Detail view of the paired columns at the garden side of the building
2 | Sketch of the garden side of the building
3 | Study drawing of the corner window and garden door
4 | View of the garden side of the building

1

2

3

1 | Close-up of the Director's cornice and the upper cornice and steel beam beyond
2 | Cornice and upper windows at the rear of the building
3 | Detail drawing of the wall, paired columns, wood windows, steel beam and GFRC cornice

1

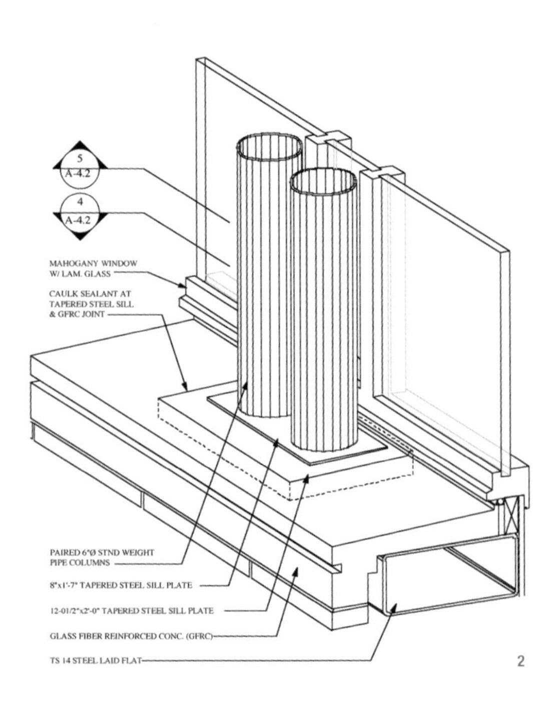

5
A-4.2
4
A-4.2
MAHOGANY WINDOW
W/ LAM. GLASS
CAULK SEALANT AT
TAPERED STEEL SILL
& GFRC JOINT
PAIRED 6"Ø STND WEIGHT
PIPE COLUMNS
8"x1'-7" TAPERED STEEL SILL PLATE
12-01/2"x2'-0" TAPERED STEEL SILL PLATE
GLASS FIBER REINFORCED CONC. (GFRC)
TS 14 STEEL LAID FLAT

2

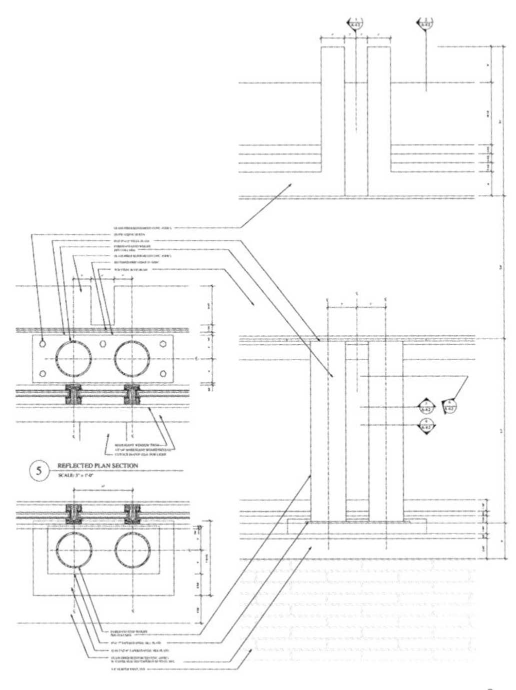

5
REFLECTED PLAN SECTION

3

1 | View of the garden wall
2 | Paired column assembly
3 | Plan, reflected ceiling plan and elevation of the paired columns
4 | Detail view of the garden wall
Overleaf full garden elevation (following spread)

4

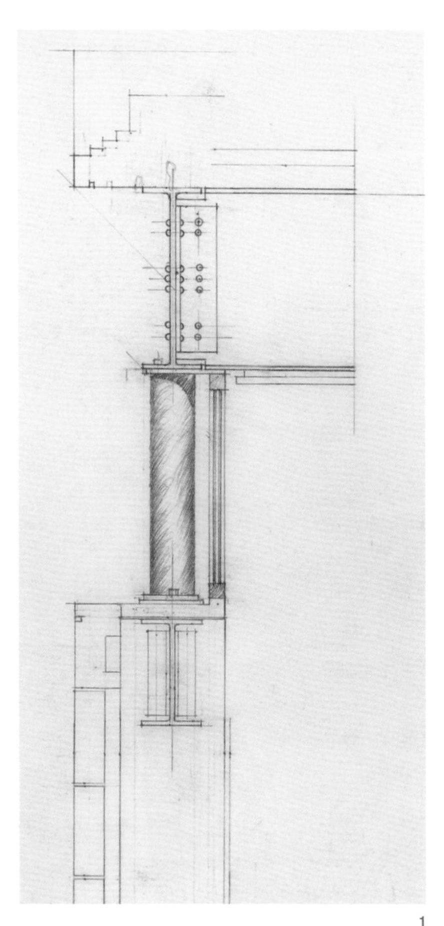

1

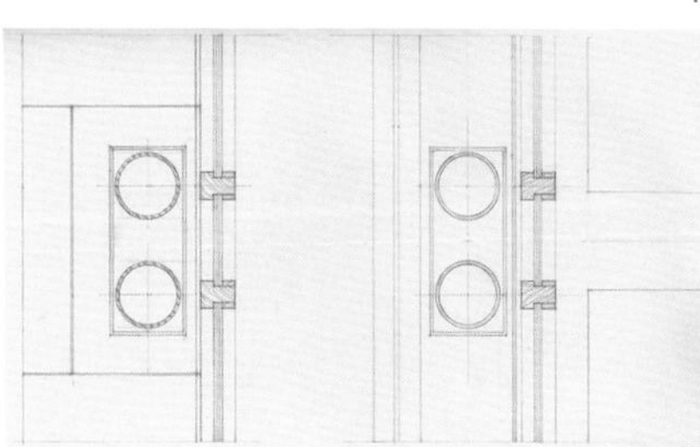

2

3

1 Study section at the paired columns
2 Plan and reflected plan of the columns
3 Garden elevation looking at the main housing block

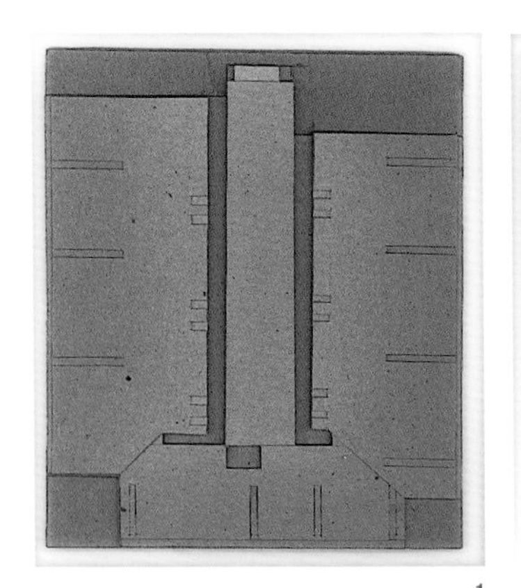

1

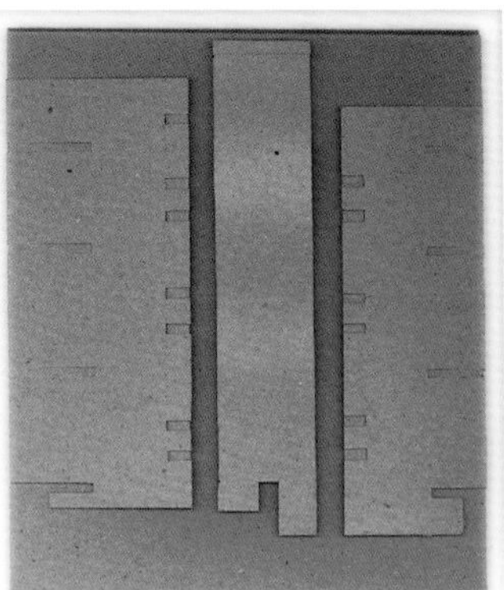

2

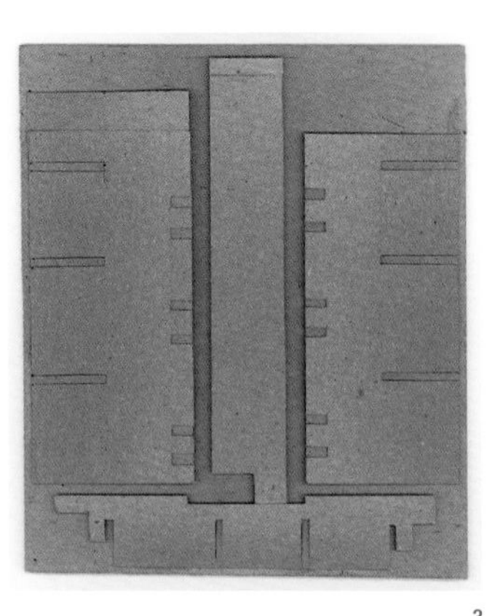

3

4

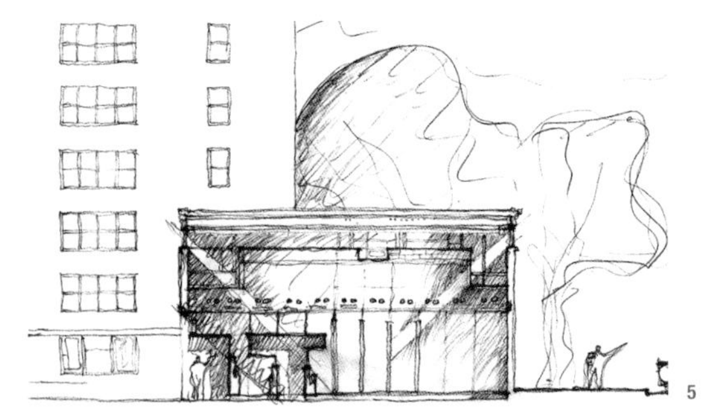

5

1 | Final ceiling model study
2 | Early model ceiling study
3 | Intermediate ceiling model study
4 | View of the shaped ceiling
5 | Section sketch through the main assembly room
6 | View of the main assembly room looking toward the service end

6

1

2

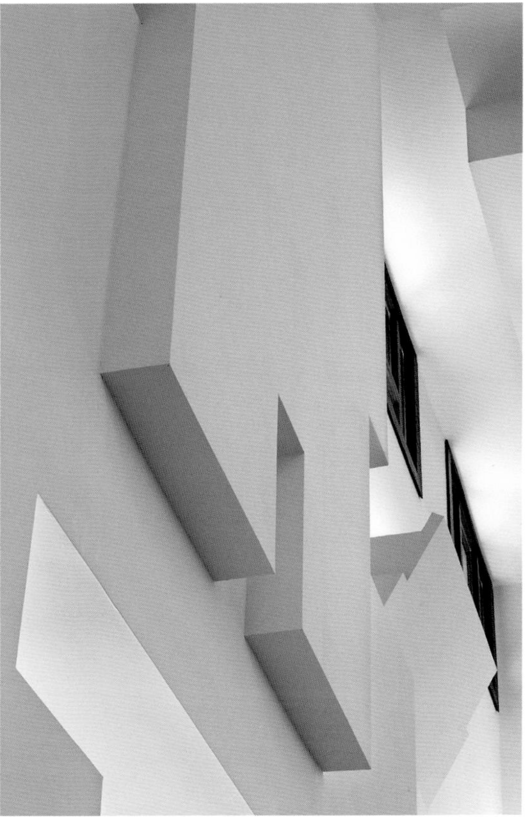

3

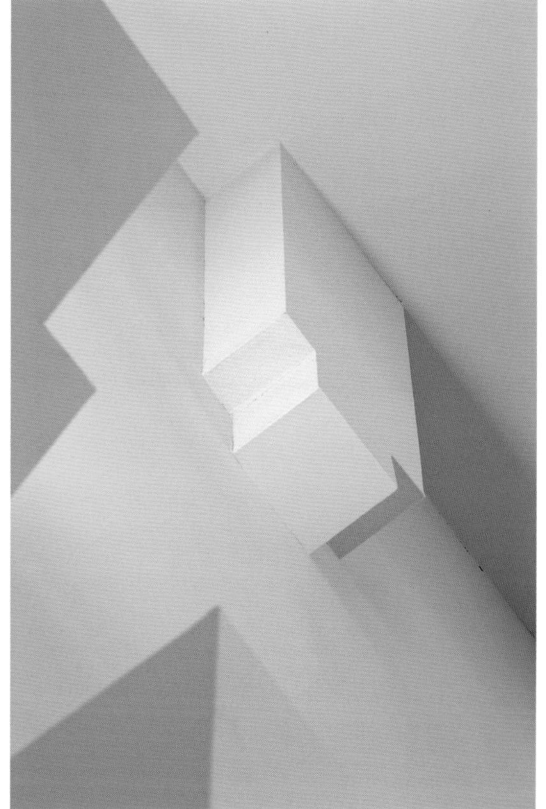

4

1 | Detail view of the main room
2 | Upper view of the windows, lighting and mechanical equipment
3 | View looking up at the rear wall
4 | View of the upper details
5 | Early sketch of the main room

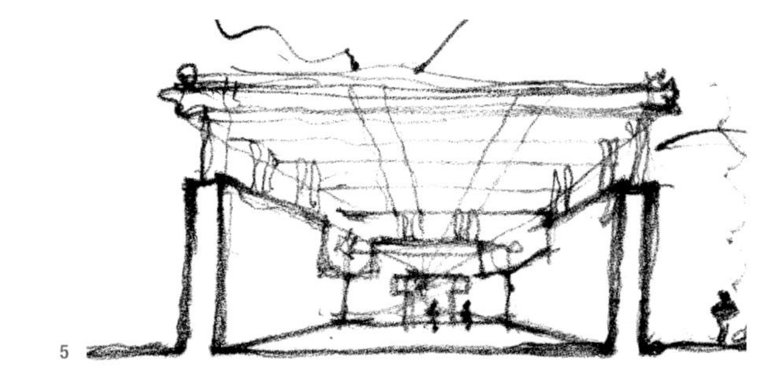

5

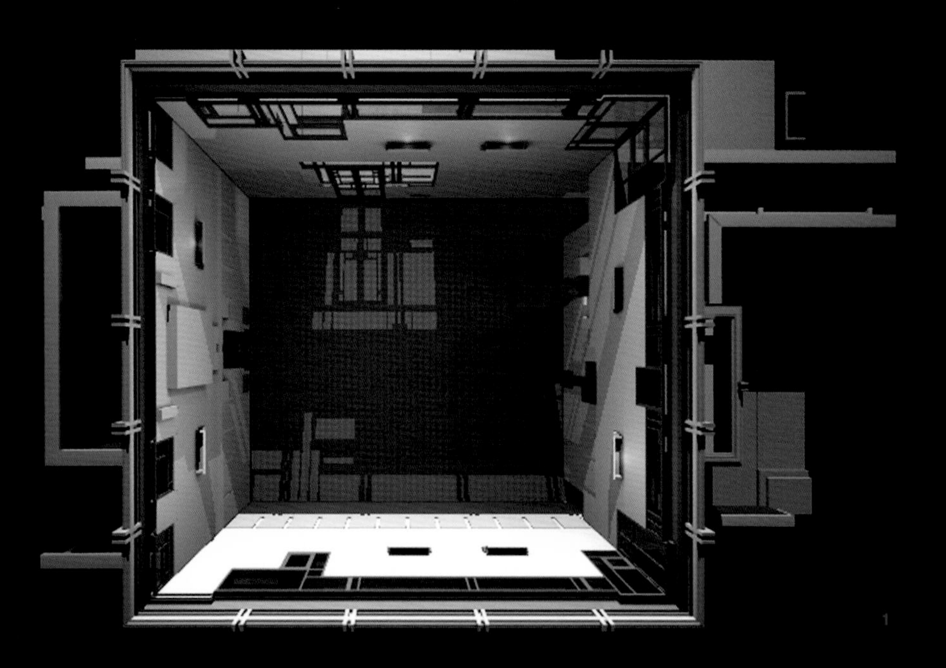

1

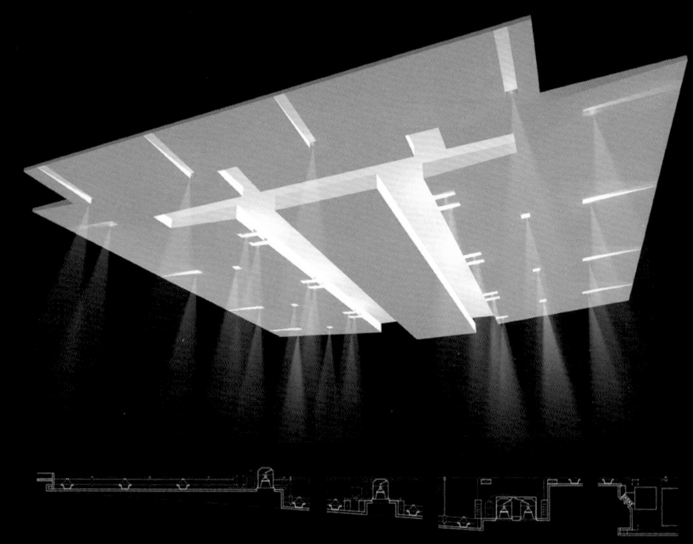

2

3

4

5

6

7

8

9

1 | Plan perspective view
2 | Lighting model and section through the shaped ceiling
3 | Interior of the main room looking toward the garden doors
4 | View of the entry and Director's office
5 | View of wall opposite the garden entry
6 | Service elevation
7 | Section through the main assembly room
8 | Wall section perspective view on the Hancock Street side
9 | Wall section perspective on the garden side

1

2

1 Corner mahogany window, plaster up-light enclosure and sunlight
2 Wall detail of plycem panels with routed lines and screw assemblies

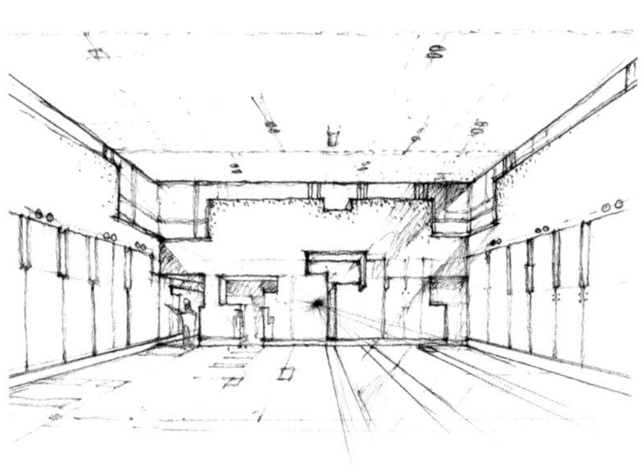

1 View of the main room from the Assistant Director's office
2 Section sketch of the main assembly room looking toward the Director's office
3 Main assembly room looking toward the entry and Director's office

ASSISTANT
DIRECTORS
OFFICE

1

2

1 View from the entry hall into the main assembly hall
2 Wall details

1

2

1 Reception room
2 Director's office

1

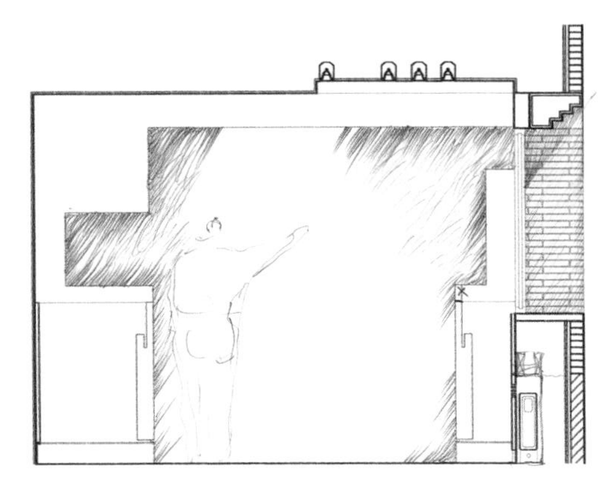

2

3

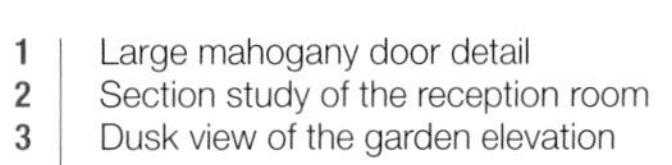

1 | Large mahogany door detail
2 | Section study of the reception room
3 | Dusk view of the garden elevation

project name	Renovation & Addition to the Queens College Student Union
location	Queens, New York
year of design	1997-1999
client	Queens College Student Union Corp., President's Office
lot size	100 x 200
project size	55,000 sq.ft.
architect	George Ranalli
associates	Robert Silman Structural Engineer
design team	Mark Dixon, Price Harrison, Fran Leadon
photographer	Model Photography: George Ranalli

Queens College Student Union

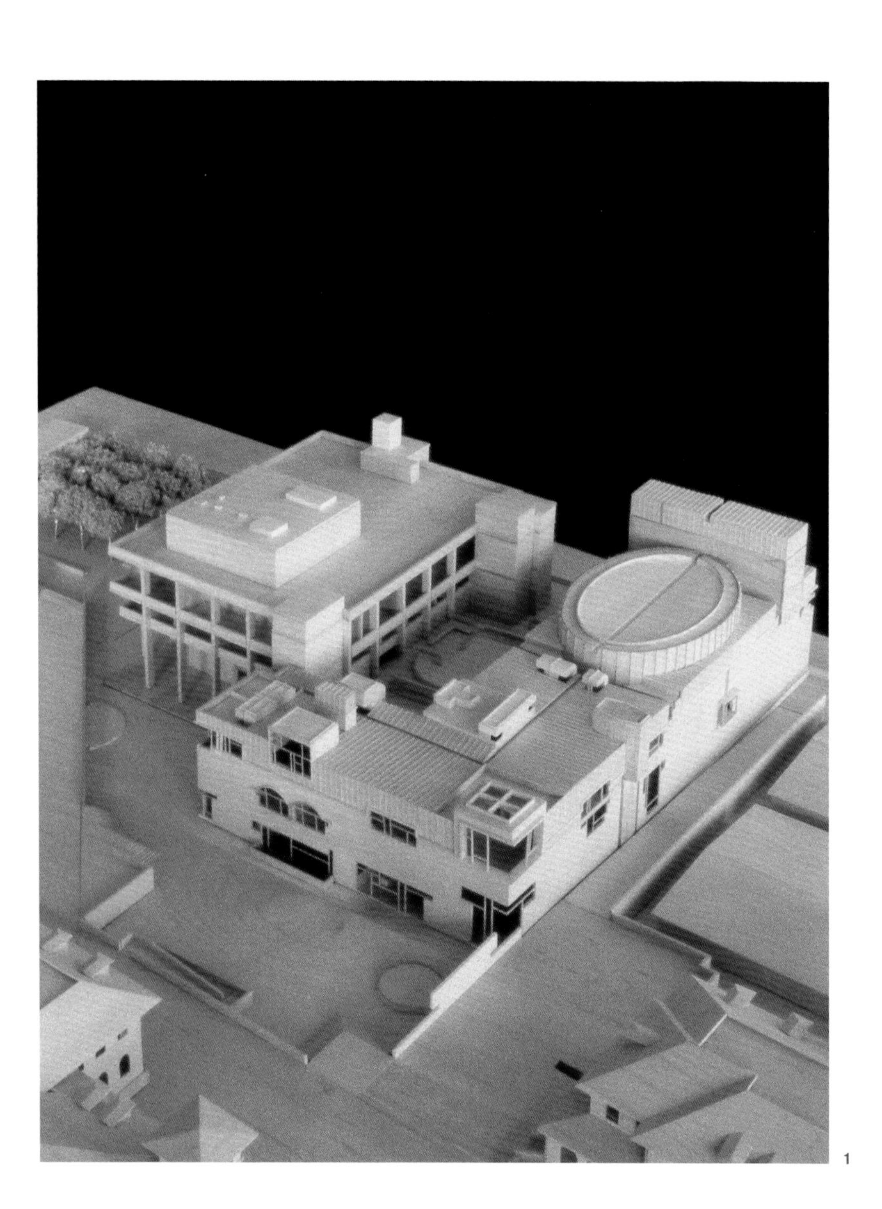

1

Queens, New York is one of the nation's most diverse counties, and Queens College students represent over one hundred countries. The college recognizes that student organizations enhance and provide opportunities beyond the curriculum for personal growth and development of leadership skills. Buildings to house such activities are not merely an afterthought in the ongoing redesign of its campus, but a central concern.

Since 1971, the Queens College Student Union, which includes student government, club, dining, and recreational facilities, was housed—with some difficulty—in a 184,000-square-foot, neo-Brutalist building that was both oppressively ugly and isolated from the main campus. We were asked to help remedy these problems with a new landscape design and a three-story, 42,000-square-foot addition.

The twin goals of the landscape design were to reconnect the Student Union complex with the rest of the campus, and to convert the area east of the existing Student Union building into a garden and park for quiet recreation. To this end, the area around the new and existing buildings is made into three interconnecting courts, each one paved with slate. The first of these, the Student Union Court, connects to the main campus Quadrangle by a stair and ramp. A large newly designed fountain is visible from a new café. The second, the Entrance Court, is placed on axis with the route to Jefferson and Kiley Halls; faced on the west and south by the entrances to the new and existing buildings. The third, the Garden Court, contains another fountain surrounded by existing trees and a newly planted grove of maple trees, surrounded by benches for students and faculty to eat, talk, read, and relax. At the east edge of the Garden Court, a stair and ramp connect the campus to Kissena Boulevard.

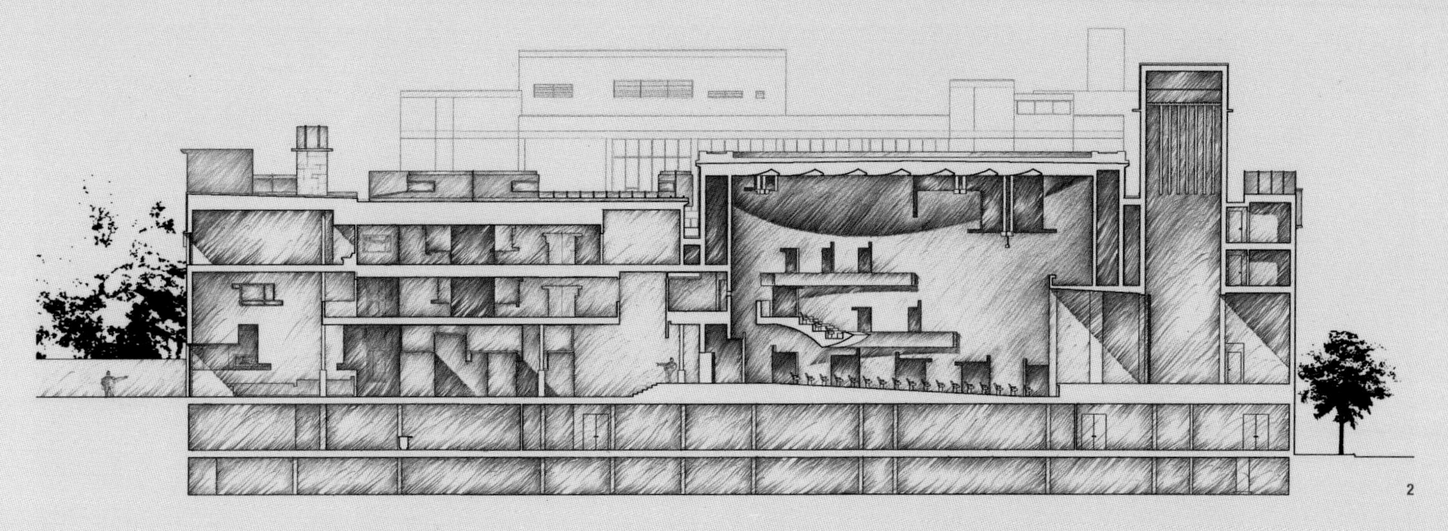

2

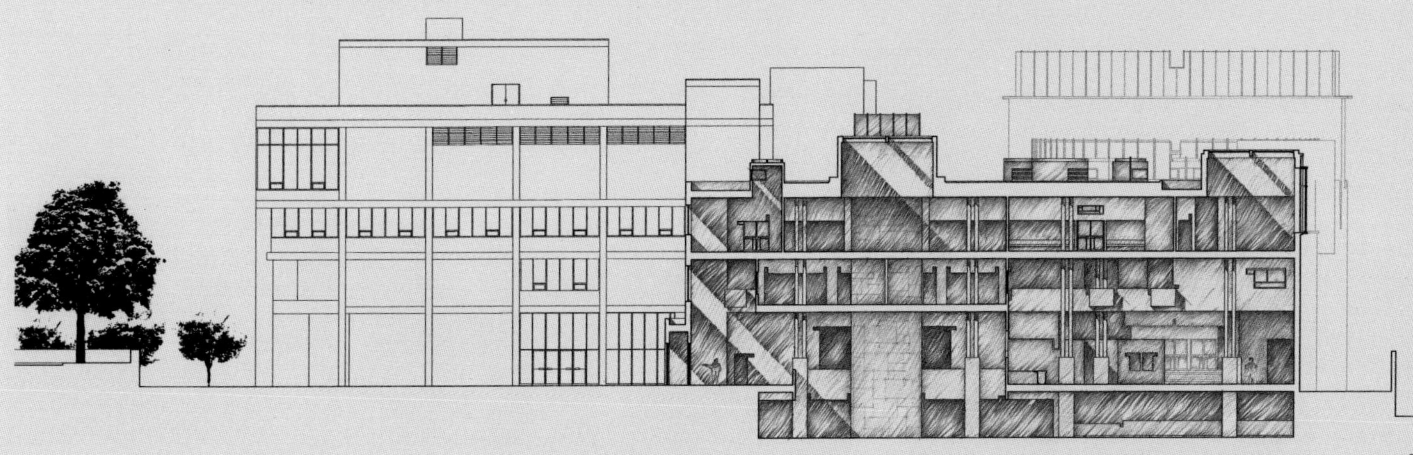

3

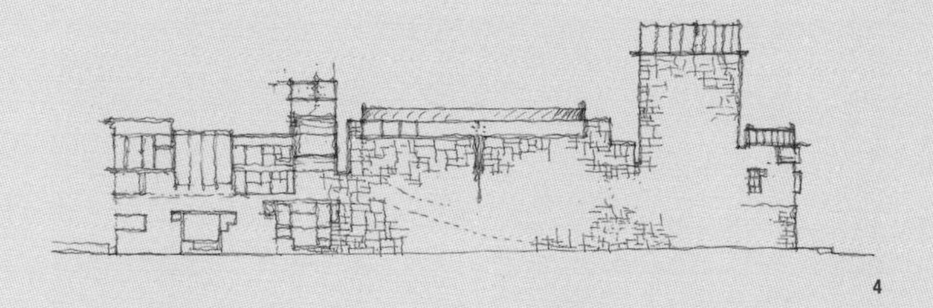

4

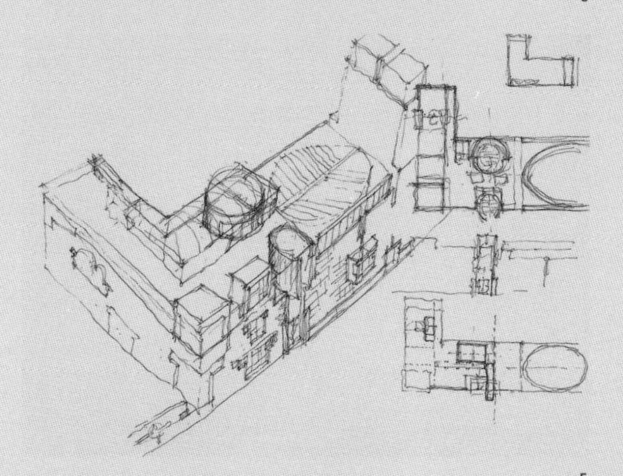

5

1 Aerial view of the addition from the main campus
2 Section through the entrance and the theater
3 Section through the entry sequence
4 Elevation study
5 Early study drawings

1

2

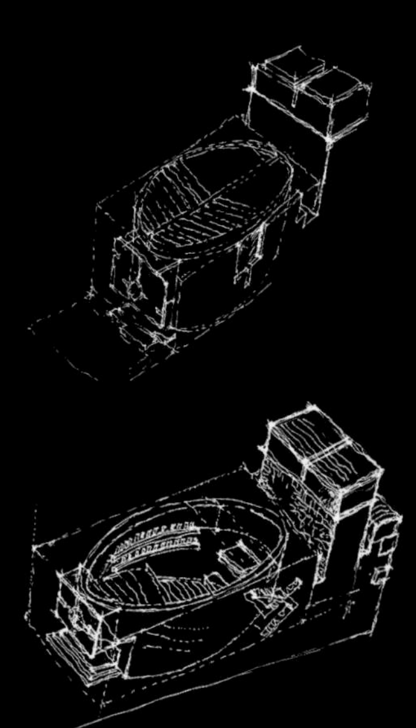

3

The new landscape design further emphasizes the co-curricular setting as a point of reference, integrating new and existing co-curricular buildings with a series of interconnecting terraces for quiet and communal seating, events, exhibits, and performances. Footpaths link to campus walkways and a new 1,900-square-foot parking facility from the terraces.

Design of the revitalized campus entrance began by considering the location of a city bus station on the public street. The city bus line connects the college to other parts of Queens, the New York City subway system, and the Long Island Rail Road. Moving the bus station a small distance made way for a prominent campus entrance featuring a welcoming grove of trees and offering a series of footpaths leading to the nearby student co-curricular facility and elsewhere.

The renovation of the existing Student Union building involves a complete program change to several floors and new architectural finishes to several other floors. The design culminate in an extensive interior makeover that helps transform the bleakness of the existing Brutalist structure into a comfortable and accessible set of spaces.

Finally, the new co-curricular building occupies a site adjacent to the existing Student Union building, currently a parking lot that is also the roof of the existing basement. It expands existing café facilities, creates twelve large seminar rooms and conferences, and provides a new 444-seat oval theater for lectures, recitals, and performances. It is functional, beautiful, and environmentally responsive, faced partly in limestone with an intricate pattern of stonework. The upper part of the building is finished in copper, with large, raised blocks containing glass openings to enhance the natural lighting in the seminar rooms. Its L shape, wrapping around one corner of the existing Student Union, softens the stark geometry of the latter without compromising functionality. Colorful contemporary interior spaces blend state-of-the-art technology with allusions to campus architecture.

The co-curricular setting celebrates the vibrant diversity of Queens College, and provides the campus with a unique setting for community events and cultural offerings.

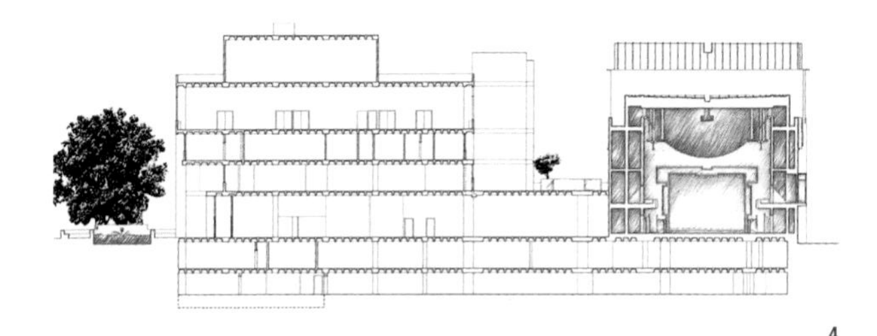

4

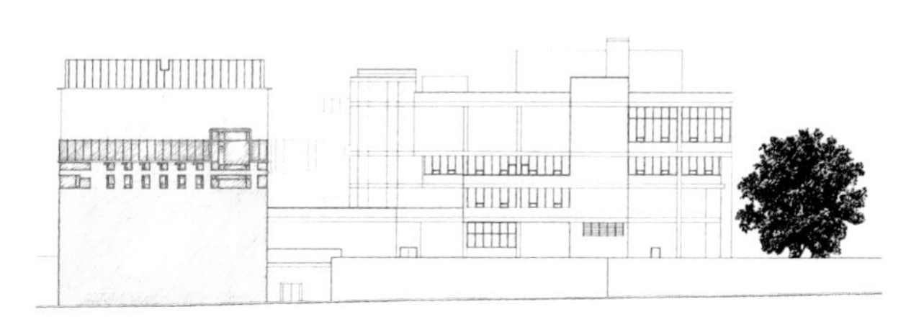

5

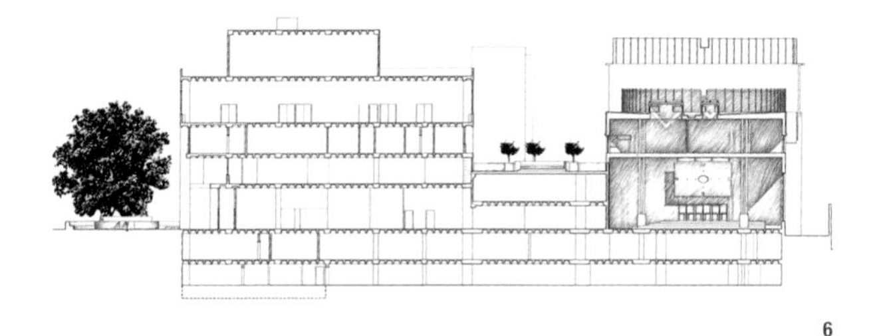

6

7

1 View of the addition from Kissena Boulevard
2 View of the addition from the main campus
3 Theater sketches
4 Section through the existing student center and the theater
5 Side elevation of the building
6 Section through the existing building and the theater lobby
7 New addition entry elevation

1. Entrance hall
2. Open to lower level
3. Elevator lobby
4. Cafeteria
5. Main hall
6. Café bar
7. Café lounge
8. Men's room
9. Women's room
10. Janitor's closet
11. Ticket booth
12. Storage
13. Theater lobby
14. Mechanical shaft
15. Theater (444 seats)
16. Stage
17. Backstage

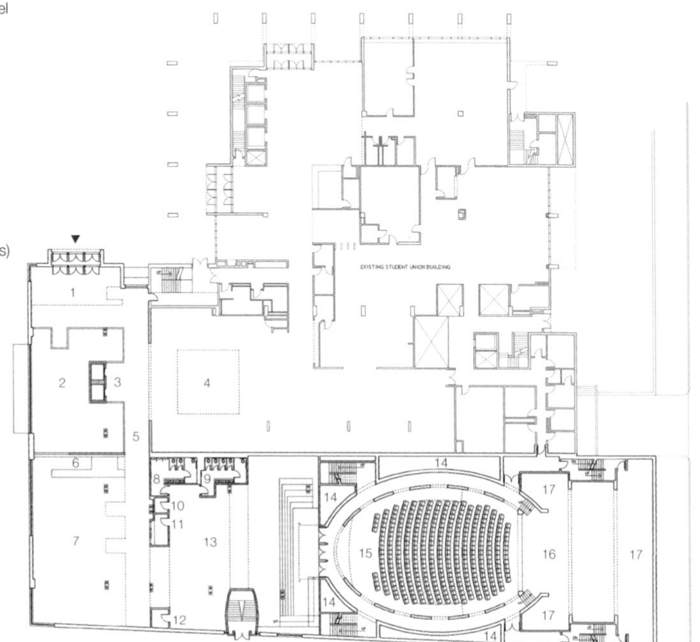

1

1. Game room
2. Lounge
3. Elevator lobby
4. Sub shop
5. Ratskeller
6. Men's room
7. Women's room
8. Mechanical room

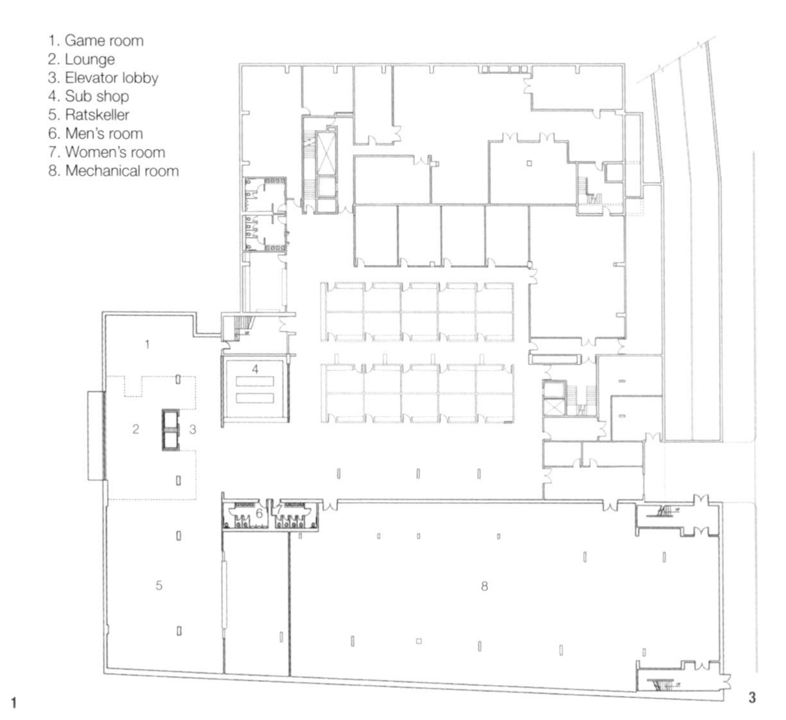

3

1. Open to below
2. Seminar room
3. Elevator lobby
4. Hall
5. Lounge
6. Men's room
7. Women's room
8. Projection room
9. Mechanical shaft
10. Theater mezzanine
11. Enclosed balcony

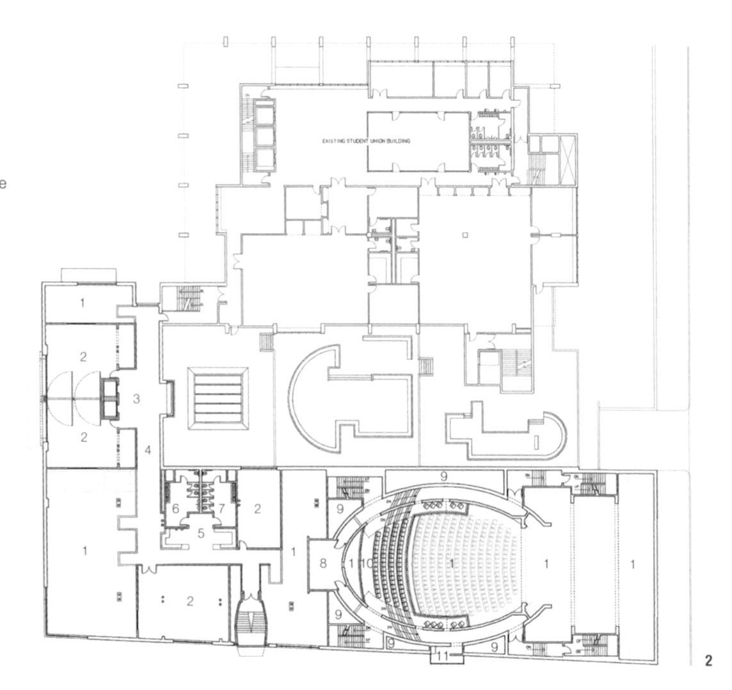

2

1. Open to below
2. Seminar room
3. Elevator lobby
4. Hall
5. Lounge
6. Men's room
7. Women's room
8. Theater balcony
9. Mechanical shaft
10. Dressing room
11. Corridor
12. Rehearsal room
13. Flytower

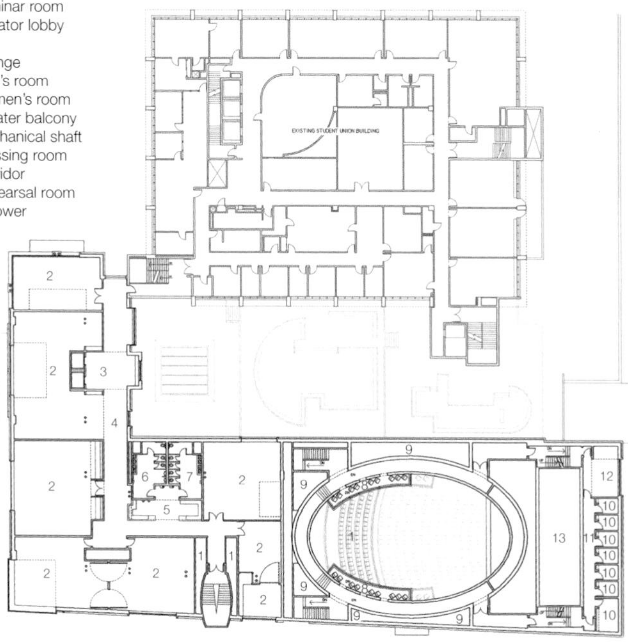

4

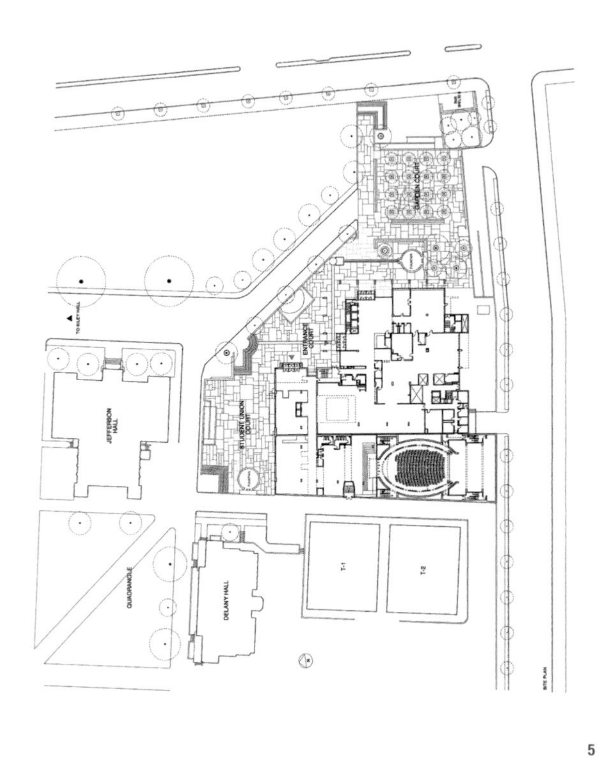

5

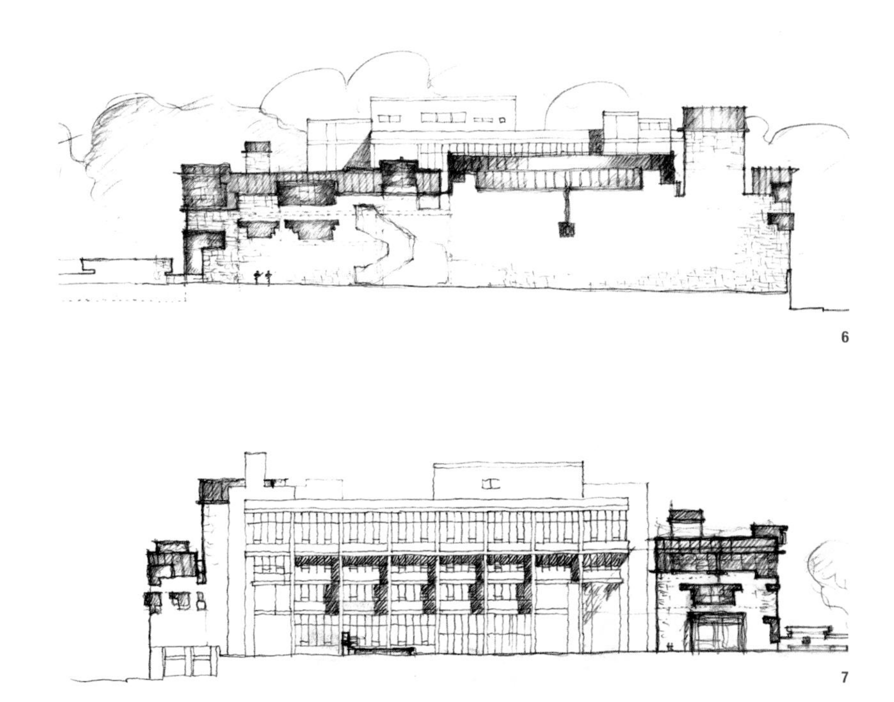

6

7

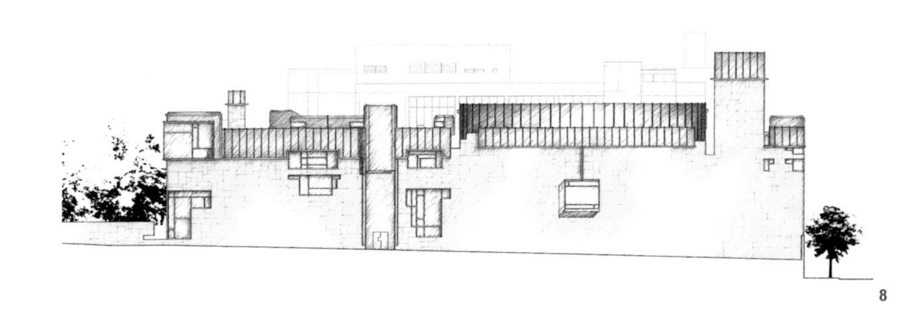

8

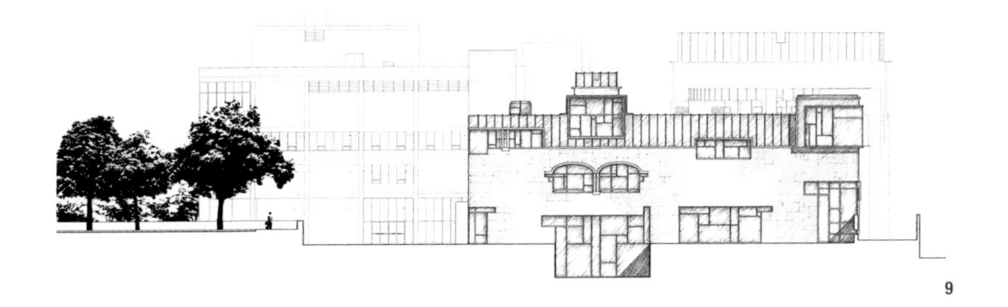

9

1 Entrance level plan
2 Second floor plan
3 Lower level plan
4 Third floor plan
5 Site plan
6 Study elevation
7 Study entry elevation
8 Final elevation on the parking side
9 Main campus elevation

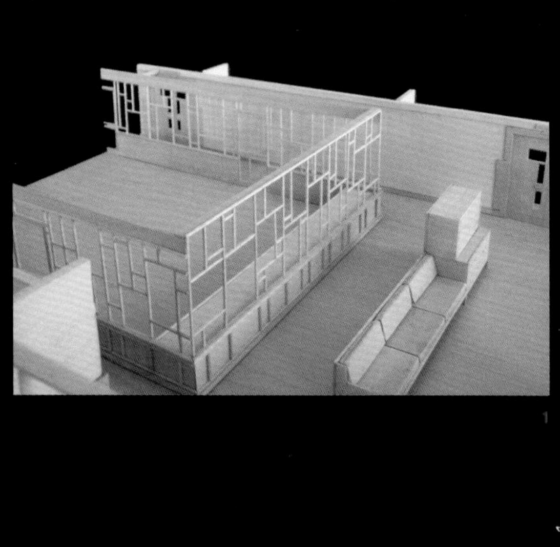

1

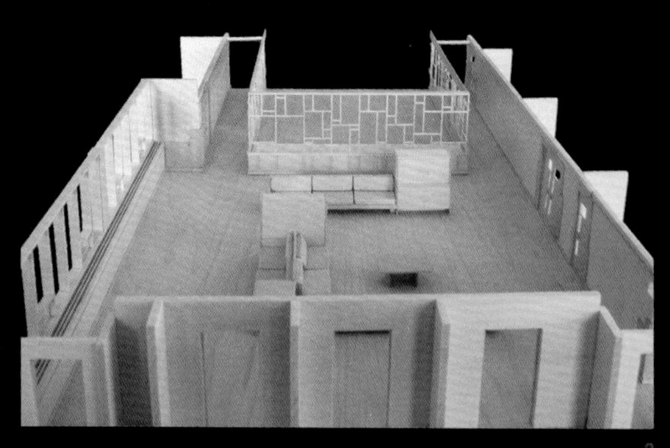

2

3

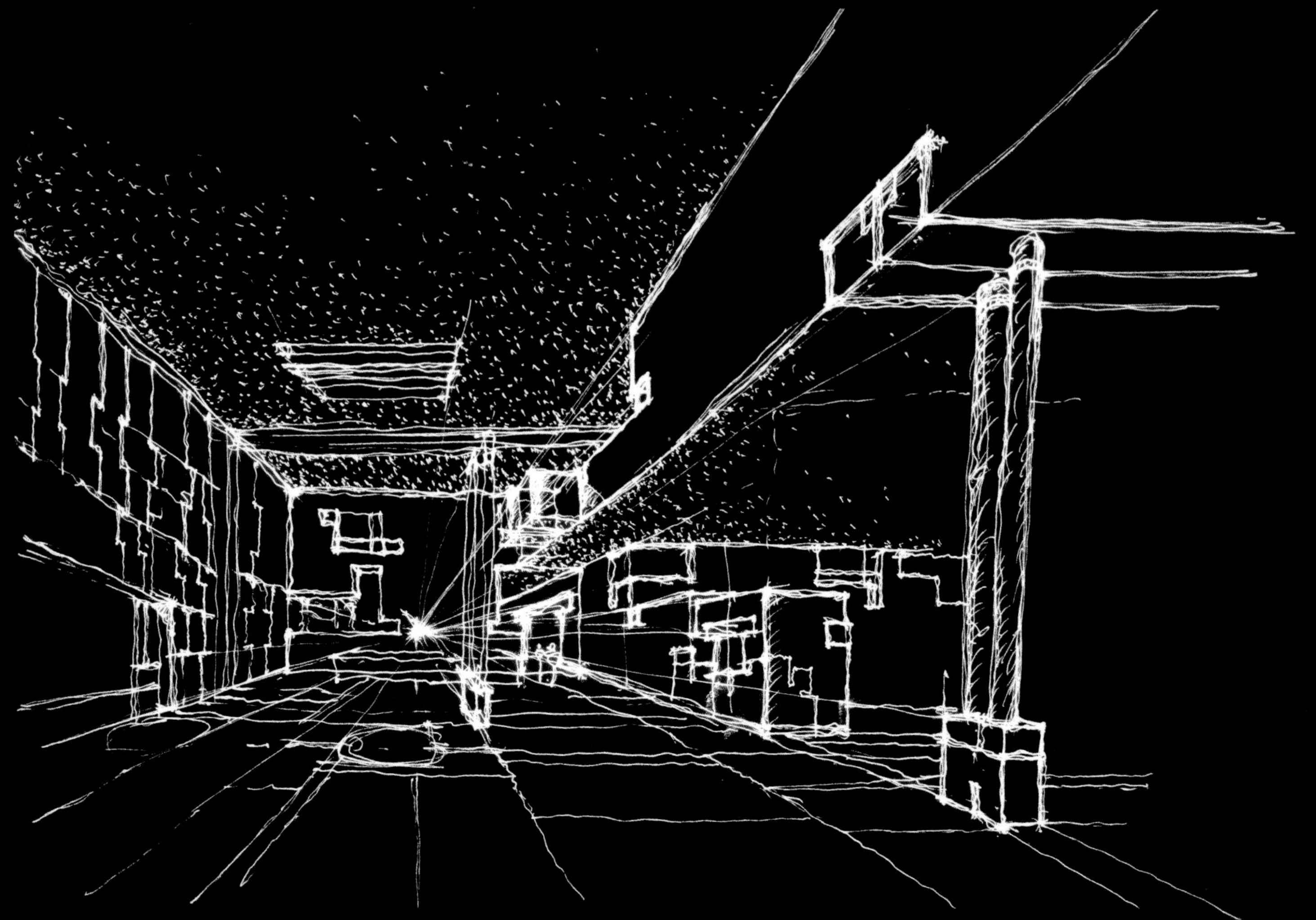

4

5

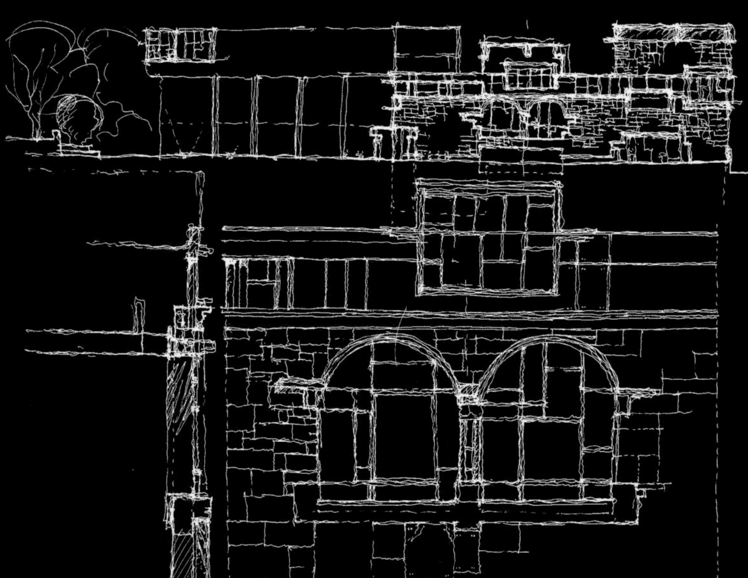

6

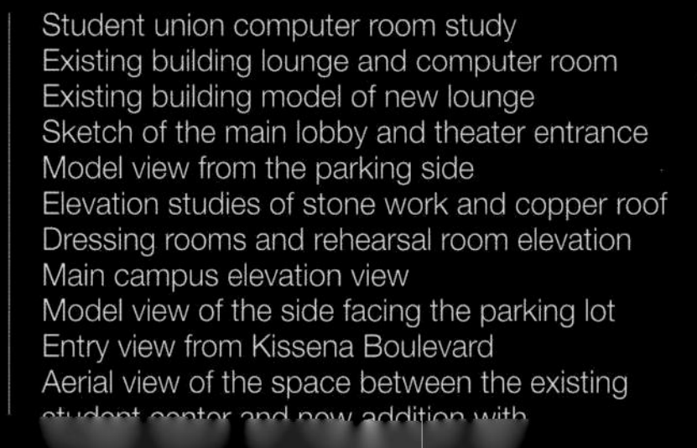

1 Student union computer room study
2 Existing building lounge and computer room
3 Existing building model of new lounge
4 Sketch of the main lobby and theater entrance
5 Model view from the parking side
6 Elevation studies of stone work and copper roof
7 Dressing rooms and rehearsal room elevation
8 Main campus elevation view
9 Model view of the side facing the parking lot
0 Entry view from Kissena Boulevard
1 Aerial view of the space between the existing student center and new addition with

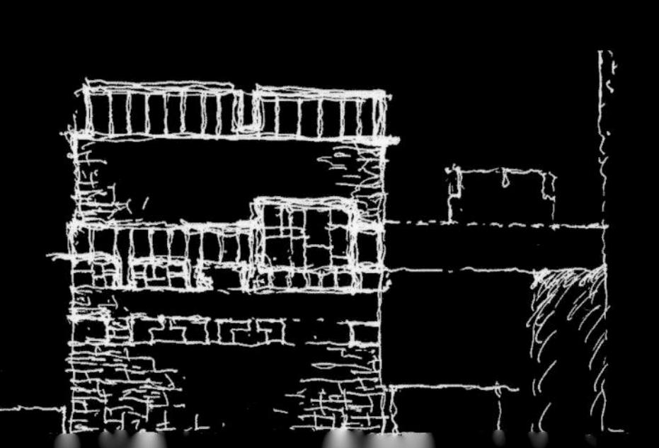

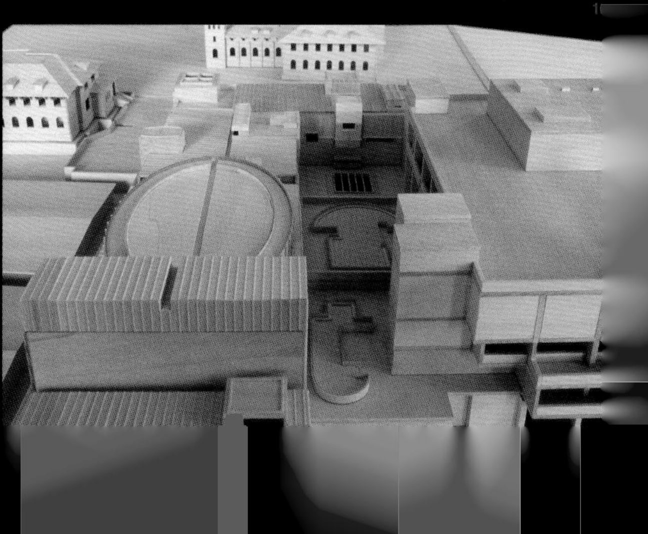

project name	Stonington Historical Society Archive Building
location	Stonington, Connecticut
year of design	1995
client	Stonington Historical Society
lot size	7.5 acres
project size	3,500 sq. ft
architect	George Ranalli
associates	Robert Silman Structural Engineer
design team	John Butterworth, Nathaniel Worden, Todd Stodolski
photographer	Model Photos: George Ranalli

Stonington Historical Society

1

This project is a 3,400 square foot addition to the existing Captain Palmer House in Stonington, Connecticut. The original structure, designated a National Historic Landmark, is an impressive period building. The addition is to contain an archive of books, letters, papers, art works, and objects from the collection of the Palmer estate. Additional material from the Town of Stonington is also to be incorporated in the archive collection.

The new building forms a small courtyard with the Palmer Mansion and the ice house to make an enclave within these disparate buildings. The new structure forms the west and north sides of the courtyard, with the two existing buildings on the south and east. It is entered from a path leading to landscape, stairs, and parking. Through the court, the front entry of the new building leads to a large entry hall. The archive is arrayed back from here, with a connecting corridor opening onto the court. At the end of this sequence is the round reading room and rectangular seminar room. Additional archive space is contained in an adjacent volume to the east.

Each space is lit by a series of windows and roof monitors. These elements help to define the space as well as admitting a special quality of light. Rooms are designed both for their use and the experience of the space; materials are selected for their ability to produce a desirable and unique atmosphere for each room. In the archive, the storage elements are designed as glass and wood cabinets, while the middle storage element comprises flat files, storage bins, and display cases.

The new building sits on a stone base on top of which sits a wood wall. The openings in the wall are designed to be a combination of window and door. The roof and all decorative elements are designed in copper. The new building asserts a strong spatial relationship with the existing buildings to form a new complex. This building is also designed to be an autonomous building with its own identity. The result is a unique blending of old and new to make a cohesive and distinctive complex.

2

1 Aerial view of the model looking toward the Palmer Mansion
2 View from the landscape toward the new addition with the circular reading room to the right
Inset: photo of the existing Palmer Mansion

1

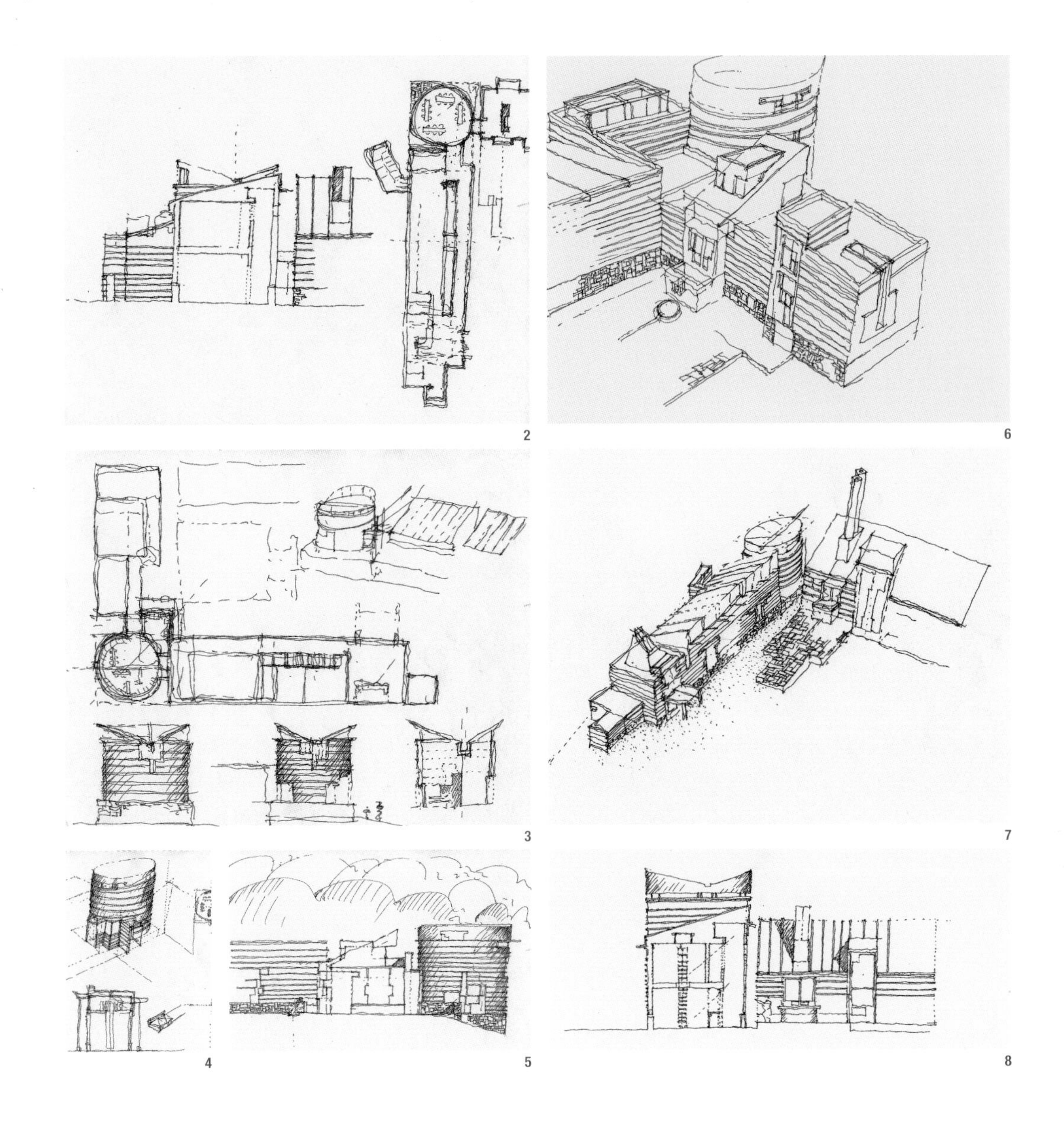

2 6 3 7 4 5 8

1	Model view of the new courtyard with the new and existing building
2	Sketch plan and section
3	Plan studies and reading room sketches
4	Reading room study
5	Section through the exhibit room
6	Pen and ink sketch of the exhibition room
7	Pen and ink sketch of the courtyard
8	Section through the archive

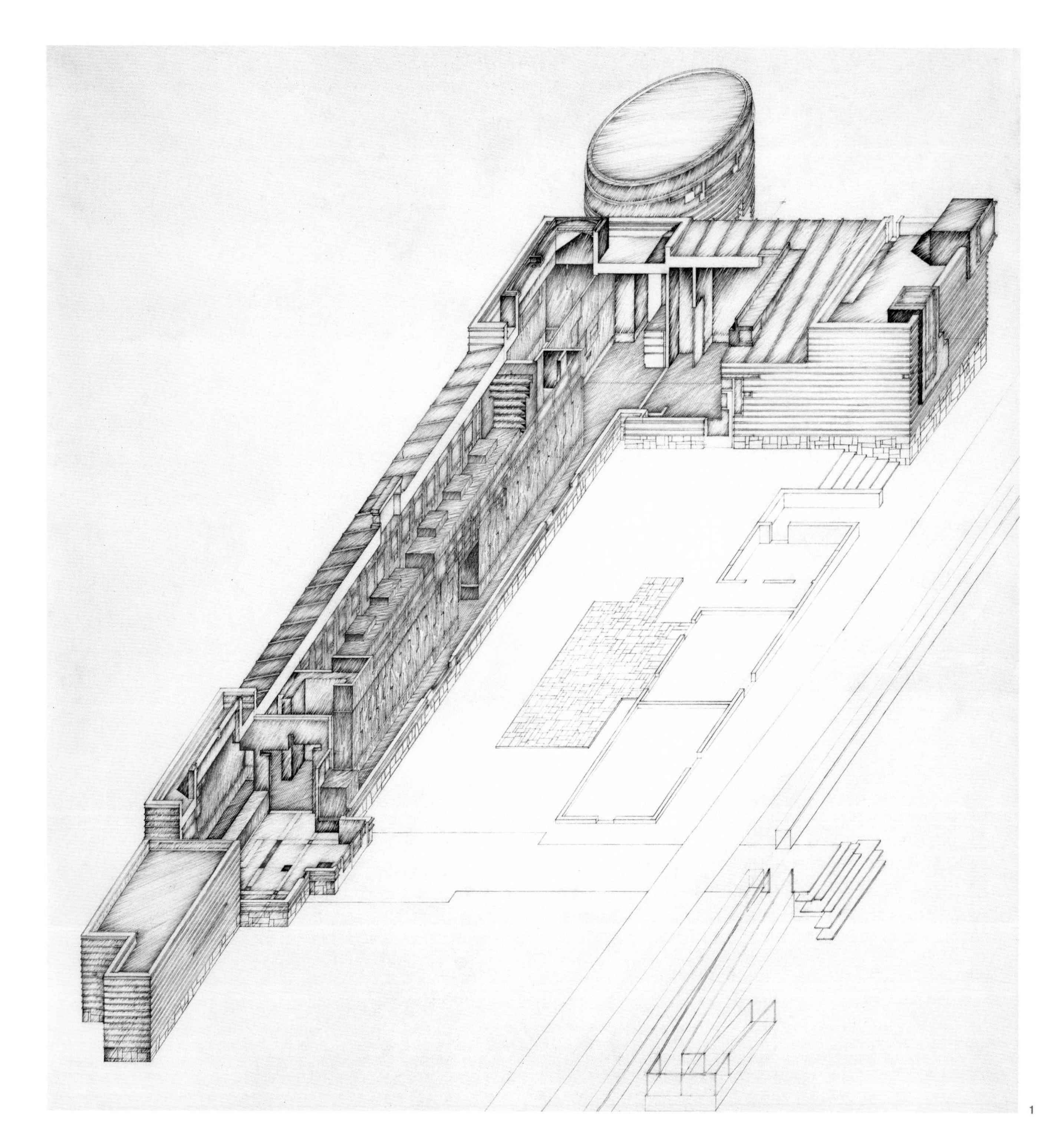

1

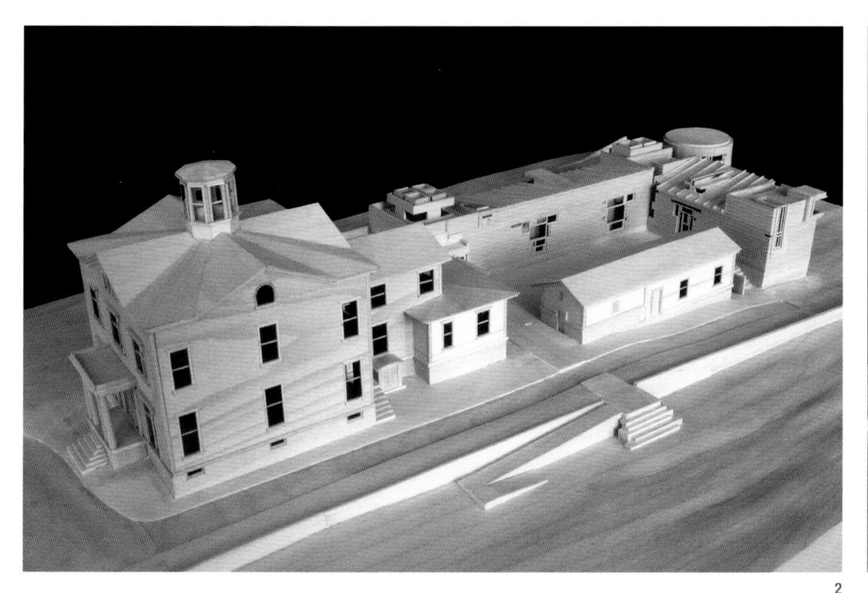

2

3

4

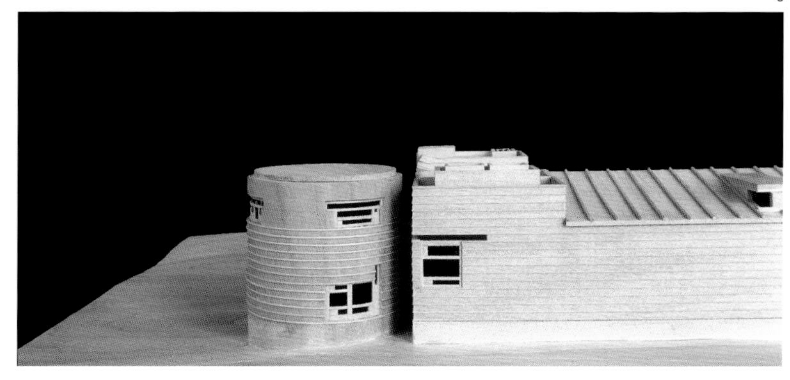

5

1 | Section oblique drawing through the entry lobby and archive
2 | Model view from the Captain Palmer Mansion end of the site
3 | Aerial view of the archive building with the round reading room in the foreground
4 | Detail view of the existing Ice House on the left and the new Exhibition room on the right
5 | View of the Seminar room and reading room and the end of the archive building

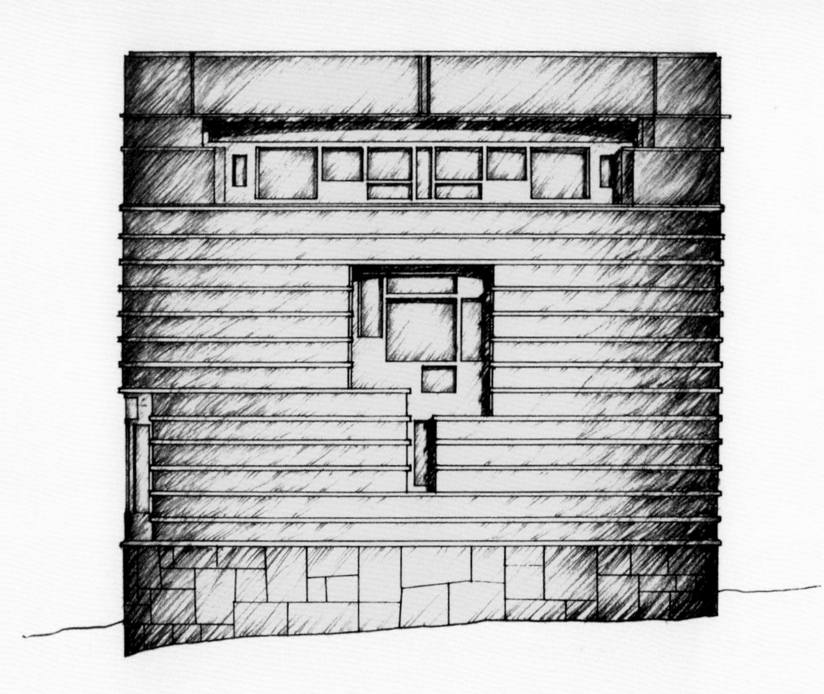

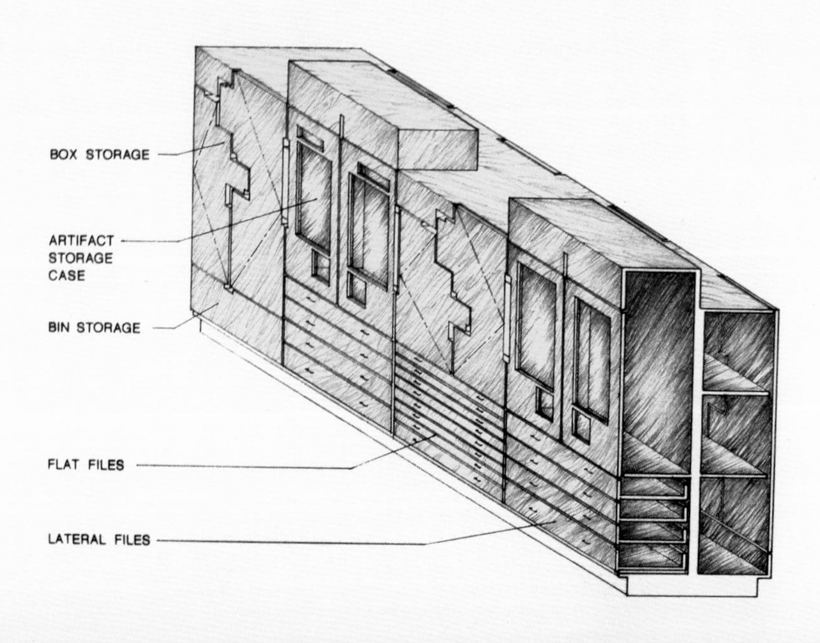
BOX STORAGE
ARTIFACT STORAGE CASE
BIN STORAGE
FLAT FILES
LATERAL FILES

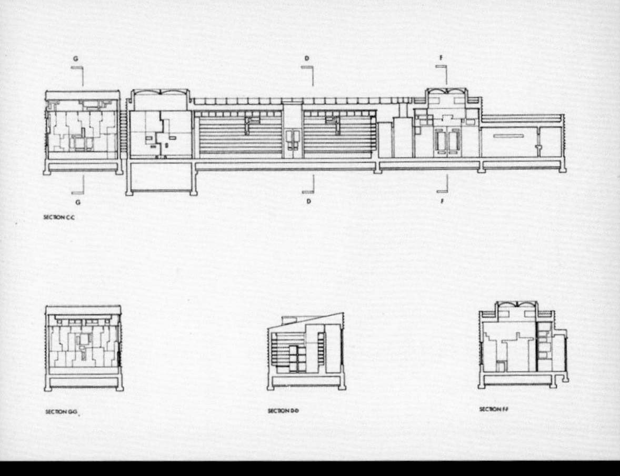

3

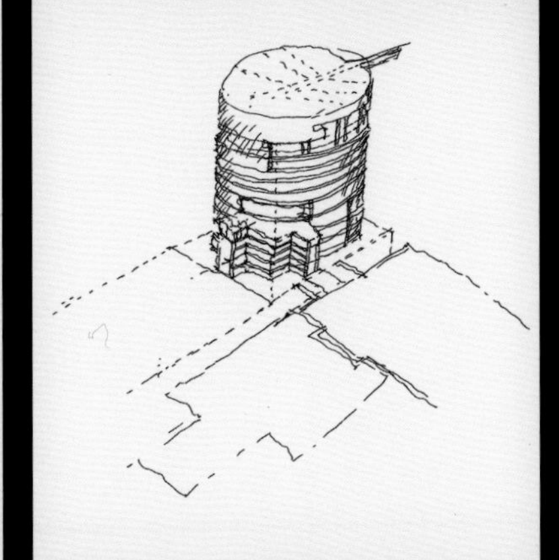

4

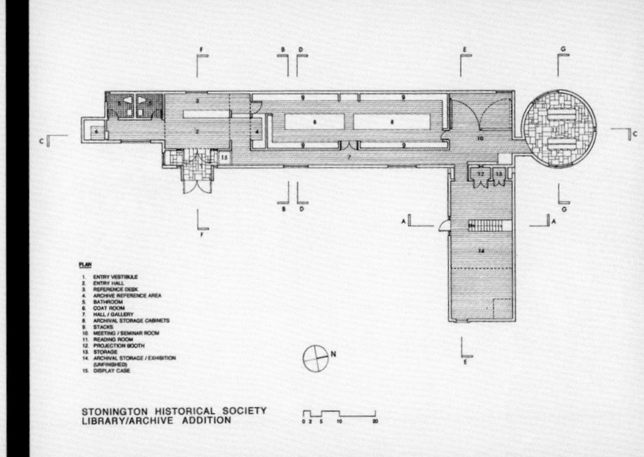

5

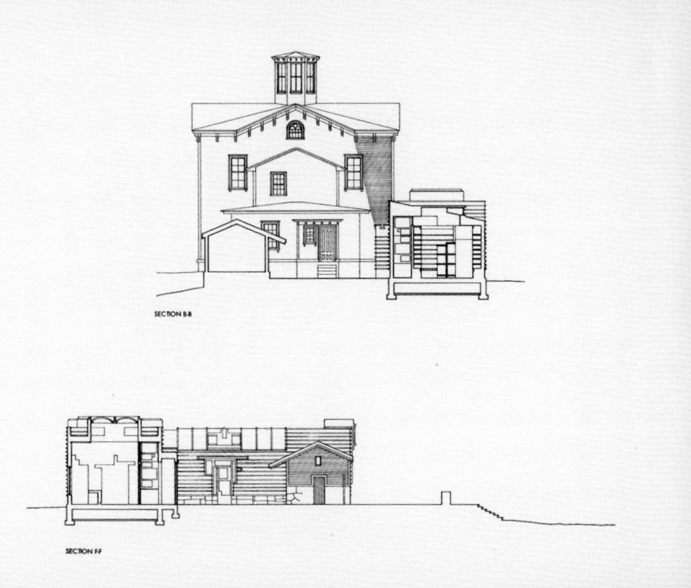

6

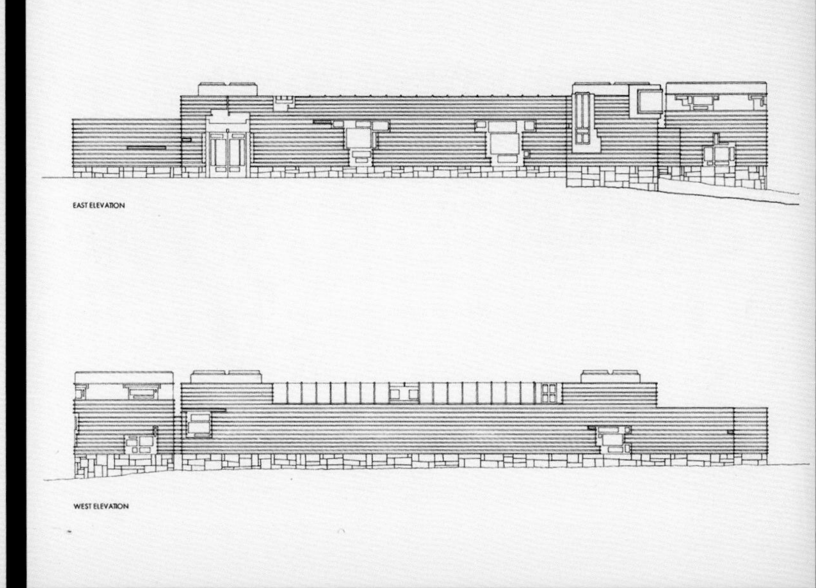

7

1 Drawing of the round reading room
2 Section oblique drawing of the wooden archive storage furniture
3 Building sections
4 Sketch of the round reading room
5 Floor plan

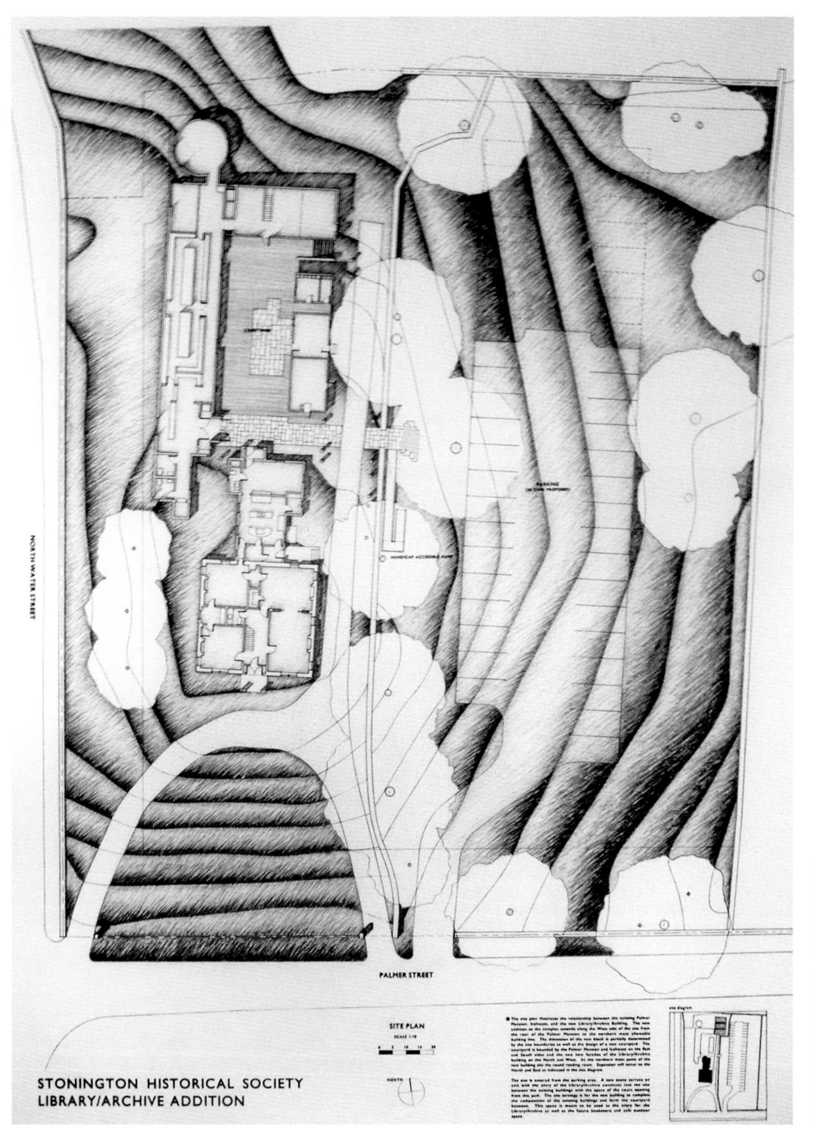

1

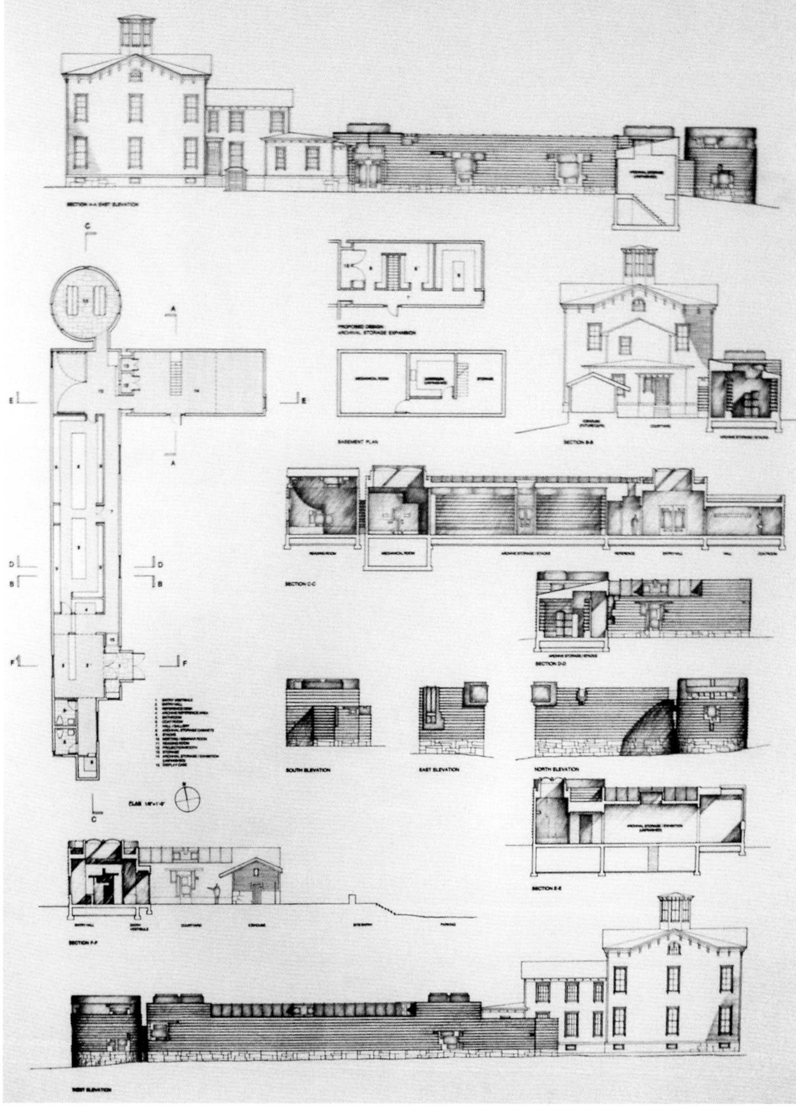

2

1 Original competition submission board of the site plan
2 Plan, sections and elevations of the original submission
3 Submission board with section perspective view, seminar and reading room details and custom storage cabinets for the archive material

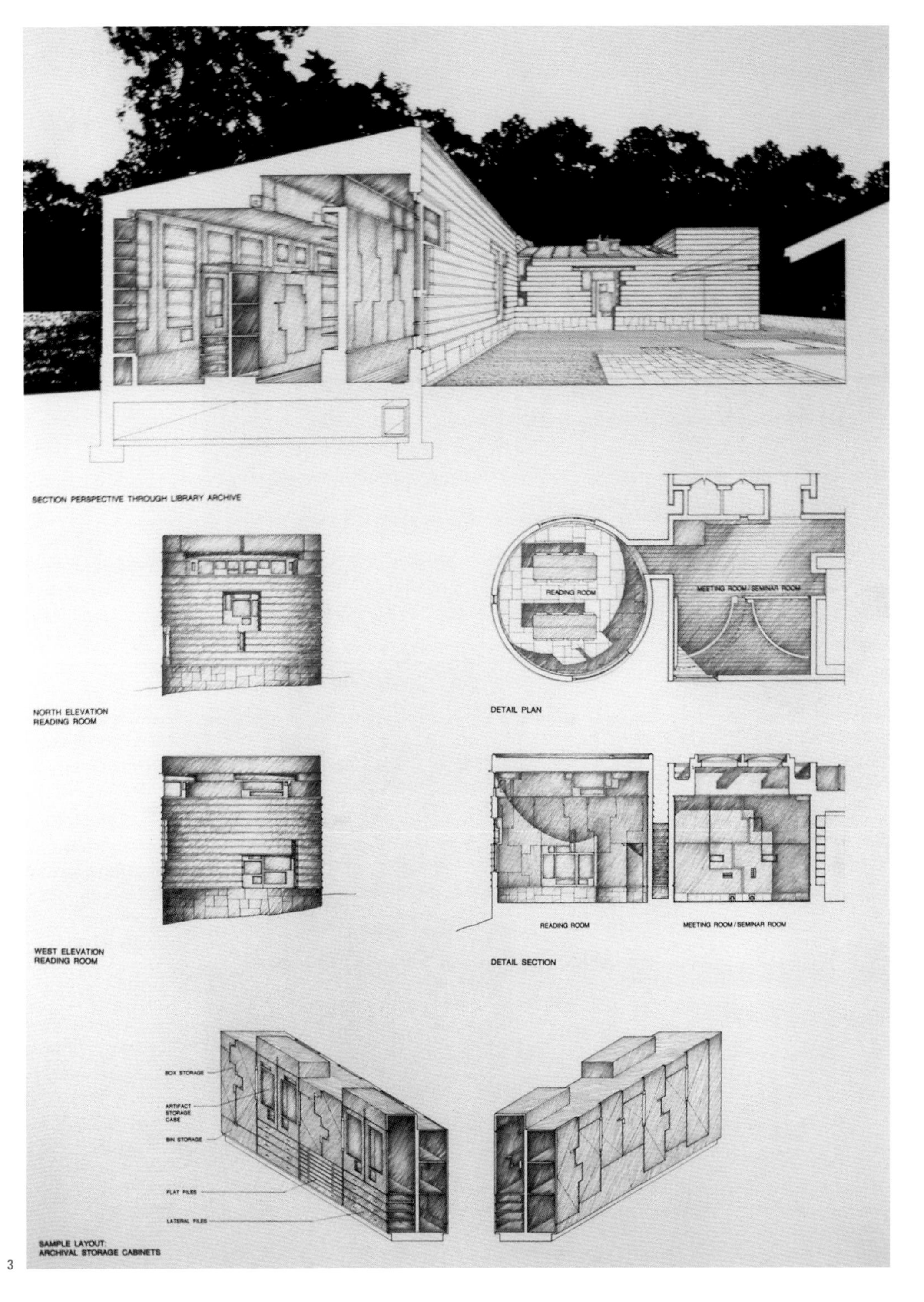
SECTION PERSPECTIVE THROUGH LIBRARY ARCHIVE
NORTH ELEVATION
READING ROOM
READING ROOM
MEETING ROOM / SEMINAR ROOM
DETAIL PLAN
WEST ELEVATION
READING ROOM
READING ROOM
MEETING ROOM / SEMINAR ROOM
DETAIL SECTION
BOX STORAGE
ARTIFACT STORAGE CASE
BIN STORAGE
FLAT FILES
LATERAL FILES
SAMPLE LAYOUT:
ARCHIVAL STORAGE CABINETS

3

project name	Paris Opera Competition
location	Place de la Bastille; Paris, France
year of design	1983
client	French Government
lot size	1/2 City Block
project size	320,000 sq. ft.
architect	George Ranalli
associates	Robert Silman Structural Engineer
design team	Nick Dermand
photographer	Model photos George Ranalli

Paris Opera Competition

1

In 1968, artists Pierre Boulez, Maurice Béjart, and Jean Vilar expressed the need for a more widely accessible opera house in Paris. In 1983, their treatise inspired President François Mitterrand to sponsor the Opera Bastille Public Establishment Competition. Its program called for an "Opera for the People" at Place de la Bastille, in the 12th arrondissement, and a redesign of the site of the existing Place monument.

The Ranalli Architect project design responds to complex zoning requirements and a programmatic goal of supporting a modest admission ticket. In particular, the sponsor believed that by increasing the number of backstage scenery storage spaces, many more operas could be performed, thereby reducing the price of admission.

The design for a new opera hall is a large cylindrical volume inside an even larger cubic mass, with all seats in the space in a radial relationship to the stage. To avoid the acoustical problems caused by curved rear walls, the back of the cylinder is opened up into the cubic enclosure. The uppermost balcony seats penetrate the cubic volume and become strong expressive elements on the facade. Access to public terraces to be enjoyed during intermissions is also through the cylinder. Administrative offices at a lower level are visible from the lobby on the south side, where the floor is pulled away from the outer wall.

Alongside the length of the site, expansive, light-filled volumes for scenery and costume shops connect to offices, scenery assembly and storage volumes, actors' dressing rooms, and music rehearsal rooms. The setbacks of the forms respond to the complex zoning requirements stipulated in the program. The project declined the option to demolish two existing buildings, opting instead to refurbish them for use as commercially viable office space for the Opera itself.

2

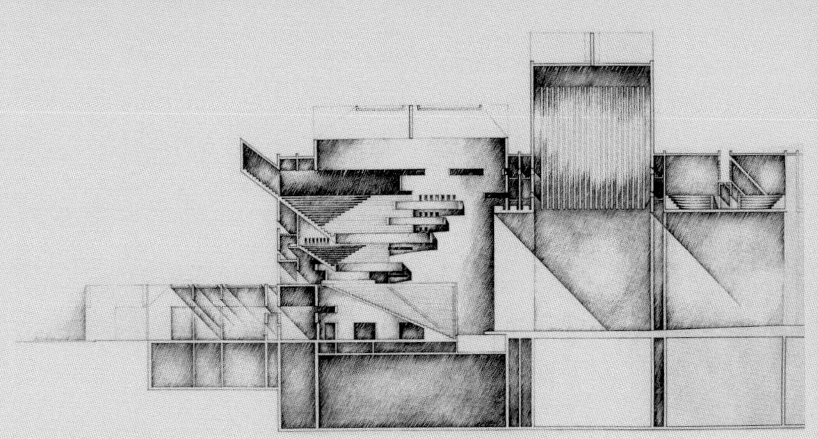

3

4

1 | Model view of the new opera from Place de la Bastille
2 | Photomontage of the site and opera model
3 | Section through the new opera
4 | Photomontage of the aerial view of the site and the model

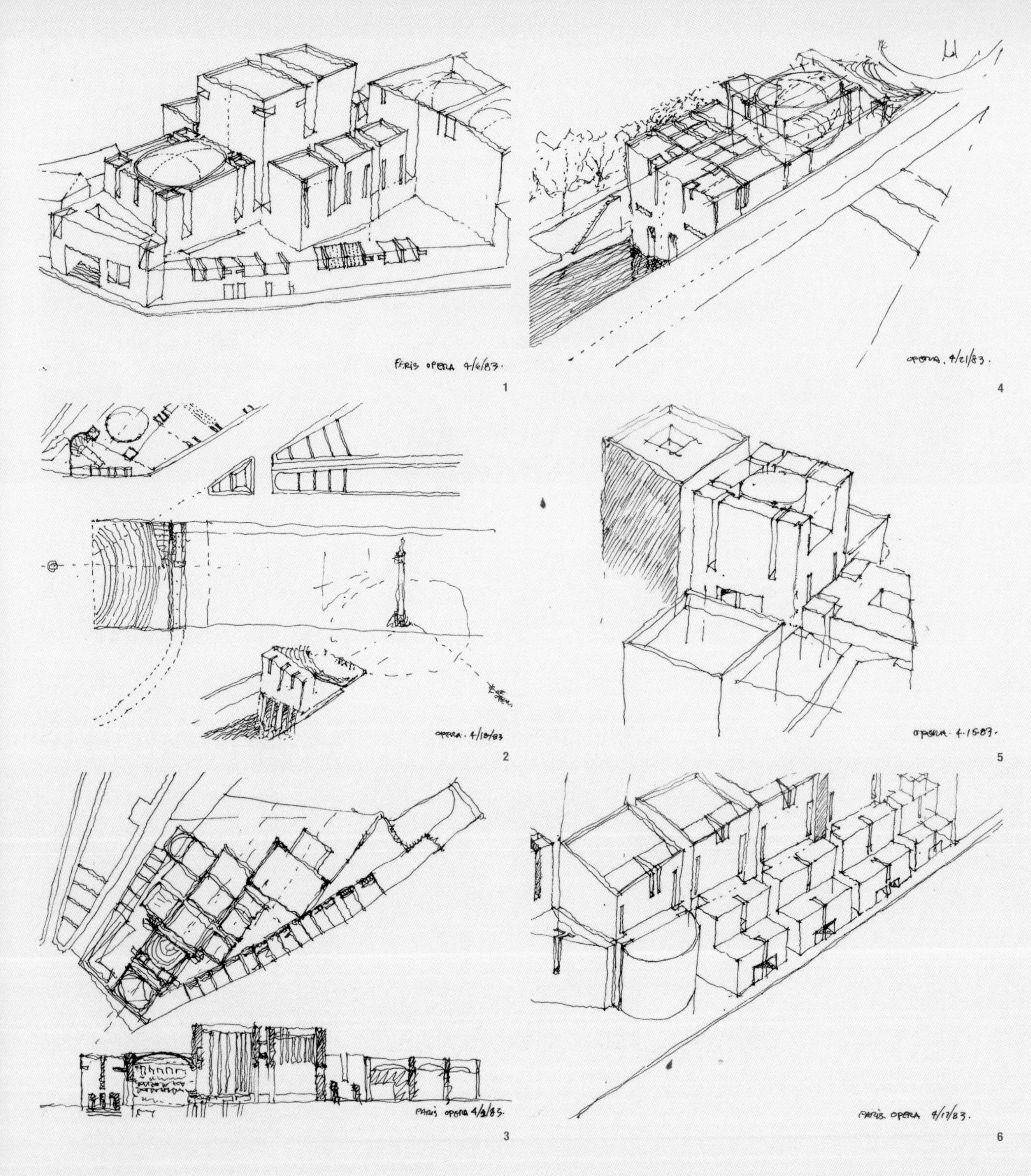
PARIS OPERA 4/6/83.
OPERA. 4/21/83.
OPERA. 4/18/83
OPERA. 4.15.83.
PARIS OPERA 4/3/83.
PARIS. OPERA 4/17/83.

1

4

2

5

3

6

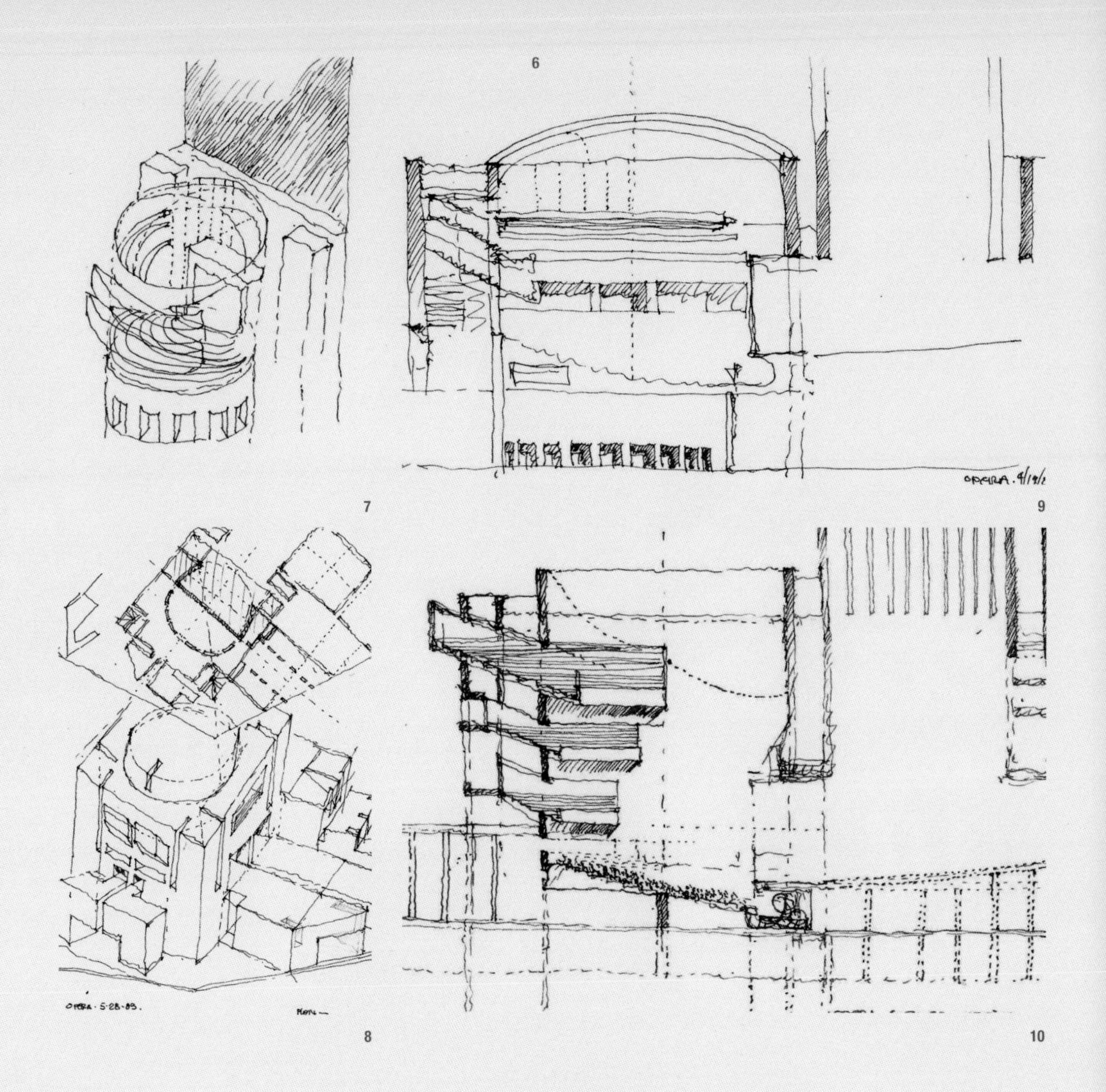

1 Pen and ink massing sketch
2 Plan and sketch study
3 Section and plan study
4 Sketch of the opera in the canal
5 Study drawing of the actor's dressing rooms
6 Massing sketch
7 Opera hall sketch
8 Plan study and massing
9 Section study
10 Section through opera hall and scenery tower

1

2

Also on site, a new open-air public theatre stands open to the outside environment, and a new subway station provides easy, relatively inexpensive access. The new interior of the subway station includes ticketing facilities, restrooms, an information/communication center, and platform-level waiting areas for theatergoers, all elegantly appointed in easily maintained floors, walls, and ceilings of marble and tile.

3

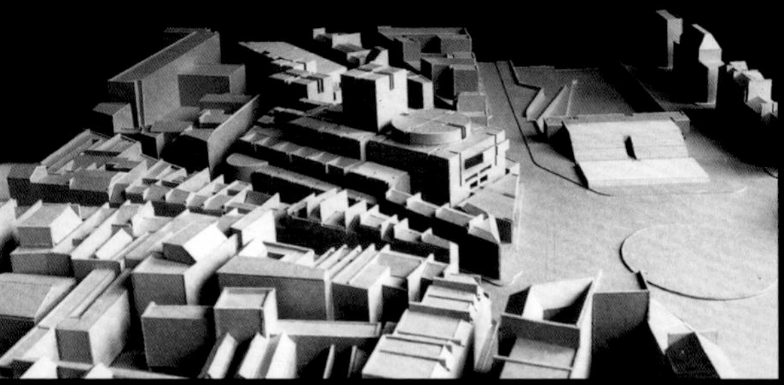

4

5

6

1 | View of the model looking toward the Opera
2 | Model view from behind the Opera looking toward Place de la Bastille
3 | Looking across the urban landscape at the Opera situated within the cityscape
4 | View in front of Place de la Bastille
5 | View from the side of the experimental theater
6 | Aerial view of the entire complex

1

2

1 Photomontage of the site photo and the model
2 Photomontage of the long view of Paris with the model photo set into the foreground

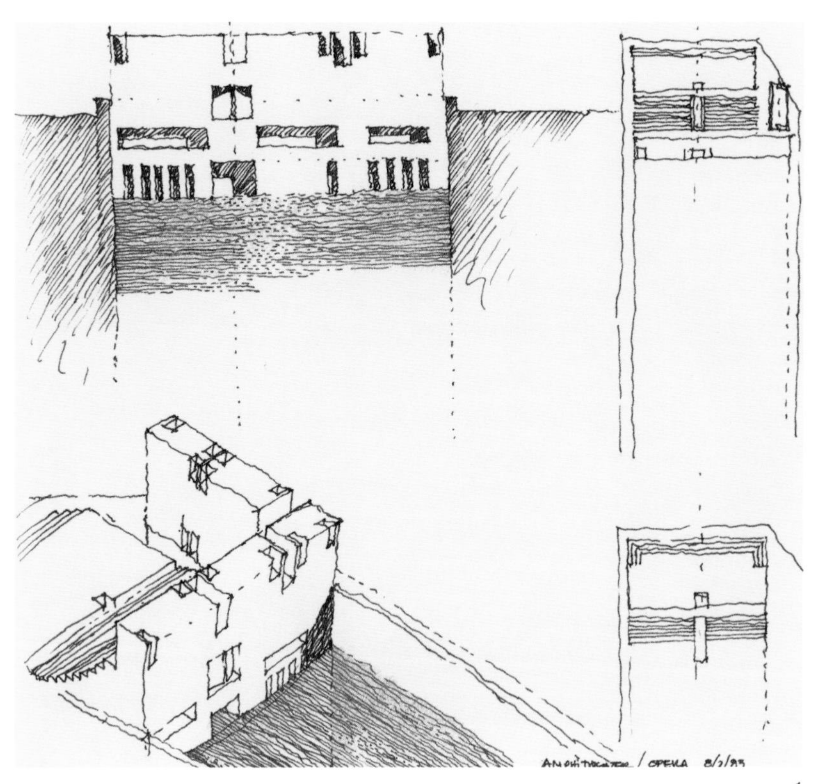

1

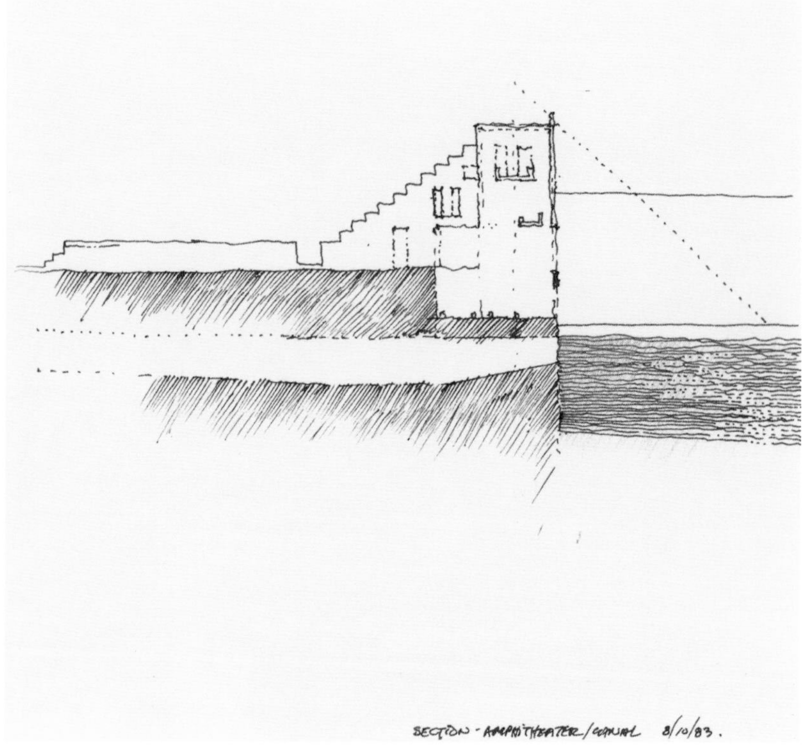

2

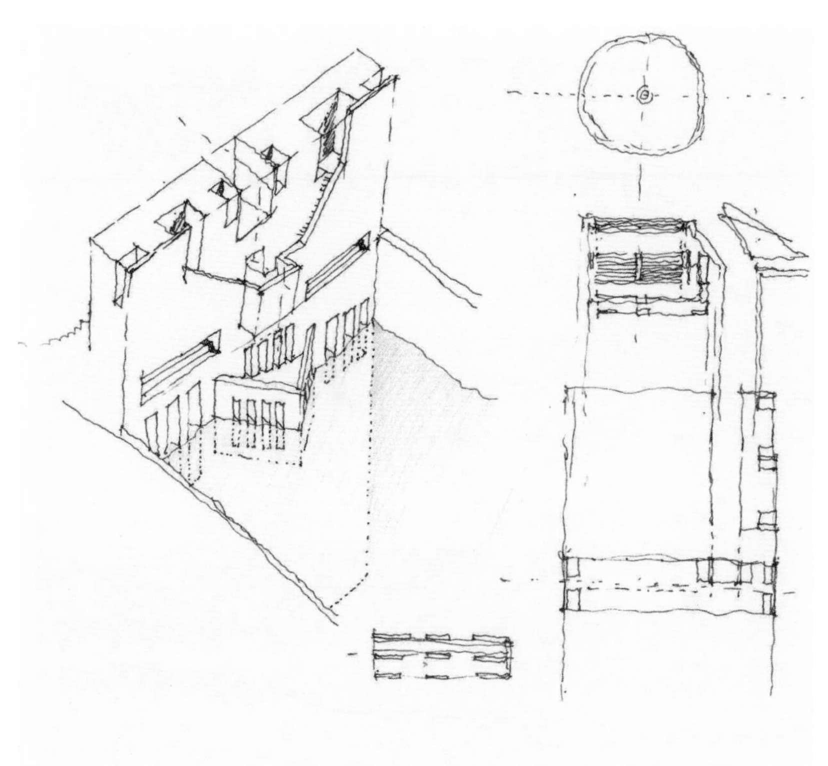

3

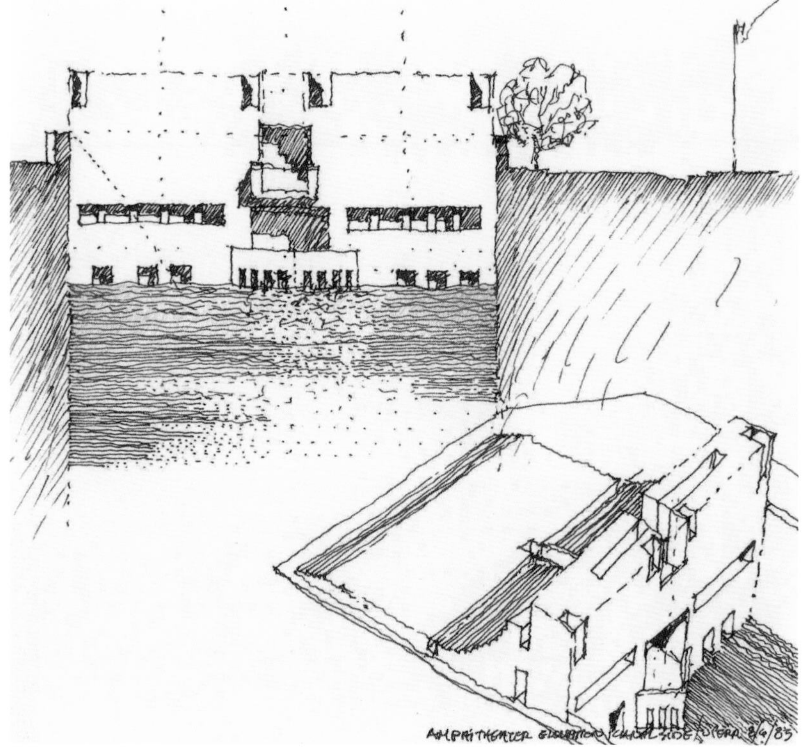

4

1 | Canal elevation and sketch
2 | Section through outdoor theater and subway station
3 | Canal sketch
4 | Elevation of canal building and outdoor theater sketch

EXHIBITS

project name	Frank Lloyd Wright, Designs for an American Landscape 1922-1932
location	Madison Avenue, New York
year of design	1995
year of completion	1996
client	Canadian Center for Architecture/Whitney Museum
lot size	7,500 sq.ft.
architect	George Ranalli
design team	Price Harrison, Fran Leadon, Aaron MacDonald
photographer	Paul Warchol

Whitney Museum of American Art

1

The Whitney Museum exhibit, "Frank Lloyd Wright: Designs for an American Landscape, 1922–1932," presented five of the architect's most ambitious and radical projects for rural sites, designed during his celebrated "lost years." Wright's projects exist only as drawings. Ranalli Architect prepared detailed models that allowed the architectural layman to immediately comprehend the scope and intent of Wright's extraordinary ideas. The installation design relies on graphic elements to organize and orchestrate the complex array of drawings and models in the exhibit. While broad bands of color run continuously around the top and bottom of each of the rooms, intricate vertical elements separate the five projects, alerting the viewer to variations within each project.

The design mediates between the museum environment and the exhibited work. The most palpable result is a warm, intimately scaled and coherent space within the gallery. On a theoretical level, the design suggests the possibility of a renewed connection between our real American present and an alternative future America represented in Wright's drawings. The exhibit is thus a presentation of historic documents, and a new design work embracing a living, vital past.

2

1 | Installation view through the gallery walls
2 | Entrance to the exhibit
View of the installation (following spread)

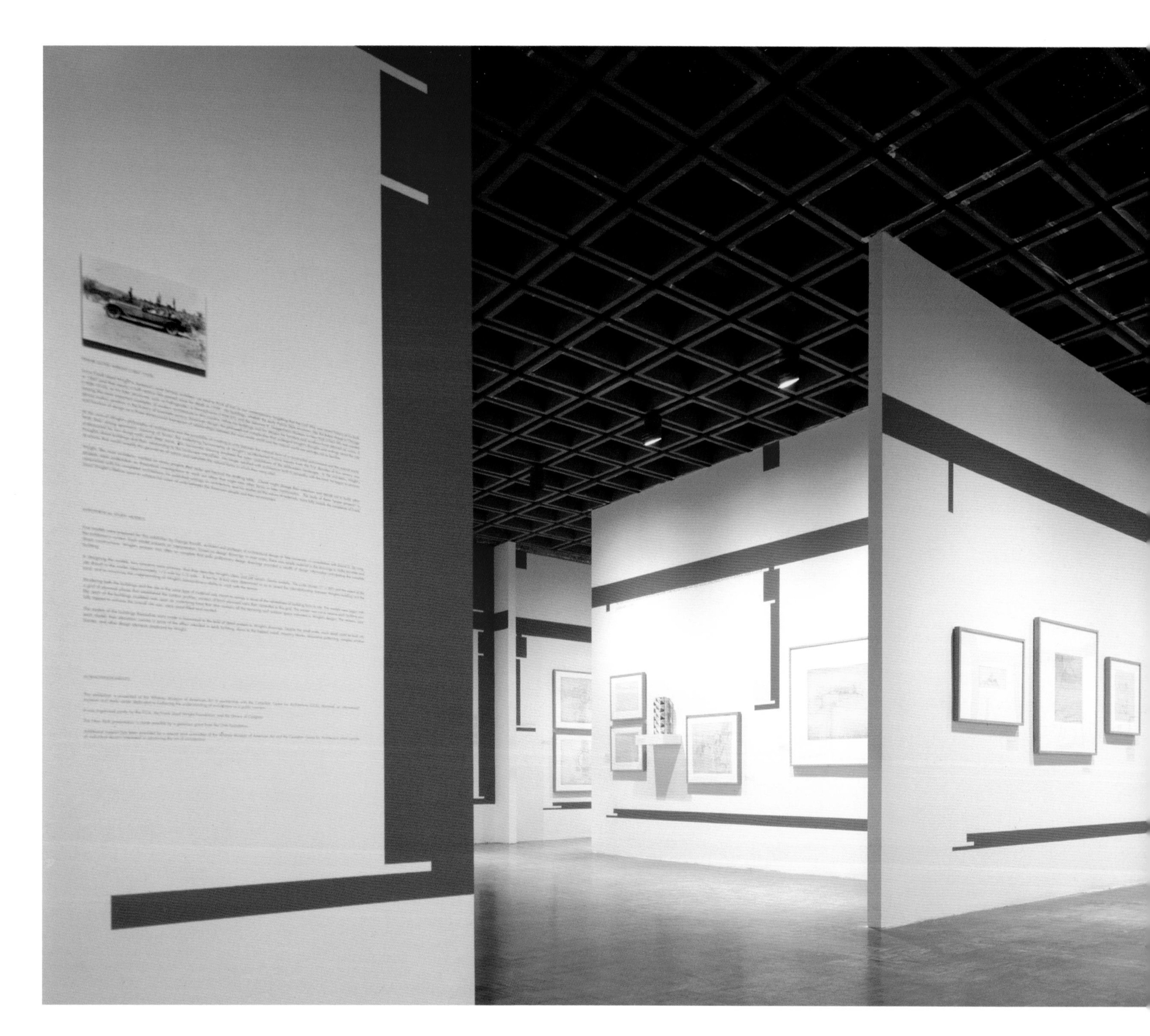

1

2

1 | Expanse of the gallery spaces
2 | Detail view of the interpretative models

project name	Carlo Scarpa: Intervening with History
location	Montreal, Canada
year of design	1998
year of completion	1999
client	Canadian Center for Architecture
lot size	7,500 sq.ft.
architect	George Ranalli
design team	Mario Gentile, Price Harrison, Fran Leadon
photographer	Michel Legendre

Scarpa Exhibit at the Canadian Center for Architecture

1

The Canadian Center for Architecture exhibit "Carlo Scarpa: Intervening With History" began with the idea to bring the work of Scarpa to a North American audience. In addition to exhibiting magnificent original Scarpa drawings, the Ranalli Architect installation design incorporates materials that represent ideas about Scarpa's work, thereby providing a comprehensive and integrated vision of Scarpa's significant architectural interventions in historic settings.

The Ranalli Architect design for the installation features materials used primarily by Scarpa. Each of the delicate Scarpa drawings is set in a custom-designed wood frame, which allowed the image to float in the body of the frame. Photography of Scarpa's built projects by Guido Guidi is placed upon steel easels with tilted tops to that accommodate the movement of viewer's gaze from the walls to the easel. In addition, Ranalli Architect provides a set of analytic wood models of Scarpa projects to help facilitate a three-dimensional understanding of these complex works of architecture. The models are set upon steel pedestals, custom fabricated in a Montreal steel shop, designed in concert with the photo easels. Each room of the exhibit is dedicated to a project or grouping of projects that revealed Scarpa's profound spatial, material, and decorative palette.

2

4

3

5

1 | Veritti House model and drawings on the wall
2 | Gallery view with photo easels contaning Guido Guidi photographs
3 | Welded steel easels containing Guido Guidi photographs
4 | View through several rooms
5 | Gallery with photo easels
View of the gallery with photo easels, interpretive model and Scarpa easel (following spread)

project name	Present Tense: The Architecture of George Ranalli
location	New York City
year of design	1998
year of completion	1999
client	Artists Space Gallery
lot size	1,500 sq.ft.
architect	George Ranalli
design team	Mario Gentile, Price Harrison, Fran Leadon
photographer	George Ranalli

Artists Space Gallery

1

As part of an ongoing series of exhibits on art and architecture, in 1998–1999, Artists Space Gallery invited Ranalli Architect to exhibit work in the Project Room. The invitation included an opportunity to design an installation. The invitation was a fascinating opportunity to explore the provocative interconnections between art and architecture through the recognition that a gallery exhibit is a work of design and architecture, as well as a primary means of communication about artistic or architectural intentions.

The exhibit, entitled "Present Tense: The Architecture of George Ranalli," occupied the Project Room for several months. The exhibit included print images, drawings of built and unrealized projects, architectural models, and photography of completed works. The latter component of the exhibit showed architectural projects in a descriptive, yet experiential manner.

The actual gallery space is utilized as an extension of works exhibited on the walls. Given the financial and temporal limitations of the gallery, a design requiring transformative construction would have been imprudent. Instead, the Project Room entrance became a large piece of spatial illusion through the application of stencil graphics. The paint, selected as a medium to satisfy budgetary restrictions, defined the space containing the exhibited work. Bold graphics and silkscreen text create a striking illusion of scale and density on the gallery walls and serve to demarcate the boundaries of the four projects exhibited. The real-time experience of the visitors to the gallery facilitates an understanding of the ideas presented by the work.

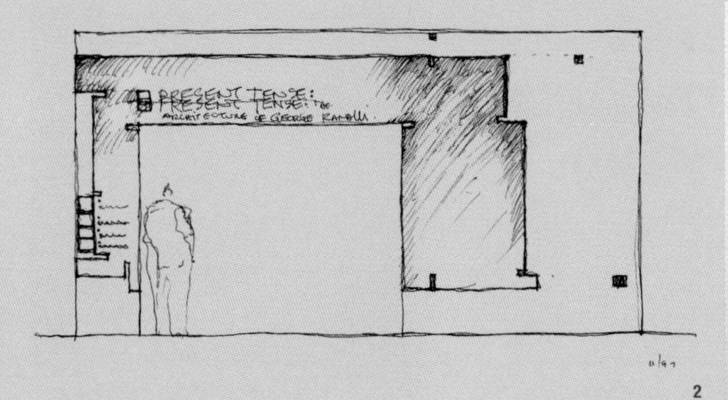

2

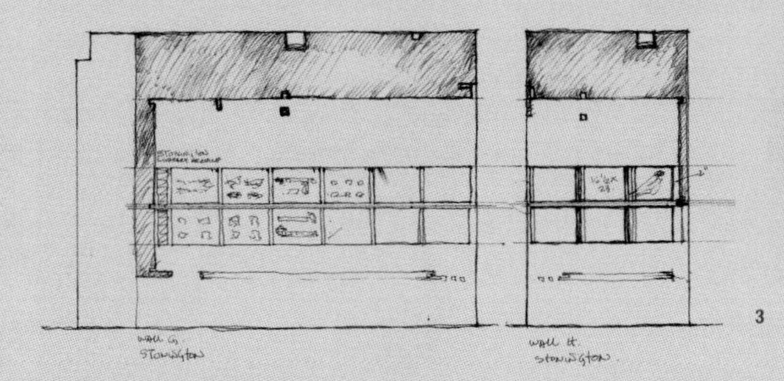

3

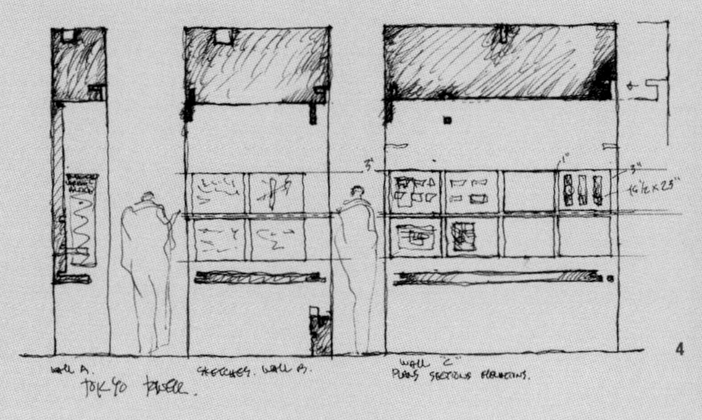

4

5

6

1 | Exhibit entry with silk-screen graphics
2 | Pen and ink sketch of the entry graphics
3 | Wall graphics and drawing layout
4 | Wall studies
5 | View of the entry wall
6 | Interior view of the exhibit

project name	17th Triennale di Milano; "Living in a Loft"
location	Milan, Italy
year of design	1984
year of completion	1985
client	Triennale di Milano
lot size	2,600 sq.ft.
architect	George Ranalli
associates	Robert Silman Structural Engineer
design team	Nick Dermand
photographer	Matteo Piazza, Stefano Valebrega

17th Triennale Di Milano (1985-1986)

1

The Triennale di Milano, Italy, has acted as a laboratory of design for decades. The premise of the show, Il Progetto Domestico, explored themes prevalent, at the time, on domesticity, the city, and history, as well as many other topical areas of theoretical discourses.

Ranalli Architect saw an invitation to participate in the exhibition as a chance to explore the principles and values of design impacting the environment of the gallery and the world beyond the exhibit room. The project for Il Progetto Domestico posited residential life in a converted industrial space as a real alternative to the normative domestic box. Industrial spaces provide practical clarity in their structure, fenestration, and spatial order. Positioning residential space into a former industrial building offers extraordinary opportunity to investigate how one lives, and how the domestic interior evolves within the architecture of former industrial complexes.

The visitors to the exhibit experience the design for 'Trienniale' by moving through the space, from the main hall, inward, for a new residential experience. Openings in the volume reveal routes through the suite of rooms, with views upwards, and through the block, until one is inside a protected enclave set between the new construction and the existing shell of the industrial container. Here the interior unfolded for the visitor, with each space dedicated to a living function, represented by a piece of furniture. Movement continues up a discrete staircase to a second floor, to a bedroom space, and beyond, to another room with a chaise longue, fabricated of molded sheet steel, projected out and suspended over the dining table. Back downstairs in the "courtyard" style open space, one end of a dining table of grey-and-white marble rests on a steel pedestal, nestled into sculpted spaces in the residential block. At the far end of the table, stands a ladder-back, black-lacquer dining chair, which was fabricated by Promosedia in Udine, Italy.

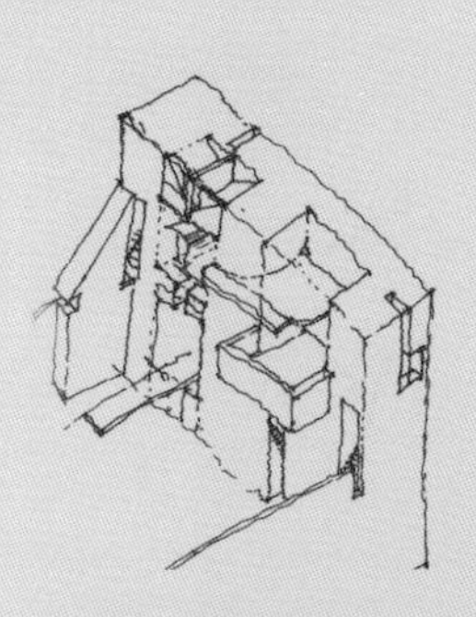

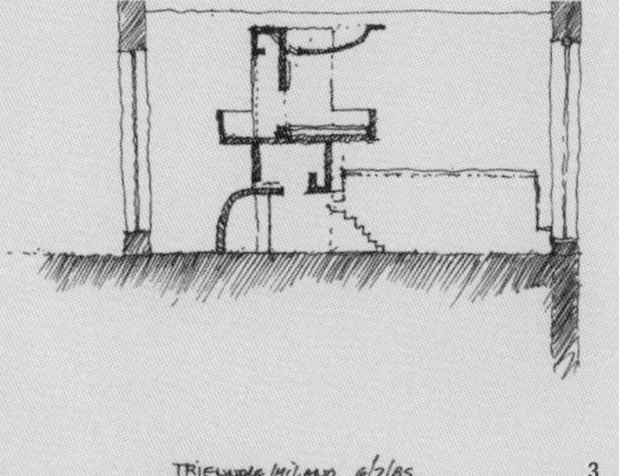

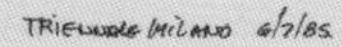

3

4

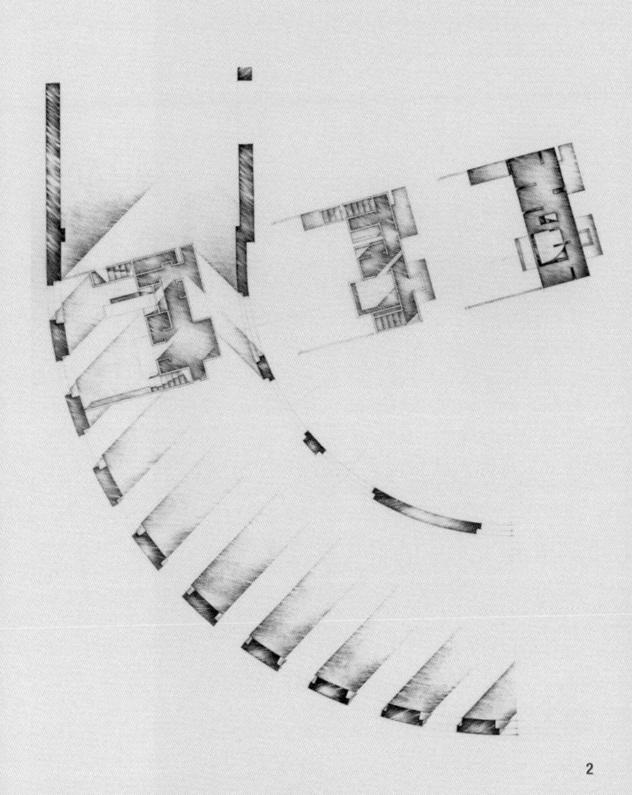

2

5

1 | Table detail in the interior court of the exhibit
2 | Plans of the exhibit, pencil and graphite on vellum
3 | Studies of the massing and section
4 | Photomontage of the space with a drawing of the exhibit
5 | View of the side of the constructed exhibit

1

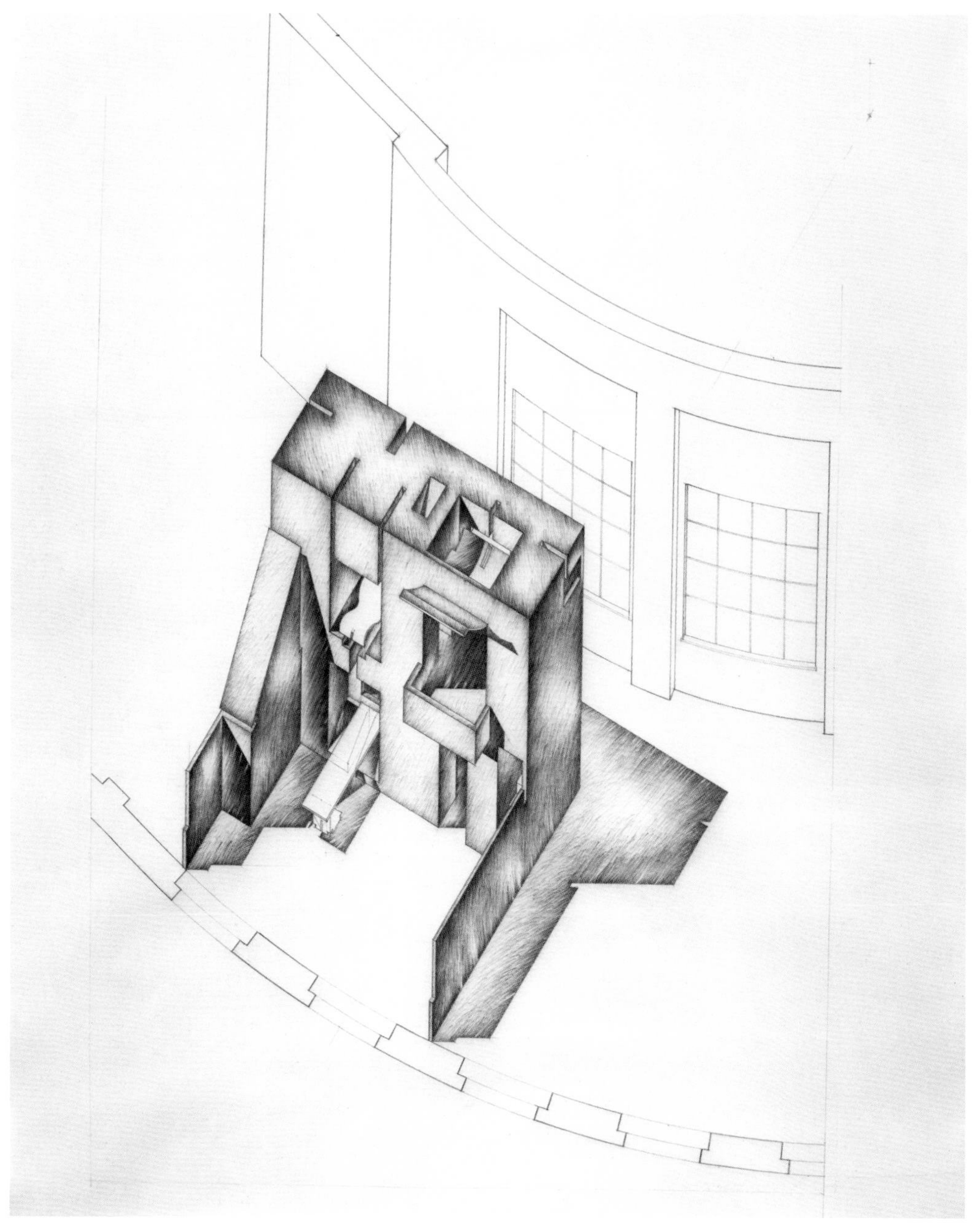

2

3

4

5

1 | Courtyard interior of the exhibit
2 | Axonometric drawing of the design
3 | Lamp design
4 | Dining chair
5 | Structural detail for the table support

1

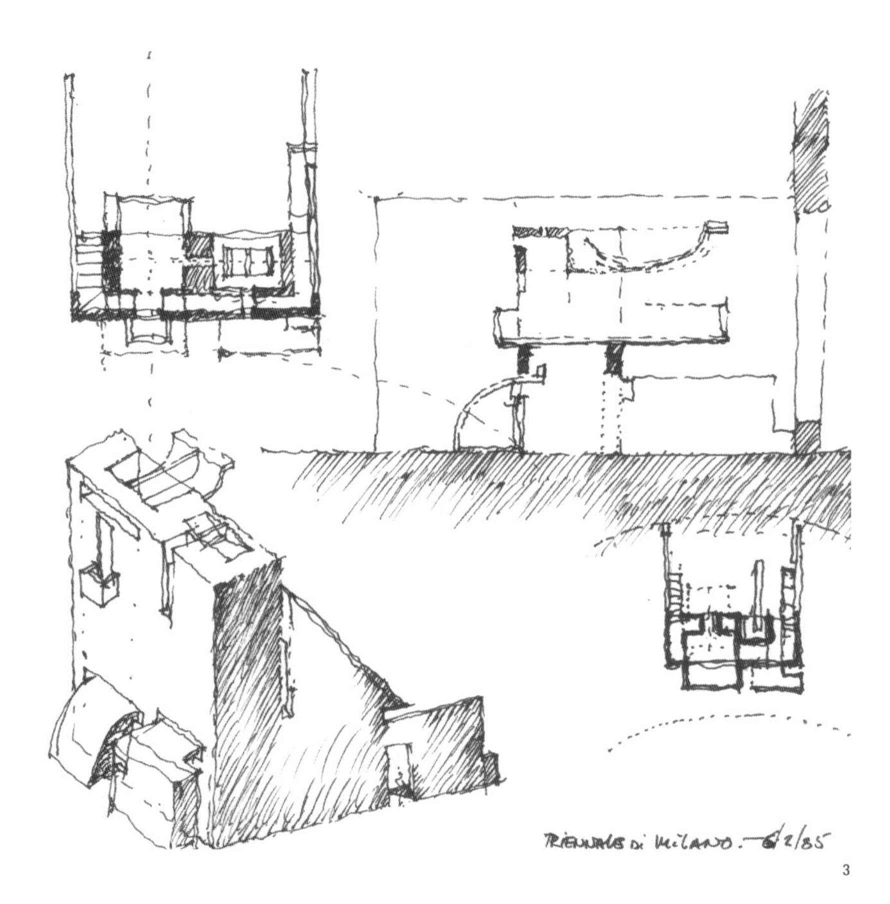

3

2

4

1 | View along the entrance
2 | View of the interior passage
3 | Plan, section and volumetric study
4 | Rotated elevation of the exhibit in the gallery
5 | View of the exhibit along the visitor's passageway

5

1

3

2

4

1 | Exit elevation
2 | Side elevation
3 | Section through the reclining chair room
4 | Section through the sleeping room
5 | Project construction
6 | View of the exhibit
7 | Early studies

5

6

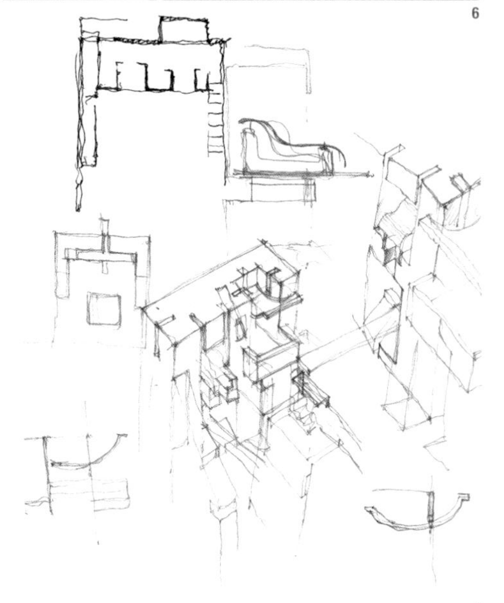

7

project name	Design at the End of the Century 1975-2000 Exhibit
location	Denver Art Museum
year of design	2001
year of completion	2002
client	Denver Art Museum
architect	George Ranalli
design team	Mario Gentile
photographer	George Ranalli

Denver Art Museum

1

In 2002, the Denver Art Museum launched "U.S. Design 1975–2000," an exhibition examining architectural projects and design artifacts seen as important points of departure for the norm during the last quarter of the twentieth century. Curator R. Craig Miller commissioned Ranalli Architects to design a full-scale work of architecture for visitors. The project was to expand visitors' awareness of the drawings and models in other parts of the exhibit. Ranalli Architect designed and installed a project representative of the firm's interest in the architectural and decorative arts, which continue as an ongoing investigation.

The built project features a full-scale wall design of wood panels with detailing similar to other interiors design projects. The Denver Art Museum project was executed for an entryway location, with all the wood panel variations corresponding to existing elements on the gallery wall. Thin strips of inlaid walnut wood separate the ornamentally arranged panels. The larger slots made by interconnecting wood sections, filled with walnut detailing, are meant to facilitate a transfer of scale from the larger full length wall panels to the more diminutive scale, relative to the hand. The transference of scale creates an experience of a design that operates at both the larger scale of the Museum and the more personal dimension, continuously engaging the scrutiny by exhibition visitors.

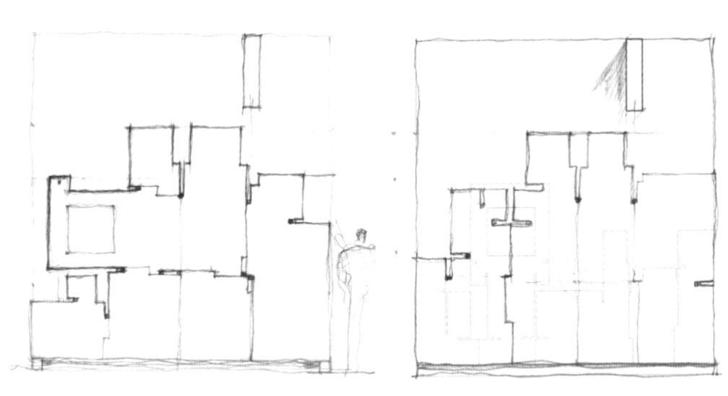

2

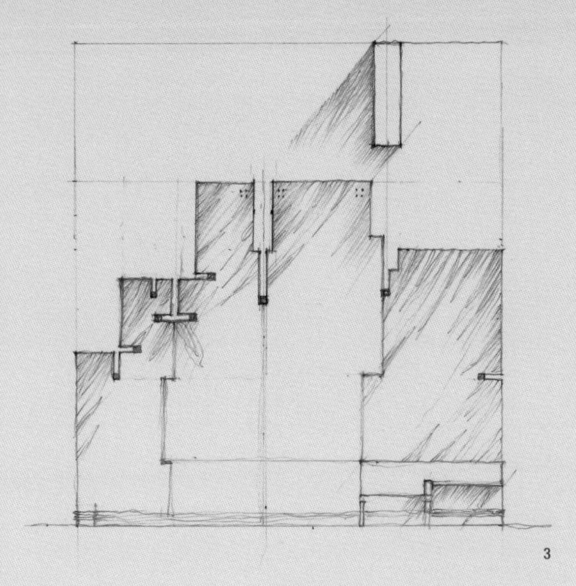

3

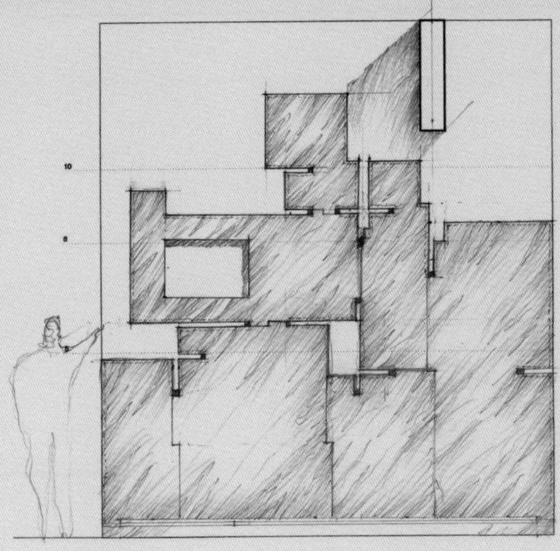

4

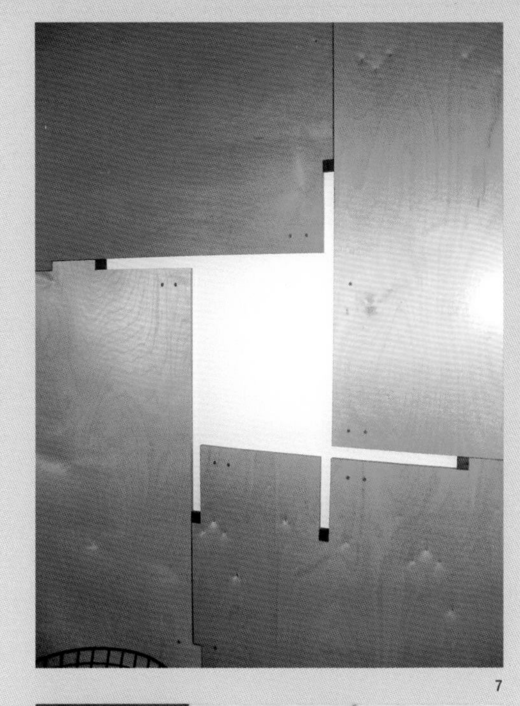

7

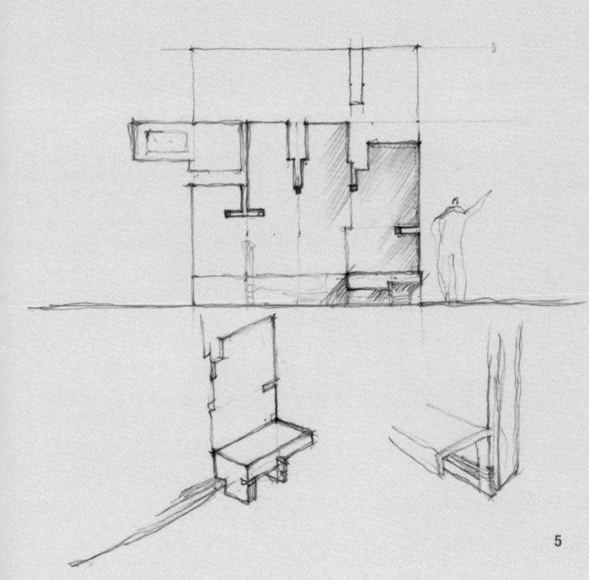

5

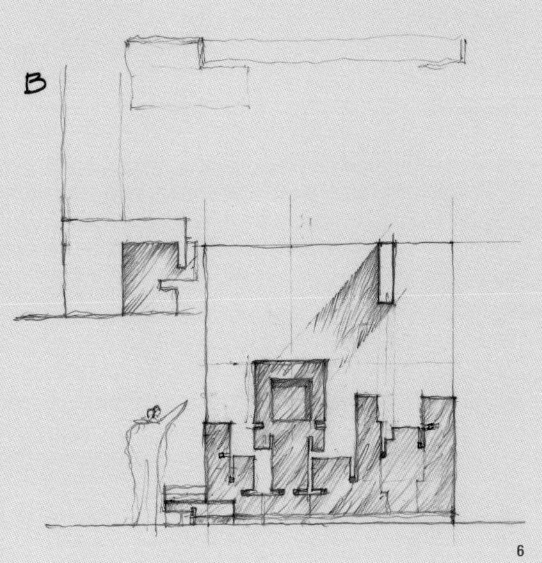

6

8

1 Wall design in the gallery
2 Sketches of the wall design
3 Wall design study
4 Final wall design
5 Wall design with extending furniture
6 Wall study drawing
7 Detail of the plywood and walnut wall system
8 Gallery installation

OBJECTS

project name	Valentine Chair 1
location	Udine, Italy
year of design	1983
year of completion	1984
client	Promosedia Corp.
architect	George Ranalli
design team	Nick Dermand
photographer	Stefano Valebrega

Valentine Chair 1

1

In 1986, the Promosedia S.R.L., Udine, Italy, commissioned the design of the Valentine Chair 1, for limited production. Another version designed for the 22nd Street Loft project differs slightly in detail and execution. Unlike the chair pictures, the 22nd Loft version of the Valentine Chair 1 was executed in plywood with a black lacquer finish and joining brass details.

The Valentine Chair 1 is a ladder-back dining chair designed for a formal setting. Situated around the table, these chairs complete a table design. Partially due to the height of the chair back, Valentine Chair 1 is perceived as forming a space around the table. The original design features exposed wood end-grain, with a final laminate layer of ebony veneer; however, the production line finish determined by the Promosedia Company was black matte lacquer. Typical for Italian furniture, Valentine Chair 1 had a limited production run.

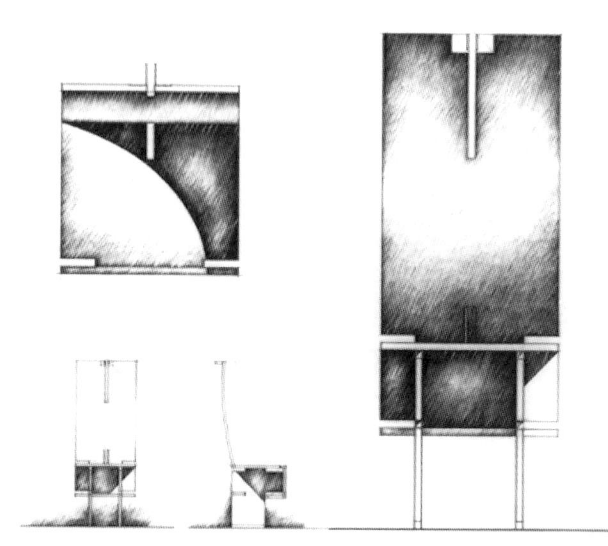

2

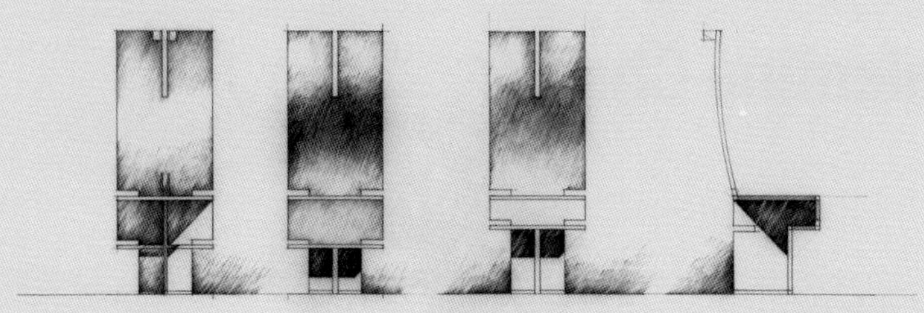

3

4

5

1 Brass detail at the top of the chair
2 Plan and elevations of the chair
3 Elevation studies
4 Dining chair from the back
5 Chair from the front

project name	Valentine Chair 2
location	Scarsdale, New York
year of design	1989
year of completion	1990
client	Formica Corp.
architect	George Ranalli
design team	John Butterworth
photographer	Richard Barnes

Valentine Chair 2

The Valentine 2 Chair was originally designed as a breakfast-room furniture ensemble for the "G" House project in Scarsdale, New York. The prototype, (pictured here), is fabricated from sheets of Surell, a synthetic sheet stock material fabricated by the Formica Corporation. The Valentine 2 chair comes in a right-hand and left- hand version to be situated on either side of a table, which for the "G" house project was placed beneath a window/skylight dining area.

Surell is factory produced in large four-foot by twelve-foot by one-half-inch panels, and available through construction supply distributors. This versatile material cuts like plywood, though its tactile properties are more like stone. Surrell is assembled using typical wood joinery techniques, such as a dado joints, but the option of applying a liquid paste of the same material, also supplied by Formica, erases all visible joints. For the Valentine Chair 2, the result is a formal composition that both expresses and conceals fabrication joints, allowing a plastic composition of surfaces, solids, and planes. Through Valentine Chair 2, Surrell reveals an extraordinary sculptural capability.

1

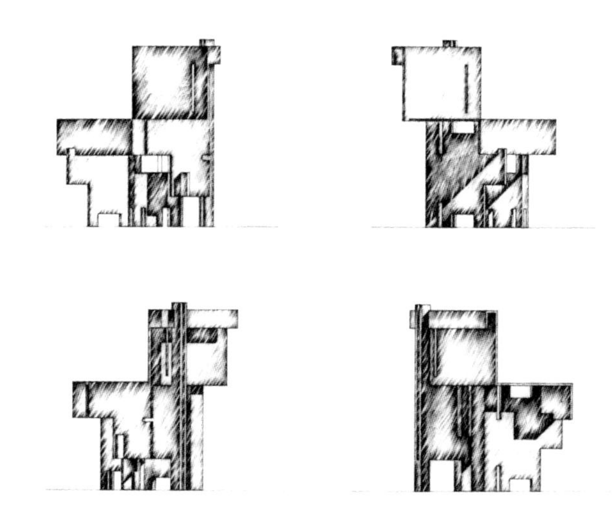

2

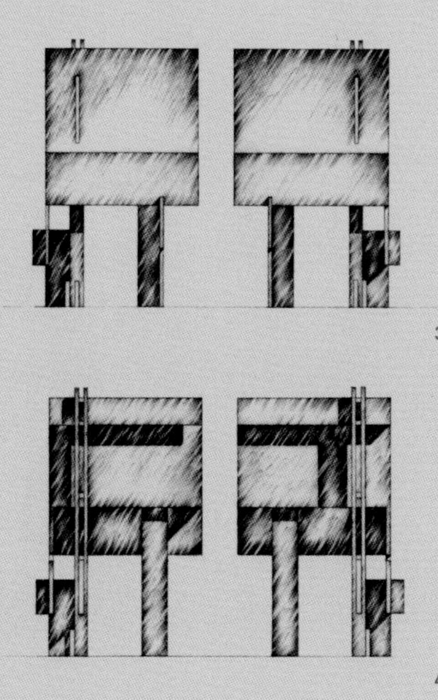

3

4

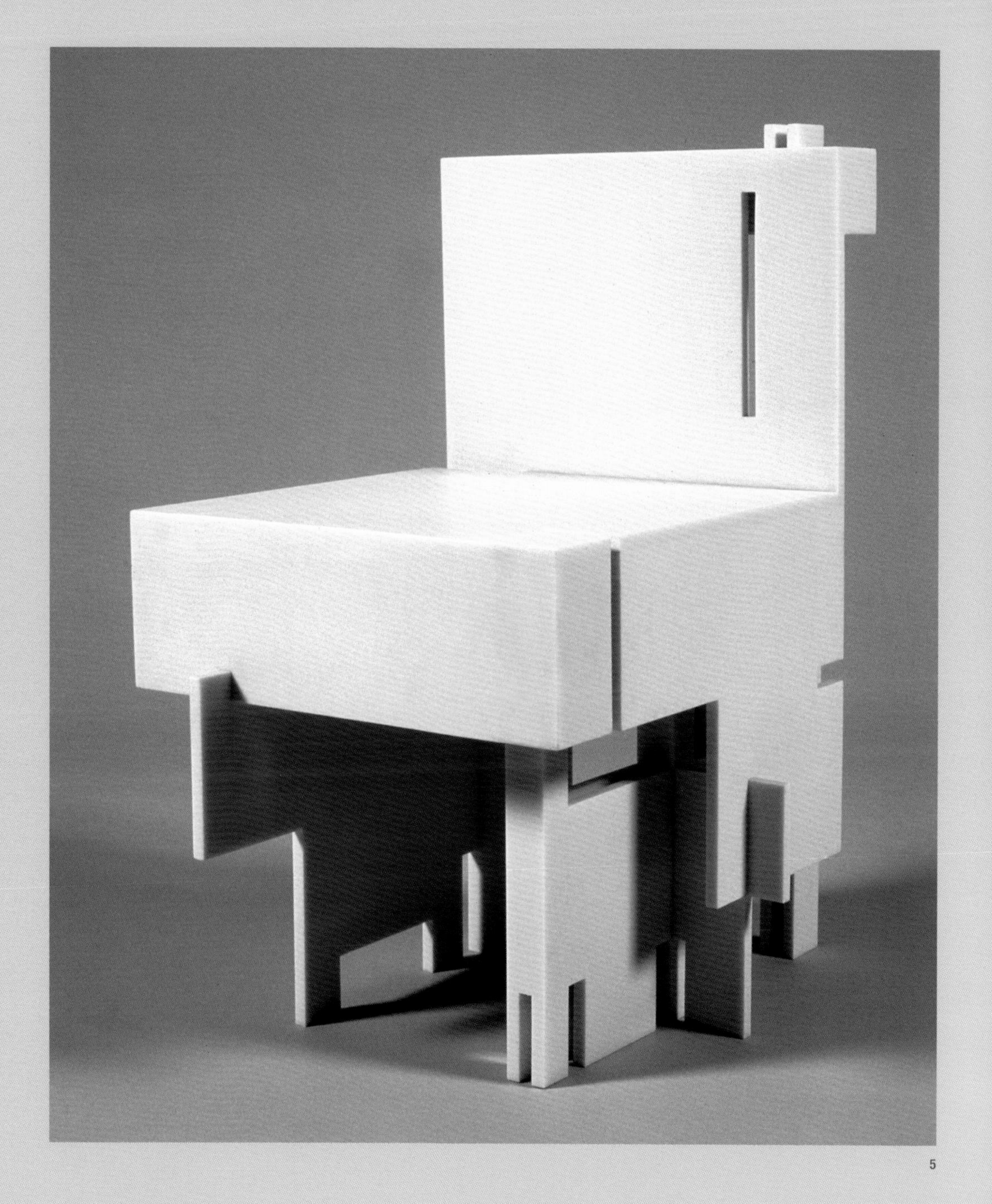

5

1 | Chair from the front
2 | Rotated elevations
3 | Orthographic elevations of the right and left hand versions of the chair from the front
4 | Orthographic elevations of the right and left hand versions of the chair from the back
5 | Chair from the corner

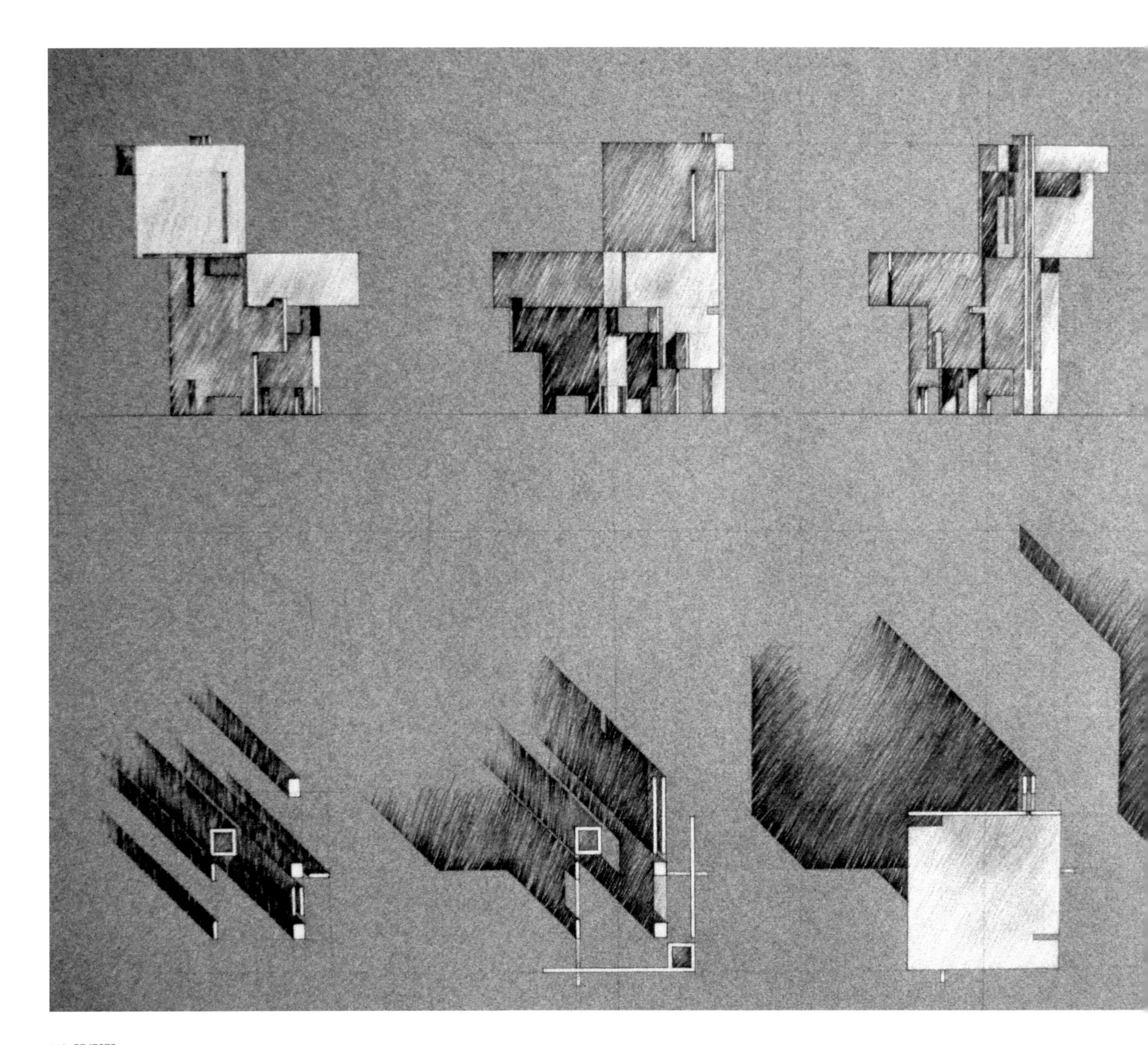

1

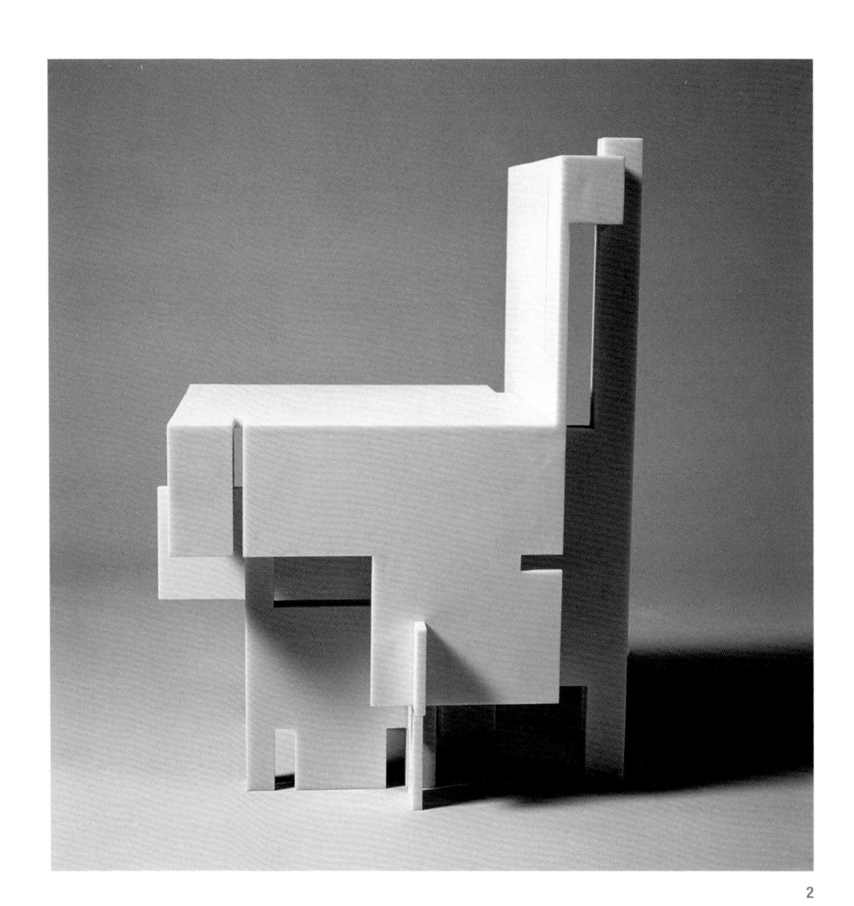

2

1 | Plans and rotated elevation drawings, pencil, white chalk and graphite on gray canson paper
2 | Side view of the chair

project name	Dinnerware Designs
location	New York City
year of design	1995
year of completion	1995
client	George Ranalli Designs
architect	George Ranalli
design team	John Butterworth, Hayden Marrero

Dinnerware Design

1

Ranalli Architect has long explored product design as an integral part of project work and as a venture into the design of everyday objects. Furniture, for example, is viewed as a natural extension of many interior design projects, including Manhattan apartments and lofts. On occasion, tableware have been designed as parts of interior ensembles, and some of these objects have made their way into commercial production.

Dinnerware patterns intended for formal and informal use were originally designed for residential clients. White and gold, often utilized for formal occasions, provide the color palate for a fine twelve-piece place setting. White, bone china, trimmed in gold leaf, and highlighted with red details cascade down the rim and into the center section of each plate. The slightly raised gold leaf details offer a subtle sensual response.

A more informal place setting, perhaps suitable for a summer table, is designed in the bold complementary colors of turquoise green with cobalt blue trim over a white center, which gives a striking presence to the table setting. For this more playful design, the accent elements are to float.

Each of the place settings incorporate fine linear elements that significantly reduce the scale to provide a pleasing ornamental presence to the table and ultimately the interior.

2

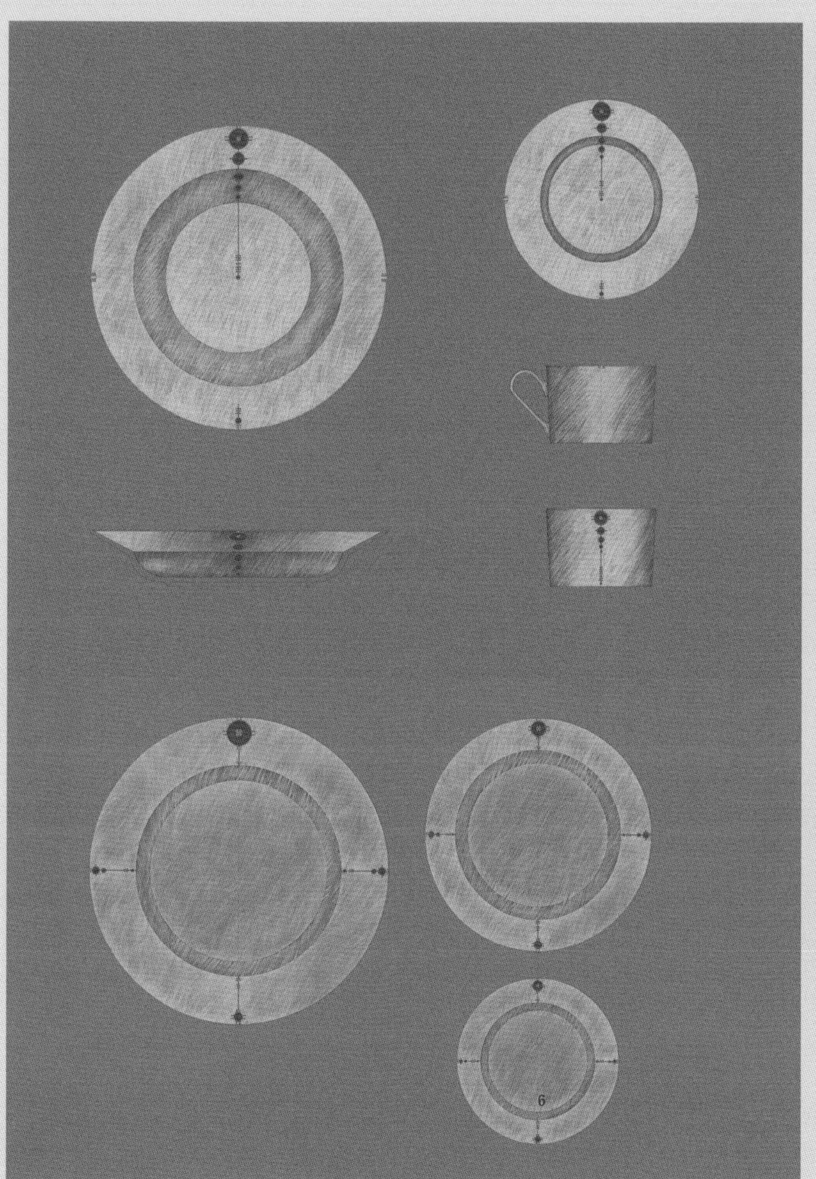

3

4

5

1 | Cup and saucer with formal dinner pattern
2 | Dinner, salad and dessert plates
3 | White chalk drawings of the full dinner ware formal set on gray canson paper
4 | Dinner plate with gold leaf trim and red enamel color
5 | Full table setting

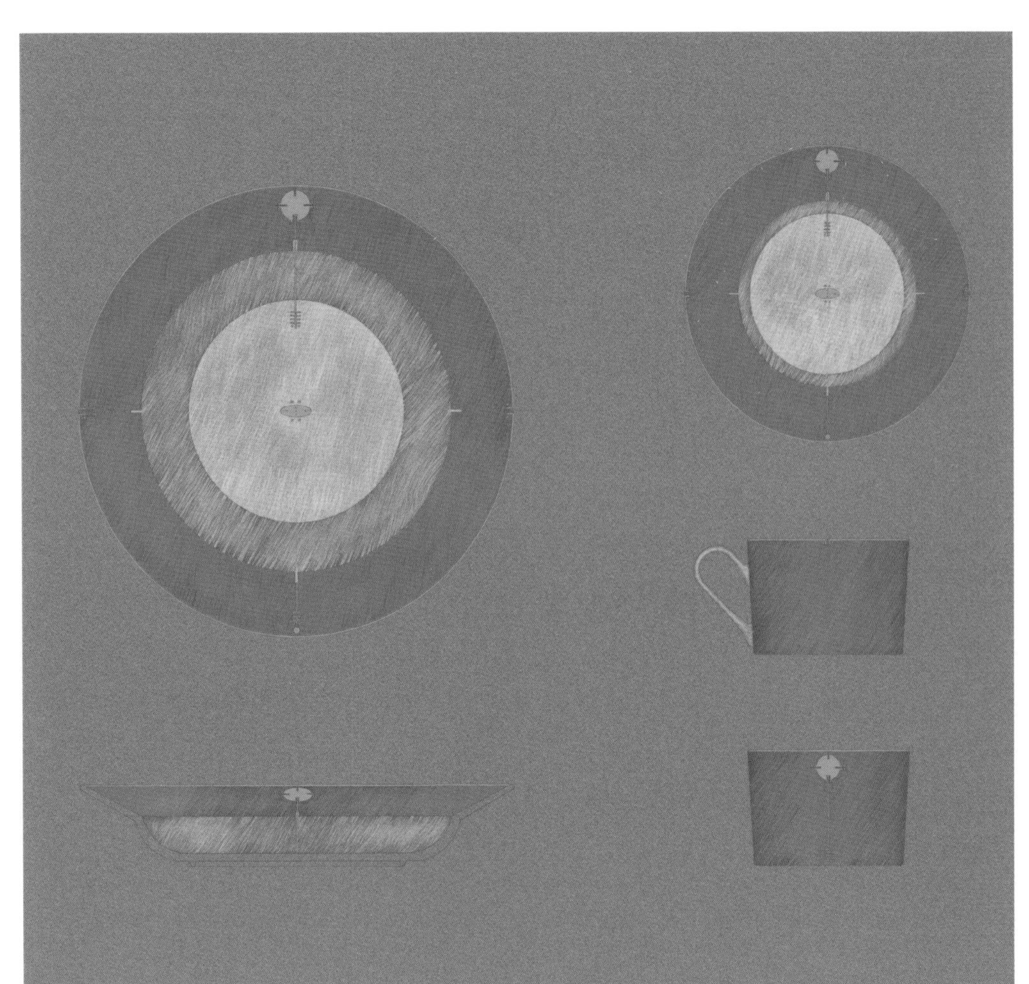

1

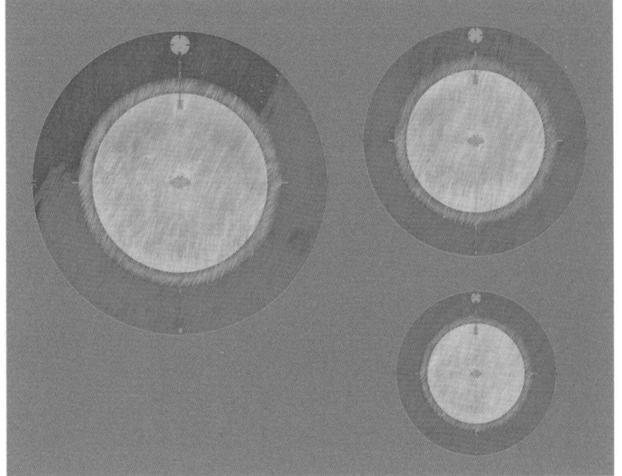

2

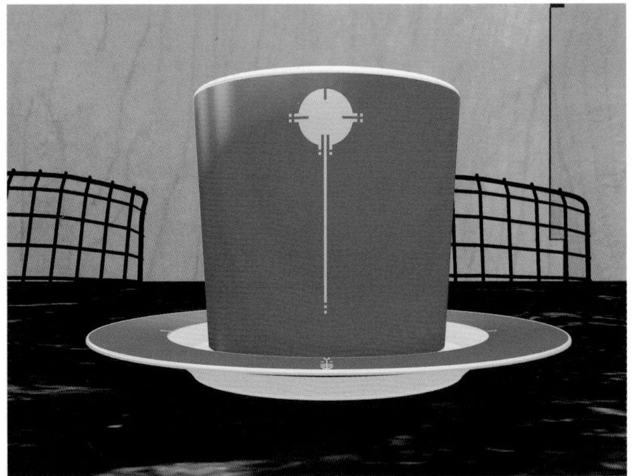

3

1	Drawing of the casual dinnerware set. Blue, green, and white color pencil on grey paper
2	Dinner, salad and dessert plate drawings
3	Cup and saucer
4	Full table setting

4

project name	Door Gems
location	New York
year of design	1989
year of completion	1990
client	Union Hardware Co./ George Ranalli Designs
architect	George Ranalli
design team	John Butterworth, Lester Yuen, Ursula Kyle Hayden Marrero

Architectural Hardware

1

The Union Hardware Company, a Japanese manufacturer, presented Ranalli Architect with an opportunity to explore mass-production techniques and the relationship between the utility and beauty for architectural hardware, by designing a set of door hardware for the beginning of the twenty-first century. The designs were conceived through a close working relationship with the manufacturer, and the end result succeeded in pushing the parameters of metal casting while remaining within a predetermined budget.

The architectural hardware designs mediate the scale of a building and that of the human hand, which is generally the first part of the body to make physical contact with any building. The door hardware designs provide visual and tangible communication about the spaces, colors, and forms that follow inside the building. Ranalli Architects Door Gems line offers a series of three different handles that represent the various elements of a building. Pendent, is a large push-plate/pull-bar handle, which accommodates the mass of a large entryway without neglecting the occupants. Pendant's push plate/pull bars are crafted in combined cast aluminum, brushed brass, and stainless steel, and the design ergonomically fit the human grip. Lock-it and Charm are lever handles intended for a variety of relatively smaller sized and scaled interior doors.

After more that a decade of production-line fabrication in Japan, Door Gems are currently manufactured in the United States. Lock-it is available as a lever handle made in cast aluminum with a nickel-dip finish through www.georgeranallidesigns.com. Charm and Pendant are available by special order.

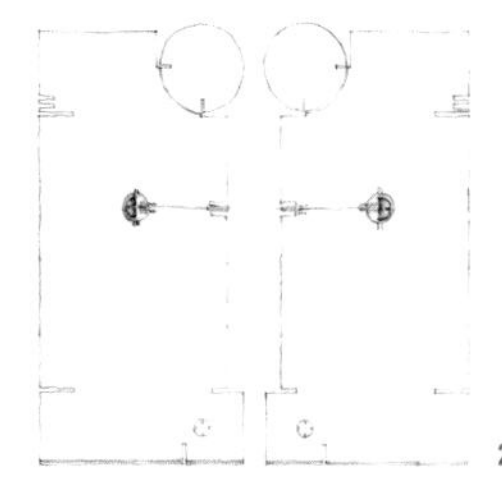
2

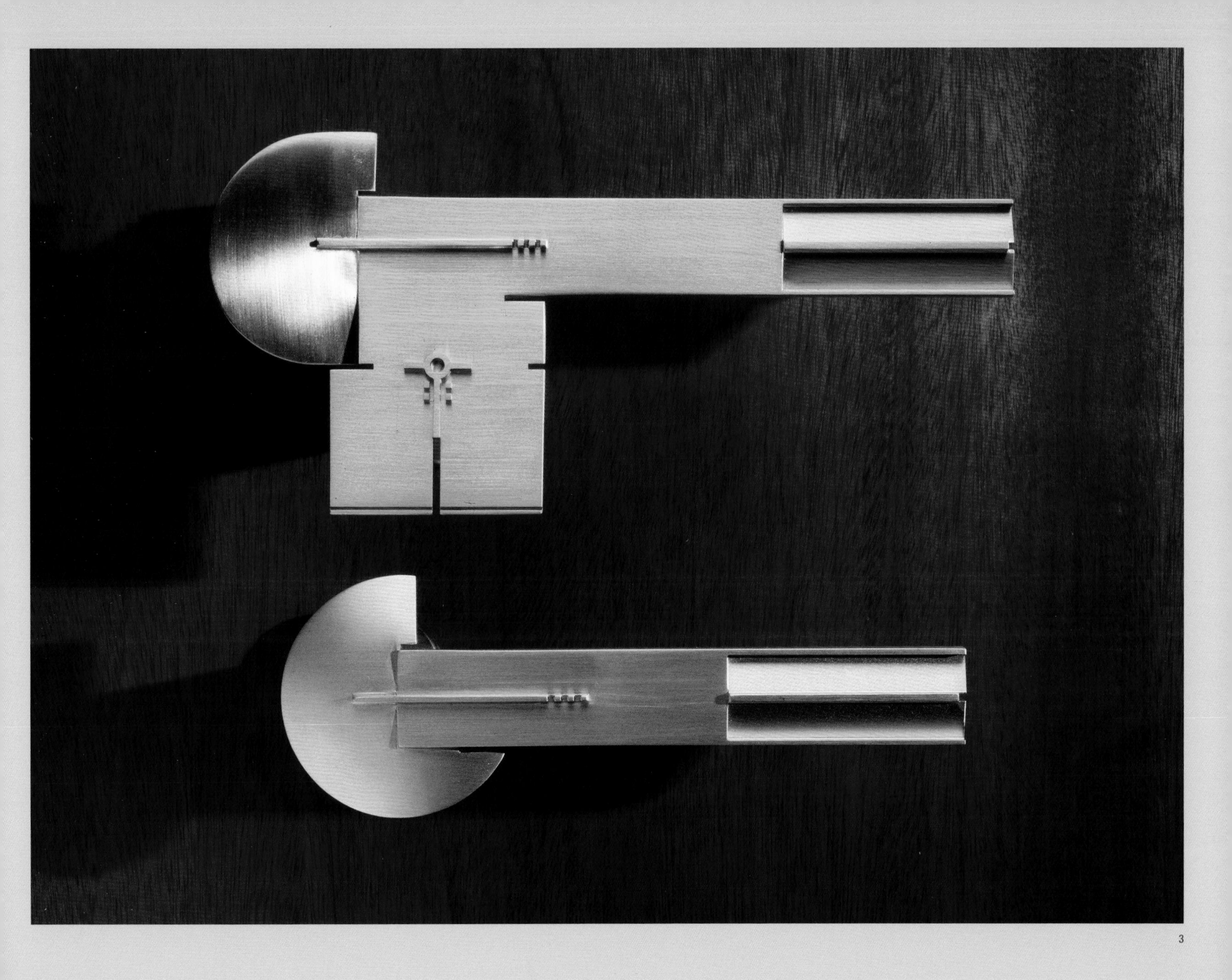

3

1 Computer model of the Pendant push plate pull bar handle on glass doors
2 Sketch of the Pendant handle
3 Photo of the Charm handle on top and Lock-it handle on the bottom

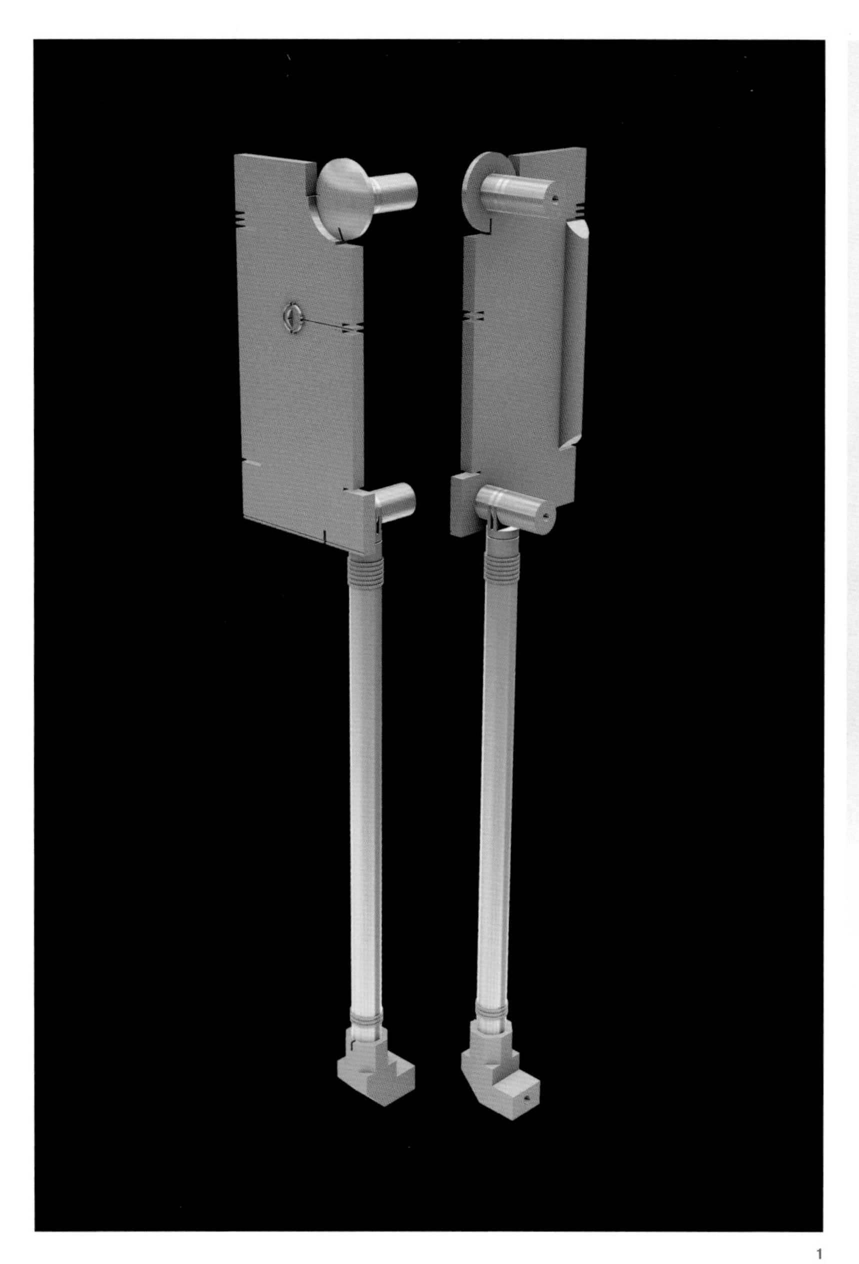

1

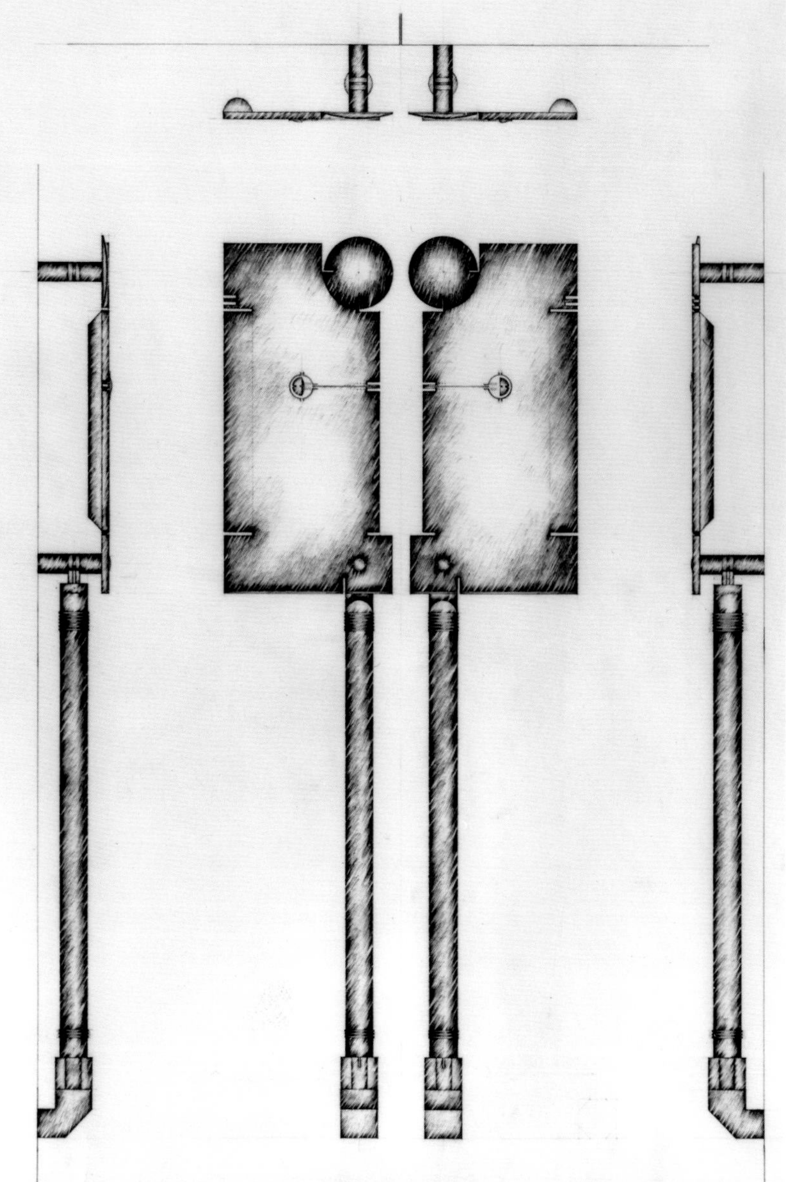

2

1 | Computer model of the back and front of the push plate and pull bar Pendant handle
2 | Front, top and side elevations of the Pendant handle, graphite on vellum drawings
3 | Isometric drawing of the push plate pull bar Pendant handle,graphite, pencil and color pencil on vellum
4 | Front view of the Pendant handle, milled bronze and stainless steel

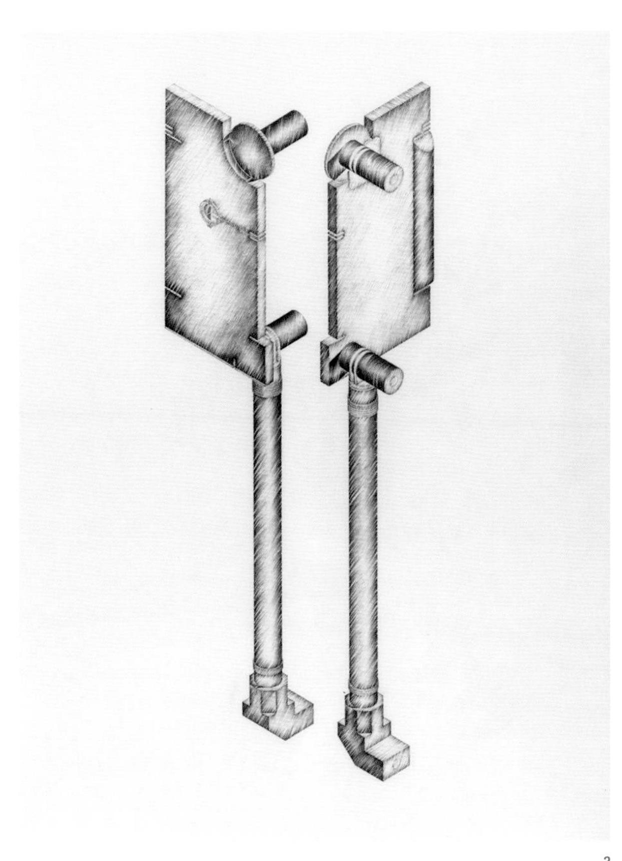

3

4

1

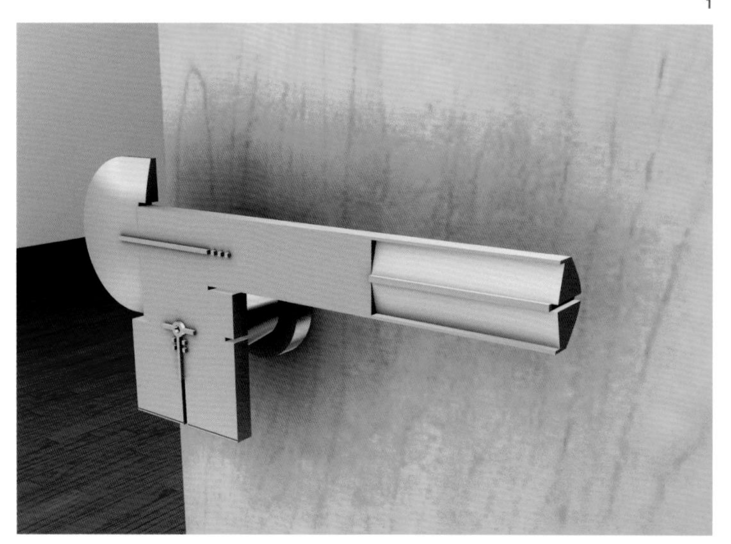

2

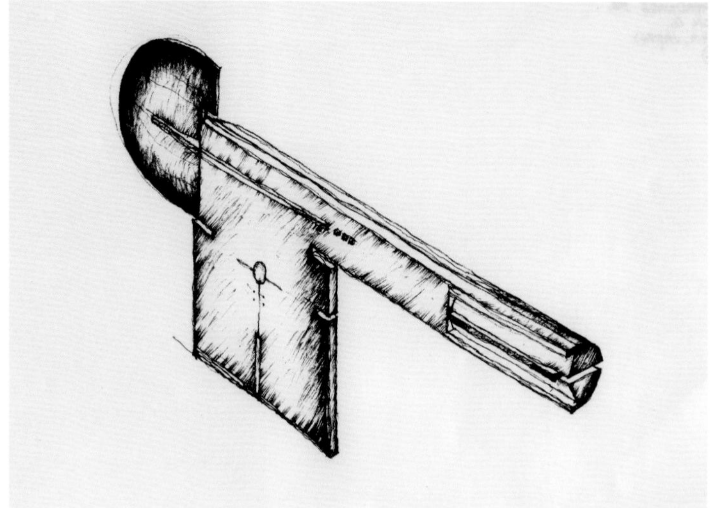

3

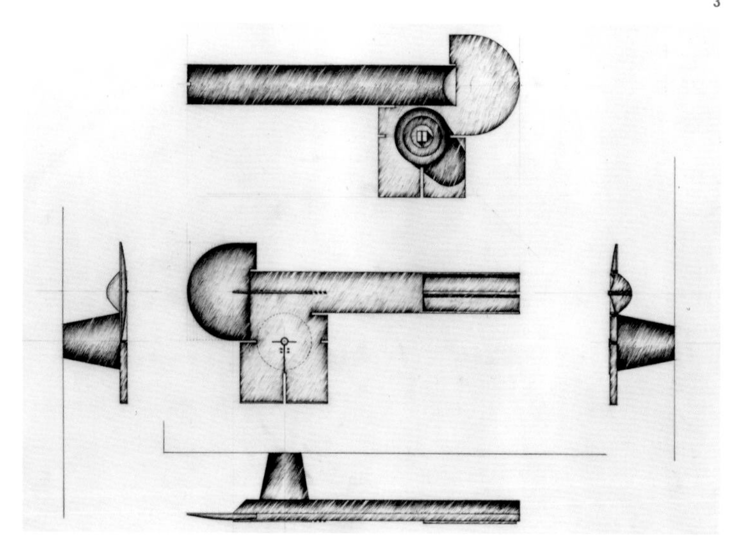

4

1 Computer model of the Charm handle shown in cast aluminum dipped nickel finish, round end
2 Computer model of the Charm handle shown in cast aluminum dipped nickel finish, grip end
3 Early sketch of the Charm handle
4 Front, back, top and side elevations of the Charm handle, graphite on vellum drawing
5 Front view of the Charm handle, cast bronze
Charm handle (following spread)

5

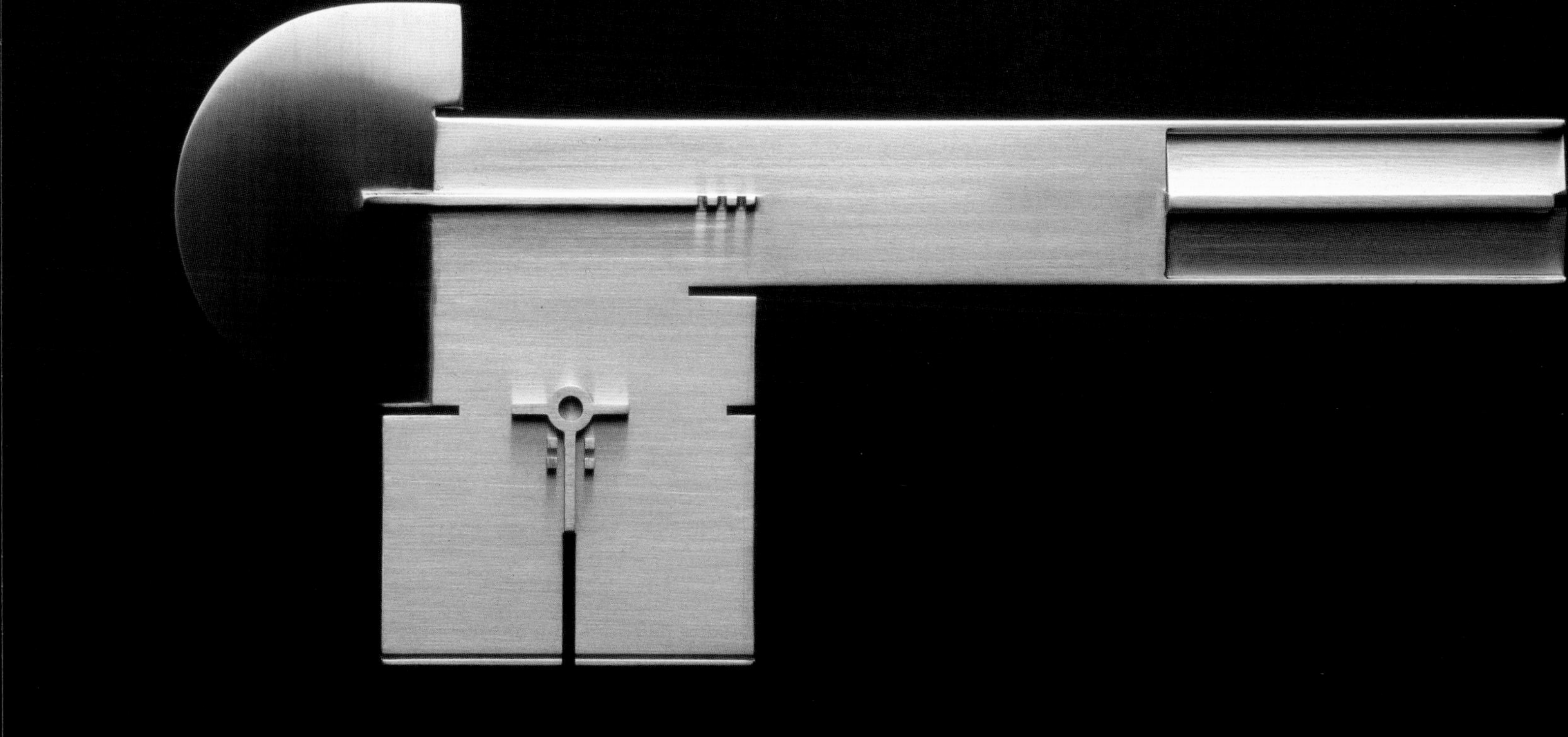

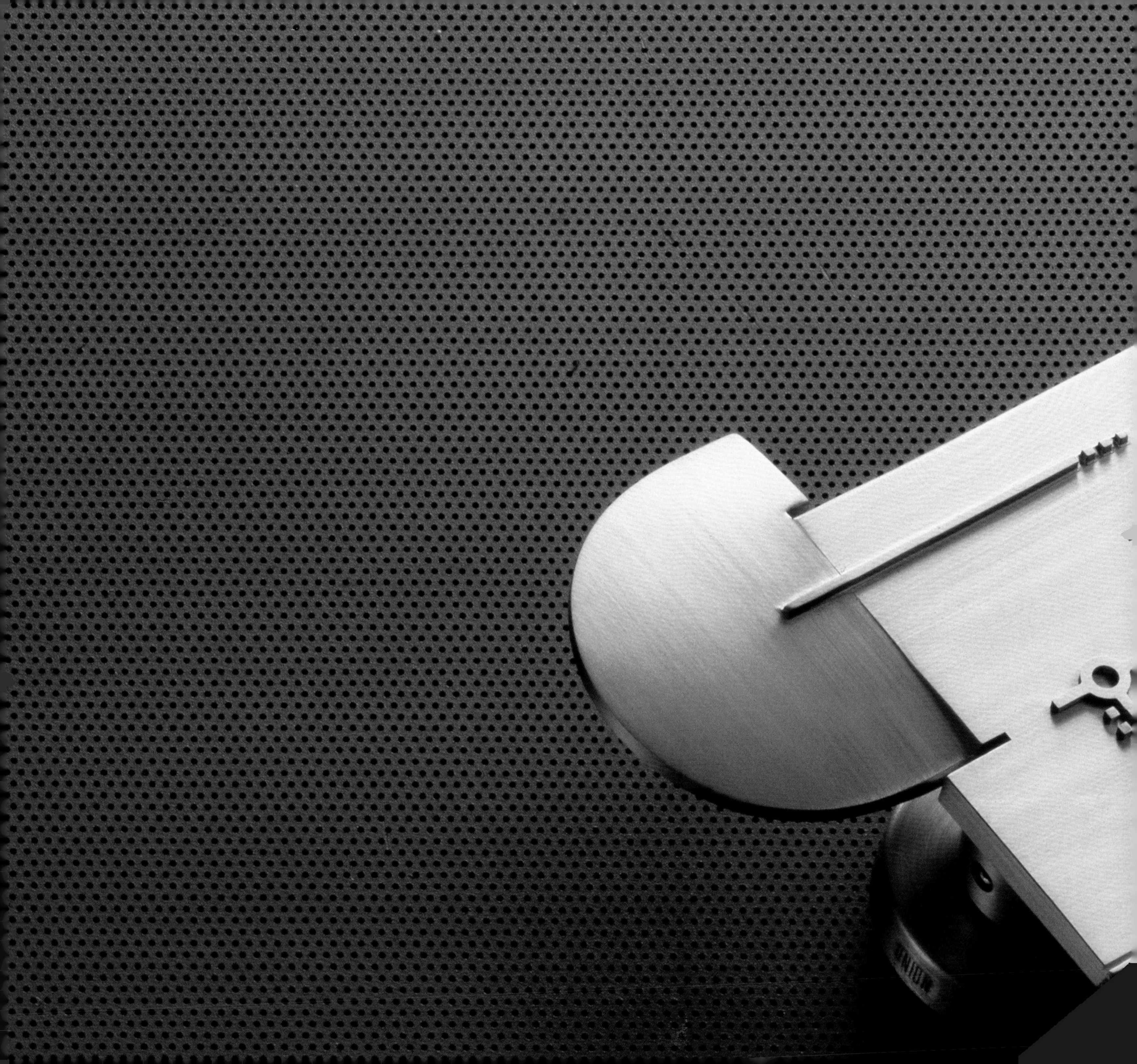
UNION

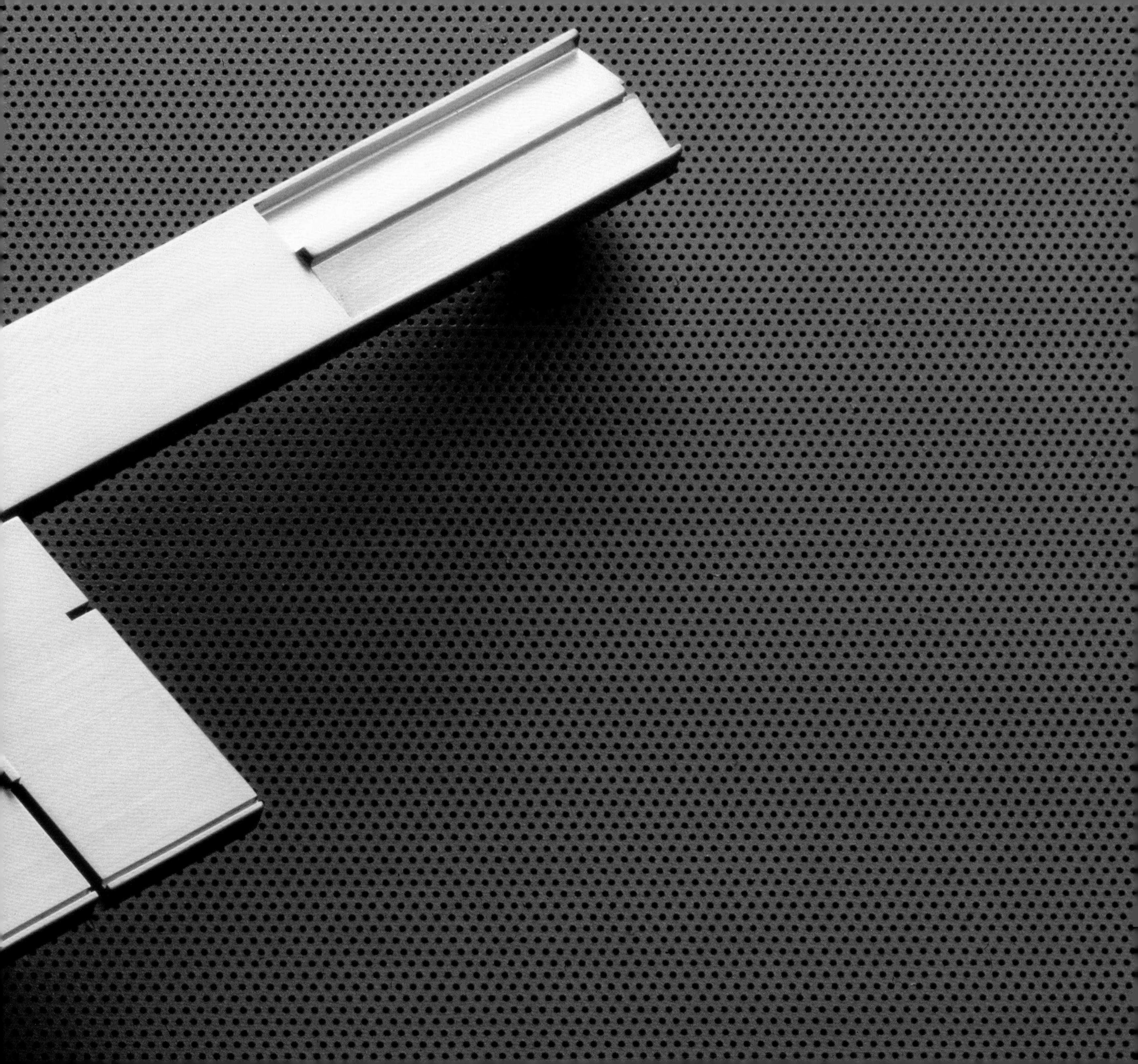

1

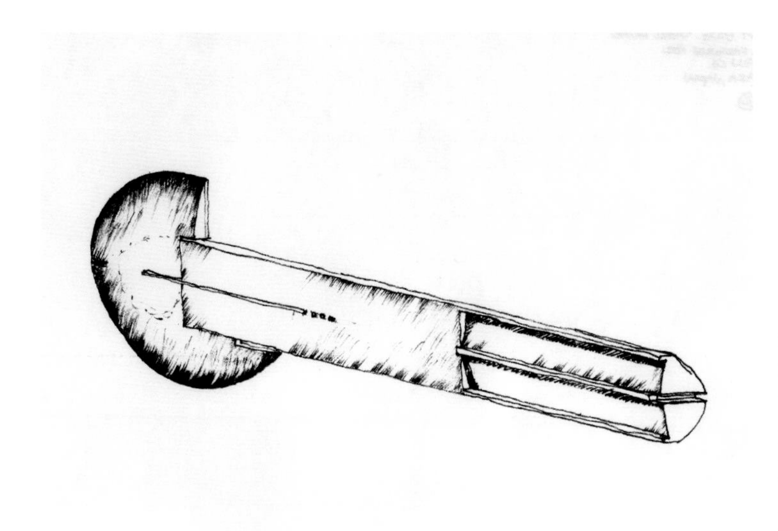

2

4

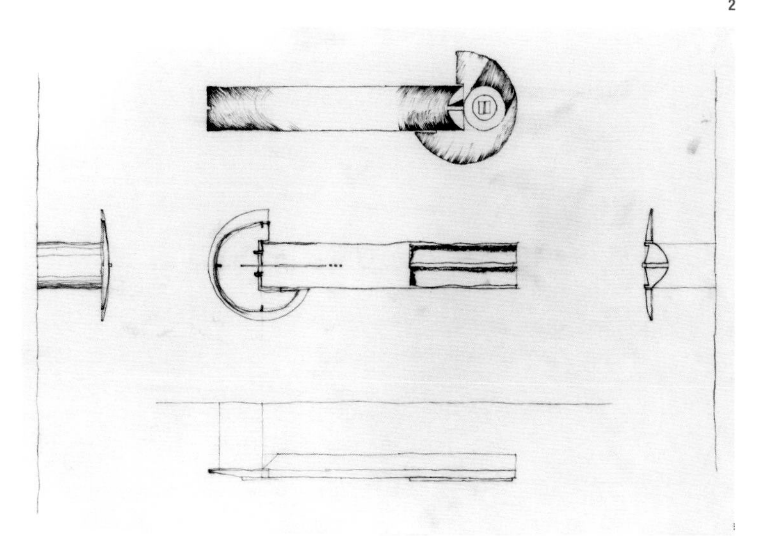

3

5

1 | Front view of the Lock-it handle, cast aluminum nickel dipped finish
2 | Early sketch of the Lock-it handle
3 | Front, back and side views of the Lock-it handle
4 | Computer model of the Lock-it handle seen from the round end
5 | Computer model of the Lock-it handle seen from the grip end

project name	AI Table Design
location	New York
year of design	1993
architect	George Ranalli
design team	John Butterworth, M.T. Chang

Atelier International Table Design

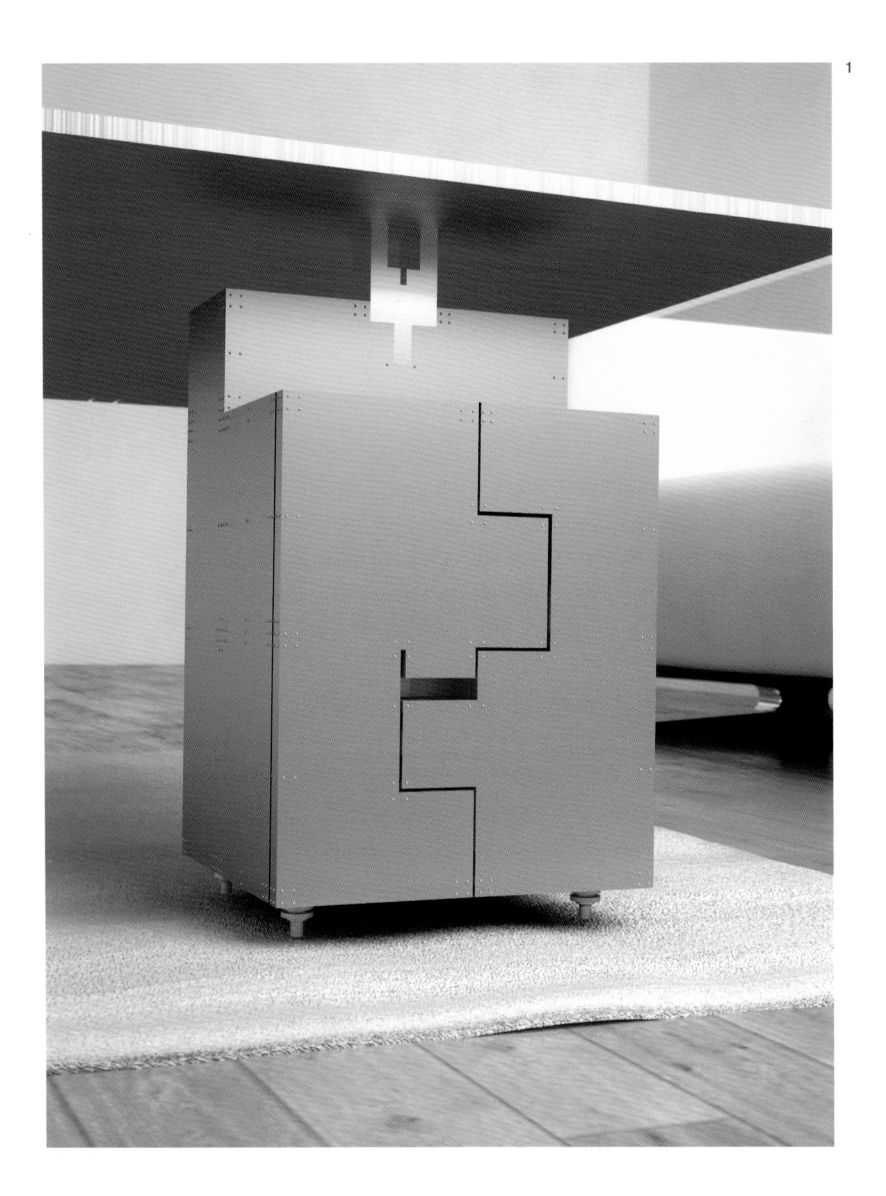

1

In collaboration with a stylish furniture company, whose products feature designs of milled, cast, and machined metals, Ranalli Architect devised the latest in a high-concept storage box coffee table design for the 21st Century. The architect had grown up around delicate Victorian cabinetry, with fragile hinges that inevitably broke from everyday wear and tear. Seeking the help and technical expertise of master craftsman, and after much sampling of mechanisms and metal work techniques, the Atelier International Table was born. The result is a modern take on a timeless classic.

The table top of Atelier International Table is composed of thin sheets of bronze, which sits atop a delicate storage box, at one end, with ample room for table accessories. At the other end, the tabletop rests on two highly sculptural legs of bronze and stainless steel, with structural elements connecting the tabletop to brass tubular legs, topped by semicircular spherical ornaments at the top. The table surface features a composition of lines, points and a fragment of a sphere at the center, which are fabricated in low relief silver. A sheet of clear glass, which provides a uniform surface for practical uses, protects the sumptuous tabletop, and the end result is charm, charm, and more charm.

1 Detail view at the storage cabinet end of the table
2 View of coffee table in a living room setting
3 Elevation oblique of the table from the storage end
4 Elevation oblique of the table from the leg end
Side elevation of the table (following spread)

2

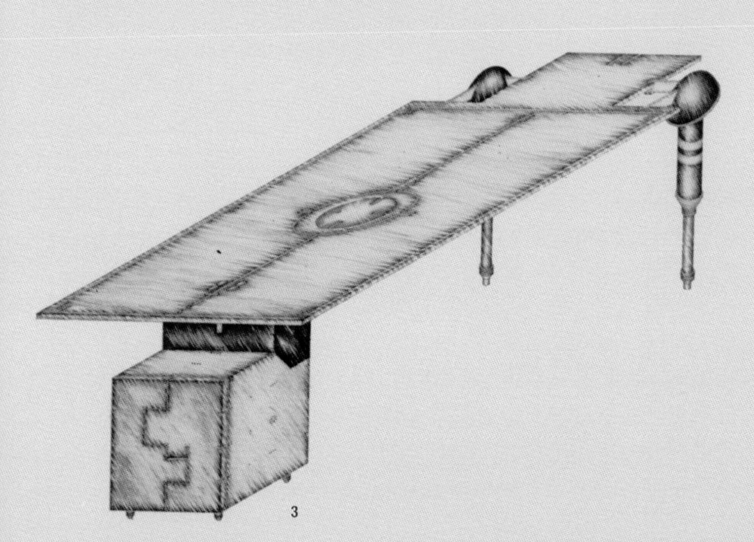

3

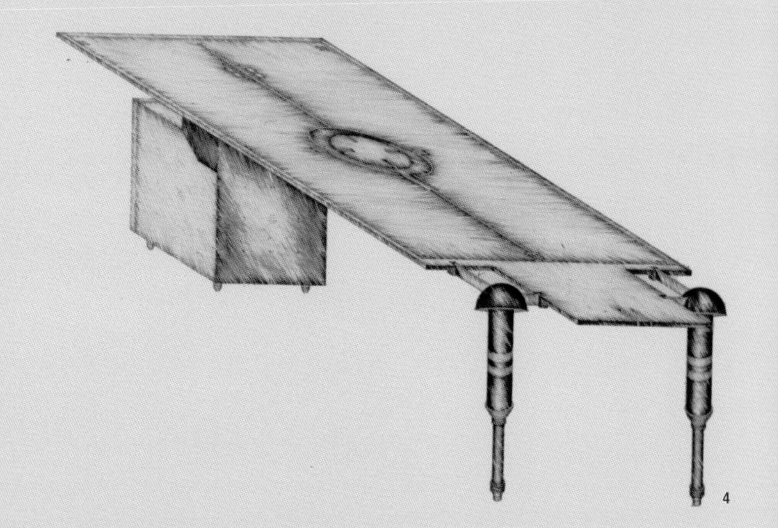

4

1

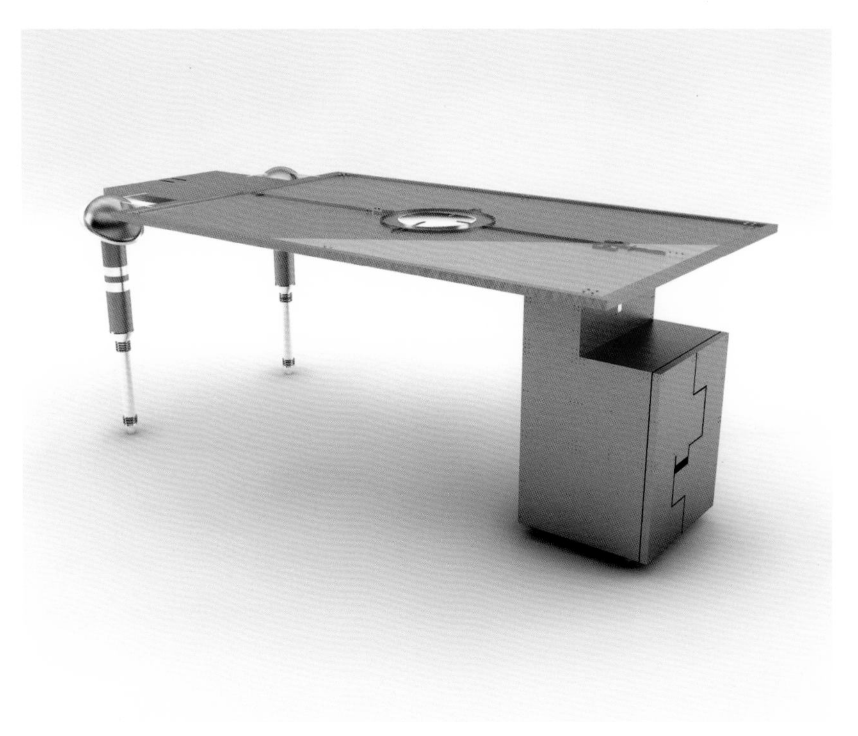

2

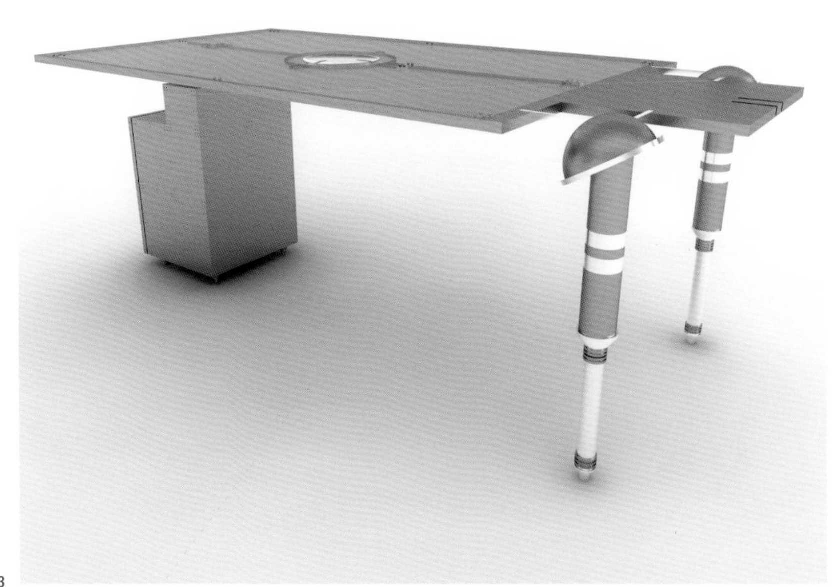

3

1 | End elevation of the table from the storage end
2 | View of the table from above
3 | View of the table front end

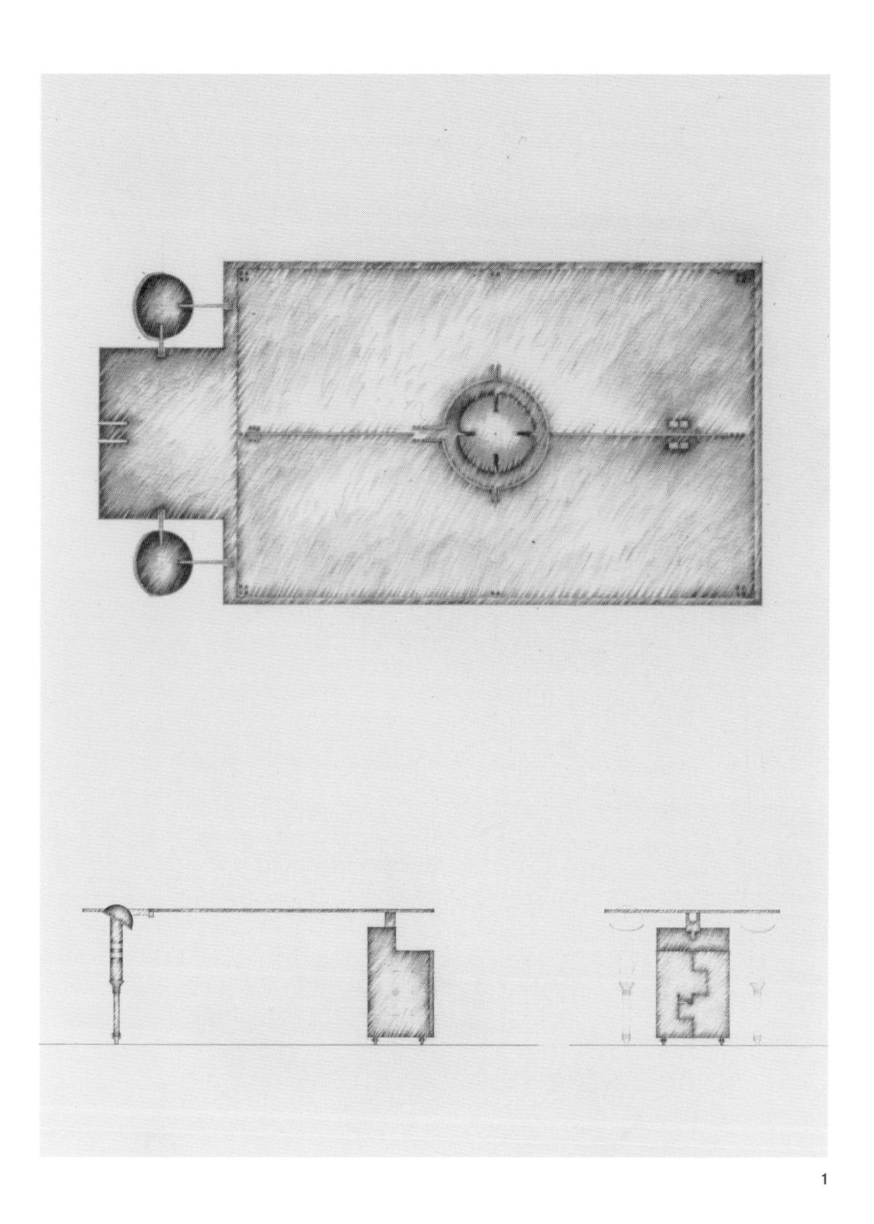

1

2

1 | Plan, side elevation and end elevation drawing of the coffee table
2 | Front elevation of the table

2

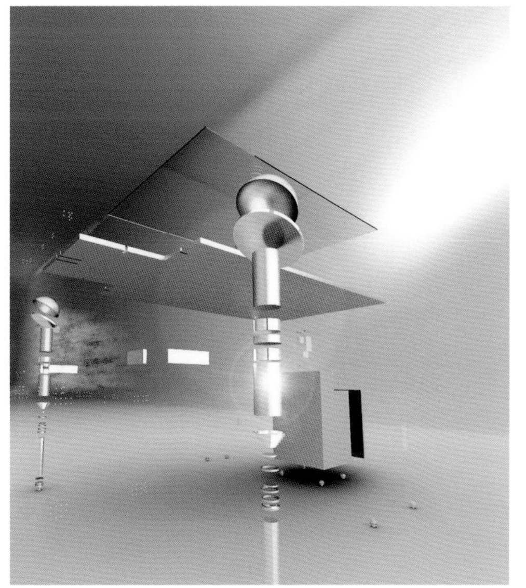

3

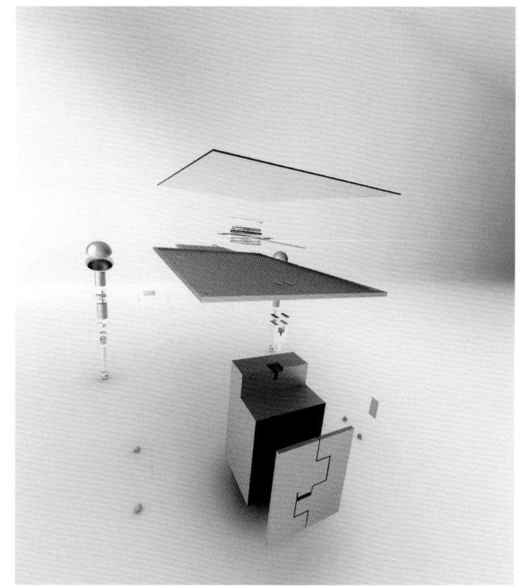

4

1 | View of the table in a custom designed interior by George Ranalli
2 | Detail of the silver element on the top of the table
3 | Exploded view of the table from the front
4 | Exploded view of the table from the storage cabinet end

1

project name	Sofia Glass
location	Venice, Italy
year of design	2002
year of completion	2003
client	Murano Glass Museum, Venice, Italy
architect	George Ranalli
design team	Mario Gentile, M.T. Chang

Sofia Glass Collection

1

Designer and Curator Cleto Munari invited Ranalli Architect to design a glass for a 2004 special exhibit at Murano Glass Factory in Venice, Italy, which features an international collection of notable glass design. The project inspired the Sofia Glass Collection, an extensive line of glassware available from Ranalli Architects.

The Sofia Glass design originally sent to Venice included specific fabrication and finishing instructions. Preliminary glass samples were evaluated before a final piece was hand-blown by a Venetian artisan. The upper bowl was made from blue glass, with amethyst gems encrusting the outer surface, while a smaller lower bowl and stem, in clear glass, completed the design. The gem colors and accent glass radiates a pink hue throughout the glass. Touching the gems when lifting the glass offers a sensuous tactile experience to accompany the taste of whatever it contains. The original piece from the Sofia Glass Collection is now in the permanent collection of the Murano Museum, in Venice, Italy.

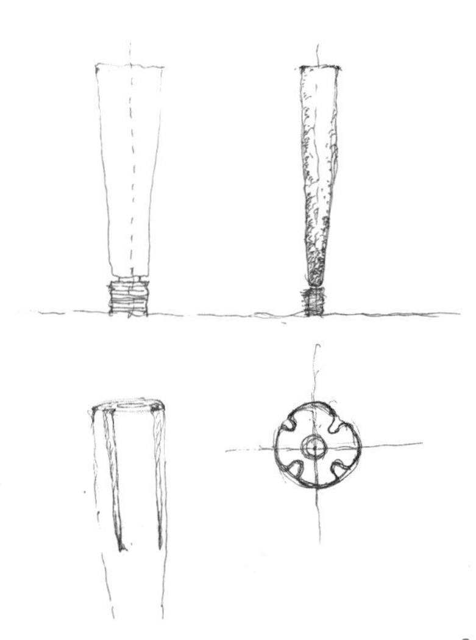

2

3

1 | Detail of tall blue glass
2 | Study of another version of the glass
3 | Four glasses in the collection

1

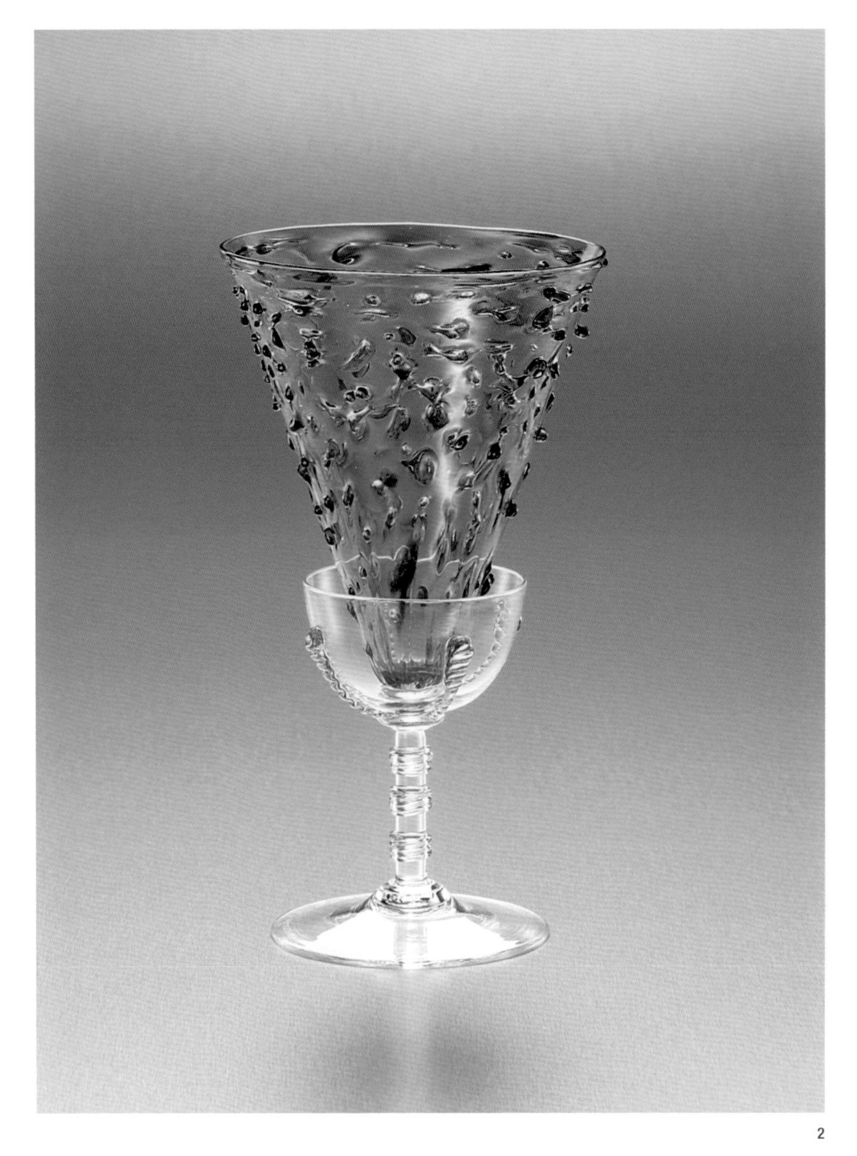

2

1 | Detail of the hand blown Sofia glass from below with amethyst stones set into the outer surface
2 | Full view of the hand blown Sofia glass

1

1 | Tall goblet
2 | Detail of the tall goblet

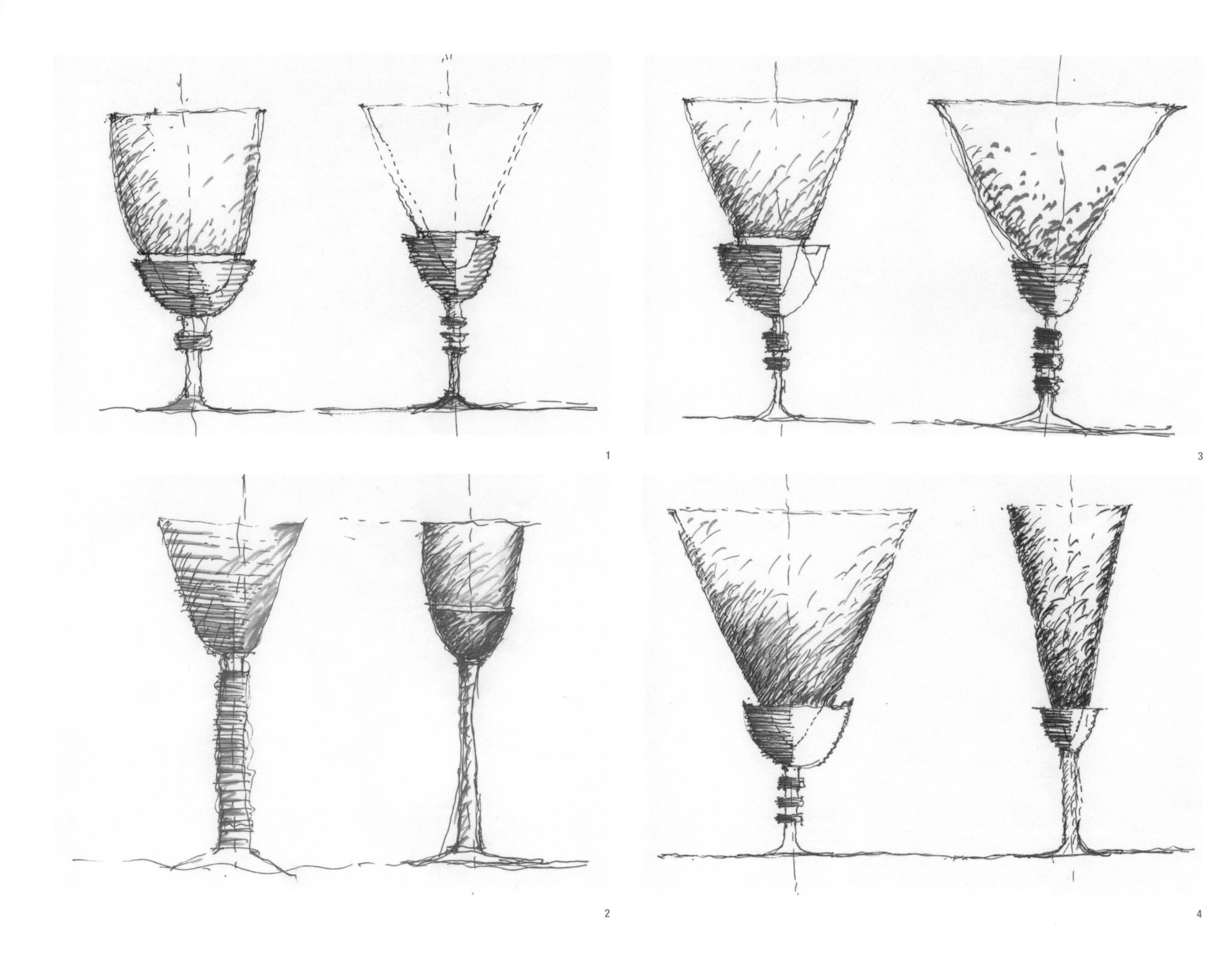
1
3
2
4

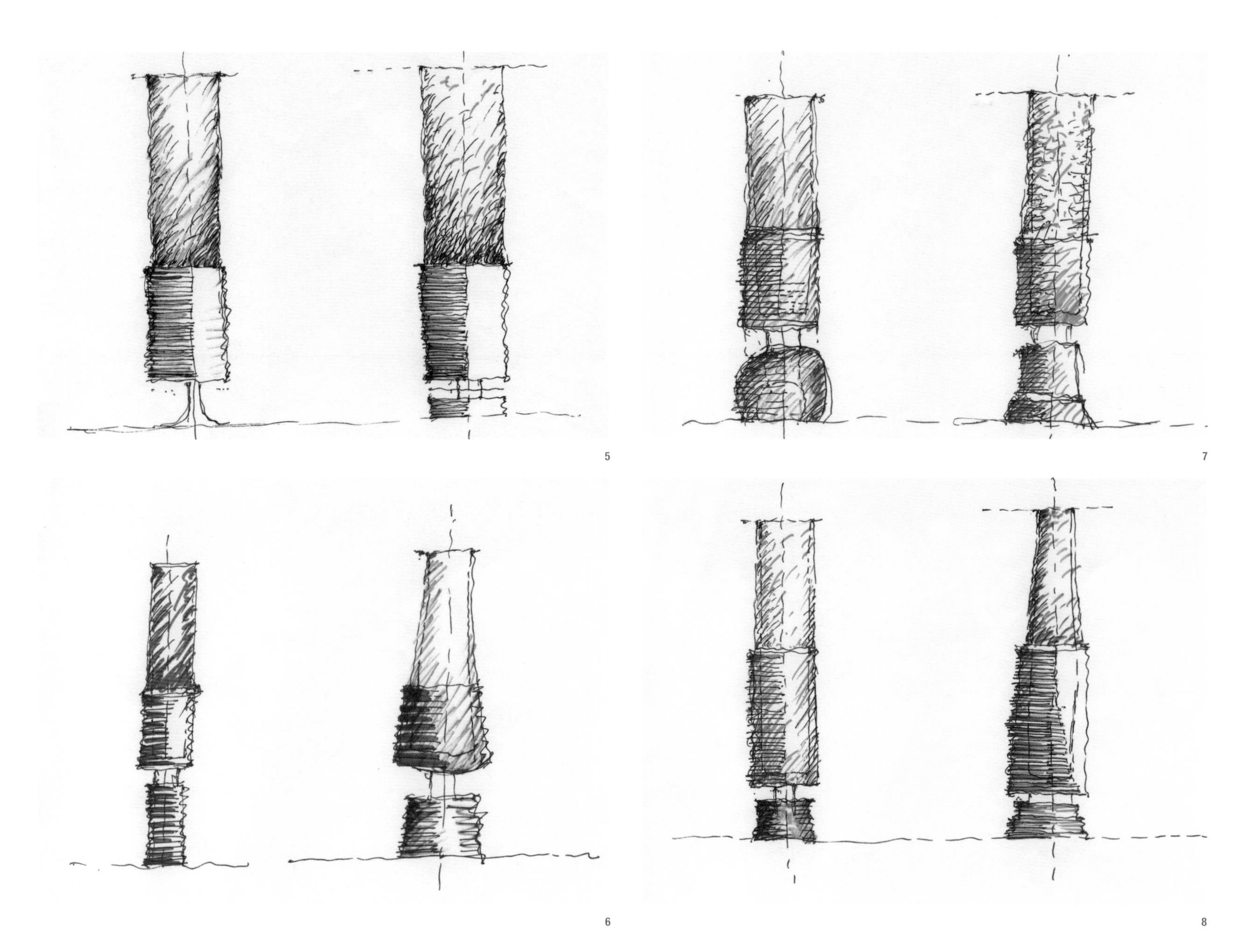

5

7

6

8

1 Studies for the Sofia glass
2 Color variations of the Sofia glass
3 Long tall drink glass
4 Tall drink glass with base variations
5 Cordial glass
6 Sofia glass studies
7 Tall drink glass studies
8 Tall drink glass color studies

1

2

1 Detail gold goblet
2 Gold goblet full view

project name	Cemetery Monument
location	Mt. Kisco
year of design	1998
year of completion	1998
client	Wendy & Lawrence Blumenthal
architect	George Ranalli
design team	Mario Gentile
photographer	George Ranalli

Cemetery Monument

1

A Cemetery Monument for a beloved residential client sits in the oldest cemetery in Mount Kisco, New York, vicinity. The client requested a memorial to commemorate the immeasurable loss with eloquence of poetry, and a monument sturdy enough to withstand years of family visits to a sacred place.

The memorial design began with a five-foot by five-foot by one-foot slab of Vermont granite. The stone is smoothed on its front face, while the back of the stone retaining a rough-hewn finish. Text is laser-cut into the smooth front. A spherical fragment on the front surface is cut away from the block to provide an appropriately modest level of detail and ornamentation to the design. Given that the cemetery is quite old, with gravestones dating back hundreds of years, it is important that a new monument not only provide modern composition, but become part of an existing legacy.

2

3

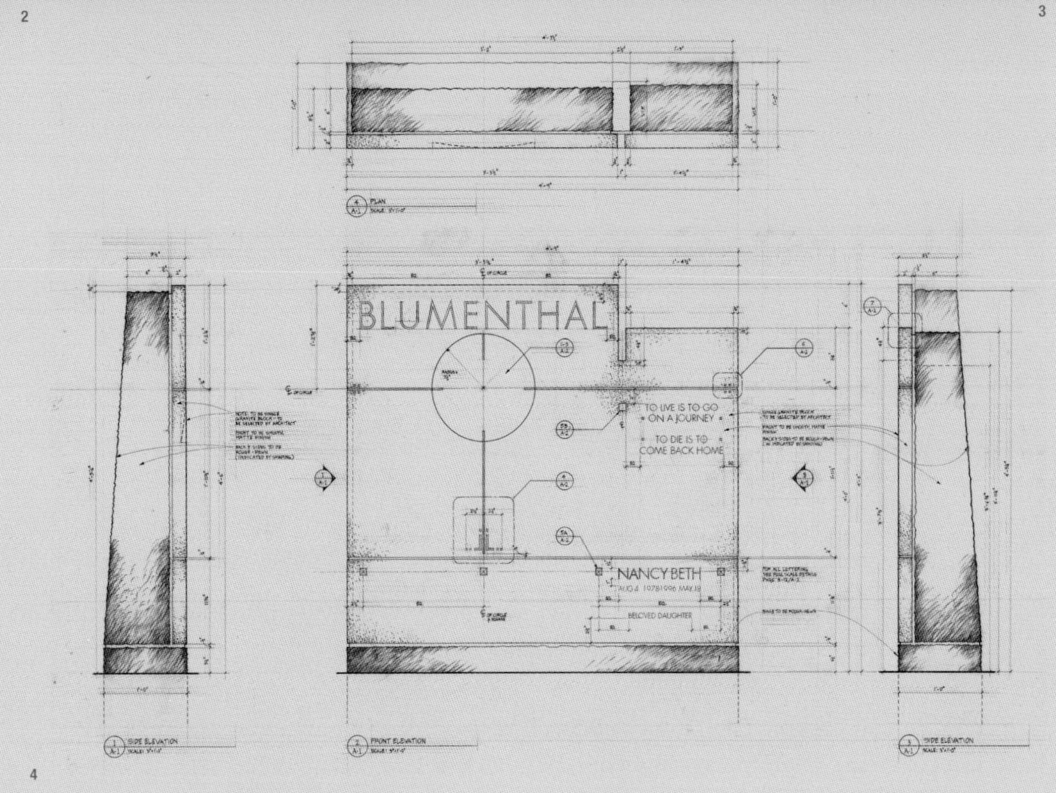

4

1 | Detail carving on the front of the monument
2 | Side view with the rough hammered back and honed front of the stone
3 | Photo of the monument in the cemetery
4 | Fabrication drawing showing the front, top and side views of the monument

ESSAYS

REDEFINING THE LOFT: INTERLOCKING FORMS ARTICULATE A MANHATTAN SPACE by JOSEPH GIOVANNINI

Artists like lofts because they can live and work in sweepingly clear spaces without drawing nine-to-five distinctions across their lives: The easy roll of a day, from pallet to palette, breeds an open lifestyle with an addictive informality. The flaw in this alternative kind of apartment, where often n=only baths merit a door, is that no matter how large the loft, two is company and three, an invasion of privacy. When children arrive, couples who had escaped rooms dedicated to the routines of standard floor plans must cope with raw space that newly necessary walls turn into that camel of dwellings, a "loftment." The loft is subdivided, and the very identity of artists seems on the line. Are the owners being domesticated along with the space? Will conventionalized space conventionalize habits and thinking, and therefore art?

Four years ago Jacque Metheny and Robert Kirschbaum had Jacob. "Before he came along we had no need for privacy," says Metheny, a sculptor. "But with one living area, we'd have to stop everything when Jake went to sleep."

Kirschbaum, a painter and printmaker, bought the downtown New York City loft seventeen years ago and over time invested considerable sweat equity. Removing the plaster on the walls and the pressed tin on the ceiling, he exposed not only brick party walls but also arching brick vaults. The loft was an open and solid volume with only a convenience wall separating the rear living space from the front studio; windows were placed across either end.
When Metheny married Kirschbaum, she also married into the loft and a way of life. Such was their bond to the space that they kept it even after he accepted a job teaching at Trinity College in Connecticut, and they bought a house in suburban Hartford. The loft became their weekend and vacation retreat.

"We come here to relax and hang out – sometimes just to order Chinese food in," says Metheny. "We even spend August here because it's air-conditioned," adds Kirschbaum, spoken like a die-hard New Yorker. "It's incredibly serene. When a car door slams on the street in Hartford, it sounds like it's happening in the living room. The loft is much more insulated."

"While we needed to renovate, we already had the experience of living in a house and didn't want to replicate that here," says Metheny. "I was fearful that we would suddenly find ourselves without what we once had in this apartment- an intimacy with our friends, a particular kind of socializing." She cites an unshaped space between the living area and the kitchen that attracted people. "It was just a little counter, but we had higher chairs, and that's where everybody always ended up sitting. Nobody used the sofas. We wanted a place where that could happen again."

The couple called New York architect George Ranalli, a friend who lives down the block in a loft that he recently adapted to accommodate his two-year-old daughter. "We turned to George because we admire his architecture, we've known him a long time, and there's a certain aesthetic compatibility between my work and his," says Kirschbaum. "Still, I was a little worried. We were very much committed to giving George carte blanche in terms of design issues, but that's not easy for people interested in the way things look. I'd always basically controlled my environment and anxiety surfaces whether this would stay *our* place."

Ranalli, who has practiced for twenty years in Manhattan, is a rock of modernism. Never had he been tempted by the soft blandishments of postmodernism or the edginess of deconstructivism. Unreconstructed, he maintains an abiding respect for the shibboleths of architecture pronounced early this century: flowing space, abstract form, expressed structure and a concern for detail that shows construction processes. His, however, is not the heroic modernism of the 1920's and 1930's caught in amber but an evolved and tempered brand – influenced especially by the work of Carlo Scarpa, the Venetian architect who conceived buildings as layers in a collage constructed over time. From the master, Ranalli learned how one element fastens to another through a third beautifully crafted and detailed piece that is the equivalent of architectural jewelry: Parts in a Ranalli building proliferate at several scales.

Kirschbaum and Metheny wanted two bedrooms, two baths and a combined living and dining area open to the kitchen so that people would congregate there. "They had no set notions about where things would go," says Ranalli, "but they were sure about preserving the expansiveness of the loft as well as its materiality – the brick walls, the vaulted ceiling that spans every four feet beam to beam, and the wide oak baseboard."

Zoning the apartment, Ranalli did something unexpected. After removing the dividing wall, which had prevented a street view, he put the kitchen and living area in the middle of the loft rather than at the front. The combined space acts as a piazza between the far ends of the floor – where he placed the sleeping and studio areas. Two bedrooms face the rear of the building, and a front area, next to a large bath, remains a workplace with a drawing table and a viewing gallery.

In other residential designs, the architect has nested smaller structures within existing building envelopes. In the loft, he created a miniature cityscape of keyed shapes and notched volumes that subtly echo the jagged Manhattan skyline. Respecting the shell, Ranalli and project architect John Butterworth made architecture out of cabinetry intricately interlocked with walls – some like cubic puzzles specifically zigged to fit the zags of surrounding shapes. The partitions that meet the ceilings follow the arched contours of the shallow vaults, amplifying their rhythm.

"I tried to integrate old and new - to establish a seamless link between the brick room and my insertions so that one flows into the other," Ranalli says about his terms of architectural engagement.

The white walls are offset by the brick and the new maple floor. The walls frame the cabinetry, which is crafted in lightly grained plywood – a handsome but unpretentious wood suited to an artist's modest construction budget. In the kitchen and bath, Ranalli used a white synthetic material that is fused at the joints to form what seem like a monolithic chunks of carved counters. The relentless sculpting of the cabinets, walls and counters keeps the eye roving across there transitive surfaces.

Like a composer, Ranalli develops his architectural variations from a few themes. He invented corner guards made of plywood to protect the plaster walls in the manner of suede patches covering the elbows of sport jackets. He extended the plywood from the corners across walls, turning it to frame doors. He punched windows through walls and filled them with a translucent glass laminate, which glows when backlit, for privacy.

With meandering edges and seams, the wood paneling ceaselessly metamorphoses to a kind of braille; The jogs in the volumes and the patches in the surfaces give an intimate scale to the loft, delivering it finally to the fingertips.
Slots and projections push and pull solids and voids, effecting a continuity between the piazza and the adjoining rooms. Even with the bedrooms, which in more standard dwellings are located behind blank, ungiving walls, Ranalli achieves a spatial porosity by creating subspaces outside. "You don't spill out of a room into a corridor but find yourself in a little antechamber where a casual conversation can take place," he says. "I designed the space to encourage these encounters and maximize a sense of community – and family."

ARCHITECTURE: GEORGE RANALLI by PAUL GOLDBERGER

It is not difficult to assume that architecture in Newport, Rhode Island, came to a dead stop over half a century ago. The great mansions by Richard Morris Hunt, McKim, Mead & White, Horace Trumbauer and others, the buildings that define this seaside resort's architecture for many visitors, were all designed in the late nineteenth century and in the early years of the twentieth. Since that time, there has been nothing of architectural distinction created here.

And Newport's "cottages," as they were called, were hardly innovative architecture, whatever their quality. But now a new project may well turn the eyes of the architectural avant-garde, at long last, toward this city. It is a set of six condominium units by New York architect George Ranalli, and they must surely rank, if not, perhaps, on so grand a scale, among the most intriguing architectural interior designs created anywhere in the last few years, let alone in Newport. This project is likely to attract the attention of historic preservationists as well as architects, for what George Ranalli and his clients Mr. and Mrs. Williams E. Boggs have done is rescue a sumptuous old Italianate schoolhouse, turning the interior into townhouses, while preserving the integrity of the exterior. These six apartments are notable not only as a work or architecture, but also as a significant gesture in the value of landmark preservation.

The Callender School had fallen vacant in 1974. William Boggs later purchased it from the city of Newport, in 1979. The building, which consisted of two stories of classrooms over a high basement, clearly called for major interior renovation- the rooms, though grandly scaled, were hardly elegant or domestic. And Mr. Boggs felt strongly that he wanted to make an architectural statement that the town of Newport would notice particularly.

To begin a project with this intention frequently leads to disaster, but here the architect's skill and the clients' expectations combined to produce a project that is at once dramatic and gracious, powerful architecturally, yet entirely suitable as living spaces. Inside, the six apartments are all variations on a single theme – they are essentially mock façades- rather like stage sets – interior structures intended to suggest the exteriors of buildings. Set into the large and high spaces of the old classrooms, each façade evolves a type of building, and together they form a symbolic city.

The mock façades are collections of walls, windows and doorways, rooflines and columns- architectural elements that are seen constantly, yet which seem to take on a new and symbolic importance here. For these elements within the Callender School serve much more than a functional purpose; they are ruminations on the nature of architecture's inner workings, studies in symmetry and proportion, openness and enclosure.

Lest all of this be thought too didactic, it should be said that the mock façades are also an entirely appropriate response to the existing conditions of the old school. The high ceilings in the classrooms made it logical to divide each condominium unit into an upper and lower story – some units even have three levels – yet, to provide a sense of grandeur, each living room was permitted to rise to a double height. The mock façades define the tall living room spaces and thus fulfill the functional purpose of dividing these areas from the two-story bedroom, and the kitchen and service areas.

Each condominium unit has its own sequence of spatial experiences, but in each case there is an interplay between the grand gesture of the mock façade and high living room area and the complex, small-scale nature of the spaces behind it. Within the large living rooms there is a sense of cut-up space active and alive behind the façade; from the smaller areas there is a glimpse of the unifying space of the main room.

All of the units are entered through intimate, low spaces to heighten the dramatic impact of the expansive living rooms. In the unit that the Boggses occupy, there is a tiny foyer, which opens on one side to the tall main living room, and on the other, to a tiny inglenook before a fireplace. The inglenooks are present in one form or another in all of the units, and they are a welcome relief from the custom of making the fireplace the focus of the largest space in a residence. Fires are much more pleasurable in intimate surroundings.

The Boggs unit is the largest, and all of its smaller spaces are grouped in its center. Beside the inglenook on the main level, there is a well- crafted kitchen and a tiny nook of an office. Master bedroom and bath are on the second level, and a library is on the level above that. To one side of this pile of rooms, rising through all three levels, is the living room; to the other side, also rising the height of the apartment, is the dining room. Thus, the unit has not one, but two walls- façades- that rise nobly in stepped-back profile. There is the same mix of variegated spaces in the other units, though each has a different feeling. For all its startling modernity, this project is an architectural experience worthy of Newport- and it connects us again to the architectural traditions of this unusual city.

ARCHITECTURE: BREAKING ALL THE RULES WITH NEW YORK'S PUBLIC-BUILDING DESIGN

by ADA LOUISE HUXTABLE

Now that the age of irrational exuberance and outrageous excess is apparently over, can we please talk about real architecture again? It has been fun seeing just how far talent can stretch itself before achieving irrelevancy, but there are diminishing returns in watching more become less in an escalating game of real-estate toys for the superrich. It has been less fun to see how easily and paradoxically in a time of extreme affluence, the social contract that is an essential part of the art of architecture has been abrogated. Or at least driven under the radar by the kind of showy construction where creativity and cost are terminally confused. You do begin to wonder what happened to the art that could build with genuine grandeur and still serve and elevate ordinary lives.

As the hype and the construction stop, there is much soul-searching talk by born-again architects about modesty, sustainability and social and environmental responsibility. But I find it hard to believe that those operating in the stratosphere of pricey self-indulgence in an undimmed celebrity culture really get it, or that they are having even a tiny epiphany. Architecture has always been the enabler of excess, for better or worse, and architects will succumb again to the same seductive pieties about cutting-edge design and a trickle-down theory that simply doesn't work.

Obviously, not all architects have been building condos and skyscrapers; some have been working quietly under the celebrity radar in ways and in places where it matters. It will be a surprise to many that this has been happening in New York (yes, New York, the erstwhile capital of architectural bling), and even more of a surprise that outstanding work is being sponsored by city departments better known for tight budgets. Byzantine bureaucracies and low-bid contracts guaranteeing bad design and shoddy construction, a process that allows elected officials to make egregiously false and enduringly ignorant claims of prudent use of taxpayers' money. The idea that a superior product can be brought in on time and on budget is a really hard sell to a public that sincerely believes no building ever comes in on budget and on time, and that the architect is always to blame. Nor does anyone get elected suggesting that the city's poor and underprivileged neighborhoods have a right to expect anything better than the dismal, degrading stuff they routinely get. Such apostasy lacks political mileage.

And so a building as good as the Saratoga Avenue Community Center in Brownsville, Brooklyn, designed by New York architect George Ranalli and built by the New York City Housing Authority, better known for its bottom-line public housing projects, deserves to have its presence shouted from the rooftops as a seriously fine demonstration of the art of architecture, and as an example of the radically revised standards that are being successfully implemented under a new city policy.

The change began with Mayor Michael Bloomberg's announcement of the Design and Construction Excellence Initiative in 2004, and the results have begun to show. An enlightened policy requires an enlightened administrator, and David Burney, the Housing Authority's director of design when the Saratoga Avenue Community Center was built, and now Commissioner of Design and Construction, has totally revamped the city's building process. The new guidelines apply to all city agencies, including those with independent programs. Jobs are awarded on the basis of talent and experience rather than to the lowest bidder, as previously mandated. The old system favored the hacks who knew how to game the system to their profit and the city's loss by bidding low and then padding costs with extras for omissions, changes and delays. Better firms were put off by the practice.

Now architects compete on the quality of their portfolios and their construction records. Building projects are grouped by cost, from high to low, encouraging smaller and younger firms to apply at the lower end; eligible architects are selected by a panel that reviews and updates the list periodically. Realistic fees are negotiated to include factors notoriously ignored in the past, such as difficult site preparation or restrictive landmarks provisions. This makes the process more open, more rational, and more fiscally controllable. It also delivers infinitely better buildings.

The Saratoga Avenue Community Center manages to break just about every deadly rule of conventional public building design. Mr. Ranalli was asked to remodel and update 1,500 square feet of an aging community center in the base of an existing tower that is part of the Saratoga Avenue housing project, and to add a new 3,500-square foot facility to include an all-purpose community room, kitchen, bathrooms, director's office, and spaces for services and storage, all on a rock-bottom budget of $2.3 million that included site preparation and landscaping, with actual construction costs at slightly less than $300 a square foot, for a total well within the Housing Authority's standard expenditure. He used the new construction to link the isolated towers and make a protective street wall that encloses two useful and attractive outdoor social areas, in a reconfiguration of the site that is a healing gesture for an open and uninviting housing superblock. At the same time, he created a building with a distinctive and elegant presence of its own. This is, in sum, real architecture.

The design could be called postmodern in its evocative recall of older models, but there are none of the bad jokes or superficial historical allusions of postmodernism's defiant denial of modernism's rejection of the past. (You've got to be defiant when you're fighting your father's belief systems.) Mr. Ranalli adheres to the logic of modernist practice, integrating its mechanical, material and structural realities with details drawn from earlier sources to create an integral ornament of abstract linear geometry. His purpose is to move modernism into an enriched and more deeply reference style. The building does what so much postmodernism of the 1980's failed to do-it reinterprets and transforms history into something completely and satisfyingly contemporary.

There are strong echoes of Frank Lloyd Wright, Vienna Secession and Art Deco-and from far more recent times, Carlo Scarpa and Raimund Abraham. This is visible in the Wrightian pattern of the mahogany frames of a continuous clerestory window at the top of the building, the Scarpa-like attention to hardware, and the cornice of glass-fiber-reinforced concrete topping the clerestory that formally completes the design and seems to float above the glass.

Below the clerestory, the building is a warm, orange-toned, iron spot roman brick laid in narrow courses above a limestone base, a total departure from public housing's featureless red or buff brick. The decorative details, assembled from precast concrete sections, are repeated in the surrounds of doors and windows, recessed, stepped back and incised to give depth and shadow to the façade. Decorative and structural elements come together where the horizontal roof line is broken by projections that reflect the presence of paired steel columns, visible through the glass, and the roof's supporting steel beams.

Inside, the white walls of the all-purpose room are patterned part way up with contrasting buff gray cement panels that embellish and scale the handsome, 23-foot-high space. Because vandalism is a continuing fact of urban life, these decorative panels are superstrong, replaceable units able to resist rough use, securely screwed to the plaster walls. The high windows are raised far enough above ground to avoid breakage, and there is bulletproof glass in the doors. But the architect's insistence on mahogany for windows and doors instead of standard steel sash, the elegant brickwork, the many thoughtful details carried out on a shoestring budget, all explode the cliché that these buildings must not only be built on the cheap but look it as well, on the principle that nothing is to be seen as wasted on anything that might raise standards or hope. In this context, beauty has been considered irrelevant and indefensible.

The Saratoga Avenue Community Center is beautiful, economical and tough. And it is no aberration; award-winning firehouses, libraries, children's museums, and arts, cultural and community centers are appearing in New York neighborhoods that combine an artist's eye with a commitment to make a difference in people's lives and environment. This is something that only architecture can deliver.

A STITCH IN TIME: RENEWING A SWATCH OF URBAN FABRIC by HERBERT MUSCHAMP

George Ranalli completed a project a few months ago that glows with the keen sensitivity to form, materials and detail that has made this New York "architect's artchitect" an esteemed figure in his profession. It's a modest work; a remodeled entrance and lobby in an old garment district loft building, along with a redesigned hallway on one of the upper floors. It is also modest in spirit, Mr. Ranalli, an architect known for spare geometric designs, has departed from his customary vocabulary and steeped himself in the style of an earlier day. He hasn't renounced his own esthetic. Rather, he's woven it into a vintage swatch of urban fabric. Synthetic blends may not be fashion's raiment of choice, but Mr. Ranalli's stylistic synthesis is a beauty.

Located at 525 Seventh Avenue (at 38th Street), the Fashion Center Building is hardly a traffic-stopping landmark. But the 24-story block of showrooms and offices is a rich part of the garment district's distinctive urban tissue. And while the building's architect, Henry Ives Cobb, is an obscure figure today, he was highly regarded at the turn of the century, chiefly on account of his master plan for the University of Chicago.

Designed in the mid-1920's in Romanesque Revival style, the Fashion Center Building is doubly anachronistic, for by the time it was completed modern architecture was on the rise. The Chrysler and McGraw-Hill buildings would reach the skyline within the decade; for the next 50 years, architects didn't look back. Still, although Cobb was out of step with changing times, the Fashion Center's lower floors- of smooth, unadorned granite, set with trim rectangular show windows- anticipated the taunt skin of the modern skyscrapers that would leave his kind of architecture for dead.

The building was renovated in the 1950's and again in the 1960's, when the International Style was at its height and respect for period styles was in the basement, and the renovators thought nothing of destroying whatever of Cobb's ornament couldn't be covered up beneath slick surfaces. Mr. Ranalli, too, at first viewed the project as a "modernization": he did not expect to depart from his accustomed minimal style. But some old photographs of the interiors, couple with the discovery that much of Cobb's ornament remained intact beneath the earlier remodelings, made him reconsider.

What appealed to Mr. Ranalli was not an old-fashioned style of ornament. It was a lapsed ideal of urban space: the belief that while lobbies occupy private property, they have a civic duty to perform. They lend dignity and drama to the progression from public street to private office. Cobb's building is a fine example of the genre. Starting with a monumentally scaled entry arch- a proscenium for the urban stage- the design escorted tenants and visitors into a soaring vestibule (open to the street), through a narrow intermediary lobby (lined with windows that looked into ground floor shops), then into the main lobby, where a chorus line of elevator operators would transport them skyward.

This is not an uncommon spatial sequence in commercial buildings of a certain age. But it's uncommon for an architect of Mr. Ranalli's day and esthetic disposition to get his hands on such a building. His design, like Cobb's, is about transition, but it creates a passage in times was well as space. Instead of emphasizing the contrast between Cobb's style and his own, Mr. Ranalli highlights the continuity between them. A seamless fusion of renovation, restoration and new design, this is, in effect, collaboration between two architects of different eras.

The team gets off to a brilliant start in the out vestibule, an outdoor room that contains the building's most robustly Romanesque decoration. Entered beneath a massive wrought iron grille (discovered in the building's basement), the vestibule is frames by four large piers of red terracotta that rise to support ornate arches. Besides restoring the damaged terracotta and removing a row of doors that had sealed the area off from the sidewalk, Mr. Ranalli has refashioned the vestibule's ceiling in a wholly new design: an ethereal cloud of white plaster ringed by circles of gold. The floor is unmistakably Ranalli; an abstract composition of circles and lines, punctuated by lamps set into recesses in the purple and green terrazzo floor. In place of Romanesque gloom, Mr. Ranalli has mounted a glowing footlight parade.

In the intermediate and main lobbies beyond, the emphasis shifts from ornate forms to sumptuous materials. Walls of cream colored marble veined with purple, are accented with black and gold marble bands. Ceiling spotlights, set into round white plaster fixtures, burnish the marble and polish a rich array of newly restored bronze heating grilles, elevator doors and window frames. The reception desk, opposite the elevators, is the remodeling's most striking contemporary feature. An inverted ziggurat of sheet bronze, the desk is Mr. Ranalli's way of welcoming design to the present. Because of a change in the building's ownership, the scope of the project was curtailed. Only one hallway in the upper stories was remodeled. This is a loss: the unified treatment of the public areas was integral to Mr. Ranalli's urban concept. The hallway's terrazzo floor, splashed with light from coffered ceiling recesses, is a simple variation on the geometric pattern of the lobby downstairs. Metal brackets, designed in a stylized skyscraper motif, frame the walls. This is a typically thoughtful Ranalli detail. Practical (it protects the walls from careering dress racks), visually bold and urbanistically savvy, it's an understated reminder that when people enter this building they don't leave the city behind. They're on their way to the skyline.

Like other Ranalli projects, the Fashion Center Building shows the influence of the great Italian modernist Carlo Scarpa. For Mr. Ranalli, history always includes the history of modern design. But in case Scarpa's influence is evident not only in Mr. Ranalli's forms but also in his display of affection for forms outside the modern tradition. The Fashion Center Building may not be Castelvecchio, Scarpa's masterpiece of historical interpretation. But New York is not Verona, nor is the Fashion Center Building a museum. It's a productive industrial building in the heart of a vibrant commercial district.

Yet change is coming to the garment district, and Nafta may well accelerate it: Mr. Ranalli expects that as sewing jobs decline there will be a proliferation of high-style showrooms. If so, his sequence of spaces has set an elegant pattern for other renovations in this quintessential New York quarter. Mr. Ranalli grasps that history, too, is a transition. It's not Then, not Now, but the way from there to here.

THE CASTLE IN THE HOUSE by ANTHONY VIDLER

Kierkegaard told the story of how, as a child, when he asked to go out, his father, refusing nevertheless offered him the alternative of going for a walk in the apartment. Hand-in-hand he and his father would stroll along imaginary paths, now passing a castle, now turning towards the beach, now pushing through noisy crowded streets. As they moved back and forward his father would comment on what they say, saluting the passers-by, shouting over the din of the traffic, relishing the food displayed in the stores. Wherever the young philosopher wished to go, there he was taken. But in this liberty, even as the interior might become the most expansive exterior, there also resided a form of imprisonment; the child was no doubt safe, but locked within the fixed relations that bound him to his father and his room, much like those bonds, also explored by Kierkegaard, that tied him to his mirror. And it was in this very condition of enclosure that lay the significance of every piece of furniture, every decorative or useful object, forced to take on themselves all the connotations of the outside world. As Theodore Adorno noted, "In the interior things do not follow an alienated existence. The interior extorts meaning from them. It is precisely thanks to alienated things that alienation is itself expressed; silent things speak as so many 'symbols'."

This perception has been a commonplace of modern thought; Rimbaud after all went for long sea-voyages while sitting in front of his fireside- the 'veillees' of his imagination; Huysmans described intricate stage-sets that emulated the cabin of a ship and the rocking of the waves; Pater and Rilke dreamed of the rooms they once inhabited in childhood; Bachelard and Heidegger nostalgically recreated the conditions of a long abandoned 'dwelling.' Interiors themselves, not unnaturally, have been equally complicit in this dreamwork. Like the department store, which, as Walter Benjamin observed, was its public complement, the bourgeois interior offered its inhabitant "a box in the world theatre," at once mnemonic device and fetish-box, the refuge of a peculiarly modern imprisonment.

Modernism, however, looked on the defensive posture of the bourgeois interior, filled with bric-a-brac and kitsch, with considerable disfavor. With sublime disdain for the needs of the dreamer, the house was cleaned; the paraphernalia of Balzac's old curiosity shop was thrown out, leaving bare walls and floors, an infinity of white space filled only with air and light. Post-Freudian man apparently no longer required the crutches of decoration and furnishing, surely the marks of the primitive or the degenerate; healthy and active, he lived not poetically but gymnastically. Punching-bags and chaises-longues, spring loaded like trampolines, formed the equipment of the room, while ramps and spiral stairs doubled as the indoor running tracks of man-on-the-move. The park outside, with its restoring breezes and athletic promises, invaded the house from bottom to top. This house on pilotis with a garden on the roof had no more room for secret cellars or cluttered attics. Such a Promethean ideal was, as we now know, generally refused and not always politely, by a middle-class who preferred to live at home and travel to their gymnasia. Only the poor, suitable objects of reform and redemption, were condemned to live in the stripped-down cells of the minimum dwelling.

The post-modern architect, fleeing from the admittedly reductive vision of total liberation from atavistic dreams and refusing a holistic heroism, seems nevertheless caught and apparently held by a relentless self-consciousness that both refuses authenticity to any "return" and originality to any invention. At its worst, the architecture of the post-modern condition turns a blind eye to cultural rupture and packages allusions to past illusions; at its best, fully conscious that post-modernity cannot ignore its essentially modern status, it provides a commentary on the paradox that within modernity the primitive still lives, that a termination of analysis is not possible; a commentary, that is, on interminability in a life without exit.

In such a state only a self-critical irony and relentless refusal of blind longing protects architecture against its degradation; where it is no longer permitted to believe in an essential truth that might be "unveiled" by criticism, only a commentary dedicated to the representation of the insignificant as well as the significant, the cracks in the wall as well as its smooth surfaces, can counter the tendency-useful solely to the market-to divide the world between those who blindly accept and those who, defeated, withdraw. Thus, where to build a "city within a city," or even a "house within a house," might, given the present conditions of urban life, simply be seen as a reaction to and reinforcement of the anti-urban pressures of contemporary economics by means of a defensive retreat. A commentary on these conditions would perhaps address the continuity in mercantile and industrial aggression against urban populations since the eighteenth century. Rather than trying, in Brecht's words, to "paper over the cracks" with utopian dreams of a restored artisan culture and a rebuilt urban fabric, such a commentary would work with the memories of previous struggles and the experience of present conflicts in order to trace their impact on the discourse of form. Here it is that the interior, for a long time unnoticed by history and criticism as the private realm of accumulation or the mere residue of big plans, becomes a privileged domain of intervention. The conditions of post-modern interiority, however, are definitely not those of nineteenth-century dreaming nor of modernist transparency. To live in the contemporary city is rather to discover the daily need for Brecht's Handbook for City-Dwellers, with its cautionary refrain, "cover your tracks." It is to live in the interstices, behind old façades and in converted rooms. The apartment is carved out of the loft, the economy loft out of this, and the studio from this. And while these successive reductions have been disguised by many architects with an efflorescence of rhetoric in pastel colours and mannerist motifs, a few have chosen to engage in strategic comment. Thus, drawing on the experiences of a century of modern domestic imprisonment, the metaphor of the "citadel in the house" takes on particular resonance. Adorno, following Kierkegaard's insight, even found meaning in the appearance of alienation this fortress mentality implied" "It is thanks to this metaphor-the fortress as the sign of a past long since completed-as it is to that of the interior as an immeasurable distance, inscribed in the here-and-now, that appearance acquires its power. All the spatial figures of the interior are only décor, strangers to the finality that they represent, deprived of their use value, uniquely the products of the isolated apartment, itself formed only by those that surround it." This comment, advanced to explain the potentiality of objects to take on a kind of exteriority, the recipients of Kierkegaard's projected desires to escape, might equally apply to the metaphoric décor of the "castle" as it appears in recent works by George Ranalli that constitute themselves as semi-enclosed "houses" placed within the spaces of other "houses," in this case, the interiors of lofts and renovated public buildings used as so many metaphoric exteriors.

Refusing the literal quotation of defensive spaces, and any direct reference to pre-modern styles and motifs, Ranalli nevertheless describes a fundamentally post-modern condition. His shelters within shelters, free-standing or attached to their containers on one side, re-enact so to speak, a primitive origin, reminiscent not of any anthropological source, but rather of those eighteenth-century myths of origin, as in that, for example, where Robinson Crusoe, model mercantile colonist, built a wooden framed structure within his cave and surrounded the whole with a palisade. Incorporating within their complex geometries recesses, shelves, hollows, even whole rooms, Ranalli's new Robinsonades refer initially, like those of the first Robinson, to the storage of objects useful and precious, with the essential difference that, in the absence of a nineteenth-century economy of accumulation, they make no provision for ostentatious display. Registering the defensive posture of the city-dweller, they deploy their abstract turrets, buttresses, and winding interior stairs, like some product of modern military engineering while all the time engaging the memory of the portcullises, bastions, arrow-slits, and city gates of Viollet-le-Duc's best medieval fantasies. They are thus entirely modern in their language, at the same time as post-modern in their range of reference and ironic in their commentary on their roles. Their uncompromising abstraction serves to awaken disturbing echoes of the past, provoking visions of long-lost exteriors, but with a self-conscious recognition of this loss. They are somewhat like those structures, described by Jacques Derrida, whose Relief and design appears more clearly when content, which is the living energy of meaning, is neutralized; somewhat like the architecture of an uninhabited and deserted city, reduced to its skeleton by some catastrophe of nature or art. A city no longer inhabited, not simply left behind, but haunted by meaning and culture.

This image appears most strongly in the renovation of the Callender School in Newport, Rhode Island, a nineteenth-century schoolhouse in which a collective assemblage of private "castles" are gathered around a space that might be either a city square or even a space outside the walls. The apartments take on the form of abandoned ducal palaces whose balconies overlook the deserted piazza below or out towards the empty countryside. Their three and four-storey elevations are designed as exterior façades and their crenellated battlements rise up with, but never touch the limits of, the found enclosure that is thereby given the aspect of an entire city: an elegant strategy for landmark renewal, no doubt, but also the deliberate insertion of another world, one that cannot adapt and mould itself to an accomplished past but nevertheless one that is changed in scale and purpose, that accepts the old as inevitable, as a fragment surviving in a world of fragments. The section of this "Callender" School renovation, itself a name that evokes the regular passing of the days, reveals a veritable archeology of such cities, each with their own particular sky, piled on each other in Piranesian profusion. But these citadels are, of course, lived in: they accommodate to all the restricted necessities of life on the run: closets, beds, rooms within rooms, nooks and crannies for privacy within the private realm, all function as precisely calculated interlocking machines, or gigantic Chinese puzzles, rock-temples for modern rites carved out of the residue of modern form. Where possible they are also wrought out of the most durable materials-welded iron, brass, marble, and hardwood. This materiality further removes them from the stage-set pastiches of a more consumable kind, forcing their angular edges on an attention too easily distracted by objects that appear as seductive gifts. Their spatiality is again different from both the academic eclectic and the modern; where the former developed what Le Corbusier castigated the "false illusion" of plans and the latter, epitomized in the same architect's Domino House prototype, floated its horizontal planes in an otherwise undifferentiated space, Ranalli's structures fold inside on outside, mirror-like inflections of their larger scale inversions. Solids and vertical surfaces, their depth revealed by diagonal cutes through apparently dense masses that from another angle of vision open up to receive objects or uses, prevail over horizontal layering; while their plans reveal no abstract logic of axes or grids, only the arbitrariness of a random horizontal cut through a complex three-dimensional sculpture. Movement through these little buildings is accomplished not be free-standing ramps or spiral iron stairs , but through narrow passages negotiated through the cliffs, the steps of which themselves become intermediate levels, habitable for a moment. Where for Flaubert the stupidity of the academic system was to be evoked by the "ide reue" of an architect "who forgets the stairs," Ranalli shows the cunning of one who perceives that the stairs might well be the only place left on which to live.

The most recent of these projects, a renovated apartment in New York, is in some ways, although not the largest of Ranalli's completed works, the most successful. Here all the themes that were announced in earlier designs, experimentally and one by one, have been brought together in a *tour de force* that is at once more controlled and yet far richer that its predecessors.

On one level the solution seems breathtakingly simple. Demolishing the wall that once separated bedroom from living room at the front of the apartment, Ranalli has created a single clear space for living and eating, lit across its full width by the metal framed windows. The loft, in this sense, has been reconstructed. Then, within the boundaries of what seems from the outside to be a unified rectangular enclosure inserted into the old shell, all the functions of sleeping, dressing-room, wardrobes, storage, study, and library have been condensed, and with dexterous ingenuity. As if interlocked in some elegant Chinese puzzle, joined by stairs and carefully places openings, each of the two major rooms in this enclosure, the bedroom and the study, is given its own character. The qualities of light, surface modeling, and proportion are so managed as to endow even the smallest alcove with a sense of particularity, while visual connections consistently work to bring unity to the whole, and, finally, to join it inseparably to the larger apartment. Thus the study to the rear, once an enclosed room without daylight, is over looked from the dressing room, a half-level above; a corresponding opening in the front wall of the bedroom allows light to filter back and reduces the sense of closure. The bedroom itself, reached by a single flight of stairs running along the side of the study but contained within its own space, is enclosed to the rear by a double wardrobe-cum-dressing room, and to the front by a thick wall of closets and alcoves. The vertical cuts in this wall angled and pitched like so many crenellations, look out to the main living space and reinforce the sense of privacy established by the raised level. The intimacy is completed by the reflective canopy hung over the bed to create a false roof to the room, enclosing without entombing. Beneath the bedroom, a roomy storage space is reached from a ladder under the double bed itself.

Such functional coherence and facility would alone mark this design as distinguished; but Ranalli, within the limits of an extremely modest budget, has succeeded in going much further on the level of detail and the use of materials. Selecting a number of important elements at different scales-the bed canopy, side lights, shelves and brackets-he has found a coherent aesthetic not in the display of metal surfaces-brass and steel. Domesticating what might seem at first a hard and intransigent material, Ranalli adds to the play of abstract surfaces exhibited by the main structure by a series of cubes, angles, and canopies fabricated out of bent steel and bolted or screwed to the walls; these either reflect the light or, in the case of the small lamps beside the bed, throw artificial light in geometric patterns that enliven the surfaces of wall and ceiling. Each piece is conceived, so to speak, as a small abstract sculpture in its own right; the ensemble gives the effect of a miniature museum of contemporary minimalism built up out of this kind of "functional decoration."

The *piece de resistance* is without doubt the bed canopy, a complex structure of two planes covered with sheet brass, suspended above the bed by a mixture of horizontal and vertical struts. The two planes are gently inclined, like the huge flittering wings of some mechanical butterfly, or, as the client would have it, a Leonardo flying-machine. Their lower and upper surfaces reflect a golden light at all times of the day, bathing the interior of the bedroom and study with a diffused glow. As in the smaller set-pieces, the design is studied literally down to the last bolt and screw; here the pattern of hundreds of round-headed brass screws that join the brass sheets to their wooden frame returns us to the age of hand crafted clocks, where every element was both useful and decorative at the same time. In this attention to detail and loving utilization of natural materials, Ranalli has been much influenced by the Italian architect Carlo Scarpa; but, influenced by an American formal tradition founded on the geometrical plays of Frank Lloyd Wright's Unity Temple period, he is perhaps more concerned with the relations of part to whole than his Venetian model. Ranalli has discovered a way to make each of his elements speak individually while contributing to the overall unity.

Inevitably, such a system of forms, although it permits surprising diversity in the objects selected by the occupants, calls for a final resolution in the major pieces of furniture. Here, Ranalli, supported by the enthusiasm of his clients, has moved successfully from interior design to furniture design, providing a steel-based, marble-topped dining table, armchairs, and sofa that, conceived within the same family of forms as the apartment as a whole, allow the architecture of the bedroom to enter, at a smaller scale, the living room. The chairs and sofa, fabricated out of bent steel sheets, covered with leather cushions, indeed, form small spaces of their own within the space as they define cubic enclosures, singly or grouped together. In this way, and without repeating the errors of a modern architecture that attempted to dominate the lives of its occupants through aesthetic insistence, Ranalli has produced that most difficult of all syntheses-a work that on every level quietly asserts its artistic presence and yet leaves its users free to go about their business, helping more than hindering, their daily lives. If this is the potential result of a carefully worked reassessment of modernism joined to individual inventiveness, then perhaps we may see in it some way out of the uncomfortable impasses of the last few years: a third way of design after modernism, neither high-tech nor historicist, but once that returns to the basic principles of good design-invention guided by the needs of the client and framed by the realities of materials, unconcerned, at least on this most tangible level, with the theatricality of nostalgia. While inevitably constrained to submit to the "cult of domesticity" that has replaced the all-too-brief flirtation with public responsibility characteristic of the seventies, Ranalli, as his larger scale, urban projects demonstrate, has utilized the enforced conditions of his practice as a laboratory that both comments on and expands the narrow confines of the urban cell.

APPENDIX

BIOGRAPHY

Dean George Ranalli has been Dean of the Bernard and Anne Spitzer School of Architecture at City College since 1999. He was born and raised in New York City. He received his Bachelor of Architecture from Pratt Institute in 1972 and Master of Architecture from the Graduate School of Design at Harvard University in 1974. From 1976-1999 he was Professor of Architecture at Yale University, and in 1988–1989 he was the William Henry Bishop Chaired Professor in Architectural Design. Mr. Ranalli recently completed his fourth monograph, *Saratoga*, devoted to his Saratoga Avenue Community Center for the New York City Housing Authority. That project has been widely praised, notably in a May 13, 2009 article by Ada Louis Huxtable in *The Wall Street Journal.*

His architectural and design work has been published internationally in numerous journals including *Domus, A+U, Progressive Architecture, L'Architettura, G.A. Houses, Architectural Digest, Architecture D'Aujourd'hui, Architectural Design,* and *Lotus*. His work has been exhibited at the Cooper–Hewitt Museum, Sperone–Westwater Gallery, the Museum of Contemporary Art in Chicago, the Museum of Finnish Architecture, Centre Pompidou in France, Deutsches Architekturmuseum in Frankfurt, the XVII Triennale Di Milano in Italy, and a one-man exhibit at Artists Space Gallery in New York in 1998.

He designed the exhibition Frank Lloyd Wright: Designs for an American Landscape, 1922-1932 for the Whitney Museum of Art in 1997, and designed the installation for the exhibition of work of Carlo Scarpa, in 1999 at the Canadian Centre for Architecture Montreal, Canada.

REGISTRATION:

Registered Architect, State of New York, October 1986

Registered Architect, State of Connecticut, May 1993

N.C.A.R.B.: National Council of Architectural Registration Boards Certification, July 1989

EDUCATION:

Harvard University, 1972-1974
Graduate School of Design; Cambridge, MA.
Degree: Master of Architecture, January 1974

Pratt Institute, 1968-1972
School of Architecture; Brooklyn, New York
Degree: Bachelor of Architecture, June 1972

New York Institute of Technology, 1967-1968

HONORARY DEGREE:

Yale University, February 1996
Degree: Master of Arts

ACADEMIC EXPERIENCE:

City College, School of Architecture;
New York, N.Y.
Dean, Bernard and Anne Spitzer School of Architecture, 1999-Present

Yale University, School of Architecture
Faculty: Professor of Architectural Design with Tenure, 1995-1999

Yale University, School of Architecture
Faculty: Associate Professor of Architectural Design with Tenure, 1991-1994

Yale University, School of Architecture
William Henry Bishop Chair, Visiting Professor of Architectural Design, Fall Term 1988-1989

Yale University, School of Architecture
Faculty: Associate Professor (Adj.) of Architectural Design, Fall 1982-1991

Yale University, School of Architecture
Faculty: Assistant Professor of Architectural Design, Fall 1976-Spring 1982

Cooper Union, School of Architecture
Faculty: Visiting Professor, 1984-1987

University of Illinois at Chicago Circle, School of Architecture
Faculty: Visiting Critic Master's Class, Fall 1980

Columbia University, School of Architecture
Guest Critic, 1977-present

New York School of Interior Design
Guest Critic: Workshops in Interior Design, 1975

New York Community College
Faculty: Architectural Drawing, Fall 1974

Rhode Island School of Design, School of Architecture
Faculty: Architectural Drawing, Fall/Spring 1973-1974

Boston Architecture Center
Faculty: Architectural Drawing, Summer 1973

Harvard University, Graduate School of Design
Teaching Assistant: Architectural Drawing, Fall/Spring 1972-1973

Pratt Institute, School of Architecture
Teaching Assistant: Design, Spring 1971 and Fall/Spring 1971-1972

AWARDS:

Stanford White Award, Institute for Classical Architecture and Art, December 2012
Design Award of Excellence in the category of Institutional, Civic and Commercial Architecture, Saratoga Avenue Community Center

Society of American Registered Architects, New York Council, June 11, 2012,
Design Award of Excellence, Saratoga Avenue Community Center

Society of American Registered Architects, Pennsylvania Council, September 22, 2011,
Design Award of Honor, Saratoga Avenue Community Center

New York Society of Architects, November 2010;
Sidney L. Strauss Award in recognition of outstanding achievement for the benefit of the architectural profession

American Institute of Architects, Brooklyn Chapter, September 2010
Award of Excellence, Saratoga Avenue Community Center, Institutional Category

Renaissance Award, City College School of Architecture, Spring 2005
The School of Architecture Alumni made this award to Dean Ranalli for his transformation of the school into a first tier design school

American Institute of Architects, New York Chapter, 1997
Projects Award for Stonington Historical Society Library/Archive Building, Stonington, Conn.; 1997 Awards Program

American Institute of Architects, New York Chapter, 1996
Projects Citation for the Indoor Lap Pool Building, Cornwall, Conn.; 1996 Awards Program

American Institute of Architects, New York Chapter, 1995
Projects Citation for the Pool & Pool House for "C" Family, Amagansett, N.Y.; 1995 Awards Program

American Institute of Architects, New York Chapter, 1994
Architecture Award for the Fashion Center Building Renovation/Restoration; 1994 Awards Program

New York Foundation for the Arts
Artist Fellowship in Architecture, 1988

Progressive Architecture, January 1980
Design Awards, Citation

American Institute of Architects, New York Chapter, 1976
James Stewardson Travelling Fellowship

New York State/A.I.A. Award, Honorable Mention, Griffiss Air Force Base Hospital, 1974
Max O. Urbahn Assoc.; George Ranalli, Designer

The Architectural League of New York, Honorable Mention, June 1974. Birch Burdette Long Show, "New York City-An Addition"

The Architectural League of New York, 1974
Birch Burdette Long Show, Illustrations exhibited

Reynolds Aluminum Prize, Harvard University, 1973
School prize for the best original architectural design with creative use of aluminum

New York Society of Architects, Pratt Institute, 1972
Matthew del Gaudio Memorial Award

Pirelli Tire Competition, Honorable Mention, 1969

PUBLICATIONS

BOOKS:

SARATOGA George Ranalli, 2009
ORO Editions, San Rafael, California

CASAS internacional #57: GEORGE RANALLI
1998
Kliczkowski Publisher, Buenos Aires, Argentina

George Ranalli: Bauten und Projekte; Constructions et Projets, 1990
Verlag fur Architetur Artemis, Zurich

George Ranalli: Buildings and Projects, 1988
Princeton Architectural Press, New York

ESSAYS WRITTEN:

Oculus, Journal of the American Institute of Architects New York Chapter, October 2005, "An Uneasy Alliance: Architecture as Art and Business", p. 33

Carlo Scarpa, Architect Intervening with History, 1999
"History, Craft, Invention", pp. 39-151 Canadian Center for Architecture/Monacelli Press

Avant Garde 6: Journal of Theory and Criticism in Architecture, 1993
"Elements of Architecture: Tower of Silence," pp. 34-41

Design Quarterly, Spring 1992
"Getting A Handle," pp. 20-23

Avant Garde 5: Journal of Theory and Criticism in Architecture, Winter 1991
"Architecture and Education," pp. 10-29

Avant Garde 4: Journal of Theory and Criticism in Architecture, Summer 1990
"ACSA, Western Regional Conference: A Commentary," pp. 9-11

Avant Garde 2: Journal of Theory and Criticism in Architecture, Summer 1989
"Autonomous Architecture," pp. 54-61

Avant Garde 1: Journal of Theory and Criticism in Architecture, Winter 1989
"Architecture and Domestic Ritual," pp. 54-61

Interior Design, February 1987
"Designer Profiles: Gaetano Pesce," pp. 288-291

Gaetano Pesce: Design & Architecture 1975-1985, May 1986. Catalogue Introduction, Musée d'Art Moderne, Strasbourg, France

Carlo Scarpa: Opera Completa, 1985
"The Coherence of a Quest," pp. 258-261

Progressive Architecture, May 1981
"Critique, Brion-Vega Cemetery by Carlo Scarpa," pp. 124-131

WORKS PUBLISHED / JOURNALS:

Urban Land, March/April 2012
Journal of The Urban Land Institute "The Power of Play" by Ron Nyren. Saratoga Community Center

Harvard Magazine, September-October 2011
"Oasis in Limestone and Brick" by Thomas Vinciguerra pp. 30-32

London Telegraph, September 18, 2010
"Brilliant Architecture Can Rescue Even Basingstoke" by Simon Heffer

New York Magazine, November 2, 2009. "Stealth by Design: How the City Is Sneaking Great Little Buildings Into Unexpected Places"
by Justin Davidson. Pp. 68-69

Chatham Press, November 2009, Chatham, New York "George Ranalli" Profile article by Rich Kraham. Pp. 16-17

Wall Street Journal, Personal Journal Section, Leisure & Arts, May 13, 2009
"Breaking All The Rules With New York's Public-Building Design" Ada Louise Huxtable. p. D1

New York Times: City Section, March 29, 2009
"On Violent Ground, a Touch of Beauty",
Front page

Architect's Newspaper, issue #04, 3.04.09. "A Bright Spot in Brooklyn" by William Menking on p. 06

ArchNewsNow, On line journal of the AIA.
"Community Building: Saratoga Community Center by George Ranalli, Architect".
January 2009

Oculus, Journal of the American Institute of Architects New York Chapter, Fall 2004 "The Secret Lives of Architects: The Sofia Glass",
pp. 12-14

ARCHITECTURE, February 2004, On the Boards, p. 41

Architectural Record, April 2002 Record News, p. 36

New York Times: Real Estate Section, February 24, 2002
"In Brooklyn, A 'Beacon' Recalls Wright".
Cover

Oculus, Journal of the American Institute of Architects New York Chapter, October 2000
"Against All Odds: The New York City Housing Authority", pp. 12-14

The New York Times Book Review, December 5, 1999
Carlo Scarpa Architect: Intervening with History, p. 44

The Architectural Review, October 1999
"Scarpa in Montreal", pp. 33-34

Art in America, October 1999
"History's Architect", pp. 148-153 & p.178

Architectural Record, September 1999
Exhibitions: Carlo Scarpa Architect: Intervening with History, pp. 61-62

Metropolis, October 1999
"Time On His Side", Carlo Scarpa, pp. 171-173

Architecture, August 1999
"The Trouble With Scarpa", pp.90-95

The New Republic, August 9, 1999
"The Interventionist", pp.31-37

New York Times: Weekend, July 18, 1997
"The Designs of a Genius Redesigning Himself," pp. 1, 29

Architectural Digest (Germany), Juni/Juli 1997
"Im Auge des Taifuns," pp. 140-147

A+U (Architecture + Urbanism), no. 318, March 1997
"George Ranalli; K-Loft in New York," pp. 40-49

ABITARE 355, October 1996
"Angoli Protagonisti," pp. 174-179

Architectural Digest, August 1996
"Redefining the Loft," pp. 80-85

BLUEPRINT, March 1996 "Intelligent Energy," pp. 32-33

DBZ (Deutsche Bauzeitschrift), March 1995
"Two Pools on Long Island," pp. 10-15

DBZ (Deutsche Bauzeitschrift), December 1994
"Autonome Strukturen," pp. 85-92

NEWSLINE, Journal of Columbia University, November/December 1994
"From Program to Detail: A Practical Theory," p. 6

Domus, no. 762, July/August 1994
"George Ranalli: Renovation of the Fashion Center Building in New York," pp. 44 49

Architecture, July 1994 "Customizing Hardware," pp. 93-99

Interior Design, June 1994 "George Ranalli," pp. 112-119

Oculus, Journal of the American Institute of Architects, New York Chapter, March 1994
"Preserving the Old with a New Twist," cover and pp. 6-7

New York Times: Arts & Leisure Section, March 6, 1994. "A Stitch in Time: Renewing a Swatch Of Urban Fabric," p. 42

Progressive Architecture, October 1993
"Projects," p. 30

Lotus #76, 1993 "The Spirit of the Collector," p. 48

A.D. (Architectural Design), vol. 62, no. 9/10, September/October 1992
"George Ranalli: Barn House and Pool House Projects," pp. x-xi

ABITARE 307, May 1992 "Maniglie di Architetti," p. 252

Building Design, March 1992 "Manhattan Projections," pp. 16-17

The Metropolitan Museum of Art Bulletin, Fall 1991 "Recent Acquisitions: A Selection 1990-1991," p. 81

Interiors, August 1991 "Door Jewels," pp. 90-91
AD 100 Architects: Architectural Digest, August 1991 "George Ranalli," pp. 196-197

Domus, no.721, November 1990"Barn for 'A' Family in Red Hook, N.Y.," pp. 12-13

Lotus #66, 1990 "The Loft Room," pp. 66-71

A+U (Architecture + Urbanism), August 1990
"Special Feature: George Ranalli," pp. 71-136

Japan Avenue, June/July 1990
"Have T-Square, Will Travel," pp. 75-84

Progressive Architecture, June 1990
"Projects," pp. 128-130

OZ Journal, College of Architecture & Design, Kansas State University, 1990
"Tower of Silence," pp. 78-79

HG (House & Garden), February 1990
"Go East Young Architect," pp. 40, 42, 44

Interior Design, November 1989
Book Review: "George Ranalli: Buildings and Projects," p. 154

Avenue Magazine, November 1989
"Have T-Square, Will Travel, " pp. 93, 98

Architectural Record, September 1989
Book Review: "George Ranalli: Buildings and Projects," p. 57

Architecture, June 1989
Book Review: "George Ranalli: Buildings and Projects," pp. 40-41

Building Design, March 1989
"Refined Inner Space," pp. 30-31

New York Times, Sunday Arts & Leisure Section, January 1, 1989
Book Review: "George Ranalli: Buildings and Projects"

Progressive Architecture, July 1987
"P/A Technics: The Uses of Steel," p. 102

Metropolis, March 1987
"Capturing Light: George Ranalli," pp. 47-48

Domus, no. 672, May 1986
"Loft, Furniture Design, New York," pp. 50-55

Casa Vogue, April 1986
XVII Triennale di Milano,"Il Progetto Domestico," p. 187

Interior Design, April 1986
XVII Triennale di Milano,"Il Progetto Domestico," p. 237

Interior Design, March 1986 "New York Loft," pp. 228-233

Lotus #46, 1985 #2 "The Castle in the House," pp. 54-61

The New York Times: Home Section, April 5, 1984
"Two Manhattan Apartments Turn Architecture Outside In," cover and p. 8

Interior Design, November 1983 "Ranalli Studio," pp. 224-227

Domus, no. 643, October 1983 "La Camera Chiara," pp. 46-48

AD: Architectural Digest (Japanese Edition), November 1983. "Architecture: George Ranalli," pp. 44-49

AD: Architectural Digest (Italian Edition), August 1983
"Architettura: George Ranalli," cover and pp. 86-91

G.A. Houses #12: Global Architecture Series
"Frehley House; Callender School Renovation," pp. 102-111

Domus, no. 631, September 1982 "Internal Architecture," pp. 40-43

New York Times: Home Section, September 16, 1982
"Emerging Young Architects: Diversity and New Directions," cover and p. 6

Architectural Digest, October 1982 "Architecture: Houses of the Future," p. 167

Interior Design, April 1982 "Geometric Progressions," pp. 212-217

Architectural Digest, December 1981
"Architecture: George Ranalli," pp. 148-153

Gran Bazaar, July/August 1981 "Una Torre nel Connecticut di George Ranalli," pp. 65-67

A+U (Architecture + Urbanism), Special Issue, no. 3, 1981
"American Architecture: After Modernism," pp. 73-78

Residential Interiors, July/August 1980
"Reading Architectural Writing," pp. 76-77, 88

Progressive Architecture, June 1980
"Chicago Tribune Competition," p. 95

Progressive Architecture, January 1980
"Design Awards," pp. 106-107

Architecture intérieure/Cree, December 1978/ January 1979
"L'école à Yale: Le dessin comme architecture," pp. 50-53

A.I.A. (American Institute of Architects Journal), July 1978
"Spaces for Selling," cover and p. 34

L'Architettura, no. 268, February 1978, pp. 590-591

A+U (Architecture + Urbanism), no. 11, 1977
"First of August," pp. 48-53

Baumeister, November 1977 "First of August," pp. 1054-1056

Architecture intérieure/Cree, May/ June 1977
"Un Été à New York," pp. 104-107

Interior Design, March 1977.
"August Too," cover and pp. 120-125

Domus, no. 572, July 1977 "Immagine Interno-Esterno," pp. 32-33

A.D. (Architectural Design), vol. 47, no. 7-8, 1977
"George Ranalli/ New York Shop," pp. 553-557

A.D. (Architectural Design), Profiles 6, June 1977
"America Now: Drawing Towards a More Modern Architecture," pp. 411, 422, 436

Domus, no. 563, October 1976 "Free Standing," p. 33

Interior Design, January 1976 "Two by George Ranalli," pp. 142-145

Architectural Record, February 1975
"Griffiss Air Force Base Hospital," pp. 122-123

Architecture d'aujourd'hui, no. 161, 1972
Habitat Collectif, "Projet d'habitat plurifonctionnel," p. 35

WORKS PUBLISHED IN BOOKS:

Guide To Contemporary New York City Architecture, John Hill, 2011
W. W. Norton Publishers, New York, London, p.195

The Visual Dictionary of Interior Architecture and Design, Michael Coates, Graeme Brooker & Sally Stone 2009, AVA Publishing SA, Switzerland, p. 204

Basic Interior Architecture: Form + Structure, Brooker + Stone 2007. AVA Publishing SA, Switzerland, p. 149

Contemporary World Interiors, Susan Yelavich 2007
Phaidon Press Inc. pp. 98-99

A Guide to Contemporary Architecture in America, Vol. 2 Eastern U.S.A.
Masayuki Fuchigami, Toto Publishers, Japan, 2007 pp. 98 & 234

New York 2000, Architecture and Urbanism Between the Bicentennial and the Millennium, Robert A.M. Stern, David Fishman & Jacob Tilove, 200, pp. 1106-1107 & p. 1190

Modeling Messages: The Architect and the Model, Karen Moon, 2005. The Monacelli Press, p. 169

Small Living Spaces, Arian Mostaedi, 2004
Carles Broto & Josep Ma Minguet, pp. 76-81

Colors: Architecture in Detail, Oscar Riera Ojeda, 2004
Rockport Publishers Inc. pp. 74-75

Glass Architecture: The Corolle d'Autore Collection, Sofia Glass, 2004. Editoriale DOMUS, pp. 122-123, 175

Materials: Architecture in Detail, Oscar Riera Ojeda, 2003
Rockport Publishers Inc. pp. 36-37

LOFT, Giovanni Polazzi, 2002
Federico Motta Editore, Italy, pp. 280-295

New York Apartments, Paco Asensio, 2001, teNeues Publishers, pp. 194-199

New York, A Guide to Recent Architecture, Susanna Sirefman, 2001
Ellipsis Publishers, pp.8.26-8.27

Manhattan Lofts, Ivor Richards, 2000
Wiley-Academy Publishers, pp. 26, 110-118

LOFTS, New Designs for Urban Living, Felicia Eisenberg Molnar, 1999
Rockport Publishers, Preface pp. 10-11

New Houses in old Buildings, Arian Mostaedi, 1999
Links Publishing, pp. 148-157

Lofts, Francisco Asensio Cerver, 1999. ARCO, Hearst, and Watson-Guptill Publishers, pp. 10-15

5000 Artists Return to Artists Space: 25 Years, Claudia Gould & Valerie Smith 1998, Artists Space Gallery Publication, p. 301

LOFT, Mayer Rus/Paul Warchol, 1998 Monacelli Press; K-Loft, pp.144-153

The New American Apartment, 30 Case Studies, edited by Oscar Riera Ojeda, 1997, Whitney Library of Design, pp. 192-199

Expressive Details, Duo Dickinson, 1996, McGraw-Hill Inc., pp. 54-57, 190-197

New Modern, Carla Breeze, 1995 PBC International Inc., pp. 14, 18-22, 166-171

Architectural Drawing Masterclass, Tom Porter, 1993 Macmillan Publishing Company, pp. 21-26

Architecture in the 20th Century, Udo Kultermann, 1993 Van Nostrand-Reinhold, p. 199

New York Urban Residence, Discover Architecture Series #13, 1992. Tokyo, Japan, pp. 40-41, 95-100

Formica & Design, Susan Grant Lewin, 1991, Rizzoli, p. 146

Architectural Politics as Seen in Competitions since 1790, Volume #5, 1991. Kodansha Publisher, Tokyo, Japan, pp. 104-105

Graphic Design Techniques for Architectural Drawing, Tom Porter, 1990. Amazon Publishing Ltd., p. 143

A Philosophy of Interior Design, Stanley Abercrombie, 1990 Harper & Row, pp. 32, 54, 117, 160

New York Architektur-Deutsches Architekturmuseum, June 1989 Frankfurt am Main, Germany, pp. 208-211

Sourcebook of Contemporary North American Architecture, Spring 1989 Van Nostrand-Reinhold, pp. 103-104

Interior Landscapes, Georges Teyssot, 1988 Lotus Documents, pp. 102-103

Center: A Journal for Architecture in America, 1988 University of Texas at Austin, "Buildings & Reality: Architecture in the Age of Information," pp. 58-61

Emerging Voices, 1986 Catalogue from the lecture series at The Architectural League of New York, pp. 22

Créer dans le Cree, May 1986 Catalogue for exhibit at Centre Pompidou, L'architecture contemporaine dans les bâtiments anciens, pp. 112-115

Il Progetto Domestico, January 1986 Catalogue for the XVII Triennale di Milano, La casa dell'uomo archetipi e prototipi: Progetti Electa, pp. 48-49

Drawing Interior Architecture, Norman Diekman & John Pile, 1983 Whitney Publications, pp. 91-93

Architecture Today, Charles Jencks, 1982 Academy Editions, London, pp. 102-103

Architectural Drawing: The Art and the Process, Gerald Allen & Richard Oliver editors, 1981 Whitney Publications, New York, pp. 148-149

Neue Laden, Karl & Eva Mang, 1981 Verlag Gerd Hatje, Stuttgart, pp. 20 & 44-46

New Architectural Drawings, Helmut Jacoby, 1981 Verlag Gerd Hatje, Stuttgart, pp. 46-47

Chicago Tribune Competition: Late Entries, Stuart Cohen & Stanley Tigerman editors, 1980 Catalogue, Rizzoli, vol. 2, p. 60

Graphic Techniques in Modern Design, William Atkin, 1979 McGraw-Hill Publishers, p. 131

Decorative Art and Modern Interiors, M. Schofield, editor, 1978 Studio Vista, London, pp. 24-31

Body, Memory and Architecture, C. Moore & K. Bloomer, 1977 Yale University Press, p. 55

Living In One Room, Jon Naar & Molly Siple, 1976 Random House, pp. 26-27

LECTURES

Center for Architecture, AIA New York, November 2012
Dean's Roundtable Discussion, Nina Rappaport, Moderator

Center for Architecture, AIA New York, November 2011
Dean's Roundtable Discussion, Sarah Whiting, Moderator

Yale Club of New York, April 22, 2010
"Saratoga, In Situ Design: People, History, Place"

Center for Architecture, AIA New York, September 2009
Dean's Roundtable Discussion, Robert Campbell, Moderator

Pennsylvania State University, University Park, PA, April 8, 2009.
"In Situ Design: People, History, Place"

Pratt Institute, Brooklyn, New York, February 12, 2009
"In Situ Design: People, History, Place"

Italian American Association of the NYC Housing Authority, New York, October 23, 2008
"Andrea Palladio, Architect for the Ages"

Center for Architecture, AIA New York, October 2008
Dean's Rountable Discussion

American Institute of Architects, Alfred W. French III Lectures in Architecture. Naples, Florida, October 10, 2008 "Iconic Form

Center for Architecture, AIA New York, September 2007
Dean's Roundtable Discussion

SCI-ARC, Southern California Institute of Architecture, Los Angeles, Calif., March 21, 2007
"Iconic Form"

Center For Architecture, A.I.A New York, October, 2006
Dean's Roundtable

Steelcase, New York, N.Y. October 2005.
"Deans of New York; 21st Century Schools/21st Century Cities"

Rice University, Houston, Texas, October 1999
"Modern Architecture: Sensuality for the New Age"

University of Southern California, Los Angeles, Calif., October 1997. "From Program to Detail: A Practical Theory"

University of Wisconsin at Milwaukee, Milwaukee, Wisc., November 1996. "From Program to Detail: A Practical Theory"

Columbia University, New York, N.Y., November 1994
"From Program to Detail: A Practical Theory"

Yale University, New Haven, Conn., October 1994
"From Program To Detail: A Practical Theory"

Italian Cultural Institute, New York, N.Y., March 1994. "The Shape of Things in the Third Millenium"

SCI-ARC, Southern California Institute of Architecture, Los Angeles, Calif., February, 1994
"Autonomous Structures"

Massachusetts Institute of Technology, Cambridge, Mass., March 1992. "Section In Autonomous Structure"

University of Southwestern Louisiana at Lafayette, Lafayette, La., Marc. "Autonomous Structures"

New York Institute of Technology, Westbury, N.Y., March 1992. "Autonomous Structures"

Chicago Institute for Architecture & Urbanism, Chicago, Ill., March 1992. "Looping the Loop," Panel

University of Illinois at Chicago Circle, Chicago, Ill., October 1991. "Autonomous Structures"

Columbia University, New York, N.Y., April 1991
"Density and the City," Panel Discussion

The Municipal Art Society, New York, N.Y., March 1991, "Writers Talk"

Washington University, St. Louis, Mo., March 1991
"Autonomous Structures"

University of Texas, Austin, Tex., January 1991
"Autonomous Structures"

American Academy in Rome, Rome, Italy, November 1990. "Autonomous Structures"

University of Colorado at Denver, October 1990
ACSA Western Regional Conference, Keynote Speaker

Designers Saturday, A+D Building, New York, N.Y., October 1990. "West Goes East: Design in Japan," Panel

The Catholic University of America, Washington D.C., November 1989. "Autonomous Structures",

Syracuse University, Syracuse, N.Y., October 1989 "Autonomous Architecture"

University of Cincinnati, Cincinnati, Ohio, May 1989
"Architecture: Imagination and Form"

Steelcase Furniture, New York, N.Y., January 1989
"Dreams + Details," Lecture/Seminar on Paul Rudolph

Temple University, Philadelphia, Pa., November 1988
"Architecture: Imagination and Form"

Steelcase Furniture, New York, N.Y., November 1988.
"Seminar on Gaetano Pesce"

Dentsu Corporation, Tokyo, Japan, October 1988.
" D-Space Project," Lecture/Seminar

Cooper-Hewitt National Design Museum, New York, N.Y., October 1988. "Architects Speak," Series

Yale University, New Haven, Conn., October 1988
"Architecture: Imagination and Form"

University of Colorado at Denver, September 1988
"Architecture: Imagination and Form," The Devon Carlson Lecture

Cooper Hewitt National Design Museum, New York, N.Y., May 1988. "The Poetics of Detail: The Architecture of Carlo Scarpa 1902-1978"

University of Kentucky, Lexington, Ky., March 1988
"On the Making of Form"

State University of New York at Purchase, November 1987. "On the Making of Form," Rosalind Kirschner Memorial Lectures in Architectural Design

Louisiana Technical University, Ruston, La., April 1987
"On Criticism," Seminar/Debate

University of Washington, St. Louis, Mo., April 1987
"Points of Departure," Seminar and Lecture

Columbia University, New York, N.Y., March 1987
"On the Making of Form"

Harvard University, Cambridge, Mass., March 1987
"On the Making of Form"

Trinity College, Hartford, Conn., February 1987
"On the Making of Form"

European Architecture Students Association, Turin, Italy, August 1986. "The Power of Form," Annual Conference

New School of Architecture, San Diego, Calif., February 1986. "The Power of Form"

Auburn University, Auburn, Ala., April 1985. "The Essential Wall"

Montclair State College of Art, Montclair, N.J., February 1985. "Recent Work"

Pennsylvania State University, University Park, Pa., November 1984. "Form, Space and Composition: Elements of Architecture"

University of Waterloo, Ontario, Canada, October 1984.
"Form, Space and Composition: Elements of Architecture"

Pratt Institute, Brooklyn, N.Y., April 1984. "Form, Space and Composition: Elements of Architecture"

Cooper-Hewitt National Design Museum, New York, N.Y., February 1984. "Other Attitudes Towards History"

University of California at Berkeley, November 1981. "Recent Work"

University of California at Los Angeles, November 1981. "Architecture: The Discreet Object of Desire"

ACADEMIC/COMMUNITY SERVICE

Yale University, New Haven, Conn., February 1981, "Recent Work"

Chicago Architecture Club, Chicago, Ill., December 1980. "The Architecture of Carlo Scarpa"

University of Houston, Houston, Texas, November 1980, "Current Work"
Rice University, Houston, Texas, November 1980 "Current Work"

Newport Art Association, Newport, R.I., February 1980
"Architectural Projects"

Graham Foundation, Chicago, Ill., May 1980 "Recent Work"

University of North Carolina at Charlotte, November 1979 "Recent Work"

Montclair State College of Art, Montclair, N.J., February 1979 "Recent Work"

Institute for Architecture and Urban Studies, New York, N.Y., May 1977
"From Pieces to Skins"

University of California at Los Angeles, March 1977 "Constructional Coloration"

A.I.A. Chicago Awards Jury, April 1992, Firm of the Year Award

Avant Garde: Journal of Theory and Criticism in Architecture, School of Architecture University of Colorado at Denver, Member of Advisory Board, Fall 1988- 1993

Yale University, Morse College
Fellow, Appointment: Jan. 1988-1999

Yale University, School of Architecture
Chairman, Design Committee, January 1989-1999

Yale University, School of Architecture
Rules Committee, 1977-1992

Yale University, School of Architecture
Chairman, Exhibition Committee, 1977-1984

PUBLIC EXHIBITS PREPARED:
Carlo Scarpa: Drawings of the Brion Cemetery, October-December 1984
With catalogue; Curator

Gaetano Pesce, October-December 1983
With catalogue; Curator

Helmut Jahn, October-December 1982
With catalogue; Curator

Raimund Abraham: Collisions, October-December 1981
With catalogue; Curator

Diana Agrest/ Mario Gandelsonas, January 1981
With catalogue; Curator

Young Architects, January 1980
With catalogue; Curator & participant

Faculty Work, School of Architecture, January 1979, Curator

The Drawings of Paul Rudolph, Fall 1977, Curator

Community Planning Board No.5, Bronx, N.Y., Dec. 1968- Jan. 1970

EXHIBITIONS

Metropolitan Museum of Art, New York, N.Y. June 2011-March 2012. *Highlights of Modern Design, 1900 to the Present, Part 2.* Valentine #2 Chair is included in the exhibit.

Architectural League of N.Y., New York, N.Y., May 8-June 26, 2010, *The City We Imagined, The City We Made.* The exhibit included the Saratoga Avenue Community Center.

Indianapolis Museum of Art, Indianapolis, Indiana, August 2008, Lock-it lever handle is taken into the Design Arts permanent collection of the museum.

Denver Art Museum, Denver, Colo., February-May 2002. *US Design 1975-2000.* Invited to construct a design for the exhibit that was built and installed in the gallery.

Metropolitan Museum of Art, New York, N.Y. June 26, 2001-January 6, 2002. *A Century of Design, Part IV: 1975-2000.* Valentine #2 Chair is included in the exhibit.

Canadian Centre for Architecture, Montreal, Canada, May-October 1999. *Carlo Scarpa, Architect; Intervening with History*. The project involved being a co-curator, the installation designer, an author for the book, and fabricator of four analytic models which are included in the exhibit. The project was installed in all 6 gallery rooms at the museum.

Yale University, School of Architecture Gallery, New Haven, Connecticut, February 1- March 5, 1999. One-man show of five recent projects.

Artists Space Gallery, 38 Greene Street, New York, November 14, 1997-January 10, 1998. One-man show. Installation design and exhibit, PRESENT TENSE: The Architecture of George Ranalli.

Whitney Museum of Art, New York, N.Y., June-September 1997. Installation design for the exhibit Frank Lloyd Wright: Designs For An American Landscape, 1922-1932. The project was installed on the entire 2nd Floor of the museum.

Denver Art Museum, Denver, Colo., July 1996. Steel side chair designed for the 22nd Street Loft Project has been included in the Permanent Collection of 20th Century Architecture & Design, Denver Art Museum.

Canadian Centre for Architecture, Montreal, Canada, June-September 1996. Five analytic models were commissioned and created for the exhibit Frank Lloyd Wright: Designs For An American Landscape, 1922-1932. These models were interpretations from drawings of 5 buildings designed by Wright which went unbuilt. The models will remain in the permanent collection of the CCA.

The Museum of Modern Art, New York, N.Y., Spring 1994. Two models of Unity Temple produced in the Ranalli Studio at Yale were included in the exhibit Frank Lloyd Wright: Architect. These models are in the permanent collection of the museum.

Denver Art Museum, Denver, Colo. Architectural Hardware for the Union Co. of Osaka, Japan, 1992. Permanent Collection of 20th Century Architecture & Design, Denver Art Museum.

The Metropolitan Museum of Art, New York, N.Y. Valentine #2 Chair, 1991 Permanent Collection of 20th Century Art & Design, The Metropolitan Museum of Art.

Communicating Ideas Artfully, New York, 1990. Steelcase Design Partnership

Deutsches Architekturmuseum, Frankfurt am Main, Germany, June 3-August 13, 1989. New York Architektur

American Institute of Architects, St. Louis, Mo., May 1989. Five Choose Five, 1989. National Convention and Design Exposition

Dentsu Corporation, Tokyo, Japan, September-November 1988. New York-Tokyo, D-Space Exhibit

From Table to Tablescape, Chicago, Ill., June-August 1988. Formica Company (New Prototype, chair)

American Institute of Architects, New York Chapter, May-June 1988. 10 On 10: The Critics Choice

Yale University, New Haven, Conn., October 1987, Faculty Work

Centre Pompidou, Paris, France, May-September 1986. Old Buildings-New Designs

XVII Triennale di Milano, Milan, Italy, January-April 1986. Il Progetto Domestico (Built Project)

America/Europe: 10 New Chairs, Udine, Italy, May 1985. Furniture Exhibit (New Prototype, chair)

Young-Hoffman Gallery, Chicago, Ill., October 1980 Architectural Projects

Museum of Finnish Architecture, Helsinki, Finland, August 1980. Creation and Recreation--America Draws

Museum of Contemporary Art, Chicago, Ill., May 1980. Chicago Tribune Competition: Late Entries

Yale University, New Haven, Conn., January 1980. Young Architects, curator and participant

Newport Art Association, Newport, R.I., March 15-April 13, 1980. Architectural Projects, One Man Show

American Architectural Alternatives, Europe 1979-1980

University of North Carolina at Charlotte, November 1979. One Man Show

Sperone, Westwater and Fisher Gallery, New York, N.Y., October 1979Elements of Architecture

New Americans, Rome, Italy, Summer-Fall 1979

Cooper-Hewitt National Design Museum, New York, N.Y., July 1979. Urban Open Spaces

Hudson River Museum, New York, N.Y., April-July 1979. Architecture for Children

Yale University, New Haven, Conn., November 1978. Faculty Work

The Drawing Center & Cooper-Hewitt National Design Museum, New York, N.Y., 1977

Otis Art Institute, Los Angeles, Calif., 1977 Drawing Towards A More Modern Architecture

CONTRIBUTORS

MICHAEL SORKIN is Distinguished Professor of Architecture and Director of the Graduate Program in Urban Design at the City College of New York. From 1993 to 2000 he was Professor and Director of the Institute for Urbanism at the Academy of Fine Arts in Vienna. Sorkin's long academic career has also included professorships at Cooper Union, Harvard, Yale (holder of the Davenport and Bishop chairs), Cornell (Gensler Chair) Columbia, Pennsylvania, Texas, Minnesota, Illinois. Michigan (Saarinen Chair), Nebraska (Hyde Chair). Sorkin lectures widely and is the author of several hundred articles on architectural and urban subjects. For ten years he was the architectural critic of the *Village Voice* and is currently contributing editor for *Architectural Record*. His books include *Variations on a Theme Park, Exquisite Corpse, Giving Ground* (edited with Joan Copjec), *Wiggle, Local Code, Some Assembly Required, The Next Jerusalem, After the World Trade Center* (edited with Sharon Zukin), *Starting from Zero, Against the Wall*, and *Indefensible Space*. Forthcoming are *Twenty Minutes in Manhattan, Eutopia, All Over the Map*, and *Project New Orleans*. Sorkin is also President of Terreform, a non-profit organization engaged in urban research and advocacy and President of The Institute for Urban Design.

SUSAN S. SZENASY is Editor in Chief of METROPOLIS, the award-winning New York City-based magazine of architecture and design. Since 1986 she has led the magazine in landmark design journalism, achieving domestic and international recognition. She is internationally recognized as an authority on sustainability and design. Susan sits on the boards of the Council for Interior Design Accreditation, FIT Interior Design, the Center for Architecture Advisory Board, and the Landscape Architecture Foundation. She has been honored with two IIDA Presidential Commendations, is an honorary member of the ASLA and AIA NYC, and the 2008 recipient of the ASID Patron's Prize and Presidential Commendation. Along with METROPOLIS Publisher Horace Havemeyer III, Susan was a 2007 recipient of the Civitas August Heckscher Award for Community Service and Excellence. She holds an MA in Modern European History from Rutgers University, and honorary doctorates from Kendall College of Art and Design, the Art Center College of Design, and the Pacific Northwest College of Art.

JOSEPH GIOVANNINI heads Giovannini Associates, a design firm based in New York and Los Angeles.
He holds a Masters in Architecture from Harvard's Graduate School of Design.
He has taught advanced and graduate studios at Columbia University's Graduate School of Architecture, UCLA's Graduate School of Architecture and Urban Planning, the University of Southern California's School of Architecture, and at the University of Innsbruck.
His projects have ranged from the adaptive reuse of a large trucking facility into lofts to house additions and apartment interiors.
A graduate of Yale University, where he did his B.A. in English, he also holds a Master of Arts degree in French Language and Literature from La Sorbonne, Paris, Middlebury College Program. Besides heading his design practice, Mr. Giovannini has written on architecture and design for three decades for such publications as the *New York Times, Architectural Record, Art in America, Art Forum* and *Architecture Magazine*. He has also served as the architecture critic for *New York Magazine* and the *Los Angeles Herald Examiner*. Published design projects have appeared in *Architectural Digest, the Los Angeles Times Magazine, The New York Times, A + U, Domus, House and Garden, GA Houses, Architekur und Wohnen, Sites*, and *Interior Design*.
He lives in New York with his wife, Christine Pittel, and daughter Isabella.

PAUL GOLDBERGER has been the architecture critic at *The New Yorker* since July 1997, writing about architecture, design and urbanism. Mr. Goldberger came to *The New Yorker* following a 25-year career at *The New York Times*, where he won a Pulitzer Prize for his architecture criticism in 1984. He joined the staff of The Times in 1972, and was named architecture critic in 1973. In 1990 he was named cultural news editor of The Times, and in 1994 he became the paper's chief cultural correspondent. He lectures widely around the country on the subject of architecture, design, historic preservation and cities, and for several years taught architecture criticism at the Yale School of Architecture. He has also served as a special consultant to several major cultural and educational institutions, including the Morgan Library in New York, the Corcoran Gallery of Art in Washington, D.C., the Carnegie Science Center in Pittsburgh and the Ross Institute in East Hampton, New York, organizing and directing the process of selecting an architect. In addition to the Pulitzer Prize, Mr. Goldberger's work as a critic and historic preservationist has been recognized with numerous awards, including the Medal of the American Institute of Architects, the President's Medal of the Municipal Art Society of New York, the Medal of Honor of the New York Landmarks Preservation Foundation, and the New York City Landmarks Preservation Commission's Preservation Achievement Award. He has also received the Roger Starr Journalism Award from the Citizens Housing and Planning Council; the Award of Merit of the Lotus Club, presented to writers of distinction; and in 1993 was named a Literary Lion, the New York Public Library?s tribute to distinguished writers.
He is the author of several books, including text for *The World Trade Center Remembered*, and *Manhattan Unfurled*. He has also written *he City Observed New York: An Architectural Guide to Manhattan, The Skyscraper, On the Rise: Architecture and Design in a Post-Modern Age, Houses of the Hamptons, and Above New York*. He is currently working on a book that will tell the story of the redevelopment of the site of the World Trade Center in Lower Manhattan, and he is also writing a book on the experience of looking at architecture.
He has been awarded honorary doctoral degrees by Pratt Institute in New York, the Center for Creative Studies in Detroit and the New York School of Interior Design for his work as a critic and cultural commentator on architecture urban design. He appears frequently on film and television to discuss art, architecture, and cities, most recently in Ken Burns's film for public television on Frank Lloyd Wright, in the PBS series "Building Big," and a program broadcast in the spring of 2002 on The Learning Channel entitled "Super Structures," for which he acted as on-camera host.

ADA LOUISE HUXTABLE is the Architecture Critic of the *Wall Street Journal*. She was Architecture Critic of the *New York Times* from 1963 to 1982, and a member of the paper's Editorial Board from 1973 to 1982. As the first full-time critic in this field on an American newspaper, she dealt with news, trends and standards in architecture, building, development, urban design and renewal, and historic preservation in news articles, appraisals, critical columns, and editorials. Mrs. Huxtable received the first Pulitzer Prize for Distinguished Criticism in 1970, the year the category was established. She left the *New York Times* after she was named a MacArthur Fellow in December, 1981. In 1999- 2000 she was a Director's Fellow of the Center for Scholars and Writers at the New York Public Library, working on new developments in architectural theory and design.
Born and educated in New York City, she is a graduate of Hunter College, magna cum laude, Phi Beta Kappa, and did graduate work in art and architectural history at the Institute of Fine Arts at New York University. She was a Fulbright Scholar in Italy in 1950 and 1952, investigating 19th and 20th century Italian architecture and design from stile liberty through rationalismo and the early modern movement. In 1958 she received a Guggenheim fellowship for the

study of design and structural advances in American architecture. She began her professional career as Assistant Curator of Architecture and Design at the Museum of Modern Art in New York from 1946 to 1950. After her return from Italy in 1952, she was a freelance writer and contributor to art and architecture periodicals and the *New York Times Sunday Magazine*, and prepared traveling and teaching exhibitions for the Museum of Modern Art. In 1963 the Times created the position of Architecture Critic for her, the first newspaper to do so in this country.
She is the recipient of more than 30 honorary degrees– doctorates of letters, fine arts, and law– from Harvard University, Yale University, New York University, Fordham University, Washington University, the Universities of Pennsylvania, Michigan, and Massachusetts, the University of Nottingham, England, and Williams, Hamilton, Colgate, Trinity, Oberlin, Smith, Skidmore, Mount Holyoke and Radcliffe Colleges and others. Among the more than 30 professional awards received for her work are the Frank Jewett Mather Award for art criticism, 1967, the Architectural Criticism Medal of the American Institute of Architects, 1969, the Special Award of the National Trust for Historic Preservation, 1970. the National Arts Club Medal for Literature, 1971, the Diamond Jubilee Medallion of the City of New York, 1973, the Secretary's Award for Conservation of the U.S. Department of the Interior, 1976, the Thomas Jefferson Medal for Architecture, 1977, the President's Medal of the Municipal Art Society of New York, 1982, the Jean Tschumi Prize for Architectural Criticism of the International Union of Architects, 1987, the Medal for Architectural Criticism of the French Academy of Architecture, 1988, the Henry Allen Moe Award in the Humanities of the American Philosophical Society, 1992, the $24 Award of the Museum of the City of New York in 1996 for significant contributions to the enhancement of the quality of life in New York City, the President's Award of the New York Chapter of the *American Institute of Architects*, 2003, the Gold Medal of the National Institute of Social Sciences in 2005, the Fine Arts Federation of New York Medal in 2007, the President's Medal of the Architectural League of New York, and the Louis Auchincloss Prize of the Museum of the City of New York, in 2008.
Mrs. Huxtable is a member of the American Academy of Arts and Letters and the American Philosophical Society, a Fellow of the American Academy of Arts and Sciences, an honorary member of the American Institute of Architects, an Honorary Fellow of the Royal Institute of British Architects, and a member of the Society of Architectural Historians. She gave the Cook Lectures in American Institutions at the University of Michigan in 1977, and was Hitchcock Professor of the Humanities at the University of California at Berkeley in 1982. She has been a member of the jury of the Pritzker Architecture Prize and of the American Committee of the Japanese Praemium Imperiale.
She has served on the Corporation Visiting Committees for the Graduate School of Design and the Department of Visual and Environmental Studies at Harvard, the School of Architecture at the Massachusetts Institute of Technology, the Board of Overseers of the Graduate School of Fine Arts at the University of Pennsylvania, the advisory board of the American Trust for the British Library, and the Rockefeller University and Smithsonian Councils. She has acted as a consultant on architect selection for the Sainsbury Wing of the National Gallery in London, the Getty Center in Los Angeles, the San Francisco Public Library, the Chicago Museum of Contemporary Art, and the Nelson-Atkins Museum in Kansas City. She is the author of *Pier Luigi Nervi,* N.Y., George Braziller, 1960; *Classical New York,* N.Y., Doubleday, 1964; *Will They Ever Finish Bruckner Boulevard?,* N.Y., Macmillan, 1970; *Kicked A Building Lately?,* N.Y., Quadrangle-New York Times Books, 1976; *The Tall Building Artistically Reconsidered: The Search for a Skyscraper Style,* N.Y. Pantheon, 1985; *Goodbye, History, Hello Hamburger,* Preservation Press of the National Trust, 1986; *Architecture, Anyone?,* N.Y. Random House, 1986, *The Unreal America: Architecture and Illusion,* N.Y., The New Press, 1997; *Frank Lloyd Wright, a biography in the Penguin Lives series,* N.Y., Viking Penguin, 2004. A volume of her writings, *On Architecture: Collected Reflections on a Century of Change,* was published by Walker and Co. in 2008.

HERBERT MUSCHAMP was born in Philadelphia on Nov. 28, 1947, the son of a business executive. He fell in love with New York in the mid-1960s while visiting the city as a freshman at the University of Pennsylvania. He dropped out after his second year to study architecture at Parsons School of Design; a year later he headed to London to study architectural history and theory at the Architectural Association.
Mr. Muschamp returned to Parsons as a teacher in 1983, where he became the director of its graduate program in architecture and design criticism. Around the same time, he began his career as a critic, writing for magazines like *Vogue, House and Garden* and *Art Forum.* He was appointed architecture critic at *The New Republic* in 1987. He was named the architecture critic for *The Times* in 1992, succeeding Paul Goldberger.
His deeply personal and wildly original reviews made him an extremely influential architecture critic in his generation. He was open to new talent during a time when architecture was in the public spotlight due to repetitive battles between modernists and post-modernists. He was equally as interested in the ideas that pushed architecture forward as the successes and failures of the buildings themselves. He died of lung cancer in October of 2007 at the age of 59.

ANTHONY VIDLER, a historian and critic of architecture, is Dean and Professor of the Irwin S. Chanin School of Architecture of The Cooper Union. Trained in architecture at Cambridge University in England, with a PhD in history and theory from TU Delft, Vidler was a member of the faculty of the Princeton University School of Architecture from 1965 to 1993, serving as the Chair of the Ph.D. Committee, and Director of the Program in European Cultural Studies. In 1993 he took up a position as Chair of the Department of Art History at UCLA, before coming to The Cooper Union in 2001. He has curated several exhibitions, most recently, Notes from the Archive: James Frazer Stirling, Architect and Teacher, at the Yale British Art Center, Yale University (2010). His publications include *The Writing of the Walls: Architectural Theory in the Late Enlightenment* (Princeton Architectural Press, 1987); *Claude-Nicolas Ledoux* (MIT Press, 1990);*The Architectural Uncanny* (MIT Press, 1992); *Warped Space* (MIT Press, 2000); *Histories of the Immediate Present* (MIT Press, 2008), and *James Frazer Stirling: Notes from the Archive* (Yale University Press, 2010). His *Scenes of the Street and Other Essays* was published by Monacelli Press in Spring 2011.

OSCAR RIERA OJEDA is an editor and designer based in Philadelphia, Singapore, and Buenos Aires. Born in 1966, in Argentina, he moved to the United States in 1990. Since then he has published over one hundred books, assembling a remarkable body of work notable for its thoroughness of content, timeless character, and sophisticated and innovative craftsmanship. Oscar Riera Ojeda's books have been published by many prestigious publishing houses across the world, including ORO editions, Birkhäuser, Byggförlaget, The Monacelli Press, Gustavo Gili, Thames & Hudson, Rizzoli, Whitney Library of Design, and Taschen. Oscar Riera Ojeda is also the creator of numerous architectural book series, including *Ten Houses, Contemporary World Architects, The New American House* and *The New American Apartment, Architecture in Detail,* and *Single Building.* His work has received many international awards, in-depth reviews, and citations. He is a regular contributor and consultant for several publications in the field.

ACKNOWLEDGEMENTS

A myriad of people have contributed not only to this book but to the ongoing work of my architectural office over these more than thirty years. Architecture is a collaborative effort involving people with various talents and gifts too numerous to list, and all are essential.

My family has been an unending source of love, comfort and joy throughout this process and I thank them for allowing me the space to produce this work. To my wife, Dr. Anne Valentino, who has engaged me in an ongoing dialogue about the relationship between architecture and culture based on her mastery of the Classics, a deep thank you. Her consummate understanding of the representational capacity of architecture has been a wellspring of clarity that has made my journey less opaque. It was she who prompted me to dig into a long-forgotten set of associations between the making of architectural works, jazz performance, my historical references, and relevant theoretical constructs that had shaped much of my early thinking about the placement of architecture into civic arenas. I thank her most of all for helping me understand that In Situ is ultimately about the making of places for the people who inhabit them.

My thanks also go to my daughter Sofia, whose talents in science and art have been a true inspiration. I marvel at her ability to inhabit both worlds with ease, and find her choreography and integrative ability in the arts astonishing.

My son Rocco's keen awareness of the narrative components of architecture has helped me see that program and form are inseparably intertwined in a most complex association. I watch in awe as he constructs complex building forms, each accompanied by a complete story about what goes where and how to get it there.

There have been several readers and editors for my text in this publication. Michael Dobbs provided a first reading of the essay, and her thoughts about restructuring it were invaluable. William J. R. Curtis provided a thorough and substantive critique, suggesting revisions that were essential to clarifying the essay's themes. He and I have been in a fertile dialogue about architecture for about forty years now, starting at Harvard University, and his incisive, tough-minded, and thoughtful contributions are greatly appreciated.

I also wish to thank Michael Sorkin, a colleague, friend, and critical thinker on architecture, urbanism, and the making of cities. Ours is a special bond that goes back to the beginning of my academic and professional life, and we share a deep and particular understanding of buildings, cities, and society. His writing on these topics is some of most eloquent ever produced, and his ethical stance and eminence in the field are above reproach. It has been a privilege to teach with him.

Erica Torres, my assistant at the Spitzer School of Architecture, has retyped essays and texts from various journals. Lastly, Larry Gilman's dogged and patient editing helped the essay achieve a much tighter and straightforward form. His help has been substantial and essential.

The relationship between academia and the practice of architecture is intimate, sacred, and filled with maze-like twists and turns. Movement between the two modes is an exhilarating process. I therefore wish to thank and acknowledge all my students over the years, who have given voice and power to the constant reinvention of architectural ideas. Their ability to understand and master this complicated art form has moved me to amazement; their questions, depth of passion, and belief in new ideas has been invigorating and stimulating. Nor can I say enough about my colleagues, those faculty members who, over all these years, have been engaging, passionate, and dedicated in their pursuit of a true dialogue about architecture. They have devoted countless hours of research, thought, and discussion to the subject of architecture. Almost all my faculty are active practitioners, yet reserve a significant portion of their precious time each week for helping students understand the complex path that is the art of architecture.

Many thanks go to Bernard and Anne Spitzer for their generous and transformative gift to the Spitzer School of Architecture at City College. Their gift has enabled me to do many things that otherwise would have remained mere dreams. My thanks also to Dr. Lisa Staiano-Coico, twelfth President of City College of New York, for her stellar leadership, unending support, and encouragement, and to Dr. Maurizio Trevesan, Provost of City College, for providing a stable academic environment conducive to intellectual growth and development. Lastly, my gratitude goes out to the Chancellor of the City University of New York, Dr. Matthew Goldstein, for his institutional support, assistance, and dedication to the cause of public higher professional education, and to Benno Schmidt, Chair of the CUNY Board of Trustees, for his consummate and impeccable stewardship of the CUNY system.

Architecture cannot be realized without strong and collaborative clients, who provide the impetus, financial support, and guidance that frames and clarifies the production of each project. My clients have been an unending source of varied sensibilities, crucial to many of the projects depicted in these pages.

Special thanks are also due to all the artisans, craftspeople, contractors, and builders who have lent their skill and acumen to constructing many of the projects illustrated herein. Each project presented different challenges, and in every case makers rose to the occasion, not merely executing the design but freely sharing their wealth of knowledge and experience. Special acknowledgement goes to the engineers and professional consultants in the structural, mechanical, civil, geotechnical, and specialties areas. My deep thanks goes to Robert Silman, who provided structural guidance and an exceptional willingness to collaborate with me on a wide array of projects. Thanks also to Joe DiBernardo for all his wisdom and skill in ensuring that each project paid careful attention to lighting, making the atmosphere of every space a truly rich experience.

Last but certainly not least, special thanks go to each and every one of my invaluable assistants. Without their tireless help over these many, many years, there would be no body of work to present. Each has generously given many hours of their time, in apprenticeship and beyond, to help me realize my projects. Several were especially critical and essential over the years, staying the course during the varied and sometimes challenging ups and downs of any practice: my personal thanks to John Butterworth, Mario Gentile, Hayden Marrero, Junko Fujimoto, Aja Garzon, Prof. M.T. Chang and Hyungjin Lim for their extra and exceptional effort.

In regard to the production of *In Situ*, I wish to make a very special acknowledgement to publisher Oscar Riera Ojeda for his dedication, tremendous talent, and wisdom in book design. His is a unique gift, which he has shared with me over several publications. He and his staff Leo Malinow and Alejandra Roman have dedicated countless hours to collecting, designing, and producing the studies that make this book possible.

UNION

IN SITU
George Ranalli, Works&Projects

Book Credits
Creative Direction by Leo Malinow
Graphic Design by Yanina Arabena, Alejandra Román
Copy Editing by Kit Maude

ISBN 978-988-15194-7-1
Printed in China by Artron.

OSCAR RIERA OJEDA PUBLISHERS LIMITED
Unit 1A 20/F.,
Far East Consortium Bldg.,
121 Des Voeux Rd Central, Hong Kong.
T: +852-5311-1625

Production Offices | China
Suit 19, Shenyun Road
Nanshan District, Shenzhen 518055
T:+86-755-8336-6138

www.oropublishers.com | www.oscarrieraojeda.com
oscar@oscarrieraojeda.com